Mimi Martin

626 284-2209

Please return !

The Sibyl Sanderson Story

Requiem for a Diva

OPERA BIOGRAPHY SERIES, NO. 16

Series Editors

Andrew Farkas

William R. Moran

The *Sibyl Sanderson* Story

Requiem for a Diva

Jack Winsor Hansen

♪ AMADEUS PRESS

Amadeus Press
Pompton Plains, NJ • Cambridge, UK

Published in 2005 by

Amadeus Press, LLC
512 Newark Pompton Turnpike
Pompton Plains, New Jersey 07444, USA

Amadeus Press
2 Station Road
07444 Swavesey, Cambridge CB4 5QJ, UK

For sales, please contact
NORTH AMERICA

UNITED KINGDOM AND EUROPE

AMADEUS PRESS, LLC
c/o Hal Leonard Corp.
7777 West Bluemound Road
Milwaukee, Wisconsin 53213, USA
Tel. 800-637-2852
Fax 414-774-3259

AMADEUS PRESS
2 Station Road
Swavesey, Cambridge, CB4 5QJ, UK
Tel. 01954-232959
Fax 01954-206040

E-mail: orders@amadeuspress.com
Website: www.amadeuspress.com

Printed in the United States of America

Library of Congress Cataloging-in-Publication Data

Hansen, Jack Winsor.
  The Sibyl Sanderson story : requiem for a diva / by Jack Winsor Hansen.--1st hardcover ed.
    p. cm. -- (Opera biography series ; no. 16)
  Includes bibliographical references and index.
  ISBN 1-57467-094-8
  1. Sanderson, Sibyl, 1865–1903. 2. Sopranos (Singers)--Biography. I. Title. II. Series.

ML420.S1419H35 2004
782.1'092--dc22

2004015945

To the memory of Carl Van Vechten

Carlo, there were two things you wished from me. The first was a tape of my Schumann A minor concerto because, you wrote, I "entered into the piano and held communion with the composer, voicing inner themes that no other artist has even been aware of." This was not to be. The last time I played it was with the WGN Symphony in their late 1960s telecast after you had passed away. I persevered long enough to honor your other request, and I dedicate this book to you with warm affection and gratitude.

Contents

Contents

Preface

Someone once said that it takes a lifetime to write a life, and it seems a lifetime ago that I first saw an autographed picture of Sibyl Sanderson on the hotel dresser of a dying man who had once been an opera singer and later music critic on the *Chicago Herald American*. I was a teenage piano student of the famed Rudolph Ganz in Chicago and had been taken to interview Herman DeVries because he had known Gounod, Thomas, Massenet, and other French composers of the late nineteenth century. He told me he had sung the role of the Count Des Grieux in *Manon* opposite her.

A few years later, after Mary Garden's autobiography made the bestseller list in the early 1950s, I contemplated doing research into Sanderson's life and career. The late American portrait painter Carroll Kelly steered me to my first literary sources. He had lived in Paris at the turn of the twentieth century and had known and painted Debussy, Anatole France, Nijinsky, and many of Sanderson's other contemporaries. Around 1910 he met Massenet when he was commissioned to design the costumes for Lina Cavalieri's revival of *Thaïs* at the Opéra.

My early efforts met with constant frustration because there was no bibliography from which to draw. Scarcely a dozen books in English contained either a chapter or more than a page about her. I had to develop my own, and Mr. Kelly guided me to music journals and newspapers of her era and assisted me with French translations.

I was fortunate to begin my research in the 1950s, for during that decade I interviewed a dwindling number of people who either knew Sanderson or who had heard her on stage. I never thought I would amass enough data to write a biography, but an unquenchable curiosity kept driving me on either to prove or disprove so many controversial statements, critiques, and stories in the press about her.

Sibyl Sanderson was determined to have it all. In the words of Robert Frone, president of the Massenet Society, she "made it big and tragically lost it big." She never possessed the physical or emotional stamina to scale the heights to which her career escalated, and its manifold pressures soon outgrew her ability to cope.

On stage she had magic—that gift of the gods to an interpreter. Her radiant presence enabled those who heard and saw her to savor the peak moments of their lives and even to relive their bittersweet memories. Nothing remained quiescent under her touch. Everything flashed, spiraled, and glowed with a burning intensity because her personality was so electric. At her worst, she was a reckless, defiant hedonist; at her best, an extraordinarily kind, sympathetic, and devoted friend. She did not merit having her boundless generosity and affability trampled by everyone from avaricious managers to duplicitous friends. Her stranger-than-fiction life was to assume all the elements of a Greek tragedy as she battled courageously, but futilely, against her self-destructive demons. The French newspaper *Le Gaulois* described it as "an adventure from a bizarre tale."[1]

Sibyl Sanderson was the first American for whom several European composers wrote operas (Massenet wrote *Thaïs* and *Esclarmonde* for her), but it is not solely for creating those roles that she should be remembered, any more than for uttering the highest notes in operatic history. Neither will she be enshrined among the legendary vocal virtuosos, but rather among that select group whose rare insight enabled them to penetrate the creative recesses of a composer's mind and reinterpret his creations. Here she ranks among the chosen few whom composers have allowed to reconstruct their scores, as she did for Massenet's *Manon*. This is perhaps her greatest musical legacy. For the first time in operatic history, she is receiving her much deserved, albeit belated, accolade.

—

I am indebted to so many people who helped me during my long years of research. So many of them are dead today; others may not have made it to the twenty-first century.

To five people I owe a special debt for the unique help they provided. First, the late Ian Fraser, head of the American Library in Paris during the 1950s when I did my research there. If it hadn't been for our chance meeting in America I never would have had the opportunity to meet Sibyl Sanderson's stepdaughter, the Princess de Faucyny-Lucinge, or study piano with his close friend, Mme Marguerite Long. His introductions to such legendary stars from *la belle Èpoque* as Cléo de Mérode were invaluable. It was Mr. Fraser who arranged for me to do private research at the Paris Bibliothèque Nationale and circumvent the red tape with which French authorities constrict foreign researchers.

At the Bibliothèque I pored over old newspaper volumes day after day gleaning critical reactions and noting evidence of the furor that Sanderson created throughout Europe, not just in Paris. I also recorded details of the period, not least the weather on the days and weeks in which the scenes of this story take place. Other libraries and archives that I have used over the years include the New York Public Library, the Newberry Library in Chicago, and the San Francisco Public Library.

I am grateful to the late Princess de Lucinge, née Natividad Terry, for her indelible memories of the two years she lived with Sibyl Sanderson. It was the princess who suspected that the unpublished letters of Jules Massenet were somewhere in America because she had heard that Marion Sanderson had returned to the United States after her marriage, and the correspondence had not been found in France. I also thank her son, the late Prince Jean de Lucinge, for sending me some of his mother's private memoirs.

After a long search I finally met Sibyl Sanderson's niece, Margaret Sanderson Nall, and was able to read the unpublished Massenet, Delibes, and Saint-Saëns correspondence for the first time. Without her assistance I could not have continued with this biography. My special gratitude goes to her for making available the unpublished letters, family photographs, her aunt's scrapbooks, the holographs of *Thaïs, Esclarmonde,* and *Werther,* the original edition of *Manon,* and most of all her mother's (Marion Sanderson's) unpublished memoirs, dating from about 1938 to 1940. These reminiscences contain a wealth of previously unpublished information: recollections of Sibyl's teenage romances, the real reasons for the breakup of her engagement to William Randolph Hearst, unpublished anecdotes involving Massenet, Antonio Terry, and the Russian royal family, and accounts of many other incidents in Sibyl's short life, including some of her most charitable deeds.

I owe the entire computer transcription of this biography to Robert Frone, someone whom I have yet to meet in person. After the hundreds of hours we spent on the telephone, though, I feel as if I know him well. His devotion to neglected French opera, his invaluable editorial advice, his patience, his dedication, and his hard work gave me the determination to see this book to conclusion.

A special niche is reserved for the author Carl Van Vechten, who had considered doing a biography of Sanderson and had even interviewed the Princess de Lucinge on one of her American visits. His generosity included giving me the notes from his interviews with Gertrude Atherton and Mary Garden. He also shared recollections of conversations with a number of people in Sanderson's life. Over and over in his letters to me he reiterated, "You must never give up on this project. Already you have probed much deeper [than others]. . . . I won't live to see its completion, but you would do me a great honor if you would dedicate it to me posthumously."

I also express my gratitude to the following people who either knew Sibyl Sanderson or heard her on the stage: Felix Borowski, Herman DeVries, Mary Garden, Marguerite Long, Florence Turner Maley, Clèo de Mèrode, Pierre Monteux, Mrs. Adolph Muhlmann, Mrs. Fremont Older, Isidor Philipp, and Muriel Atherton Russell. Today they have all passed on, but their memories are now preserved for posterity.

In the case of Mary Garden I soon realized that any additional interviews were futile. I returned from Europe in the late 1950s fully aware of the fiction she had created about the circumstances and date of her own debut in 1900, not to mention the various canards she had recounted to me.

I am also indebted to Dr. George Anteblian, Tony Altamirano, Ann Barzell, Louis Biancolli, Ralph Bishop, Mme Boschot and Mlle Briquet of the Bibliothéque Nationale, Lawrence Calloway-Henry, Louis and Jean Clément, Mr. Castelaggio of the San Francisco Public Library, Deborah Chapman, Renè DeVries, Quaintance Eaton, Arland Grant, Mary Emily Grant, Ruby Winsor Hansen, Barre Hill, James Hinton, Earl Horner, Carroll Kelly, Jonathan Kilbourn, Robert Lawrence, Prince Jean de Faucyny-Lucinge, Esther Leger, Bill Lynch of the San Francisco Public Library, David Mendenhall, Mireille Massot of the Nice Bibliothéque, Linda Naru of the University of Illinois Research Center, Bidù Sayão, Harold Schonberg, Ellis Schuman, Patricia Steinhaus, Richard Schwegel of the Chicago Public Library, Carleton Sprague Smith of the New York Public Library, Evelyn Wells, Frances Winwar, Kathleen Zachary, and the librarian of the Paris Opèra. Last but not least, I wish to thank the irrepressible Marion Davies for recalling her conversation with William Randolph Hearst about his broken engagement with Sanderson: "They [Hearst's sons] tied me up legally so I can never tell a word about my relationship with their old man, but they sure as hell can't stop me from talking about a few of his old flames before he met me."

Prologue

"Extra! Extra! La mort de Sibyl Sanderson, la belle cantatrice!" (Extra! Extra! The death of Sibyl Sanderson, the beautiful opera star!) Under the striped awnings by the little round tables, men pay a few sous to learn of the untimely death of one who was beloved by the French public. The setting sun is raying through the closed shutters of the windows, closed against the turbulence in the Avenue of the Bois de Boulogne below. She lies in final peace on a luxurious Louis XV bed. The glow of a small grate fire reflects on the smooth surface of the soft blue striped satin wallpaper; it reflects the exquisite features of one whose talent, beauty, and charm have been the acclaim of Paris. Only the soft step of her maid breaks the silence of the room—her fiancé Count Tolstoi, kneeling in prayer beside her bed, has not moved. Over the bed are strewn his beautiful appointments, masses of American Beauty roses, symbols of her homeland.

I must prepare for the few favored to attend the last rites. Newspaper men are repeatedly begging for admittance at the door. Messages are pouring in from all over the world—messengers are coming and going, a thousand and one details—and then, a page out of the past. The doorbell rings again, and a tall, distinguished man in flowing cape and sombrero begs audience. I agree and receive Count de Fitz-James, some time since gone from these familiar surroundings. He looks about, terribly moved. He tells me he has come to say farewell and asks that she be given a private mass of the Catholic religion, her adopted faith. I agree—Count Tolstoi does also.

Soon the door opens to clouds of incense. Two altar boys lead a small, silent procession—priests in colored stoles, sisters of charity in their long black robes. As they enter Count Tolstoi rises from his place of prayer and, crossing himself, acknowledges the procession—the last rites for one who has been the center of dramatic action in life—close now to her bed—the final prayer. In silence the procession withdraws, leaving behind the closest few. Then suddenly the two counts, both contenders for her hand, arise and clasp hands in mutual sorrow and understanding over the bed where lies the woman they loved. Thus is the curtain lowered on a life which has been so full of joy, sorrow, drama, success, love, and generosity.

—From the diary of Marion Sanderson

The Sibyl Sanderson Story

Requiem for a Diva

Chapter 1

The Silver Spoon

The day was 15 April 1865—a catastrophic one in American history. President Lincoln, so recently elected to his second term, had been fatally shot the night before while attending a play in Washington, D.C. Rumors of a conspiracy were already searing the newspapers. The president's assassination was received with shock and alarm throughout the North. Everyone from congressmen to small-town ministers was eulogizing the fallen leader. Fears of anarchy and reprisal gripped many parts of the country, particularly the border states of the recently war-torn nation.

In faraway California, the legislature was convening in Sacramento to hear a speech by the chief justice of the state supreme court, Silas Woodruff Sanderson. The deliberate, unhurried gait of the stocky jurist and his slight limp were a familiar sight around Sacramento's Capitol Park. This morning he left his home across the park a little later than usual. Having been asked to deliver a short eulogy for the late president, he had taken time to draft some hasty notes before his departure.

When Sanderson arrived at the capitol building, he found the assembly in turmoil. Secretary of State William H. Seward had been wounded by the conspirators—no one knew how seriously—and Vice President Andrew Johnson had narrowly escaped death. Soon, however, Sanderson's forceful oratory reassured the worried senators, and his eulogy was promptly printed in the leading California papers. He had done much to steady emotions and cool tempers during this crisis.

Even in California, Silas Sanderson remained the quintessence of rock-ribbed New England. Born in Sandgate, Vermont, on 16 April 1824, the son of lawyer and assemblyman John Sanderson, he attended Burr Seminary and Williams

College, where he ranked among the foremost scholars of his class. The youngest in a family of four boys, he had been forced to shun athletic activity in his youth because a fall while skating left him permanently lame. In 1846 he graduated from Union College in New York State and was soon admitted to the bar.

Rather than practice in the North, however, he moved to Florida, where he became an apprentice to his older brother John, an attorney in Jacksonville. The Sandersons practiced together for two years before news of the 1848 gold strike promised to turn California into the Elysian Fields. Realizing the opportunities for legal practice in such a state, Sanderson emigrated to the West Coast in the fall of 1850 via the Strait of Magellan. He arrived the following spring and went immediately to Coloma,[1] the scene of the first big strike.

From then on his ascent was meteoric. He was elected district attorney of El Dorado County, and his prosecution of brigands who preyed upon travelers to the Washoe Mines finally made that area safe for everyone. He became a member of the Breckenridge Convention of California in 1861, where a few fellow Democrats hoped he could stay the secessionist proclivities of their party. As a member of the committee on platforms and resolutions, he found himself single-handedly fighting against the right of secession. Frustrated and angry, he bolted the party, and at the next election threw his support to Leland Stanford, the Republican candidate for governor.

Serious, introspective, and of a thoroughly investigative nature, Sanderson fell headlong in love upon his first meeting with a young local belle. Her name was Margaret Beatty Ormsby, and he was introduced to her at Charles Crocker's dry goods store in Marysville. As she concluded her purchases of dress material and swept out the door, he turned to the friend who had introduced them and confided that within a week he would propose to this lovely creature of the honey-blond curls and heavy-lidded blue eyes.

Margaret's parents, Dr. and Mrs. John Ormsby, had come from Pennsylvania in 1850, crossing the plains by covered wagon. She and her brother Oliver were old enough to recall the ferocious winter their wagon train had endured, the disease and starvation, the savage Indian attacks, and the death of a baby sister, whom her parents buried on the plains. When the Ormsbys arrived in California, peace still eluded them for a while. After being routed by floods from their first home in Marysville, they moved to Sacramento, only to cope with the disastrous fires that periodically ravaged the town. Finally they settled in Healdsburg. By this time, another daughter, Mary, had been added to the family.

Margaret was only seventeen, but she was astute enough to realize this square-jawed attorney from Placerville would go far. That he was exactly twice her age posed no barriers; his courtship represented the flowering of his maturity. Nor did she mind that he wasn't among the most romantic swains who pursued her. His other attributes erased this questionable shortcoming. Thoroughness, sincerity of purpose, and honesty were apparent in every action. So was another trait she admired: ambition. At the end of the week, when he proposed, she unhesitatingly accepted.

His love letters to "my dear Maggie"—now yellowed by the passage of more than a century—discussed their impending union as soberly as a legal treatise, but she preserved them all in a little box until the end of her life in Paris. One month before their marriage in Healdsburg on 5 March 1858, he wrote that he was "busy whitewashing and fitting up the mansion"for them. The letter, however, closed with a typical example of his wry humor: "The farther I get from you the more I love you, but I beg you not to wish me in China merely for the purpose of increasing my love for you."

They began their new life together in the little Placerville frame house that he affectionately called a "mansion." But it soon became apparent that Placerville was too small to hold this ambitious pair for long. Margaret, whose warmth and charm won friends everywhere, was equally aspiring for her brilliant husband. Sanderson's colleagues had urged him to run for state legislature in 1862, and they took advantage of his shift to the Republican Party to get him elected. During his brief membership in the assembly he burst into national prominence as the originator of the Specific Contract Act, which authorized gold as legal tender in California to combat the inflationary spread of paper money. The unqualified success of this law set Sanderson's reputation soaring. It was undeniably responsible for his election to the California supreme court a year later. As was expected, the Sandersons lost no time in moving to Sacramento.

The new crop of judges drew their terms by lot, and Sanderson, drawing the shortest time of two years, became chief justice of the court for the period of 1864 to 1866. Although he was the youngest of the magistrates, Sanderson had now risen to the very zenith of power.

He had arrived at the bench during an era when California was still in a formative stage. There were entanglements with Spanish and Mexican land titles, a tendency to avoid strict enforcement of the law, and general social disorder. Sanderson proved to be a man of integrity and impartiality whose decisions commanded the respect of the citizens and of the immigrant horde that was pushing into California. By nature he was bold and aggressive, and it was only natural that he would press his views at times with a belligerence that bordered on the tyrannical. Joseph P. Crocket, one of his associates on the bench, wrote that he would "rip and snort around the consultation room, when he got his dander up."[2]

A single opinion unexpectedly catapulted him into the national limelight of American jurisprudence—his historic decision in the case of *People v. Sanchez,* in which he clearly defined murder in the first and second degree for the first time in America. When he traveled to Washington, D.C., over the coming decade to appear before the Supreme Court, it would be no surprise for Sanderson to hear a justice quote one of his own verdicts.

Since coming to Sacramento, the Sandersons had purchased a handsome three-story brick house at the corner of 727 Ninth and H streets. Margaret had her mansion at last. Their immediate neighbors were Governor and Mrs. Leland Stanford, Mrs. Redington and her two sons, and Mrs. Carroll and her daughters. A close relationship grew among the families of the four corners, and their various members reappeared from time to time in the lives of the Sandersons both in America and abroad.

During their first years in the state capital, Margaret's pregnancies kept her confined a good deal of the time. Sibyl Swift was the first to arrive, on 7 December 1864. The judge proudly entered her name in the large Sanderson Bible where births had been registered in New England for over a century. Less than two years later, on 13 June 1866, Jane Stanford was born.

Sibyl and Jane (to be affectionately called "Jennie") were baptized in a joint ceremony duly reported in the 1866 society columns of the Sacramento newspapers. The Reverend Mr. Hall performed the ceremony, using water that had been brought from the river Jordan, no less, by Sibyl's godparents Mr. and Mrs. John Swift (Swift was later to become American ambassador to Japan). Jane's godparents were Governor and Mrs. Stanford.

On 19 July 1868 Marion Woodruff was added to the family, and on 13 December 1870 the birth of Edith Lawrence completed the quartet of Sanderson girls. By this time, Margaret had given up all hopes for a boy.

At the expiration of his tenure in January 1866, Judge Sanderson was reelected to the supreme court as associate judge for the full term of ten years, but circumstances were soon to intervene.

The coming of the railroad drastically changed California's history and concomitantly the fortunes of the Sanderson family. Thomas Hill's famous painting *The Driving of the Golden Spike,* copied from photographs taken on 10 May 1869, commemorated the final linking of east and west at Promontory Point,

Utah. In the painting, Associate Justice Sanderson stands close to his good friend former governor Stanford, now president of the Central and Southern Pacific Railroad Company. Stanford, who had worked so tirelessly to help the young nation realize this transcontinental dream, was given the honor of delivering the first blow at the spike. The railroad terminated in Oakland, just across the bay from San Francisco, and in terms of safety, speed, and comfort, it had rendered the wagon train obsolete. Although Sacramento still remained the state capital, it was no longer the seat of power. The millionaire locomotive kings—the Crockers, the Huntingtons, the Stanfords—were abandoning the town to erect gilded palaces on top of the steep San Francisco hills.

Margaret had long dreamed of living in San Francisco, and to her it seemed as if all their friends were deserting them for the Bay City. She constantly lamented that provincial Sacramento was no place to educate their growing family. When a lucrative offer arrived from the Big Four—Huntington, Stanford, Crocker, and Hopkins—for Silas Sanderson to become chief legal advisor to their Central and Southern Pacific Railroad Company, Mrs. Sanderson multiplied her arguments. Even though her husband held a distinguished position in the state legal system, she argued that his annual stipend was not adequate to provide the proper social and educational advantages for their daughters. The four most powerful men in the state had offered him a salary of $25,000 a year. This was a chance of a lifetime!

For himself, Judge Sanderson would have been perfectly content with Sacramento and his esteemed position on the bench, but he respected his wife's ambition for their children's future. He knew the railroad monarchs well. This notorious quartet had been running California's government for a decade. Governor Stanford had unashamedly used his public office to browbeat the legislature into diverting $850,000 of public funds into his own, all for the good of the state, he rationalized. Now the West Coast colossi were requesting Sanderson's legal expertise to protect the precious company that had made them so rich. It would be the most important decision of his career, but this was one time he had to think of his family first.

Reluctantly the judge accepted the offer the first week of January 1870. His resignation from the bench, after serving less than half of his ten-year term, created a whirlwind of controversy. His political enemies accused him of selling out to big business, and Sanderson would have been the last to deny it. On 5 January 1870, in the midst of the uproar, the editor of the *Sacramento Daily Record-Union* summarized his resignation in a more philosophical vein. "While the Supreme Court will sustain a serious loss by the withdrawal of one of the ablest jurists in the state, Mr. Sanderson will secure a position more lucrative, if not more honorable."

Margaret felt the heady flush of triumph. A year later the family sold their house and moved to the South Park area of San Francisco, although they did not remain there long. They soon moved to a larger dwelling at the corner of Van Ness and Bush streets where the mansions stood four stories high behind a graceful row of eucalyptus trees.

Like many California women of pioneer stock, Margaret could adapt to whatever circumstances the family faced. These women could cope with poverty, drudgery, even danger, if they must, but given wealth, they promptly expanded like peacocks in the sun. They had been reared on family legends told by mothers homesick for the East or on their own memories of beautiful clothes and elegantly appointed homes. When these pioneer girls grew to maturity and married men who prospered, they sought to re-create the genteel atmosphere of the East in their new homes. They ransacked Europe for antique treasures, and their obsession with owning the best of everything in the finest Victorian fashion often turned into unbridled greed. Margaret Sanderson was a woman of sensitive taste who would acquire her possessions with discrimination.

She enrolled Sibyl and Jennie in various private schools in San Francisco for a while and supplemented their education with a battery of private tutors and governesses at home. A Miss Morse taught the girls music—a subject for which only Sibyl showed any aptitude. As far back as her parents could remember she loved to sing. When only a tiny girl in Sacramento she used to cover her father's legal cap with mysterious scrawls, which she gravely assured him were original compositions. As a first-grader in school she would oblige the teacher by climbing on a chair to sing for visitors. By the age of ten she felt that she was destined for a musical career.

Margaret engaged an Italian professor for drawing lessons. He taught the girls how to sketch still lifes in charcoal, using grubby little pellets of bread for erasing. A surprisingly good sketch of a small statue entitled "The Boy and the Thorn" proved to be Marion's masterpiece, and both her parents and teacher decided that she was the only one in the family with any talent in this medium.

The four Sanderson girls enjoyed an idyllic childhood. They loved to rollerskate on the sidewalks and to walk on perilously high stilts. The three younger ones often played store, selling pinwheels made out of stolen covers to Sibyl's music. Schuyler Cole, son of their neighbor Senator Cornelius Cole, would whittle the sticks for them, and they would barter their creations to other children for pins, which in turn they would sell to their mother. When the first bicycle arrived in their neighborhood—one huge wheel with a tiny one behind—the girls rode it excitedly with many a fall.

In the summer the judge would rent a beautiful estate down the peninsula in Menlo Park. It blazed with acres of yellow poppies and a burgeoning orchard on the grounds brimmed with apricot, pear, and fig trees. When the girls weren't lost in the golden glow of the poppy fields, they would be playing base tag with the Mills brothers, who lived on the neighboring estate.

In the summer the Sandersons often went to Santa Cruz, which at that time boasted the finest bathing beaches in northern California. Sibyl and her sisters adored frolicking in the ocean and collected unusual pebbles or moss agates in the sand. Then there were drives through the steep ravines of the redwood forest in a coach and four with Mr. Goodman, the splendid driver, cracking his whip as he careened around perilous curves on the mountainsides or drove right through manmade arches in the giant redwood trees. Impressed by the hush and majesty of this primeval forest, the family would often stop to picnic, grilling steaks and, as related in Marion's memoirs, "marveling how the aroma of freshly brewed coffee could blend so mysteriously with all the forest odors." The girls also looked forward to visiting California's Petrified Forest and thrilled to its haunting silences and ghostly shapes. They would gather bits of glistening bark that had turned to stone millennia ago, imagining that once upon a time this had been a pagan garden for exiled gods.

Sibyl was a vivacious child blessed with a sparkling personality and talents for forming fast friendships and for not telling tales. For a while she was enrolled at Miss Denman's school and Miss Foster's cottage, where she was always ready to help her classmates when they got into trouble. She was not a particularly bright scholar, and it was always easier for her to share a lunch with such friends as Ruth Holladay or Jennie Hooker than to help them with a difficult example in long division.

Sibyl's special weakness was the candy store opposite Miss Foster's school, and she treated the other girls to cakes and candy nearly every day. A classmate later recalled that she would manage to get permission to go to the candy store even if the rest of the class was in disgrace. Her special favorites were the "red hots"—spicy little candies filled with cinnamon and cayenne pepper—and she would bring back a bag full of these or chocolates.

There was never anything shy about the oldest Sanderson girl. Sibyl even got herself expelled from a boarding school in the East because she was caught jumping over a fence one day to meet a boy. In contrast, her sisters were extraordinarily timid. Their parents had instilled in them the proper Victorian belief that children should be seen and not heard. At the dinner table, when not eating, they would sit with their hands primly folded. A family friend was so amused by Mrs. Sanderson's three little models of behavior that she once inquired whether they were drugged. The girls all possessed Dresden-china features enhanced by golden hair and eyes that were varying shades of blue-gray. If any of them could have been classified as an ugly duckling at this period, strange to say, it would have been Sibyl. Although her cheeks were tinted with a rosy blush, she was inclined to be painfully stout. The only characteristic that might have heralded her later physical transformation was the graceful arch of two dark eyebrows in marked contrast to her blond hair.

San Francisco continued to mushroom as the result of the railroad. Elegant department stores such as the House of Shreve and Gump's sprang into existence. Margaret's sterling flatware and rococo tea set were from Shreve and hammered from the famous Comstock Lode, and the girls each had monogrammed sterling tea sets as well. The oriental carpets that Mrs. Sanderson chose were often piled three to four deep on the floor, as rug pads were unknown at this time. The china for her dinner table—Spode, Sèvres, and Royal Crown Derby—came from either the White House or the City of Paris, two of San Francisco's most exclusive stores. Like other fashionable West Coast hostesses, she never bought one set at a time, always two or three, with serving pieces and place settings for at least twelve. There were dozens of everything: embroidered linens and rare laces, gold and silver frames for family photographs, and small boxes and bibelots of precious metals scattered throughout the house. The password for the successful society queen, as Margaret learned, was extravagance.

Among the girls' greatest pleasures was sharing part of the journey when their father traveled across the continent in his private railroad car on his trips to Washington, D.C., to argue railroad taxation cases for the Central Pacific Company. His car was always at the end of the train. There was a drawing room with seats made into beds for the children, a bedroom for their father and mother, a dining room, and a tiny kitchen. After being tucked into bed, whenever they heard the train stopping at a water tank, the girls would raise the window shades to peep at the Indians with their long hair hanging under slouch hats and blankets wound around their bodies. The next morning they would awaken to the delectable aroma of hot cakes, which the black chef was making in the kitchen. It was always a treat for Sibyl and her sisters to take turns riding in the engine beside the engineer. Upon arrival in Omaha or Chicago, they were put on a westbound train, and the judge would continue on his journey to Washington, D.C., with his secretary, Fred Lake.

In 1876, when Sibyl was not quite twelve, her mother joined a party of San Francisco women eager to visit Europe. It had now become the rage for affluent American matrons to descend upon the Continent and, as Edith Wharton observed, "pursue Culture in bands, as though it were dangerous to meet alone."[3] Margaret's group included her former Sacramento neighbor Mrs. Redington, who drafted her teenage son Henry as their sole male escort.

It was the first time Margaret had ever been away from her family, and the departure was a momentous occasion. Her mother, Mrs. Ormsby, had arrived from Healdsburg to take charge of the household. She was a kindly old lady, with her white hair parted in the middle and drawn back severely over her ears. Mrs. Ormsby was proud of her handsomely corseted figure, and she wore tight-fitting black cashmere dresses with a row of tiny jet buttons down the front. A black onyx brooch was always pinned at her neck with an accompanying spray of lilies of the valley. The girls would beg her to tell them tales of her exciting 1850 pilgrimage across the Oregon Trail. On Sundays, after attending services at a local Presbyterian church, she would stay in her room for the rest of the day reading the Bible. This always amused the judge, who remained an agnostic all his life.

He wrote his wife that her mother was not being overworked, a most unlikely possibility in a house teeming with servants, and that he had fixed up a room in the basement with desks and blackboards for the children. A Miss Hooker had been engaged as their governess. She proved to be a strict disciplinarian. If her charges did not learn their lessons, they were placed in a corner with a dunce cap on their heads. The girls despised everything about her, from her regimental approach in the classroom to the way she braided their hair. Periodically the judge would descend the basement stairs to look over his daughters' lessons and admonish them for not studying harder. Although he was always bitterly disappointed in their scholastic achievements, it probably never occurred to him that the family decision to opt for private tutors might have been at least partly responsible. Only Sibyl and Jane had ever been sent to private schools. Marion and Edith were completely cloistered at home, and the judge, who was so eager to obtain the best education possible for his offspring, never realized that for lack of competition from their peers, the girls remained poorly motivated students. Edith proved to have the most inquisitive mind in the family, and as soon as she was old enough could always be found in her father's library.

Mrs. Sanderson and her party traveled with a guide, and the girls treasured the postcards that came from various European cities. When his wife returned to America in early 1877, the judge took his private car to New York and met her at the docks. If he thought she had departed with an ample amount of luggage, he was overwhelmed by the number of trunks with which she returned. Margaret had spent her husband's entire $5,000 letter of credit. She and her companions had brought back gifts, jewels, perfumes, and brand-new wardrobes designed by Charles F. Worth, a foremost French couturier.

It was often said in old California that when San Francisco women died their souls went to Paris instead of heaven. Margaret Sanderson was a perfect example. Now she began planning for her girls to finish their education in the French capital some day, imagining that they might even find titled European husbands. A French governess was quietly installed in the Sanderson home, and all conversations at the dinner table were henceforth conducted in French. Margaret was determined to study the language alongside her daughters. The situation could not have been a pleasant one for her husband; he didn't understand a word that was spoken. But he acquiesced to his wife's wishes and even fined the girls a quarter from their allowances if they reverted to English. Ever since leaving Sacramento, the judge had maintained a lenient rule for his household. Whatever "Maggie" decided was automatically right.

Neither did he make any formal objection when his wife inveigled him into purchasing a large, rambling residence at the corner of Octavia and Sacramento streets, actually a double house with a tower, spacious grounds, a garden, and a stable in the rear. The tower, painted light blue with stars on its ceiling, became Marion's studio, where she would spend hours painting and laboriously copying old engravings. Margaret ordered black satin chairs studded with yellow satin buttons and finished with a black-and-gold cord fringe. She also bought cherry satin chairs to match her cherry satin drapes. The living room boasted a boldly designed floral carpet, an impressive crystal chandelier, and an upright Steinway piano. Over a sofa in the parlor hung an enormous oil painting of a sunset.

Judge Sanderson enlarged the house by adding an ample dining room, whose walls he paneled in redwood. The windows contained alternate panels of beveled amber and clear glass. Huge Gothic chairs were upholstered in embossed leather, and at the far end of the room stood a large fireplace with a stained-glass window over it, inlaid with the figure of an armored knight wearing a plumed helmet. Low bench seats were found on either side of the fireplace, flanked by two doors leading to the conservatory.

The household was run exclusively with Chinese help, including an aristocratically dressed butler in fez and green or blue brocade blouse over pantaloons. The cook had a foul disposition and would hurl anything within reach at the judge's little angels if he caught them dipping into his raisin jar. Margaret communicated with the kitchen help through a Victorian intercom known as an ear trumpet. This device consisted of a tube through which she would first blow to attract the servants' attention by a sort of whistling sound. At the other end in the kitchen was a receiver for listening. After obtaining his instructions, the cook would go to the back door and bargain with Chinese merchants whose baskets of vegetables hung from long poles that they carried on their shoulders.

Nothing delighted the girls more than a trip to Chinatown with their butler. They would peep into the lurid dens where opium addicts lay in bunks smoking their long pipes. After several hours of sightseeing, they would return home laden with silk fans, sweetmeats, exotic teas, and lichee nuts.

Chinese servants, willing to work more cheaply than the Irish after the railroad was finished, were extremely popular in San Francisco during the last quarter of the nineteenth century. The perceived injustice of this situation aroused the ire of an agitator named Dennis Kearney, who threatened to burn down every home that employed Chinese help. For a while San Francisco was gripped in a reign of terror, as Kearney and his thugs were determined to drive the Chinese out of the city. A white cross would be chalked on the door of every house that was slated to be burned. Each morning the Sanderson girls would rush downstairs to their front porch to see if it had been marked. Miraculously the house remained untouched, and Kearney was eventually arrested.

Judge Sanderson could usually be found in the billiard room after he came home from the office, often instructing his daughters in the game because he considered it a necessary accomplishment for young ladies. He also insisted that they become proficient riders. He had them fitted out in tight black satin riding habits and would order Charles, the coachman, to take them to the park for instruction.

Following her husband's death, Mrs. Ormsby was now living permanently with the family, but there is no record of her clashing with the judge over his atheist beliefs. The girls attended Sunday school at a local Episcopal church, not because their parents insisted upon it, but because all their peers did likewise.

Mrs. Sanderson rapidly assumed her position as a leading hostess in San Francisco, holding afternoons at home and musical soirees. Since Sibyl was diligently pursuing her piano studies during this period, she either performed at the Steinway upright or sang for the guests. More and more she was allowed to stay up past the other girls' bedtime and help her mother entertain. By now she had lost her baby fat and was fast turning into a ravishing young lady. From the long lashes of her enormous star-sapphire eyes to the top of her forehead she resembled Mrs. Sanderson strongly, but more and more she was developing her father's firm, square jaw. Little by little, her freckles were fading, and the golden glint of her hair had darkened to a rich chestnut.

On New Year's Day she was allowed to help her mother receive callers, a charming Victorian custom whereby young men called upon women in groups to extend the season's greetings. For this occasion the gentlemen invariably donned cutaways and top hats. They would partake of the eggnog and fruitcake served by teenage girls who assisted the hostess. Then they would graciously take their leave and go to the next house to repeat the ritual. As the eggnog had been liberally laced with liquor, the city's gallants were in uproariously high spirits at the end of the day and sometimes too inebriated to get home without assistance.

By the time she was approaching her sixteenth year, Sibyl was among the most popular girls in San Francisco. She was in demand to sing at various functions, and she made afternoon calls with her mother on Tuesdays and Thursdays. The carriage, lined in royal-blue satin and studded with buttons, would be at the front door promptly at 2 P.M. with a pair of sleekly groomed horses, and Charles, the mustachioed coachman, waiting in his best livery.

During 1879, 1880, and 1881, San Francisco's society columns fairly hummed with the social activities of Judge Sanderson's oldest daughter. Sibyl was seen in theater boxes, in the opera house, at this ball and that cotillion. Her gowns and diamond accessories were duly reported. She was visiting friends in Santa Cruz or "weekending" down the peninsula. Already a flirtatious smile or glance threw more than one male heart into turmoil. The city dowagers were prophesying an early marriage for her and perhaps a European title as well.

Few girls had received such heady attention at so early an age. So far it did not seem to mar two of her most appealing assets, her frank sincerity and engaging personality. Truly the gods had smiled upon her. She appeared to have been given everything: beauty, wealth, charm, social prestige, kindness, and, above all, a golden untrained voice.

With San Francisco already succumbing to her attractions, what more could she want? Strange to say, there was a good deal more. Ever since her mother's trip abroad, Paris had begun to occupy an increasingly important position in her daydreams and fantasies.

On their trips across the country in the judge's private railroad car, father and daughter talked as they had never done before and never would again. Sibyl confided her secret dreams: "I want to go on the operatic stage when I grow up, and to do this I must begin studying voice soon in Paris."

The judge maintained that she had been reared for a very different kind of life. The stage was fraught with perils, and she had no idea of the insecurity to which a career before the footlights would expose her. He would be unable to protect her in this alien territory. In the hothouse environment of the pampered rich, she had been sheltered from life's evils. But Sibyl remained adamant. She rejected the idea of marrying a dull scion of San Francisco's millionaire set and presiding over boring receptions and charity bazaars for the rest of her life. She argued that she had known she was destined for the stage since she was a little girl. She would become a great singer some day and nothing would dissuade her.

As they spoke, her father raised a trembling hand over his graying beard. Marion Sanderson's memoirs reveal that he also raised his voice, and its sonorous tones echoed through the Pullman car. There would be no more talk about the stage. She would return to San Francisco, take her rightful place in its society, and eventually make her debut. Perhaps she would have a future season in Paris to finish her education, but it would be in the field of general humanities only. For the moment nothing more was said. Sibyl felt as though Moses had descended from the Mount and hurled the sacred tablets at her feet.

As for the judge, he had glimpsed something he hoped never to find among his offspring—the determination to live a life of one's own. Perhaps this was just a passing fancy. After all, his high-spirited daughter had changed her beaux as fast as her perfumes. "Constancy," he would later write to his wife, "is not a strong point in Sibyl's character."[4] From that hour on, though, he feared for her: the longest case he was ever to plead would be Sanderson versus Sanderson.

Chapter 2

Hearst and the Violet Rainbows

It was inevitable that the future queen of the French stage should meet the coming Napoleon of journalism. Their tragedy was that they met too soon.

William Randolph Hearst told his official biographer, Mrs. Fremont Older, that he was introduced to Sibyl Sanderson at the Hotel Del Monte in Monterey after he arrived home from Saint Paul's prep school in New Hampshire in 1881. They could have had a slight acquaintance as children, but the boy spent most of his time in private schools in the East or on his father's 45,000-acre ranch down the coast at San Simeon. When they encountered each other in their late teens, it seemed to them as if they had never met before.

Young Will had returned to his home turf in January, yet approximately four months went by before their meeting in Monterey. Their parents certainly rubbed shoulders in the interim, dancing together at Hattie Crocker's February party where Sibyl was surrounded by a bevy of beaux, but there is no mention of young Hearst in attendance.

Will was already dropping in on the weekend "hops" at the Hotel Del Monte as early as March of that year. His parents invited all his friends to a birthday party for him on 29 April. He had just turned eighteen, a slender, awkward six-footer with a shock of sandy hair and intensely probing steel-gray eyes. His voice had not changed completely and on occasion would omit embarrassing boy-soprano squawks. He loathed the regimentation of the prep schools and was delighted to be finished with them, home and free to make his own choices in life for the first time, or so he thought.

Boarding the *Daisy* for the train trip to bucolic Monterey on Friday night was a popular pursuit for the San Francisco social elite. Mrs. Sanderson, accompanied by daughters Sibyl and Jennie, descended upon the Monterey

15

hotel the last week in May with the intention of staying for a few weeks. As it turned out, the future lord of the tabloids was spending some time there also, ostensibly to relax and prepare for his Harvard entrance exams later in the year.

The Hotel Del Monte was the weekend playground for the wealthy and the most luxurious place of its kind on the West Coast. Built a year before by the railroad kings as the "Newport of the West," it was an enormous edifice set in the pine woods not far from the beach. Its grounds covered 126 acres of unparalleled beauty with vistas of mountains, forests, bays, rivers, and ocean. Guests relaxed on the veranda, strolled in the gardens, and walked or rode along the pine-forested paths. There were croquet and tennis, card games, gossiping on the terrace, and the endless ritual of changing one's clothes. In the evening, dancing in the ballroom was a popular pastime, and elaborate Victorian gowns designed by Parisian couturiers whirled about the floor.

Sibyl had no idle moments. She was surrounded by the young men of her set, with whom she rode, danced, and flirted vivaciously. Henry Redington, an old family friend from Sacramento, escorted the Sandersons that last weekend in May. It was either then or the following weekend that Will and Sibyl became aware of each other's existence.

The hotel was preparing to celebrate its first anniversary, and San Francisco's beautiful people had turned out to make it a gala occasion. When the musicians in Ballenberg's orchestra took a break, the management announced some impromptu entertainment: Judge Sanderson's daughter had agreed to sing a few numbers. The sixteen-year-old paragon walked to the piano perfectly aware that her small but voluptuously formed figure was considered a work of art. She sang with an infectious self-confidence born of the bravado that cloaks an amateur's insecurities.

Whatever else she may have warbled that night, it was "Il bacio" (The Kiss) that short-circuited the heart of young Hearst. He wasn't the only electrified male present. The gilded youth of San Francisco present that night cheered her wildly. The ardent Hearst had no trouble pursuing an introduction, but when he gazed into the eyes of this extraordinary girl, he was bewitched. Were those huge, luminous orbs gray or blue? If the light struck them at a certain angle, an arc of soft violet mists seemed to span their azure surfaces.

For the rest of the evening Will danced every number with Sibyl. The next week they saw each other constantly except for the time he spent trying to study for his Harvard exams with Harold Wheeler. Even when he practiced his tennis with Dick Hammond and Jerome Lincoln, Sibyl sat under an umbrella on the sidelines watching him. The enamored youth found it impossible to concentrate on either activity.

They boated, swam, and rode together. They took a carriage drive to the nearby crumbling Mission of San Carlos in Carmel. They walked hand in hand through the cobblestoned streets of old Monterey, in the 1880s still a slumbering little red-tiled adobe town steeped in the legacy of the Spanish families that founded California in the colonial era. They followed in the footsteps of Robert Louis Stevenson, who had once lived there. Arm in arm, they thrilled to a blazing sunset under a wind-gnarled cypress that defiantly clung to the rocks of the Monterey peninsula.

Within a week or two they were hopelessly in love. Sibyl had known infatuations before, but Will was badly smitten. Under the moonlit Monterey pines, he asked Sibyl to marry him; forgetting all her future plans for Paris, she accepted.[1]

Young Hearst was a matrimonial prize. His father's wealth was legendary. George Hearst had made millions from his famous mines: Ophir, Homestake, Ontario, and Anaconda. He had already bought his first newspaper, the *San Francisco Examiner;* later he would become a United States senator. It was said that when George Hearst spoke a few complimentary phrases to anyone, the person addressed felt as if he were participating in history.

Like Silas Sanderson, the elder Hearst had arrived in California in 1850, but by wagon train rather than by sea. In 1862 he returned to his native Missouri to marry Phoebe Apperson, a schoolteacher. Eschewing the dangers of the Wild West, they took a boat to Panama, crossed the Isthmus, and then boarded another steamer for San Francisco. The honeymoon trip took about a year, and Mrs. Hearst suffered through a trying pregnancy. In 1863 she gave birth to twins, Will being the only survivor. It had been a difficult labor, and the Hearsts decided not to risk having more children.

Mrs. Hearst now lavished her attention and affection on her only offspring. She was one of the reigning beauties in San Francisco society, but as young Will grew older he bore little resemblance to her. She taught him the correct Victorian precepts: honor and obey one's parents, love one's country, fulfill one's obligations and duties, and respect the powers that be. Since her laconic husband cared little for the superficial refinements of their social position, Phoebe Hearst found her teenage son a handsome substitute. He was mother's ideal equerry. He escorted her to parties and balls that bored his father. He danced with her regularly at the Hotel Del Monte, and more than one newspaper columnist gushed about the stunning couple they made. He was always at mother's side, ready to assist her as a dutiful son when she threw her own lavish balls. He had idolized her above all other women until now.

In some ways Will and Sibyl were much alike. His fun-loving and impetuous nature appealed to her own high spirits. Both possessed ardent romantic temperaments, neither being inclined toward scholarly pursuit. But Sibyl discovered that this complex young man was extraordinarily sensitive to nature and beauty. Everywhere they went, Will would stop to pick her favorite flowers—violets. Nightly she wore them as a corsage. He genuinely thrilled to her soprano voice. He adored animals, and he was a collector, forever picking up odd and fascinating seashells, agates, and abalones when they strolled along the beach. He would discover bits of exotic seaweed abandoned by the tide that he asked Sibyl to press for him. Every rainbow-colored starfish they found seemed to embody the magic of the time they shared together.

They also had in common a passionate love for the theater. Will was a born mimic. He had seen all the great stars of the era and could give clever imitations of them. He enjoyed putting on minstrel shows with friends in a small theater constructed in the coach house behind his Van Ness home. Will introduced Sibyl to these affairs as soon as they returned to the city. Later he continued the amateur performances after his parents moved to Taylor Street.

San Francisco's reigning black minstrel at the time was Billy Emerson, known as "Big Sunflower" because he was never without one in his lapel. Will took Sibyl to the Bush Street Theater to hear him, and she was captivated by his rendition of "Are You There, Moriaritee?" After they left the theater, young Hearst amazed her by imitating Emerson's singing down to the exact inflections of his dialect. She was convinced he should go on the stage.

Unfortunately, reality was already intruding upon their private covenant. The lovers had excitedly told their parents of their betrothal, and both families received the news with frosty reservations. The Sandersons would have been thrilled to have Will as a son-in-law, but marriage would interfere with plans for Sibyl's education. Margaret intended to take her to Paris later in the fall, and the girl had announced proudly that she would enter the Conservatoire even though her father had no such intentions for her. What would Will do if they were married before she left? Neither Judge Sanderson nor his wife wanted him to sacrifice his future education at Harvard just to marry their daughter.

As for Phoebe Apperson Hearst, she became nearly hysterical. She had rushed back to the Del Monte by the third week in June to keep an eye on her son's amorous proclivities. She adored the Sanderson family, particularly

Jennie, but she could not tolerate the thought of any sixteen-year-old rival stealing her darling Billy. Besides, the girl had a rather "fast" reputation for her age. Sibyl told daring stories with a naiveté that would have excommunicated her from every San Francisco drawing room had it not been for her parents' social position.

Will was too young to consider marriage—particularly to someone who wanted to go on the stage. In its classification of the various sins, Victorian society looked upon acting as one of the most degrading. Venereal disease was a private family tragedy; having a daughter-in-law flaunt herself before the footlights was a public one. Yes, any marriage now would ruin their plans for his brilliant future. George must be persuaded to do something—anything—to rescue their precious Billy from the clutches of this shameless young siren.

When the youngsters felt the full impact of their parents' opposition, painful scenes occurred in the Octavia and Van Ness households. The lovers were obdurate. If they did not receive their parental blessings, they would elope to Europe and perhaps go on the stage together. To hell with Harvard. Ironically, Hearst was never to graduate from that institution.

Hearst did not tell Mrs. Fremont Older that his parents were united against his engagement to Sibyl. His authorized biography left the stage-struck girl preferring vocal study in Europe to matrimony, and no biographer since has ever questioned this misrepresentation.[2] For the rest of Hearst's life he suppressed the facts about his father's next actions. According to both Margaret Sanderson Nall and Hearst's longtime inamorata Marion Davies in personal interviews, George Hearst visited Silas Woodruff Sanderson at his office and displayed a copy of his new will. In the event of an elopement, he had cut his son off except for a tiny income to keep the pair on bread and water.

The barrister was in complete accord with Mr. Hearst. Marriage was out of the question at this time for both offspring. There would be no elopement, Judge Sanderson assured the publisher, even if he had to lock Sibyl in her room. He and his wife planned to whisk their daughter off to Europe immediately, before news of the betrothal leaked out in the press. On 10 July the society columnist of the *Examiner* titillated the Nob Hill set by hinting that the couple's engagement would be announced shortly:

> One of our first young society ladies is about to become engaged to a wealthy young man she first met here [at the Del Monte], are you not aware that there is only one young lady of society of that description? . . . Suffice it to say that the story has leaked out and is known to many.

The two mothers were never more cordial to each other than during the Fourth of July festivities at the Del Monte, Mrs. Hearst in a cream-colored gown with panniers of rich Belgian lace and the judge's wife in a blue silk gown also trimmed with lace. Sibyl, who, according to the *Examiner,* wore "a short costume of white bunting," had been joined by her friend Ruth Holladay for the weekend.

The hotel was deserted that morning, for everyone had gone swimming in the surf until noon. After lunchtime, a crowd of several thousand people gathered along the Monterey road to watch a military parade. Two platoons of soldiers had arrived from San Francisco by train to march from the hotel into Monterey and back. Spanish grandmothers, with black-fringed shawls draped around their shoulders, ensconced themselves on the hotel grounds with their families to watch the procession. Local equestrians galloped back and forth along the road on their handsome chargers. At the appearance of the soldiers, women threw their dainty perfumed handkerchiefs into the air in the most noble Victorian manner.

That evening the hotel had to provide dinner for the 850 guests in shifts, as the dining room only seated 250. The veranda was romantically lighted with Chinese lanterns, and from time to time fireworks exploded in the night air. Again there was dancing in the ballroom until after midnight. Sibyl watched the fireworks from the balcony. They came blooming out of the darkness only to die away as softly dripping colored stars, blooming and dying, unpredictable as love and ephemeral as life. She had had a private talk about those eternal verities with Mrs. Hearst that week in San Francisco. History has not been privy to what Mrs. Hearst told her,[3] but it was persuasive enough to make her reluctantly break her engagement to Will.

Mrs. Sanderson, now wearing a corsage of red roses, had organized a musicale for the guests. The program was notable for Sibyl's conspicuous absence, although Ruth Holladay and other local talents had been corralled to perform. Afterward, a select audience congratulated the judge's wife on such a lovely concert. It had been such a perfect holiday. Perfect for everyone but Will and Sibyl; their hearts were quietly breaking.

There were tears, emotional scenes, and a final parting as the two realized that parental authority and Victorian conventionality had triumphed. By the middle of July, the trunks were packed, and Mrs. Sanderson had swept her daughter onto their private railroad car and off to New York. There they boarded a steamship for Europe, where Sibyl would enter into a new love affair—with Paris.

Had it been merely a youthful summer romance? John Tebbel commented in his 1952 biography of Hearst, "At least one of the people who knew Hearst well doubts it. He believes, and there is some confirmation, that W. R. Hearst never really got over Sibyl and that if they had married, the course of Hearst's life and the history of American journalism might have been different."[4]

Hearst recovered in time, but he had been hit hard. As Tebbel noted, he did not enter Harvard that fall. Nor did he take the breakup of the engagement "philosophically," as W. A. Swanberg wrote dismissively about the affair in his 1961 biography.[5] No Hearst biographer to date has written about his activities in that nebulous period of 1881 and 1882—the lost year in which he should have attended Harvard.

Mrs. Hearst was determined that her darling Billy pursue his Harvard matriculation on course, and the *Examiner* announced the two had left the Bay City for Boston at the end of August 1881. What occurred immediately afterward is a matter for conjecture. Perhaps Hearst failed the entrance examinations that year. Perhaps the pair never got any closer to the Cambridge portals than New York City. Will was despondent and in no mood for study. It is known that they returned to San Francisco a few weeks later, for Judge Sanderson, in his letter of 14 September 1881 to Sibyl, disclosed that Hearst was back in town and had called at the house the night before with mutual friend Annie Head to take Jennie to dinner at the Holladays'.

Will brooded off and on for nearly six months at his father's country estate at San Simeon. He wanted desperately to follow Sibyl across the Atlantic and never return, later confiding to Marion Davies that he seriously considered running away and boarding a steamer for France.[6] He was a lovelorn Orpheus who had had his Eurydice torn from him. Somehow he must follow and find her again. Unfortunately, he was Orpheus with an umbilical cord. Even a visit to a ranch in New Mexico failed to dispel his despair.

His solicitous mother felt he needed a complete change of scene. The *Examiner* announced that he and a friend would embark upon a yachting trip to the Orient, where they would see the ancient splendors of Japan for the first time. If his mother insisted they book passage upon a commercial steamship, at least she could relax about one rankling worry—he would be sailing in the opposite direction from Sibyl. When he returned, Hearst had recovered sufficiently to enter Harvard on 24 September 1882. His mother again escorted him from California to make sure he didn't change his mind.

Although Hearst was to fall deeply in love several times later in his life, there would never be another summer as magical as the one of 1881, when he proposed to the beauteous Sibyl under the moon-haunted pines of Monterey. Their families were to remain the best of friends, and once having offered her his heart, Will would always pledge his friendship. Hearst's loyalty to his friends was legendary, and he and Sibyl were to see each other often on his later visits to Europe. It was particularly touching that in 1903, when he arrived on his honeymoon in Paris the very week Sibyl died, he would steal away from his new bride for a few hours to order a wreath of violets to be placed on her grave.

Chapter 3

Sanderson Versus Sanderson

"Cheer up, Sibyl, don't be homesick." This was the far-from-comforting advice in a letter written on 8 August 1881 by Jane—the sister who had become so neurotically ill in an East Coast private school that she didn't last a semester away from her family. In his postscript to the letter, Silas Sanderson quoted a familiar Victorian adage: "Don't give up, Sibyl. One must take hold of the plough and never look back." If Hearst's biographers allege that Sibyl was cold and career-obsessed in her relationship with him, this exhortation suggests that her father knew otherwise.

Sibyl was dreadfully unhappy about spending a year away from her family in a strange country. Margaret had taken her first to London, where they were royally entertained by John Bright Jr., son of the distinguished English states-man. Although young Bright showed them the sights of the British capital, the girl longed for the sunsets and fir trees in Monterey. She was even less thrilled with Paris when she and her mother arrived a few weeks later. Her first impres-sion was of a collection of dreary, gray stone buildings sliced in half by an equally dreary river. On 23 August she wrote her father begging him to let her come home after three months of exile in France.

Three weeks later, the judge sent her a stern but affectionate reply: "I should like to yield to my selfish wishes and order you to come home with your mother, but your interests forbid it. . . . We must deny ourselves the pleasure of your society for the present so as to enable you to make it more agreeable to us in the future." Her father also listed a number of young men who had called at the house asking to be remembered to her, but if this temporarily warmed the heart of a lonely girl thousands of miles from home, a malicious visit by a San Francisco matron would soon leave a chill.

Mrs. Leland Stanford, the ex-governor's wife and Jane's godmother, couldn't wait to call upon the Sandersons during one of her frequent European visits. Making tactless comments and queries about the way the Sandersons had terminated Sibyl's engagement to Hearst, Mrs. Stanford managed to offend both Sibyl and her mother. In his letter of 31 October to Sibyl, Judge Sanderson defended their action.

> Mrs. Stanford seemed to have done nothing but mischief to yourself and your mother. . . . I think she might have at least held her tongue and not made your mother miserable by its too frequent use. Your mother ought to have had enough sense not to allow herself to be influenced by anything she had to say upon the subject of which we alone are the most competent to judge.

Although Margaret had a list of several exclusive schools, she took her time in selecting one for her daughter. Throughout the fall, Sibyl's unstable health seemed to reflect her depression, and her mother grew uneasy when the time came to leave. As she planned to return to America around the first of November, Margaret finally decided to place Sibyl in a French *pension de famille* because she needed the atmosphere of a home more than that of a boarding school. After this she could continue her studies in Mme Bazault's school. It was John Bright Jr. who provided her with a letter of introduction to just such a family, the de Forcades.

The de Forcades were pillars of old French aristocracy, de Forcade having once been minister of the interior under Napoléon III. After the fall of the Second Empire he had died, leaving his widow, Edith, and their children virtually penniless. The family consisted of one son and three daughters, two of whom lived with their mother at 23 rue de Moscou, one of the dreariest streets in Paris.

Mme de Forcade was a typical warm French mother, a tiny woman with a huge nose and a bun of hair done up in a net. Margaret liked her at once. The son had recently married, so the family saw little of him. The oldest daughter had married an ex-officer named de Bonfils and had inherited her mother's charming personality, an attraction that more than compensated for her appearance. The two younger girls, Marguerite and Madeleine, were unquestionably ugly.

Sibyl discovered that she would not lack for Anglo-Saxon companionship. Two English girls were also pensionnaires in the household, one of them soon to become the bride of her friend John Bright Jr. Having already espied the grand piano in the parlor and learning that Madeleine de Forcade was an excellent pianist, Sibyl was determined to profit by the situation. Once she received permission to enroll for voice lessons in school, the girl had no difficulty in convincing her mother that she could successfully adjust to her new surroundings. With a sigh of relief, Margaret made plans to sail for New York from Liverpool. Before she left, she arranged for Sibyl's monthly checks to be forwarded to the bank of Seligman Frères and limited her to a strict allowance of $3.00 a week. Mme de Forcade promised to write the Sandersons periodically about Sibyl's progress in her studies.

After her mother's departure, Sibyl realized that her major problem would be communication. Her formal textbook training in French proved to be of little value. She needed a lot of experience in mastering idioms and verb tenses. Her immediate goal was to win over the de Forcades, and the two pathetic-looking daughters represented a formidable challenge.

Marguerite, the older, was tall and big-boned, with the enormous de Forcade nose and protruding upper teeth. The English girls nicknamed her le gendarme, because she spied on them to make sure they weren't conversing in English. Madeleine, the youngest, was pathetically hunchbacked and displayed a huge twisted nose above a mouth full of crooked teeth. Sibyl perceived that she was really quite vivacious and kind. Once they shared their mutual love for music, the two established a fine rapport.

Sibyl learned that although the de Forcades had been reduced to taking in foreign girls as boarders, it was kept sub rosa that they were paying guests; otherwise all chances of a profitable marriage for the two family Medusas would be ruined. A certain percentage of the money was automatically set aside for their dowries.

Sibyl continued to follow the family into the parlor at night and eventually made her way into their hearts. She chattered away in her unintelligible fashion, but so perseveringly that they all became interested in her progress. Madame would lay down her knitting in the evening to correct her. Madeleine would stop her incessant piano practicing to help this lovely foreigner express herself accurately. In turn, they were rewarded by the ray of California sunshine that Sibyl brought into their drab lives, not to mention the gifts she began to lavish upon them.

The de Forcade apartment lay several flights up some highly polished marble stairs. Upon entering it, one stepped back into the faded splendor of the Second Empire. The chairs and mirrors dating from the 1860s were covered carefully with linen slips every week. As in most French homes there were no bathing facilities. Sibyl was told that the average Parisian indulged in the luxury of ordering a bath once or twice a month. In the meantime she followed the practice of spraying herself heavily with cologne.

There was one old servant, called Bobonne, whom the family had retained from their halcyon days. Marion described her face as "a relief map of dirt-creased wrinkles; her hands crisscrossed with a thousand weathered lines." Her enormous apron was soiled beyond redemption. Every morning she shuffled into the girls' rooms to bring them their pitcher of hot water and draw the musty curtains that kept out the night air. Then she set down the breakfast tray of hard rolls, confiture, and café au lait served in a dirty cracked bowl. When Sibyl's conservative sisters stayed in the place a few years later, they were horrified that she could have enjoyed living in such unsanitary conditions. They dreaded the moment Bobonne would pull back their bed covers after her filthy hands had scratched at some coke and fagots in the fireplace to start a fire.

The good china, like everything of quality in the home, was saved for Madame's receptions. On those days the slipcovers were removed from the chairs, which would be placed in a formal row on either side of the fireplace. Sibyl was invited into the parlor and introduced to the guests as Madame's *petite amie américaine* before taking her place on a chair. As a coke fire sputtered reluctantly in the hearth, she had a certain length of time to practice her conversational French before the lethal combination of body odor and stagnant cologne would become asphyxiating. Everyone sat in two rows stiffly facing each other and talking to their neighbors in hushed tones. How different French receptions were from her mother's, where Americans periodically moved from room to room conversing informally with everyone. All Madame's friends belonged to conventional "old" society, including some aristocrats and others whose fortunes, like her own, had gone down the drain with the Second Empire.

Sibyl would listen to the platitudes about the last opera or play seen. At first she was overwhelmed by the names of new poets and artists and their individual schools—the impressionists, the symbolists, the naturalists, the Parnassians, and the Barbizons, among others. She had no idea what their particular credos were, but she knew that Paris was brimming with artistic movements rebelling against the crass materialist society of the Second Empire. No wonder Madame's reactionary friends found them shocking and immoral. Their world was being exposed to ridicule. Although she had not read any controversial authors nor seen exhibits by any radical painters, Sibyl concluded that she had come to Paris during an exciting time in the arts.

Sibyl's mastery of the language grew rapidly, and she was asked to sing for the guests with Madeleine at the piano. She proved to be such a success that the de Forcades began to invite her into exclusive Faubourg St. Germain circles as their little cousin from the country.[1] There were many who weren't fooled. This girl's patrician manners and regal carriage did not belong to any provincial urchin. The de Forcades were really harboring a foreign princess in disguise.

At these receptions Sibyl's vivacity and beauty invariably drew a crowd of young men whom she insisted upon introducing to her "cousins," Marguerite and Madeleine. The girls were utterly enchanted with their American angel. They had never known any male attention before.

Sibyl had not yet seen anything of the theatrical and musical worlds that made Paris so famous. She was merely one among hundreds of foreign students hurrying between their classrooms and pensions, carrying their books as shields against the flirtatious glances of the boulevardiers. She may not have been ready for Paris, but she was convinced of one thing: Paris must wait until she was.

The week of her birthday, in December, a small, neatly wrapped package arrived from San Francisco. As the excited de Forcades watched her unwrap it, Sibyl held up a small, exquisitely engraved gold watch. Under the cover, with its ornately scrolled S, was an affectionate message from home: "Papa to Sibyl on her seventeenth birthday, 7 December 1881."

Throughout the winter of 1881–82 her father continued to worry about her. He would chide her humorously in his letters for confusing the preposition to with the adverb too. He would remind her not to spend so much time on her music and singing, but "pay more attention to the rest of your curriculum." He continually exhorted her to concentrate upon literature, history, and grammar.

Sibyl, though, was working hard at the only subject that really interested her—music. She practiced voice several hours a day, and piano as well. Throughout the year Sibyl's letters contained little news other than the progress of her musical studies, to the exasperation of her parents. In view of all the money they were spending on her, Margaret complained that the least she could do was to write them in French.

Sibyl had finally cajoled her father into increasing her allowance to four dollars a week. With the rate of exchange at seven francs to one dollar, Judge

Sanderson thought that it would be an excellent opportunity for Sibyl to learn bookkeeping. He asked her to maintain a ledger of her expenses and send it home at the end of each month. Several months were to pass before he realized that she was incapable of fulfilling his request. Her drafts were becoming more and more frequent, and never once did he suspect that she wasn't spending the money on herself. The rooms of the de Forcade sisters were stacked to the ceiling with boxes full of hats, gloves, purses, shoes, and perfumes.

By the summer of 1882, Sibyl's expenditures had gotten out of hand. She had been allowed to spend a few weeks in London after assuring her parents that she would be properly chaperoned by John Bright and his fiancée. Never once did she bother to explain her urgent need for more and more money. Her father, who had been seriously ill with rheumatoid arthritis for three months, wrote an exasperated letter on 11 August.

> In respect to handling of money you have disappointed me. You have been extravagant in your expenditures . . . your course has compelled me to take the handling of money out of your hands and place it in the hands of Mme de Forcade. If this is mortifying to you, you have by your own conduct made it necessary.

In his next letter less than a week later, Judge Sanderson confessed, "I love you too much to remain angry with you." His health was failing. He dreaded the thought that his daughters would be pursuing their studies abroad in a few years and he would spend his last years alone. Because he was due in Washington to expedite a favorable piece of railroad legislation before the Supreme Court, it was decided that his wife would sail in October and bring Sibyl back to the American capital for the winter. Grandmother Ormsby could look after the other girls during their absence.

Sibyl's new experiences had already made the year of 1881–82 the most exciting in her young life, but the most memorable event of all occurred shortly before her mother arrived that fall. Mlle LaFond, a distinguished soprano, visited the school one day, and Sibyl was among the students chosen to sing for her. Mlle LaFond was impressed with the young Californian and praised her highly, according to a story in the San Francisco Examiner years later, on 17 May 1889: "But she is gifted, cette petite. She ought to study seriously because she can go far!"

Mlle LaFond tried to persuade Sibyl to enter the Conservatoire and work with her singing teacher, the renowned professor Saint-Yves Bax. The girl replied sadly that her year in Paris was drawing to a close and she must return to the United States. But secretly Sibyl was more determined than ever to return and prepare herself for the stage. One day her name would be on marquees beside those of Sarah Bernhardt and Adelina Patti. She would be as big a star as any of them.

—

Although Margaret had arrived in Paris on 22 October, she didn't return to America with Sibyl until the middle of December. For a month and a half she enjoyed a social binge with her friends the Charles Crockers, who were also visiting Paris. While Hattie Crocker was entertaining Sibyl, Margaret and Mrs. Crocker were undergoing fittings for new wardrobes at Charles F. Worth's salon.

By the time the judge met them in New York and all the trunks had been loaded onto the train, he was convinced that his wife had bought out Worth's entire collection. As Margaret was quick to point out, however, if they were going to spend the winter in Washington, D.C., he would want them to make a favorable impression. Sibyl's formal society debut would take place in a few weeks at Dora Miller's ball. Dora was Sibyl's old friend, the daughter of California's Senator Miller. The debut seems to have been a smashing success. Attired in "a robe which follows the requirements of youth," Sibyl captivated everyone with her exquisite grace and charm, including ex-president Ulysses S. Grant and his diamond-bedecked wife, Julia.

Victorian fashion was enjoying its gaudiest era. Decked out in one of her most spectacular Worth creations, Judge Sanderson's wife was wearing a gown of terra-cotta and white satin embroidered with variegated silks and iridescent beads among which Worth had actually introduced real stuffed hummingbirds—a horrifying thought to those living a century later. Judging by the amount of newspaper space devoted to its description, Margaret Sanderson must have created a sensation.

Sibyl and her mother were introduced to everyone worth knowing in the capital. At the White House ball, Sibyl was presented to President Chester A. Arthur and his wife. The French ambassador lauded her perfect command of his language and invited her to be his unofficial translator at various receptions.

The judge, however, wrote to Marion on 22 January 1883 that he was less than enthusiastic about the continual rounds of socializing:

> Sibyl and her mother are on the go, morning, noon, and night. Their time is
> so occupied with parties, balls, and receptions that they can't attend to

domestic duties such as writing their family. . . . I dodge as much of it as possible but cannot escape it all. When I do have to participate, I pretend I am having a marvelous time.

Once he had won his tax case before the Supreme Court, the Sandersons departed for California by way of the southern route. Stopping off in New Orleans, they were joined by Truxton Beale, one of Sibyl's old beaux and later American ambassador to Persia. When Sibyl arrived home, she was surprised to see that her father had redecorated the house to celebrate her return. The halls had been tiled in terra-cotta with a frieze of Egyptian figures, which was the current rage. All the bedrooms were redone with elaborately molded ceilings. The guest rooms contained ebony furniture with mother-of-pearl inlay and boasted a ceiling design with wild roses and spider webs in low relief.

But Judge Sanderson soon learned that it would take more than beautifying the family nest to content his oldest daughter. Sibyl had not been home long before she began studying voice with a Professor Galvani. Later she worked with other teachers, including Alfred Kellcher and Mme Caroline Zeis-Dennis, who lived at the Palace Hotel and advertised herself as a "contralto lyrique." When the prodigal siren returned to the Hotel Del Monte in the spring of 1883, she created a *succès fou* in the ballroom by singing with Ballenberg's orchestra again. Once more the gilded youth of San Francisco were at her feet, and many a young man offered her his heart.

It was not only her voice that brought Sibyl such a rush of male admirers, but also a steaming sexual magnetism that attracted men of all ages and types. Her heavy-lidded violet eyes seemed simultaneously to conceal and betray two smoldering fires on some exotic altar. The bewitching shrug of her shoulders, the inviting rise and fall of her firmly molded breasts, the infantine pout of her upper lip, the caressing tones in her voice—all contributed to a sexual intensity that stamped her as totally different from her equally attractive but timid sisters. Once a man had succumbed to her seductions, she became the storybook heroine of his fantasies. This magical ability to conjure illusions was later to become her primary asset during her stage career.

It didn't take her friends long to detect subtle changes in her personality. They noticed that she had become a bit affected since her return from Paris. She appeared with her mother at afternoon teas invariably dressed in black with a small bunch of violets pinned to her left shoulder. Someone asked her if it was the latest Parisian craze. "Oh, yes," replied Sibyl calmly, "but only among the demimondaines. They are far smarter than the respectable matrons." High society reeled at that daring observation.

Her English began to acquire a slight Continental accent. She now bleached a peroxide streak through her bronze tresses. And she was always practicing her operatic entrances and exits. She would come into a room singing a phrase, apparently unconscious that anyone else was present. After a feigned start of surprise, she would immediately recover her self-possession. There could be no doubt that she was obsessed with the stage.

Her mother subtly encouraged Sibyl's aspirations by entertaining every opera company that visited San Francisco. Colonel James Henry Mapleson's troupe was always feted in the Sanderson home, and by 1884 Sibyl had met such world-famous prima donnas as Etelka Gerster and Adelina Patti. Other celebrated guests included Oscar Wilde, John Bright Jr., and Arthur Sullivan of operetta fame.

One of Sibyl's friends was blonde and willowy Gertrude Atherton. She had been enduring a loveless marriage to George Atherton, scion of the wealthy Chilean Atherton family who lived on Octavia Street just below the Sandersons. She desperately wanted to become a writer, but her Spanish mother-in-law, Dominga de Goni Atherton, refused to allow it. Gertrude was constantly reminded that "ladies in Spain do not write." For the time being she had to be content with penning articles for the local papers and promoting her own literary salon.

Mrs. Atherton and Sibyl used to take long, despairing walks over the steep hills of the city, wondering if they would ever escape it. Gertrude felt that Judge Sanderson might succumb to Sibyl's pleas in time, but that for herself there was little hope, shackled with husband George and their little girl, Muriel.

So far, the judge showed no signs of relenting. True, he allowed Sibyl to sing at various charity musicales, and even in a concert at Saint John's Presbyterian Church, where her grandmother was active. He voiced no objections when she joined the Saint-Cecilia club with her friends, the Holladay sisters, to study vocal scores two hours a week. When Sibyl appeared in a comic opera benefit at the Mission Street opera house, he was in his box beaming with pride. The entire audience was composed of people he knew and approved of—Sibyl's social equals. His darling was not being subjected to the vulgar gaze of the masses.

It was the world of the pedestrian and the common from which he wished to shield her. She would not know how to cope with it. Sibyl had once shocked friends at a dinner party by announcing that she intended to savor life "from its heights to its depths." When the remark was quoted to her father, he merely shook his head and made no comment. As long as he lived, she would never have an opportunity to experience life from the latter perspective. For the present her vocal aspirations were restricted to limited amateur activities; he had no intention of allowing her to return to Europe and study for the professional stage. She had had her fling in Paris, he reminded her, and now it was only fair that her sisters be given their turns.

"You know that patience is not one of my principal virtues, therefore, do not subject it to so great a strain," he had written to her. Usually, she knew just how far to push before dropping the subject. It remained a constant source of friction between them, a continual locking of wills. In some ways they were very much alike. Sibyl had inherited her stubborn determination and ambition from her father, and he knew it. She also realized that with his increasing attacks of rheumatism, which sometimes crippled him for weeks, sooner or later his resistance would crumble. Time was on her side.

For the next few years she played the role in society that her parents expected of her. She attended a monotonous succession of balls, cotillions, weddings, and parties and helped preside at charity bazaars. She dutifully marched in the dull Fourth of July parades with other society belles. Every time an old calendar was discarded, she felt more and more robbed of what she wanted in life.

Since Will Hearst had entered Harvard she saw him only at various social functions when he was home on vacation. Their feverish affair had burned itself out, and in its place grew a devoted friendship. His mother was giving her exclusive midweek musicales, but there is no record of Sibyl being asked to sing at one of them. Mrs. Hearst still regarded her as a permanent threat.

Sibyl felt like a bird in a cage, free to warble only within the confines of its bars. But even caged birds rebel occasionally. Dr. Hugh Tevis, one of her more ardent suitors, took her for a carriage ride down the peninsula one day. Following the current vogue, Sibyl was wearing a row of artificial spit curls pinned under the rim of her hat. When a sudden gust of wind took her hat and curls into the air, young Tevis stopped the carriage and got out to chase them down. Sibyl suddenly leaped into the driver's seat, whipped up the horses, and galloped back to the city. Poor Hugh Tevis had to walk home. "I was bored," she explained to her horrified parents.

When Sibyl found herself in the doldrums, there was nothing like a heady flirtation to elevate her spirits. After an incident in the San Mateo home of Mr.

and Mrs. John Parrot Jr., San Francisco gossips were convinced that Sibyl was born to play Amina in *La Sonnambula*. The Parrots had given a delightful party, but everyone noticed that the host had been overly attentive all evening to the fair Sibyl. After the guests had retired, Mr. Parrot remained in the library to smoke a cigar. Some time later, his wife, irritated by his delay in coming to bed, decided to go downstairs to see what was the matter. She had no sooner reached the top of the stairs when she espied the judge's daughter, gowned in a transparent negligee, going into the library with candle in hand. At the wife's query, the girl came to an abrupt halt. Wheeling toward the stairs and blinking, she emitted a feeble "Where am I?" Then, blushing a deep scarlet, Sibyl hastily explained that she must have been sleepwalking and hadn't the slightest idea of how she arrived at the library door.

A French baron and lady-killer named Aaron de Bonnemains was the next object of Sibyl's affections. He had come to San Francisco as the suitor of the eccentric heiress Mabel Pacheco, but the madcap Mabel had grown bored with his questionable attractions. He lingered on for some time hoping that a lady of means would adopt him. For about nine months he was lionized by society. Feeling maternal sympathy for the rejected baron, married women fought for a turn to ask him to the theater and shower him with parties. By February 1884, when Margaret Sanderson invited him to a reception, his popularity had crested. Sibyl was ripe for a torrid romance, and it didn't take much encouragement for the baron to demonstrate that he was far more skilled in this field than she. Their relationship came to an abrupt termination that summer, although two different explanations later broke in print.

According to the first story, the baron judged a beautiful woman with the same care as a blooded horse. In order to survey Sibyl's physical attributes objectively, he encouraged her to have some photographs taken in flesh-colored tights and send them to him. It was a daring thing for a society lady to do in 1884. Only showgirls, dancers, and prostitutes ever admitted to the practice. When Sibyl's father was informed of this latest escapade, he was furious. No gentleman would think of suggesting such a thing, and no lady would consider doing it. In the end, as other fathers did in similar situations, he had to pay off the baron to redeem his daughter's risqué photographs.

The second version had the affair expiring unhappily at the Hotel Del Monte that summer. Every morning Sibyl received a box of beautiful roses with a fervent note from the baron. On one particular day, a friend of Sibyl's was present when the flowers arrived. Because Sibyl was temporarily occupied, the young lady volunteered to open the box and put the roses in water. As luck would have it, she also picked up the florist's bill from the bottom of the receptacle along with a personal note pleading for Miss Sanderson to settle the baron's delinquent account. It took all of Sibyl's pin money to make restitution. In the meantime, her "dear" friend couldn't wait to spread the story all over San Francisco.

By the end of 1884, Sibyl's love life was mired in a rut. Judge Sanderson observed this when he wrote to his wife, "she is particularly unfortunate in matters of the heart. It seems to be her fate to fall in love with the wrong men, and her matrimonial prospects . . . are not bright." Neither were her chances for going on the stage. She was already twenty years old and still trapped in fogbound San Francisco. Would Paris still be waiting? She began to have nagging doubts.

Chapter 4

Final Decree

If 1884 had been a frustrating year for Sibyl, the beginning of 1885 seemed worse. Her father was growing progressively more irritable because she continually rejected the homegrown suitor for the dubious charms of visiting foreigners. Every time an eligible European admirer called upon her, Judge Sanderson became slightly more paranoid. Perhaps it was only natural that he should regard foreigners with suspicion. San Francisco attracted more than its share of fortune hunters, and for good reason: in the 1880s it boasted more millionaires than any other American city.

Sibyl's admirers descended upon Octavia Street in droves. According to the reminiscences of an elderly Gertrude Atherton, the house looked like

> a florist's shop; the candy stores flourished as never before. But the huge boxes of sweets were devoured by her sisters and the servants. Sibyl never forgot her figure or lost it. The gossips must have subconsciously loved her, she contributed so generously to their mill. Her many flirtations were considered outrageous![1]

Musically speaking, the new year was filled with a variety of stimulating events. In February Emma Nevada, California's first soprano to make a successful Parisian debut, returned to take the city by storm.[2] The Sandersons were in the audience, and Sibyl was filled with inspiration at the singer's accomplishments and awed by the reception she received from the wildly cheering San Franciscans.

When the Mapleson troupe arrived for a four-week season in March, opera fever was running high. The male roster featured a new young Italian tenor named Cardinali, who had sung the first performance of Wagner's *Lohengrin* in Italian in Buenos Aires a few years earlier. But the star attraction, advertised as "the greatest event of the decade," was the reengagement of the world-famous soprano Adelina Patti. Crowds pressed around the Palace Hotel and surged into the lobby to catch a glimpse of the legendary diva.

The Sanderson family always took a box at the opera house for the Mapleson performances. After the second night, Mrs. J. W. Brown gave a reception for the artists at her Pine Street mansion, to which the Sandersons were invited. Sibyl could hardly wait to meet the darkly handsome Cardinali. His high C-sharp had set her spine tingling. After the Continental kiss, there was a smoldering glance from the tenor, the pressure of his hand, and a request for Sibyl to join him in a duet. The invitation was conveyed with the aid of an interpreter, because Cardinali spoke no English or French; for the moment Sibyl wished she had studied Italian. Before the party was over, they had sung several duets, and Cardinali enthusiastically predicted that this lovely girl would achieve an even greater success in Europe than her compatriot, Mme Nevada.

The following week, Cardinali was a constant caller at the Sanderson home. He sang more and more duets with Sibyl, while in the library behind locked doors he professed his love for her in rapturous hemorrhages of Italian. Sibyl ignored her mother's frantic entreaties to open the doors, and a weeping Margaret Sanderson begged her husband to order the tenor off the premises. The judge calmly replied, "I have perfect confidence in Sibyl."

Sibyl was momentarily smitten. She informed Cardinali that she was already studying the role of Cherubino for an amateur production of Mozart's *The Marriage of Figaro*. Seeing her chance to flee the family coop, she promised to marry him as soon as he formally petitioned her father for her hand.

The following week, accompanied by Mme Scalchi's husband, Count Lolli, as his interpreter, the C-sharp Adonis called upon Judge Sanderson. He announced that he was really an Italian baron, a man of great landed wealth in Italy. The judge smiled and said nothing. He could understand why the singer's dazzling white teeth and beautiful wavy hair had turned his daughter's head. But he noticed something else that had escaped Sibyl's attention. Cardinali's hands and feet more closely resembled those of a lumberjack than those of an aristocrat. When the impetuous Italian had finished his plea for the judge's permission, the latter slowly lighted a cigar and gave his answer, later disclosed in both the *San Francisco Chronicle* and *Examiner.*

"Young man, you have a pleasing appearance, and I have heard nothing ill of you, but I don't know you well enough to give such a consent."

"But I have excellent references," insisted the tenor.

"I can give my daughter no dowry," the judge countered.

Cardinali drew himself up. "I have no wish for money. It is your daughter that I love."

"Fine. Then you won't mind waiting for six months. I will give you my answer by that time," the judge concluded. "Meanwhile I intend to make the necessary inquiries."

Sibyl was ecstatic. She confided to all her friends that within six months she would be singing a duet for life with her ardent Italian. Gossip columns in the San Francisco papers were already twittering about it. When the last perform-ance of the Mapleson season was over, Cardinali was pursued by a barrage of reporters as he escorted Sibyl and her mother to their carriage. Through his interpreter the handsome tenor announced they were officially engaged. After his season in Chicago and Boston, he would return to San Francisco to marry Signorina Sanderson. It was the last time she ever saw him. Within two months the judge's spies in Italy had discovered that he was no baron but the son of a humble cobbler instead. Toward the end of the year, a brief news item in several New York papers noted that he had eloped with a chorus girl. Sibyl was still des-tined to remain a signorina.

About a month after Cardinali's exit, the next blow to the girl's ambitions occurred when her father inexplicably pulled her out of the amateur cast of *The Marriage of Figaro*. Perhaps he made the decision because of her constant succes-sion of colds. At any rate, all of San Francisco society turned out to cheer Ruth Holladay in the role of the Countess, including her biggest boosters, the Sanderson family.

Ruth Holladay seemed to have all the luck. Not only had she won a resound-ing success in the Mozart production, but she was engaged to marry one of England's most eligible bachelors, William E. Blackwell, heir to the Cross and Blackwell pickle fortune. Dora Miller announced her engagement that summer as well, to a navy lieutenant. One by one, all Sibyl's friends were capturing prize matrimonial specimens, while she would soon be twenty-one and still single.

Her sisters had now reached the respective ages of nineteen, seventeen, and fourteen. Jane was about five foot one, Sibyl's approximate height, and while she resembled her sister strongly, her eyes were grayer, and far more copper shone in her hair. The only other characteristic she shared with Sibyl was an unpredictable temper. At five foot five, Marion was the tallest in the family and the only true blonde. Her swan-like neck and delicate features were so exquis-itely modeled that many a visitor pronounced her the reigning beauty in the family. Edith was short, with eyes that rather squinted and an impudently tilted nose, seemingly not inherited from either parent. Already she was showing marked promise at the piano. Jane, the only one who displayed no artistic inclination, was nicknamed the "salad mixer" because of her love for cooking.

Margaret planned to take her three younger daughters abroad in the fall of 1885 and give them their year of schooling in Paris. The problem was what to do with Sibyl. Already, Ruth Holladay had asked her and Jane to be bridesmaids at her lavish society wedding that fall in London. Afterward Margaret expected to be occupied with settling her other daughters in Paris, and there would be no one to escort Sibyl back to New York. In the Victorian age, it was taboo for a young, unmarried lady of genteel breeding to cross the ocean without an older escort.

Tearfully and dramatically, Sibyl begged her father to let her stay with the family in Paris and study voice at the Conservatoire. In a sudden and astonishing change of heart, he granted her request. This did not mean permission to go on the stage, far from it. Judge Sanderson was simply worn out by her incessant entreaties and irritating emotional scenes. He never denied that cultivation of one's vocal talent was a desirable social attribute for a young lady, and in case she should remain a spinster, she might be able to earn a respectable livelihood teaching music.

It was a far-reaching decision. The family would be gone for a year, and Margaret disliked leaving her husband for long because of his declining health. Privately, the judge dreaded seeing them go, for it meant he would be alone except for his mother-in-law. His married life had been a constant succession of sacrifices for his family.

Sibyl couldn't wait to share her triumph with Gertrude Atherton. "I shall succeed," she calmly declared as she stood in Mrs. Atherton's parlor. "I shall become the rage of Paris. All I have to do is to find a composer who needs my voice, and the rest will follow." In 1931, when Gertrude Atherton was writing her memoirs, she recalled that visit as if it had happened only a week before:

> I have never known anyone quite so poised, so self-possessed, so sure of herself as Sibyl. She had the lightest of lyric voices; she knew no one of influence in Paris; the opera houses were besieged yearly with aspirants from all over the world; and yet she had no more doubt of conquest than if her voice had been as great as Patti's and impresarios were scrambling for her favor.
>
> Sibyl, although she had the reputation of a beauty, was not one in the strict sense of the word. The lower part of her face was too heavy . . . but her large luminous blue-grey eyes expressed all things, her skin was smooth and

white and brilliantly colored, her hair like burnished bronze, and her figure perfect; I doubt if a more beautifully formed woman ever lived. And she had a style and a carriage both haughty and graceful. . . . She entered a room with the air of one born to be stared at and admired, and no one thought of doing anything else.

"Of course you will succeed, and get everything else you want," I assented warmly. "What else was Nature thinking of when she made you? But I could hate you, all the same. You'll get there long before I do."

"Cheer up!" she said. "One never knows what's around the corner. Yesterday papa was as pig-headed as ever. You may have a book published before I make my debut."[3]

Since Judge Sanderson had to be in Washington, D.C., on business the first of October, the family accompanied him in his private railroad car and spent as much time with him as possible before they left for Europe.

Sibyl had stars in her eyes. Not only would she shortly be returning to the city of her dreams, she was in love again, this time with a bona fide member of the landed European gentry. His name was Lord Sinclair, and his family occupied Castle Thurso in Scotland. They had met that summer in San Francisco, and he was a constant visitor in her home. From the night he appeared in kilts carrying a bagpipe, there could be no doubt about his physical appeal. The Sanderson girls thought him the most handsome man they had ever seen. Years later, Marion recalled him as the personification of Sir Walter Scott's kilt-clad heroes. Although the stalwart young lord returned to Scotland in September without giving Sibyl a ring, the couple considered themselves unofficially engaged. It was understood that if Sibyl should accompany her sisters to Europe that fall, she must visit his parents at their ancestral castle.

The Sandersons sailed for Europe the second week of October, and aboard ship they again encountered the English composer Sir Arthur Sullivan and his business partner, Richard D'Oyly Carte. Sullivan, who had been a guest in their home in California, professed to admire Sibyl's voice and temperament. After hearing her sing in the ship's ballroom, he advised her to study in London for a year or so; then she should be ready to appear in his operettas. It was a tempting thought, but Sibyl distrusted English voice teachers. Furthermore, as her sights were set on "grand opera," she felt Paris was the logical place to pursue her studies.

Once they arrived in London, Marion later recalled, Sullivan found the Sandersons comfortable lodgings on Half Moon Street, and not a minute too soon. Edith promptly succumbed to typhoid fever and had to be put to bed at once. As Margaret would be confined with her for some weeks, a Miss Clemmons, whom they had met on the ship, agreed to chaperon the other girls around the city. Tall, slender, and blonde, Katherine Clemmons had appeared as Buffalo Bill's niece in his famous road show. Privately, she was said to be his mistress. The group visited all the important museums, the Tower of London, and other points of interest including Mme Tussaud's waxworks, which completely enthralled the girls, much to their mother's disgust. Decked out in elaborate gowns of white tulle, Sibyl and Jane walked down the aisle as bridesmaids at Ruth Holladay's sumptuous wedding. By the end of November, the girls had been on such a social merry-go-round that only Jane had taken the time to write to their father. Once Edith had recovered, Margaret finally crossed the channel and escorted her brood to Paris.

Upon Sibyl's glowing recommendation, her mother deposited Marion and Edith with Mme de Forcade, and Jane was placed with her oldest daughter, Mme de Bonfils. Margaret and Sibyl took an apartment on the rue de Tilsitt. While Edith pursued her piano studies and Marion attended Felix Barrias's painting classes, Sibyl entered the Conservatoire on 25 November to join the class of Saint-Yves Bax, the teacher whom Mlle LaFond had recommended. Jane, meanwhile, devoted herself to sightseeing with her congenial hosts.

Before long Marion and Edith came to despise living at the de Forcades' and eagerly looked forward to weekends at their mother's apartment. The dainty trays of hot chocolate and croissants that Margaret brought them on Sunday mornings were a welcome contrast to the cracked bowl of café-au-lait in Bobonne's filthy hands.

Before Judge Sanderson returned from Washington, D.C., to San Francisco, he wrote to Jane, reminding her to make certain that his girls spoke only French when they got together. The rheumatic attacks in his right arm were becoming so severe that he could barely hold a pen in his hand. He was aging fast. His writing had deteriorated, and what was worse, for the first time in his life he had begun to misspell words. It was a bad sign.

Her father's health, however, did not occupy a prominent place among Sibyl's current priorities. She never informed him that she had boldly procured an audition at the Opéra-Comique with its director, Léon Carvalho, and his celebrated wife, retired prima donna Caroline Miolan-Carvalho. If the judge had suspected what she was up to, his wrath would have known no bounds. There is no record of what she sang, but it was most probably some of her San Francisco repertoire: Isabelle's Aria from *Le pré aux clercs* by Hérold or the "Ballata de Guerny"—vocal works that long ago passed into extinction. A few years later the French journals revealed that the reactions of the Carvalhos seemed to have been one of patronizing kindness. They pronounced her to be "gifted," always an innocuous compliment, and wisely counseled her to continue her studies at the Conservatoire.

Besides her theatrical aspirations, she chiefly wrote to her father about wanting to marry Lord Sinclair. She loved him passionately even though all his quarrelsome family was united in opposing their marriage. The Scottish laird and his parents had visited her in Paris and brought the chill of the North Sea with them. Making it clear that they expected her father to furnish an extravagant dowry, Lord and Lady Sinclair received her with frigid politeness. Sibyl learned that outside of his eventual inheritance of the ancestral castle, her Scottish suitor didn't have a farthing to his name and no means of earning one. When Margaret sent her husband a list of the impossible demands made by his family, the judge declined to give his consent.

He outlined some basic reasons for his refusal in a letter to Marion on 15 May 1886.

> So you have all gone stark mad over the possibility of a marriage between a descendant of Scotch pirates and Sibyl? Pedigree and poverty make very good alliteration, but they will not suffice to buy a good dinner. We can live with the latter, but we cannot fill an empty stomach with the former . . . but joking aside, you all seem to have so set your hearts upon Sibyl's marrying Lord Sinclair that I am made to feel more and more regret that I have been compelled to decline my consent to the conditions imposed by his father. To have consented to those conditions would have been to undertake more than I can perform. Besides, to have done so would have been unjust to the rest of you whose claims upon me are equal to those of Sibyl.

In his 28 May letter to Margaret he expanded on the subject.

> In view of the fact that all of the members of his family are opposed to the match, I am glad that I said "no" while I was ignorant of the fact. . . . She certainly cannot wish to enter a family who do not wish her presence among them. I think she should drop all intercourse with him or them. . . . Constancy is not a strong point in her character and I shall be greatly disappointed if her fancy for Sinclair survives long after a final separation.

In his last surviving letter to Sibyl, he had presented some serious questions that demanded the utmost self-evaluation. Knowing her as well as he did, he must have had second thoughts about how much attention she would allot to them.

San Francisco
13 March 1886

My dear Sibyl,

Your letter of the 20th of February came in due time,. I am sorry you have been ill but you have never exercised much care in looking after your health and I do not suppose you ever will. Yet, you must know that nothing can be of more importance than good health to any one, and especially one who hopes to become a successful singer. . . . I want to know how you stand in the estimation of your teachers with other pupils. I want to know whether you are to take rank with some of the great singers of the world. Unless you have a fair prospect of equalizing such singers as Kellogg, Carey [presumably American contralto Annie Louise Cary], and Van Zandt, I shall be unwilling to see you on the stage . . . if such are your prospects, there are reasons . . . which might induce me to consent to your going upon the stage. But if the chances are that you will not be able to attain a higher level than that of a second or third class singer I should much prefer that you abandon the idea. . . . Think of those who have tried and failed. Those who have succeeded can be counted on your fingers, while those who have failed may be counted by the hundreds. The question which you are now to consider is one of vital importance—for your decision will affect your future life and the whole of it.

Your loving father,
S. W. Sanderson

The judge was perturbed about his wife's plan to bring their other daughters home after a trip through southern France while leaving Sibyl to continue her studies in Paris. Knowing how irresponsibly she took care of herself, he believed it to be a grave mistake. On 28 May 1886, he sent his wife $430, which she immediately exchanged for 3,000 francs at her Paris bank. Once she was equipped with sufficient funds, Margaret and her offspring began their last tour of southern France and Switzerland. When they arrived at the Hotel Nationale in Lucerne, she received an urgent telegram from her mother. Silas Woodruff Sanderson was dead.

He had been ill the previous week, spending much of the time in bed. One of his physicians, "Doctress" Jaquith, called upon him at 4 P.M. on 24 June. After her departure, the judge drank a cup of tea and went upstairs to take a hot bath for his gout. At 5:30 P.M., Mrs. Ormsby, noticing that his presence in the bath had been prolonged, entered the room to find him dead of an apparent heart attack.

The San Francisco newspapers paid tribute to his brilliant career. The *Morning Call* hailed the late judge as "one of the ablest jurists in the United States." The California *Daily Alta* described his decisions as "models of style, diction, and exhaustive research which made them the admiration of the bench throughout the country . . . . His recent management of the great cases for the railroads have crowned the efforts of a brilliant professional career."[4]

Mrs. Ormsby and Joseph Redding, the judge's devoted secretary, arranged for the funeral to be held in his home. The remains rested in a heavily draped casket in the drawing room. A large floral Bible from ex-governor and Mrs. Leland Stanford lay on the lid of the casket with an inscription in purple larkspur: "The Highest Court has Called our Friend." Reverend Meldrum, the pastor of Mrs. Ormsby's church, read from the fifteenth chapter of the First Epistle of Paul to the Corinthians. Redding had enlisted some of the judge's colleagues from the bench to act as pallbearers. Interment was in Lone Mountain Cemetery. Later, Redding saw to it that the cryptic epitaph that the judge had requested was carved on his tombstone: Final Decree.[5]

Although the California papers had dutifully eulogized the judge, they mentioned little about his personal life except that he was "a man of few words," a man "averse to display." Silas Sanderson truly lived for his family. He always placed their welfare before his own needs. In the final analysis, he sacrificed his own life and career for them.

The important cases that he had won in Washington, D.C., for the Southern Pacific Railroad Company had given the Big Four unprecedented power on the West Coast. It would be no exaggeration to say that they controlled the lives of every inhabitant of California through their regulation of all forms of commerce and transportation in and out of the state. Their growing abuse of authority must have gnawed at Sanderson's vitals, but what he really thought of them will never be known. He was an intensely secretive man, according to his daughter Marion, with "deep, hidden emotions."

After purchasing their mourning outfits in Paris, the Sanderson family began their sad journey home aboard a French liner. Trouble, however, continued to snap at their heels. On 4 July 1886, just beyond Fire Island, a spark from the rockets saluting America's birthday alighted in the ship's laundry and set fire to the clothes within. All the passengers were roused from their cabins in the middle of the night and ordered on deck immediately. The entire hold was being rapidly destroyed by fire and water, and already the ship was tilting. Once the passengers were on deck, they were lowered into the lifeboats. All their luggage had already been destroyed in the hold. Officers stood by the rope ladders with drawn pistols, threatening to shoot any man who attempted to enter a boat before the women and children. Because of the captain's strictly enforced disciplinary code, pandemonium was avoided, and all the voyagers were safely deposited into the boats below.

Years later Marion recalled that everyone managed to maintain a sense of humor as the lifeboats were tossed about on the murky waves. Meanwhile, officers aboard the blazing ship frantically continued to signal for help. The Sanderson girls giggled at their own ludicrous appearance, with pigtails dangling down their backs and each other's hats pulled over their ears. The catastrophe took on the aura of an exciting adventure, and they competed to catch the rolls and chocolate bars the officers threw down to them. Toward morning a ship from New York City finally appeared to rescue the weary refugees as well as the gallant crew.

Margaret's brother, William Ormsby, was at the dock to meet them, much relieved to see that they were none the worse for their near disaster. He took them immediately to the Fifth Avenue Hotel, and once in their rooms, the Sanderson clan soon realized what a pathetic lot they were. As their cabins rapidly filled with smoke, they had grabbed any clothes they could find and put them on helter-skelter. Marion discovered that she was wearing no drawers at all, but Margaret found herself clad in two pairs, each tied around her waist, and not a leg in either one.

Once rested, the family commenced the last stage of their unhappy pilgrimage to San Francisco. Marion described the homecoming in her memoirs as "sad beyond words." Only Mrs. Ormsby was at the depot in Oakland to meet them, and Margaret wept softly in her mother's arms. It should have come as no surprise to them that San Francisco society did not rush to their Octavia Street home to console them.

Inevitably, there was malicious gossip about the fact that Margaret Sanderson had been gallivanting about Europe when she should have been home caring for her husband. The family couldn't help but notice a chill developing among some of their former friends. Plagued with feelings of remorse for not being at her husband's side when he died, Margaret was haunted by the shadow of her own guilt for years afterward. Of course she had been aware that he was in poor health before she had taken their daughters to Europe, but it was at his insistence that she went in the first place. The judge always concealed his real feelings—even from her.

As for Sibyl, who knows what was coursing through her active mind? Although torn by mixed emotions, she must have secretly exulted that time had decided in her favor. Her hard-fought battle with her father was over. Gone was the man who had tried to protect her from a world she had never known and, in his eyes, a life certain to bring cruelty, suffering, and deprivation—a life she could only envision as glamorous and thrilling. Now the door to the gilded cage was open.

Chapter 5

Beaucoup des Dumbbells

A short but momentous family conference was held in the Octavia Street mansion not long after the Sandersons arrived home. Papa was dead; whither lay their destinies now? Since all the girls had begun their studies abroad, it seemed no less than a crime not to continue with them. If they pursued this course, it would be impossible to remain in San Francisco any longer. Everyone appeared to be in perfect accord. The time had come to pull up stakes in America and join the burgeoning expatriate colony in Paris.

Margaret knew it was a move that her late husband would not have approved. It had been a crucial decision; she could only pray it was the right one. For her, Paris had always been the ultimate in musical culture. Filled with a strong parental sense of obligation to develop any artistic talent in the family, she could justify the move to herself. She realized, sadly, that she was cutting all ties, quite possibly forever, with her past life in America, and Margaret was now a middle-aged woman.

It was arranged for Sibyl and Marion to go ahead to Paris while Jane and Edith remained with their mother until she settled her husband's estate in San Francisco. Sibyl was ecstatic to know that the family would soon be reunited in Paris. The judge's death had been a devastating blow to her mother and sisters, but if it left any serious scars on Sibyl's psyche, the effects were not visible. With her father gone, all obstacles were removed from her path. Sibyl had long known that her mother secretly sympathized with her frustrated ambition for an operatic career. She lamented constantly to Marion during their voyage that she was nearly twenty-two and still had not made her debut.

Upon their arrival in Paris, the two sisters accepted temporary shelter with the American ambassador's family, Mr. and Mrs. McLane, in their embassy apartment on the avenue Montaigne. Mr. McLane soon found a suitable place for his wards at a small finishing school run by a Mlle Lantz. Mademoiselle allowed only French to be spoken under her roof so that all her charges might perfect their knowledge of the language. Most of the pensionnaires were either English or American, and in a short time the Sanderson girls had made friends with many of them.

Sibyl lost no time in renting a piano and reentering the class of Saint-Yves Bax at the Conservatoire. In a daily ritual, he drilled her on vocal exercises, and insisted she enroll in harmony classes as well. The experience would improve her musicianship, increase her ability to memorize, and be of invaluable assistance if she should ever sing with orchestra. Marion was pursuing her studies in art. She took lessons from Felix Barrias and attended night classes at Julian's Academy, studying with Robert Fleury and William-Adolphe Bouguereau.

One day a young Australian woman arrived at the pension from England. Mlle Lantz told her boarders that the new guest would be studying voice with Mme Marchesi, perhaps the most celebrated teacher in Paris. The young woman was decidedly buxom and physically unattractive, and she wore the dowdiest English clothes. She refused to speak French and at first seemed so distant and uncouth that it took everyone some time to warm up to her. The Sanderson sisters decided that one reason she created such a negative impression was because her basic command of the language was so insecure. If anyone at the pension could succeed in thawing her out, it was Sibyl, and gradually they grew to be fast friends. Her name was Mrs. Nellie Armstrong, but when she opened her mouth to sing, opinion was unanimous that this gauche Australian possessed one of the most glorious voices of the day. In less than a year she was to burst upon the musical horizon as Nellie Melba. Since Mlle Lantz gave occasional musical soirées, both Melba and Sibyl were called upon to perform.

As their mother and sisters were expected soon, Sibyl and Marion could no longer delay their quest for a furnished flat. They found an attractive apartment on the rue de Bassano at a very select *pension de famille* run by a charming English couple, Mr. and Mrs. Stark. There were always congenial Americans coming to the Starks' for dinner, among them the Boston painter Oudinot with his protégée Miss Greenough and her brother Horatio, both offspring of the neoclassical sculptor Horatio Greenough Sr. It was a relaxed atmosphere where everyone was interested in the arts and felt free to converse in English.

Tony de Navarro, the wealthy American owner of Navarro Flats, a New York City apartment complex, often dropped by. He was a dapper little man, immaculately dressed, with a long flowing mustache and heavily pomaded hair. A good amateur musician, he would sit down at the piano in the parlor to entertain the guests after dinner. He began to accompany Sibyl and soon became one of her most enthusiastic fans.

Tony had many acquaintances in Parisian artistic circles and squired the girls about the city to museums, galleries, and concerts. He introduced Sibyl to everyone as his protégée and confidently predicted stardom for her. He informed her that Opéra-Comique really meant opera with spoken dialogue and not necessarily comic opera. Actually, there were as many tragedies as comedies in its repertoire. Sibyl also learned that opera and theater were state supported in France, as in most European countries, and that the directors' policies must meet with the approval of the state department of fine arts.

Among those to whom Tony introduced the girls were Dr. and Mrs. Shepard, who occupied an elegant apartment on the avenue Montaigne. The Shepards were extremely cultivated people and prominent members of the English-speaking colony. Sibyl's voice soon became a familiar sound in their parlor. The Shepards agreed with the American playboy: this beautiful girl was destined to go far.

Shortly before their mother's arrival, the two sisters met the wealthy French family of Gustave Dreyfus, apparently no relation to the unfortunate officer whose court-martial was later to become the cause célèbre of the 1890s. The Dreyfuses took the girls into their home at once and introduced them to their son Karl and their four daughters, Juliette, Emma, Edwine, and Marcelle. The young ladies got along famously, and the Dreyfus family treated the Sanderson girls like their own flesh and blood.[1]

A banker by profession, Dreyfus was also an avid art collector. The family entertained on Thursday evenings, and many important Parisians called regularly. Sibyl often sang at their soirées, and they told her that the composer Jules Massenet was a close family friend. He had taught their daughters piano some years before and at one time had been considered practically a member of the household. His own daughter was an intimate companion of the Dreyfus girls. Recently, they hadn't seen him so often; his frenetic schedule now imposed strict limitations upon his time. However, Sibyl and Marion met numerous other celebrities at the Dreyfus receptions, including Italian author Gabriele D'Annunzio.

With the arrival of Margaret, Jane, and Edith shortly before Christmas of 1886, the entire family had a joyful reunion. After settling her husband's affairs, Margaret had sold their San Francisco home, and the family possessions were en route to France by steamer. Her sister, Mrs. John Yost, had agreed to care for their aging mother. The fact that her late husband had invested their money shrewdly came as no surprise to Margaret. His $200,000 legacy in no way approached the exaggerated accounts of the "fortune" Sibyl later flaunted before the European press, but it did provide a comfortable income for his family for the remainder of their lives. Margaret continued to mourn his death for several years and always appeared in public wearing widow's weeds. She never dreamed when she left her native land that she would not see it again until eighteen years later.

When the furniture arrived in the spring of 1887, the Sandersons had to seek larger quarters. Sibyl was thrilled to see her beloved Steinway upright again. Incredibly, after a seven months' voyage the Steinway remained reasonably in tune, certainly an omen that the family had made the right decision.

But Sibyl had a confession to make to her mother: she had left the Conservatoire in November 1886 after less than a year of study. It seemed such a waste of time, she rationalized, to spend hours of labor over tedious harmony exercises and endless attacking of tones. Besides, she had been extremely disappointed by Mr. Bax's official prognosis about her future. According to the candid professor her voice was now of sufficient volume for *opéra bouffe* (comic opera), but it would never be powerful enough for grand opera. This was an affront to her self-esteem. She felt certain she was destined for a great operatic career. Obviously she was wasting her time and the family largess on an institution that didn't have the discernment to recognize her potential. The next teacher she chose must have at least one important prerequisite: powerful connections to the lyric theater.

A delightful American girl, Grace Mosher, often came to the Stark pension that fall to dine with the New England painter Oudinot and his circle. Sibyl and Marion struck up a friendship with her and learned that she was studying painting with Carolus Duran and Jean-Jacques Henner. Her widowed mother and two sisters, Florence and Maude, were planning to join her soon from Boston. Florence wanted to study piano, and Maude, violin. When the rest of the Mosher family arrived, they took a quaint flat on the top floor of a rue Washington building with a spectacular view of the city.

Once the two families met, there was an instant rapport that was to last a lifetime. The Moshers existed on a very limited income, but Marion wrote that "never did a cheese omelet or a fresh, crisp salad taste so good as when one was seated around the Mosher supper table looking out over the lights of Paris."

The Moshers had courted the arts in Boston, and their salon back home had collected a colorful entourage of assorted New England painters, poets, and other writers. Having migrated to Paris over the years, many of these same artists once again gravitated to their former sanctuary, now transplanted to the rue Washington. The Mosher circle included the painter Oudinot; Phillip Hale, son of the famous author Edward Hale and later a distinguished Boston music critic; Episcopal bishop Phillips Brooks, then at Trinity Church, Boston; and the eccentric Canadian poet Bliss Carman. Carman recited his poetry in a high, shrill voice, and Sibyl was often called upon to sing, with Florence Mosher at the piano. The Lithuanian-born art authority Bernard Berenson, who had known the Moshers during his immigrant days in Boston, would often sit by the intimate coke fire, sipping coffee and expounding on European Renaissance art before an enthralled audience of American expatriates.

A year later the Sandersons were to meet the American playwright Clyde Fitch at the Mosher residence. Fitch was on his first visit abroad and had arranged to join his mother, who was staying with the Moshers. He had been writing poetry and short stories and was haphazardly supporting himself at the time by publishing tales for children in various magazines.

It was undoubtedly at the Shepard home that the Sandersons first encountered Fanny Reed, a grande dame of the American expatriate colony. Of indeterminate middle age, Miss Reed was a handsome, well-groomed woman whose prominent nose reinforced her dominant personality. She still wore the faded pink and blue ribbons of her halcyon days in the white hair that was piled high on her head. When she entered a room it was with such commanding authority that one imagined an invisible platoon marching behind her.

It had taken a lifetime of self-denial and sacrifice to achieve such self-possession. She and her sister, Mrs. Marietta Stevens, had started their long climb up the social ladder from the bottom rung some thirty years before in Boston. Marietta eventually captured wealthy hotel magnate Paran Stevens, and the couple produced a daughter, Minnie, who became Mrs. Arthur Paget of England. The death of her husband left Mrs. Stevens with the bulk of his fortune, and entrée into the best homes of international society. Fanny, on the other hand, devoted much of her time to caring for their aged mother and positively gloried in spinsterhood. She had no income of her own and derived an annual stipend from her generous sister, plus gifts from wealthy Americans anxious for their daughters to meet eligible titled Europeans. A few years later, in 1894, her influence peddling reached its zenith when she introduced multimillionaire Jay Gould's hunchbacked daughter Anna to France's Count Boniface de Castellane.

The Sandersons were told that Miss Reed was *the* person in the American colony who could make or break you. Besides operating under the illusion that she had once been a great beauty, she also suffered from the delusion that she possessed a voice even more ravishing than her looks. At various social functions she would terrorize guests with the prehistoric sounds issuing from her petrified vocal cords. Somehow the captive audience managed to survive and recover enough to feign the proper adulation.

Sibyl sang for her and for some inexplicable reason captured her fancy. The girl had talent, poise, temperament, and beauty—all the qualities Fanny fatuously told the Sandersons she herself had possessed at Sibyl's age. When Sibyl asked her to recommend a voice teacher, Miss Reed unhesitatingly chose the legendary Mathilde Marchesi. As she knew the lady personally, she offered to arrange an introduction, and with the starry-eyed girl in tow soon bore down upon Marchesi's studio on the rue Jouffroy.

Marchesi was an autocratic little German woman whose Sicilian husband, Salvatore Castrone, had adopted the title Marquis de Castrone. Her sharply pointed nose was complemented by an equally truculent lower lip. Her tiny, beadlike eyes missed nothing, and if their pupils were observed closely, it was said they would turn into miniature dollar signs through spontaneous generation. She was a veritable Prussian field marshal who had made a fortune on American mothers with stagestruck daughters. Ironically, money was never discussed once Madame deigned to accept a girl as a pupil. It remained for her husband Salvatore to handle such mundane matters. From then on the cash was to be deposited in an envelope and left on a table in the vestibule on the first of every month. Marchesi had coached many celebrities, including the American opera star Emma Nevada and, more recently, Sibyl's good friend Nellie Melba, who was on the way to becoming Marchesi's prize protégée. Autographed pictures of Gounod, Saint-Saëns, Massenet, and all the other great French musicians graced the walls of the hallowed studio.

After Sibyl's audition, Marchesi soberly informed her: "Mademoiselle, your voice has not been brought out properly. I cannot take you in hand unless you consent to study at least two years with me."

"Two years?" Sibyl echoed incredulously. "But that is too long. I have lost too much time already." And with that naive response, she committed the unpardonable sin of walking out on the vocal empress, leaving Miss Reed speechless.

Sibyl now began a frantic trial-and-error search for a voice teacher that became a constant source of irritation for her mother. There would be the usual audition, the usual promise, a lesson or two, followed by the usual cancellation.

She is said to have studied for a while with the noted Anna de la Grange, but this has never been confirmed.

It was inevitable that about this time she should become attracted by the reputation of the Polish matinee idol Jean de Reszke, whose highly successful teaching career would extend from the turn of the century to his death in 1925. The handsome tenor stood six feet tall, and his brother, famed basso Edouard, six foot four. They were accepting a limited number of students between their long tours. Women in the audience screamed and fainted when Jean sang to them. In addition to his splendid voice, his leonine head of dark, wavy hair, impressive physique, and magnetic eyes kept his fan mail overflowing with marriage proposals.

Sibyl was determined to charm him with the same wiles that had mesmerized Cardinali back in San Francisco. Her beauty was a weapon that she had long ago learned to use to full advantage. At present its potency was far more lethal than her lyric prowess. She could almost picture de Reszke on his knees, begging her to costar with him in his next opera.

Preening herself to perfection, the violet-eyed ingenue paraded a series of vocal and physical charms before him. Although he was impressed by the latter, his verdict on the former was basically the same as Marchesi's. Somehow he survived the audition without groveling at her feet, but he and his brother did agree to tutor her for several months before they left Paris on their next tour.

As it turned out, de Reszke's departure was not an irreparable loss. His ability to teach did not begin to rival his singing, and most of the principles he espoused seemed to belong to one of his former teachers, Giovanni Sbriglia. For now Jean de Reszke appeared to have no sensitivity to, or understanding of, the female vocal mechanism. "Draw back the uvula," he would order imperiously. "Pinch the tonsils, and push—PUSH from the diaphragm! Never will I allow you to use any nose or head resonance. Keep the abdomen expanded as long as you can so that your breath may be kept under compression as long as possible." Sibyl discovered she didn't have the strength to last through his torturous voice-forcing sessions. She could barely produce an audible whisper when she left his studio.

It did not surprise her to learn that his ruthless methods of tone forcing had crippled many an aspiring young singer.[2] Furthermore, de Reszke appeared to be an egomaniac who surrounded himself with a legion of sycophants. Foremost among them was his worshipful valet Moufflard. Years later, the valet even opened a voice studio, claiming that only he knew the "true method" of the great de Reszke.

Sibyl learned that the celebrated singer was originally a baritone who had gone to Giovanni Sbriglia on a dare. Sbriglia bet him six months of free tutelage that he could open his top voice register and turn him into the world's number-one tenor. When Sbriglia succeeded, the vocal transformation skyrocketed both of them to international fame. From then on the professor was overrun with almost as many famous students as Marchesi. The great bass Pol Plançon publicly announced that he owed everything to Sbriglia, and the American dramatic soprano Lillian Nordica also coached with him.

After the de Reszkes left Paris, Sibyl was determined to continue her studies with the Italian professor. His home was located on the rue de Provence, and the Sandersons learned that his wife was an American who acted as his secretary. As Sibyl and her mother were ushered into his studio for an audition, a resonant high C flamboyantly announced the maestro's presence in the doorway; he was a small man with an enormous, almost disproportionate chest, dark thinning hair, and thick, furry eyebrows. After hearing Sibyl sing, he excitedly rushed forward to unbutton her dress and, to Margaret's horror, began to behave with embarrassing familiarity toward her daughter. However, the volatile professor was merely explaining his breathing methods to both of them as he pressed and probed Sibyl's rib cage.

"I don't breathe," he emphatically proclaimed to his students, "I build up ze chest!"[3]

Despite the novelty of this approach, Margaret decided that the little pouter pigeon was serious. He insisted that Sibyl purchase a pair of dumbbells and start working out at home. "Beaucoup des dumbbells" became his weekly sermon.

Sbriglia labeled his method "diaphragmatic." He sat at an upright piano in his studio with a mirror on the wall before him, while she stood in back of the piano during the lesson. In this way the professor claimed he could keep a watchful eye on his pupil's breathing and his own at the same time. He sang exercises to demonstrate his theory of singing against the diaphragm, carefully watching his expanding chest in the mirror. He showed her how to sing forward against the chest for support. The stronger the chest, the stronger the diaphragmatic support.

The theory made sense to her, and she noticed a certain increase in her vocal strength. Yet even though Sbriglia was gentler than De Reszke, basically he was pouring the same wine into her glass—camouflaged by a different bottle. He was still forcing tone. The professor assured her that her compatriot, the great Lillian Nordica, had spent hours building up her chest. Sibyl glanced in the mirror and shuddered. The idea of becoming an Amazon repelled her.

Next she entered the studio of Mme Duglé for some coaching. Although the lady did not have the reputation of either Marchesi or Sbriglia, Mme Duglé was Charles Gounod's niece. It wasn't long before she had introduced Sibyl to the old gentleman. Gounod was by this time in the twilight of his life, but still revered as the indisputable high priest of the French operatic school. A little man with remarkably expressive eyes and a luxuriant white beard, his appearance gave the impression of a curate. There was something distinctly ecclesiastic about his manner. When he lifted a hand, he became an abbé imparting a benediction. His speech flowed with melodious intonation; his diction was precision itself. Even his studio resembled a miniature sanctuary. It contained a stained-glass window that diffused the light, baptizing both the organ and an upright piano with a spiritual glow.

Sibyl adored the master the minute she met him. She announced that she wanted him to coach her on his roles of Marguerite (*Faust*) and Juliette. After a preliminary audition, Gounod sat down at the piano to work with her. She discovered that he possessed an exceptionally high and true tenor voice that, curiously, had not grown old. Its strength had long since waned, yet as he sang his tenor parts opposite her in subsequent lessons, he could still modulate his voice well enough to bring out many beautiful inflections, which continued to amaze her. She found him to be a perfectionist in matters of interpretation and style, and also strict with enunciation. He often used metaphor as a valuable teaching device. Marion's memoirs reveal that he told Sibyl to feel the mood of each operatic scene: "You must see, only then can you be taught to express." Several times Gounod took her to the Opéra to hear his works performed, and after one performance of *Faust* he introduced her to the cast as his "coming Marguerite."

Like most of Gounod's students, Sibyl was somewhat astonished the first time she met his wife, whose Brobdingnagian proportions seemed to dwarf the pipe organ in his studio. She was acquainted with a few details about their stormy marriage. She knew of their long separation when the composer went to England to live with soprano Georgina Weldon. Nevertheless, Sibyl found Anna Gounod to be a warm and sympathetic person who was to remain a loyal friend even after her husband's death.

After the Sandersons' furniture had arrived from San Francisco, Margaret rented a large mezzanine apartment on the rue Lincoln. Here Sibyl had a music room in which to practice. There was a salon large enough for entertaining and a good-sized dining room, where Margaret was soon to begin her Sunday-evening receptions.

Following the move, Sibyl was closer to the American bar just off the Champs-Élysées where she could order her special brand of American cigarettes. It was an age when ladies concealed habits of this sort and usually delegated the task of purchasing such items to their maids. The American colony was shocked at this liberated girl for having the audacity to walk into a bar and personally leave an order.

Little by little everyone grew used to Sibyl's eccentricities. One day she would don a black crepe mourning outfit in memory of her father; the very next afternoon she would appear dressed entirely in crimson, all the way to her red parasol. The American community was soon to learn, as were the French, that the good fairies had given this unpredictable girl everything at birth except self-control and stability.

She was becoming more and more Parisian every day. In spite of a slight accent, there was an infantine lilt to her speech much like that of French children. Her vivacity and joie de vivre seemed so Parisian. All she needed now, or so her well-meaning friends thought, was to find some magic lamp at a flea market from which she could conjure up a genie to open those theatrical doors. What they didn't realize was that she already had all the magic she needed in her throat, and that her genie was about to appear.

Chapter 6

The Genie

"To the sound of heavy hammers of brass, so I was born," Jules Massenet once confided in an interview.[1] He was a trifle poetic in his description of the event, but nonetheless accurate. His father, Alexis Massenet, a graduate of the Polytechnic School in Paris, had been a military officer during the First Empire and later became an iron master at Saint-Étienne in the Loire district of France. He was the inventor of huge metal hammers that crushed bars of steel into sickles and scythes by heavy, rhythmic blows. So it can be said that the future composer made his worldly entrance on 12 May 1842 accompanied by the cyclopean timpani of the iron foundry. Massenet's later interviews reveal that his father had sired a veritable rabbit warren of a family—twenty-one children by two wives. Jules was the youngest of the last four born to the second wife, Éléonore Adélaïde Royer de Marancour. According to Demar Irvine's biography of the composer, however, the combined family totaled an even dozen.[2]

Six years after Jules's birth, declining health forced Alexis Massenet to sell his iron foundry and move the family to Paris. His wife, a piano teacher, elected the fatal day of 24 February 1848 to initiate her son into the world of music, and the boy's first steps at the piano proved to be no more melodious than his birth. His lesson was interrupted by gunfire in the city, which lasted for several hours. The revolution had begun, and that evening the frightened five-year-old gazed out of the window at the carnage in the streets. The grim scene would make him abhor violence for the rest of his life.

The youngster's progress at the piano was so rapid that shortly after his ninth birthday he was accepted at the Conservatoire. His teachers were encouraging, and the youthful prodigy soon became the unofficial "laureate" of the institution.

When his father's ill health forced the now impoverished family to move to Chambéry for a climatic change, Jules continued to work hard at his musical studies. But after a ten-month absence, he missed his teachers in Paris so much that his parents allowed him to return. Contrary to his statement in his auto-biography, he did not remain away from Paris for "two whole years." The Conservatoire records reveal that he was gone only from January to October 1855.

Once back in Paris, he stayed with an older sister, Mme Julie Cavaillé, and reentered the Conservatoire to study piano again with Adolphe-François Laurent. As his father could no longer afford to send him an allowance, he was dependent upon his sister's charity. Massenet loathed his constant state of penury and in later life could see nothing romantic whatsoever about poverty.

Upon entering puberty, he began pursuing composition studies under François Bazin and Ambroise Thomas, whose protégé he was to become. Although his two greatest successes, *Mignon* and *Hamlet,* were yet to be written, Thomas was a man of vast learning who gave young Massenet a solid technical foundation.

The ambitious youth displayed a demonic capacity for work and won first prize in piano as well as in counterpoint and fugue. In 1863 his cantata *David Rizzio* was submitted to the Académie des Beaux Arts, which awarded him the Prix de Rome. As its select recipient, he was granted a four-year term of study in Italy and Germany plus an allowance of 3,000 francs a year.

Massenet was enchanted to be visiting a country as rich in ancient culture and art as Italy. After considerable sightseeing he began his studies in Rome, where he met Franz Liszt, who was living in the monastery of the Madonna del Rosario. While attending one of Liszt's receptions, he was introduced to a pretty French piano student, Constance Louise de Gressy (alias Orry de Sainte-Marie, alias Ninon de Saint-Marie), whom he had noticed a few days before on the church steps of Aracoeli. A good deal of confusion exists about her multiple names because her birth records were destroyed in a fire. Perhaps her mother was married three times, first to an Orry, then to a de Gressy, and finally to a Monsieur Saint-Marie, since her brother Abel Orry was only two years older than her.[3] According to Massenet's unreliable memoirs, Liszt was unwittingly playing Cupid when he suggested that Massenet coach her. Massenet learned to call the girl "Ninon," an affectionate family nickname.

They played duets, they took drives in the country, they went sightseeing with eyes only for each other. Massenet and Louise were falling in love. When they returned to France, in spite of some opposition from his fiancée's family (who may have hoped for a more ambitious union), they were eventually married in the little church of Avon outside Fontainebleau on 8 October 1866. Two years later, their only child, Juliette, was born.

The young musician now faced the struggle to earn a living. He accompanied choruses, gave piano lessons, and played triangle and kettledrum in theater orchestras. Fortunately, as the recipient of the Grand Prix, he was awarded a temporary stipend of 3,000 francs a year that enabled him to survive. He soon met a young publisher, Georges Hartmann, who took a chance on many unknown French composers, and it was he who published Massenet's first song cycle, *Poème d'Avril*. In 1867 his first operatic work, a one-act opus entitled *La grand' tante* (The Great Aunt), received its premiere at the Opéra-Comique— another benefit of winning the Prix de Rome. He was soon to learn the exasperating trials of writing for the stage.

In his debut opera the scene opened in Brittany on a wild, stormy night. A servant girl had to build a fire and at the same time face the door through which the hero, played by the celebrated Victor Capoul, was to enter, singing, "What a country! What a wilderness! Not a face soul in sight!" Truly, there wasn't. The girl was so nervous on opening night that she forgot to turn toward the door. When Capoul made his entrance, he abruptly encountered her protruding derrière as he wheeled and sang, "Thank God! At last a face!" An uproarious outburst of laughter swept the entire house. After the close of the performance, just as the stage manager was about to introduce the composer and the librettist, a cat stole the applause by strolling nonchalantly onto the stage.

Massenet identified closely with animals throughout his life. "He who loves animals loves people," he wrote in his memoirs. Cats were his particular favorite. He communed with them, sang them his themes, and told them his dreams. His affinity for the feline species approached that of a Pied Piper. As late as one year before his death, according to accounts found in the files of the New York Public Library, stray cats were still following him home in a mesmerized trance. In a cold Milanese winter he shared his food with some thirty shivering pigeons perched on his balcony. On one Christmas Eve in Rome he found himself in the midst of a procession of animals before the church of Santa Maria Maggiore. Like Saint Francis, Massenet entered the church with the herd, embracing a goat who refused to leave his side.

In the beginning of his career it was only natural that the budding Orpheus should meet with a certain amount of rejection from critics as well as conductors. When his *First Suite for Orchestra* was given its premiere by Jules-Étienne Pasdeloup's orchestra, the hissing of an enemy claque became so infectious that the entire audience burst into audible displeasure. It was a devastating experience for the hypersensitive composer, and for the rest of his life he avoided the premieres of his works as often as he could. The second performance of this suite sparked a hostile review by Albert Wolff in *Le Figaro*, which, in turn, generated a donnybrook between composer and critic for a while in the same paper.

But Massenet refused to be defeated. After a stinging rebuff by Pasdeloup, his first oratorio, *Marie-Magdeleine*, was heard in 1873 with the legendary Pauline Viardot creating the title role. Two years later, a second oratorio, *Ève*, helped to win him the Légion d'Honneur. When his opera *Le roi de Lahore* was given its premiere in 1877 at the Paris Opéra, Massenet's reputation was secured. He was nominated for an appointment as professor at the Conservatoire in 1878 by his teacher Ambroise Thomas and held the position until 1896 (when Thomas died) despite considerable absenteeism. As Massenet's interests became increasingly involved with the theater—his first love—he was forced to neglect his classes shamefully. By 1890 they were often left to various assistants for weeks at a time.

In the 1880s Massenet produced some outstanding operatic works, notably, *Hérodiade*, 1881; *Manon*, 1884; and *Le Cid*, 1885. With the brilliant success of *Manon*, Massenet assumed his well-deserved position as crown prince of the French operatic school. Venerable Charles Gounod, with his long string of operatic successes, still wore the royal mantle, but Jules Massenet now stood at his right hand as heir apparent.

The composer has written in his memoirs that during his youth he had an insatiable appetite. Like any ambitious man he was also insatiable for financial success. Now that his theatrical works were enjoying popular runs at both Parisian opera houses, Massenet was basking in prosperity and all its concomitant rewards for the first time in his life. Making personal checks on ticket sales became part of his daily routine. Later, when telephones were installed, managers grew accustomed to his daily calls. He invested his earnings cleverly at the Bourse and developed into such an astute stock-market speculator that even the brokers became impressed with his inquiries. Having grown up on the periphery of poverty and never forgetting his starving student days, he was determined never to find himself in the tragic pecuniary straits of Mozart, Schubert, and other famous predecessors. He died a millionaire, probably the wealthiest French composer of the nineteenth century.

His early struggles undoubtedly were responsible for his later miserliness. The composer Gustave Charpentier, who once studied with him, has related a youthful incident about falling ill in his little room in Montmartre. One day he was pleasantly surprised to discover Massenet had climbed five or six flights of stairs to visit him. Charpentier was lying in bed with nothing over him but his overcoat, utterly destitute.

Massenet recalled that when he, himself, was a young man, ill and penniless in a similar situation, he had been touched by a visit from his teacher Ambroise Thomas. He related dramatically how Thomas, moved by his poverty-stricken condition, immediately offered him money for food and medicine. Before Charpentier could open his mouth to inquire about the outcome, Massenet added in deadly earnest, "Of course, I proudly refused!"[4]

In his memoirs, Léon Daudet recalls the painful fact that for all the free hospitality Massenet enjoyed at his parents' Thursday-night dinners, the latter were never once accorded an opportunity to savor Mme Massenet's culinary specialties. Daudet was especially bitter because his father, distinguished author Alphonse Daudet, had collaborated with the composer.

Later in Massenet's career there was a certain Argentinean impresario who had produced the Frenchman's operas for years throughout South America without paying him any royalties. It was a constant source of irritation to him. One day the composer was surprised to receive a photograph from the gentleman with a request for an autographed one in return. Massenet obliged, but sent the picture C.O.D. instead. "I am keeping the three francs which you enclosed for postage," he wrote to the producer. "It will always remain that much to my credit in our little account."

Massenet's work ethic was relentless, his self-discipline compulsive. The composer would labor unceasingly for twelve to fifteen hours at a time if necessary to finish an operatic act. Since he seldom required more than four or five hours of sleep, he would rise in his red dressing gown and work through the early morning hours on his compositions. Even when he was ill, he would demand to be propped up in bed so that he could continue to compose.

He was extremely well organized. His study at home reflected an orderliness that bordered on the neurotic. The room contained his piano, his composition paper, and always, on his desk, well-sharpened pencils. Bookcases lined the walls; paintings, precious vases, photographs, and other memorabilia of his career were also neatly arranged.

The same systematic orderly atmosphere prevailed in his little workshop of an office, more a cabinet than a room, in the publishing house of his editor, Georges Hartmann. Here a stained-glass window threw a rainbow of color over the composer and his music as he wrote at a low, counterlike desk that looked more like a workbench. Every article was in place, manuscripts piled neatly, scores arranged with an almost fanatical fastidiousness. Massenet never needed a piano to compose, and his librettos were always memorized beforehand. He could be found jotting down phrases in cabs, on trains, on buses, and in restaurants, wherever he might be when the muse summoned him. In later years, after he had purchased his Égreville château, he kept several spinets concealed in specially constructed desks—whether he admitted it or not, the composer did need a piano to work out orchestral counterpoint. His hobby was collecting fine bookbinding. He loved nothing more than to take guests through his library and proudly point out the exquisite bindings on display.

He was Saint Francis with an impish smile: half faun, half angel. Recollections abound of this small, febrile man burning with nervous energy. Gertrude Atherton described him as "volatile, effervescent, yet playful as a child at times." Descriptions of his features at this period mention a face sparkling with an admirable pair of hazel eyes and festooned with a dark, pointed mustache. His long, black, thinning hair was brushed straight back from a sculptured forehead. His finely chiseled nose was set above the most mobile of mouths. Although he seldom looked anyone straight in the eye, when he did his gaze was like flashes of sheet lightning upon a landscape.

Massenet's efforts to cope with his waning sex appeal in middle age were not only pathetic but degrading. In his *Souvenirs* Léon Daudet has left posterity a devastating description of the birdlike courtship dance the aging composer would perform when introduced to a pretty young woman in Alphonse Daudet's home.

His first object, upon entering the room, was to compliment everyone present on his or her appearance and accomplishments, after which he would collapse in an armchair, acting like mama's spoiled boy who's thirsty or mother's little doggy who's hungry. Tea and cake would be forthcoming, and while he lapped up one and sprinkled the crumbs of the other, he maintained a steady flow of simpering trivialities always intended to flatter the particular listener. Among the guests were always certain old ladies who "just adore music," exhibiting the decayed remains of their former physical glories. Massenet would treat them as if they were still twenty, literally smothering them with compliments. Meanwhile, his roving eye, glancing beyond these venerable relics, would discover some really young and lovely woman modestly staying in the background. At once he would drop to his hands and knees, crawl over to her while executing some sort of a Pyrrhic war dance; in short, he would perform any antic likely to amuse—or annoy—the chosen one, who, for the time being, had become his Dulcinea. . . . His shallow but swooning glances seemed to implore, to demand, the immediate gratification of his desires. His eyes would urge, beseech: "Here, now at once." He had all the inflammable sensuality of the lyrebird, or the peacock when it spreads its tail. . . . Invariably the husbands of these love objects were present, and . . . Massenet would be obliged to quickly allay his fever. Resigning himself to seek diversion in music, he would tell his woes at the piano. There Massenet became transfigured, really great—in fact, incomparable.

The *Musical Courier*[5] and other publications carried accounts of Massenet pretending to be a chimpanzee, dexterously scratching himself, grunting and begging for a banana (a kiss on the forehead), and leaping from chair to chair with amazing simian grace. Or he would become a dog, seated on its haunches, panting and entreating the new mistress for the ultimate reward: an affectionate caress on the forehead.

Massenet loved his practical jokes, his crude little pranks. Marion Sanderson has left posterity some hitherto unpublished anecdotes about them. "Massenet's moods would change at the twinkle of an eye," she wrote, "one minute bubbling over with merriment, the next, filled with tears."

He would espy the exquisite Marion, trudging home from her studio in the rain on the Champs-Élysées, paint box in one hand, the other holding up her long skirts. Then pulling his fedora over his eyes, he would sneak up behind her, seizing her by the arm, whisper menacingly, "Ah, Mademoiselle, I've got you now, don't I?" and chuckle heartily over the fright he had given her.

One night after he had taken Sibyl's three sisters to hear Yvette Guilbert at a little outdoor garden theater, he purposely fell behind them on the way home. Then he crumpled up a piece of paper and threw it at their backs, at the same time gruffly expectorating on the pavement to give the effect of having spat upon them. The infuriated trio wheeled in outraged precision, according to Marion's reminiscences, only to discover Massenet "hiding behind a nearby tree convulsed with laughter and delighted with his success."

Part of his chameleon personality was his rapier wit, which fascinated everyone who came in contact with him. The periodical file on Massenet at the New York Public Library contains the following selected anecdotes from *Musical America* and other journals:

A young composer once went to him with the intention of playing his first opera for the master. "You know," began the neophyte, "Molière used to read all of his plays to an old woman in the belief that scenes which evoked applause on her part would produce a similar effect in the theater. Hence, I have decided to perform my work for you feeling sure that whatever pleases you will appeal to the public in like manner."

"You are very kind, very kind indeed, my dear sir," interrupted Massenet, "but since you are not Molière, you will pardon me for not being your old woman."

Once a petulant lady rebuked him for not having glanced in the direction of her box the previous night when he was on the podium. He responded graciously, "I am so sorry, but you see, my dear, while conducting I have the bad habit of looking now and then at the orchestra."

On another occasion a young woman gushed, "I am so thrilled to meet you, dear Maestro, at last. I have often thought I would give five years of my life to make your acquaintance." A roguish twinkle gleamed in Massenet's eyes, and he purred, "Mmmm, to whom would you give those five years?"

Colleagues, nevertheless, knew for a long time that they could not trust his leprechaun smile or sympathetic handshake. Massenet was a master of duplicity. Mary Garden wrote in *Collier's Magazine* years later that "one could not believe a word he uttered."[6] He would stop a soprano backstage at the Opéra-Comique at the most inopportune times, declaring there was no one with such marvelous gifts as hers. Then, after virtually burying her under an avalanche of flattery, he would announce his intentions of writing his next work for her alone. The singer learned not to take him seriously. Heaven only knew how many artists had been forced to listen to the same expressions of adulation that day.

Saint-Saëns and Gounod learned of Massenet's little chicaneries early in their associations with him. In 1880, an important musical festival took place at the Concert du Châtelet. All three composers were invited to conduct some of their works. Massenet, who was an excellent conductor, decided upon a scene from *Le roi de Lahore.* He secretly arranged for a heavily reinforced brass section to augment the orchestra at the last minute. Saint-Saëns, who lacked his colleague's dexterity on the podium, was enraged at this deceitful maneuver, but the discovery came too late for any countermeasures. Needless to say, the decibel level of Massenet's performance was ear-splitting, and the audience was totally overwhelmed by such massive waves of sound. The composer had more than achieved his purpose: to steal the show from his competitors.

Massenet's hypersensitivity and jealousy at the success of others were well known, too. At a rehearsal of *Manon* in 1883, the tenor Jean-Alexandre Talazac, who was creating the role of Des Grieux, decided to play a "spiteful" joke on Massenet.[7] During this same time he was also rehearsing Delibes's *Lakmé*, which he was to sing a few months earlier than *Manon*. One day he encountered Massenet in a rehearsal room at the Opéra-Comique.

"Eh, bien, this *Lakmé*," asked Massenet, filled with apprehension as usual, "is it going well?"

"Admirably," replied Talazac, who not so innocently began to sing a theme from *Manon*, substituting the name of Lakmé: "Lakmé! Lakmé! Astonishing sphinx! Veritable siren!"

"What's that?" shouted Massenet, turning crimson from shock. "That is a phrase from *Manon*, one of the most beautiful!" "Ah, cher Talazac, what a catastrophe! What a disaster!"

For a moment he thought that Delibes had stolen one of his precious phrases and plagiarized the words as well. To calm the composer's soaring blood pressure, friends thought they would have to resort to a sedative.

It was one of the few times he had been caught off guard. Generally, he had an uncanny ability to outguess, outmaneuver, and outwit his competitors. Did he have moments of prescience? The fact that he possessed an extraordinary imagination is well known, but all his biographers have overlooked his tendency toward the psychic. Just how gifted he was in this particular area is a matter of speculation, for Massenet himself was always careful to disguise these uncanny moments as flights of poetic fancy.

"Love, and your flower will be brought to light." These are the words that the dead poet Alfred de Musset supposedly whispered to Massenet in the Forest of Fontainebleau on his wedding day. Whether Massenet believed this communication actually occurred is difficult to determine. In his memoirs he is constantly hiding such quasi-psychic experiences behind phrases such as "I seemed to hear" or "I have always fancied that I saw."

He mentions that when he was nine years old he "imagined" he saw Napoleon and Josephine in the front-tier box of the small theater during his conservatory audition. At this age he probably did not know that both monarchs had attended such occasions in the past and sat in that very box. Did he really believe he had seen such a vision? The impression was forceful enough to have been included in the memoirs of his old age, but always carefully cloaked to suggest nothing more than the overzealous workings of a youthful imagination.

Psychically gifted people differ in their approach to a subject, but one thing they have in common is the fact that they prefer to have some object, some souvenir of the person or topic upon which they are concentrating. Massenet disclosed in several interviews that he always wanted some memento, souvenir, or picture of the story he was setting to music. While writing *Le roi de Lahore,* he kept caressing an intricate gold-and-blue-enameled Hindu box that rested upon his desk. During the creation of *Les Érinnyes,* his gaze shifted back and forth from the manuscript to an exquisitely sculptured group of dancing figurines that stood nearby.

He never kept a sketchbook of themes for future use as did Beethoven, who was constantly reworking and reshaping them. He never endured the agonies of thematic birth that Chopin suffered, rewriting a phrase over fifty times, chewing his pencils to pieces, and tearing the buttons off his shirts. Once Massenet caught the mood of the subject, or perhaps its vibrations, musical ideas quickly welled up in his mind, breaking the floodgates of creation, and poured out faster than he could set them down on paper.

Identifying with the author's surroundings often sparked remarkable musical creativity within him. Much of his Louis XV masterpiece *Manon* was written at The Hague in the very room in which the author of the novel, the Abbé Prévost, had lived. Massenet even slept in Prévost's gondola-shaped bed.

A visit to the house in Wetzlar, Germany, where Goethe had written his immortal romance *The Sorrows of Young Werther* proved to be a deeply moving experience for the composer, who soon afterward began setting the story to music. Marion Sanderson wrote in her memoirs that Massenet would go to the Trocadéro Museum in Paris to gaze hypnotically at the mummy of the "ancient Egyptian dancer Thaïs, mistress of Alexander the Great," when he was composing the score about another Thaïs for Sibyl. (Thaïs was actually a Greek courtesan and the mistress of Alexander's general, Ptolemy.)

Massenet never clarified the frustrating statement in his autobiography that "an invisible, secret power directed my life." If anything, he tried to obscure it. In an interview in the *New York Tribune* a few weeks after his death, soprano Bessie Abott recalled an unusual incident that happened to them. They were both standing by the edge of a pool before the palace of Versailles one autumn day watching the dead leaves fall into the water. Massenet seemed to be in a reverie, or was it a trance? Suddenly, he grabbed Miss Abott's arm, pointing to the surface of the pool, and cried excitedly, "Look! Look! Don't you see them?

There are the faces of all the dear, dead women which were mirrored here in the great days of the past. Look! There is Louise de la Vallière as blond as wheat and plump as a vineyard quail. There is Pompadour magnificently beautiful, and there—there is a supremely lovely face, but sad as the mother who turns from her first born's grave. It—it is the face of Marie Antoinette."

Miss Abott admitted she could see nothing but the floating leaves. She described Massenet's state as "uncanny" and said that she had to take him by the arm and "drag him away." Was this perhaps a hallucination similar to those which, according to biographers, afflicted Chopin periodically? Again, we don't know.

On the night he was to meet Sibyl Sanderson at a dinner party, he didn't really want to go. At the time he was depressed by the fact that the director of the Opéra-Comique had recently rejected one of his operas. Yet, he wrote in his memoirs, "It seemed to me perhaps my afflicted heart might be meeting something there which would turn aside my discouragement." Was this another hint that he knew something extraordinary was about to happen to him?

Chapter 7

Pygmalion Appears

Massenet wrote in *Mes souvenirs,* originally published in newspaper install-ments in 1911, that his first encounter with Sibyl Sanderson took place at a din-ner party in the home of a rich American family. If the hostess really was an American, she had to have been either Mrs. Walden Pell, who maintained an elegant musical salon in Paris, or Mrs. Ples Moore, better known as Mrs. "Plus" Moore, or just plain "mother Moore." Of the two hostesses Kate Moore was by far the more colorful. Despite her various nicknames, Mrs. Moore was the rich-est, most obese American in Paris and a charitable, impulsive woman, if not a particularly erudite one. In an ambitious climb up the social ladder to attract the rich, the titled, and the famous to her door, she spread her extravagant gifts munificently. One example of her largess was the distribution of thirty grand-tier boxes at the Italian Opera House to her retinue of sycophants every season. Small wonder that her parties were frequented by princes, bankers, diplomats, and artists from all over the world. She died just as she had lived, faithfully rewarding her social lackeys in her legacy. Fanny Reed had introduced the Sandersons to Mrs. Pell and probably Mrs. Moore as well. Fanny knew everyone in Paris who belonged to the beau monde. Yet Fanny seldom entertained; she maintained a symbiotic existence by having others entertain her.

A different version of events has been given by Marion Sanderson, who wrote in her unpublished memoirs that it was the Gustave Dreyfus family who intro-duced Sibyl to Massenet for the first time. The four Dreyfus girls had been stu-dents of Massenet and were good friends of his daughter Juliette. The first French newspaper accounts of the fateful meeting mention the home of a Parisian banker. Mr. Dreyfus was a banker and a lover of the arts. This account is consistent with Marion's recollections.

Still a third version exists in a letter Massenet wrote to Ruggiero Leoncavallo on 2 January 1892: "What great success for Mlle Sanderson ever since the day when, recommended by you, I first heard this artist to whom I owe more than 100 performances of *Esclarmonde* and again more of *Manon*."[1]

Wherever the meeting took place, their separate stars came into conjunction during a summer night in 1887. Massenet recorded a detailed account of that dinner party in his autobiography. He mentioned that he was seated between a lady composer and a French diplomat. After dinner, the guests were ushered into the drawing room for some music. Massenet was doing his best to escape from boredom when two ladies, an older and a younger, both dressed in black, entered the room. The master of the house hastened to greet them, and Massenet was presented to them shortly.

The composer described the scene that followed:

> The younger was extraordinarily beautiful; the other was her mother, also lovely, with that thoroughly American beauty which the republic of the stars and stripes often sends us.
>
> "Dear master," said the younger woman with a slight accent, "I have been asked to this friendly house this evening to have the honor of meeting you and to let you hear my voice. I am the daughter of a supreme court judge in America and I have lost my father. He left my mother, my sisters, and me a fortune, but I want to go on the stage. If they blame me for it, after I have succeeded, I shall reply that success excuses everything."

Without further ado, Massenet ambled to the piano to accompany the neophyte.

> "You will pardon me," she added, "if I do not sing your own music. That would be too audacious of me."
>
> She had scarcely said this when her voice sounded magical, dazzling, in the Queen of the Night aria from *The Magic Flute* (Mozart).
>
> What a fascinating voice! It ranged from low G to the counter G—three octaves—in full voice and in pianissimo. I was astounded, stupefied, subjugated! When such voices occur, it is fortunate that they have the theater in which to display themselves; the world is their domain. I ought to say that I had recognized in that future artist, together with the rarity of that organ, intelligence, a flame, a personality which were reflected luminously in her admirable features. All these qualities are of the first importance on the stage.[2]

So wrote Jules Massenet of that first encounter, although by 1911 he had taken a certain amount of poetic license in recalling it. In reality he had not been overwhelmed by the ambitious foreigner. He told Fanny Edgar Thomas of the *Musical Courier* just a few years later that upon first hearing, her voice had not impressed him particularly. It was her dramatic temperament that sent seismic waves through him. Her sensuous way of moving, the sinuous grace of her speech and gestures, the magnetism of her rain-blue eyes—she seemed to be an incarnation of all the famous temptresses of history.

He made no mention in his autobiography that Sibyl wanted to study his scores with him, and that his iron willpower vanished when she turned a seductive array of charms upon him. Despite whatever may or may not have occurred, the shaken composer left the house with the firm conviction he had caught a glimpse of Manon herself. The young siren departed with more self-assurance than ever. Sibyl was convinced that once Massenet made good his promise to coach her, he would be her "open sesame" to stardom.

In his memoirs the composer exaggerated his next actions. He stated that he rushed to Hartmann's office the morning after their momentous meeting, stridently trumpeting his discovery of America. Hartmann seemed preoccupied with another matter. It concerned a new libretto for an opera to be given at the Universal Exposition the following year. Would the master compose the music? Massenet wrote that he had scarcely glanced through a couple of scenes when he exclaimed enthusiastically, "I have the artist for this role! I heard her yesterday! She is Mademoiselle Sibyl Sanderson! She will create *Esclarmonde!*"

This scene probably never happened except in his imagination, for Massenet neglected to say that he had had the libretto of *Esclarmonde* in his possession since December 1886. He later recorded Sibyl's first lesson with him as occurring on 16 September 1887, in an elegant leather-bound volume of *Manon* that he presented to her on her birthday in December of that year. It was no accident she had sung scenes from that opera for her preliminary instruction.[3] By the time she had finished the second lesson, the extent of her interpretative capabilities was dawning upon him. He later told Fanny Edgar Thomas that one audition had not been sufficient. By October he was completely bewitched. Here was the Manon for whom he had been waiting and searching for over two years.

Manon was Massenet's masterpiece. Inspired by the Abbé Prévost's famous novella *Manon Lescaut* (or, more fully, *The Story of the Chevalier des Grieux and of Manon Lescaut*), the opera had been written at The Hague in 1882 and finished in Paris the following year. In the winter of 1883 the composer played the score for Léon Carvalho, director of the Opéra-Comique at that time, and his collaborators Messrs Meilhac and Gille. Carvalho and his wife Caroline, a famous prima donna, were tremendously impressed with the score, and Massenet saw no harm in advancing his cause by discreetly dedicating the work to Madame Carvalho. After a long search for the right soprano to create the title role— nearly every diva in Paris had been auditioned, including some legitimate stage actresses with a modicum of vocal training—Massenet finally decided upon Marie Heilbronn, who had originally made her debut in his first stage opus, *La grand' tante.* By this time, Heilbronn was in her early thirties and rapidly growing buxom. She had retired from the stage to marry a wealthy nobleman. However, she was still a handsome woman, and she had shrewdly maintained her vocal technique in retirement. After the brilliant premiere of 19 January 1884 at the Opéra-Comique, *Manon* was to run for eighty-eight performances over the next two years until Heilbronn's untimely death in 1886. Massenet was disconsolate, writing in his memoirs that he withdrew the work from the footlights rather than entrust the role to another.

In fact, he failed to mention that the once lovely Marie Roze, who had sung the London premiere in 1885, was residing in Paris at that very time. According to Marion Sanderson's notes, the reason he would not allow her to succeed Mme Heilbronn was that she had grown alarmingly overweight. Massenet knew that the critical Parisians would laugh the work off the stage if they saw her in the title role. From then on, the composer scrutinized every debutante who auditioned for him, but until he met Sibyl, he had found no one with the necessary qualifications for the role.

The composer paraded his new acquisition through the salons and offices of important friends, impatiently awaiting their reactions. Comments were generally favorable. Alfred Bruneau, a Massenet pupil, recorded his impressions of Sanderson's voice the first time he heard her in Hartmann's office as "accurate, flexible, wide ranging, agile, ethereal, and notable for its crystalline limpidity and voluptuous tenderness."

But not everyone burst into applause. Massenet next procured an audition for Sibyl with Louis Paravey, the new director of the Opéra-Comique. It was obvious to this gentleman that Massenet was too emotionally involved to understand the risks he was proposing. The youngster had no experience on the professional stage, and Paravey was not fool enough to jeopardize the reputation of the venerable Opéra-Comique by featuring an unknown, untried foreigner in an important new production during an Exposition year. Contrary to later reminiscences by Massenet that were uncritically repeated by his various biographers, Paravey did not rush to sign Sibyl to an exclusive contract. He cleverly left the door open until he could see more evidence of the American's prowess. Of course Massenet assured him that the Sanderson girl could well afford the customary fee of 10,000 francs for the privilege of making her debut with the Opéra-Comique.

It was then that the young aspirant took the initiative, putting the proposition squarely to her mentor: it was up to him to use his influence and expedite a trial performance elsewhere. Once the debut had been arranged, Paravey could be invited to judge her attributes for himself. After all, Massenet had important connections in all the French provincial theaters. But the more the composer considered the idea, the more he preferred a foreign country, a place where his protégée would be completely unknown.

After secret negotiations with some powerful officials in the Netherlands, Massenet arranged for her debut at The Hague in the title role of his *Manon*. The performance was scheduled to take place with the Théâtre Royal Français de La Haye at the Koninklijke Schouwburg, a former palace converted to a theater, toward the end of January 1888. Both the composer and director Lucien Desuiten were delighted at the prospect. Massenet advised Sibyl to use an assumed name for the occasion. In case of failure it would not affect her budding reputation in Paris. A Sanderson friend in the French capital was Ada Adiny, an American soprano at the Opéra, and it was she who suggested that Sibyl take *Ada* from her name. *Palmer* was selected for the surname because it was so unlike Sanderson.

Sibyl now needed the experience of trying out her role as often as possible at various social gatherings. The Dreyfuses hosted the first private performance in their salon on Tuesday, 10 December 1887. Massenet accompanied his heroine at the piano and recorded the occasion modestly in her *Manon* score under the words "grand success."

Among the guests were his good friends, the Paul Poirsons. They next arranged an important soiree for the aspiring prima donna at their home opposite Sarah Bernhardt's on the Place Malesherbes. The Poirsons occupied an unassailable position in the top echelons of Parisian society. They invited two hundred distinguished guests to hear Massenet's American discovery. Mme Poirson, of Anglo-Saxon parentage, was among the reigning queens of Parisian society. An accomplished musician, Mme Poirson would accompany Sibyl at the organ in several scenes from *Manon*. Massenet had successfully lured his first Des Grieux, Talazac, to sing. Madame Massenet, almost as enthusiastic as her husband over the singer's possibilities at this stage, even volunteered to turn pages for Mme Poirson.

Radiant in a white satin gown trimmed with sable, the young soprano scored a scintillating triumph in the dual realms of art and pulchritude. Describing the event in her *Manon* score, Massenet listed Alexandre Dumas *fils*; librettists Henri Meilhac and Philippe Gille, his collaborators on *Manon;* Campbell-Clark, the English ambassador; the De Blowitzes; and Ganderax, the editor of *La Revue de Paris,* as among the important guests. He excitedly described all the ovations Sibyl and Talazac received, but selfishly failed to mention that fellow composers Gounod and Saint-Saëns were present also. Fortunately, the French newspapers noted their attendance. In fact, Gounod himself accompanied Sibyl at the organ as she sang his *Ave Maria* and the Waltz Song from his *Roméo et Juliette.* The Sanderson girls sat next to Massenet's daughter Juliette, and author Marcel Prévost was seated directly in front of them. Years later Marion recalled the evening as "a brilliant success for Sibyl, artistically and socially."

Massenet had made certain that reporters from *Le Figaro, Le Gaulois,* and the Paris edition of the *New York Herald* were there. The next day a short but enthusiastic article even appeared in the *New York Times.* Sibyl had registered her first glimpse of her mentor's genius for publicity—an art in which Massenet remained unexcelled.

After the concert Mr. Poirson presented Sibyl with a lovely bouquet , and the Sandersons had a delightful surprise when they returned to their apartment on the rue Lincoln. A check lay buried among the flowers. It was typical of Sibyl that she would spend the first money she had earned on someone else. The fledgling soprano immediately took sister Marion down to the rue de la Paix and bought her a stunning ruby and diamond wristwatch.

Although the French press was aware that Massenet would leave for The Hague to oversee the revival of *Manon* after the new year, it was a carefully guarded secret that the leading soprano, one Ada Palmer, was really his new protégée. Her costumes had already been ordered from the house of Doucet and fitted before Christmas. Massenet had invited his publisher Hartmann and the Opéra-Comique director Louis Paravey to attend. Dr. and Mrs. Shepard were in the Sanderson party that left for The Hague the last week in January 1888. They stopped off in Brussels, where Melba was singing at the Théâtre Royal de la Monnaie. As Sibyl was not feeling well, Margaret attended the performance without her and afterward procured an autographed picture of the diva for her daughter. Upon arriving in the Dutch capital, they all took lodgings at the Hôtel de l'Europe. Marion and Edith shared one room, Sibyl and her mother, another; but Jennie did not come. So far, she had not liked living abroad, and she refused to exist on the periphery of Sibyl's expanding career. The second Sanderson girl opted for a trip to the Riviera instead.

The first rehearsal was scheduled for Thursday, 26 January, after which Massenet recorded an annoying setback in Sibyl's *Manon* folio.

Thursday, January 26. First rehearsal with orchestra—the first reassurance, we are happy and delighted, but also anxious about a menacing cold which is aggravating 'S.' The orchestra applauded her first act aria, Voyons Manon, plus de chimères. The second rehearsal is excellent and everyone prophesies success—but her cold has not abated.

Saturday, January 28, the date set for the first performance—it will be impossible to perform if the cold is no better—a sad day for "S" and me.

Because of Sibyl's indisposition, the premiere had to be delayed until the following Thursday, 2 February 1888. Dr. Shepard remained in attendance and tried to cheer up his discouraged patient. Massenet was beside himself with anxiety. He was constantly sending his card to the Sanderson room with comments such as "Monsieur Massenet begs to inquire about the state of Mlle Palmer's health."

The fates seemed to have conspired against him ever since his arrival in the Dutch capital. Just after the first rehearsal the composer received a telegram that nearly sent him into cardiac arrest. His son-in-law's well-known Parisian store, Le Bel Jardin, had caught fire the night before and burned to the ground. As much as he wanted to catch the next train for Paris, it was impossible. His immediate obligations were to the Dutch company, his opera, and his ailing protégée.

When at last the glorious event was over, the debutante had lived up to his high expectations, and an ecstatic composer wrote the following comments in his running diary of marginal notations on Sibyl's score.

Finally, Thursday, February 2, 1888—at 7:30 P.M. the curtain rises—it is the premiere of *Manon*—it is THE DEBUT. Dr. Shepard and his wife, Hartmann and his wife are in audience—there is great wealth in the dress circle—at a quarter of eight, I enter upon the scene to direct the orchestra—flowers, ovations, and curtain calls—the success is complete! We sup in my room—we are seven at the table—it is midnight—on est content. The first evening has been so beautiful!

Margaret Sanderson had managed, with difficulty, to survive the trials of her daughter's nerve-wracking debut. Just a week before, she had written Jane that despite the thrill of hearing Sibyl's first orchestra rehearsal, she was terribly worried over her condition. Now she could relax and write Jennie another letter.

> I feel today as if I have gone through seas of trouble and am exhausted after all is over. If you could have seen Mr. Massenet, he wept for joy afterwards. Hartmann and his wife are here, they cried also. Many of the audience were in tears at the "Adieu, notre petit[e] table." Telegrams of congratulations are coming in from all sides. We both prayed to your dear father for help, neither knowing what the other had done. Had supper in Massenet's room afterwards. There were beautiful flowers from the king's secretary, and others. . . . Oh, Jennie, if you could only have seen and heard it all! No other time in her life will be so exciting! Sibyl is cool and calm and less excited about it than Massenet and me. She had no fear last night and was not in her best voice (still has the cold).

Two reviews of "Miss Palmer's" debut have survived in the family. One from the *Dagblad* appeared in French after the second performance:

> The greater part of the success of the performance was due to Mlle Palmer who was chosen by Massenet for the role of Manon. With an advantageous appearance and the most charming physical characteristics, she possesses a great deal of talent both as an actress and as a singer, . . . Her voice is not loud or powerful, but it penetrated and attained the extreme limits of the upper register to the contra E with ease and facility of airy lightness. . . . Her singing could not have been improved upon in the morceaux of sentiments in the first act; in the Adieu of the second act; and in the Grand Aria of the third act. Only in the portamenti and the staccati was she less sure, probably the result of her recent indisposition which had disappeared by the second performance.

The other review is an excerpt from the *Handelsblad* copied in French on a piece of stationery from the Hôtel de l'Europe, evidently by Margaret herself, and translated by the latter's granddaughter:

> Mlle Palmer obtained great success, and we predict for her the most beautiful future. . . . Her partner, Mr. Barbe, played with fervor and sang very well, but

we cannot forget the unhappy timbre of his voice sometimes and the bad production of some of his sounds . . . after the fourth act, both of the singers were called before the curtain and each received a garland of gold leaves. . . . Mr. Massenet was saluted with fanfares when he took the podium, and after the fourth act he had to come on the stage between Mlle Palmer and Mr. Barbe who were both recalled more than ten times between acts. Mr. Barbe presented him with a crown of bronze flowers in behalf of the company, and Massenet thanked him with some well-chosen words.

After the second performance at The Hague, the troupe left for Amsterdam, where even an incessant downpour couldn't dampen the enthusiasm of the audience. Sanderson's debut was a decided hit. Massenet described the trip in his diary annotations in Sibyl's music:

Tuesday, 7th, February, depart for Amsterdam—large theater—ugly and cold—a great many people in the audience—in spite of a little stage fright, more than the first performance, the evening is a success, and we return at 2 A.M. to The Hague.

Mrs. Sanderson wrote to her daughter Jane in more detail on 9 February after her return to The Hague.

Since I wrote you, dear Jennie, Sibyl has sung twice. She made a great hit in Amsterdam. Recalled twice after each act—After the 4th scene people stood up all over the house and cheered, some throwing up their handkerchiefs. She had a handsome bouquet given to her, and Mr. Massenet a superb bronze flower stand by the subscribers of the Amsterdam opera—We expected to spend the night there but on arriving we found the hotel so poor that we returned that night with the rest of the company. It was a bad day . . . fine rain all of the time . . . and that along with so much water everywhere made anything but a favorable impression on me. I took a carriage and visited the art museum, but returned early to the hotel where I left Sibyl resting. I *never* leave her when Massenet is in the hotel; he is as anxious as to what people may say as I, and she is never alone with him. He is always in our room when in the hotel, so you see I am really confined. Sibyl has never been so much frightened as the night at Mme Poirson's. She gets very excited in changing her dresses, I gave her a little Anti Peryn's [a Victorian patent medicine] between some of the hardest scenes if she gets nervous. . . . The gala concert at The Hague came off last night. There were 1,700 people present. Sibyl had a great success. She sang the Waltz Song from *Roméo et Juliette,* accompanied by Mr. Granier and an orchestra of 70 pieces. Massenet got to hear her from the audience for the first time. He is simply MAD about her voice. She sang two of his songs later accompanied by him at the piano and was encored. We had many callers in the foyer during the concert when M Massenet led the orchestra for *Phèdre* overture and the fourth act of *Hérodiade.* We sat in the box of the President of the Society of Music with his wife and daughter.

After the concert Massenet and the Sandersons were driven to the palace of the late Prince of Orange, at the time occupied by T. Hora Siccama, the President of the Netherlands Society of Music, for a gala supper. Twenty guests were invited to the reception, and the dining room was resplendent with crystal chandeliers and servants in red livery and powdered wigs. After a superb meal, M Siccama made a speech, first addressing the proper panegyrics to Massenet, then hailing Mlle Palmer as "the fair diva" and predicting a glorious future for her.

When the last performance of *Manon* took place, on Saturday, 11 February, Sibyl seemed to be completely recovered and once more in excellent voice. An exuberant teacher proudly eulogized the farewell appearance in his pupil's score.

> Saturday 11 February, 1888
>
> —The third and last performance of *Manon* at The Hague. It is no longer hindered by stage fright or a cold—it is a superb performance—it is a consummation of success—the Adieu to the petite table was encored again as on the evening of the premiere.
>
> Return to Paris Sunday 12th of February, one minute before midnight, and now—Paris and *Manon*—
>
> I add to these souvenirs the expression of my admiration and affectionate acknowledgments—
>
> J. Massenet

Sanderson had begun her European career in the Netherlands as Miss Ada Palmer, and after four performances of *Manon* and one gala concert, the Dutch had received her with open hearts. Still, her success had been a costly one with constant doctors' bills, telegrams to Paris for medicine, and meals in the room.

The budding soprano had received only five hundred francs a performance, and when her mother figured the bills, they had just made expenses.

From then on, her career was to adhere astonishingly closely to the same pattern: for every triumph there was a parallel misfortune of some kind with its concomitant expenses. For every success there was a corresponding adversity. Her life was doomed to this accursed cycle for the rest of its short span.

Chapter 8

A Night of Anguish

Sibyl's unstable health did not improve upon her return to Paris. Her temperature shot up to 104 degrees, and the doctor confirmed fears that this time she had contracted scarlet fever. When Massenet heard the news he was desolate. As Paravey had been unable to leave his duties at the Opéra-Comique to attend the performance, he entrusted a contract to Hartmann, upon whose judgment he relied. The latter was so bewitched by the trial debut at The Hague that he signed the young soprano immediately. There had been a tentative plan to star her in a Parisian revival of *Manon* that spring, but now the project was abandoned.

Sibyl was confined to bed for approximately six weeks with one of the most virulent strains of the disease that the doctors had ever encountered. They had to burn ulcerated spots out of her throat many times. Gradually she improved, only to be struck down again by tonsillitis. After her tonsils were removed that spring, she was never to know good health for the rest of her life.

Massenet bombarded the Sanderson apartment with a barrage of notes, not through the mail but by courier and always marked "Very Urgent, Respond Immediately!" The messenger would wait for the reply from Margaret, who knew the composer was not a patient man. He kept a daily check on Sibyl's health and the state of affairs in the entire household. On 8 March 1888, his message to Margaret showed serious concern for Sibyl: "The dear, sick one— hope for good news—*tell me the truth even if it causes me grief.* The little package enclosed is for Mlle Sibyl, if you will permit it."

On 3 April, learning that Margaret was suffering from an eye affliction, he dispatched a note of condolence: "I am sorry to learn of your great pain. My wife joins me in expressing my great sympathy." Other communications were utterly trivial, merely reflecting his whimsical moods, which changed from minute to minute. One began: "What beautiful weather! How sweet life can be!" Yet this, too, was marked *Very Urgent, Respond Immediately.*

The master tried to cheer up his recovering invalid. He presented her with the holograph of the first song he would write for her, labeled simply "Feuillet d'album" (Album Leaf), which he had composed during their sojourn to The Hague. He would write at least three others for Sibyl, and probably more. Blanche Marchesi's memoirs disclose that Massenet "wrote song after song for her."[1] Unfortunately, some of these remained in manuscript form and are lost today.

Fortunately, the young singer had the natural resilience of youth, and on 11 April 1888, she was well enough to receive the Chopin-Rossini award at the Conservatoire. Massenet, beaming with pride, sat in loge sixteen with Margaret to watch the proceedings. As he was a distinguished faculty member, he undoubtedly had his fine Gallic hand in the selection, for Sibyl had left the Conservatoire in the fall of 1886 after completing less than a year of study. She had done nothing whatsoever on the premises to merit any citation, but more than likely the honor was for her recent achievements in the Netherlands.

That same spring found the composer hard at work on the chivalric tale of *Esclarmonde.* The story was originally inspired by a medieval romance entitled *Parthenopoeus of Blois,* which Massenet's librettist Alfred Blau had discovered in the library of Blois nearly twenty years earlier. Blau, realizing it had all the elements of an operatic fantasy, persuaded the gifted Louis de Gramont to collaborate with him on the libretto. The plot abounded with all sorts of medieval trappings—sorcery, chivalric combat, magic, exorcism.

By 1882 they had finished the first version, entitled *Pertinax,* and offered it, curiously enough, to the Belgian composer Gevaert. At that time Gevaert's duties as director of the Brussels Conservatoire occupied all his attention, and he had to decline the honor. The two collaborators then reworked their libretto and retitled it *La fée mélior.* From the second revision emerged the draft for which Massenet started preliminary sketches as early as December 1886.

The action alternated between ancient Byzantium and France. Phorcas, the Byzantine emperor and a practitioner of sorcery, has decided to abdicate in favor of his daughter Esclarmonde, whom he has also instructed in the arts of magic, but upon the condition that she conceal her physical beauty from mankind until her twentieth birthday. At this time, her hand shall be the prize in a tournament. Esclarmonde takes the sacred vow and is warned that the penalty for breaking it is the loss of both magical and temporal powers.

Unknown to her father, Esclarmonde has been using her supernatural prowess to learn of life in other realms. She has seen a handsome French knight named Roland in her visions and has fallen in love with him. Employing her sorcery, she casts a spell upon him and transports him to a magic island. She enters into a mystical marriage with him, still concealing her identity. He is told she will come to him every night no matter where he is, but he must never look upon her face.

Meanwhile, France is invaded by the Saracens, and Esclarmonde gives Roland the magic sword of Saint George, which is invincible in the hands of a true knight but useless to a perjurer. Armed with the sacred weapon, Roland saves the city of Blois from the invaders and is rewarded by the king with his daughter's hand. To the shock and amazement of everyone, Roland declines the honor, but the curious bishop of Blois coaxes Roland's secret from him in the confessional. That night the bishop lays a trap for the secret lovers and, tearing off Esclarmonde's veil before he exorcises her, reveals her incomparable beauty to Roland.

Esclarmonde invokes the spirits of fire and air to rescue her and, as she is carried away, laments to Roland that he has seen her for the first and last time. Now the penitent princess has to pay the double penalty of which her father had warned her. However, he agrees to restore her temporal powers if she will abandon Roland—otherwise, the knight will perish. Esclarmonde resigns herself to the sacrifice, and her father arranges a tournament to choose a husband for her. Unknown to them, a heartbroken Roland has come to Byzantium to seek death in this tournament, but instead emerges as the victor. The plot comes to a rapturous close when the prize of the contest turns out to be Esclarmonde, who unveils herself to Roland as the fairy princess he has loved.

The story was the quintessence of medieval Gallic romanticism. Massenet knew that its fragile credibility depended upon the resplendent beauty of its heroine, and the Californian had all the physical requirements: the hypnotic, star-sapphire eyes; an astonishing eighteen-inch waistline; and alabaster skin so clear that "one could see the blood pulsing through the veins."

As was his habit, the composer kept a day-to-day memorandum of his intimate feelings and thoughts in the margin of the holograph. In one entry that spring he reflected, "hailstones are falling hard enough to break the window and I am sad." On 28 April he was "uneasy, filled with inquietude, for it is the day of her operation, the treatment for tonsils"; 29 April was "a more cheerful day with the first blue sky"; 30 April: "sad. I wanted to end this act today and play it tomorrow after lunch with Mlle S."

Massenet came to the Sanderson apartment almost every day to rehearse his muse. He would arrange the salon like a stage, setting it for each scene, as he always wrote with the staging in mind. Then assuming the tenor role, the composer would work with his heroine in minute detail on subtle dramatic points.

He also began to steer Sibyl to the right public places. Aficionados of an intimate second-floor restaurant called Vions often saw him with his vivacious pupil, always in the company of her solemnly dressed mother. Massenet seized every opportunity to sing Sibyl's praises to the many newspaper correspondents who just happened to frequent the place. One night he introduced the drama critic of the *New York Herald* to the young lady, proclaiming her to be the new Patti. After meeting mother and daughter, many a French reporter remarked that Mme Sanderson, dressed in her habitual mourning, seemed to embody all the sadness of life following in the trail of its joy.

That summer the Sanderson family went to Vevey, Switzerland, where they vacationed at the Grand Hotel. Leaving his wife behind, Massenet turned up promptly, complete with manuscript paper, score, and portable keyboard. In his 1912 autobiography the composer wrote that every evening from five to seven he rehearsed his future star in the particular scene upon which he had been toiling that day. However, the composer seems to have had a memory lapse; except for the orchestration, the opera had been completed in Paris, 6 July 1888, at 1 P.M. in the Sanderson apartment, according to his final note on the holograph.

The rehearsals went on ad infinitum, whether in Paris or Switzerland. A fanatic for work, Massenet would drill his songbird on a single passage for hours at a time, until she fell to a sofa fainting, screaming, and rebelling in violent fits of temper. Gertrude Atherton has recorded these emotional eruptions in her autobiography and observed that often a solicitous mother would have to intervene and beg for clemency.

Mrs. Atherton was not the only witness to such scenes. Sibyl's health had not stabilized during the spring of 1888, and in his manuscript the composer was already noting their frequent clashes in addition to her periods of despondency. A musical soirée given by the California millionaires Mr. and Mrs. Ben Ali Haggin on 6 June was the occasion for another outburst of hysterics after a surfeit of Massenet's carping. On this particular night, Mrs. Haggin consoled the girl by explaining that her mentor demanded such perfection only because he knew she was capable of it.

Massenet was a stubborn taskmaster; according to Mrs. Atherton he showed no consideration for his pupil's precious instrument. Furthermore, he was not a voice teacher. The most foolish thing Sibyl had done at this point in her career was to discard Sbriglia, placing herself completely in the hands of the composer. The mistake was a critical one, and she was to pay bitterly for it.

Furthermore, Massenet was writing a virtuoso role for his pupil—a Gallic *Turandot,* one that bristled with all kinds of fiendish difficulties, and one she should not have attempted at this particular stage of her vocal development. The title role demanded that the heroine's vocal color modulate from lyric to coloratura to dramatic, sometimes requiring all three categories within a single scene. He was ruthlessly exploiting her phenomenal upper register and had revised his cadenzas to include the highest vocal utterance in musical history: the G in alt.[2] Massenet was perhaps writing with as much attention to future historical perspective as any immediate vocal relevance to his American discovery. It is quite possible had she still been studying with Sbriglia, he would have forbidden her to sing the new opera.[3]

The rehearsals turned into a series of nightmares for Sibyl, and at one critical point she was ready to abandon the project. But she wasn't reckoning with her mentor's wiles. He would bite his lip, shed a few tears, and accuse her of cowardly desertion and ruination of all his lofty aspirations for them both. The crafty Frenchman refused to admit defeat. As for Sibyl, never had she allowed any teacher to treat her so tyrannically before, but neither had she been so close to her long-sought goal of stardom. The manuscript notations from this period are filled with such intriguing expressions of the composer's anguish as: "a painful evening last night . . . sad end to the 'S' evening . . . a sleepless night . . . role abandoned; role reclaimed . . . a dismal future."

In August the Paul Poirsons and their son arrived at the Grand Hotel and invited Massenet and Sibyl to join them for a drive to Clarens. In spite of all the emotional trials and tribulations at Vevey, including an eye operation Margaret Sanderson underwent on 25 August, Massenet finished orchestrating his first three acts by the end of the five-week stay. Sibyl managed to cling to her role; she had survived.

She had not only survived; somehow she had mastered it, even despite a nearly disastrous fall, of which no details are available. Of course Sibyl was aware that what Massenet had done for her was unprecedented in the history of music drama. She was the first American for whom a major European composer had written an opera. True, her compatriot Marie Van Zandt had created the role of Delibes's Lakmé at the Opéra-Comique in 1883, but it was the director who had chosen her for the part. Delibes had not conceived the role to display Van Zandt's particular vocal talents.

Sometime that fall or winter Sibyl almost derailed the Byzantine Express when she was rushed to the hospital with appendicitis. Massenet was beside himself with alarm and maintained daily courier contact between his office and the Sanderson apartment. Dr. Joseph Michel, his personal physician, performed the operation. The composer ordered flowers to be sent to his young protégée's bedside daily, and his wife even made daily inquiries to Dr. Michel on his behalf. Sibyl recuperated at home for a couple of weeks before she felt well enough to resume rehearsals.

The manager of the Opéra-Comique had given Massenet carte blanche to control the production, which meant that all sets and costumes had to meet his personal approval. The Opéra-Comique was spending an immense sum of money for scenery; the four hundred costumes alone cost 20,000 francs. Eugène Grasset created the seven visions in the Incantation Scene, which were projected onto a screen at the back of the stage by means of a magic lantern.

Massenet finished orchestrating the opera in Paris on 14 October 1888, and on Sibyl's birthday, 7 December, arrived at the Sanderson home, ringing the doorbell in a frenzy. When the maid told him the Sandersons were at lunch with guests, he strode toward the dining room door and pounded violently on it. Gertrude Atherton wrote in the *California Argonaut* that everyone eating lunch "jumped as if shot." Upon entering the room he announced with mock solemnity that he had something of grave importance to announce.

Pulling up a chair, he sat down beside his disciple with portfolio in hand and said to her: "Mademoiselle, when I first saw you and heard you sing, I offered to give you lessons, and have done so. Then you wished to make your debut in *Manon,* and I arranged it. After that you desired an engagement at the Opéra-Comique, and I said you should have it, and you are now engaged; so I have kept my word in every case. Today I come to show you that I have kept my latest promise—that I should write an opera especially for you. It is in this very portfolio, and I intend to sign the last page now in the presence of your mother and family. Here it is, and I hope you will be satisfied."

Sibyl was more than satisfied; she was thrilled. She had a major European composer at her feet handing her stardom on a silver platter. Already she was the envy of every ambitious young singer in France. Massenet formally presented her with the holograph and, dedicating the work to her, insisted that she should add her signature next to his.[4] From then on he traced the history of the rehearsals in the margin of Sibyl's manuscript.

On Monday, 17 December 1888, at 2:30 P.M. the first reading of *Esclarmonde* took place in the green room of the Opéra-Comique. According to Massenet's notes those present included the composer, his wife, Mrs. Sanderson, the directors, the authors, Massenet's publisher, and Monsieur Bourgeous, the director of the chorus. Other members of the cast who convened that day included Émile-Alexandre Taskin (Phorcas), Mlle Herbert (Énée), Jeanne-Eugénie Nardi (Parséïs), and young tenor Étienne Gibert, a graduate of the Conservatoire, who would be making his Parisian debut as Roland. Massenet added in the holograph that "Mlle Sibyl Sanderson sang nearly the entire role of Esclarmonde— *great success*—the foremost hopes for the future."

There were twentytwo rehearsals in the theater foyer, and on Saturday, 17 February 1889, Massenet recorded in Sibyl's manuscript that the first onstage rehearsal had occurred. This was to be followed by fifty-six more, including ten with orchestra. Probably no opera in the history of the Opéra-Comique to that time had received more assiduous preparation. One would have thought that Massenet had his hands full with the elaborate stage rehearsals, but he still found time to meddle in the lives of others, especially if their accomplishments might encroach upon those of his interpreter.The career of the American soprano Emma Eames was a case in point. She had obtained a contract with the Opéra-Comique in 1888 and was successively assigned roles in *La traviata, Mignon,* and *Les pêcheurs de perles*—always to learn but never to sing, as the dates for her debuts would be mysteriously postponed and dropped. In her memoirs Eames placed the blame upon the machinations of Massenet for "the wily old fox resolved that I should not make my debut before Sibyl Sanderson . . . especially as the great international exhibition was coming in 1889 with its power to enhance the glory of any singer who might be appearing while it endured." Although Eames and Sanderson began their careers as rivals, Eames wrote of Sibyl: "She was a very beautiful and a greatly talented woman . . . one of the kindest and most generous of people, incapable of meanness, and probably knew nothing of the real import of Massenet's maneuvers . . . and afterwards became a very dear friend."[5]

After a frustrating year at the Opéra-Comique, Eames demanded and received her release. She secured an audition at the Opéra and was engaged to make her debut in Gounod's *Roméo et Juliette* on 13 March 1889.[6] Ironically, the first note of congratulation she received the following morning was from Massenet, "who must have been in a perfect rage at seeing all his good work on behalf of Sibyl Sanderson at the Opéra-Comique overthrown."

In a letter to her daughter Jane on 2 March 1889, an excited Margaret Sanderson was already overcome with the heady attar of Sibyl's expected triumph: "Her voice reaches into every part of the house as clear as a bell . . . no doubt whatever of her success now in my mind . . . a tenor at the Opéra-Comique told Mr. Blau, Mr. Massenet, and me that such a voice has not been heard there in twenty years. Say nothing about this to anyone, however."

Neither was there any doubt in Gertrude Atherton's mind about Sibyl's conquest of the French. Mrs. Atherton had arrived in Paris that spring for a visit to her inlaws, the Rathbones, Major Rathbone being the American vice consul. They lived on the Champs-Élysées, just a block from the Sanderson home on the rue Lincoln, and every day Gertrude visited Sibyl and shared the singer's hopes and fears. She discovered the American colony was divided into two camps: Eames versus Sanderson. She learned that Sibyl also worried about the critics because their wives resented an American's capturing a French composer's "personal affections" as well as his professional interest. The aspiring prima donna introduced her mentor to Gertrude,[7] and she joined them on picnics in the country accompanied by Manon, a grotesquely shaven standard poodle, Massenet's latest gift to Sibyl.

As the premiere of *Esclarmonde* approached, hordes of people from all over the world poured into Paris for the Exposition. Massenet was constantly being interviewed by reporters from many countries and invariably seized the opportunities to extol the virtues of his American discovery. "Her voice is that of a nightingale; her beauty is that of a goddess," he rhapsodized in an interview with the *New York World.* To another paper he described his pupil as "gifted with a miraculous voice, capable of rising to any height."

On 12 May, he released to the press a letter he had written to Sibyl the day before.

11 May 1889

Chère Mademoiselle,

You show that I was correct since it is for you I have written *Esclarmonde.* I had faith and you proved at the rehearsal today, Saturday, 11 May 1889, that I have confided my role, unique in its difficulties, to a *unique artist.* You are making your debut, but I predict for you a future also unique. Later on, *when speaking of theatrical glory, people will mention Sanderson!*

Yours with highest recognition,
J. Massenet

Massenet's publicity campaign was reaping fertile results at the box office. By the first of May, *Esclarmonde* was already sold out for the first fifteen performances. Scalpers were hawking tickets at incredible prices. Louis Aublet had done a huge portrait of the composer at the piano coaching Sanderson in *Manon,* and the painting was conveniently unveiled at the salon that summer.

The night of 13 May 1889 was chosen for the *représentation générale,* a public dress rehearsal. On such an occasion the fate of a new theatrical work could be decided by the press in Paris. The event was not truly public: attendance was by invitation only, and the elite of politics, society, arts, and letters all fought over tickets. The Rathbones held four tickets for the highly coveted event, but as Mrs. Rathbone disliked Sibyl and refused to go, Mrs. Atherton suggested taking Mrs. De Young, the wife of a San Francisco newspaper editor, instead.

At 7:55 P.M., the three customary poundings backstage at the Opéra-Comique meant that the performance was about to commence. Then the house was plunged into darkness for a few minutes. This was followed by a cymbal crash from Jules Danbé's orchestra, and when the stage lights flashed on, the handsome basilica of the Prologue was revealed. Mrs. Atherton described the occasion in her autobiography:

> The opera was very gorgeous in decor: Romanesque-Byzantine. Sibyl . . . was breathtakingly lovely in a crown a foot high and gowns as gorgeous as the scenery. There was not a tremor in her sweet, pure voice, and it soared like a bird's. . . . The audience seemed interested and responded obediently when the hired claque led the applause. But I kept one eye on the critics, who all sat together, and I saw no enthusiasm in those sharp faces. They sneered, they looked bored, and I feared for the morrow. . . . I went behind the scenes after the performance was over, but Sibyl was too nervous and exhausted to talk beyond asking me in a hoarse whisper to come over in the morning.[8]

The jealousy and enmity that Sibyl had feared were very much present at the *représentation générale.* There was a growing cabal against American singers in Paris. After Eames's debut in March, one writer in *Le Figaro* commented: "In order to be successful in Paris, it looks as if a singer must first of all be foreign, then pretty, if in addition to this she possesses some talent, her future is assured." When Melba made her sensational debut at the Opéra in the first week of May, the critic of *Le Matin* erroneously assumed that she was an American also.

But Massenet's wide-ranging publicity campaign for his protégée overshadowed these other debuts and in its own way backfired at first. Curiosity was undoubtedly the reason for several hundred people crashing the performance, but in no way did the uninvited crowd approach "two thousand," the number reported in American papers. The audience had expected to witness a revelation, and they refused to admit anything miraculous had occurred to justify the extravagant predictions. Just another pretty American with another pretty voice pleading her case before a jury of jaded Parisians.

Massenet felt the hostility was aimed toward him as well. His constant intrigues and his dictatorial policies in all aspects of the rehearsals had made him extremely unpopular. Two perfunctory curtain calls after the epilogue constituted the greatest excitement the performance had generated. The composer wrote on the margin of Sibyl's manuscript:

Monday, 13, May, 1889—*représentation générale*—a great many people—a few friends—from 8 P.M. to 1 A.M. I experienced an evening of anguish.

Chapter 9

Paris Capitulates

Le rêve, malgré vos alarmes,	The dream in spite of your fears
Est devenu réalité,	Has become reality, master,
Maître! les cœurs ont palpité,	Our hearts have beaten faster,
Les yeux se sont mouillés de larmes.	Our eyes are moist with tears.
A l'interprète pour ses charmes	To the heroine for her charms
Comme (à l'œuvre) pour sa beauté	(As in the opera) to her beauty
Ce tout-Paris si redouté	All Paris so fearsome
A du rendre humblement les armes.	Will humbly surrender its arms.
Demain laissez hurler les loups	Tomorrow let the wolves howl,
Des impuissants et des jaloux	Let the cries of the jealous and untalented
Poussez du pied la troupe immonde.	Expel this gang so foul!
Qu'importe ce qu'ils penseront?	What does it matter, the thoughts of this crowd?
Soyez fier, levez haut le front,	Lift high your head, be proud
Et dites: "J'ai fait *Esclarmonde!*"	And say, "I have written *Esclarmonde!*"

Mercredi, 19 Mai '89
1 A.M.

An unpublished poem sent to Massenet by historian Charles Malherbe at the premiere of Esclarmonde, *15 May 1889.*

The morning after the premiere of Esclarmonde, Mrs. Atherton was awakened by her sister-in-law Alejandra Rathbone, who jubilantly dumped all the morning papers on her bed.

"Read these! This is the last of Sibyl!"

Mrs. Atherton snatched the papers and hastily glanced over the articles. She claimed the entire lot was nothing more than a carnivorous orgy offering Sibyl up on a platter "disemboweled and dismembered." She jumped out of bed, dressed, and rushed to the fallen debutante's side.

One wonders to which reviews Mrs. Atherton was referring. In a city of more than thirty newspapers, not all the notices could have been expected to be raves. Most of the major French critics did not publish their reviews the day after the performance. They were not pressured by the constricting American system of deadlines. French editors allowed their journalists to pocket their reviews, take time to contemplate a performance, and often see a second one before publishing their oracular pronouncements.

Mrs. Atherton exaggerated not only the number of hostile reviews but also their importance. There were some second-rate critics such as "Willy," Colette's first husband,[1] who did not grovel in the dust before Massenet's score or his protégée, but their newspapers were not among France's most influential.

Nevertheless, Mrs. Atherton insisted that the Sanderson apartment was in complete pandemonium when she arrived. Margaret was weeping, and terror seemed to have turned the three sisters into pillars of salt. Newspapers were scattered all over the floor. In the midst of the debris, Massenet was striding up and down like a lunatic, "literally tearing his hair." When he caught sight of Gertrude, he sprang forward and seized her by both arms. Mrs. Atherton has recorded the electrifying scene that followed:

> "Sibyl is ruined—ruined—ruined!" he shouted, and then his voice broke into a wail. "This is the most terrible day of my life!" He began pacing up and down again, waving his arms. "Ruined! Ruined! Her career ended last night! And I too am ruined! All my hopes were on her and she has failed me!" I could stand no more and stamped my foot at him. "You are a brute!" I cried. "A selfish male brute. Instead of bucking her up you think of nothing but yourself. YOUR work is over. SHE has to make the same effort four times a week. And you blame HER! You know she was exquisite last night. Even you could find no flaw. . . . " I turned to Mrs. Sanderson. "Where is Sibyl?" The prostrate mother waved a feeble hand, and I opened the door of Sibyl's bedroom and closed it behind me. She was lying on the bed, on her face, in an

attitude of complete abandon, sobbing convulsively. This was no time for sympathy. I gave her shoulders a vigorous shake and exclaimed, "Sibyl! I am ashamed of you. Why should you—*you*—care for the worst those miserable hirelings can do? You know their motives. You expected this. So did everyone else. Who will pay any attention to them?" "Oh, you don't understand!" she wailed. "No singer, no actress, can survive with the critics against her. I don't know anything about American critics, but they rule our destinies in Paris. I am ruined! I'll break my contract! I won't—won't—sing to empty seats!"

I leaned over and pinched her throat. "When they slit this and cut out your vocal chords you will be ruined but not before. Now, listen to me. I don't know what power they may have in an ordinary season, but Paris is so packed with visitors to the Exposition that they are sleeping wherever they can find a bed. Every theater, both opera houses, will be filled nightly. You have a God-given opportunity to make your own reputation. Americans never read the French newspapers, and the others will be too busy. They'll make up their own minds about you and pass the word on. There can be only one verdict. In a month you will be the fashion, and the critics will be gnashing their teeth. You will not only conquer but you will establish a new precedent . . ." I heard a noise behind me and turning saw Massenet in the doorway. I hissed at him and he was about to retreat when Sibyl sprang from the bed. For a few seconds I had the impression of being in the path of a cyclone. Flying ornaments and furniture. Raucous shrieks. Whirling arms. Massenet shaking as if he had been attacked by paralysis agitans, and gasping for breath.

"I hate you!" screamed Sibyl. "It's all your fault! You could have bribed those men! And you have done nothing but whine over your stupid old opera!" She flew at him. He gave a leap backward, pulled the door to behind him, and an instant later I heard the sound of racing feet and a distant slam.

Sibyl dropped into a chair, tears running down her face, rocking herself to and fro. "Mon maître! Mon maître!" she wailed. "He'll never forgive me! He'll never come back! He'll hate me!"

"No, he will not," I said. "He'll come cringing back like a whipped dog to lick the hand of the master it adores. And it will do him good. He's acted like a brute . . . "

"He's not a brute,!" Sibyl glared and screamed. "He's a great man and I won't hear a word against him."

"Well he's an angel then. But go to bed now and stay there until tomorrow night, and then do your best."[2]

Among the early minor reviews, Tisserand's diatribe in *La Bataille* was the worst of the lot and sufficiently insulting to have thrown Massenet into a rage:

> It was difficult yesterday to judge M Massenet's new work because it was completely strangled by Mlle Sanderson, whose engagement can only be explained by the fact that the young lady is beautiful. . . . Mlle Sanderson parades herself out on the stage to flay the skin off our ears with much imperturbable aplomb . . . She has typical American taste and "Yankee brass" . . . There is a certain air about her which seems to say, "You know me, but what do I really care about you? I am rich with plenty of dollars in my pocket. Isn't it just too droll to sing in a French government-subsidized theater? And it is even more fantastic to think that I get paid. But then, am I not very pretty?" Yes, it is true that she is très jolie. But if I wish to see a really lovely woman I can go to Chez Fatima for twenty sous where I don't have to listen to beautiful music being despoiled.

There were a few condemnations which appeared several days later in the important papers. On 16 May in *La Revue des deux mondes,* Camille Bellaigue thoroughly excoriated the opera without going out of his way to cast stones at the prima donna. He lamented that the composer had forsaken his Gallic birthright to compose a small "French *Tristan,*" and further chastised Massenet for abandoning the natural for the artificial in musical thought.

Léon Kerst's pontifical blast in *Le Petit journal* of 17 May depicted Sibyl as "a spoiled child by nature . . . who is not a singer for the theater . . . nor an actress for the stage." He further complained that "Gibert offered some good qualities that one attributes to a blackbird when obliged to do without a thrush."

Most of the laudatory reviews did not appear until after the premiere. It can only be assumed that Massenet was on the edge of nervous exhaustion, and the first adverse reactions to this latest opus triggered his reflexes prematurely.

Whether the humorous petit bleu[3] from librettist Louis de Gramont helped soothe his wounded psyche is not known, but the composer immediately sent it to his interpreter as a token offering of contrition.

Mon cher Massenet,
Bravo and *merci!* Now calm yourself, you highly nervous man. I have written *Esclarmonde* also. All will go according to your desires. As for your dear inter-

preter, tell her well that we are charmed with her and that she will capture the whole world just as she has subjugated us—now stay calm! Please try to like me a little; I love you a great deal.

Gramont

A violent storm shook Paris on the day of the premiere, May 15, complete with freak hailstones and lightning, as if the spirits of fire and air were demanding revenge for the intemperate treatment of their sister Esclarmonde. However, the deluge subsided before evening, and by the time the elegant crowd arrived at the Opéra-Comique only the monotonous dripping of raindrops from roofs and trees was heard.

There had been receptions and balls ever since the Exposition opened, but nothing compared with the star-studded audience that assembled for the operatic premiere. Among the celebrities filling the theater were President Sadi Carnot and family; composers Reyer, Delibes, and Godard; author Alexandre Dumas fils; and even two of Sibyl's former teachers, Giovanni Sbriglia and Mme de la Grange. Christine Nilsson, Emma Calvé, Nellie Melba, and Martha Duvivier were among the prima donnas who descended upon the hall to judge the latest aspirant.

The American colony, led by social matriarchs Fanny Reed and Mrs. Walden Pell, turned out *en masse*. Other prominent Americans included the William Vanderbilts and their party. Even Mrs. Mary Yost, Sibyl's aunt from California, put in an appearance.

Also present was Mme Marchesi, who made a last-minute disclosure to the press that the young American was no longer her student. This eccentric remark was hardly necessary, since Sibyl had rejected her tutelage some years before. But Marchesi was well acquainted with the controversy surrounding the dress rehearsal and, expecting a genuine fiasco, didn't want her reputation stained by any part of it.

Marchesi needn't have worried. None of her famous students could rival the sensation that Sibyl Sanderson was to create by the end of the evening. Albert Carré, future director of the Opéra-Comique, recorded his indelible memories of the occasion in his memoirs:[4]

> I shall never forget the wave of enthusiasm which filled the hall on the night of her debut. When the golden doors opened on the Byzantine iconostase and the young artist appeared lifting her jewel-studded veil (before the emperor) to reveal a beauty almost super-human, a gasp of adoration ran

through the house, and when that pure and limpid voice began to lift itself to incredible heights, it was one of the joys of art that is rarely experienced in a lifetime.

Glittering like an exotic idol, Sibyl had brought Paris to its knees by the end of the first act with a dazzling display of vocal and physical charms. A common whisper criss-crossed the house: "The woman is seductive." She was gowned in salmon-rose silk embroidered with Byzantine crosses and cloaked in turquoise-blue silk and gold lamé inlaid with sunbursts of diamonds and sapphires. On her head she was wearing a high crown surmounted by a Byzantine cross of nine huge diamonds. The French had never seen anything like her.

When the rain of roses began to fall upon the lovers in the Magic Isle scene, Massenet's music had won its approval as well. One critic remarked that his voluptuous themes had aroused the audience to "an erotic paroxysm . . . the men's eyes narrow in rapture; the women hide theirs behind their fans."

But Sanderson's vocal and histrionic talents were to be fully revealed in the exorcism scene. After the performance, Christine Nilsson admitted to reporters that never in her lifetime had she seen anyone on the stage make such dramatic use of her arms. When the debutante began her phenomenal "Eiffel Tower" cadenza offstage, the audience was spellbound. Reports to both the *New York Herald* and the London *Times*[5] stated that she scaled the heights up to a high F-sharp, "holding it with imperturbable confidence," and then passed on to the G in alt, remaining at that dizzy height "for an incredible length of time, not as a shriek or a scream, but bell-like in its clarity." This unprecedented feat aroused the house to a frenzied acclamation. Sanderson had broken all records in musical history.

From then on the evening was an indisputable victory for the California nightingale. Enthusiastically cheered after the final scene, she returned to the stage hand in hand with her mentor, haloed in triumph. The Opéra-Comique heard their names echoed together for the first of many nights to come. Their joint reign over the Parisian heart had begun. President Carnot even came backstage afterward to congratulate both the composer and the soprano. For the next two days press notices continued to appear, most of them highly complimentary to the new prima donna.

Alphonse Duvernoy wrote in *La République Française* on May 20 that "Mlle Sanderson, absolutely ravishing with or without veil, has conquered the public not only with her eyes, her shoulders, and her arms, but also by her dramatic intelligence." He did not admire her counter G. "It is an eccentricity—nothing more."

Auguste Vitu pronounced his blessing in *Le Figaro* on 16 May:

> This young girl of such exquisite features and limpid eyes possesses a crystalline voice, a trifle thin in the medium register, but which becomes round and full-bodied as it rises to the higher register; she ought to remind herself of Fouquet's maxim: "To what heights should I not ascend?" . . . Her counter G in altissimo has up to now never emerged from the throat of any other singer in history. But at the beginning of the first act she sang with simple majesty the lament of Esclarmonde (Comme il tient ma pensée), meriting more lasting and enviable applause than that of the counter G, which has been nicknamed "the Eiffel Tower note."

Ernest Reyer added his seal of approval in *Le Journal des débats* on 19 May:

> Her voice is slightly pinched in the middle register, but extremely brilliant and flexible in the upper one. Mlle Sanderson will do well not to abuse her voice, since she will soon discover that her talent and dramatic temperament will permit her to go not only higher, which gets her nowhere, but further. The success of the young debutante was indeed genuine and very well earned. She is truly very lovely with the tiniest waistline, yet admirably proportioned, elegant, regal, with her cascades of dark faun-colored hair, her *enfantine* mouth, her enormous violet eyes, and her arms of such pure, sculptured delineation.

Backstage, immediately after the premiere, the composer had recorded a few terse words in Sibyl's manuscript: *"first performance—revenge—hope."* But the next morning it was a jubilant Massenet, now engulfed in waves of praise, who sent her a rapturous telegram:

> ALL OF MY LIFE—FOR THE REST OF ITS JOURNEY—MERCI! MERCI! FROM THE DEPTHS OF MY SOUL—YOUR SUCCESS WAS ABSOLUTELY THE MOST DESIRED ACHIEVEMENT OF MY LIFE—THIS TRIUMPH WHICH OCCURRED LAST NIGHT FOR YOU—I NO LONGER CAN ALLOW MYSELF TO WRITE YOUR NAME "SIBYL." YOU WOULD THINK ME TOO FAMILIAR.
>
> YOURS WITH THE HIGHEST ESTEEM,
> J. MASSENET

Other telegrams, slightly less effusive, were pouring into the Sanderson household as well. Sibyl received congratulatory messages from divas Christine Nilsson, Emma Nevada, and Emma Abbott; from American author Willard Mathews, and a host of admirers, friends, and relatives. Nellie Melba wrote a warm letter of felicitation adding that she could hardly wait to come and visit. The San Francisco Bohemian Club cabled their congratulations, and Sibyl and Massenet, in return, sent the club a jointly autographed copy of the operatic score.

Her director's congratulatory letter has been preserved in her scrapbook.

> Chère Mlle,
> I am taking time to send you all of my congratulations for your great and legitimate success last night. You have entered triumphantly upon your career, and you have had the great glory of having assumed the very soul of this most beautiful stage work of your dear Massenet. No one has been more moved than I by last night's performance, and I want you to know well the important part you have played in its creation.
> > Kindly accept my most devoted sentiments,
> > Paravey, Director of the Théâtre National de l'Opéra-Comique

Because *Esclarmonde* was unlike anything Massenet had previously written, most French critics found it an enigma. Many of them detected the influence of Wagner, Meyerbeer, Berlioz, and Gounod. Jean (Johannès) Weber[6] and L. de Fourcaud were among the prescient writers who defended Massenet's musical experimentation and hailed the work as a splendid example of "the music of the future." On the other hand, Kerst, Pougin, and Wilder accused the composer of having sold his soul to Bayreuth.

Ernest Reyer had the insight to recognize "the delicious surprises in the orchestration" and considered the Love Duet in the Magic Isle scene to be "one of the most passionate and voluptuous examples of amorous music ever heard on the stage."

Massenet had written his first symphonic drama that elevated the orchestra to the same level of importance as the singers. He had introduced a complex system of leitmotifs that were woven through the weft of the work, and the horns were given an important role in interpreting these motifs.

Wagner's influence is undeniable in *Esclarmonde,* but this is true for all the late-Romantic composers, including Strauss, Mahler, Bruckner, and even Debussy and Scriabin. The mystery of the work is not the degree to which it is permeated by Wagner's techniques, but how Massenet absorbed and made them his own. Massenet frankly worshipped the German titan and made no attempt to disguise the fact. When one of his detractors labeled him "Mlle Wagner," he retorted, "I consider myself worthy to reach the man's ankles."

But Massenet's treatment of his leitmotifs—whether in *Manon* or *Esclarmonde*—is far different from Wagner's. Whereas in Wagnerian music drama the leitmotif is an integral part of the work that forces the vocal line to become an immutable, complex series of measured recitatives, those of Massenet are supporting thematic ideas that still allow room for conventional arias in which their use is optional.

It is true that *Esclarmonde* is far more chromatic than *Manon,* but if Wagner's shadow can be seen in this, it must be pointed out that Chopin's daring experiments in chromaticism strongly influenced Wagner, and that Berlioz also predated him in the use of the leitmotif.[7] In turn, Massenet's mastery of the long vocal phrase and supple melodic line influenced Puccini. Thus is the fabric of musical history interwoven with reciprocal influences.

Esclarmonde holds some of Massenet's most thrilling music even though it regrettably contains no outstanding arias for either hero or heroine, the solos being too similar in character. Instead, it is a cornucopia of masterful vocal ensemble writing. The duets between soprano and tenor rank with those in *Manon* as the finest Massenet ever conceived. The composition of such an astonishing work for a twenty-four-year-old debutante remains without parallel in operatic history.

Chapter 10

La Vie en Rose

Sanderson had uttered the note that was heard 'round the world, and reactions to it in newspapers on two continents ranged from awe to skepticism. William Randolph Hearst scooped the singer's life story in his *Examiner,* but understandably omitted the fact that he once had been in love with her.

Irascible Ambrose Bierce outdid himself with a choleric sermon in the same newspaper on 26 May 1889, admonishing the public not to be carried away with the young artist's press puffery and warned Sibyl to abstain from "the locusts and wild honey of praise." The paths of "the friendly critic, the professor, and the manager," added Bierce, "are strewn with the bleaching bones of wrecked singers." He prophesied doom if Sanderson dared to cross the Sacramento River and sing for her own people. Years later when she returned to California, that grim augury was to hover over the singer's head like the shadow of a sinister bat.

In Paris, for the present, everything remained la vie en rose. On the day after the premiere of Esclarmonde, master and muse exchanged autographed pictures, both dating them 15 May 1889.[1] After the eighth performance, the composer presented Sibyl with the manuscript of "Pensée d'automne" (Autumn Sentiment), an art song he had composed for her after they met for the first time in the summer of 1887.[2] Written to the verses of Armand Silvestre, the work was to become Massenet's most famous song during his lifetime. The holograph bears the following inscription:

> To Miss Sibyl Sanderson, the divine Esclarmonde
> 31 May 1889 at midnight—
> In as much as you are today the acclaimed and recognized artist, I am sure

that this manuscript will receive your sensitive reception. It was written almost the day after I saw you and heard you for the first time. Before long this souvenir may seem insignificant to you, but of that I am doubtful because you are the soul of an artist and a woman. To you, Mlle, my most respectful admiration.

J. Massenet

The song became tremendously popular in Europe, and French sopranos considered it a must on their programs. In his *L'art du lied et les mélodies de Massenet,* Jean D'Udine ranked it among the composer's finest art songs, together with *Poème du souvenir* (a cycle of six songs) and *Crépuscule.* He described the "pre-Debussyian" harmonies in the introductory recitative as creating "a certain feeling of languishing in space, masterfully handled, which brings the superb enthusiasm of the principal melody into full bloom."

A week after the premiere, Massenet and Sanderson were guests of honor with Alexandre Eiffel, the architect of the new tower, at a reception given by President Carnot in the Élysée Palace. Singing arias from the opera and a few of her mentor's songs, Sibyl was duly feted with the worshipful Frenchman accompanying her at the piano.

The Exposition was drawing capacity crowds from all over the world. European audiences were spellbound by the show that Colonel Cody (Buffalo Bill) and Annie Oakley put on nightly at the Hippodrome with their troupe of American Indians. Americans thronged the various exhibits, and some of them recorded their impressions of *Esclarmonde* and its heroine that summer. Not everyone was overwhelmed. In their reports to the *Musical Courier* Otto Floersheim and Octavia Hensel felt that Sanderson's voice was being abused by nightly efforts to attain the stratospheric notes.

Henry Peurner, writing to The *American Musician,*[3] deplored her unpleasant vibrato and remarked that "she sings as if she had worked hard for forty years when she has only sung about three months." Everyone commented upon her rather deficient middle register. It was obvious that Sbriglia, if he was actually coaching her at this time, had done nothing to correct it.

But Sanderson denied in countless interviews that she was anyone's pupil but "Massenet's alone." The debutante's contract called for four performances a week, which were much too strenuous on her voice. Today, no star's operatic contract would permit such enslavement.

Later, in her memoirs, Marion Sanderson recalled one vocal problem that, not surprisingly, beset her sister at this time:

102

One afternoon while vocalizing, Sibyl discovered the Eiffel Tower note would not materialize for one reason or another. She was frantic. The house was sold out and there was no substitute for her. She sent for the doctor and dispatched one of us in a fiacre to the Opéra-Comique, miles away, to tell Mr. Paravey that she could not sing that evening. But with the aid of a doctor and repeated efforts, the note came back. Another sister was dispatched to tell the management she would be able to sing after all.

There was no understudy for Sanderson because every young singer the Opéra-Comique sent to audition for Massenet was rejected for one reason or another. The composer claimed to have despaired of ever finding another vocal instrument like the American's. In an interview with the *New York Herald* that year,[4] he had some discouraging words for other sopranos who hoped to interpret his new heroine.

This role of Esclarmonde, which is certainly the most difficult of all my feminine roles, demands an artist of especially original talent. To sing it well, one must have both a light voice and a heavy one. . . . It is not easy to unite these two qualities of lightness and dramatic sentiment. . . . "Impossible!" all the artists tell me who come to ask advice about the role. "Go to the Opéra-Comique tonight and see for yourself," I reply. And when they return the next day, all, without exception, confess that the impossible has been achieved and recognize the superiority of Mlle Sanderson. . . . So true is this that, despairing of finding many voices like Mlle Sanderson's, I have been obliged to make numerous changes in my score. . . . But they pervert the work, and audiences who see *Esclarmonde* after all these alterations will be much surprised, if at some later day, they hear Mlle Sanderson sing the role as I originally conceived it.[5]

In a conversation with American author Louis Elson,[6] Massenet mentioned how difficult it was to find someone with the necessary physical allure for the role and how he refused to have "one of those monsters who yearly disfigure *La traviata* just for the sake of a beautiful voice. When Mlle Sanderson sings, 'Am I not beautiful and desirable?'it fits the situation exactly," the composer sighed, singing the appropriate phrase himself at the piano. He confessed to Elson that he had not missed a single performance of *Esclarmonde,* something which had never happened with any of his previous operas.

Sanderson's popularity in Paris had completely eclipsed that of Eames and Melba. Parisian newspapers were labeling her "the California nightingale" or "the American linnet," and the affectionate nicknames identified her for the rest of her career. Crowds thronged the stage door on nights after her performance. Margaret, writing to her daughter Jane in America during the winter of 1889–90, remarked that "there were at least three hundred people on the sidewalk of the Opéra-Comique, the last time Sibyl sang, to see her when she came out on the street. They crowded up around her carriage screaming, 'I won't move until I see her!' 'We must see her!'" *Vive la belle Sibylle!* was the common cry of a wildly adulatory public. The demand for her pictures became so great that her first photographer, Benque et Cie., was constantly in arrears printing them.

If her voice scaled the heights of the Eiffel Tower, her heart surpassed it. In spite of her numerous faults, her exquisite acts of kindness and appreciation were to become legend. Irénée Bergé recalled later that, at a performance, she and other pupils of Massenet pooled their resources to send Sanderson a superb crown of silver leaves. The next school day the students were astonished to see the "divine Esclarmonde" appear in the doorway of their classroom. She had come to thank them personally for their gift. Afterward Massenet sat down at the piano and, in a reverie, began to play the score. His mood became hypnotic. In a few moments the soprano rose from her chair and for the next several hours sang the entire role to her private audience. Bergé wrote that "the students were spellbound . . . never had they enjoyed their professor's opera so much, and never had they heard such artistic singing."

If Sibyl had not succumbed to influenza that fall, she would have reached her hundredth performance at the Opéra-Comique by Christmas. Because of this setback the centennial presentation of *Esclarmonde* was delayed until Thursday, 6 February 1890. All of Paris turned out for the gala occasion. There were so many floral tributes to the singer that the artist's loge could not hold them all. A huge tree completely sheathed in ruby roses and baskets of other flowers had to be deposited in the concierge's quarters. Parisian newspapers announced that Sanderson had brought in 600,000 francs to the coffers of the Opéra-Comique, breaking all box office records in French operatic history. The government presented her with an enormous cobalt vase made of Sèvres porcelain and inscribed in honor of the occasion. The soprano found herself being feted at a series of receptions including one given by Mrs. Whitelaw Reid, the American minister's wife, at the Hotel Continental.

Massenet was in a euphoric daze. At the centennial performance he wrote the following tribute in Sanderson's manuscript:

Thursday, 6 February 1890

A lack of words is caused by the disappearance of this work from the bill-boards of the Opéra-Comique. But of what importance! The memory of Sibyl Sanderson as Esclarmonde will remain unique and ineffaceable as long as there is a human being left on earth.

On 16 March 1890 he was at no loss for words when he wrote to Louis Lombard, director of the Utica, New York, Conservatory of Music.

I love your marvelous country!

To it I owe my greatest theatrical success! *Esclarmonde!* On Thursday the centennial performance of *Esclarmonde* took place in Paris—the centennial performance of Mlle Sibyl Sanderson, without a day of rest!—The *fact has never before existed!* And what a role! This young girl has an extraordinary voice! [Massenet wrote the uppermost and lowest notes on the letter: the G below the treble clef and the G on the fourth line above] But it is not only the compass which is extraordinary, but the art of singing, the originality of interpretation, and her dramatic ability!

The singer's mother, on the other hand, was surprisingly sober about the sit-uation and frankly relieved the ordeal was over. Sibyl had barely made it to the centennial performance. Tension had been building between the two for months.

In the summer of 1889 Jane Sanderson had left for America with her aunt, Mrs. John Yost, who had been on an extended European visit. Jane had been invited to stay in San Francisco for the winter by Mrs. George Hearst, whose fondness for her contrasted sharply with her antipathy to Sibyl. Writing to Jane that fall, Margaret complained that "Sibyl spends her money as fast as she gets it, and she already has a considerable sum of bills to pay . . . soon she will know what it means to be called upon for money . . . I do not look to her for anything that could give me happiness, but I hope you will do something for me and marry a man whom you and I can be proud of."

On 28 January 1890, Margaret Sanderson wrote another letter to Jane confess-ing to overt friction between her wayward offspring and herself. Obviously, she was not sharing Massenet's ambrosial vision of the Elysian fields.

Sibyl has had a bad cold and sang twice on it. Her voice was not touched by it then, but I fear for tomorrow. She is frightfully done up. We have had a doctor daily for her. Three more performances and the 100th will have passed, but as I am a pessimist, I cannot feel it coming . . . She has this cold from pure carelessness, but I have been coughing for two months. The doctor tells me that the fatigue of the last year is telling on me now. That is true, but it is also true that for three weeks Sibyl has done much to trouble me, and now that she finds me very much down, says she will *never* do it again. She simply refused to listen to me when I asked her to wrap up her mouth and remained out far too late. Her friends told her also that she was imprudent, and now she is paying the penalty for it and *so am I.* Alas, I must have rest, but how? She can give it to me if she will. But she will not! She now thinks she will never say *no* to me again, but *she has no power over herself* . . . I feel quite sure that Sibyl will have trouble with her director. Mr. Paravey is very much taken with Mlle Simonnet, and she has all the power at the theater. *Massenet is not liked at the theater at all,* and therefore I believe *Manon* will not be put on this winter. . . . I must tell you that Sibyl and I do not get on together. She wants more freedom and feels she cannot have it. I wish dear Mrs. Hearst could see her and talk with her again. She is nervous and so am I. And so it goes Jennie, in the same old way. Never come back to it if you can help it! . . . The American newspaper rumor about your becoming an actress is as true as the current [Parisian] one about Massenet's divorce.

The letter clearly revealed the difficulties Margaret was having with her head-strong daughter. While she admitted she was a "pessimist," she already harbored a foreboding presentiment that Sibyl's lack of control would eventually bring both of them nothing but misery. Her prediction about Sibyl's future at the Opéra-Comique also contained a clairvoyant ring. Paravey had had his fill of the multiple machinations of Jules Massenet. The wily Frenchman had not only prevented Emma Eames's debut at the Opéra-Comique, but he had also plotted to replace Taskin as Phorcas in his own opera because of the singer's excessive vibrato.

The proposed revival of *Manon* was now postponed indefinitely. However, Sanderson's stardom had been firmly established. Offers were pouring in from England, Russia, and Belgium, not to mention a request from the Opéra to create the lyric soprano role in Massenet's next opus, *Le mage.*

Margaret Sanderson was evidently among the few people in Paris that spring who scoffed at the rumor that Massenet was about to become her son-in-law after his wife divorced him. The entire musical world knew of his incandescent feelings for his disciple. He could not decide which he admired most: the woman or the artist. But Massenet slyly exaggerated these sentiments for good reason. They meant soaring box office returns. His beatific praise, his effervescent letters, his breathless interviews were well calculated to create the illusion of the grand affair, even though he would have been the first to deny it. There is no evidence that the composer's romantic penchant for his songbird ever progressed beyond platonic portals, even though Gertrude Atherton admitted in her memoirs Massenet was undeniably infatuated with Sibyl. Infatuated he was, but not so inflamed that he had to possess her physically. The fact remains that he was terrified of the potentially far-reaching consequences of any sexual overture toward his pupil.

Massenet viewed his goddess as a femme fatale: demanding, self-possessed, and self-indulgent, a woman to be worshipped from a safe distance only. He was aware that men lose their willpower in the presence of such women, and his whole life was dedicated to self-control. If he had dared cross the sacrosanct bounds of that control, he would have left his wife and daughter and given up everything he held sacred—even his precious respectability—for the American sybarite. On Massenet's list of priorities, this middle-class virtue ranked close to the top. Once having trespassed into that no-man's-land between self-control and self-indulgence, he feared that he and his protégée would destroy all the artistic aspirations they cherished, all the goals toward which they had worked so hard.[7]

The French revered Massenet as the composer for lovers. To them he was the "Alfred de Musset of Music." But unlike Musset, he chose his art as the realm in which to make love to the female sex and seldom strayed from that medium. Within the cherished security of his operatic manuscripts, the composer could indulge his passions respectably; he could safely seduce his heroines within the erotic world of tone.

The students at the Conservatoire idolized what the late André Benoist described as "their master's liaison with the reigning queen of song and beauty."[8] Their illusions would have been destroyed if they had known the truth. All of Paris was prey to the same illusions, as was, in fact, the entire European musical world. Albert Carré, a subsequent director of the Opéra-Comique, wrote in his memoirs, "I do not think it is a secret to anyone . . . that the composer was hopelessly in love with the ravishing American soprano."[9]

The fact that Massenet was neurotically possessive of his pupil convinced colleagues their relationship was a clandestine one. Gibert, Sanderson's tenor, has recounted that every night at the Opéra-Comique the composer hid in the wings during the Magic Isle scene, just to make sure his two interpreters, who were lying in each other's arms behind a curtain of roses, didn't take advantage of the situation.

In a personal interview, Pierre Monteux related that Massenet would come early to the Opéra-Comique on the nights of her *Manon* performances and let himself into her dressing room before she arrived. Then, according to the concierge's delectable observation, he would go through the flowers, reading all the cards, and remove those from every bachelor or roué with whom he was acquainted. Invariably, Sibyl would arrive to contemplate the nightly dilemma of the vanishing cards. A few discreet inquires promptly solved the mystery, but whether the singer ever confronted him with the issue is not known. She must have realized that Massenet was a compulsive creature whom nothing could deter from his obsessive ritual short of an edict barring his presence backstage.[10]

Outside of the fact that their temperaments were both highly inflammable, the two were total opposites. The soprano was prodigal in her acts of kindness toward others; the composer was parsimonious, to say the least. While he remained envious of the success of colleagues, Sibyl did not understand the meaning of the word envy. According to Blanche Marchesi's memoirs, her psyche never possessed an atom of jealousy. Unstable and vulnerable, she completely lacked a self-protective instinct. In marked contrast, he worked overtime to create professional, financial, and emotional security for himself. Massenet reminded Sibyl, at least in one respect, of her late father; he was the quintessence of self-discipline. One part of her personality struggled every day to attain it; the other side rebelled thoroughly against it. He lived for his art; to Sibyl, art was merely one reason for living.

Massenet adored the entire Sanderson family; in turn, Margaret looked upon him as the foster father of all her daughters, and the composer basked in this relationship. "I want you to know I am faithfully attached to you with all my heart," he had written to Margaret. He sent her a rose every year on her birthday, and his roses to daughters Marion and Edith increased by one with every birthday. He wrote Margaret humorous notes, sad notes, and fretful ones worrying over Sibyl as if she were his own daughter. Excerpts from these letters read like a dizzying kaleidoscope of paternal advice with words underlined not once but often twice:

> Tell Mlle Sibyl not to tire her eyes . . . tell Mlle Sibyl not to forget to write M
> Paravey a word of gratitude for his lovely and charming letter and also a card
> to Mme Paravey—tell Mlle Sibyl to be careful of the perfume of these flowers,
> I am sick this morning and the bouquets are from my room—I come to ask

for news about her: how did she spend the night? What about morale? My wife has told me that Dr. Michel has spoken of his intention of using a vessacatoire [drain] on Mlle Sibyl and then decided against it. This is reassuring but speak to the doctor anyway, just a simple question, without any undue insisting, only to know the reason . . . answer me in English if you wish—Tell Lina not to forget the package for Mlle Fleuriette—How I think of you! I fear you are really ill!—I am leaving for Vienna tomorrow to oversee the rehearsals for *Werther,* any messages for Mlle Edith? I think of *all* of you!

The Sanderson apartment on the rue Lincoln displayed various gifts from the composer to his muse. On the fireplace mantel stood a lyre-shaped, crystal-looped clock that chimed on the half hour, and the singer wore the hand-chased gold watch he had given her on one of her birthdays. They lived in an age when presents of silver were always inscribed with a personal message. A little silver honey pot bore the inscription, "À divine Esclarmonde—J. M." A silver spoon and the sugar container were both engraved with a similar souvenir, "À l'incomparable Manon—M." Under no circumstances did Massenet permit anyone to call him Jules; he despised his first name and refused to use it. The silver demitasse spoons Sibyl gave him were inscribed, "To my master—S. S."

The composer's most precious gifts, however, were the holographs of the operas he was to write for her. Several times on the manuscript of *Esclarmonde,* he noted that in spite of the heat and other irritations, "I continue to labor on our opera." Massenet had never used this expression before. On 7 December 1888, when he asked Sanderson to add her name to his on the final page of *Esclarmonde,* he had joined her in a symbolic marriage she never fully comprehended. He dreamed of writing operas for her that only she could sing. He would immortalize her name. In return she was to place her musical future in his hands. The gift of *Esclarmonde* would seal their artistic union. Inside the title page he inscribed a few lines that, as usual, revealed his emotions only peripherally: "You have the right to such a large part of the creation of this opera that I permit myself to offer you the manuscript as a small expression of my affectionate gratitude."

The popular new star was in constant demand for appearances with her mentor. In the summer of 1889 they triumphed together in a concert at the Ministry of Fine Arts, where France put its most celebrated musicians on display to honor some important foreign visitors to the Exposition. Thomas, Godard, Gounod, Delibes, and Saint-Saëns were the major composers, besides Massenet, who turned out to welcome America's Edward MacDowell and Russia's Rimsky-

Korsakov among others. Sanderson received an ovation for singing the premiere of Massenet's "Pensée d'automne."

Singing one of the Queen of the Night arias from Mozart's *Magic Flute,* a few of Massenet's songs, and the Love Duet from *Esclarmonde* with tenor Albert Vaguet, she enchanted Parisian society at another soiree given by the Paul Poirsons. Whether she sang at a reception in the American embassy or at a concert for the Union of Parisian Artists, the audience was mesmerized. After her two April appearances in Gounod's cantata *Gallia* at the Conservatoire, the committee-in-charge sent her a special medal to commemorate the concerts.

In June 1890 she stole the honors at a brilliant soiree given by the De Blowitzes in their elegant mansion on the rue Tilsitt. The entire literary, artistic, and political elite of Paris had assembled to hear a star-studded program on which divas Eames, Sanderson, Artôt de Padilla, and Baudé shared vocal honors with male idols Albert Vaguet, Jean-François Delmas, and Delssart. Among the guests were the ambassadors from England, the United States, Spain, and Persia and last but not least, the three Juleses—writers Simon and Claretie, and composer Massenet. Dinner was served at 8 P.M.; two hours later the guests moved into the enormous salon where a forty-piece orchestra was hidden behind a massive embankment of flowers. According to *L'Écho de Paris,* in spite of the stellar competition, "the divine Sanderson" was in superlative voice and carried off the evening's highest accolades. For the grand finale Sibyl was joined by Vaguet (tenor) and Delmas (bass-baritone) in the trio from the last act of Gounod's *Faust,* and their rendition brought a screaming audience to its feet.

Massenet was so excited that he wrote Sibyl's mother the following note in the early morning hours, sending it by courier, and rousing the entire family from its slumber:

> To Mme Sanderson, 7 rue Lincoln
> *Réponse Urgente!*
> Her success was very great at this performance
> *Love Duet* from Esclarmonde with Vaguet *encored*
> Two of my songs—
> *Minuet* in the style of the 18th century [Marquise] encored
> *Pensée d'automne encored*
> *Trio from Faust encored*
>   What tremendous enthusiasm on the part of the audience!!!! All of this
> delayed me from having news of you and her. I was so anxious to accompany

her home but even with Lina I couldn't do so because of propriety. Please send me news. From a heart overflowing with pride and happiness.

Massenet

The Lina to whom Massenet referred was Sibyl's lifelong maid, Lina Bournie. The Sandersons had somehow acquired her when they moved to the rue Lincoln, and Margaret had not found her satisfactory at all. Several times she was at the point of dismissing her for laziness and obstinate disrespect when a sympathetic Sibyl would interfere. Finally, the young artist volunteered to keep Lina on as her personal maid.

Sibyl resigned from the Opéra-Comique after it became obvious that director Paravey had no intention of reviving *Manon*. She told a reporter from the *New York Herald* that she had not made up her mind about the offers she had received, but one thing was certain: she would definitely accept the invitation by Messrs Ritt and Gailhard to create the leading soprano role in Massenet's *Le mage* at the Opéra for the coming season.

The plot of *Le mage* (The Magician) was to be based on the life story of the famous Persian general Zoroaster, who, circa 1000 B.C., became the involuntary creator of a new religion because of circumstances over which he had no control. Jean Richepin had written an original libretto. Sanderson was to create the lyric coloratura role of Anahita, queen of the Touranians, whom Zoroaster conquered and carried back to Persia with her captive people before he lost his heart to his prisoner.

In June 1890 with pen and manuscript paper packed away, Massenet took the train for Vevey, Switzerland, where it was announced he would be staying at the Hôtel des Trois Couronnes. Furtively, he checked into the Grand Hotel, where he knew the Sandersons were due to arrive the following day. Of course, his wife was aware of his intentions, but she would say nothing to compromise his all-important propriety.

Now the composer was looking forward to several weeks to drilling his queen of song in her new role—the second he had written for her. Besides periods of intense creativity, there would be at least one drive up Mount Jorat with her, at least one excursion on Lake Geneva with her, the inevitable picnic in the park with her, as always under the protective shadow of her mother's presence.

Because she knew that Mrs. Sanderson would be chaperoning Sibyl at all times, Mme Massenet said absolutely nothing about these periodic desertions. She was used to them; after all, she had come from an artistic family too. Her cousin Jules Armingaud had founded a well-known chamber music group with the composer Édouard Lalo. Her brother Abel Orry, a painter who belonged to the Barbizon school, was often gone from the family on some artistic expedition. She was a tiny, retiring woman of infinite kindness and patience. Early in her marriage to the volatile composer, she realized there was room for only one prima donna under their roof. Massenet adored her, and at the same time still loved to dally with the ladies. His flirtations usually did not cause her serious discomfort because she understood how much he esteemed the sacred bulwark of his home. "My wife is a saint," he constantly proclaimed, and anyone who knew them both did not argue the point. For the present she was forced to bide her time and hope her husband's burning infatuation with his pupil would run its course in due time.

Sanderson had already signed a contract to go to Brussels in September where she was engaged to be leading chanteuse légère (lyric soprano) at the Théâtre Royal de la Monnaie. She planned to return to Paris for rehearsals of *Le mage* at the end of the year. Cognizant that she would be exploring the French repertoire in Brussels and be expected to have full command of it, the cantatrice had spent considerable time coaching the roles of Marguerite and Juliette with Gounod, besides working regularly with Léo Delibes on his *Lakmé*. Sibyl knew she could not exist for long merely functioning as a Massenet specialist, but unfortunately, she was coasting without a voice teacher and falling prey to unhealthy vocal habits.

Her appearance at the Conservatoire with the Polish pianist Ignacy Paderewski in June 1890 was not a critical success. While Paderewski's performance was lionized in Paris, the critic for *Le Guide musical* wrote of Sanderson's solo from Gounod's *Gallia:* "The well-earned success of the woman's stunning beauty still cannot make up for the insufficiency of her vocal powers."

Had she gone to Mme Marchesi and immediately sought lessons, she might have averted the tragedy that was soon to commence. Unhappily, the soprano was intoxicated with the "locusts and wild honey of praise." By the time she finally sought Marchesi's tutelage it was too late.

Chapter 11

The Belgian Conquest

The Sandersons arrived in Brussels before the end of August 1890 and were fortunate to find a reasonable first-floor apartment in a pension directly across the street from the Royal Opera House. Margaret promptly rented furniture for it, acquired a reliable maid named Sophie, and proceeded to make their new home as comfortable as possible. The apartment consisted of a large salon overlooking the boulevard Ausbach, a small dining room, a kitchen, and two good-sized bedrooms, plus a dressing room for the star. The only other occupant of the house was the owner, who, with his family, lived on the main floor.[1]

The singer and her mother lost no time in calling upon the directors of La Monnaie, Oscar Stoumon and Édouard Calabresi. The former was a Belgian; Calabresi, a French subject born of Italian parents, had lived for some years in New Orleans, where he managed the French Opera House from 1867 to 1873. Together they operated the theater under a government grant of 300,000 francs per year, half of it coming from the royal exchequer, the other half from the city treasury.

Massenet appeared the last weekend in August to superintend the final four rehearsals of *Esclarmonde.* He took the Sandersons on a carriage ride through the city, pointing out its various sights. The Belgian capital had always occupied a special niche in his affections, for it was here that one of his earliest operas, *Hérodiade,* received its premiere nine years before, when he was struggling for recognition in Paris. The whitewashed city fairly gleamed, with bilingual signs in Flemish and French on its main boulevard, and no end of stores filled with lace. Massenet ordered the driver to take them a few miles out of the city to the palace of Laeken where the Coburgs, Belgium's royal family, resided. He explained that the queen had been an Austrian archduchess before her marriage and was not only an ardent music lover, but one of his most enthusiastic fans. By the time he dropped them off at their apartment (and Margaret paid the fare), mother and daughter were in agreement on one point: they liked the city far more than they had expected to.

Sibyl's leading tenor in *Esclarmonde* was a darkly handsome young giant named Dupeyron who was also making his debut at La Monnaie. Max Bouvet was re-creating his role of the bishop. The rest of the cast consisted of Jean Vallier in the part of Phorcas, Challet singing King Cléomer, and Anna Wolf as Parséïs. Concert cellist François Servais was to be the principal conductor, assisted by Franz (Édouard) Baerwolf. Mme Zina (Marguerite) de Nuovina, a superb Romanian soprano who had created the opera's title role in Brussels the previous season, gracefully relinquished it to its Parisian originator.

The royal theater opened its doors the first week in September with Nuovina in a resounding production of *Faust.* Sibyl's highly publicized debut in *Esclarmonde* was slated for 6 September 1890, and the night of her first appearance found the hall jammed to capacity. All of Brussels was anxiously awaiting the American phenomenon.

The enthusiastic anticipation felt by the spectators, however, was conspicuously absent backstage. The star, in the throes of stage fright, was suffering a violent attack of nerves and dysentery. An agitated composer, smoking incessantly as he strode back and forth in the dressing room, didn't help her composure. Sobbing hysterically that she couldn't go on, Sibyl had good reason to be distraught. Everyone in the audiences would be comparing her to the highly admired De Nuovina. The dark-eyed Romanian had a larger voice; she had more experience on the stage in her native country; and her creation of *Esclarmonde* in Brussels, even with Massenet's simplified cadenzas and omission of stratospheric notes, had been highly acclaimed. Margaret had to ply her daughter with some patent medicine before she calmed down and the curtain could be raised.

The magical results were described in Margaret's letter to Jane on 10 September 1890.

> Sibyl made her debut on Sept. 6 to a cold audience which soon warmed up, and her success was far greater than even in Paris. She sang again on the 10th and had from her first aria an ovation . . . her second performance was a great success . . . She has all but one paper in her favor, and articles such as only great artists can have . . . She has had stage fright for ten days. Never did I see her so down. She was ill with dysentery and I also. It is the illness preva-

lent here, and that along with her fright told on her . . . Sibyl does not eat well, and I cannot have beef tea and such things when I want them . . . 15 Sept. I have been to the station to get the girls. They were met at Antwerp by M Massenet who had been there on a concert.

He saves me in every way and when he leaves us, I do not know what we shall do. No one to ask advice of, and we have so much need of that . . . He is greatly liked in Belgium, and is a *great man.* He is very proud of Sibyl. Her success here proves him to be correct in his judgment of her . . . I did not send any dispatches simply because I did not have any money. I am in very *narrow straights [sic]* for money owing to such great demands on my purse by Sibyl for her costumes.

Margaret's maternal pride can be forgiven for a rather exaggerated account of Sibyl's debut. Actually, the only thing Brussels gleaned from the highly advertised event was the fact that the soprano seemed to be immobilized by stage fright, although glimpses of her vocal virtuosity shone through the score in isolated moments. In the exorcism scene she wisely omitted the famed G in alt from her offstage cadenza, because her voice had cruelly betrayed her by cracking on the high F just moments before.

However, the audience appeared to be an exceptionally understanding one and, realizing her obvious terror, kept trying to encourage her with recalls. By the end of the opera Sibyl had recovered sufficiently to leave "an honorable impression," but in no way did she erase the memory of Nuovina's stellar interpretation of the previous season. Dupeyron's rapturous singing had captured the real ovations of the evening.

The local critics even forgave the poltergeist in her throat for playing that evil trick on her third-act cadenza, but most of the papers agreed she had achieved little more than a succès de beauté. Her exquisite face and figure were accorded their due tribute, and her star-sapphire eyes had already cast their hypnotic spell over the Bruxellois. Nevertheless, *La Reforma,* on 7 September 1890, complained that "after we were promised marvels, it was somewhat disillusioning. Mlle Sanderson's voice is clear but pinched and further impaired by a quasi tremolo."

Lucien Solvay's September 18 report to *Le Ménéstrel* in Paris was probably the most accurate.

Mlle Sanderson was suffering from la peur bleue [stage fright]. She who had displayed, at the premiere of the work in Paris, so much confidence, was here

more dead than alive. Fortunately, the public . . . realized all of her conflicting and terrifying emotions and gave the lovely American such an encouraging hand of applause . . . at times she seems to have made real progress since
her Parisian debut . . . we hope that the cantatrice-phénoménale will soon be
replaced by the artist-singer when *Roméo et Juliette* is given next Monday
night.

Every day the new soprano was rehearsing Gounod's *Roméo et Juliette* opposite Emmanuel Lafarge, a Paris-born Belgian tenor of enormous girth. Sibyl was
fully aware that the press was depicting this occasion as her "real debut." It
would be the date of her first encounter with the standard repertoire, the decisive test by which she rose or fell before the jury of public opinion.

Sanderson's Shakespearean heroine had been as eagerly anticipated by the
Belgians as her Byzantine sorceress, and the night of 23 September again found
La Monnaie sold out. Coaching the role with Gounod that summer should
have bolstered the soprano's confidence, but again her nerves betrayed her in
the dressing room. Once more Margaret found it necessary to tranquilize her
daughter with an ample dosage of patent medicine—a habit that was becoming
a most unwise ritual.

Shortly after the curtain rose on the ball scene, a murmur of admiration
greeted the exquisite Californian. She entered the stage in a gown of white-and-
silver brocade paneled in pink and adorned with pearls. Her bodice was embroidered in silver and diamonds, and topping the ensemble was a cherry-colored
toque over Juliette's blond wig.

In spite of a well-executed Waltz Song, which evoked enthusiastic applause,
Sanderson seemed to be sleepwalking through the first two acts, her voice continually throttled by stage fright. On the contrary, Lafarge's impassioned
singing in the balcony scene created a sèche of bravos from all over the house.
However, the rest of the performance saw the newcomer grow much stronger
in emotional warmth and color. The scenes in Juliette's bedroom, Friar
Laurence's cell, and finally the tomb revealed "strong and unexpected dramatic traits" in Sibyl's interpretation, as one review noted. By the end of the
evening, the ovation was spontaneous; she had come through the ordeal triumphantly.

The *Bruxelles soir* of 24 September observed that "her interpretation became a
highly moving one in the last two acts . . . at last the lovely statue came to life
and her soul revealed itself . . . her flame shone most brilliantly in the death
scene, and the evening ended victoriously for her."

Nearly all the Belgian critics agreed that what began as a rather pallid Juliette had bloomed into an emphatic success, and Sibyl earned some additional accolades for piping the Waltz Song (Act I) in G major, its higher original key. Reams of print were devoted to her bewitching appearance. The *Chronique Bruxelles* extolled her as "the *plastique* incarnation of sixteen-year-old Juliette in the flesh."

News of the young American's conquest of Belgium quickly reached Paris, and Massenet responded with an ecstatic telegram: MY JOY IS WITHOUT LIMIT—NEVER HAVE I EXPERIENCED GREATER HAPPINESS—YOUR TRIUMPH PLACES YOU AMONG THE FIRST RANK OF GREAT ARTISTS—MY FAITH HAS ALWAYS BEEN JUSTIFIED—AFFECTIONATE GREETINGS TO YOUR DEAR, BELOVED MOTHER. Contrary to the hyperbolic sentiments of her mentor, Sibyl's success as Juliette did not catapult her into the category of such operatic divinities as Patti and Nilsson, but it had secured the singer's hold over her new subjects.

The following Sunday, Queen Marie Henriette arrived to hear the young artist repeat her performance and was so impressed she personally communicated her satisfaction to the managers. An excited mother described the occasion to daughter Jane in her letter of 27 September.

> You are always in my thoughts Jennie, all of you, not alone Sibyl . . . Marion and Edith are in Antwerp for a visit to Mrs. Dyer. They all came up to hear Sibyl in *Romeo and Juliet* and returned after twelve . . . The Queen came up to hear Sibyl, she and the Princess Royale came on the train arriving at the theater *in their traveling dresses.* The Queen sent for her before the performance commenced and talked very sweetly to her. She said, "I have come from Spa expressly to hear you." She congratulated her on her success afterwards and all during the evening she and the Princess applauded Sibyl vigorously. She sent for the director (Mr. Stoumon) to say she was very pleased with Miss Sanderson, and the director told Sibyl she has not done this for anyone else. She returned at midnight to Spa on the special royal train. Sibyl found her to be very much queen-like, except she allows everybody to stroll up before her . . . Sibyl is now the *one person* talked of [in Brussels].

Sanderson had caught the fancy of the Belgians, who were avidly thirsting for more information about her. The press had enlightened a somewhat puzzled segment of its readers that in America it was not considered unusual for a young heiress to choose a theatrical vocation. In European countries, on the contrary, it was verboten for any woman of social prominence to embark upon a stage career.

The newcomer was now singing three nights a week besides rehearsing a new opera every other afternoon. Some of the more astute journalists feared she might overtax her voice, but Messrs Stoumon and Calabresi were no different from managers anywhere else in the world. A star was a marketable commodity, and they would have been fools not to take advantage of her soaring popularity. Her voice, her beauty, her ravishing costumes, and her extraordinary witchery on stage were a rare combination of attributes for one woman. Together, they made a marvelous aggregate for exploitation.

Already the publicity department of La Monnaie had sent releases to the Brussels papers promising that Mlle Sanderson would be "a revelation" in her next revival, Massenet's *Manon*. Dupont's photographs of her as Manon and Juliette were causing a furor in the Belgian capital. Her Manon costumes, which had been created by Doucet in Paris, were described as having cost a little under 18,000 francs, an unheard-of sum for a single operatic role. Massenet, recovering from a recent liver attack, arrived in Brussels for the final rehearsals under the watchful eye of his son-in-law, Léon Bessand. Wrapped up in an enormous poultice tied around his body, he still deftly supervised the rehearsals.

The *représentation générale* was postponed from the afternoon of 2 November to 8 P.M. at the request of the queen. The delay did not assist Belgian railroad authorities in their fruitless search for a missing antique jeweled fan, a gift from Mrs. Ben Ali Haggin to Sibyl for the occasion.

On Tuesday night the queen and several members of her suite entered the royal box. Still thoroughly poulticed, Massenet shared a box with his son-in-law. The opera went off with jeweled precision, and the silver-haired monarch frequently applauded. At the end of the Saint Sulpice scene, she rose from her chair, vociferously shouting "Brava!" The orchestra also sprang to its feet, echoing her majesty's sentiments.

After the performance the queen invited the heroine to her box for some complimentary words. "Mlle., you are perfection! No wonder M. Massenet holds you in such high regard. I must confess you are fast becoming my favorite soprano also."[2]

The first public reprise of *Manon* occurred on Saturday night, 6 November 1890; La Monnaie had been sold out for some weeks. When Americans from Paris arrived at the theater, they found themselves surrounded by an excited horde of Belgians clamoring to obtain tickets from scalpers.

Massenet had to leave for Paris with his son-in-law right after the Cours-la-Reine scene, but he congratulated his disciple in her dressing room before he departed. Making his adieu with a kiss to her hand, he predicted, "Mlle . . . if you sing the chapel scene as well as you did at the dress rehearsal, you will achieve a real success!"

From all reports, the young artists surpassed his expectations. Jean Delmas's interpretation of "Le rêve" and Sanderson's "farewell" to the petite table evoked storms of applause in the second act. When the curtain came down on the highly emotional Saint Sulpice scene, the feverish Belgians were on their feet screaming "Brava!" and throwing their programs into the air.

Sanderson's voice was showered with encomiums by the Belgian press: "ravishing in quality . . . pure . . . exquisite as to intonation and dramatically expressive." Her stage personality was said to be "touched by the divine Judic."[3] Delmas was praised for "singing the role of Des Grieux with superb finesse." Only the orchestra was thrashed by the critic of the *Étoile belge* on 8 November, for not achieving enough subtlety, but by now the papers abounded with remarks about the insensitive conducting of Franz Baerwolf.

Audible gasps of disbelief greeted the prima donna's much-publicized costumes.[4] In the gambling scene she looked like "a Greuze figure come to life," observed the critic for *La Gazette de Bruxelles* on 8 November. Manon had swept onto the stage in a magnificent gown of green satin embellished with silver lace and strewn with mastic roses, over which was worn a velvet rose-pink overdress embroidered with antique gold. A white powdered wig adorned with a rose and a diamond aigrette completed this eighteen-century vision. In the second act, another idolator described Sibyl as "having stepped out of a Watteau painting in a pale blue Louis XV satin peignoir trimmed with silver lace."

The craze for the California nightingale was spiraling in the Belgian capital and simultaneously bringing her mentor's popularity to its crest also. When the Association of Artists-Musicians announced that they would honor Massenet at their December concert, it came as no surprise. The Frenchman seemed to be in Brussels as much as Paris that season. There would be two symphonic offerings on the program conducted by the composer, his overture to *Phèdre* and his suite *Les Érinnyes*. Lafarge was engaged to sing a group of Massenet's songs, and for his aria he chose the Farewell from Wagner's *Lohengrin*. Sibyl would perform her mentor's "Pensée d'automne" and Menuet before she closed the program with one of the Queen of the Night arias from Mozart's *Magic Flute*.

The night of the Association's program, which took place on 2 December, the star and the composer received a series of ovations from a large, elegantly dressed crowd at La Monnaie, including the queen and her retinue. Sanderson's "merveilleuse et richissime toilette" was described by a reporter for *L'Indépendence belge* as "the despair and envy of every woman in the audience."

119

He further remarked that "the gracious soprano . . . obtained a double triumph—a *succès de lorgnettes* as well as an artistic one."[5] The following evening the pair attended a glittering soirée organized by Les Cercles des Arts et de la Presse, and again they were cheered to the echo. Although other artists appeared on both programs, the public had come to hear Jules and Sibyl. The names of the legendary couple would remain inexorably linked in the memories of all who heard them and saw them bow together on stage. The Belgians as well as the French had romanticized the relationship as one of the grand passions of the century.

A far less pleasant task awaited Massenet upon his return to Paris, one that would demand his combined talents for strategy and diplomacy. Chorus rehearsals had begun the previous month at the Opéra for *Le mage,* which would receive its premiere soon after the beginning of the year. With Sibyl bound by her contract to La Monnaie until spring, it was the first time in his life he desperately wanted to delay one of his productions.

For the moment Sibyl had her hands full in Brussels, having emerged from a dismal production of Verdi's *Rigoletto* shortly before Christmas. The opera was given in French, and she was forced to learn the part of Gilda in little over a month. Bouvet sang the title role of the court jester, and Lafarge appeared as the Duke of Mantua. The critics awarded Bouvet the few laurels that were tossed, whereas both the Duke and Gilda seem to have left decidedly negative impressions. Since much of the singing took place in the shadows, the soprano was without one of her most precious assets: her beauty. The Belgian papers were amused and slyly suggested that for her own protection, she should avoid roles in which the action transpires in the dark.

Sanderson could not have been expected to shine with any particular radiance in her first excursion into the Italian repertoire. She had hastily learned the mechanics of the role without proper time for interpretive maturation. More than a year had elapsed since her lessons with Sbriglia, and during that time the young artist had deceived herself into believing that she could learn new roles independently. It was a serious error. Her vocal development was rapidly reaching a plateau. Already her pro-Wagnerian adversary, Maurice Kufferath, was sneering in *Le Guide musical:* "This artist is having more and more difficulty every day in sustaining her Parisian reputation."[6]

Happily, her next assignment—*Lakmé*—would see the cantatrice returning to the French operatic school. Rehearsals were to commence shortly after Christmas. Ever since Sibyl had arrived in Brussels, her entire life seemed to be nothing but an interminable round of rehearsals. Four roles in four months.

She felt trapped. Never did she dream that learning the repertoire would involve so many hours of repetitious drudgery. The fair Californian had not been reared for this kind of existence. More than once she recalled her joyous, carefree youth spent sweeping through San Francisco ballrooms followed by a train of infatuated beaux.

With the holidays approaching, Sibyl counted the hours until she and her mother could escape the relentless pressures of La Monnaie for Christmas in Paris. She could hardly wait to see her sisters and friends. More urgently, she must meet with Massenet and the directors of the Opéra about postponing her rehearsals in *Le mage*. When the train pulled out of the Brussels depot for the French capital, Sibyl and her mother dropped into their seats half dead with exhaustion. Finally they could relax for the first time in weeks. Rummaging through her purse, the diva accidentally came across a calling card she had mislaid in her hasty packing: Baudouin de Flandre.

She had forgotten all about him. The prince's equerry had brought a message written on it to her dressing room between acts of a recent performance with a bouquet of flowers. "Chère Mademoiselle, Kindly accept these flowers as a token of my highest esteem. You would do me the greatest honor by allowing me to call upon you at your earliest convenience." Absentmindedly, Sibyl gave the aide a tentative date when she could receive the prince, completely forgetting that she and her mother had planned to leave a few days early for Paris.

The prince of Flanders, oldest son of the king's brother, the count of Flanders. Wasn't he the heir to the throne? She had met his mother at the dress rehearsal of *Manon*. Her son was said to have the face of a Christmas angel, with a shock of flaxen hair, the palest blue eyes, and the most cherubic features. What a gaffe! Somehow she would have to rectify her mistake after the first of the year.

Chapter 12

A Winter for Duels

Europe had been struck by the coldest winter of the nineteenth century. Icy blasts swept down from the Arctic Circle as far south as northern Algeria. Blizzards blocked all mountain passes in Austria, paralyzing train service. The roofs of some English cottages collapsed under an unusually heavy accumulation of snow, and hundreds of people froze to death.

Among the victims of that Arctic cold wave was the French composer Léo Delibes. Already in precarious health, he caught a chill on the evening of 8 January 1891 after paying a call upon his librettist, Philippe Gille. He succumbed to pneumonia eight days later, five weeks short of his fifty-sixth birthday. The portly, bearded, near-sighted composer was always described by contemporaries as an "affable, buoyant, and thoroughly unassuming personality." Like Massenet, he was a gifted youngster who studied piano and composition at the Conservatoire, where they shared some of the same teachers. The untimely death of his father forced the youth to seek employment as an accompanist and church organist. His early experience playing with theater orchestras instilled in him a lifelong love for ballet. Indeed, among his best-remembered compositions are the ballets *Sylvia* and *Coppélia*.

Honors had come his way in an unostentatious manner. In 1877 he was made a Chevalier in the Légion d'Honneur, and in 1881 he was appointed professor of composition at the Conservatoire. Three years later Delibes was duly elected to the Institute.

In spite of his prolific legacy—everything from male choruses and operettas to religious works—he left behind only one major music drama, the opera *Lakmé*. The American soprano Marie Van Zandt had caused a furor in the title role at the Opéra-Comique in 1883. Perhaps it was not surprising that a successful foreigner should become embroiled in feuds with native divas. The singer was well on her way to becoming the toast of Paris when she is said to have appeared intoxicated on the stage one night, only to be booed and hissed with such ferocity (at least partly at the instigation of her enemies) that the manager was forced to ring down the curtain. Her contract was revoked, and she sued the Opéra-Comique, claiming that, in reality, she had been very ill. Although she won her suit for slander, her career was irrevocably finished in Paris for the rest of the decade, and she found it necessary to seek engagements elsewhere. Fortunately, the opera's popularity quickly spread to other cities, including Brussels, where it received a successful premiere in 1886.

When Sibyl's study of *Lakmé* commenced in the spring of 1890, Delibes opened the doors to an exotic world of Hindu symbolism. She was enchanted with the words; no opera has ever contained more beautiful poetry and Oriental imagery. Gradually she came to realize that the basic conflict in the story consisted of more than the spurious clash between western and eastern civilizations. It was deeply involved with competing philosophies of life and death. *Lakmé* was indeed the precursor of *Madama Butterfly,* Puccini's later operatic hit.[1]

It was Sibyl who requested the current Belgian revival, a fact Delibes had acknowledged in a letter of gratitude earlier that fall. Jean Delmas was cast as Gérard, the English soldier with whom the priestess Lakmé falls in love. Vallier was assigned the part of the Brahmin priest Nilakantha, and Badiali would sing Frédéric.

Delibes's admiration for Sanderson had grown enormously in the months she coached the role with him. As early as 13 May 1890, he wrote her that he was "eagerly looking forward to completing your study of *Lakmé* which has begun so well." On 6 November 1890, we find the composer writing the diva that he had been confined to bed in the country for "a slight indisposition" and his strength weakened by a milk diet imposed upon him by his physicians. From then on his condition steadily deteriorated. In spite of his serious decline, Delibes's last unpublished letter to Sanderson revealed that he was still planning to leave for Brussels no later than the twenty-first of January.

Wednesday evening, 7 January 1891

Chère Mademoiselle,

Two or three days ago I received a little note from M Stoumon with the excellent news about *Lakmé* and he tells me the opera will be performed currently this month right after the Belgian premiere of *Siegfried.*

. . . I have been wretchedly ill in recent weeks, and it has been a torment I must confess, but now that I am getting better, I hope to persevere in recovering my health.

Now when will rehearsals begin? When do you think I should appear on the scene? . . . When do you think it will be ready?

Unless my doctors *absolutely* forbid me to come to Brussels because of the terrible cold, I certainly want to arrive in time for one or two rehearsals.

I am busy at the Conservatoire until the 13th in the evenings. Other chores will detain me until the 20th, but I plan to leave no later than the 21st, and I am placing myself completely at your disposal . . .

. . . When you see the managers, tell them that I have written you at length and am looking forward to taking part in the preparations for the revival . . .

Kindly accept, dear Mademoiselle and friend, for your mother and yourself my best, and most devoted wishes for the new year.

Léo Delibes

Nine days later, on 16 January, Sanderson was rehearsing at La Monnaie when she received the tragic news of Delibes's death, which stunned the musical world. Deeply shaken, she wrote a memorandum into her score of *Lakmé* in a large, flowing hand:

In rehearsal when Delibes died—a great loss to all—and to me a great shock—only a few days before he had written me that he would come on the 21st—how little we then thought the sad end was so near—the first performance is scheduled for Monday, 25 January [sic] 1891.

But the unhappy demise of the composer wasn't the only adverse occurrence to plague the production. On Saturday morning, 24 January, Belgium was thrown into shock and consternation by the announcement of the sudden death of the king's nephew, twenty-two-year-old crown prince Baudouin de Flandre, the very prince who had requested permission to call upon the young American prima donna just a month before. The first official stories in print asserted that he was the victim of the extremely cold winter and had contracted a chill about a week before. Every paper in Brussels carried a different version of how the "chill" was contracted: by a walk a few days earlier; by a prolonged review of his regiment two weeks before; by sitting at the bedside of his sister Princess Henriette, who was confined with influenza.

The royal family's homeopathic doctors had been in constant attendance. Later in the day they drew up a death certificate declaring that the prince's death was caused by "violent hemorrhages in the kidneys, followed by four days of pleuro-pneumonia."[2] The official statement in *Le Moniteur belge* was met with instant skepticism—and for good reason: no bulletins about any suspected illness had been forwarded to the public, a custom highly unusual, to say the least.

Malicious whispers were not slow to incubate. European newspapers lost no time in speculating about all sorts of auxiliary factors, everything from small-pox to a ruptured love affair. Did the prince kill himself over a German governess with whom he had been intimate? Was it true that she was pregnant and had been banished from the palace by the king? Was foul play involved? If the curious Bruxellois wished to acquaint themselves with the latest rumors, they had to procure foreign papers. Strict censorship was immediately imposed upon the Belgian press by the government.

The *New York Times* revealed that the prince's engagement to the youngest daughter of the king and queen, Princess Clementine, would soon have been announced. Leopold's only son had died as a child in 1869 and female members of the royal family were excluded from the succession by the Belgian constitution.

The whole country was plunged into mourning. Flags over all government buildings in Brussels were flying at half staff. Shops were closed and blinds drawn. The doors of the royal opera house were padlocked for a week, and the revival of *Lakmé* was postponed until after the first of February.

On Friday, 30 January, the day of the state funeral, houses along the streets where the cortège would pass were draped in black, and in a welcome thaw in the weather, crowds began to form along the designated route by seven in the morning. Guns fired periodic salutes and church bells tolled. Shortly after 10:30 A.M., the cortège left the palace of Flanders for the Cathedral of Saint Gudule in a long and lugubrious procession. Bringing up the rear was the flower-smothered funeral carriage drawn by six black-draped horses and led by footmen in mourning livery.

Inside the cathedral the coffin was placed on a catafalque surrounded by a triple row of candles. A solemn funeral service was conducted by the Cardinal Archbishop of Mechlin, who was enthroned on one side of the altar with the bitterly grieving king on the other. Afterward the royal family and foreign dignitaries entered state carriages for the final journey to the Cathedral of Laeken where the prince was interred with relatives in crypts below the church. There was no mention in the Belgian press that several august members of the nobility—the Prince and Princess de Ligne, for example, and the Prince and Princess de Caraman-Chimay—had hastily left the country the previous week without plans for any imminent return. Some observers found this rather strange.

Even after the funeral, rumormongers refused to let the unfortunate Baudouin rest in peace. Less than two months later an odious story was printed in several Parisian papers that the late prince had been killed in a duel over a ravishing American—who else but the siren Sibylle? According to unidentified sources his royal highness was said to have been wildly enamored of the singer, and calling unannounced one day at her hotel, he unexpectedly encountered her mysterious "ducal protector." A duel ensued over the prima donna's affections, and the crown prince was wounded. Aides thought his wound could be treated and his death averted, and it was thought wisest to keep his infatuation with the beauteous opera star from the public. Mlle Sanderson was rumored to have fled to Paris on the very night of the fatal duel and remained there until the funeral.

Sibyl and her mother were stunned by the libelous fabrication. At the very moment of the prince's demise the singer was immersed in rehearsals and would not have known him on sight. She didn't even have time to send him her apologies for her unintentional slight. Now it was just as well. No doubt such slander would be suppressed in the Belgian papers, but sooner or later the tale would reach the directors of La Monnaie. The scandal could ruin her.

Massenet excitedly telegraphed her not to let the foul calumny go unchallenged. Legal counsel must be consulted at once. The very fact that he appeared to show implicit faith in her innocence was amusing. One can be sure that he checked with all possible sources in Brussels for any hint of veracity.

Sibyl had no choice but to consult an attorney about salvaging her shattered reputation. A prompt lawsuit was threatened against the offending Parisian journals if they did not print an immediate retraction. Surprisingly enough, the guilty papers complied most apologetically.

No sooner had the French press retracted the canard than it surfaced again in a London newspaper, with a variation or two. This time it was the story of the enamored prince who shot himself in the diva's boudoir because of his unrequited love. Again Sanderson's attorney had to threaten the British paper with appropriate action, which brought about another retraction. The thrilling tale of the prince and the diva soon reached American shores, and the Hearst papers had a field day. "Think of it," the *New York Journal* whispered luridly to its readers, "a royal life gone out on her account . . . but then royalty has become commonplace to her." THE WOMEN MEN DIE FOR was the provocative headline the *Illustrated American* ran above an equally provocative picture of the soprano. So many stories were popping up in print that any attempt to combat them would have been futile. Sanderson had become a maligned princess of yellow journalism.

In fact, she had remained in Brussels during the entire episode. The very afternoon of the prince's funeral, the singer received an important visitor from Paris: Léon Carvalho, former manager of the Opéra-Comique, who had just been reinstated following M Paravey's departure. Sibyl was aware that Paravey had been embroiled in a fiery contretemps with the ministry of fine arts over his administration of the Comique. Once he submitted his resignation, the directors, oddly enough, recalled Carvalho, whose false conviction for embezzling state funds had been overturned after he served a short prison term. Because he had been at the helm of the Opéra-Comique for so long and his name had been cleared, the cabinet of fine arts sheepishly offered him his old job once more.

Carvalho's first act upon reinstatement was a journey to Brussels. He was determined to bring Sibyl Sanderson home to Paris once her contract with La Monnaie expired. One of Carvalho's reasons was his intention of reviving *Manon* that fall. They discussed the singer's imbroglio with the Paris Opéra. Massenet had tried to delay the premiere of *Le mage* as long as he could, but both mentor and protégée realized the futility of the situation. Gailhard and Ritt, the directors, had become so annoyed with the composer's daily meddling that they informed Massenet that the Opéra had no alternative but to procure a substitute for Sanderson. She had already been notified by wire of her replacement. Massenet was crestfallen.

Sibyl realized there was no way to circumvent her La Monnaie contract, which now would be extended one week further into May because of the prince's death. If she formally broke her contract with the Paris Opéra, which, after all, ran only for the length of *Le mage,* she would be free to sign with the Opéra-Comique for the following season. Jubilantly, Carvalho watched the prima donna add her signature to his own. The Opéra's loss was certain to become the Comique's bonanza.

On Monday night, 2 February 1891, the Théâtre de la Monnaie reopened its doors, and the long-delayed revival of *Lakmé* took place without further rehearsal. According to all the papers, the performance was such a catastrophe that Léo Delibes was fortunate to have been paged by the Grim Reaper beforehand and spared additional suffering.

"The choruses sang dreadfully out of tune," complained *L'Indépendance belge*.[3] "The orchestra played at random and seemingly at cross-purposes with everyone else," the *Chronique belge* grumbled.[4] "Even the principal roles were inferior to what had been expected of them," lamented *La Gazette de Bruxelles*.[5] *L'Art musical* accused the directors of "shocking negligence" and Baerwolf of "heavy handed and stultifying conducting." Lucien Solvay, however, was completely enraptured with Sanderson's interpretation. His tribute in *Le Ménéstrel* acclaimed her as "so much more than a totally charming Lakmé . . . her portrayal of the tragic Hindu priestess was always dramatically moving, brimming with melancholy tenderness and emotion, filled with the utmost lyric sensitivity."[6]

In the audience that night was a bereaved spectator torn by mixed emotions—the composer's widow. Her congratulatory note to Sibyl must have moved the singer profoundly after all the sabotage she had been forced to endure.

3 February 1891

Chère Mademoiselle,
Kindly permit me to send you my highest compliments for the pleasure—
extremely sad as it was for me—that I had yesterday in hearing you perform
the role of Lakmé.—I still cannot disentangle my joy from the deep chagrin
of thinking that the dear, late composer did not have the good fortune to live
long enough to hear you in what would have been his ultimate rapture.

Mme E. Léo Delibes

La Monnaie held no monopoly on musical misfortune that winter. Fate seems to have been stalking not only the spirit of Léo Delibes with unusual vengeance but a viable Massenet as well. At the Opéra in Paris, the rehearsals for *Le mage* were continuously beset by ill luck. The composer had met with constant frustration for nearly a year in casting the work. In the summer of 1890 he had been rebuffed by Jean de Reszke after asking the tenor to create the title role of Zarastra. When Opéra officials refused to delay the production any longer for Sibyl Sanderson, she had indignantly broken her contract with them. Mme Lureau-Escalaïs was chosen to replace her as Anahita. Next, the composer had sought Mme Renée Richard to create the role of Varedha, but she, like Sibyl, was shackled to La Monnaie in musical servitude, so the part passed to Mme Fierens. Then the famous baritone Lassalle, who had originally been contracted for the role of the high priest, walked out of rehearsals after a row with the management, and baritone Jean-François Delmas was hastily summoned to substitute. It was not surprising that Massenet had become despondent over the situation.

The premiere finally came off on 16 March 1891 and appears to have created more excitement offstage than on it. Lassalle and Massenet were at loggerheads because of a few vituperative and ungentlemanly remarks the baritone supposedly made about Sanderson's absence. Massenet was so furious that, according to *Le Figaro,* he had challenged Lassalle to a duel. Paris held its breath. Would the romance of the decade come to such a melodramatic denouement? Lassalle was not only a giant of a man but an expert swordsman. During his entire life the composer had never held anything more lethal in his hand than a baton. With duels nearly obsolete in France by this time, it was not surprising the whole affair was settled with an apology from Lassalle and lunch for two, with the baritone picking up the bill. Then the American novelist Marion Crawford accused Massenet's librettist, Jean Richepin, of plagiarizing one of his novels and threatened legal action. How this matter was resolved has never been made public, but one thing seems certain: it never went to court.

Sanderson had been fortunate to escape the opera. The critics annihilated the work, and after thirty-one performances it was given an unceremonious burial in the Opéra archives. A few journalists found the oft-recurring leitmotif of Anahita to be of haunting beauty. They had no idea that it was borrowed from Massenet's *Albumleaf,* his first unpublished song for Sibyl, and incorporated into the opera as Anahita's love theme.[7]

If the Parisians were disappointed by her absence during the production, they were gratified to know she would return to Paris during the Lenten season to sing the title role in Massenet's oratorio *Ève,* 26 March 1891. The unsavory publicity surrounding the singer in recent weeks had been more than sufficient to sell out the entire Hippodrome.

Paul Viardot, the director, had given Sibyl top billing over her co-artists, and with the composer conducting a fifty-voice choir in the background, the mystery play held the audience spellbound. When they returned to the stage for encores of two of his songs, the audience became ecstatic. Jules and Sibyl together again! The pair remained a unique musical and romantic duo unparalleled elsewhere in fin-de-siècle Europe.

Upon her return to Brussels Sanderson barely had time to unpack her luggage before rehearsals commenced on her last production of the season—a revival of Gounod's *Mireille* that was to be presented in April. Because Sibyl had cajoled the directors into staging the original version of the opera, the composer was delighted with the project. He had always detested his diluted edition, particularly the happy ending Léon Carvalho had forced him to impose upon Mistral's tragic poem for its Parisian premiere. Having coached the title role with Gounod on her recent trip to Paris, Sibyl planned to interpret the Provençal maid with both a simplicity of style and purity of faith. Delmas was cast as her lover, Vincent, and Badiali as the villain Ourrias.

Unhappily, the Belgians were familiar only with the revised edition and did not react any more sympathetically to the original conception than the Parisians had. On opening night Baerwolf's pachydermous conducting again scuttled the production. Gounod's poignant creation seems to have been further mangled by a cumbersome chorus. The restoration of the two scenes in the third act, "The Valley of Hell," and "The Rhône," met with a frigid reception from the press as well as the public.

The critics also observed that Sanderson's voice had deteriorated in quality since the beginning of the season, although tribute was paid to her dramatic sensitivity. About six performances seemed to have been offered, and they marked her only encounter with this elusive opera during her career.

Shortly before her Belgian indenture ended in May, Sibyl's future return to the Opéra-Comique was jointly announced in the French and Belgian papers with considerable lament in the latter about her impending departure. What an exhausting year it had been. Her vocal cords were worn nearly threadbare from constant rehearsals and public performances three times a week for the entire season. Nevertheless, the young artist had accomplished her mission: she had come to Brussels to learn the repertoire.

Moreover, she would be departing as the heroine of a mysterious tragedy. At the tender age of twenty-six, Sibyl found herself undeservedly enshrined by the press among the famous sirens of history. The news media had molded her in the image of the temptresses she played on stage, and no amount of converse publicity would ever eradicate their conception of her as a femme fatale.

To the end of his days, Belgium's beloved King Albert, the successor to the ill-fated Baudouin, denied the sinister whispers about his brother's death. On an American tour in 1897 he refused to discuss the subject with the press. As late as 1930 he declared in an interview, "My brother led an exemplary life, he was a saint, and public malice has tried to make him the victim of a passionate affair . . . the truth is more simple.—He died of pneumonia contracted during an outing with his company of carabineers . . . these lies . . . have never ceased to spread about Baudouin's untimely death!"[8]

King Albert may have spent most of his life trying to whitewash his brother's character, but according to privileged information obtained by the author, his own children did not entertain the illusion that Uncle Baudouin was any candidate for sainthood.[9] King Leopold had spent hours affectionately training him for his upcoming duties and doted on his youthful emulation. Unfortunately, he inherited his uncle's prodigious sexual appetite without being in the latter's impregnable position. Chasing after both single and married women, from servants to princesses, he became the terror of the court.

Five years after the prince's death, Clara Ward, the beautiful American libertine, was to titillate Europe with a shocking tale of how her ex-husband, the Prince de Caraman-Chimay, had been forced to challenge Baudouin to a duel because of his lascivious attentions to her. The Detroit heiress to the Eber Ward fortune had earned quite a scarlet reputation on the Riviera by putting her nymphomania on display. It was there she met the Prince de Chimay. A whirlwind courtship and marriage to the Belgian aristocrat in 1890 didn't reform her in the least. She couldn't resist inviting her current paramour, a German captain, to the wedding. Her new husband swept her back to the Chimay castle in Belgium and introduced her at court. That proved to be a mistake; twice she ran off with the Chimay coachman, and other times she didn't even bother to run. It was only natural that her brazen affairs would arouse the hostility of the court ladies, particularly when the local wolf pack was now led by the heir to the throne himself.

According to her 1896 interviews with the Pester-Lloyd papers and the *Neue Freie Presse* in Budapest, the crown prince's bold advances toward Clara at a Laeken garden party created such a scandalous scene that they were forced to leave Brussels not long afterward because of her husband's "subsequent course of action." The story proved to be the sensation of 1896, but there was just one thing wrong with it: Whatever his intentions, the Prince de Chimay never killed the royal Casanova. That onerous task was reserved for someone else.[10]

On a stormy winter day, either 18 or 19 January 1891, a secret duel had occurred in the ballroom of a deserted villa on the outskirts of Brussels. The crown prince had been severely wounded by his adversary—the Prince de Ligne. When the agitated Prince de Ligne—a man some years older than his opponent—arrived at his château, his mind was undoubtedly overwhelmed by a dizzying whirl of conflicting emotions. Only yesterday he had been the Belgian ambassador to the Netherlands, scion of a prestigious noble family far older than the Coburgs. Now his career was finished. He faced immediate resignation and exile. Over and over he must have asked himself, "Why did I do it?"

But the answer was always the same: his honor was at stake. He had no recourse after making an unexpected trip home a few weeks earlier only to discover that the royal satyr and his wife were involved in a passionate affair. About a year later, the *New York Herald* announced that the scene of the tragedy had been boarded up and was subsequently demolished.

Baudouin's family was stunned. Their son had successfully hidden all evidence of the fatal confrontation from them. At first the homeopathic physicians thought they could save his life, but unfortunately hemorrhaging in both lungs and kidneys soon became serious. On 22 January Dr. Rommellaere expressed his alarm to Dr. Mélis over the prince's rapidly deteriorating condition. By this time, pneumonia was exacting its toll also. At 6 P.M. the last sacraments were administered. The king and queen, as well as the premier, M Beervaert, were summoned and remained with the count and countess of Flanders until midnight. Cupping glasses were applied at 10 P.M. without any noticeable improvement, and shortly after midnight the patient feebly bade his weeping family farewell. The prince soon slipped into unconsciousness, his respiration growing more labored every moment. There was a sudden, last flow of blood from his lungs, and at 1:45 A.M. the heir to the Belgian throne breathed his last.

Chapter 13

The Diva Meets a God

Sanderson wisely chose her biggest hit—*Manon*—for her last appearance in Brussels on 9 May 1891. It was an emotional evening with cries of "Ne partez pas!" (Do not leave us!) echoing through the opera house. Time and time again a wildly cheering public recalled the cast before the curtain, but when the prima donna and the composer appeared together, hand in hand, for a final bow, the audience was in a state of frenzy.

Massenet had rushed back to Brussels for the gala farewell and relished every bow he took on stage with his heroine. After thoroughly inspecting the magnificent floral offerings to his songstress, he discovered a singularly exotic gift buried deep among the bouquets and included it in his long account of Sibyl's triumphs in her *Manon* folio.

> 9 May 1891
>
> Farewells are made to the Brusselites in *Manon*—backstage, an avalanche of flowers—among the souvenirs I found a lovely bird cage which contained an adorable nightingale from Japan, the gift of a child in admiration of our *Manon*.

It was common knowledge among the more astute Belgian opera lovers that Sibyl's voice had lost much of its purity and brilliance because of constant rehearsals and performances all year. The Belgian critics were even discussing it in the newspapers. Sanderson had sung six different roles in one season, only two of which she had really mastered before she left Paris. She had worked harder on new roles than she ever would again in her life, but her reward was an enduring knowledge of the French repertoire.

Now the soprano and her mother found it necessary to pack quickly and leave for London, where Sibyl would soon make her Covent Garden debut in the French-language premiere of *Manon*. The first London performance of the work had taken place at the Drury Lane Theater on 7 May 1885[1] with Marie Roze and (Joseph) Karl Maas singing the leading roles in English. This time, at Massenet's insistence, the spectacular Belgian heldentenor Ernst Van Dyck had been engaged to make his London debut as the Chevalier Des Grieux. Jacques Isnardon was cast as Des Grieux's father, and Eugène Dufriche in the role of cousin Lescaut.

If Sibyl's mother had been in total possession of her wits, however, she would have canceled the engagement at once. The number of things that were to go wrong in the next few days would have been interpreted as an adverse augury by anyone except these two besotted devotees of Apollo's lyre.

Margaret withdrew a thousand francs from the bank and gave it to someone to pay a bill for her. The culprit promptly absconded with the money, leaving the Sanderson exchequer temporarily depleted. Next, Sibyl, following her usual pattern every time she had to prepare for an important debut, came down with a severe cold. By the time they arrived in London to rent a house at 13 Margaret Street, Cavendish Square—yet another ill omen—they were both completely exhausted, and the singer had to be put to bed.

On 16 May Margaret wrote a letter about their recent misfortunes to Jane in California:

> Your last letter has not been answered, Jennie, owing to my other great worries and anxious moments before we left Brussels. To get packed up, to pay the bills, and try to arrange to get off, and the excitement of the last night there. Sibyl sang *Manon* for her adieu. The *salle* was such as one sees rarely in America, a crowded house, and the stage covered with flowers, as well as flowers all around the hall . . . almost like her first night in Paris. She has every reason to be proud of her success. But she has had a bad cold ever since we came, and I have been uneasy for her, for she has only a certain time to sing. I feel strange to be in that theater (Covent Garden) where I have heard Christine Nilsson and Patti, and other great singers and now to see my own daughter standing on the same stage. Goodness knows what her success will be. I know what it would be in *Romeo* as it is known here, but *Manon* is not known, and a public not understanding the opera may not take it favorably. We are in a small house by ourselves. It is very *poor,* not comfortable . . . and the table is poorly served. We do not feel at home and I am trying to find

another place, but we have a very short purse and have trouble to make ends meet . . . 17 May, this is Sunday morning, cold and sad without and terribly so within this house. Sibyl has had some invitations for lunch, but she is not well enough to accept. She has not been out in two days. London is grand and interesting as ever no doubt, but all is so changed for me that I don't care. Your uncle Will [Ormsby] seems to think that to have a singer of some renown in the family is a reward for *everything else!* I do not feel that way, but Sibyl would give me anxious moments under any circumstances—*it is her nature!*"

Margaret Sanderson was learning something of the trials and tribulations that accompany fame. Back in California, she had been so ambitious for her stagestruck daughter that, were she able, she would have built a theater for her, brick by brick, with her own hands. Before Sibyl's career was over, this same mother was to be led through a maze of incredible trials and heartbreak.

Massenet had departed for London with Belgian critic Lucien Solvay the day after Sibyl's emotional farewell to Brussels. Rehearsals commenced as soon as she arrived, and once the diva gazed into the enormous hall, she was beset by worry and anxiety. Covent Garden was the largest theater in which *Manon* had been performed to date.

Oddly enough, Van Dyck's voice seemed to blend with Sanderson's at first. She had no idea that he was singing in half voice to save his throat from additional strain—a common practice in operatic rehearsals. Massenet himself remained strangely ignorant of this fact even though he knew something of Van Dyck's enormous vocal reserves, having heard him create the role of Des Grieux in the Viennese premiere of *Manon*, 9 November 1890. He even noted on Sibyl's score that the rehearsals "were succeeding brilliantly." Coming from a composer who, just three years before at The Hague, had been frantic with anxiety over Ada Palmer's indisposition, it is a curious comment. Now, while the heroine struggled to sing with an inflamed throat and clogged sinuses, he appears to have deluded himself with a false sense of security.

He may have been so preoccupied with the unexpected bankruptcy of his publisher, Hartmann, that he was unable to give the rehearsals his full attention. Massenet had good reason to be concerned. He feared that all his scores from the past two decades would be scattered among many different publishers.[2] He wrote Quinzard at Hartmann's firm on 14 May that he was "deeply sad and alone, and discouraged, and unnerved."

All the London papers were aflame with publicity for the artists' twin debuts. A full-length picture of Sanderson in an opulent Doucet costume graced the cover of *Piccadilly Portraits* that week, and prolific sketches of her fabulous operatic wardrobe were on display in all the magazines.

On Tuesday night, 19 May 1891, Covent Garden was jammed with a spectacular audience. Among the celebrities were several members of the royal family, including the Prince of Wales (the future Edward VII) and his wife, Princess Alexandra, sister to the czarina of Russia. The boxes were filled with the peers of the British Empire and such social lionesses as the duchesses of Manchester, Wellington, and Newcastle, Lady Randolph Churchill (America's Jennie Jerome and mother of Sir Winston), Lady de Grey, and Sibyl's old acquaintance Sir Arthur Sullivan.

The stalls and orchestra were no less glittering, with composers Isidore De Lara and Augusta Holmès in attendance, writers Oscar Wilde and George Bernard Shaw, opera stars Emma Eames and Victor Maurel, and California actress Mary Anderson, who had recently married Sibyl's friend Antonio de Navarro.

Sanderson had slipped the management the required sum to hire the usual claque who obediently applauded when she stepped out of the carriage in Act I. By the end of the ill-starred evening she was to discover that she could have used the entire Buckingham Palace guard. Her leading tenor had not been on stage for more than five minutes before he was greeted with spontaneous ebullitions from the gallery. By the end of the first act, according to George Bernard Shaw in the *London World,* "he was in the position of a lyric Caesar, having come, and sung, and conquered."

While Sanderson was changing costumes in her dressing room after Act I, Van Dyck's waves of Herculean sound were still ringing in her ears. "How am I to sing against a voice like that?" she gasped to her mother. The opera had not progressed far when it became obvious that the lyric match of Sanderson and Van Dyck was not made in heaven. In fact, it was the musical crime of the decade, pairing a light, Parisian-trained coloratura with a Belgian heldentenor who had already been acclaimed as a great Parsifal at Bayreuth. But this time the management could not be held responsible. It was Sibyl's ever-vigilant pedagogue—the omniscient Massenet himself—who had insisted Harris draw up the disastrous contract, the very man to whom the soprano had entrusted the care of her precious vocal cords since 1887.

Van Dyck, aware that his tremendous lung power was overwhelming Sanderson's efforts, whispered to her during an intimate moment in the second act, "Let out your voice!"

"This is all the voice I have!" came the desperate reply.[3]

From then on Van Dyck knew the evening belonged to him. He had misjudged her completely during the rehearsals. She had not sung in half voice as he had done, but rather in full strength. For the duration of the performance, the tenor poured forth such voluminous cascades of sound that he all but obliterated the heroine.

The hall was roused to screams of hysteria when he sang "Le rêve" (The Dream) with bold Wagnerian bravura, completely disregarding the composer's gossamer anticlimaxes in the score. He sang as though a truly French Des Grieux was the last thing the English wanted. They craved the stentorian power of a Teutonic hero, and he couldn't resist the opportunity to turn the sensitive Des Grieux into another Tristan.

By the end of the opera the house had become frenetic over the Belgian. Massenet joined his artists on stage for the curtain calls, but the Frenchman and his exhausted protagonist both were aware that the ovations belonged to the new "Meistersinger." Sanderson received numerous baskets of flowers, bowed gracefully, and realized her hopes for a fortuitous debut had been exterminated. Friends poured into her dressing room to gush the usual stereotyped compliments. There were the Navarros, Arthur Sullivan, and the John Brights assuring her that she was a success. The Prince of Wales was introduced to her and while ogling her beauty, he became rhapsodic over her interpretation. Sibyl's cousin John Yost from California had been visiting London that month and was thrilled to hear his celebrated relative for the first time.

Quite the contrary was true for Massenet, who quickly congratulated his interpreters and staged a remarkable disappearing act. Fearing that the wrath of a California squall might be blowing in his direction, the composer hastily retreated to his hotel. By sunrise he had already packed and fled the British Isles for the safer shores of the Continent.

The next day all the London papers confirmed Margaret's worst fears. Van Dyck was not only showered with accolades, he was practically deified by the critics as "a manly tenor with lower notes so powerful they almost approach baritone quality" and "a magnificent voice of the utmost robustness and great compass," one who "possesses every gift to place him in the front rank of operatic tenors."

On 27 May in the *World*, George Bernard Shaw ignored the outrage perpetrated against the soprano that night, despite what he certainly knew from having reviewed the opera's London premiere six years earlier. Shaw went down before the heldentenor like grain before the scythe, extolling him as "dignified," "virile," and "irresistible," and saying that "he was surely born to play" Siegfried, adding

> I own that I waited for the second act with some apprehension as to the effect of the charming air [Le rêve (The Dream Song)] which Des Grieux sings to Manon at the dinner table, where they literally dine off love. It seemed only too likely that a Belgian tenor would resort to the conventional artificial French mezza-voce and thus spoil the pathos of the air for English ears . . . I reckoned without Van Dyck's genius. Nothing would be more unstudiedly original and natural in conception, more skillful and artistic in execution, than his performance of this number, which brought down the house.[4]

Shaw was an unabashed Wagnerite, a journalist with no formal music training whatsoever, who founded his pronouncements on knowledge gleaned from the performances he attended. He failed to understand how crucial the sensitive high pianissimos are to this aria and how much more difficult they are to control in comparison to fortissimo climaxes. He was wickedly condescending to the soprano, constantly using the old English spelling of her name ("Saunderson"). He dismissed her superciliously as "having a pretty talent for imitating French singing of the Opéra-Comique genre." But it must be remembered that Shaw had written equally scathing phrases about the great Melba's debut as Juliette the year before: "She was shrill and forward, the waltz-ariette coming out with great confidence and facility, which I think Mme Melba mistook for art."

Evidently, Shaw and his colleagues also mistook Van Dyck's musical perversions for art. It was a travesty that not one London critic castigated the Belgian singer for the rape of The Dream Song.

As for the heroine, all the local savants, from the *Times* to the *Saturday Review*, agreed that the American singer was a shocking disappointment. Their colleague on the *Monthly Musical Record* offered one of the more objective appraisals on 1 June.

> She is graceful and sympathetic and acts with intelligence. But the want of greater volume of tone was sadly against her . . . she has also adopted the Parisian vice of the tremolo, and in consequence was frequently defective in her intonation . . . yet we have not the least doubt that an ample measure of success awaits Miss Sanderson in opera houses where her physical powers are not so heavily taxed.[5]

Sibyl knew there were four basic reasons for her London failure: 1) fatigue from a season of overwork in Brussels; 2) laryngitis from an aggravated cold; 3) miscasting with a Wagnerian tenor thanks to the blundering of her musical guru; and 4) lack of any competent vocal training for the past two or more seasons. She realized only too well that her voice had deteriorated and upon her return to Paris she must seek a new teacher for serious study.

As for the opera, the London sages agreed on one point: the work would be heard to better advantage in a smaller hall.[6] They did not know how to react to the exquisitely spoken dialogue Massenet had written over a running orchestral accompaniment. Pure *opéra comique* was a rarity in the British Isles. By the time *Faust* and *Carmen* had reached English ears, their original spoken dialogue had been supplanted by musical recitatives. Londoners were still accustomed to the old Italian form of opera in which the audience waited patiently during the singers' interminable jabbering of endless polysyllabic phrases until the recitative was over and the long-awaited aria got under way.

Commenting upon this subject, *Punch* wryly observed that "there is far more spoken dialogue in *Manon* than a Covent Garden audience is accustomed to, and this superfluity is resented by those who come for the music, and who, if any talking is to be done, like to do it themselves."[7]

In 1955, Felix Borowski, composer, teacher, and distinguished critic of the *Chicago Sun-Times,* conjured back his own special memories of the event to the author:

> I don't think it was the premiere but rather one of the following performances that I first heard Sanderson and Van Dyck . . . I don't remember exactly . . . She had a very high voice, as I remember, and the upper register was remarkably pure and crystalline. One could almost describe it as angelic in quality. But her medium was weaker, as I recall, and completely obscured by Van Dyck who simply electrified the hall. Women screamed and fainted when he sang "Ah, fuyez douce image." He had a marvelous voice, yet he sang the role like he was singing Siegfried, with total disregard for the composer's intentions, and all the subtle nuances of the score were lost. But the work was so new to London at the time, no one knew the difference then. One thing I've always remembered was the chapel scene. When Sanderson started her seductive aria, she ran her hands little by little all over him. Then she grew bolder, and when she unbuttoned his priest's collar, you knew Des Grieux was lost to the church for all time. With the possible

exception of Patti, Sanderson was the most beautifully gowned soprano I saw in my youth.

The soprano now felt well enough to accept some of the social invitations that were pouring into the house on Cavendish Square. Mrs. Leinster, better known as London's sapphire queen, gave a brilliant breakfast for Sibyl that was attended by such aristocrats as the Duchess of Manchester and Lady Randolph Churchill. Sibyl also lunched with the six-foot London goddess Lady de Grey, whose word was becoming law at Covent Garden.[8]

A staunch bond was formed between the diva and the Oscar Wildes. They invited Sibyl and her mother to dinner, and the playwright nostalgically recalled the warm hospitality he had enjoyed in the Sanderson home on his San Francisco visit. But immediately after the dessert Oscar asked to be excused, pleading a previous engagement. Sibyl was determined to cement a friendship with his obviously neglected wife. A summer or two later, Constance Wilde was to spend a few weeks in Paris visiting the Sandersons, and Marion subsequently stayed overnight with the Wildes on a trip to Scotland.[9]

London society was panting to find out anything at all about the coruscating rumor that the Belgian crown prince had shot himself in Sibyl's boudoir. The story, which surfaced in a London newspaper about six weeks before her debut, would have been sufficient to sell out Covent Garden by itself.

Scores of worldwide journals reported the following amusing incident at Peter Martin's. The Marchioness of Ripon went into ecstasies over the diva's performance and then queried maliciously, "And your jewels, my dear Sibyl, they're ravishing! Entrancing! Where did you get such a marvelous collection? You've only been on the stage for a few years. I just know you've had some exciting, secret admirer in Brussels."

"You liked them—really?" purred the soprano.

"Like them? My dear, I have never seen their equal."

"You mean you thought they were real?"

"Real? Why certainly," exclaimed the marchioness in tones of rising indignation. "Now don't tell me they are nothing but paste?"

"But they are indeed, my dear marchioness," Sibyl lamented with simulated distress. "And to think you imagined all of those splendid necklaces, sunbursts, and brooches were real! How could you? How could you think me so wicked as all that?"

Nevertheless, the young singer had so slavishly devoted herself to her art all year that she was tingling with the need of some male divertissement. After the second performance, Van Dyck began to show an unusual offstage interest in his leading lady. Sanderson was flattered but not surprised; his tempestuous lovemaking in *Manon* had been a bit too realistic. Van Dyck's appetite for women ranked on the same scale as his highly famed appetite for food. Physically, he could not be labeled an Adonis. Prematurely balding and of only medium height, he was husky and inclined toward a protruding belly. But his magnetic personality, his infectious smile, and his tremendous virility left female fans gasping. He took a woman with the ease of an after-dinner cognac. It would be difficult for any soprano not to succumb to such extraordinary charm.

The sparks their incendiary love scenes were generating in the opera burst into flame for a while offstage. Van Dyck took her out to dinner one night between performances. He whispered ardently to her that she was the most beautiful soprano in the world and he had to possess her. Sibyl remained in awe of him on or off the stage. When her daughter didn't arrive home at a respectable hour, Margaret was frantic. Tossing fitfully in her bed until nearly sunrise, she finally heard the wheels of Sibyl's horse-drawn cab grind to a halt in front of the house. Within a few minutes her worst fears were realized. The singer candidly admitted that after some drinks the rage of Covent Garden had seduced her in his hotel suite. What was more, she hadn't offered a centimeter of resistance.

Shaking with anger, Margaret struggled to control herself. "What would your dear father say if he were here tonight and heard what you have just confessed? Do you think I am going to ask the girls to come over now, only to have them learn that their sister has been seduced by the very man who humiliated her on the stage? Now you have been twice dishonored by him—a tenor, of all people—and still you stand there and say 'I couldn't help myself!'"

"But, mama," came the all-time classic response. "He is not a tenor, he is a god!"[10]

When the Sandersons returned to France on 13 June, Margaret breathed a sigh of relief. The alarming behavior of her oldest daughter had deepened several furrows in her forehead. Sooner or later, she told herself, it was bound to happen. She had learned to expect the worst from her unpredictable offspring.

When Van Dyck returned to Paris in the fall of 1891 to sing at the Opéra, the couple renewed their intimacy over Margaret's pleas and protestations. The tenor was married to the sister of Franz Servais, the principal conductor of the Opéra Royal de la Monnaie, and she doubtlessly bore her husband's many amorous conquests with silent stoicism. Remaining in London after his *Manon* appearances, Van Dyck was offered a flood of future roles. Nothing of this sort happened to the soprano. As a weary mother dragged her unrepentant sinner onto the boat, Sibyl promised herself that someday she would sing *Manon* again with her Olympian seducer and try to balance the scales of success.

The summer of 1891 found Sibyl at the Aix-les-Bains festival, where she was engaged for a single performance of *Roméo et Juliette* and a performance of *Manon,* which would be receiving its local premiere.

Aix-les-Bains was a fashionable resort in southeastern France, located in an Alpine valley about fifty miles southwest of Geneva, Switzerland, on the shores of Lake Bourget. Famous for its warm alkaline and sulfur springs since Roman times, it had become a celebrated spa once its bathing facilities were rebuilt by Napoleon III. During the latter part of the nineteenth century, emperors, statesmen, and international high society flocked to its bathhouses every summer. Massenet had not told Sibyl that Aix-les-Bains was also known as "cocottesville," but it didn't take her long to discover this fact for herself. The Grand Hotel literally swarmed with them, as did the local casino at night. Nearly everyone at the hotel was having an illicit affair while spouses were elsewhere behaving in a like manner.

DeGenne had been engaged as Sibyl's leading tenor for both operas, and Gréteaux signed for the dual roles of Des Grieux's father in *Manon* and Friar Laurence in *Roméo et Juliette.* Édouard Colonne's superb orchestra had been brought from Paris for the occasion, and Colonne himself would conduct both performances. The Théâtre du Grand Cercle in Aix was far smaller than Covent Garden, so Sanderson did not have to worry about forcing her voice.

The night of Saturday, 18 July, found the theater sold out to the cream of international society and some of its clabbered milk. Sanderson walked off the stage victoriously in a trail of bouquets and bravas, reducing most of the audience to tears in the powerful Saint Sulpice scene. So great was the clamor for another performance from visitors who could not obtain tickets that the management asked the artists to repeat the opera Monday night with all box-office proceeds going to charity. DeGenne and Sanderson agreed, and the soprano decided to donate her salary to the Society for the Orphans of Poor. When a second performance was announced for 20 July, it was sold out within hours.

On Monday Sibyl repeated her previous success. After the final curtain both stars were summoned to the box of King George of Greece. First the king warmly congratulated the artists, then before the entire house, the tall Nordically sculpted monarch[11] pinned the medal of Saint George onto the diva's bosom; it was the highest award of his government. Sanderson's charitable gesture had earned her an unexpected royal citation and a six-minute standing ovation from the audience. On Saturday night, 25 July, the popular stars scored another triumph in *Roméo et Juliette*. Afterward Sibyl and her maid left for Vevey to join her mother and sisters for a much-needed rest.

Massenet had arrived at Aix-les-Bains on Friday, 17 July, just in time to hear the dress rehearsal. The next day, however, he dashed back to Paris to settle affairs before joining the Sandersons again at Vevey for a few weeks' vacation. Incomprehensible as it seems, Sibyl refused to blame him personally for the London catastrophe. Instead, she went over the score with him, note by note, pointing out various places where the vocal advantages fell to the tenor, and requested certain alterations.

More important, Sanderson showed him latent facets of Manon's character he had not realized were still hidden in the score. If the audience were to understand that Manon loved Des Grieux in spite of the fact she planned to leave him in Act II, her brief ariette "Adieu, notre petite table" ought to be lengthened into an important aria. If Manon was to show the world that she was the dazzling queen of the Parisian courtesans in Act III, she needed certain sustained high notes that would glitter like the diamonds she wore. Manon's first-act aria "Je suis encore tout étourdie" (I am completely bewildered) had to be completely rewritten to make the girl sound more like an excited, babbling teenager on her first trip away from home. There were a myriad number of small changes the composer would find himself making, as he began to rewrite the role for the woman whose musical insight had convinced him she was born for the role.

It was unfortunate that Massenet could not stay over on the night of July 20 to watch the king of Greece decorate Sibyl. He had discovered her, made her a star, and nurtured her career. Nothing gave him greater satisfaction than seeing her talent extolled by others.

The distinguished singer Marie Sasse wrote to him on 18 July 1891:

Cher maître,
Tonight, I attended the premiere performance of *Manon* here sung by Mlle Sanderson, and it is with the greatest pleasure that I address these lines to you to read of her great success . . . She has shown such extraordinary grace and range of talent in the entire role; she is the perfect actress and an exquisite singer. But I found her remarkable beyond all limits of expression in one instance. That was the great duet from the Saint Sulpice scene. There she moved me to tears, and it was necessary for her to have been totally sublime

to have affected me so. But through my tears I noticed there wasn't a dry eye in the rest of the audience either. The remainder of the opera was no less superb. She had a tremendous triumph and justly deserved it.

Marie Sasse

Grand Hotel, Aix-les-Bains

Massenet proudly saved the letter and gave it to his protagonist upon their return to Paris in September. After all, weren't Sibyl and his operatic heroine two expatriates at large? More and more they were being identified with each other. They had been cheered enthusiastically in Brussels, reviled in London, and wept over in Aix-les-Bains. How would Paris receive them on their return?

Chapter 14

Immortal Manon

By the fall of 1891 anticipation had gripped the entire Parisian musical world. One of its favorite tarts was returning, having been banished for six years by her own creator—Jules Massenet. The courtesan was Manon Lescaut, foolish and adorable, and Parisian to the tips of her lacquered fingernails. She was to be reincarnated in *la belle Sibylle,* who, though born in faraway California, could, as natives of the city would soon learn, be more bewitching, more fickle, and more Parisian than their own cocottes.

According to the notes Massenet left in her *Manon* folio, he and the Sandersons elected to take a scenic excursion through the Grande Chartreuse and the Simplon Pass on their way home from Switzerland.Upon her return to Paris the first week in September, Sibyl found herself involved in daily rehearsals for *Manon.* Massenet sat in the front row of the orchestra beside Léon Carvalho.

Behind a huge waxed mustache in the viola section sat a young musician who would later become known as a world-famous conductor: Pierre Monteux. The memories of the rehearsals he shared with the author sixty-eight years later are unforgettable ones.

> Every day Massenet ran the gamut of a thousand moods. One minute he would be in tears over one of Sibylle's exquisite phrases, wiping his eyes with a huge handkerchief, the next, he would be raving to Carvalho over some nuance she had spontaneously added to her interpretation. I can still see him crying copious tears into that enormous handkerchief. Everyone was thankful Mme Massenet decided to remain home. You see, everyone in the theater, everyone in Paris, knew how madly in love he was with that gorgeous woman![1]

Léon Carvalho was sparing no expense to make the revival as opulent as the premiere. The second act, which takes place in the lovers' apartment on the rue Vivienne, would feature the same Louis XV furniture, with its gilt, bronze, and marquetry, used in the 1884 production.

The gambling scene was a masterpiece of staging, with the sharpers, croupiers, and chorus all blocked in interchangeable formations around the tables. Several magnificent porcelain chandeliers were hung from the ceiling of the Hôtel Transylvanie, each glittering with scores of crystal prisms. Gilded rococo sconces lighted the walls of the main gambling salon, while in the rear, huge French doors opened upon another room silhouetted by flickering candelabra to reveal shadowy figures around other gaming tables.

Jean Delmas, Sibyl's young chevalier from her Brussels season, would be making his Parisian debut in the same role. The gifted Lucien Fugère had replaced Cobalet at the last minute as Count Des Grieux. Massenet was as solicitous over the upcoming revival as he had been about the premiere of *Esclarmonde.* Everyone was aware that he had been grooming Sibyl for this day ever since they had met in 1887. To him no one else possessed all the subtle, childlike variations in temperament so necessary for the role. Now his long-awaited dream was about to become reality.

There had been many changes in the score since 1884. However, the chief interpolation was the bewitching Gavotte that the composer had added to Act III, originally entitled a "minuet" for the English-language edition (Novello) in 1885. He borrowed the theme from one of his earlier songs, *Sérénade de Molière,* which, in turn, traced its origin to a risqué street tune. After Sanderson's death (but not before), Marie Roze claimed she had sung it in the original 1884 English production, but no confirmation of this can be found in the English papers. Based on the accounts in all print sources consulted, the revival of *Manon* on 12 October 1891 marked the first publicly recorded performance of this Gavotte.

When the doors of the Opéra-Comique opened that Monday night, an enormous crowd poured into the loges, the orchestra, and the balconies. The sold-out theater was filled with the upper echelons of Paris society—literary, social, and artistic. A nervous intensity usually present at an important premiere held everyone in its throes. An announcement was made before the curtain that Jean Delmas was suffering from a cold. The critics were briefed about his condition, and they made allowances for it in their reviews. Before the evening was over, however, the radiant Sibyl was to steal this performance as completely as Van Dyck had done in Covent Garden.

"Enthusiastically recalled after the first two acts," Arthur Pougin wrote in *Le Ménéstrel* of 18 October 1891, "she stopped the show with Manon's aria, 'Je marche sur tous les chemins' (Act III), which received a torrential ovation."[2] Once the applause abated, the diva introduced her gavotte. As the chorus sang its lines, "Let us profit by our youth," she coquetted about the stage, flirtatiously answering them phrase for phrase. Paris took leave of its senses. Never had it seen such witchery. Pougin described her cadenza as executed "with a brilliance, a flair, a boldness, and a bravura which literally tore the audience right out of their seats."

From then on, he observed, "Her success assumed the proportions of a triumph!" The greatest artists, writers, and musicians of France flocked to the artists' loge to congratulate her after every act. In the Saint Sulpice scene, where Manon lures her former lover away from his vows to the priesthood, Sanderson's powers of seduction were so enthralling that a correspondent for *L'Indépendence belge* later recalled, "If any priest had been in the audience that night, he would have defrocked himself immediately."[3]

Following his usual custom, Massenet planned to stay away from the theater, but anxiety overcame him and he arrived shortly after 11 P.M., just in time for the final curtain calls. The agitated composer trembled with joy as he witnessed a delirious audience giving his performers a standing ovation, throwing their programs and handkerchiefs into the air. The stage was strewn with flowers. The next day he recorded his impressions in Sibyl's private edition.

Monday, 12th October 1891

first *reprise* at the Opéra-Comique
GRANDISSIME SUCCÈS!!!!
The most open-hearted, warm, scintillating,
and *unique evening!*
I arrived at the theater at 11:15 and
found the stage *jammed with thrilled and
enthusiastic friends*
There were Ambroise Thomas and
Saint-Saëns offering their warmest
congratulations to Mlle Sanderson
Yesterday, 8,000 francs—the maximum—
The next six performances are sold out!

Massenet neglected to mention just how warm the felicitations of his teacher were, although the press described the occasion as one of "unforgettable sentiment." The trembling, old Ambroise Thomas attempted to embrace the prima donna but was so overcome with excitement that he fainted in her arms instead. It took someone's fan and Margaret Sanderson's smelling salts to revive him.

When the star and her mother finally emerged from the stage door, cries of "*Vive Sibylle,* long live the queen of song!" rang through the night air. Scores of youths from the gallery had been waiting impatiently for her appearance. Unhitching the horses from her carriage, they fastened ropes first to it, then to themselves, and pulled her home through the city streets. Behind them came Lina and the coachman in a hired fiacre loaded with magnificent floral offerings.

Paris could not sleep that night. A new generation was extolling its American goddess to the skies. Time and time again the students chorused the words of the Gavotte, "Let us profit by our youth," with the soprano answering them, "Let us love, laugh, and sing, for we shan't be young again." Although this scene was to repeat itself many times during Sanderson's reign in the French capital, James Gordon Bennett later wrote in the Paris *Herald* that "of all her triumphs, probably none was more exhilarating than the night she victoriously revived *Manon.*"[4]

Sanderson had retaken Paris by storm, and Massenet now realized that the three additional years of waiting had not been in vain. In 1891 she was a far more experienced artist than she had been in 1888, when he had failed to persuade Paravey to revive the opera.

Despite the columns of praise that were to erupt in the press, a few French critics did not succumb to Manon's new interpreter. Was it the fact that this audacious American had dared to usurp a uniquely French role? Ernest Reyer wrote indignantly the next day in *Le Journal des débats:*

> It would be absurd to establish a comparison between the late Marie Heilbronn and the new interpreter of *Manon.* The former made the heroine of Abbé Prévost's novel a passionate woman who gave herself (to Des Grieux) with all of her soul; the latter sings like a student, albeit an excellent student, however, gifted with a remarkable vocal virtuosity; endowed with a fresh, sparkling voice of agreeable color and *timbre,* but she turns Manon into a well-bred lady who amuses herself with reservations and loves Des Grieux with discretion.

On October 14, the sachem on *Le Temps* sneered chauvinistically: "Is this really the mistress of Des Grieux that we saw last night? Although she has powers of extraordinary sentiment, Mlle Sanderson is an American who teases and flirts; she is NOT a French woman who loves!"

Fortunately, a few isolated objectors could not stop the avalanche of favorable criticism. Arthur Pougin painted a far more objective and less prejudiced picture in *Le Ménéstrel*.[5]

> She has made enormous strides in the development of her talent. Her voice has taken on more body, equality of registers, and if her vocal agility was always breathtaking, the phrasing has become more distinct, the articulation more supple, and the notes of the lower register are more solid and full-bodied.

The famous pianist and pedagogue Isidor Philipp agreed with Pougin in *Le Monde musical* of 30 October, adding, "She is a fascinating artist and an astonishingly perfect one . . . Her Manon is a different woman in every act. . . . Her superb interpretation of such a complex role does her the greatest honor."[6]

Even Sibyl's old antagonist Camille Bellaigue had to own up in *La Revue des deux mondes* that week:

> Since *Esclarmonde* her progress is undeniable. She knows her role to the very letter; her diction and pronunciation have improved; and the voice has become more equalized in its various registers . . . in the brilliant arias her voice literally explodes into showers of a thousand golden sparks.[7]

On 13 October in *Le Figaro,* Charles Darcours predicted that the opera was destined for immortality.

> If one is to judge by the tremendous reception given to the revival of *Manon* last night, this work would have victoriously overstepped the boundaries of survival even outlined by [composer] Auber . . . the *Manon* reprise of last night was an *actual triumph* in every sense of the word . . . Mlle Sanderson has returned to us a more experienced and brilliant cantatrice with an exquisite speaking voice, and, at times, a most adroit actress; her voice is of extraordinarily beautiful quality; she handles it with surprising assurance in attacking the most difficult passages, then in scenes of expressive tenderness she brings out inflections of infinite loveliness. Laughing and curious in the

first act, dreamy in the second, brilliant in the Saint Sulpice scene, Mlle Sanderson continued to evoke thunderous applause and constant recalls . . . We haven't forgotten Mlle Sanderson's predecessor but we are no longer obsessed with her memory, so different are their means of expression and interpretation.

The day after the revival, the composer seized upon Sanderson's soaring popularity to dedicate a new song to her, "L'âme des fleurs" (The Soul of Flowers). Once tenor Albert Vaguet introduced it at his concerts and the public learned of the dedication, it became Massenet's best-selling opus for the season. Written to the verses of Paul DeLair, this sentimental ditty was conceived for commercial purposes and does not compare to "Beaux yeux que j'aime" (Beautiful Eyes That I Love), another song he dedicated to her that same year.[8] Massenet obviously held the same opinion because he only gave Sanderson the holograph of the latter.

For the rest of the season *Manon*'s popularity remained unchallenged in Paris. Performances were sold out three weeks ahead, with the American linnet triumphing three nights a week. President Carnot attended the third performance and requested that the diva come to his box between acts for his personal congratulations. It became a nightly ritual for all of Parisian society to troupe to the artist's loge between acts and pay homage to the heroine. Only one person in the capital was conspicuous by her absence: Louise Massenet. She had had more than enough of Sibyl Sanderson—the gossip, the innuendoes, and her husband's rapturous recitals of his protégée's virtues. On the other hand, it is doubtful whether she ever objected to all the royalties Sanderson was bringing into the family coffers.

The managers of the Opéra were certainly alarmed over the success of the revival. Messrs Ritt and Gailhard were biting their nails as they watched their attendance dwindle to half-empty houses by the first of November. From 25 October to the end of the year the Opéra was forced to offer tickets for Melba and Lassalle in *Hamlet* at half price because none of its singers could compete with the charisma of the very soprano its directors had dismissed earlier that year.

The perfidious charmer of Abbé Prevost had not only come back to reconquer Paris, this time she was home to stay. But by now her identity had undergone a considerable transformation. The score from which Marie Heilbronn created her role in 1884 had been changed for all time. Composer Reynaldo Hahn, Sanderson's own protégé and Massenet's pupil, believed that the alterations the master later incorporated into the revised edition (1895) for her were decidedly unwise. In his *Thèmes variés* Hahn discussed the two versions at length and concluded that the composer had committed "serious and regrettable errors" by copyrighting the changes he made for his votary.

In the first phrase of Manon's opening aria, "Je suis encore tout étourdie" (I am completely bewildered), Sanderson wanted the appoggiatura lengthened on the last syllable of *étourdie* (I am completely be-*wil*-dered) to better express Manon's naiveté. In order to sustain this rallentando, she would need an eighth-note rest for a new breath before "tout étourdie" (see example 1).

Example 1. First phrase of Manon's opening aria, Act I

In subsequent repetitions of that phrase, Massenet inserted rallentandos over similar appoggiaturas along with new eighth-note rests. At the end of the aria, she asked Massenet to alter the rhythm in the passage "Pardonnez à mon bavardage, j'en suis à mon premier voyage" (Pardon my chattering, this is my first journey) to create a more spontaneous impression of a babbling teenager. To achieve this effect, Massenet wrote tenutos over both the "*par*donnez" and the extra grace note he added to the penultimate syllable of "bavar*dage*," which was followed by a breath (see example 2).

Example 2. Final phrase of Manon's opening aria, Act I

In the middle of the aria she suggested the addition of coloratura passages to convey Manon's laughter as preferable to the dull one-note series of "ah! ah! ah!'s" (see example 3).

Example 3. Alternate coloratura passages in Manon's Act I aria

Massenet also obliged her by adding a higher ending to the aria and included these alterations as ossias (alternate choices) in the 1895 edition.

In every scene she suggested subtle changes in the melodic line by the employment of an occasional échappée, appoggiatura, or suspension—all skillful devices to make Manon more seductive. Hahn felt such alterations were musical perversions of the original score. He also disputed Massenet's lengthening the dramatic section before "Adieu, notre petite table" (Act II) into an "interminable lament" because Sanderson felt the aria needed an intensely moving introduction.

In the Cours la Reine scene Hahn accused Massenet of momentarily turning Manon into an asthmatic by breaking the phrase "Suis-je gentille" (stop and breathe) "ainsi?" (Am I not—stop and breathe—pleasing?), so his heroine could dramatically sustain the high G on ain-*si*. If Hahn disapproved of the alternate cadenza Massenet wrote for Sanderson in the final passage of the "Je suis reine" aria (Act III) it is not on record. But he did object to the presto vocalise Massenet interpolated into the Saint Sulpice aria after the words "n'est-ce plus ma voix?" (isn't this still my voice?). Sanderson felt that Manon, desperate to lure her ex-lover away from the priesthood, would employ every wile she could muster. Hahn considered it a clever trick really intended to say "Isn't my own light, coloratura voice ravishing?" Massenet obviously agreed with his interpreter; Pierre Monteux confided that the composer used Sanderson's extemporaneous example in the rehearsal almost note for note in the revised edition (example 4).

Example 4. Vocalise interpolation in Manon's "N'est-ce plus ma voix?" from Act III

N'est-ce plus ma voix? ah _____
Is   it not my voice? Ah! _____

Hahn concluded:

> All these changes were made after the revival of *Manon* at the Opéra-Comique in 1891 for Sibyl Sanderson. That brilliant artist was a spoiled child. She demanded and received, without any effort, in fact, with the flash of a mere smile, the modifications and changes which the master was justified in according perhaps to her, for talent and prestige always allow certain liberties. But he was wrong to consecrate in any way the privileges accorded to one person as an exception and impose them on posterity.[9]

Sanderson herself felt she was justified in requesting the alterations.[10] In several press interviews she reflected on how Massenet had unwittingly weighted the score heavily in favor of the tenor. She was determined to tip the scales just enough to even the balance by securing a greater share of vocal advantages for the heroine.

Pierre Monteux agreed with her. He thought Massenet was decidedly correct in passing his changes for Sanderson on to future interpreters.[11] "We in the orchestra watched that opera change before our very eyes during the rehearsals," Monteux recalled in 1959.

> Massenet was in awe of her extraordinary musical perception. We all were. Every day Sanderson would request the addition of a fermata, or a suspension, or some rhythmic alteration in a phrase which would so delight him that he'd order us to copy them into our scores. . . . You know Massenet was a very clever man with admirable instincts for what was dramatically right for the theater. He wouldn't have incorporated all her changes into the score if he hadn't felt they were an improvement upon the original edition.

Having seen all of the famous Manons in my lifetime with the exception of Heilbronn, and having conducted the opera for many of them, I have never known any soprano who could compare with her. Sanderson was simply the greatest of them all. She *was* Manon, you know. In the second act, when she was on her knees by the little table as she sang her "Adieu," she ran her fingers over the edge of the glass trying to retrace where both lovers' lips had drunk from it. You knew Manon loved Des Grieux with every fiber of her being, but she couldn't help herself, she was dazzled even more by the riches Brétigny offered her.

I have never seen anyone sing and dance such a bewitching Gavotte. When the chorus sang "Profitons de ta jeunesse," she would whirl so gracefully and caress the cheek of some boy with her fan. Then she would turn to the audience, peeping so coyly over her fan, only to wave it aside in time to answer the same phrase. She could make that fan speak with a language all its own. Although she never played the role quite the same way twice, she was always seductive and elegant, never gauche at any time.

When describing her voice, Monteux fairly beamed.

She was a beautiful woman with a beautiful voice! What more can I tell you? Her voice was a lyric soprano, almost coloratura, but not quite. In spite of the fact she sang coloratura roles, I never felt she was really a true coloratura . . . but she was born for that part [Manon], and there has never been anyone else like her. And what an enchanting Phryné [Saint-Saëns] she was!

Unhappily, Monteux had fallen victim to the common canard of the day. He believed she was Massenet's mistress. "Of that there was no doubt," he insisted. "It was known to everyone in the theater, everyone in Paris. I can still see him clutching her arm tightly in his as he escorted her to her carriage after rehearsals, and he would wave to her in a trance."

With all due respect to these priceless recollections, such sentimental gestures were hardly evidence of a grand passion. However, they did make for sensational gossip. And, more important to Massenet, sensational box office. Monteux never became acquainted with the highly complex personality of the composer. He was too young to know about Massenet's obsession with publicity. He knew nothing of the composer's steely self-discipline or his rigid middle-class morality. He was unaware of the paternal role Massenet played in the

Sanderson family because he knew none of the parties intimately, nor had he any idea of the warm relationship between the two families.

Happily, master and disciple were both dedicated artists with neither the time nor the inclination to pay attention to the gossip about them, and there was plenty of it. *Manon* had made Sanderson the indisputable queen of the French lyric stage—a queen, unfortunately, with a throne on quicksand. Her worshipful public knew nothing about her nightly fits of panic backstage because of the instability of her voice, or about the pernicious habit to which she had fallen prey in order to allay those fears.

Sanderson realized all along, but chose to ignore, the crucial fact that she should be studying with a voice teacher. Four years had passed since she worked with Sbriglia. The latter may have been an excellent male coach, but outside of Lillian Nordica, he wasn't noted for producing outstanding female singers. He had done nothing about Sibyl's sporadic, troublesome tremolo.

During those four years the soprano had become painfully aware that her vocal technique was not dependable. One night she would sing exquisitely, but during the next performance, her voice might fail her at some unexpected moment. This faulty production was the result of not studying long enough with any one professor to properly develop a solid technical approach and test its validity before the public. Overly ambitious for stardom at any price, she committed the gravest error in her career by dropping all of her teachers to work solely with Massenet; France's champion star maker could not equip her with the sturdy technical foundation she needed. Instead of selling her soul to Mephisto for eternal youth like Faust, Sibyl Sanderson had indentured her voice to the composer in exchange for fame.

Discussing this situation with him, she found that he still recommended Mathilde Marchesi as the best technician for women in Paris. The Mother Superior of the female voice claimed men knew nothing about feminine vocal production and worked only with singers of her own sex. Her reputation was greater than ever. She had done wonders for both Eames and Melba, and many great sopranos of the day seem to have studied with her at one time or another.

Sibyl decided to swallow her pride and return to the teacher she had rejected some years earlier. At her insistence, Massenet agreed to act as intermediary. With his anxious protégée in tow, the composer descended upon Madame's studio in the rue Jouffroy about a month after the *Manon* reprise and asked the old autocrat to work with her.

If Mathilde Marchesi had expected a supercilious attitude from the diva, she was pleasantly surprised. Sibyl's words were the essence of sincerity. "Madame, will you not take me as a pupil who must begin at the beginning; who will be the most obedient of pupils; who will do anything you bid her to do; who will, if you insist, leave the stage until she really knows how to sing?"

Astonished by the singer's disarming humility, Madame assured her it would not be necessary to quit the stage. She knew that adding Massenet's exponent to her stable of stellar pupils meant a reciprocal increase in her own fame. She had always been careful to leave the door open by sending the young star occasional congratulatory notes and telegrams. Now Sibyl Sanderson's alliterative name would join her list of notable American students.

Sibyl later confessed to an American reporter that she was to suffer agonies from her tutelage with Marchesi as she started over with the basics to rework her entire method of voice production. "Toujours la voix de la tête [always use the head voice]," Madame would insistently reiterate. At first this was difficult for Sanderson, who had been employing a totally different approach from the diaphragm.

> It was not the easiest or most pleasant task in the world to take a singer who had been before the public and had some success and assume the responsibility of rebuilding her voice all over again. Her treatment at first seemed very hard, and many a tear I shed over it. I even looked upon myself at times as having made a great sacrifice and used to say to myself: "Why, here I am, I who have had success, working just like another beginner." But though her discipline seemed awfully hard to me at times, I have lived to bless her for it. I always found her sweet and kind and sympathetic, and have the deepest affection for her.[12]

The singer realized it was hardly necessary to mention the glorious rewards she reaped from their musical association. Marchesi was to eradicate every trace of tremolo from her sustained notes, to equalize her various registers from top to bottom, and to bring out powers of projection she never dreamed she possessed.

It had been a long, arduous journey from the Hotel Del Monte in California to the footlights of the Opéra-Comique, but the California nightingale had triumphantly achieved her goal. "I shall become the rage of Paris. All I have to do is to find a composer who needs my voice, and the rest will follow." Nearly a decade had passed since she uttered those prophetic words to Gertrude Atherton back in San Francisco. At that time she had no idea of the hours of slavery that would be involved, or of the bitter price she was to pay for stardom without technical security.

By the hundredth performance of *Manon* on Saturday, 7 November 1891, Sanderson had become the reigning prima donna in France. She had eclipsed every other lyric star in the Parisian firmament and sent the box office at the Opéra into a tailspin. For the next two years *Manon* would remain the number one drawing card at the Opéra-Comique, and Massenet allowed no other soprano to sing the title role in Paris. After the revised edition was published in 1895, Sanderson's interpretation would be indelibly stamped upon the score for all time, yet Massenet would go to his grave without giving her any published credit whatsoever.[13]

Chapter 15

Nights from Shéhérazade

Margaret had her hands full the fall her daughter reconquered Paris. Van Dyck's return to star in the Parisian revival of *Lohengrin* had added a few more gray hairs to her head. Try as she might, she could not prevent Sibyl from renewing her intimacy with him. Edith Sanderson recorded in her diary in November that "Mama can breathe easier now that Van Dyck has left town. . . . Poor mama! Is there ever to be any peace for her?"

The same month, Margaret was busy getting Edith packed up and off to Vienna, where she and Florence Mosher were going to study piano with famed pedagogue Theodore Leschetizky. Next she had to get ready to accompany Sibyl to Russia. The soprano had signed a contract with the Mariinsky Theater in St. Petersburg to star in the Russian premiere of *Esclarmonde* in January 1892. Sibyl had also received an imperial command to perform for the czar. In addition, she was scheduled to sing the title role in *Manon* and Marguerite in *Faust,* a role Sibyl would be performing for the first time, although she had coached it off and on with Gounod for some years.

Margaret continued to worry about Sibyl's frenzied attacks of stage fright and her neurotic spells of anxiety before curtain time, but she no longer had to give her any patent medicine for nerves. The prima donna now found temporary courage in more and more nightly glasses of wine before a perform-ance.[1] She decided the ritual relaxed her throat muscles and stimulated her at the same time. Margaret watched with concern as her daughter grew steadily more dependent upon this habit.

Sibyl was excited about the prospect of appearing before Alexander III. She had heard fascinating stories about him. He was said to be a human colossus; he slept on a army cot, dined like a peasant on yogurt for lunch, and sawed a cord of wood a day to keep fit. His physical strength was tremendous. In 1888, when the imperial train derailed near Kharkov and slid down an embankment, the Romanov titan lifted the collapsed roof of the dining car on his shoulders and held it up long enough for his wife and family to crawl free, miraculously unhurt.

On 6 January 1892, the diva and her party boarded the Paris–St. Petersburg express with all the necessary credentials as a traveling ambassador for French opera. Sibyl's entourage consisted of mother and maid, five fox terriers, and piles of luggage complete with the fabulous Sanderson costumes, jewels, and a floor-length sable cloak. They had their private car, for it was an era in which divas and actresses traveled in grand style.

St. Petersburg at that time was anything but a typical Russian city. The "Venice of the North" was built on nineteen islands, gracefully spanned by bridges and interlaced with canals. Bisecting the capital was the Neva River, which flowed for hundreds of miles from the Russian interior to empty into the Gulf of Finland. The architects who designed the city for the Romanovs were Italian, and it was not surprising that many of the public buildings looked more Mediterranean than Russian.

Visitors discovered that St. Petersburg was surrounded by some of the flattest plains in all Europe, and daylight hours in the wintertime were short and understandably precious. A stygian darkness descended upon the city in the middle of the afternoon and held it captive until the middle of the following morning. Ferocious Arctic blizzards and icy winds came sweeping in from the desolate plains to lash its baroque spires, walls, and windows with their frozen fury. The city would be a gray monochrome for weeks.

When Sibyl and her mother descended from the train they were amazed to see altars with burning candles in the huge St. Petersburg railroad station. There were pictures of the Madonna and Child everywhere—in the depot, the restaurants, and hotels. The Sandersons even noticed an icon on the dining room wall of the Hotel de France, where they were staying. The entire city seemed to be consumed by a religious intensity that they were soon to discover was as much façade as fervor.

Its upper-class attitudes and mores were strictly Western and had remained so ever since the reign of its famous Francophile, Catherine the Great. The social whirl, which commenced after New Year's Day, was probably the wildest and giddiest in Europe. There was a perpetuum mobile of parties, balls, receptions, banquets, concerts, operas, plays, and ballets that orbited the clock at a frenzied pace until Lent. By that time an exhausted society had buried its casualties, and the survivors were only too glad to atone for their sins.

Nevertheless, certain characteristics of the city stamped it as distinctly Russian. The Sandersons were amused at the horse-drawn cabs with their multi-colored worsted reins of green, blue, yellow, and red. The horses' harnesses were elaborately ornamented with silver and brass; stationed above their heads was the ubiquitous high brass hoop, looking like a suspended halo. Scarlet and gold seemed to be the favorite local colors. Everywhere spires, domes, and statues were completely gilded. In all the commercial establishments from depots to hotels and restaurants, the porters, waiters, and other public servants were gaily bedecked in bright scarlet or pink blouses. Scarlet and gold. Gorgeous and bar-baric. The Sandersons wondered if the flamboyant colors weren't a psychologi-cal attempt by the natives to elevate their spirits and counter the depressing winter elements.

The arts were thriving in the Russian capital that season. The Italian ballerina Virginia Zucchi was enchanting balletomanes with her dance recitals at the Petit-Théâtre. Anton Rubinstein and Mme Timanoff were giving piano con-certs to standing-room-only audiences. The Italian Opera Company at the Alexandrinsky Theater was playing before packed houses nightly. French operetta was represented by singers Marie Grisier-Montbazon and Clara Lardinois (later known as Blanche Arral). And now the California nightingale had arrived for rehearsals at the Mariinsky Theater.

Aside from Sanderson, the cast included all native artists. The tenor Mikhail Mikhailov was to sing Roland; Leonid Yakovlev was assigned the bishop's role; and Maria Slavina would portray Esclarmonde's sister, Parséis. The production was to be a bilingual one. The prima donna would sing in French; the others would perform their roles alternately in Russian and French. A new conductor, M Krouschewsky, had been assigned the performance, and everyone was impressed with him. For breathtaking fantasy and imagination, the stage set-tings even surpassed the ones at the Opéra-Comique.

Although an elderly Mathilde Kshesinskaia wrote in her memoirs that the public dress rehearsal ("in which the beautiful Swedish *[sic]* singer, Sanderson, had a triumph") took place on 4 January 1894,[2] it had to have occurred some-time during the second week of January 1892. The singer never set foot on Russian soil in 1894, and Edith Sanderson's diary reports 6 January 1892 as the date of Sibyl's departure for Russia.

Unfortunately, Kshesinskaia's memories of that event were recorded in her advanced years and are hopelessly inaccurate. She recalled that "the Emperor and the Czarevitch were in the front row. The Empress and the Grand Duchesses were in the Imperial Box in the middle of the grand tier," while she herself "was in the grand tier," presumably after she finished dancing in the ballet of the Magic Isle scene.

On the contrary, Lydia Paschoff wrote to *Le Figaro* that the royal family was in mourning, though some of them attended the *répétition générale* incognito. This meant that they sat behind closed lattice windows in their boxes and listened quietly to the music. Observance of court mourning procedure was very strict, and under no circumstances would the emperor and the czarevitch have been sitting in the front row of the grand tier on public display.

According to Sibyl's January letter to Edith in Vienna, there were fewer than a hundred spectators in attendance and "it was a terrible ordeal to sing before such an enormous, empty house, especially all of those closed boxes in the grand tier." When the soprano was later interviewed by American reporters, she again underscored the fact that the royal family was in mourning and confessed that she "had dreaded the whole ordeal."

In spite of the hearty reception she received from the sparse audience, her first taste of opera in St. Petersburg was a negative one. Her reception by the press was a chilling Arctic blast. Without exception the journalists in the Russian capital declared war on the French composer and his American exponent. The leading critic of the *Journal Petrogradskaia* openly scoffed at the Wagernian influences alleged to have infiltrated the score.

Attacking the work as "lugubrious, boring, and tasteless," the archbishop of the St. Petersburg press railed against the monotony of "the endless choral chanting."[3] He decided that "the four major arias of Esclarmonde are too similar in character," though he regarded "Regardez ces yeux" as the most outstanding. The same observation held true for the three passionate love duets. Strangely enough, he melted before the Mendelssohnian witchery of the Magic Isle ballet. He cited Esclarmonde's two fiendishly difficult cadenzas as the sole virtuoso moments in the score, and admitted they had stopped the show "thanks to the soprano, not the composer."

Nor was the star treated any more kindly by the sage commentator. "Mlle Sanderson does not belong to the great dynasty of coloratura singers," he carped, and then proceeded to cite three from another age whom he probably had never heard: Catalani, Sontag, and Persiani. The writer catalogued her as "typical of the group of miniature coloratura warblers which America has been exporting lately, such as Marie Van Zandt, who possesses more lightness of vocalization than Mlle Sanderson, and Mme Nevada, who shows more suppleness of phrasing than Mlle Sanderson." In fact, Mademoiselle's pulchritude remained her only redeeming feature. "Très jolie, exquisitely proportioned, elegant, piquant, she has all these qualities, and aren't they enough to turn the heads of the St. Petersburg jeunesse doré just as they have in Paris? In this particular area she is one step ahead of her rivals."

The other critics shredded both singer and score just as mercilessly and complained bitterly that the Mariinsky Theater never presented any works of native composers "who, as everyone knows, are superior to French ones." The Russian press relished attacking any cultural import, particularly one of French origin, because the St. Petersburg nobility was infected with Francophilia. The upper classes ordered their wardrobes in Paris; their hairdressers were Parisian; and some even sent their laundry to be properly finished in Paris. The court spoke only French, but when communicating in Russian became necessary, it managed to affect a foreign accent. The press, made up of members of the lower middle class, vehemently hated the wealthy echelons. Sanderson had been totally ignorant of the class war being waged in Russia, as native artists, playwrights, and composers fought for recognition. She began to realize that as a representative of American gentility, she was the latest pawn in this class struggle.

Because the court was in mourning, the first public performance was postponed until Tuesday, 18 January 1892. Sibyl discovered that the social life of the Russian capital was a dizzying whirl; she could not begin to accept the never-ending invitations to parties, banquets, receptions, and teas.

A new acquaintance, the Duchess of Leuchtenberg, introduced her to Crown Prince Nicholas at one of these functions. Sibyl found him to be a charming, affable young man who spoke excellent English and French. He was only of medium height and totally unimposing stature in comparison to his gigantic father. But his handsome face possessed exceptionally symmetrical features, sparkling blue eyes, and a bashful smile half concealed under a brown mustache.

As for young Nicholas, he found himself drawn to the violet-orbed diva like a magnet. Her skin was as luminous as Meissen porcelain. The poise and grace of her carriage were regal enough to make her the envy of every titled head in the room. Like the others, he had heard rumors about the late Belgian prince and the singer and wondered about their veracity.

The czarevitch told her that his family was looking forward to the premiere of *Esclarmonde*. Some of them, he admitted, had secretly attended the dress rehearsal but were bound by court protocol to remain incognito. Sibyl swallowed hard; so there had been some life behind that long, dreary row of closed boxes. She giggled and retorted that with her present luck perhaps two hundred people might show up for the first public performance. Nicholas laughed and promised her he could fill at least two tiers of the theater with just his relatives alone. As they chatted about her first impressions of St. Petersburg, the czarevitch promised her a personal tour of the capital once she had made her debut.

The soprano need not have worried about attendance at the premiere of *Esclarmonde.* When the curtain went up on 18 January 1892, the opulent gold-and-azure Mariinsky Theater was packed to its gilded ceiling. All St. Petersburg had read the vitriolic reviews and had come to decide for themselves. Nobility was there in mass, and when the imperial family entered their boxes, the audience stood while the orchestra struck up the national anthem, "God Save the Czar."

As the magic lanterns threw a series of projected visions onto a scrim, Sanderson's vocal acrobatics in the first-act incantations brought a torrent of bravas across the footlights. When Act I was over she received a prolonged reception. It was obvious that the public and the press had had opposite reactions to their American visitor.

Sibyl had just returned to her dressing room when an aide of the czar was announced. Her presence was requested in the royal box. Excited and apprehensive, the prima donna was escorted to the grand tier, where she curtsied before the six-foot-four emperor Alexander III. And what an awesome monarch! He was nearly bald, with just a few strands of dark hair left on his head. His square jaw suggested a bulldog tenacity consistent with his autocratic behavior. His thick neck resembled that of a wrestler. Low brows protected eyes deeply set in a wide face, and his hands were so enormous they seemed to begin at his elbows and fan out into five fingers. At any moment Sibyl expected his massive chest to burst the seams of its bemedalled uniform.

The czar was extremely cordial to her and congratulated her profusely in French. The petite and exquisitely jeweled czarina Maria Fedorovna also greeted her warmly. They apologized for having to miss the *représentation générale.* The grand duchesses were anxious to see her at close range, having devoured columns of newsprint about her fabled beauty.

The rest of the evening was an unqualified triumph for the singer and for her mentor, "the Alfred de Musset of French music." Sanderson's stratospheric cadenza in the exorcism scene excited the house to a frenzy, and she was recalled some thirty times at the end of the performance. The czar stood up in the imperial box and ordered a shower of jewels to be thrown to her on the stage. Sibyl had already been clued that if this should occur (and it hadn't to Melba), stagehands would discreetly enter from the wings afterward to collect them for her. Under no circumstances was she to stoop over, as a few other foreign divas had done, and gather them herself. Again His Majesty summoned her to the imperial box, where he and his family were vociferous in their compliments. He kept her this time for twenty minutes, and a whirlwind of gossip was already circulating through the house that the mighty autocrat was smitten by *la belle Américaine.*

A letter to *L'Art musical*[4] in Paris from Monsieur Giaconne, its Russian correspondent, claimed that "Mlle Sanderson had enjoyed a double triumph as both a singer and an actress." The journalist paid tribute to the excellent vocal support she received from her partners but felt that in the realm of acting Sanderson was far superior to all other divas who had ever trod the stage of the Mariinsky. The sets were described as "an exotic fairyland, which shimmered with the splendid decor and the dazzling richness of the costumes."

The following performances of *Esclarmonde* drew sold-out houses, and the emperor's nightly attendance became a ritual. His enthusiastic approval only infuriated the press, which kept raining acerbic barbs on Alexander's new American pet. But the critics could not dampen the furor she was creating with the public. Russian theatergoers were infected with the same epidemic of Sanderson fever that had decimated Paris. Every night the students mobbed the stage door entrance. They threw their coats and jackets down in the snow like an Arctic brigade of Sir Walter Raleighs for the diva to cross to her carriage. Then, unhitching the horses, they pulled it through the streets of the capital, singing her praises.

An invitation had come to the Hotel de France commanding Mlle Sanderson to sing for the royal family at the Winter Palace. An imperial carriage would arrive to fetch her. Swathed in her sable cloak, with her mother and maid, the star was driven along the frozen Neva to the enormous edifice. It could not be mistaken at night, for its baroque walls were illuminated in a flood of light three blocks long that reflected upon the icy river below. It had been built at the turn of the eighteenth century for the Empress Elizabeth by the Italian architect Rastrelli.

Once inside the imperial residence, mother and daughter gasped at the incredible luxury that surrounded them. They were conducted up a magnificent carpeted marble staircase to an enormous gallery. Gigantic columns of jasper, malachite, and marble supported the ornate, gilded ceilings from which were hung colossal gold and crystal chandeliers. Never had the Sandersons seen so much malachite and marble. There were malachite doors and marble floors. Huge pairs of malachite urns stood at the sides of gilded rococo doors. Along the walls stood potted palms in marble jardinières and malachite planters filled with fresh orchids transported daily from the Crimea. Framed by the potted trees were rococo mirrors shining in yet more gilt. Soldiers from the Chevaliers Gardes in white uniforms with silver breastplates and silver eagle-crested helmets were stationed at intervals along the corridors with scarlet-clad cossack guards. Scarlet and silver. Gorgeous and barbaric.

Sibyl had been informed that she and the orchestra would perform behind a screen. When the royal family sent for singers they seldom wished to have their privacy or illusions disturbed. It was a strange custom, but too often the world's most beautiful voices repose in the throats of the world's least glamorous people. The proud, disdainful Romanovs did not want their auditory rapture marred by any visual unpleasantness. When she arrived in the concert salon, Sibyl was delighted to discover the screen had been removed. The hall was resplendent in eighteenth-century decor and gilded furniture in the French style.

The entire Romanov clan had convened for the concert—the czarevitch, the grand dukes and duchesses, and finally their imperial majesties were announced. The emperor's stride was so enormous that his tiny Danish wife seldom could keep up with him. The cossacks were used to seeing him stop, bend over, and with one powerful arm lift the czarina into the air and carry her from room to room.

Regally gowned in cream-colored peau-de-soie with a lace-inset train,[5] the diva walked out on the stage, creating a visual sensation. No jewels covered her matchless décolletage; instead three small diamond sunbursts were pinned to her beaded satin bodice. Her program consisted of arias from *Manon, Roméo et Juliette, Faust, Lakmé,* and *The Magic Flute.* In marked contrast to their reception of other artists, to whom they usually listened in silence, the royal family cheered her enthusiastically. When the encores began, the grand dukes rose like caliphs from the *Arabian Nights* and began throwing jewels at her feet. Exotic and unreal, it was like a scene from *Shéhérazade* itself.

After the concert Sibyl presented her mother to the royal family. With her natural grace and poise, Margaret Sanderson captivated the Romanovs as much as her daughter did. Later, everyone moved into a magnificent dining room where supper was served by scores of servants costumed in eighteenth-century livery. Seated at tables gleaming with French porcelain and crystal, the Sandersons remained blissfully sheltered from the fact that thousands of his majesty's subjects would be sleeping on frozen dirt floors that same night.

The festivities came to a close at 1:30 A.M., when the emperor and empress retired for the night, and the Sandersons were driven back to their hotel in the royal carriage. As the exhilarating events of the evening flashed through her mind in retrospect, Sibyl must have been grateful that his majesty had requested the removal of the screen. It had to have been frustrating for her colleagues Mmes Nevada, Melba, and Calvé to sing to such an impersonal barricade, never once permitted to experience personal contact with their audience. The next day a messenger from the Winter Palace arrived at the hotel. Among the gifts he brought from Alexander III were an enormous cabochon emerald ring, a large emerald-studded bracelet, and a diamond-and-pearl necklace.

The grand dukes fascinated Sibyl. They were all gourmets, bon vivants, and spent their time on "slow horses, fast women, and strong athletes." Indifferent to money, they had run up such enormous bills in Paris that their creditors were on the verge of suing them. The gray-bearded Vladimir, the oldest and most cordial of the three, had been infected thoroughly with the craze over the American diva. He cheered himself hoarse at all her performances and deluged her hotel suite with orchids. His German wife, Grand Duchess Marie Pavlovna, also adored Sibyl. Vladimir was the commander of the imperial guard and president of the academy of fine arts. Like all Romanovs he was an excellent musician, a member of the royal athletic club, and a patron of the famous weightlifter George Hackenschmidt.

His dark-bearded brother Alexis was a two-hundred-and-fifty-pound example of royal overindulgence. His titles included Grand Admiral of the Russian Navy—which would later find itself woefully unprepared to meet the Japanese fleet at Port Arthur. For over fifteen years his highness had been blatantly and systematically plundering the royal treasury by submitting periodic reports of enormous expenses and equal demands for reimbursements while the imperial navy didn't have one additional battleship or cruiser to show for it. His mistresses, on the other hand, could not complain of similar neglect. The jewel caskets on their boudoir tables were truly overflowing cornucopias.[6]

Serge, the youngest, who was governor general of Moscow, occasionally put in an appearance at the scene of his duties when the Parisian ritual of tossing gold coins at Maxim's grew monotonous. He, too, had his lady friends, usually ballerinas who were passionately desirous of stardom and equally undesirous of the work necessary to achieve it.

Young Crown Prince Nicholas could not resist seeing the soprano and often picked her up in the royal troika for a whirl about the city, with tea at some exclusive little restaurant and a party afterward where they would sing duets together. He even confided to her that he wrote poetry and had attempted to set some of his verses to music. Sibyl was impressed with his mellifluous tenor voice. His shy, tender smile touched her heart. Nicholas was so different from his father; the prince never seemed to become accustomed to the fact that one day he would rule an empire of more than eight million square miles.

Since all the Romanovs had requested autographed pictures of the singer, the Duchess of Leuchtenberg took Sibyl to Helena de Nrosovsky's studio, where she was photographed in a variety of poses that ranged from cuddling two of her dogs to reclining in some of her sybaritic costumes. With her hectic social schedule, it was no surprise to her mother that Sibyl was waylaid by influenza for a week, and *Manon* had to be canceled. When she recovered she went immediately into rehearsals for the role of Marguerite in *Faust.*

Her partner was the well-known tenor Nicolai Figner, and they both scored a pronounced success in the opera on 23 February 1892. Marguerite's "Jewel Song" had to be reprised as an encore. The St. Petersburg public had no inkling that she was singing the role for the first time and suffering from a severe attack of stage fright. Reports to the French papers stated that in the prison scene she had broken with tradition and worn a simple gown of coarse gray cloth bound with a rope girdle instead of the usual ludicrous nightgown of virginal white.

Sanderson's farewell to Russia had been billed as a scintillating gala with scenes from *Manon* and *Roméo et Juliette* and one act of *Esclarmonde,* but there is no record of this affair ever taking place. After the performances of *Faust* the Mariinsky closed its door, together with the other theaters, for Lent had descended upon the city.

A few days before the singer's farewell in *Faust,* Grand Duke Vladimir had organized a concert at his palace and a spectacular banquet for her. The royal family and most of the nobility turned out for the occasion. Sanderson again sang arias from the French repertoire and some of Massenet's songs. The applause was deafening; once more she was showered with uncut jewels. Sibyl found herself toasted and feted extravagantly, for she had captivated the Romanovs as no other lyric artist had ever done.

The next day the empress sent the soprano an unrecorded gift and her autographed picture. Grand Duke Vladimir and his wife also dispatched tokens of their appreciation: an exquisite cloisonné mirror inlaid with Russian enamels, and autographed pictures of themselves. An unrecorded gift also arrived from Grand Duke Alexis, but the note that accompanied it has been preserved in the family.

Monday

Chère Mlle Sanderson,

The Grand Duke Alexis sends you this bauble and again thanks you for the delicious evening last night. He wished to write you himself, but being exceptionally busy this morning, has begged me to do it for him. I take this opportunity with pleasure to reiterate how delighted I have been to make your acquaintance, of which I shall treasure always the most charming memories.

Please do not forget me, with a thousand amitiés.
The Duchess of Leuchtenberg

When the prima donna left Russia she was so laden with booty that it would not have been surprising if the railroad officials had added an extra car to the train. Sanderson succeeded where Napoleon had failed; she had conquered the hearts of the people as well as their rulers.

Constellations and Black Holes

Margaret Sanderson was fast becoming a much sought after hostess in the American colony in Paris. She had started "at homes" on Sunday nights as early as 1888, during the first year that the Sandersons lived on the rue Lincoln. At this time Sibyl and Edith often prevailed upon amateur musicians and students to perform at their informal gatherings, and Marion would ask American art students from Julian's Academy.

The Massenets were invited during those early years, and the fingers of the middle-aged Orpheus could often be heard improvising themes at the Steinway upright. Because of her growing antipathy toward Sibyl, Louise Massenet finally declined to accompany her husband although she was very fond of the rest of the family. The composer didn't object in the least. The Sanderson Sunday-night soirée was an important social hub that provided him with the perfect opportunity to meet wealthy American music students in Paris and their ambitious mothers as well.

Massenet was not the only musical celebrity to cross the rue Lincoln threshold. Some of the leading musicians of France were among the regular Sunday-night coterie: Saint-Saëns, Godard, the Gounods, the Édouard Colonnes, and Ambroise Thomas and his wife. Nor were foreign opera composers strangers to the Sanderson home. During his many trips to Paris, Italy's Ruggero Leoncavallo often called upon Sibyl.[1] Every time Isidore De Lara was in town, the reputed lady-killer looked forward to dining at the Sanderson home and singing duets with the soprano.

Among the other guests were the three American Emmas: divas Eames, Nevada, and Abbott. The last-named soprano became a fast friend of Sibyl's before her 1891 death in America, and the latter was asked to sing at a memorial service held for her in Paris. The experience proved to be such a tearful one for the Californian that never again would she sing at a funeral. Nellie Melba always enjoyed herself at the Sandersons'. Marion recorded that once, on a drive through the Bois in a hired fiacre, she turned to the Sanderson sisters and exclaimed, "Oh, girls, how often I have wished myself back in your sweet company."

Marion also recalled a dinner party to which the Massenets, the Carvalhos, the noted painter Edouard Detaille, and the California millionaires Mr. and Mrs. Ben Ali Haggin were invited. Mrs. Haggin had successfully told a risqué but witty joke in French that shocked Marion's proper Victorian sensibilities but provoked hearty guffaws from Massenet. Marion was to discover that the composer, like most Frenchmen, relished an off-color story. The Hungarian baritone Zoltán Döme would often make an appearance, invariably accompanied by his monstrous Great Dane. "A big, handsome fellow with dazzling white teeth," the singer would wander into the parlor, sit down at the piano, and accompany himself. Often he sang duets with Sibyl.[2]

Among the guests who came to the rue Lincoln soirées in the fall of 1891 were the American composer Ethelbert Nevin and his wife Anne. Nevin was a slender young man with a mass of wavy brown hair parted in the middle and a long, sensitive face. Sibyl invited Massenet to meet him, and Nevin played some of his compositions for the master. Massenet was always delighted to meet new American talent and even more delighted when Nevin announced that he wanted to study composition with him. The project collapsed when the funds were not forthcoming from America, and Massenet, as usual, did not volunteer any scholarship aid.

One Sunday evening a handsome youth arrived at the apartment with a letter of introduction to the prima donna. He was a swarthy lad with hair the color of ebony and eyes inlaid with jet. An older sister, who looked sultry enough to be a flamenco dancer, accompanied him. Their names were Reynaldo and Maria Hahn, and their land of origin was Venezuela. They explained to the Sandersons that their wealthy father, Carlos Hahn, had emigrated to Paris when they were mere youngsters for the sake of their education. Reynaldo had entered the Conservatoire at the precocious age of eleven; now he informed Sibyl that he wanted to be a composer and later in the evening sat down at the Steinway upright to perform some of his compositions for her. The soprano was so enthusiastic about his talent that she couldn't wait to share her latest discovery with her mentor. He was equally impressed. Massenet suggested that young Hahn study directly with him at the Conservatoire. Meanwhile, Sibyl took the spirited Venezuelan under her wing as a sort of protégé. Hahn was a born mimic, and she found her own vivacious nature irresistibly drawn to his sense of humor. He would snatch a scarf off the piano and, stomping on the floor, perform a riotous imitation of an aging Spanish dancer until the singer would collapse on the sofa with laughter. She introduced him to many influential friends, including one of Paris's most beloved and eccentric hostesses, Madeleine Lemaire.

A hopelessly mediocre talent who fancied herself a still-life painter, Mme Lemaire was a big woman with a highly rouged face and coarse features who boasted that she once had been the mistress of Alexandre Dumas, père. She turned out canvas after canvas of nauseating lilies and roses, rumored to fetch up to five hundred francs apiece. "Only God has created more of them," observed Alexandre Dumas, fils.

Her little house at 31 rue de Monceau was always open on Tuesday evenings and jammed with the most unlikely combination of people in Paris. Her receptions took place under a glass-roofed studio annex where dukes and duchesses rubbed shoulders with writers, composers, artists, actors, and anyone else who had anything the least creative to offer the world. One would meet the titled aristocracy of the de La Rochefoucaulds, the Greffühles, and the Uzes, all the Parisian theatrical world from Réjane to Mounet-Sully, writers like Zola and Daudet, and such celebrated artists as Rodin and Degas. Around these luminaries swarmed dozens of lesser lights who were all treated with equal respect by their hostess. Somehow Mme Lemaire managed to circulate through this kaleidoscope of humanity without seeming to make real contact with anybody. She demanded and received absolute silence when an actor or musician was performing. At 31 rue de Monceau the artist reigned supreme.

Sibyl introduced her aspiring discovery to this bohemian world and suggested that Mme Lemaire engage him for a musical evening. The painter agreed. When the handsome youth sat down at the piano to perform, the hostess kept shouting "Bravo!" after every number. Once the diva had sung some of his songs, the acclamation of the guests was unanimous. Reynaldo Hahn had become an overnight celebrity thanks to the combined efforts of the queen of roses and the queen of song. Sibyl's generous nature led her to sponsor a wide variety of protégés; if it wasn't a girl with the unlikely cognomen of Mlle Shanck, it might be a soprano from America named Minnie Tracey. The star was particularly impressed with Miss Tracey's voice and lost no time in introducing her to Massenet. Later she helped the girl procure an engagement at the Nice opera. When Sibyl left the Opéra-Comique in the fall of 1893 the entire chorus signed a poignant farewell missive wishing her happiness and success in her new venture and expressed their gratitude for "the many kindnesses and favors" she had shown them in the past.

For all the purported camaraderie within the private Sanderson sorority, tiny cracks began to appear. Jane had remained in America for over three years trying to discover her own identity away from the blinding aura of Sibyl's fame. Marion managed to secure an honorable mention in a painting contest, but otherwise her efforts to pursue a career in the graphic arts had met with little success. Edith took out her frustrations on the piano every day for four hours, but even her teacher, Monsieur Fissot, could not inculcate the self-confidence necessary to appear in public. Both girls suffered from periodic bouts of depression and more and more from headaches undoubtedly caused by an unhealthy proximity to the family star.

Sibyl encouraged her youngest sister to join their mutual friend Florence Mosher, who was planning to leave for Vienna to study with the famous keyboard authority, Theodore Leschetizky. Edith had never been away from home for any extended length of time, and the experience would be invaluable to her. Although Margaret seems to have been hard pressed for money that fall, somehow she found the necessary resources to finance the budding pianist, who agreed to share an apartment with the Mosher girl.

Edith continued her diary in the Austrian capital, and on 28 December 1891 she proudly mentions that she refused to receive Van Dyck when he attempted to call upon her. A few weeks later we find her worrying about Massenet's lack of attention.

> Vienna, 20 January 1892. M Massenet is in Vienna staying at the Hotel Sacher and supervising the rehearsals of his forthcoming premiere of *Werther*. He has not taken the trouble to come and see me. I must say I think he *might* find time.

Despite Edith's pique, the composer had not forgotten her. In the midst of his frenetic schedule he managed to obtain a favorable report of her progress from Leschetizky, which he promptly relayed to Margaret upon his return to Paris. On 15 February, Edith exulted in her diary that complimentary tickets had arrived by messenger for the dress rehearsal.

> Vienna, 15 February 1892. M Massenet's tickets arrived yesterday, and this morning we went to a *répétition générale* of *Werther*. We were simply over-

come. It is a perfect thing from beginning to end, but so frightfully sad. Van Dyck is *superb,* and one cannot say enough about him. I don't think he can be equaled. How I do wish Sibyl could have sung the role of Charlotte, although it lies a little low for her, she would make a much better Lotte than Marie Renard. The latter has a good voice but acts vilely and does not move well . . . Floss [Florence Mosher] and I heard it repeated on Saturday and on leaving the theater nearly went into hysterics and had to enter a house to control ourselves and put our veils on. Last evening we took a ticket to Leschetizky . . . He could not go but Dominirska [his wife] went instead. She was delighted, and so was Brahms who sat right behind me. M Dreyfus and M Bessand [Massenet's son-in-law] were there and spoke very nicely to me . . . Eduard Schütt [the Viennese composer] liked it on a whole very much and thought the orchestration fine and the first act exquisite. Brahms raved over the moonlight music in the first act where Van Dyck and Renard come walking home together from the party . . . says it is a *dream!*

Vienna had shown the courage to host the premiere of *Werther* when Paris had rejected it. Carvalho's disparaging opinion of the score still burned in Massenet's memory: "I had hoped you would bring me another *Manon!* This dismal subject lacks variety. It is doomed from the start!"[3]

The reason for the French disdain toward Massenet's opera was obvious. Massenet's libretto closely adhered to Goethe's novel, and to its overriding theme, with hardly any respite. Basically, all four acts are dominated by unrequited love. Only at the end of the death scene does the audience finally see the good hausfrau Charlotte break from her dauntless bourgeois morality and confess that she loves the dying Werther.

However, a more sympathetic climate was to be found elsewhere. The successful Viennese premiere of *Manon* on 9 November 1890 encouraged Herr Jahn, the director of the Imperial Theater, to request another work from the Frenchman. Massenet naturally lost no time in proposing his spurned child. Herr Jahn couldn't have been more amenable. Van Dyck, who had been such a thrilling Des Grieux, would create the title role, with Marie Renard interpreting Charlotte.

The world premiere of *Werther* took place on 16 February 1892 and was accorded a brilliant reception. The Viennese press proclaimed that the Frenchman had produced another masterpiece. His superior command of orchestration was highly acclaimed by the critics, and the innovative use of a mournful saxophone intrigued the Viennese. In spite of the morbidity of the subject, the Austrians found the work to be filled with an unexpected sweep of power and pathos rarely encountered in Massenet's writing.

Van Dyck's interpretation of the tormented hero alternately generated paroxysms of sobbing and explosive ovations. One cannot fail to be amused by the fact that even Edith Sanderson, who had gone to the performance thoroughly prepared to loathe the tenor for personal reasons, had left the theater reduced to tears.

Sibyl and her mother arrived in Vienna the first week in March fresh from their Russian campaign and took a suite at the Hotel Continental. For the next week the Sandersons and the Leschetizkys seem to have spent every evening together, and on 5 March they went to hear *Werther.* It must have been a painful night for Margaret. She not only had to applaud Van Dyck on stage but be civil to him at a party afterward.

Sibyl's career was ascending rapidly that spring. She made a brilliant return to the Opéra-Comique in March, and on 1 May 1892 was invited back to Brussels for a star-studded benefit concert at the Théâtre de la Monnaie. Massenet was engaged to conduct Acts I, III, and IV from *Manon* for her. The opera house was sold out, and the Belgian monarchs even put in an appearance for the occasion. Melba, Lassalle, Alvarez, and Mme Deschamps-Jehin had been promised in the *Rigoletto* quartet, but when Melba failed to appear, Sibyl went on in her place to save the evening. The Belgian papers described the public reception as "tremendous" with "Massenet, Mme Deschamps-Jehin, and, above all, Sibyl Sanderson receiving thunderous ovations . . . with Massenet's sympathetic conducting, Mlle Sanderson stole the entire evening."[4]

On 26 May 1892, she scored another triumph in her first Parisian *Lakmé* with Gibert again her tenor. The "Bell Song" aroused a volley of bravas and had to be encored as did the Act I duet. The next day Serge Busset wrote in *Le Figaro:* "Once again Mlle Sanderson has proven herself by the exceptional virtuosity and charm she brings to her new role."

In spite of the fact that Carvalho continued to alternate *Manon* and *Lakmé* for the rest of the season, the romantic mystique of Jules and Sibyl held the French capital in its thrall. The last week in May a few papers gleefully announced that Massenet would personally sing the baritone role in his sacred work *Souvenez-vous, Vierge Marie* opposite his protégée in a religious concert. It will never be known who put the press up to this hoax, but on the night of 27 May, the hall was jammed with a throng of breathless Parisians expecting master and muse to unite their voices in public harmony for the first time. The more skeptical were not surprised to see a baritone student from the Conservatoire on stage with the star, flanked by a chorus of more students from the same institution. Except to acknowledge the applause, the composer remained obliterated in the orchestra pit.

Carvalho, now belatedly encouraged by the successful Viennese premiere of *Werther,* decided to risk a production of the work before the 1891–92 season closed. Press releases were sent to all the papers announcing that the French premiere would be scheduled for the first week in July with Gibert and Sanderson in the leading roles. It was a curious time to program such an important premiere, because the beau monde was already beginning its exodus from Paris for the summer.

For some unpublished reason, Sanderson suddenly bowed out of the production one week before the *représentation générale.* Having realized all along that the part of Charlotte lay too low for her voice, she now urged Massenet to procure a bona fide mezzo-soprano instead. It was a bitter blow to the composer, but he reluctantly acquiesced, and the premiere was postponed until the following season. Neither he nor the Opéra-Comique subscribers objected to her closing the season as Manon instead.

The summer of 1892 found the Sanderson family in Switzerland united for the first time in several years. Jane had returned to Paris in the spring and was trying hard to adapt to a city that she loathed even more intensely than Edith. Margaret's sister, Mary Yost, and her daughter Mabel were vacationing in Europe that summer and joined them at Vevey for a few bucolic weeks. Other friends arrived including the Shepards and May Palmer, accompanied by her mother.[5]

Relations seem to have been cordial in Vevey's little American colony. There were scenic drives up Mount Jorat to St. Denis, a quaint little village, where the young ladies enjoyed some delicious beer at the Hotel of the White Horse. There were also some enchanting afternoons boating on Lake Geneva with two gentlemen staying at the Grand Hotel named Strange and Balavin. The former managed to extricate his emotions when his vacation ended, but Balavin was smitten with Sibyl. In less than two weeks he asked her to marry him.

Edith Sanderson has left some indignant comments about the affair in her diary.

> 10 August 1892 . . . this youth is very nice, in fact, has an exceptionally fine character for twenty-one years, but Sibyl has fallen in love with him and has made a frightful fool of herself and to my mind has made him propose; they are to have six months to consider the matter, and at the end of that time if

they still *love* each other, there will be a wedding in the Sanderson family! What laughing stock we will all be. Sibyl the great! Ha! singer marrying a boy twenty-one years old whose father is a dyer. But to my mind it will never come to anything.[6]

A month later, the outcome predicted by Edith was rapidly materializing. When the Sandersons returned to Paris the final week in August because of Sibyl's rehearsal schedule, young Balavin followed on their heels. He and Mr. Strange arrived in Paris the first week in September to hear Sibyl sing. They dined with the Sandersons on the eleventh. In spite of the fact that the prima donna inundated the dyer's son with presents, Edith shrewdly observed: "Sibyl has not the slightest intention of marrying him." It came as no surprise to the family when both parties soon severed their matrimonial plans and pledged to remain "the truest of friends." The Sandersons were well aware that Sibyl's perpetual adolescent ego still needed to be nourished by periodic infatuations.

As Parisian temperatures soared to their summer highs, Sibyl opened the new Opéra-Comique season the first week in Septembe r with the 151st performance of *Manon*. A capacity audience convened to greet her. On September 11, *Le Ménéstrel* portrayed her as "beaming like a lark, radiant with joy, in more superb voice than ever" and "the object of the crowd's ovations."

Throughout the fall Sanderson alternated her Thursday- and Saturday-night performances of *Manon* with *Lakmé* on Monday nights. By the end of 1892 she had established herself as the leading Parisian exponent of Delibes's heroine. But her director had other plans for her. A lifelong Mozart devotee, Carvalho was organizing a stellar revival of *The Magic Flute*. With Fugère and Mlle Éleven as Papageno and Papagena, he cast Monsieur Nivette as Sarastro and Cécile Simonnet as Pamina. Edmond Clément and Jean Périer, a recent graduate of the Conservatoire, were assigned the roles of Tamino and Monostatos. He reserved the role of Queen of the Night for his queen of beauty and gave her top billing on posters and billboards throughout Paris. If Sanderson really was a pure coloratura, the casting would seem to fit her like the proverbial glove.[7] Mozart wrote the part for his sister-in-law and had included the F in alt for her—the highest note in vocal history before Massenet conceived *Esclarmonde*.

The first performance was scheduled for Friday night, 16 December 1892, and every seat was sold. Many of the old subscribers remembered the legendary appearances of Christine Nilsson as the Queen of the Night, not only from the Théâtre Lyrique in 1865 but also from the glory days when the Opéra-Comique was enshrined at the Salle Favart.

The day after the revival most of the critics were still sighing for those halcyon days, although they admitted certain allowances had to be made for the present cast encountering the score and working together for the first time. The only singers who were awarded unanimous accolades were Fugère and Mlle Éleven, while Nivette and Mlle Simonnet received most of the critical barbs. The "Queen of Beauty" was handed mixed notices, but she had the critics groveling before the "magical apparition" she created on stage.

The following day both Georges Street in *Le Matin* and Bicouqet in *L'Écho de Paris* lauded her accurate and brilliant execution of the high-pitched passages but devoted more space to gasping over her "ravishing" appearance than to critiquing her singing. On December 17 Ginistry wrote in *Le Petit Parisien,* "Mlle Sanderson, sufficiently icy in her role, triumphed over the difficulties of the formidable coloratura passages." On the other hand, Henri de Curzon claimed in *Le Théâtre* that she "lacked the Mozart style," and Émile Péssard declared in *L'Événement* that "Mlle Sanderson did not attain the success in the role that was expected."

Perhaps Charles Darcours, the savant on *Le Figaro,* pinpointed the reason for her controversial reception with the most accuracy on 17 December:

> Mlle Sanderson scaled the difficult pyrotechnics of the famous air ["Der Hölle Rache kocht in meinem Herzen"] with a glittering audacity, not missing one of her stratospheric notes, but in spite of this achievement, the public remained cold, following her hesitation in the final, crucial passage.

Only her family knew that she was suffering from throat trouble that week and had had to fortify herself with copious draughts of wine before stepping into Christine Nilsson's shoes. The next week her physician ordered her to bow out of subsequent performances for the rest of the month, and she was replaced by Mme Landouzy.

Edith Sanderson's diary sheds more light on the reason why Sibyl suddenly abdicated her new role: "30 December 1892. I received a letter from Marion today. Sibyl has not sung *Flute* since the first night as she is in bad voice. She is not well at all and is ruining herself from banting [liquid dieting]."

So far, the young soprano's life had been plagued by a constant succession of physical obstacles: colds, influenza, sore throats, scarlet fever, and operations for tonsillitis and appendicitis. In the near future she was destined to undergo still another one. Clearly, nature had not physically equipped her with the proper stamina for a stage career. But she had taken destiny into her own hands and altered it. Now her growing career and its concomitant glory were rapidly escalating out of control. The decision to work with Mme Marchesi had been among the few wise ones she had made, but it came too late. Marchesi's efforts to rebuild Sibyl's vocal technique on terra firma could have provided the artist with a solid foundation for her career had she retired from the stage for two years. Tragically, Sanderson's glittering fame outpaced her new training, and self-destructive forces within her psyche would hasten the burnout and ultimate collapse of her star.

Her mother had long fancied a small private home on the avenue Malakoff, not far from the Bois de Boulogne. Located a stone's throw from Paderewski's domicile on the avenue Victor Hugo, it was constructed of brick, three stories high, and resembled a small English house. In the rear there was an intimate garden with a single tree and a few flower beds. The main floor consisted of two salons, a large dining room and small kitchen, and an adjoining library. Upstairs were the individual bedrooms and a studio, which Marion immediately claimed for herself.

Shortly before Christmas of 1892, Margaret purchased the house, and the family moved to 46 avenue Malakoff in March 1893. The wide hall on the main floor, which divided the two salons, was amply festooned with ferns and palms. Sibyl and her mother reigned over the "grand salon"; Marion and Edith received in the "petit salon."

In 1896 Léon Bessand, Massenet's son-in-law, wired Margaret that he had found some exquisite Louis XVI furniture in Rouen that he thought she might like. Trusting his judgment, Margaret immediately sent him a check for two thousand dollars to buy the entire collection. Paris, with its rich cultural heritage of art, theater, and music, was now to become the permanent Sanderson home, and California would fade into the past for this expatriate family.

Chapter 17

Delicately Brutal

Although *Werther* had been canceled in Paris the previous season because of Sanderson's defection, Carvalho was determined to reschedule its first presentation there for the winter of 1892–93. Sibyl had urged her mentor to procure a true mezzo-soprano, and the composer chanced to hear a remarkable one at the home of the Alphonse Daudets that summer. She was a buxom damsel by the name of Marie Delna.[1] No one knew much about her. She was reported to have been discovered in her native village of Meudon, where she worked in a small inn owned by her grandparents. Overwhelmed by the rich luster of her voice, Massenet impetuously begged her to create Charlotte. However, he vacillated the entire fall between Jean Delmas and Guillaume Ibos, a former Opéra tenor, for the creation of the title role. When Delmas fell ill for a few weeks, Carvalho announced to the papers in December that Massenet had decided upon Ibos. With Max Bouvet cast as Albert and Jeanne Laisné debuting in the part of Sophie, Carvalho postponed the Parisian premiere from 12 December to 16 January 1893. The first performance met with a tremendous reception from the public, rave notices for the cast, and unanimous critical praise for a work the director once had predicted was destined for failure.

One week later, Sibyl and her mother arrived at the Hotel Luxembourg in Nice, where the artist was engaged by the Nice Opera Company to debut in *Roméo et Juliette,* sing Gilda in *Rigoletto,* and then create Charlotte in the Riviera premiere of *Werther.* On 30 January with Auguste Vianesi in the pit, she made her Nice debut singing Juliette to Gabriel Gandubert's Roméo. The artist was described by local critics as "in excellent form" and "the recipient of constant ovations and floral tributes."

The following day, in her interview with a correspondent from the *New York Herald,* Sanderson shared some serious reflections about her forthcoming appearance in *Werther.*

> No, I have not yet appeared as Charlotte; the role does not exactly lie within my vocal range, but it is so challenging I cannot resist a chance to perform it. M Massenet is coming in a few days to superintend the rehearsals, but he will not conduct the performance. I consider the score of *Werther* the most beautiful opera M Massenet has yet written. It is sad, yes, but sympathetic. It is full of the most extraordinary harmonies and is thoroughly capable of holding a music-loving audience. It is my favorite opera and would have been given for my opening performance in Nice except for the fact there were too many preparations to be made.

After a week of rehearsing *Rigoletto* with Guillemot in the title role and Gandubert as the Duke of Mantua, Sanderson again ravished the Niçoise with a poignant interpretation of Gilda. The critics agreed that the role was ideal for her voice and with some more coaching she could make the part uniquely her own throughout Europe.

Massenet arrived on 4 February, and everyone plunged into rehearsals for *Werther* with a maniacal fervor. In fact, the sessions proved so grueling that Sanderson was too fatigued from singing in chest register to repeat her performance of Juliette on 11 February.[2] The temperamental Émile Cossira, who had recently been fired from the Paris Opéra for chronic truancy, was to create the title role. With the excellent young Vianesi again in charge of the orchestra, the cast included Frédéric Boyer singing Albert and Mlle Alboni as Sophie.

On Monday night, 13 February 1893, *Werther* received its first performance on French soil outside Paris. The next day, the critic for *L'Éclaireur de Nice* hailed the Riviera premiere as "superb in every respect." Sanderson's interpretation of Charlotte was lauded as one of "great artistic intelligence," and Cossira was showered with equal superlatives. The more jaded members of the audience who customarily deserted the hall after the third act for the gambling casino were the losers this time. Sanderson and Cossira poured a torrent of emotion into the death scene. When an impassioned Charlotte finally kissed the dying Werther and confessed she had always loved him, there wasn't a dry eye in the theater.

In spite of her Riviera triumph in *Werther,* Sanderson was never to sing Charlotte again. She knew she had been forced to employ too much chest register for projection of the low notes, and that ultimately it would be injurious to her voice. But not for a moment did she regret all the fruitless campaigning she had done for the work when she was in Brussels. New performances of it were now springing up all over France. Upon her return to Paris, Sanderson received a surprise gift from her mentor—the holograph of the opera, to which Massenet had pasted a small, complimentary review from the Nice correspondent for *Le Ménéstrel*. It was his way of thanking her for her unwavering belief in a score universally condemned by the prophets of doom.

After singing the role of Charlotte, the American soprano did not have long to wait before encountering a part tailor made for her talents. Camille Saint-Saëns had been toying off and on with a spicy tale about the ancient Greek courtesan Phryné, a friend of the sculptor Praxiteles and model for his legendary statues of Aphrodite. Augé de Lassus had given him the libretto of a three-act play back in 1888. Although he was intrigued by it, other plans forced Saint-Saëns to shelve the project for the next few years. Then Mme Détroyat, the wife of a former collaborator, called upon the composer in the fall of 1892 to request a new musical work for her husband, who was assuming the directorship of the Théâtre de la Renaissance in January 1893. Saint-Saëns promised her a score and at the gentle prodding of de Lassus decided to revive his play about the legendary courtesan.

Born in 1835, Saint-Saëns had been a child prodigy in piano and a student at the Conservatoire, where he won first prize in organ as well. Outside of the school, he pursued studies in composition for a while with Gounod. Twice he tried but failed to win the Prix de Rome. For twenty years he was organist at the Church of the Madeleine and later was to tour Europe as a concert organist and one of the brilliant piano virtuosos of his day. In 1868 he was awarded the Légion d'Honneur and was elected to the Institute in 1881. Even in his old age, he was concertizing throughout America in the dual capacity of pianist and conductor.

With Romain Bussine, Saint-Saëns was a founder of the Société Nationale de Musique, whose object was to encourage a school of Gallic composition. He had developed a violent antipathy toward Wagner because he feared the latter's insidious Teutonizing of French music. As a composer there was hardly any musical area he left untouched. With his amazing versatility, he far outshone his rival, Massenet. He produced symphonies, songs, symphonic poems, secular as well as religious choral works, chamber music, organ literature, and an abundant output for the instrumental repertoire, including concerti for various solo instruments and orchestra.

In the field of opera, however, his success always trailed that of Massenet with the exception of his masterpiece, *Samson et Dalila.* Nevertheless, in his day some of his other opera scores—*Henry VIII, La Princesse jaune, Ascanio,* and *Proserpine*—met with varying degrees of success.

Bald and bewhiskered at this stage of life, Saint-Saëns was a tiny man with remarkably small hands and feet. He was an extremely nervous individual with fingernails that were always bitten to the quick, and under tension his soprano lisp would soar to a screaming falsetto. Mary Garden once described him as "delicately brutal and brutally delicate." At receptions the antisocial satyr delighted in playing an obnoxious Cain to Massenet's unctuous Abel.

The fifty-seven-year-old Frenchman loathed the Parisian winters and usually avoided them by opting for sun and sin in the Canary Islands with some teenage girl whom he had invited. The older he grew, the younger the girls became, and if they were not available, teenage boys were equally welcomed. This time he took off for Algiers, frantically trying to complete the opera before Détroyat's opening. He reduced the score to two acts and changed the role of the male slave, Lampito, to that of a mezzo-soprano.

Nevertheless, when the Théâtre de la Renaissance opened on 31 January with an expensive revival of *Les contes d'Hoffmann,* Saint-Saëns had barely finished the first act. He forthwith dispatched it to his ex-pupil, composer-conductor André Messager, to be orchestrated. A few weeks later he was stunned to learn that Détroyat's theatrical venture had been such a financial disaster that the impresario was forced to close his doors on 28 February. Following this unexpected announcement was a jubilant telegram from Carvalho insisting that *Phryné* now belonged to the Opéra-Comique. The composer quickly succumbed when the wily director further disclosed: "There is only one woman in Paris today who can properly interpret Phryné, la divine Sanderson . . . now hasten the wedding!"

De Lassus had also been depicting Sibyl as ideal for the role in his letters to Saint-Saëns. He subsequently wrote of her: "Sanderson still retained a slight accent of her native country. It may have caused a fleeting smile, but she, herself, smiled little, as little as a lovely marble escaping from the trembling hands of Pygmalion . . . this Britannic *[sic]* Phryné seemed an Athenian even to the soft curve of her lips. One would have sworn that the Athenians talked that way."[3] Saint-Saëns was instantly receptive to his collaborator's suggestion. He immediately revised the score for Sanderson's vocal prowess, adding a copious sprinkling of vocalises, scales, and arpeggios.

On 5 March 1893, Saint-Saëns finished the score under a clump of date palms on a sheltered Algerian beach. We find him writing Messager on the 11th:

> I have finished my second act . . . but will not send it to you as I intend to orchestrate it myself while you finish the first one. You realize that it is to be performed immediately, therefore there is no time to lose. I shall leave you only the finale, which is composed of themes from the first act with slight modifications.

Carvalho was no less judicious in his choice of the remaining cast. The young tenor Édouard Clément would debut in the role of Nicias, and Lucien Fugère, perhaps the greatest singer/actor of the French stage, would create the baritone role of the roguish judge.

With the casting completed and rehearsals scheduled to commence the first of April, the only cloud on Carvalho's horizon was the state of Sibyl Sanderson's health. She had been struck down by a gallbladder attack in February right after her return from Nice and forced to cancel all Parisian performances. About the twenty-first of February she underwent emergency surgery and was on the operating table four precarious hours. Massenet reinstated his courier communication with the Sanderson home, and his short notes reveal his concern. Dr. Michel insisted that Sanderson take a month to recuperate before returning to the Opéra-Comique on March twenty-first to sing *Manon* again.

Phryné has been described by Jean Bonnerot as "a delightful artistic whim ranging from fantasy to familiarity,"[4] and critic Adolphe Julien affectionately referred to it as an *opérette*. Recalling the work, Pierre Monteux described it as "one of the most enchanting moments ever to flow from the pen of Saint-Saëns." He was perplexed about why it had remained an unknown entity in America and even more astonished to learn that in 1893 the *Musical Courier* had labeled it "pornographic opera" and waged a self-righteous campaign to quarantine it from the Western Hemisphere.[5]

The plot concerns Phryné, the beautiful Greek courtesan, who is in love with Nicias, a young man deeply in debt. The latter's uncle and guardian, Dicéphile, is a hypocritical old magistrate who is secretly conspiring with Nicias's creditors to seize his estate and jail his nephew. Phryné is determined to thwart Dicéphile's plans. She orders her slaves to drive off the bailiffs in the public square when they arrive to arrest Nicias and offers him refuge in her home. Then she persuades her servants to sing ribald songs before the judge's bust, which has just been unveiled before the gullible Athenian public. Her slave, Lampito, even pours wine over the statue and crowns it with the half-empty bottle.

When night falls, the old magistrate appears in the square with lantern in hand. Seeing the desecration of his bust, he swears that he will be revenged for this outrage. With a menacing shake of his fist in the direction of chez Phryné, he suddenly hears the offstage echoes of the salacious tarantella that the slaves had sung earlier: "Dicéphile! Dicéphile! Dicéphile is a dirty old scoundrel!" Between acts, Phryné is summoned before the Athenian tribunal and convicted for her brazen conduct, and she is awaiting sentencing.

In the second act, the lecherous judge, having feasted his eyes on Phryné's beauty at the trial, is determined to call upon her the following night for a more personal inspection. The courtesan, seizing the opportunity to reverse their fortunes, plans to trap the old rogue. She seduces Dicéphile into compromising himself, and then at the critical moment, Nicias rushes in with a number of witnesses. Together, the lovers successfully blackmail the judge under threat of exposure to reverse their sentences and loan Nicias the money to pay off his debts.

Saint-Saëns orchestrated his score in the most original manner, reviving the ancient Greek usage of harps, timbrels, and flutes. In Phryné's "Invocation to Venus" he employs exotic harp arpeggios in the lower register to depict the murmur of waves and a persistent pedal point of low Es to create the impression of an archaic Greek hymn. Bassoons jeer at the old judge when he sings, and an offstage chorus chants the charms of Venus-Aphrodite as her statue is lighted.

The composer dealt cleverly with the sense of propriety that inhibited Sibyl from completely disrobing in the seduction scene. After enticing the judge to clasp some bracelets around her arms and comb her hair, the courtesan asks him to bring her a rose from behind the curtain. When the infatuated old roué stumbles to the other side of the stage to open the curtain, the stage lights are suddenly blacked out, and a blue spotlight focuses upon the altar, little by little revealing the contours of the naked statue of Phryné behind it. The astonished Dicéphile, believing she has actually appeared to him as Venus-Aphrodite, grovels before the statue in carnal subjugation while the courtesan, her lover, and her slaves are hiding on the opposite side of the stage in darkness. When the magistrate has totally debased himself, the lights are turned up again, and the triumphant witnesses appear to draw their snare around his despoiled reputation.

The stage settings were constructed by Chaperon and Rubé, longtime designers in the Parisian theatrical world. The noted painter Joseph Thomas designed the costumes, and the popular sculptor Daniel Campagne was commissioned to create the naked statue of Sanderson in the guise of Venus-Aphrodite.

A thoroughly tanned and enthusiastic Saint-Saëns arrived from Africa early in April to begin overseeing rehearsals. Augé de Lassus later recalled the composer's inexhaustible energy:

> I still can remember him at rehearsals. He kept running, jumping up and down, leaping from one singer to another. First he reached out and caught one dancer, then another, he made them pivot and turn about. The very devil was in his body. He would not quit until they were all panting, almost exhausted. Finally, he would retire to his suite which Carvalho had given him and fall on a couch, dripping with perspiration. Then all at once he was up, standing behind a screen, changing his shirt, laughing heartily, and ready to go again.[6]

Saint-Saëns's lyric comedy was advertised on billboards throughout Paris under its full title: *Phryné or the Diversion of a Noble Spirit.* The premiere was scheduled for Wednesday, 24 May 1893, and posters all over the city depicting Fugère on his knees before Sanderson's nude statue were more than sufficient to pack the Opéra-Comique on opening night.

From her first appearance on stage, in voice and person, Sanderson seemed to capture "the shimmering radiance of sunlight on the Aegean sea" according to Georges Street in *Le Matin,* 25 May 1893. She moved across the stage like "A Tanagra figurine resplendent in beauty and warmth of personality. . . . With her enormous violet eyes where unknown troubled lights may blaze, her golden hair with its mysterious glints, her mouth full of seduction and cruel mockery, she miraculously evokes the image of the ravishing courtesan whom the ancient Greek poets have so glorified."

The "Invocation to Venus," in which Phryné retells the tale of Aphrodite's apparition on the seashore, received such acclamation that Sanderson was obliged to repeat it. The couplets of Dicéphile also had to be repeated as the statue of Venus-Aphrodite was lighted in the last scene.

By the end of the evening the American sorceress had seduced Paris with the same ease with which the Phryné of old had subjugated Athens. Saint-Saëns came on stage afterward between Sanderson and Fugère, to be inundated with a blizzard of flowers, crowns, and laurel wreaths.

All the Parisian critics agreed with Georges Street on 25 May that "the success of the composer's musical satire constituted a stunning revenge of French music against that of Germany." De Fourcaud wrote in *Le Gaulois:* "This work, without any officious grandeur, makes us forget many gigantic works of the

German repertoire. The great talent of the master has run away with itself in this coquettish intermezzo." "A total triumph . . . a piquant subject enhanced by a delicious orchestration and the most lovable interpreters." This was how Charles Darcours described the premiere in *Le Figaro.*

As for the heroine, all the Parisian journalists hurled bouquets at her feet. They praised her "rare virtuosity" and her "marvelously pure and facile voice," and lauded her interpretation as "simply perfection." Ernest Reyer noted that "never did she sacrifice quality for volume,"[7] a sacrosanct precept in French aesthetics. Fugère was hailed as making the knavish judge "one of his most important creations,"[8] and columns of newsprint extolled the erotic charms of the diva's nude statue.

Saint-Saëns was so delighted with Sibyl's interpretation that he bought her an exquisite necklace of semiprecious stones. His few surviving letters to her are all addressed "my beautiful Phryné." Reutlinger, the famous Parisian photographer, photographed Sanderson in a series of Phryné poses. Afterward he observed to Augé de Lassus: "Her beauty is not only statuesque, but chaste. One could undress that woman and she would still seem clothed."[9]

Toulouse-Lautrec also succumbed to the spell of this Art Nouveau princess and sketched her one night at the Opéra-Comique. The lithograph, entitled *Phryné—an American singer* and dated 1893, was first published in 1898. An edition of about four hundred impressions was printed three years later.

Phryné became so popular that the Opéra-Comique presented it four times a week until the close of the season in July. Already overworked at the Comique, she still found it impossible to decline constant invitations to sing before the Parisian beau monde. One week she might be heard at Mme Pulitzer's garden party, the next at the Hotel Continental ballroom singing the Berlioz *Nuits d'été* on one of Mme Marchesi's programs. Following that would be a reception at the American ambassador's residence.

At an elegant reception given by Mme Campbell Clarke, wife of the editor of London's *Daily Telegraph,* Sanderson was once again accompanied by Massenet and Gounod in a program of their songs before the cream of international society. She also introduced two offerings by a contemporary composer, Ella Kopékink. Clapping unenthusiastically in her seat, a granite-faced Louise Massenet must have presented an amusing contrast to the standing ovation by all the ambassadors, dukes, and princesses.

At least once during her hectic career the artist was unable to enter the very hall where she was scheduled to sing. Sanderson and Massenet were engaged to appear together at a musical fete in the Cathedral of Notre-Dame de Lorette, and the church was jammed to capacity hours before the concert. Arrangements for controlling the crowd that surrounded the church were hopelessly inadequate. The mob grew belligerent and smashed the iron railings bordering the church on the rue Flechier. In the melee, no one recognized the star and the composer trying in vain to reach the door. After circling the church three or four times, they abandoned all efforts to penetrate the unruly horde.

Sanderson's roles of Phryné and Thaïs (1893–1894), by perfect timing, made her a major influence in the revival of classical Greek fashions at the end of the nineteenth century. Photographs of the singer in flowing Hellenic costumes were constantly being copied on various Art Nouveau posters and calendars; her face and bust appeared on innumerable sets of Bavarian china, for which she never received a cent of remuneration. It is also doubtful whether she made any money from the hats and gowns "à la Sibyl Sanderson" that were beginning to appear on the international market. Copyright laws were regrettably nonexistent during this period. Nevertheless, she must have been compensated for endorsing such products as Hoff's Malt and Pond's Extract with her personal signature.

La belle Sibylle had become the spoiled child of Paris. Although she would always lack self-control and business acumen, few singers had been blessed with so many gifts. No matter how she struggled to attain personal discipline, as all artists must, the goal always eluded her. Carvalho, taking advantage of her tremendous popularity, overworked her shamelessly. She was the aurora borealis of his marquee. No other star could guarantee a sold-out house night after night. Her guileless affability, in fact, made it all the easier for him.

Yet, the theater caused her untold suffering. It was her ecstasy and at the same time her crucifixion. After the curtain calls, the flowers, and the applause, Sanderson would leave the stage physically and emotionally exhausted. Success had overwhelmed her, and her efforts to cope with it proved futile. Night after night, she gave all of herself to a carnivorous public that could not get enough of her. Like Moloch, they would devour her, and subconsciously she must have begun to resent their constant drain upon her vital resources.

Sarah Bernhardt, Ellen Terry, Modjeska, and other stage luminaries of her era always divorced themselves from the characters they portrayed.[10] Sanderson never learned how to control her emotional expenditure on the stage; this was to play an important part in her downfall.

Maurice Halperson later wrote that there were nights when she so identified with Manon that she would become "hysterical" in the Saint Sulpice scene, "which didn't do the music any good."[11] Des Grieux's love seemed more real to her than the leather-bound volume of the opera with her mentor's lengthy inscription. In rebellion against the bondage imposed by her art, another personality was gradually emerging from her subconscious, that of a self-destructive hedonist. Like Odile, the black swan in Tchaikovsky's famous ballet, she arose insidiously to destroy the achievements of Odette, the lyric swan queen. Before long, these two personalities would be locked in continual conflict.

Sibyl's family did everything they could to see that she was not disturbed on mornings after performances. The maid even sat beside the door until noon to prevent any visitor from ringing the bell and awakening her. But how could the singer continue to recharge the invisible battery that supplied her unique kind of charisma when the audience wanted to consume more than she was capable of producing? It was becoming an impossible task, and she began to resort to artificial means of coping with it.

During the first years of her career, she suffered dreadfully from stage fright. In *Esclarmonde,* Massenet had demanded superhuman feats for which her voice was not yet technically prepared. These gymnastics were not incorporated as a permanent part of the score, and other interpreters of the role were not required to execute them. She became terrified at the thought of going on the stage and being expected to outdazzle her pyrotechnics of the previous night. Basically, she was competing with herself, and she could not cope with this age-old dilemma of the performer's existence. Someone suggested a glass of wine between acts to relax her nerves and throat muscles. Innocently, Sanderson complied. The results were almost magical; it seemed to be the ambrosial elixir—at first. Nightly, she began to rely upon alcoholic stimulants to overcome anxiety attacks and fortify her debilitated energies with false strength.

Now the habit was growing upon her offstage as well. She was rebelling against the tyranny of her art, which did not allow her to enjoy a normal life. She could lie in bed, indulge in alcohol, and fantasize about the ordinary pleasures of life her routine would not allow. At first it seemed the ideal sanctuary, the perfect shelter where she could secretly regenerate her strength and recharge her emotional vitality. No one could intrude upon this secluded refuge, this hermetic world, and demand her heart.

Her mother grew disturbed over Sibyl's offstage drinking. Margaret may not have understood the psychological reasons, but she did know that Sibyl could not manufacture courage, magnetism, and other emotional intangibles from a liquor bottle. She began to argue, even implore, but Sibyl would retreat into that silent fantasy dimension, and the door to reality would be closed. Neither

Massenet, Carvalho, nor the pressures of her career—not even her family could reach her there. She felt safe at last.

Margaret suffered agonies over this alarming trend in Sibyl's behavior; it had begun as early as the winter of 1891–1892. In a letter to Jane dated 1 March 1896, she wrote: "I have such a sinking in my heart since poor Sibyl is never to be well I am sure, and I dread the years left to her . . . I think I may be able to say no other child has caused me such sorrow . . . she suffers so deeply and yet cannot help herself or will not."

Chapter 18

The Monk and the Courtesan

"Virtue is not dramatic in the least because it has no range of development,"[1] Francis de Croisset once remarked. The Belgian playwright further observed that no one really wants to see a play about a good woman because she is a one-dimensional character, a person of a single color. But evil continues to have an enormous range when it comes to character development. De Croisset believed that the multifaceted nature of a villainous life would always be great box-office insurance in the theater.

Throughout history innumerable playwrights and novelists have agreed with him. Shakespeare had his Lady Macbeth, Dickens his Madame Defarge, Robert Hichens his detestable Ruby (*Bella Donna*), and Lillian Hellman her scheming Regina Giddens (*The Little Foxes*), to mention only a few.

French author Anatole France was also intrigued by the topic—and by one sinful woman in particular. In 1867 he first published his *Legend of Saint Thaïs* as a poem. It recounts how Paphnutius, a fourth-century Egyptian monk, converted a ravishing pagan harlot named Thaïs into a saint. Historically, there is little veracity in the tale. The woman seems to have been mentioned first in a seventh-century collection of Syrian legends, where the monk's original name is recorded as Sarapion. The tale of her conversion found its way through various Latin and Greek manuscripts to Germany, where it became the subject of a tenth-century drama by a Benedictine nun, Hrosvitha. In 1839, the play was first translated into French by Charles Magnin and published in *La Revue des deux mondes*. It drew Anatole France's imagination like a magnet.

There was also another Thaïs in Egyptian history, a very real harlot who had accompanied Alexander the Great on his Asiatic conquests in the third century

B.C. as General Ptolemy's mistress. At the turn of the twentieth century her mummy was on display in Paris at the Trocadéro Museum.

Remaining obsessed by the legend of Saint Thaïs, Anatole France was not content to leave it as a poem. In 1888 he decided to transform the story into a full-length novel. Now, however, there were enormous changes in character development. The holy man saves the eternal soul of the sinner only to lose his own when he is overcome by lust for his convert. It was typical of France that he should so sardonically portray the monk as an overzealous hypocrite. The author thought most priests were hypocrites. In spite of the fact that he had been reared in the Catholic faith, France carried on a running feud with the church for decades. "I have only two enemies," he is reported to have said, "Christ and chastity."

The decision to transform his original poem into a novel may have been influenced by his recently acquired mistress, Mme Arman de Caillavet, who was the hostess of an important literary salon in Paris and an ambitious woman with powerful connections. Once the story was finished, the lady brought enormous pressure upon the editor of *La Revue des deux mondes* to publish the work, first entitled *Paphnuce*. The editor quickly realized that its controversial theme provided a potential bonanza. Cleverly, he changed the pedestrian title to *Thaïs,* and the novel appeared in serialized form. It created a sensation in the literary world, and when the opus was reborn in hardcover shortly afterward, it became an instant bestseller. The subsequent condemnation by the church served to further kindle its fame.

But the fascinating story of a monk and a courtesan who reform each other in reverse was not destined to remain solely in novel form. There was something distinctly theatrical about its appeal. Massenet wrote in his memoirs that shortly after his return from the Viennese premiere of *Werther* (16 February 1892) he received a visit from Gallet and Heugel, his librettist and publisher. They both proposed a lyric dramatization of France's explosive novel for his next project.[2] The composer could already see the California siren in the title role. All three gentlemen were in complete agreement. No one else in Paris had the glamour, temperament, and seductive charm necessary to portray the Egyptian strumpet.

As a matter of record, this visit actually occurred in the fall of 1891. The Parisian papers announced the first week of January 1892 that Massenet's next opus would be *Thaïs.* By that spring Massenet had decided to compose the leading male role for a baritone rather than the usual tenor. There were specific reasons for doing this. The figure of the fanatical monk was not the usual romantic lead, and for more than half the story he remains the adversary of the heroine. In general, monks and priests are traditionally cast as basses in opera, so the composer's decision to use a baritone struck a happy medium.

The powerful American baritone Eugène Oudin had been a guest in the Sanderson home that winter, and Massenet may have met him there at that time if not before.[3] He auditioned for the role of the monk in the spring of 1892, and after hearing a few candidates, Massenet enthusiastically announced his choice of Oudin in May. Next, the singer was heard by Carvalho, who also was impressed by the unusually dark timbre of the baritone's voice. He offered Oudin a special engagement in the opera, which was to premiere at the Opéra-Comique the following year. Now the two leading roles had been cast, and, curiously enough, with American artists.

But the composer's journey to the ancient Nile was to be plagued with constant trials and irritations. When librettist Gallet read his completed text to France, the author argued that it was so changed he didn't even recognize his own novel. Paphnuce, he argued, had been transformed into a "cavalry captain" with the name of "Athanaël." Thereafter, he angrily refused Gallet permission to adapt any more of his works for the stage.

Massenet left Paris in the late spring of 1892 to spend part of the summer on the Brittany coast with his family. Heugel had offered him the use of his villa at Pourville, where the composer could concentrate upon writing the opera in complete privacy. His departure marked the first time in nearly four years that he had failed to accompany Sibyl and her family to Switzerland.

The composer finished orchestrating the first two acts at Pourville and by the following winter had completed most of the score in Paris. Although other projects intervened until late 1893, Massenet had given his pupil her copy of the manuscript to study that summer, having already completed all the vocal parts. In addition to *Thaïs* Massenet was laboring on two other scores during the summer of 1893. After the cataclysmic events that occurred in early June, however, it was amazing that he ever finished the opera. The irresponsible Sibyl nearly wrecked the Egyptian safari.

Ever since 1891, the managers of the Opéra, Messrs Bertrand and Gailhard, had suffered in silence at their half-empty houses on nights when Sanderson packed the Comique. Neither Rose Caron nor Albert Alvarez nor any of their other stars could compete with the charisma of the "divine American." They were faced with the humiliating prospect of either closing their doors certain nights of the week or wooing this exotic Lorelei from the footlights of "Chez Carvalho." Knowing that her contract would expire at the end of September

1893, the Opéra directors decided to offer Sibyl a far more lucrative one. By now their mutual ill will over the *Le mage* episode had faded.

Sanderson was thrilled at the chance to appear on the stage of this much larger and more prestigious theater. At last she glimpsed the opportunity to realize her long-sought ambition: to be accepted as a versatile artist in the standard repertoire of Gounod, Thomas, and Verdi instead of remaining merely a Massenet specialist. She eagerly signed the contract in Gailhard's office, sub rosa of course. Carvalho would eventually have to be informed, but she would deal with that problem when it arose.

Sibyl had been reviewing both *Faust* and *Roméo et Juliette* with Gounod that spring. Now she boldly petitioned Gailhard to make her debut as the Shakespearean heroine. The soprano's request was overruled, this time by Gounod himself, who insisted she was ready for Marguerite (*Faust*). Outside of the Opéra directors, this musical veteran was among the few people in Paris who happened to be aware of her secret negotiations, and his lips were sealed.

Although Sibyl knew that Massenet was writing *Thaïs* expressly for the Opéra-Comique, she was not capable of understanding how her impulsive decision to play musical chairs was about to throw the whole production into chaos. The diva had already concocted a convenient rationalization: she would simply inform her director and her mentor that she was abdicating the role of the Egyptian tart, and they would have to find a new one. They might be a trifle vexed, but so what? They would get over it.

Vexed was hardly the proper word. Both Massenet and his publisher Heugel were stunned when an impetuous Gailhard quickly informed them that the Opéra would produce *Thaïs* instead with the California nightingale in the title role. Years later, Massenet confessed in his memoirs that all he could say was: "You've got the artist; the work will follow her."[4] The words must have stuck in his throat at the time. Now he was biting his nails at the thought of relaying the news to Léon Carvalho. The prized songbird was about to flee the cage, and a miracle would be needed to conjure an equally ravishing duplicate.

Massenet realized only too well how the director of the Opéra-Comique would feel about losing his top box-office attraction. He knew that Carvalho had unashamedly exploited Sibyl's popularity, but he had been equally guilty in never once objecting to it. Every sold-out performance of *Manon* helped to augment his own lucrative investments at the Bourse.

Carvalho, who had not been in good health for the past year, nearly went into cardiac arrest after Massenet detonated the bombshell in his office. His face vacillated between the pallor of a calla lily and the crimson of amaryllis.

Alternately pounding his fist on the desk and shaking a recriminating finger toward the composer, the enraged manager accused Massenet of duplicity and chicanery, and most unfairly blamed the composer for engineering the entire maneuver behind his back. Only ten years ago it was he, Léon Carvalho, who had given the budding composer the opportunity of a lifetime when he agreed to produce *Manon.* And now he had been ruthlessly betrayed! What despicable ingratitude!

Choking and gasping for breath, the crusty veteran next aimed his artillery at the singer. He furiously indicted her as a woman without principle and denounced her for breach of faith. Sanderson was speechless before such an outburst. The composer struggled to defend his innocence but found himself also trying to shield his guilty disciple. Nevertheless, when his back was to the wall, Massenet always came up with his most brilliant ploys. Nervously gesticulating with one cigarette after another, he tried to placate Carvalho with a two-point proposal: first, the Opéra-Comique could keep *Thaïs* if auditions were held at once for a new interpreter, one who would be satisfactory to each of them. Carvalho's stomach churned. If the Son of God appeared at the Trocadero and resurrected the mummy of the real Thaïs, Massenet would find fault with her.

The second suggestion was equally repugnant to the manager: release *Esclarmonde* in place of *Thaïs,* and transfer the work to the Opéra for its creatrice. Massenet knew Carvalho was not about to relinquish his rights to the greatest box-office triumph in the history of the Comique. By presenting the director with his choice of two impossible conditions, he managed to escape from an embarrassing situation. He would be exonerated of any malfeasance, and, of more critical importance, his delinquent muse would retain her role. But she was fortunate not to have been in his studio right after Carvalho's onslaught. He was so angry with her that, like Coppélius in *Les contes d'Hoffmann,* he might have broken his unpredictable Olympia into a thousand pieces.[5]

The unhappy Carvalho had no choice but to send notices to the newspapers that auditions would be scheduled shortly for a new Egyptian courtesan. Whether they were ever held is extremely doubtful. After contemplating the composer's proposal for a week or so, Carvalho capitulated to Massenet's handful of trumps. The singer could leave in the fall and take his despicable trollop with her. Somehow the Opéra-Comique would survive.

Unfortunately, Eugène Oudin would not. He was the next casualty of *l'affaire Sibylle.* It was a bitter blow when Carvalho canceled his contract; the gifted baritone immediately returned to London to seek engagements. Unexpectedly, he was to die in England just a year later.

When Sanderson left for Switzerland in August after summer appearances at the Vichy, Royan, and Dieppe festivals, Massenet and his wife must have breathed a sigh of relief. The diva's capricious caper had jeopardized the composer's relationship with Carvalho and his staff. Now they could depart for Avignon, where he would spend the month of August working on his next opera, *La navarraise,* under the protective eye of his beloved Ninon. How fortunate he was to have her. She was his Gibraltar of stability and understanding— the total opposite of the spoiled California princess.

Chapter 19

Thaïs at the Opéra

When the Opéra-Comique opened its doors in September 1893 with Sibyl's return as Phryné, tempers had cooled. It was arranged between Carvalho and Gailhard that she could remain at the Comique for the celebration of *Manon's* two hundredth performance there that fall. Harmony between master and pupil was restored, with the devoted Frenchman as publicly enthusiastic as always over the gifts of his favorite interpreter.

In an interview with Alexander McArthur of the *Musical Courier,*[1] Massenet revealed that he had not heard the Californian in her new role yet, but he was eagerly looking forward to it.

> One of the greatest pleasures I receive after writing an opera is to hear how others interpret my ideas. Artists like Mlle Sanderson who have a distinct personality often reveal to me hitherto concealed beauties in my works, and when this occurs, my personal gratification is immense.

When McArthur pointed out the composer's affinity for American talent, Massenet replied between puffs of his cigarette: "Ah! Mon cher! It is true. But without your American prima donna what would I, what would art, be today?"

Neither master nor art had any complaints when the bicentennial performance of *Manon* occurred on Monday, 16 October 1893 at the Comique. The house was sold out with box-office receipts of more than 8,000 francs. Throughout the evening the singers were constantly feted and recalled before the curtain, but when the composer joined his heroine for a special bow, the audience became hyperemotional. Their mystique had won a special niche in every Parisian heart. Again and again the same romantic platitudes rippled through the hall: "What devotion! She has his pen and his love! *Quel bel sentiment!*"[2]

Sanderson continued to sing her two courtesan roles for the rest of the month. Friday night, 3 November, marked her adieu to the Opéra-Comique as Manon. Comments about her departure proliferated in the French press, but Alexander McArthur in his November 2 letter to the *Musical Courier* observed that the soprano "has worked like a slave at the Opéra-Comique, in fact, she is in anything but good health, suffering from overwork." Between France, Belgium, England, and Holland, Sanderson had already sung 250 performances of *Manon* in five years, approximately 120 of *Esclarmonde,* and 37 of *Phryné,* besides numerous ones of *Lakmé.*

Sibyl still refused to recognize that she was being crucified by her own ambition, as though she sensed her existence would be a fleeting one, and she was determined to savor as much success as she could in the short time allotted to her. Her interpretations had been showered with abundant praise, but no critic had called her a great artist so far. Blindly ignoring all danger signals, she entered the Opéra immediately to begin coaching her new role with the well-known Edouard Mangin. Massenet often came to Marchesi's studio that fall to accompany Sibyl's lessons at the piano.

In fact, Mme Marchesi devoted so much time to training the diva for her forthcoming debut that a rebellion erupted in her classroom. Eighteen American students became so incensed at the unfair amount of time the old German *Feldmarschallin* devoted to Sibyl's lessons that they signed a round-robin letter of protest. Future star Suzanne Adams and several others bolted the ranks and sought other teachers.

Massenet finished orchestrating the last act of *Thaïs* in November 1893. He had already given Sibyl her copy of the holograph. His inscription on the title page read simply: "À Mlle Sibyl Sanderson, une grande artiste.—J. Massenet." All the leading roles were now cast by the Opéra directors. The baritone Jean-François Delmas, not to be confused with Sibyl's tenor at the Comique, would create Athanaël. The part of Nicias went to tenor Albert Alvarez. Laure Bauvais was assigned the role of Albine, the convent prioress, and François Delpouget that of the old monk, Palémon. Crobyle and Myrtle, the two slaves, would be sung by Jeanne Marcy and Meyrianne Héglon.

Rehearsals ran throughout December and January with the entire cast assembled in the foyer of the Opéra, but preparations for the complex stage machinery were lagging. The directors postponed the premiere until March because Massenet was dissatisfied with the ensemble.

Massenet may be forgiven for his perpetual dissatisfaction; he was under tremendous pressure that season. In addition to *Thaïs,* two other operas by the composer were receiving premieres within a space of three months: *La navarraise* in London and his one-act *Le portrait de Manon* at the Opéra-Comique. A constant trail of cigar and cigarette smoke was always the clue to his whereabouts in the rehearsal rooms at the Opéra. If journalists were able to fend off a shower of burning cigar ash from his excited gestures, they could depend upon him for some fast quips.

Apropos *Thaïs:* "Anytime a monk meets a courtesan, one should get marvelous results somewhere."

About Sibyl Sanderson: "She is the only singer I know at present who has any temperament."

Concerning rehearsals: "Of all the hells, they are the worst! To write an opera is child's play, but to put it on the stage—zut!"[3]

Arriving at a rehearsal in late February, a journalist from *L'Illustration*[4] soon learned why Massenet existed in a state of constant agitation. Everything seemed hopelessly chaotic. First, the composer was agonizing over the scarcity of acolytes in the first scene. When the stage manager blamed the influenza epidemic, Massenet retorted, "It is strange that none of the one hundred machinists on the Opéra payroll have succumbed to it." Next, he was infuriated because the curtain got stuck at the end of the first scene. "You'll see!" he stormed. "You'll see! On opening night everything will come down but the curtain!" Then he was fuming over the puny sound of the gong. By the end of the afternoon, the reporter heard him moaning, "In the name of God! This affair will never be ready! Never! Never!"

Although the diva was rehearsing in street clothes that particular day, a week later she nearly caused the police to raid the establishment by trying out an original idea about costuming the Egyptian sinner. An Opéra official, later interviewed by a correspondent for the *Musical Courier,* described Sibyl as "sending shivers through the house during rehearsals. Her voice was electrifying and her acting even more so. She was not playing Thaïs, she was Thaïs! She came onto the stage one day [nude] under an ethereal costume of mosquito netting into which she was gummed. She was indescribably the most beautiful sight in female form I have ever seen, but that gown had to be suppressed for public performance at all costs!"[5]

Fortunately, the composer's wife was not present to witness this apparition, or Massenet could have expected more trauma at home. The controversial costume, however, created no less havoc with the orchestra. *Town Topics* reported that the musicians were so distracted that "the sight of Sibyl made it impossible to play—save at the most feverish tempo."[6]

Sanderson's forthcoming debut at the Opéra had created a furor among the city's artistic elite. Enemies were predicting that her high, liquid soprano would never carry to the rear of Garnier's auditorium. The *répétition générale* was slated for 13 March 1894, and the upper echelons of art, literature, and politics were fighting over invitations. Overcome by panic and self-doubt, Massenet hastily released a statement to the press that he was not satisfied with the complimentary tickets allotted to him and declined to attend.

> My share of author's tickets for the *répétition générale* of *Thaïs* remains, in spite of the good intentions of the directors, so inadequate in comparison to the requests I have had, I feel I must decline them. Please accept all of my regrets and apologies.
>
> J. Massenet

By the time Massenet's letter was printed, he and his wife had packed their bags and fled the city until the ordeal was over.[7]

The composer's last-minute disappearance scarcely caused a ripple among the excited Parisians. High society turned out en masse on the night of the thirteenth. The grand staircase at the Opéra was the scene of an extravagant fashion parade. Beau monde watchers were agog over the celebrities in the foyer: barons and baronesses, counts and countesses, princes and princesses, the director of the state department of fine arts, cabinet ministers, and the president of the chamber of deputies, who arrived early to welcome his guests. Everyone from Ignacy Paderewski to Madeleine Lemaire had turned out, making the audience the most brilliant of the decade. Sibyl Sanderson's name was on every lip. Would she meet her downfall?

When Paul Taffanel lifted his baton at 8 P.M. and the performance got under way, it soon became apparent why the composer had fled the scene of the crime. Evil furies were working overtime to sabotage the production. The chorus sang off pitch, stage hands kept having accidents, and the ballet dragged on interminably.

At the end of the first act, an acolyte accidentally stepped on the cloak of his predecessor, tearing it off his shoulders. The audience howled when the "monk" was revealed to be a woman clad only in flesh-colored tights. So many cenobites had been laid low by influenza that a certain dancer named Mlle Mante was drafted as a last-minute replacement. The audience was aroused by the vision of Thaïs dancing naked before the populace but still irritated because she did not appear onstage.[8] Then the curtain, just as Massenet had predicted, refused to budge at the beginning of the second scene.

Finally, the moment arrived for which everyone had been so impatiently waiting. Amid clouds of incense, the chorus acclaiming the divine Thaïs, a spotlight focused on top of some marble stairs, revealing the idol of ancient Egypt to be a glamorous blonde. According to *L'Écho de Paris*, she paused a second and "floated down the stairs like a winged Nike," throwing roses to each side of the crowd.[9]

One attendant who followed the sybarite was the lovely Cléo de Mérode, waving roses in one hand and a mask in the other. She described the diva's effect upon the audience in her memoirs: "Her beauty, her plasticity of movement, that voice of pure gold, and the joy and magnetism which emanated from her created overwhelming admiration."[10]

At the end of the first act, Thaïs did a lascivious dance entitled "Les Amours d'Aphrodite" before the monk in Nicias's palace. To accompany this pantomime, which, according to a note on the holograph, "was performed yearly at the festival of Adonis in fourth-century Alexandria," Massenet had written a seven-page symphonic poem. The highly chromatic music, which he regrettably cut from the revised edition, was the most erotic in the score. After the second page Athanaël fled the palace with a hand shielding his horrified eyes. For the rest of the poem the courtesan mounted some steps and leaned seductively against a marble pillar to watch his departure.

On this ill-fated night an incident was to occur that has become a part of opera's treasured stage lore. As the diva lifted a matchless white arm, glittering with two gold bracelets, to encircle the column, the attendants heard a light, ripping sound. One of Sanderson's shoulder straps had broken. Astonished, the girls called softly, "Mademoiselle!" But in the tumult of the whistling and screaming from the audience, Mademoiselle could not hear their voices. The frenzied spectators began to behave as if they were at the Folies Bergères, and the dancer wrote in her autobiography that "all the young girls on stage were horrified for poor Sibyl, the victim of such an awful catastrophe."

However, "poor Sibyl" was evidently enjoying herself too. There she stood against the pillar, "not moving an arm or an eyelash, holding the pose of a naked goddess." De Mérode concluded that "she was probably laughing on the inside at our childish horror."

Though everything that followed seemed anticlimactic, the evening was far from dull. A few words of the libretto, with their double entendre, provoked the next round of guffaws. Thaïs entered the stage in Act II singing, "Ah, I am so tired" after her debauchery with Nicias had run its course. But those who expected Sibyl Sanderson to fail witnessed an electrifying performance. They heard a voice that floated easily through the vast hall, one that could not only laugh effortlessly on the high Ds and E-flats, but one whose "low notes projected marvelously," according to *La Revue de Paris*.

The musical and literary controversy that ensued dominated the press for the next few days. *L'Écho de Paris* and *Gil Blas* belonged to the minority that vigorously defended the opera as "a superb work . . . a direct result in the evolution of our contemporary musical art."

The majority of the reviews condemned Massenet's harlot to the stake. Much of the hostile criticism was aimed at the libretto and the joint failure of Gallet and Massenet to retain the satiric philosophy so indigenous to Anatole France's original story.

Léon Kerst pronounced his sentence in *Le Petit journal* on 17 March.

> *Thaïs* is an enormous mistake . . . and the error springs from the false perception of the novel on the part of both the librettist and the composer. They were not aware that *Thaïs* is a satirical work. The complex character of Athanaël becomes untranslatable into the language of musical tone.

Charles Darcours complained in *Le Figaro* on 17 March that "the new opera lacks contrast and relief . . . Massenet forced his inspiration to flow too regularly this time with the repetition of stereotyped formulas." In *Le Temps* Jean Weber predicted "nothing but failure" for *Thaïs*,[11] and Félix Grenier agreed with him in *Le Journal* adding, "it is hardly probable that curiosity to see the ballet in the third act will suffice to keep this opus in the repertoire."[12]

Not all the hostile reviews blamed Louis Gallet for the failure. In *La Revue des deux mondes*[13] Camille Bellaigue declared that "if the opera didn't achieve the level of its worthy subject, it wasn't the fault of the librettist." He sneered that the work was "shabby, of vulgar paltriness, with the seedy rhythms of a dance hall composition . . . the ballet was a mediocre paraphrase of the Temptations of Saint Anthony . . . The Méditation sounded like a weak phrase from Chopin—what a nocturne for such an emotional night!" The rest of the score was dismissed as "nothing but exaggeration of artifice and manner."

On the contrary, the prima donna arose from the ashes like the phoenix itself. She was lauded as never before. The French critics unanimously admitted that the perilous debut was a triumph for the American soprano.

Le Gaulois praised the artist's enunciation as "the most perfect of any foreigner ever heard on the Parisian stage." Darcours acclaimed her interpretation in *Le Figaro*[14] as "absolute perfection, unexpectedly so." He admitted "it was feared that her voice would be too small for the huge hall, but, on the contrary, it seemed to develop into larger proportions than ever before." He praised the "spirited brilliance" with which she sang the Mirror Aria and was no less impressed by the "profound simplicity" with which she interpreted the death scene.

Charles Widor pulled out all stops in *La Revue de Paris*:

> It not only has been said that the voice of Mlle Sanderson would never carry in the Salle Garnier, but also that only her high notes would be heard in the boxes directly facing the stage . . . yet not only was the middle register of the young virtuoso strong enough in volume and fine enough in timbre, her low notes also came through marvelously. . . . Mlle Sanderson belongs to the family of great artists now, and the progress she has made during the last few years places her in the top-drawer category today.[15]

Even the soprano's old adversary Léon Kerst agreed with Widor.[16]

> We must henceforth place Mlle Sanderson in the enviable rank of true and great artists . . . her success was assured by a very exact vocal technique and merited even more by an irreproachable style . . . the exquisite doll, which is what she merely used to be, has now arrived to take her place among singers of the highest rank.

After the accident to the soprano's costume, it was expected that at least one critic would indulge in a little word play. Willy recorded the audience's unexpected delight in perusing "Mlle Seinderson [sic] naked to the waist," *sein* being the French word for breast.

Delmas was generally praised for handling his unrewarding role with "authority and intelligence," but he must have felt undeservedly stigmatized by such critical jeers as "the character of Athanaël (as conceived by Massenet) fails to exist, musically speaking."[17]

When the composer returned from Dieppe and read of Sibyl's sensational debut, he immediately sent a congratulatory telegram to Mme Marchesi. The day after his arrival in Paris, he received a summons from Messrs Bertrand and Gailhard. Filled with apprehension, he entered their office only to be greeted with vague, inaudible sighs about the disastrous dress rehearsal—"the press—immoral subject—it's done for." Gailhard managed a few coherent words.

"Alas, master," he lamented, "your beautiful *Thaïs* has made only a succès d'estime." The composer swallowed hard, trying to fight back tears of disappointment and defeat. To his credit, Massenet didn't waste any time on self-pity; he had only forty-eight hours to make serious revisions suggested to him by both the managers and the press. The scene with Athanaël alone in the desert was drastically changed. The monk's pantomime with his cup of life's impurities under the Star of Redemption was dropped because of complaints about its ambiguity.

As for the ballet of temptation, Massenet had wanted a fantasy of macabre specters and apparitions with a constantly changing play of light on the stage to haunt the monk in his dream sequence.[18] It was a scene of allegorical pantomime, not the divertissement that had been the standard conception of ballet in Paris ever since the time of Louis XIV. Gailhard argued that Massenet's complex lighting demands made the stage too dangerous for his swirling dancers to perform on, and too nebulous for the audience to follow the action. Massenet quickly shortened the ballet, only to drop it permanently on 9 April. Opéra officials substituted an exotic one from their own repertoire, *La Korrigane,* which was used for the rest of the year. After the managers informed him of the derision that greeted Thaïs's opening phrase in Act II, Massenet changed the words to "Ah, I am alone at last . . . "

The March 16 premiere was far more successful than the *représentation générale,* and charged with excitement because the directors were known to have received an anonymous bomb threat if they did not halt the performance. Taking no chances on certain religious fanatics who objected to the "immorality" of the opera, Bertrand and Gailhard packed the fifth tier of the house with plainclothes policemen from the arson squad. They need not have worried; no anarchists appeared. Everything went off smoothly this time. The stage machinery functioned well, and Massenet's modifications to the score were praised by Charles Widor as "making the work more cohesive." Again the production was hailed as an "immense success" for its heroine who resembled "an animated marble figurine" according to *La Revue de Paris.*

In 1959 Florence Turner Maley, who had attended the premiere, recalled to the author that when the composer appeared onstage afterward clasping his prima donna's hand, the audience gave them a standing ovation. "There were four of us American girls in a box," she reminisced, "thanks to the largess of a French doctor, and we just clapped our hands off! My! She certainly put that role over. . . . She seemed so natural on the stage . . . We were so thrilled that an American could receive such adulation from the French . . . I remember going back to my little room and writing her a fan letter."[19]

The press was no less feverish than the public. French newspapers were convinced that Sibyl was born to re-create all the famous courtesans in history. They erupted with so many superlatives about her mastery of such plastic poses as the contrapposto (S-curve) that today one can only conclude she had become one of the art nouveau deities of Paris. The following appeared in *Le Figaro* the day after the dress rehearsal:

> Thaïs-Sanderson—she is the goddess of kisses—a goddess whose milk-white arms of such perfect symmetry open and close for irresistible raptures . . . her shoulders are a delicate cluster of rose-white flesh tinted by the painter, Gérôme, himself . . . her breasts are two endless fountains of pure intoxication . . . her eyes dart their fires more brilliantly than the opal . . . within their enormous violet orbs even new ecstasies lie dormant and waiting . . . her head is crowned with golden tresses as radiant as those of Aphrodite herself when she rose from the waves in days of old.[20]

While Paris was burning incense before its American idol, misfortune continued to prey upon the cast of *Thaïs*. In the latter part of March, Alvarez lost his young bride to diphtheria, and the tenor was replaced by Vaguet in the role of Nicias.

A few weeks later, Giuseppe Verdi and his librettist Arrigo Boito arrived in Paris for the French premiere of their *Falstaff*, a visit duly noted by the Parisian press. The dean of Italian opera was now eighty and looking more distinguished than ever with his tall, spartan figure crowned by a head of flowing white hair and framed by a meticulously trimmed beard. During the final weeks of his operatic rehearsals, he accepted an invitation from the Opéra managers to hear Massenet's controversial opus. After the final curtain the Italian composer and his collaborator were taken backstage to meet Massenet and the cast. Verdi cordially autographed Sibyl's score of *Rigoletto,* and both musicians gave her autographed pictures. Verdi's private opinion of the work, however, has not been recorded for posterity.

Perhaps Verdi was fortunate to have heard the opera when he did. Four years later Massenet published his revised edition, which contained some curious changes—not always for the better. Besides witnessing the heroine's erotic dance to *Les Amours d'Aphrodite,* the Italian master listened to Thaïs softly utter her supplication to Venus in the Mirror Aria as she warbled those haunting roulades later to be transposed for the clarinet. He heard a short but impassioned aria, "Oui, je suis fou," sung by a deranged Athanaël, which Massenet would soon eliminate. But beyond this, Verdi was present for the most controversial moment of all, a startling, dissonant conclusion to the opera that the composer later chose to dilute. As the frenzied monk hurled himself upon the dead Thaïs, screaming "pity me," a high male voice offstage sang "Away with you, vampire, away!" A second later a harsh female voice from the opposite wing echoed the words an augmented seventh above the tenor. It was one of Massenet's most powerful and original ideas, yet he allowed his accursed desire to please to supersede a moment of theatrical genius merely because it shocked the public.

In contrast to those who faulted Massenet's librettist for the critical failure of the opera, a singular voice stood out—and an American one, at that. In a provocative letter published 4 April 1894, Miss Fanny Edgar Thomas, the new correspondent for the *Musical Courier,* chastised the composer for painting his picture to fit the frame.

Thaïs is not a feeble work. There is some beautiful inspiration . . . and much that is above the ordinary . . . but you leave disappointed, and the causes undoubtedly are that Massenet has written his opera for one woman. Inspiration brooks no control, it must have freedom, and Massenet, believing otherwise, shows his folly in *Thaïs* . . . I wish you could see Sibyl Sanderson in her courtesan roles of Phryné and Thaïs. Sense and reason give way before it. You can stand it while she sings, you can even criticize a voice far from perfect, but when (you fancy so, as you see her act, it is so real) she turns to you in her own admirable way and begins to bring one after another of her charming tricks of seduction into play, you have no other alternative but to fly—if you can! Figuratively speaking, Massenet has not flown, *he has laid genius at the feet of the beautiful California siren!* I doubt if anything lovelier in the shape of woman could be imagined . . . It is a pity, since outside of her adorable beauty Sibyl Sanderson is but a mediocre actress and far from great as a singer . . . To write an opera for her, Massenet is forced to descend to her level. He paints his picture to suit the canvas and cripples his inspiration and his art thereby . . . but Massenet needs to forget himself and all outside influences . . . I feel sure if he could . . . go off to some retired spot and write what his inspiration guided him to, our art would gain and his would be great.

Miss Thomas's powerful remarks had given her American readers a mouthful to digest. Although determined to resist the siren's enticements, it wasn't long before she would reverse her opinion and become one of the soprano's most militant champions.

If the score as a whole measured up to the duet in the last act, which the composer set against the background of the Méditation, *Thaïs* could rank with *Werther* and *Manon*. Besides too many sequential formulas and too much dialogue between the protagonists on a single note, the basic problem with the opera is its stark dichotomy of character: the monk's unrelenting austerity versus the cloying sensuality of the harlot, with scarcely any middle ground between these polarities.

On the other hand, Massenet need not apologize to posterity for the monk's exciting aria, "Voilà donc la terrible cité," and Thaïs's seductive hymn to love, "Qui te fait si sévère." They rank among the opera's most worthy moments, in addition to the superb Oasis tableau, a later addition to the work.

Any discussion of the opera cannot be concluded without a word about its world-famous melody, the "Méditation." Suffice it to say that in spite of its frankly saccharine theme, Massenet developed it with consummate skill and craftsmanship. Ernest Newman annihilated its detractors when he wrote, "It is precisely in some such silken, caressing terms as these that a Thaïs would embrace a new faith."

Thaïs is far from a dated period piece. The lyric drama of the penitent who gains her soul and the evangelist who loses his is as relevant today as it was at the turn of the twentieth century. The pagan temptress is still awaiting many exciting reincarnations.

Chapter 20

The Golden Calf

The Grand Prix commenced on Friday, 17 June 1894 and lasted for three days. All society flocked to the opening of the races at Longchamp, then to a spectacular ball on Saturday night. On Sunday afternoon the fashionable carriage parade known as the Grand Prix de Drag took the rich and famous from Longchamp to the Bois before they left the city on vacation. The side-walks were jammed with the less favored: merchants, artisans, the petit bourgeois, children, and visitors all straining to catch a glimpse of the passing celebrities.

Returning from the racetrack that afternoon in the stream of elite carriages was a dark-blue landau with stern lackeys and a sleekly groomed pair of prancing horses. With its violet-eyed occupant, gowned in shades of gentian blue that complimented her bright blond hair, it was attracting attention rivaling that paid to President Carnot's carriage. The tip of a patent-leather pump could be seen peeping coyly from beneath the hem of her skirts, and a graceful arm was supporting her parasol in the most approved fashion. Beside her sat a tall, dark gentleman in top hat and cutaway coat. The two carriages continued at a parallel pace, then stopped because of traffic congestion. When the president rose and bowed to the lady, the crowd emitted a roar of recognition and cries of "Vive!" to both parties. "It was the reigning queen of song," wrote Fanny Edgar Thomas to the *Musical Courier,* 12 July 1894, "the Lillian Russell of Paris—Sibyl Sanderson!"

Sanderson had all but burned Paris to the ground that spring. Her one-woman campaign had successfully nullified the adverse criticisms of *Thaïs* and saved the work from extinction. Every performance was sold out and the Opéra continued to bask in unprecedented ticket sales. "All Paris," admitted

Miss Thomas, "crowds to see her remarkable beauty (on stage) as much as to hear her."

Newspapers and magazines from all over the world were clamoring for interviews. Jules Huret tantalized Parisians in the 17 March 1894 edition of *Le Figaro* by mentioning that she had received him "in a form-fitting negligée of black lace with ropes of rare pearls hanging over her ravishing bust." The public learned such breathtaking trivia as the fact that she was one hundred and fifty-two centimeters in height; she wore a five-and-three-fourths-centimeter glove; her favorite authors were de Musset and de Maupassant; and she refused to sing at funerals or tell the name of her perfume.

When asked who her favorite people were, she replied, "The French, at present, I adore them . . . you know it is because I am very Parisian at heart, myself. Much more than many real Parisians." Whose music did Mademoiselle prefer to sing? Laughing, she replied, "Everybody's, of course." Her favorite country would be anyplace where there are "no cows, pigs, or manure." As for romance, Huret made a mysterious reference to "a grand American gentleman with a bouquet of cornflowers in his lapel who interspersed remarks in English from time to time and laughed heartily at some of the questions."

Fanny Edgar Thomas seemed surprised at her first interview to discover that "she is not nearly as tall as she looks on the stage . . . every line on her is a curve, her expression is enfantine. She has the same satisfactory fitness of clothing and perfect figure that are some of Lillian Russell's chief claims: the same complexion, the same self-contained conscious unconsciousness of being observed at all times, and the same surprise of bright intelligence in a pretty woman. Even the few sentences in a drawing room show a mind active, not forceful certainly, but not weak either. Whatever she may be on intimate acquaintance, she certainly can be all that is charming in manner. Costumer, teachers and photographers all adore her . . . Massenet tells me that at first hearing he had no idea she would become the diva she is today."[1]

Emma Bullit of the *Brooklyn Eagle* described Sanderson as having "a will which removes mountains of difficulties and if there are some mountains which do not allow themselves to be removed, she merely jumps over them . . . near her favorite chair in her drawing room stands a reduction of the famous Victoire de Samothrace . . . I told her that in the first act of *Thaïs* when she floats down the stairs with a light dancing step, she reminds me instantly of that winged woman."[2]

An English reporter from the *St. James Gazette* found himself temporarily barred from the Sanderson parlor by Sibyl's standard poodle, Manon, until he had shaken her paw. "The more I succeed, the more my audiences expect of me, and, naturally, the more nervous I become, "she confessed after ordering Manon to stop pestering the writer. "It frightens me to realize how much more is expected of the creator of *Esclarmonde* and *Thaïs* than Ada Palmer, the unknown girl who sang *Manon* at The Hague just a few years ago."

When the emissary from the *California Argonaut* arrived, he was conducted on a tour of the soprano's home together with reporters from Boston and Chicago. The house was set so close to the street that there was scarcely room to stand inside the little gate before the maid opened the door. The writer noticed that all the windows consisted of tiny panes, each with a border of red glass. In the hall he espied a newly installed luxury, the telephone, as well as a gong that Sibyl's mother used to communicate with the servants. On the right of the foyer were two reception rooms; one contained an Érard piano; resting on a little table beside it were two volumes of music bound in blue Moroccan leather—the original edition of *Manon* with a three-page dedication from the composer. The furniture was described as "massive pieces of rosewood in the Gothic revival." A sweet but subtly mysterious perfume pervaded the entire main floor. On the floor above the rez-de-chaussée were the bedrooms of the singer and her mother. Above that were the apartments occupied by the younger sisters. The first room was Marion's studio, the next her small boudoir, and the others were bedrooms. If any of the reporters stumbled upon the fact that the siren of old Alexandria was secretly imbibing, they made no allusion to it in their articles.

Offstage, the diva reigned over military balls, appeared with such stars of the legitimate stage as Réjane (Gabrielle Reju) and Sarah Bernhardt on benefit programs, and sang at receptions for the Faubourg-St. Germain aristocracy. When she endorsed a corset called "Phryné, the One and Only," the boulevardiers snickered in amusement; rumor had it that she never wore any.

It would be inaccurate to believe that there was never any jealousy or enmity toward the American soprano in the French capital. To the majority of Parisians Sibyl Sanderson dwelt on Parnassus, but there always existed a small core of envious artists, students, and teachers. They claimed her success would last only as long as Massenet continued to write roles to fit her voice and temperament. They jealously thirsted for the day when she would appear in a standard work from the Opéra repertoire in which she could be compared to past interpreters. What a disaster she would be! Sibyl Sanderson unmasked as an inferior artist at last!

The envious did not have long to wait before Sanderson put their hypothesis to the test. Opéra officials announced that she would make her Parisian debut in Gounod's *Roméo et Juliette* on 1 June 1894. The performance was sold out within hours; at last she faced the decisive test of her artistry.

When the soprano received a reporter from *Le Gaulois* two days before her debut, she announced she "had worked very hard on the role," that she was "enormously fond of it," and that "to sing it constitutes a true joy for an artist." Sibyl confided that Gounod had "adored" her and that she had last worked with him just ten days before his death on 18 October 1893. She also disclosed that Mme Gounod had attended the last rehearsals (at her request) to advise her on interpretative details. When the interview was over, Sibyl invited the reporter and her colleague Emma Eames to the house of Doucet, where she was to be photographed in her costumes by acclaimed portrait photographer Léopold-Emile Reutlinger.

The reporter gasped at her ball gown, which was a ravishing specimen of Genes velvet, almond and green, embroidered all over with lotus flowers and strands of pearls, and cinctured with a large, jewel-studded belt. For the balcony scene Sibyl donned a flowing violet and turquoise creation. After glimpsing the raiment designed for the tomb scene everyone present agreed that no Juliette in history had ever died in more splendor, and that none ever would. Doucet had created a gown of brocaded silver lamé, embroidered in turquoise, and emblazoned with diamonds and pearls. Over it would be worn a rich court robe of brocaded satin. The costumers seemed determined that Sibyl's audience should gaze upon her through the eyes of none other than Romeo himself. No mention was made that Sanderson's entire salary that year would barely cover the cost of such a luxurious turnout.

On Thursday night, 1 June, a brilliant audience crowded the Opéra for the revival, eager to see how their lyric goddess would compare to the great interpreters of the past: Mme Miolan-Carvalho (who created the role), Patti, and Nellie Melba. A superb cast had been assembled. The lusty-throated Alvarez was to sing Romeo, Jean-François Delmas would portray Capulet, Gibert was cast as Tybalt, and Noté as Mercutio. It was no wonder that the box-office receipts were reported to be over 22,000 francs, the largest sum ever recorded for the work to that date. In spite of a temporary indisposition that gripped the soprano in the middle of the performance, Sanderson scored a pronounced success with an avalanche of bouquets hurled at her feet, ovations, crowns, and recalls.

On 2 June 1894 the critic of *L'Éclair* observed that "shortly after a brilliant execution of the Waltz Song, which took the audience by storm, Sanderson was suddenly seized with a vocal constricture which seemed to partially throttle her middle register for a while and produce some notes of dubious pitch, but she recovered to sing the final scenes like the consummate artist she is." Charles Darcours wrote on the same day in *Le Figaro:* "This young lady, already so well received and beloved by the Parisian public, conquered an even greater place in its favor yesterday by the charm and grace with which she interpreted the role."

Le Gaulois of 2 June 1894 paid her the following tribute: "The actress and singer were exquisitely combined last night—this adorable historical figure for which the poet and musician could not dream of a more perfect interpreter from all points of view." Alvarez was praised as "a truly magnificent Romeo." Acclaiming her "dramatic recitatives" and her "unusually expressive gestures," in *Le Journal* of the same date, Félix Regnier pronounced Sibyl "a captivating Juliette" but admitted that "she was not always in complete possession of her vocal powers."

In spite of a few minor reservations, not one critic had denied the diva's victory. Only Sibyl herself knew how narrowly she had avoided disaster. All spring the soprano had been drinking precariously while treading the perilous tightrope of success. It is quite possible that after her brilliant first act, an anxiety attack may have caused her to resort to stimulants in her dressing room, followed by nausea and stomach cramps. It had happened so many times before that even her maid had lost count. The more the audience demanded from her, the more compulsively she rushed to her flask to seek the solace of its perfidious strength. At any rate the next performance was postponed until 13 June because of Sibyl's mysterious "indisposition."

On Sunday, 12 June, she was well enough to accept the Countess Greffuhle's invitation to appear at a star-studded memorial concert for Gounod at the Opéra, and the following night she again sang Juliette with Albert Saléza replacing Alvarez as Romeo. The latter had hastily departed for London, where he was shortly to costar with Emma Calvé in the world premiere of Massenet's *La navarraise.*

Albert Saléza, a Sephardic Jew from southern France, was an operatic Adonis who kept challenging Jean de Reszke's unrivaled suzerainty over the feminine heart. If his lyric art could not match the power of the Polish tenor, he did not deserve the epithet of "Mlle Jeanette de Reszke," which he was given by the latter's sarcastic fans.

Saléza's first appearance with Sanderson held the audience spellbound. Rarely had two artists interpreted their roles so sensitively; rarely had the blending of two voices revealed so many hidden beauties in a score. Hailing them as "the ideal couple to portray the ill-starred lovers from Verona," the press acclaimed their interpretation as "a veritable triumph for both singers." The spurious predictions of the diva's enemies had been sealed in the very tomb where Juliette expired. Her brilliant portrayal of Shakespeare's heroine had placed her among the foremost artists in Europe. The lips of the jealous were silenced, it seemed, for all time.

Sibyl Sanderson was now at the height of her career, the first American singer to conquer Paris. The city was worshipping her as its Golden Calf. The press burned incense before her altar; the public lavished its shekels upon her temple. The Sanderson cult had become the topic of newspaper discussion on two continents. It was only natural that New Yorkers were clamoring to hear her. Why hadn't this queen of French lyric drama ever been heard at the Metropolitan? She had been voted one of the twelve best-dressed women in France and hailed as one of the most polished actresses on the European operatic stage, but still she was an unknown quantity in her native land.

It was no surprise in international theatrical circles when Maurice Grau, the shrewd little manager of the Metropolitan, bowed to public pressure and made a trip to Paris to engage her. Negotiations were opened the last week in May, and Grau was extravagant in his promises. He would produce *Manon, Thaïs, Esclarmonde,* and *Phryné* for her. She could have her choice of any other role she wanted. He was prepared to offer her a handsome fee. After several previous proposals from him that she had deemed unsatisfactory, Sibyl felt both flattered and elated. The drawbridge to the Metropolitan was being lowered at last. Overwhelmed by his lofty assurances, she signed a contract in June to take her first bow at the Metropolitan the following season and tour the United States afterward with Grau's company.

Romantic hearsay also kept her in the international eye. On 24 May 1894, *Le Journal* created a sensation when it announced that Sibyl Sanderson would shortly reveal her engagement to a member of the Vanderbilt family. The news threw the American colony into an uproar and was reprinted in all the New York papers the next day. The prima donna was forced to call a press conference in her home on the 25th. "I have never known anyone named Vanderbilt and I am not betrothed to anyone," she insisted. Then the singer laughingly added, "You may say I am wedded to my art and hope to remain so."

Massenet returned from London, where he had spent the greater part of June overseeing the rehearsals for the triumphant premiere of his *La navarraise.* To stop the boulevardiers from observing that his inspiration needed the constant spur of Sibyl Sanderson's charms, he discreetly dedicated the new work to his wife.

The composer, flushed with victory over the success of his newest opera, had not been home long before he received a *petit bleu* (message by pneumatic post) from his lyric priestess. She wished to see him on some urgent business in his studio. The master was simmering with curiosity when he received her. His spies (Heugel employees) had informed him that the carriage of Sibyl's suitor was at the Opéra stage door every night she sang.

Sibyl informed her mentor that she had signed a contract with the Metropolitan, where she was scheduled to appear in the French premiere of *Manon* the following winter. She requested musical recitatives from him to replace the old spoken dialogue; under no circumstances did she wish a repetition of the Covent Garden fiasco. Massenet was all smiles and assurances. Of course, he would construct special recitatives for her.[3] Inwardly, he was torn by mixed emotions on the subject. While he wanted the opera to succeed on the large stage of the Metropolitan, he was secretly opposed to altering the original structure of the work.

Massenet could hardly wait to question her about the matrimonial rumors that had received such wide circulation. Sibyl denied them, explaining that too many problems stood in the way. Currently she was bound by her contract at the Opéra and in the midst of negotiations to obtain a leave of absence for her upcoming American tour. The composer remained skeptical. He had met Sibyl's swain at the premiere of *Thaïs,* and now the couple were reported to be altar bound by summer.

After her final appearance in *Thaïs* the first week in July, Sanderson left for Switzerland with her wealthy admirer and the Massenets departed for Brittany. It seemed strange not to accompany his protégée to Vevey anymore nor to be drilling her in her latest role. In his unique way the composer had loved her above all other women. He had worshipped at her shrine and laid his genius on its altar. Now he was losing her, and he couldn't help feeling resentful and bitter. Knowing only too well how Massenet reacted when he felt betrayed, his enemies could have issued a collective warning: *prends garde* (beware)!

Chapter 21

Grape Leaves and Fillies

When the news of Sibyl's betrothal hit the Paris edition of the *New York Herald* the last Saturday in August 1894, it came as no surprise to Massenet. The *Herald* had scooped the romance of the year: SIBYL SANDERSON IS ENGAGED TO A WEALTHY CUBAN—THE WIFE OF ANTONIO TERRY PLANS DIVORCE PROCEEDINGS. In a few hours cables to the American papers were relaying a hundred breathless details:

> Mrs. Silas Sanderson has announced the engagement of her daughter Miss Sibyl Sanderson to Don Antonio Terry, son of the late Tomaso Terry y Adan . . . Mr. Terry is an enormously wealthy Cuban planter. The news has come as a genuine surprise to the many friends and numerous acquaintances of the bride-groom elect in New York City.
>
> For some time Mr. Terry has lived abroad, principally in Paris. It was reported a few days ago that Mrs. Grace Dalton Terry, wife of Mr. Terry, who has also lived in Paris for some years but apart from her husband, has begun divorce proceedings in Paris naming two correspondents. The next hearing of the case is fixed for 31 August.
>
> Mr. Antonio Terry is one of the sons of Señor Tomaso Terry who left, at his death in 1886, a fortune amounting to something like fifty or sixty million dollars to be divided among his six surviving children . . .
>
> By the terms of his father's will, Antonio will come into the possession of a large sum of money in Spanish gold, a sugar plantation in Cuba known as "Juragua a la Caudal" and a residuary in the estate with the other surviving children upon the death of their mother.
>
> Mr. Terry was married in 1876 in New York City to Miss Grace Dalton Secor, an orphan niece of lawyer William H. Secor. The bridegroom was only

twenty years old at this time and his bride was two years younger. For some time the young couple lived in apparent happiness, and a daughter was born to them in 1881. The husband, however, had always been accounted a "high liver," and rumor soon began to link his name with that of actress Sadie Martinot. By an agreement made 4 February 1887, a separation by mutual consent was affected between Mr. and Mrs. Terry; he, agreeing to settle $6,000 per year upon her, with an extra $2,000 yearly to cover the expenses of his daughter's education. Later Mrs. Terry decided to bring proceedings for divorce and an action was begun on 12 September 1887, but in a few days the suit was dropped. Both Mr. and Mrs. Terry went abroad soon after this and have lived apart ever since.

Sibyl, who had been dividing her vacation between Switzerland and the Brittany seacoast, was besieged by reporters at the American Club in Dinard. They quoted her as saying, "I only expect to be in Paris a short time before sailing for America . . . but if the divorce suit should be concluded before my New York engagement, I will marry Mr. Terry immediately."

In an interview with the *New York Herald,* Mrs. Terry confirmed its report that she would consent to a quiet divorce if "proper settlements were made upon herself and her daughter." The word "proper" covered a vast abyss of speculation.

It is not known how the diva met her Prince Charming. His own daughter was never informed, and neither did Marion Sanderson mention it in her private reminiscences. In its subsequent story on Sibyl's romances, the Hearst syndicate disclosed that Terry first heard the singer at the premiere of *Esclarmonde* in 1889 and promptly lost his heart to her.[1] It is possible they could have met at that time, but not until the winter of 1893–94 did Terry begin his courtship. It is more probable that they were introduced in the artists' loge of the Opéra-Comique during the two hundredth performance of *Manon* on 16 October 1893. Undoubtedly, Terry was the gentleman who escorted her a few weeks later to a Thomas festival at the Opéra-Comique.

Antonio Eusebio Terry was a six-foot Cuban lady-killer and one of the most lavish spenders of his time. Marion Sanderson has described him as "simply the handsomest man in Paris." His mustache was meticulously curled into two handlebars of jet; his heavily pomaded hair was usually parted in the middle. Two flashing dark eyes dominated a square-jawed face of olive complexion, and they were truly the *ojos negros* of Latin lore. He exuded an indolent sensuality, and his female conquests were flaunted as boldly as the cornflowers he wore in his lapel.

The New York newspaper accounts of the Terry family history were far from accurate. Tomaso Terry had been the prototype for his playboy son with one single exception: he was a shrewd businessman. The old Irish Cuban had not only accumulated a fortune; he knew how to hold on to it. Every time a rebellion erupted on the island, he managed to stay on the winning side of the uprising. Although thousands of acres of sugar cane might go up in flames, his fields were never touched. Tomaso's known progeny by his wife numbered somewhere close to a dozen. His illegitimate offspring were rumored to comprise at least another dozen. He was an avid devotee of the stage, and before his death had bequeathed an exquisitely designed theater (which still stands today) to the inhabitants of Cienfuegos. Among his legitimate heirs were sons Alfonso-Francisco, Andres, Juan Pedro, and Emilio, and a daughter, Mrs. Perina, most of whom now lived in Paris. Francisco and Emilio were negotiating to buy the famous Château de Chenonceaux, which Henry II originally built for his mistress, Diane de Poitiers. After a scandalous marriage, Juan Pedro had recently died. Another daughter, Natividad, had married the Baron Blanc, the longtime Italian ambassador to United States, during the 1880s. At present, the Baron was the minister of finance to the Crispi government in Italy. Antonio, the youngest, was born 14 August 1857 in Cienfuegos. Thoroughly spoiled by his older brothers and sisters, the mischievous youngster was his mother's raison d'être.

The fact that various family members had not been summoned to sit at the right hand of God was a mere celestial oversight in Señora Terry's mind. Teresa Terry y d'Orticos was convinced her offspring were of divine origin. No son- or daughter-in-law, if not of Spanish blood, was even worthy to wash their feet. Throughout her extraordinarily long life of ninety-seven years, the Terry matriarch instilled in her children the concept of Latin supremacy and an instinctive hatred of Anglo-Saxon culture.

As a teenager, the Baroness Blanc had attended an exclusive private school in New York City thanks to the insistence of her half-Irish father. One of her classmates was a beautiful orphan girl with periwinkle blue eyes and windblown hair the color of corn silk. Her name was Grace Dalton, and she was the ward of her uncle, William H. Secor, a prominent barrister. One fatal weekend, Natividad Terry introduced the girl to her impetuous brother, and from the moment Tony gazed into those blue eyes he was lost. The excitable Latin began an ardent pursuit. After a whirlwind courtship, their lavish wedding at the church of Saint Vincent de Paul was one of the big social events of 1876. The newlyweds made their home in a handsome brownstone on New York's fashionable Fifth Avenue, just a few blocks from the gigantic Vanderbilt palace in the sixties.

It was there in 1881 that their only child was born. Named after her aunt and godmother, the Baroness Blanc, she was christened Natividad Marta Maria Dolores Mercedes Terry. After saddling his daughter with such a lengthy list of names, it was not surprising that Tony later decided upon "Natica" as an affectionate sobriquet.

For a while, the young parents were a highly popular couple in New York society. No fashionable party was complete without them. They often went to the theater, and it wasn't long before Tony's roving eye began to ogle one lovely actress after another. He became increasingly bored and irritated with his domestic tranquility. The glamorous star Sadie Martinot provided just the kind of diversion Tony was seeking. Their flaming liaison soon became the scandal of New York. Only when the avaricious Sadie had taken her lover for a fraction of her weight in diamond bracelets did the affair grow stale. By then the pattern of Terry's love life had been established: he was chasing every female whose name happened to adorn a marquee.

Although Mrs. Terry had been reared a strict Catholic, it was inevitable that her humiliation sooner or later would reach the saturation point. In February 1887 she sued for separate maintenance. By that time Tomaso Terry had died, leaving his heirs a virtual monopoly on the sugar trade of Cuba. The entire clan immediately forsook the shores of the American continent for permanent residence in Paris. Even New York had become too provincial for them. Of course, it was necessary for the sons to make periodic business trips back to Cuba, which was still the source of their income. Years later, Antonio Terry's daughter, the Princess de Lucinge, made no apologies when, in a personal interview, she summed up the Terrys as "a thoroughly dreadful family." According to her, they were always quarreling and fighting among themselves over three commodities: money, horses, and women. And precisely in that order.

It would seem as if the first Mrs. Terry, now legally separated from her husband, should have been delighted to be separated from him in terms of distance as well. This was not to be the case. Instead, the neglected woman astonished her friends by joining the collective exodus to Paris with her young daughter. She seemed to derive some kind of masochistic pleasure from remaining on the periphery of her philandering husband's turf.

In Paris Tony's behavior grew more profligate every year. His entire life was devoted to playing the horses by day and wooing stage beauties by night. He had won the acclamation of the international sporting world by introducing the first trotters to France and soon began to breed them at his stud farm in Vaucreson. Every night his elegant victoria was at the stage door of some young starlet such as Mlle Aymand or Marie Alemayne. It wasn't long before he boldly climbed the theatrical ladder to pursue more famous names. He wrangled an introduction to the beauteous Lillie Langtry, whom he temporarily distracted with a shower of diamond-sprinkled bouquets and diamond-studded corsages. The toast of the British Empire was impressed. For a while she found him not only an amusing spender but also a highly entertaining suitor.

After their affair had run its course, the stagestruck Cuban began devoting all his attention to another "pearl diver," the notorious Spanish dancer, *la belle Otero*. At least they had one thing in common: the same explosive Latin temperament. When their tempestuous liaison was over, Tony was lucky to have escaped with his life. Not only had her expensive tastes bankrupted several European fortunes, Otero watched one of her discarded lovers commit suicide in her boudoir while she heartlessly filed her fingernails.[2]

Perhaps it was inevitable that the California Venus and the Cuban Casanova should succumb to a mutual attraction. Each of them possessed a warm, impulsive personality. Both were generous to a fault.[3] Not only did they share a mutual disregard for frugality, they also seemed to radiate a mutual, if fatal, magnetism. Her star was at its zenith in the lyric firmament. She was an exotic jewel he must add to his collection, no matter what the cost. As for Sibyl, her hard-won position as queen of song deserved a lavish courtship by someone with Terry's means. He was her Lancelot, her Galahad—a composite of all the legendary romantic heroes of literature.

It wasn't long before Tony's impetuous charm and generosity were working their spell upon Sibyl's family. Anything the Sanderson girls liked in his home on the rue Villajuste was theirs for the asking. If Marion admired some spectacular antique picture frames, they would arrive at 46 avenue Malakoff the next morning by messenger.

In addition to his famed appetite for women, the prodigal Latin was also a splendid epicure. His table boasted the finest in food and wine. Showing guests the rare vintages in his wine cellar was a constant delight to him. His reputation as a raconteur invariably rivaled his image as a bon vivant. Tony's pet theory about the creation of the world had its origin in the tale about a giant monkey called "The Great Komonka" who sported a ruby in its tail.[4] After dinner while sipping coffee in the drawing room, Tony would entertain Sibyl's sisters with the latest installment of this legend.

Had Sibyl been at all capable of self-preservation, she would have fled as far as Bora Bora if necessary. The man she envisioned as a knight of King Arthur's court was really a follower of Dionysus in a perpetual quest for pleasure and sensual delight. Sexual indulgence may have been the least of his derelictions. His penchant for alcohol and overeating could debilitate him more thoroughly than any recourse to a brothel. He was exactly the type of suitor her late father would have abhorred.

By September she had yielded to one of Terry's most adamant demands and announced her intention of retiring from the stage after their marriage. There can be no doubt that her future plans wounded Massenet to the core. His worst fears were about to come true, but he bore his anguish in uneasy silence. This Cuban menace had to be removed from his protégée's life at all costs. Already his Machiavellian brain was concocting the most diabolical scheme of his career.

After approximately four months of idle socializing in various resorts, Sanderson returned to the Opéra on 7 November in *Thaïs* with Jean Bartet as her new Athanaël. One of her most faithful admirers, Charles Darcours, did not exactly turn somersaults in *Le Figaro* the next day: "While the queen of beauty warbles with a certain charm which is hers alone, she has sung the role with a fuller and more ample voice earlier this year."

His shrewd observation confirmed the opinions of more than one musical sophisticate. Sanderson had strayed from Mme Marchesi's fold and was backsliding toward some of her old, faulty musical habits. Just a season before, she had gratefully sworn allegiance to her mentor in these lines:

> Dearest Madame,
> I am indeed happy to be able to add my name to the long list of pupils who have profited by your precious counsels, but unlike them I hope never to say adieu to my lessons with you. I shall always come to you, dearest of friends to me, for the guidance in my art which you have so generously given me, and which I do so deeply appreciate.
>
> Ever yours, lovingly and devotedly,
> Sibyl Sanderson

No one could have been more sincere than Sibyl when she wrote these lines, but the singer should have omitted the word "never" from her vocabulary. Too often, she would do exactly what she had sworn not to do. She hadn't set foot in Marchesi's studio for months, and since spring Madame had witnessed a disturbing change in her behavior. Ever since the beginning of her relationship with Terry, Sibyl seemed to be assuming more and more of Manon's personality in real life. When the diva should have been practicing hard and reviewing this operatic score to adapt her role to a large stage, she was indulging herself on the social circuit: the races in the afternoon, followed by dinner in some terribly chic place such as the Jockey Club, where Tony was a charter member. Hadn't Manon sung to her admirers, "Let ours be sweet love and fair roses now . . . who knows if we shall live to see tomorrow?"

Marchesi had warned Sibyl that she could not serve both Mammon and art. But her protestations went unheeded; already the seeds of self-destruction were being sewn. A few years after Sibyl's death, Madame was to comment sadly, "She took her career and threw it out the window with both hands."[5]

Massenet was not present for Sanderson's return to the footlights. He and his wife were in Milan, where he was overseeing rehearsals for the Italian premiere of *La navarraise* that month. If he was perturbed about Sibyl's future matrimonial plans, he did not betray it in his letter to Margaret dated 26 November 1894.

> Chère Madame,
> I have been thinking since I am far from Paris that you may have forgotten me, so I have decided to come knocking at the door of your memory. I am anxious to know if you and your daughters are well, particularly Mlle Sibyl. I am busy at the theater here every day. I am aware that Mlle Sibyl has already played Thaïs twice since her return. I am so happy about it. My wife and I have congratulated her by letter and with roses. It is nothing, but it will serve as a token of my regard.
>
> > With all my heart,
> > Massenet

Hastily scribbled on the back of the letter was this postscript:

> TO READ FIRST
> At the moment when I was ready to post this letter I learned of the schedule of Mlle Sibyl; the Opéra announces *Thaïs* again for tomorrow evening. What courage and devotion are hers, and with what gratitude I send my thoughts to her. Tell her this quickly before the time of her entrance onto the stage.

In spite of the composer's reference to his wife, Margaret was well aware that Louise Massenet had not participated in her husband's congratulatory gesture to his lyric goddess. And his polite inquiry about Sibyl's health was a veiled expression of his concern about her sobriety. All year he had watched her increasing alcoholic sprees with growing concern.

It is interesting to note that Massenet made no mention of whether he had completed the new *Manon* recitatives that Sibyl had requested for her New York debut. Shortly after his return to Paris in early December, Sanderson visited his studio only to receive the most fervent reassurances. The recitatives were not only finished but had been personally expressed to Maurice Grau at the Metropolitan. Massenet had already given her the holograph to study. Lulled into a false sense of security, Sibyl could almost sense an American victory within her grasp.

The soprano continued to keep *Thaïs* before the public until her last appearance on 28 December, which marked the twenty-seventh performance of the work in its first year. Bertrand and Gailhard had granted her a six month's leave of absence for her American sojourn, and she was not due to return until 1 June 1895.

On 14 December, Sanderson attended an event celebrating the one thousandth performance of *Faust* at the Opéra, costumed as Juliette. Afterward she joined Rose Caron, Lucienne Bréval, Alvarez, Delmas, and other artists who were to impersonate Gounod's various operatic characters at the unveiling of his statue by Falguière in the foyer. For one indelible hour the audience witnessed a spellbinding scene. All Gounod's heroes and heroines—from Baucis and Sapho to Friar Laurence and Mireille—were incarnated about the figure of the composer, singing his most beloved themes.

Early on the morning of 30 December, Sanderson departed for Le Havre, where she would immediately sail for New York. Her party included her maid Lina, her sister Jane, and Fanny Reed's sister—an internationally known society queen—Mrs. Paran Stevens. Margaret's health had been too unstable that fall for her to attempt the ocean voyage, but she adamantly demanded that Sibyl enlist the company of this famous doyenne because Sir Lancelot had also insisted upon joining the lyric crusade. Mrs. Stevens had known Terry and his former wife in New York and was expected to see that the shining knight of Sibyl's court maintained a virtuous decorum.

Fun-loving and jovial, Tony looked forward to his fiancée's American tour as an exciting new adventure. He would be at her side to share in her triumphs, meet new people, and see new cities. He could not anticipate the hours he would have to spend alone while she was in rehearsal. Nor was this spoiled darling of the gods capable of understanding her highly disciplined routine of quietude and practice.

The fact that Tony demanded her acceptance of the Catholic faith before their marriage posed no predicament for Sibyl. She was so enamored that she would have become a Shintoist to please him.

Sibyl was vaguely aware that her health was in jeopardy. In her climb to international stardom, she had been treading blindfolded along a precipice. The soprano adamantly refused to be dissuaded from her expedition to the New World; neither would she bow to her mother's wishes and consult a doctor about her growing alcoholism. Physically and mentally, she was in no condition to undertake the tour. The last thing she needed at the moment was the distraction provided by the Cuban charmer, who kept assuring her that as soon as his lawyers had completed the divorce settlement, nuptial bliss was merely a couch or two away.

By now Sibyl was aware that she and her fiancé shared one weakness in common—an addiction to the grape. It had become almost a nightly ritual for Adolph Bonnet, Tony's valet, to undress his inebriated employer and put him to bed. Of the two, it was obvious that the millionaire was far more flagrant an imbiber. He drank openly with fraternal conviviality, she in the closeted terror of her insecurity. After all, no one expected a playboy to behave like a monk, but the New York public did demand that its lyric goddesses manifest divinity, not to mention sobriety.

Chapter 22

Fall from Olympus

After a storm-tossed passage, the *Champagne* docked a day late in New York on the morning of 7 January 1895. This complicated Sibyl's schedule because now she would not be able to rest before her first American news conference. Both the singer and her fiancé had suffered severely from seasickness.

Although newsmen were scheduled for a mass interview at five o'clock in the afternoon, Sibyl had acceded to William Randolph Hearst's request to grant some extra time to his representative from the *San Francisco Examiner.* He was planning to devote one whole page to her American debut that would be reprinted in his *New York Journal.*

When the prima donna arrived in her suite at the St. James Hotel,[1] she discovered a bouquet of roses on the table from her upstairs neighbor Emma Eames and a fire crackling in the parlor hearth, also ordered by the singer. Jane immediately telephoned Hearst's New York office to suggest his reporter come an hour early.

Ned Townsend, a veteran Hearst writer, accommodated her request by arriving nearly two hours early. Once Lina opened the door, Townsend's attention was fixed upon the silhouette of a plump little lady standing on a large white rug before a blazing fireplace. Sibyl was dressed in a dove-gray broadcloth gown trimmed in black and a low-cut white blouse finished with a large black satin sash. Her chestnut hair was parted in the center and brushed to each side in unruly waves. A cape of black monkey fur hugged her shoulders.

Refusing to turn on the electric lights above, the singer paced up and down until a heavily shaded oil lamp was brought and placed next to Eames's roses. Then she relaxed on the divan beside her fox terrier, Maggie, while gales of winter rain furiously pelted the windows. Sibyl spoke of being confined to her cabin for nearly the entire voyage by seasickness. Then the doorbell rang again, and a six-foot porter, tucking the edge of his calico shirt into his trousers, appeared to announce the arrival of several dozen trunks.

Passing her hand dramatically across her forehead, Sibyl feigned total help-lessness over the situation and begged Townsend to stay and assist her sister in supervising the proceedings, as Lina spoke no English. Soon afterward the hotel manager called to inform Sibyl that the lobby was overflowing with reporters—forty of them, to be exact, an unheard-of number for an interview with any prima donna.

Discarding her cape, she donned a gray broadcloth jacket with dramatically flared sleeves trimmed in black, to complete her ensemble. Bellboys were called, and extra chairs brought in. Within fifteen minutes the parlor was swarming with newsmen from all over the country. They were standing, sit-ting wherever they could find a chair, and many more were seated cross-legged on the floor. Paper and pencils were in every hand.

With the soft lamplight and the glow from the hearth working their magic as they cast shadows about the room, Sibyl held her interviewers spellbound. The *New York Journal* reporter described her rich contralto speaking voice as "low, luscious, and languorous, almost voluptuous—a voice never to be forgot-ten." Her voice reminded another writer of Shelley's famous line, "When music, moonlight, and feeling are one." Her beauty conjured Goethe's "What a rich heaven with star upon star." The radiance of her complexion was com-pared to that of a "peachblow vase." Amid this extravagant outpouring, only the emissary from the *New York World* noted the considerable amount of addi-tional weight she had acquired since he last saw her in Paris.

All the newsmen were anxious to learn the latest developments in her engagement to Antonio Terry. She confidently predicted that his divorce would be finalized before her Metropolitan engagement was over, and she expected to be married in America.

Where was he staying?

"Why right here in the St. James Hotel, but on a different floor, of course. Until we are married, I can't count Mr. Terry as one of my party."

Some muffled sniggers greeted this comment.

In regard to her art, she confided: "Expression and diction are the two points of which I think most. I act a part as much as I sing it. I try not only to sing, but to be my role. Perhaps this is not appreciated in America, I don't know as yet."

Discussing her approaching debut in *Manon,* she declared that the reason the opera failed in London was because "the delicately spoken recitatives did not carry in the enormous hall of Covent Garden."

"There is no danger of repeating that mistake here," she naively told the reporter from the *New York Herald*. "Massenet, after I signed my contract, especially revised *Manon* for me and has written musical recitatives for the parts originally spoken. . . . These recitatives are really excellent and follow the inflection of the speaking voice in the most admirable manner."

Sibyl concluded the interview with a parting request to the representative of the *New York Times:* "I would like to be judged by what I do at my first appearance in my native country, and I ask for frank criticism." At the moment she had no idea how literally this statement would be taken.

The California comet had returned at last, and her reentry into the American hemisphere was highly touted. Scantily clad photographs of her had not only graced the front page of the *New York Sun* as well as the covers of various musical journals but were turning up in such magazines as *The Illustrated American* and *Munsey's*. Sibyl had come back to a country where thousands believed the stage to be Satan's domain. Her scandalous "love affair" with Massenet was still being publicized in American newspapers. She had been criticized for playing mostly ladies of easy virtue. A typical diatribe appeared in the *Rhode Island Gazette* that very week: "Sibyl Sanderson has arrived in New York with thirty trunks full of clothes but what she wears on the stage would rattle in a hatbox."[2]

On 17 January her uncle William Ormsby unwittingly added fuel to the fire by releasing to the California papers some maudlin prose that he had just received from Massenet.

> Cher M Ormsby,
> If the dream of your life is realized in learning of the great success of Mlle Sibyl Sanderson, you can know from me that this success has been the *first great joy* of my whole life! Picture to yourself a woman in the plentitude of her beauty, an artist in all the luster of her genial talent, a being with all the strength of goodness, grace, and frankness. It is adoration which we all have for her . . .
>
> J. Massenet

Such a letter merely confirmed the suspicions of West Coast readers. Massenet and Sibyl were still lovers. It never occurred to Ormsby that America's philistine hordes considered the family star anything but another shameless hussy who had slept her way to fame.

Now Sibyl had crossed the Atlantic with a married man whose wife, so far, had refused him a divorce. Few newspapers bothered to mention that she was properly chaperoned not only by her sister but by such an internationally recognized bastion of respectability as Mrs. Paran Stevens. On the contrary, they eagerly revealed the fact that her "tightly married" fiancé had taken up residence in her very hotel.

For two Sundays in a row, W. J. Henderson, the *New York Times* critic, had warned Metropolitan subscribers not to be carried away by Sibyl's "extravagant [press] puffery" or their expectations would suffer "some disappointment." Sarcastically referring to her as Massenet's "parrot," he added that her Parisian popularity was not only owing to her mentor's powerful influence (an untrue statement), but also due to the fact that "she is the possessor of potent physical charms which she is said to exhibit with uncommon generosity." Needless to say, the latter remark didn't exactly hinder a three-day stampede at the Metropolitan box office. But neither did it make Sibyl realize that only the greatest vocal artistry could overcome these newspaper indictments. At a time when she should have redoubled her efforts to stay in top physical condition and refute her accusers, she seldom bothered to read the papers.

Massenet's new recitatives, on which the soprano was counting heavily, failed to arrive at the Metropolitan. Each day her frantic inquiries to Mr. Grau's office elicited the same negative response. Believing her mentor's assurances that he had mailed them before Christmas, she confided her suspicions that they had been stolen to Reginald de Koven of the *New York World* and later to the correspondent of the *Musical Courier.*[3] She wondered if she had fallen victim to some cabal from the powerful German wing of the Metropolitan.

Although the orchestra and chorus were heavily saturated with Germans, significant changes had occurred in just a few years. The *Manon* production of 1895 was undeniably multinational. The conductor, Signor Bevignani, was an Italian. The Chevalier Des Grieux was Sibyl's onetime Polish professor, Jean de Reszke, still the foremost operatic matinee idol. Pol Plançon, a tall, handsome Frenchman, was singing the Comte Des Grieux, and Mario Ancona, another Italian, was interpreting Lescaut.

Totally devoid of duplicity herself, Sibyl had refused to believe the many tales she had heard about Massenet's betrayal of other colleagues, but by now she certainly was aware of his treacherous plot (soon to be revealed) to scuttle her engagement to Tony. The fact that she indignantly requested that his letters be returned to him that winter indicates she was finally viewing her Svengali in a more accurate light.On the night before her debut, which was scheduled for 15

January, Sibyl invited her author friend Gertrude Atherton and Atherton's teenage daughter Muriel for a quiet dinner in her suite. It was snowing heavily when they arrived, and Lina helped them take off their coats, scarves, and muffs. Mrs. Atherton greeted Sibyl affectionately while mentally noting her recently acquired embonpoint. Then she introduced her daughter.

"So this is Muriel. The last time I saw you, you were just a tiny thing back in San Francisco. Why, you're practically a grownup young lady!" Sibyl exclaimed.

Years later when Muriel Atherton Russell recalled the visit and helped to reconstruct the conversation,[4] she remembered Sibyl as dressed in a pale-pink silk peignoir. Mrs. Russell remembered her expression as "listless and sad," but the soprano explained that she was "exhausted" after the dress rehearsal at the Metropolitan.

Once they had settled themselves on a sofa before the fire, Mrs. Atherton admired the enormous canary diamond that Sibyl announced was Tony's engagement ring. Only a few minutes of conversation were necessary to ascertain that the diva was in a fractious state of mind. She was plucking the petals of a rose and idly scattering them across the white rug while she paced up and down. Tony had disappeared; no one had seen him since Sibyl began rehearsals. Both Jane's and Mrs. Stevens's inquiries had met with failure. Only his roses continued to arrive every day.

Jane ordered tea to be sent up as Mrs. Atherton expressed her regrets at not meeting him. Quickly changing the subject, she continued, "Sibyl you're the most talked-of person in New York! Are you aware that John Mackay has bought over a thousand dollars' worth of tickets to your debut?" John Mackay was a San Francisco multimillionaire and owner of the famous Comstock lode.

"So, I've been told," Sibyl admitted. "Since I'm the first Californian to sing at the Metropolitan he insists upon doing his part to make it a success. He's been so sweet and considerate."

"Everyone who is anyone will be there tomorrow night. I hear Will Hearst left San Francisco by train last weekend to get here in time. I bet he still has a soft spot in his heart for you. Does he ever call upon you when he visits Paris?"

"Every time he's there," was the reply.

Mrs. Russell remembered her mother taking one or two society-page clippings from New York newspapers out of her purse and reading them to Sibyl.[5]

"I suppose she did this to cheer her up, but she didn't have much success," Mrs. Russell commented.

The conversation eventually turned toward the encouraging reception the English were giving Mrs. Atherton's recent novels. Tea arrived, and as Jane began to pour, the doorbell interrupted Mrs. Atherton's monologue.[6] Jane excused herself to join Lina and act as interpreter. A moment later she returned with a sealed envelope exuding a subtle, mysterious perfume.

"Who's it from?"

"I don't know, but it smells like Auntie Paran's perfume." "Auntie Paran" was the affectionate nickname for Mrs. Stevens.

Sibyl took the envelope and opened it indifferently. No sooner did she start to read the contents than she began to tremble convulsively.

"Sibyl! What is it?" chorused Jane and Mrs. Atherton.

"It—it can't be true! I don't believe it! Why that fickle, two-timing—" Sibyl was shaking so badly she dropped the letter. With a sweep of her hand, she sent the silver teapot crashing to the floor, and her fox terrier bolted across the room.

Jane snatched the note and hastily read it. Of all people, Lillie Langtry had returned to New York and was appearing in Brooklyn at the Columbia Theater in a play entitled *Esther Sandraz*. She had also made a few appearances in the St. James Hotel, and Tony's carriage had been seen at her stage door every night.

"How could he?" Sibyl cried. "Chasing after that dreadful woman again! Why, she's old enough to be his mother!" (Actually, Mrs. Langtry was not quite four years older than Terry, but Sanderson was too distraught at the moment to think clearly.)

"Sibyl, the note's only printed. We don't know who it's from!" Jane interrupted.

Mrs. Russell recalled that Jane tried to placate her sister, but her voice was lost in a cacophonous din as Sibyl proceeded to hurl china and silver against the wall. Then she tore the note to shreds.

"Mother seized her by the shoulders and shouted, 'Sibyl, control yourself! Don't allow yourself to get worked up over an anonymous note that may not be true!'"

"Sibyl insisted the perfume smelled like Mrs. Stevens's, but mother argued that whether the message was true or not, she shouldn't go to pieces on the night before her debut."

Ignoring Mrs. Atherton's logic, the soprano upset her chair, flew hysterically toward the door and out into the hall. As both women raced after her, Muriel followed them to the open door, speechless at the diva's antics.

"Sibyl! Come back here! Where are you going?"

"To order a cab. I'm going over to Brooklyn right now and tell him he'll have to choose between us—or we're—we're through!"

"You lunatic!" Mrs. Atherton shouted breathlessly as she caught up with her friend. "Have you lost your senses? You can't go out in this storm! You'll catch your death of cold!"

"Oh, Sibyl think of your debut tomorrow night! You're not even dressed," Jane urged as both women put their arms around the overwrought singer and slowly led her back to her suite. "Now come in and sit down. If you must go, please let Lina or me come along," Jane continued. "You've no business going out by yourself in this storm. You don't even know how to get there."

"Jennie's right," Mrs. Atherton interposed. "You can't go out like this. At least put on some warm wraps! Why don't you send him a telegram saying it's crucial he contact you immediately?"

Jane explained that all their messages had remained unanswered. It was apparent that Tony had not been back to his suite for some days, and now it was obvious where he had been spending his nights.

Reluctantly, Jane ordered Lina to bring Sibyl's floor-length sable cloak. As they draped it over her shoulders, both women made a last-minute plea for the diva to change her mind. Sibyl stubbornly refused to listen. It was something she had to do and do alone. She even rejected her sister's offer to call for a cab. There were always plenty of fiacres in front of the hotel. Lina would see her off, she continued. Gertrude and Muriel could stay and have dinner with Jane. Surely, the cab driver would know the address of the Columbia Theater, and how to get to Brooklyn.

Five minutes later the tall, gaunt, snow-covered figure of Lina Bournie reappeared in the doorway. Wearily, she told Jane that when they got downstairs there weren't any cabs in front of the hotel. The wind-whipped snow was turning into a raging blizzard, and Mademoiselle had ordered her inside so she wouldn't catch cold. The last she saw of her mistress was a pathetic little figure wandering aimlessly into the storm to search for a cab. Years later, an elderly Muriel Atherton Russell admitted she couldn't remember whether Sibyl got to Brooklyn or not (Gertrude informed Carl Van Vechten that she didn't).[7] Too upset to eat any dinner, Muriel and her mother left shortly afterward.

Sibyl's attempt to reach Brooklyn was unsuccessful, and she was to pay dearly for one of the most irrational acts of her life. Some years later Mrs. Atherton discussed the consequences with Carl Van Vechten, who recorded her reminiscences and gave his notes to the author.

She single-handedly wrecked her American tour running out into a blizzard that night, but we couldn't stop her! She was wild with jealousy and rage!

The next afternoon when she arose, she had caught cold. Her throat was inflamed and her sinuses clogged with mucous. Her sister tried to persuade her to postpone the debut, but she insisted upon going through with it. After all, it wasn't the first time she had sung with a cold. They called the hotel doctor to treat her, and the Metropolitan doctor was in her dressing room that night, spraying her throat with some vile smelling solution between acts. But she wasn't up to par and failed to do herself justice.

On Wednesday evening, January 16, 1895, a large and brilliant audience converged upon the Metropolitan Opera House. The Rockefellers and the Harrimans were in their boxes early. The Perry Belmonts and the August Belmonts arrived with their Parisian guest, the old Marquis de Castellane, a fervid admirer of Sibyl's art. Attired in white tie and tails, Clyde Fitch looked handsome enough to star in his own plays. Removing her opera cloak in Mr. and Mrs. Maurice Grau's box, Emma Eames appeared radiant in a crimson velvet gown.

There was a sizable delegation from California also. Leading the San Francisco contingent were multimillionaires Mr. and Mrs. John Mackay, their son Clarence and his family, and Mrs. L. L. Baker, a longtime friend of the Sandersons. Hattie Crocker Alexander and her husband, now living in New York, had brought flowers to throw on the stage, and so had Hattie's brother George and his family. While Gertrude and Muriel Atherton were nervously fidgeting in their orchestra seats, William Randolph Hearst was turning heads in the dress circle because of his inappropriate tweed suit.

Also seated in the dress circle, beside the Spanish consul, was a tall, dark gentleman in tails, sporting a flashy yellow diamond stickpin. Antonio Terry was reported by his neighbors to be chewing compulsively on the ends of his long mustache. Unbeknownst to them, he was undoubtedly wrestling with his conscience.

Probably no one in the audience knew that the original edition of *Manon* that Sibyl was forced to sing that night was obsolete in Paris. There were still no orchestra parts available in America that had all the changes Massenet had directed the musicians of the Opéra-Comique to pencil into their scores. Neither would New York be hearing Manon's bewitching Gavotte.[8] A few months were to pass before the composer's revised score was finally published.

In either version, however, Manon still steps out of a coach at the Amiens inn, unhappily bound for the convent. When Sanderson made her entrance in the courtyard, a few critical observers were disconcerted to see her wearing a single strand of brilliants around her throat. It never occurred to her that Americans were not familiar with the old European custom of a girl selecting one precious gift upon entering the convent to become the bride of Christ. Moreover, this California princess never realized that few European peasant girls of the eighteenth century would have had the means to obtain any jewels in the first place.

Sibyl's performance, nonetheless, was a vivacious one in the first act, and her voice seemed warm and vibrant in the duet with Des Grieux. By the time Manon and her chevalier had stolen a carriage and run off to Paris, the audience broke into spontaneous applause, hurling bouquets and laurel wreaths. So far, everything was going surprisingly well.

But as the opera progressed through five more scenes, critics noted that the debutante could not always sustain the beautiful work she had done in the first act. Her voice sounded increasingly nasal, and her high notes grew progressively shriller. Parts of the spoken dialogue failed to carry in the large hall.[9] In spite of the ovation she won for her highly emotional singing in the Saint Sulpice scene, Sibyl's powers of projection were waning irretrievably. It was amazing she lasted through the final scene. Although the performance marked Jean de Reszke's debut in the role of Des Grieux, his Olympian reserves of strength and passion garnered the lion's share of the applause.

Visually, Sanderson had created a sensation. The day after her debut, the *New York Herald* observed that "no woman has ever been so minutely scrutinized on the stage of the Metropolitan." When the diva stepped out of her sedan chair in the Cours-la-Reine scene, lorgnettes went up in unison all over the house. Sibyl was gowned in a Louis XV creation by Doucet with a diamond-sprinkled petticoat of white satin edged with pink and silver roses. Over it was a ravishing affair of pink mirror velvet studded with gold paillettes, looped up high at the hips with iridescent butterflies, then falling in folds to the back. The ensemble was completed with a powdered wig topped by a garland of pink roses and a diamond-studded pom-pom.

No less dazzling was her costume in the gambling scene. A gown of rose-pink satin fell over a petticoat of white satin, the train embroidered in gold and embellished with clusters of white ostrich tips. A deep fall of point lace adorned the corsage and sleeves. Another powdered wig ornamented with feathers and flowers completed this eighteenth-century portrait.

After the curtain calls, admirers poured into Sibyl's flower-banked dressing room to congratulate her. Except for a few, no one knew she had given a far more dramatic performance offstage the night before. As for Tony, he hovered over her so possessively, no one would have suspected that the slightest rift had occurred between them. With so many old friends present, it was inevitable that Sibyl's past would overtake her present. William Randolph Hearst, beaming from ear to ear, strode into the room to offer his congratulations. Intoxicated with all the excitement, Sibyl introduced him to her fiancé. Hearst extended a warm handshake to Terry, but his cold gray eyes held another message in reserve. Sibyl could not have divined that in this blissful moment the forces had been set in motion for her past to chart her future. Within a few years the American newspaper mogul would play a considerable role in the destruction of the Cuban sugar king.

Given the circumstances under which she had appeared, the reviews, as a whole, were far better than would have been expected. Jean de Reszke's performance was hailed as one of "power," and "full of passion and exquisite tenderness" by various New York papers. As for Sibyl, the majority of the critics were guarded in their praise but confessed that she had won their hearts.[10]

The *Sun* admitted that "she was well received and certainly made a favorable impression. Her performance was a finished one both vocally and dramatically. . . . Her personal charms, which are far more than any ordinary mortal possesses, go far to create illusions about her."

The *Journal* pronounced her lower register "good, the middle, delightful, but the upper sometimes defective and trembling . . . nevertheless, her vocalization was always good, and she made a strong impression during the third and fourth acts."

Finding her high notes occasionally "shrill and wiry," Reginald de Koven aired his opinions in the *World*. "Thoroughly trained is Miss Sanderson with voice, gesture, and expression all obedient to her will and portrayal of the character . . . She played the part to perfection . . . she sang her 'Je suis reine' aria in finished style and rose to real heights of emotional and dramatic power in the Saint Sulpice scene."

The *Herald* declared that "of all the American songstresses who have achieved fame abroad, she is incomparably the most talented actress . . . a splendid example of this artistic training she gave in her aria "N'est-ce-plus ma main" in Saint Sulpice . . . there you did not feel any limitations of the artist's voice and that it had appeared to be a small voice in the beginning (first act). But it is a sweet and true voice and sufficiently penetrating in quality to assert itself even in the ensembles. A flexible voice too, and one that commands a variety of colors."

Critics of all the secondary papers were in agreement: based upon her work in *Manon* she was not an artist to rave over but one to hear with genuine pleasure.

However, the two most powerful arbiters of musical opinion in New York, W. J. Henderson and Henry Krehbiel, found little to admire.[11]

Following his previous attacks upon her, Henderson was not expected to shout hallelujahs in the *Times*. Chiding her for wearing her jewels to the convent, he damned with the faintest praise.

> Miss Sanderson's voice lacks warmth and emotional character. It is pretty, but it is much too small for the Metropolitan. It frequently runs to the quality called "white," and this characteristic is increased by faulty placing at times. Her high notes are thin and strident but the upper part of her middle register is good. . . . Her staccati are extremely sharp and wooden. Of course, she has a good comprehension of the role of *Manon* . . . and at the end of the third scene, in the duet with Des Grieux, she sang with a good deal of feeling . . . Her acting is graceful but it is not convincing.

Sanderson's attempted conquest of the New World had been dealt a serious setback. If Henderson had wounded it with a damning blow in the *Times,* Henry Krehbiel was to fire an equally crippling round in the *Tribune.*

> Of Miss Sanderson's performance it is possible to speak with kindly recognition if not with enthusiasm. Her voice is not one of the kind to be associated with serious opera. It is pure and true in intonation . . . but it is lacking in volume and penetrative quality. It is pleasant in timbre and fairly equable through its natural register when not forced, but it becomes attenuated as it goes up and its high tones are mere trickles of sound. It is afflicted, moreover, with an almost distressing unsteadiness, and is deficient in warmth. These things must be said in view of the rank which the world has been told Miss Sanderson has taken in Paris among the singers of today.

Today Sanderson's Metropolitan debut is considered a failure by all musical historians because of two adverse reviews. If she had been in decent vocal condition and able to sing the revised edition, would the treatment she received have been any better?[12] Although Carl Van Vechten later recalled Gertrude Atherton to be of this opinion, I cannot agree with the latter. The New York critics of the day were too enamored of conventional Italian opera to understand the radical new French concept of a singing actress. Sanderson's interpretation of Manon at the Opéra-Comique had been a series of exquisite vignettes (in every scene Manon was a different woman with a different voice) linked together by her consummate skill as a diseuse. Nothing comparable had been heard at the Metropolitan before, and Sibyl had neither altered her conception of the role nor adjusted her vocal palette to the larger American stage.[13] When Henderson and Krehbiel later tried to crucify Mary Garden in a similar manner, she was fortunate to have such powerful champions as James Huneker and Carl Van Vechten rally to her defense. In 1895 no knight appeared on the horizon to rescue Sibyl.

On 20 January 1895, Henderson launched a vindictive attack on the plot of *Manon,* stopping just short of a few other critics who had already condemned it as "immoral." He found the "shallow lovers" to be "devoid of any strong human sympathy" and regretted that Manon had "no grand vices, no masterful follies." She was a mere "Dresden china sinner" who bored him, and her spineless lover was intolerable.

Composer Reginald de Koven, a knowledgeable critic in New York at this time, rushed to defend Manon's honor in the *World* a week later.

> It is absurd to say that *Manon* is not of sufficient importance, musically speaking, to warrant its representation on the stage of the Metropolitan. The work is certainly *not* light enough in either texture or theme to debar it from those august precincts. Neither does it strike one as necessary at this day and age to comment unfavorably or object seriously on moral grounds to the somewhat questionable propriety of its story—Compared to *La traviata, Carmen,* and the incest in *Die Walküre, Manon* is a story for boys and virgins.

If Sibyl had been in respectable voice, she might have been able to champion Manon's cause even more effectively. But the cold she had so foolishly contracted now triggered a new and more dangerous menace—laryngitis. There was little time for rest and recovery with a parlor full of admirers and autograph seekers every afternoon, not to mention reporters trying to get interviews for their newspapers.

In any case, she used her opportunities with the press to defend her interpretation. "My friends will find out when the role demands it, my voice can roll out as large a volume of sound as almost any singer of the day," the soprano informed a deputy from the *New York Journal.*[14] She grew even more emphatic in her utterances to a writer from the *Musical Courier.*[15] "If I had sung my part with a tremendous voice, I should have failed to interpret the role as the composer intended it to be sung . . . I sang Massenet's instructions to the letter!"

Terry seems to have been conspicuously devoted all week and escorted her to the tea that Hattie Crocker Alexander gave in her honor. He even tore himself away from the charms of Mrs. Langtry long enough to hear Sibyl sing the first performance of *Manon* with the company in Philadelphia on 22 January 1895. On the morning of the performance she had been coughing so badly it was feared she would not be able to appear at all. As the day wore on she improved enough to insist upon singing that evening. Georges Mauguière was singing the role of Des Grieux for the first time. Even though an apology was made at intermission for Sibyl's below-par condition, the local critics did not feel that it was necessary.

While the *Philadelphia Ledger* envisioned Sanderson as "a Dresden china shepherdess," the *Philadelphia Times*[16] declared that "she sang with a purity of enunciation and delicacy of sentiment that very few singers have approached . . . of her vocal skill there can be no question of the understanding, the charm, and finesse with which she sang her part."

Unfortunately Sibyl's laryngitis did not improve when she returned to New York for three more appearances, including one at the Brooklyn Academy of Music on 29 January. Because of the public's tremendous curiosity to see both the woman and her fabulous wardrobe, the performances were sold out. De Reszke alternated with Mauguière as her chevalier.

In his newspaper review of 1 February,[17] the Brooklyn critic observed, "Her voice is of agreeable timber and well modulated, her enunciation clearness itself. She uses it very skillfully and artistically. As an actress she is very clever, quick, and graceful in gesture and motion, and her diction is specially admirable."

Nevertheless, a few newspapers in New York continued to distort her every move. Gossip columnists likened the image of Sanderson as Manon to "an overdressed Christmas tree" and denigrated her reputation to the status of a "mere amateur" in the company of world-famous professionals. When she gallantly refrained from sharing a final bow with Jean de Reszke so his fans could cheer him alone, several journalists gleefully leaped to the conclusion that she was jealous of her costar. It didn't require much time for her to realize she was the victim of a smear campaign in New York. Nothing delighted a few hostile scribes more than the suspicion that this expatriate goddess might have feet of clay.

Chapter 23

Love and the Locksmith

Sibyl fully realized that as long as she sang *Manon,* New Yorkers were not going to change their view of her as a "divette" instead of a diva. Since no one at the Metropolitan knew the scores to any of her recent creations, her chances of being heard as Esclarmonde or Thaïs were nil. This left her with one alternative: to appear in a standard role from the repertoire.

Descending upon Mr. Grau's office, she requested the opportunity to sing Juliette. Grau replied that his hands were tied. The part belonged to Melba this season, and unless the Australian singer was taken ill, he could not, in good faith, ask her to relinquish the role to another soprano. In addition, when Melba had been indisposed a few weeks before and he had asked Sibyl to pinch-hit in *Rigoletto,* she claimed that she was too ill to oblige him.[1]

Sanderson returned to the St. James, smarting with disappointment. Her dream of an American conquest was fast turning into an ignominious defeat. Her physical condition was so noticeably below par that her laryngitis would improve one week only to be aggravated by a new cold the next.

To placate her growing dissatisfaction with the Metropolitan, the management asked Sibyl to sing two arias at a concert on Sunday night, 3 February 1895, under the baton of Anton Seidl. Hoping this would be a chance to display her full vocal virtuosity, she chose Esclarmonde's aria, "Regardez ces yeux" and the Waltz Song from *Mireille.* Under normal circumstances it would have been an ideal opportunity, but she was so indisposed on the night of the performance that New Yorkers left the Metropolitan believing her concert appearance showed her to even less advantage than her operatic ones had. By now the singer was reverting to a dangerous remedy for her various tribulations—her silver flask.

In February several events reduced Sibyl's retinue. First, Tony found it necessary to leave for Cuba because a recent rebellion on the island had jeopardized his land holdings. Then, just before her departure for Baltimore with the opera company on 17 February, Sibyl and Jane received the second of two telegrams from Marion in Nervi, Italy. The first had intimated that their mother was slightly indisposed but resting comfortably. This one announced that she was bedfast with pleuro-pneumonia and in critical condition. Both sisters were stunned. As Sibyl was bound to her American contract, it was decided that Jane would sail for Europe as soon as possible on the *Gascogne*. Sibyl asked Mr. Grau for permission to stay over and see her off on the morning of 20 February. Then she would immediately board a train and still arrive in time to sing that evening.

After a tearful farewell to Jane at the pier, Sibyl and Mrs. Stevens reluctantly departed for Baltimore. The company had scheduled four operas in three days: *Lohengrin, Otello, Faust,* and *Manon.* As it turned out, *Manon* and its exotic exponent were the most intriguing novelties of the week. While the audience gasped at her gorgeous costumes, the critic on the *Baltimore Sun* found the performance "the least brilliant of all four" and Sanderson "pleasing though not imbued with any special depth." Damned with faint praise in print, Sibyl had her own critique of the janitorial staff. In a letter to her family, she complained that no one had bothered to scrub the dirty stage in months.

When the company arrived in Washington, D.C., the next day, Sibyl learned that her old nemesis Phoebe Hearst was planning a gala reception for the stars. She was aware that the Hearsts had been making their home in the nation's capital ever since George had been elected senator. The soprano sent her regrets and wisely chose to rest at the hotel. To help pass the time, Mrs. Stevens began teaching her how to knit. The weather was unusually warm that week, and the singer noticed a decided improvement in her throat trouble.

On the evening of 23 February, Sibyl felt even more encouraged by the brilliant audience that had assembled to hear the local premiere of *Manon.* The hall was crammed with foreign diplomats and their wives, who gave her an enthusiastic welcome. Constantly recalled before the curtain, she received armloads of flowers, and in the midst of all the bravas, no one noticed that the senator's wife had not attended.

Although the *Washington Post* prudishly objected to the morality of the opera, it admitted that "anyone more chic or coquettish would be difficult to find for the title role."[2] The *Washington Times* extended a genuine rave, lauding her as a "rarely gifted lyric artist. . . . Hers is a pure, high, bell-like soprano, ample in compass, and abundant in volume. Her voice is so perfectly trained that the most exacting demands upon it are responded to without any apparent effort."[3]

Such a warm review offered encouragement that Sibyl's reception in America might improve if she could avoid further physical setbacks, but upon returning to New York, she was again the victim of bad luck. The parlor cars on the train were overheated, and when all the company clamored to board the New Jersey Ferry, there weren't enough carriages to convey the artists into Manhattan. In the midst of the confusion, Sanderson and Mrs. Stevens were forced to stand in the bitter cold for nearly twenty minutes before a cab could be found. When she finally arrived at the St. James Hotel, Sibyl discovered that she had not been expected until the following day; consequently, her suite was not heated. By this time she had caught another chill. Once the doctor arrived and examined her throat, he confirmed that her laryngitis had flared up again.

This was the final blow! There was no sense in staying in America any longer if she was unable to sing. Sibyl sent an urgent message to Grau requesting him to call upon her at once. When he arrived the following day, she presented him with a medical certificate and reluctantly asked to be released from her contract. Grau was perturbed but not exactly surprised. It was obvious from her bloodshot eyes, her nervous, excitable gestures, and her slurred phrases that the doctor had not listed all her ailments. He begged her to stay with the company until she had sung *Manon* in Boston the following week. By then she would have fulfilled enough of her contract to warrant releasing her—and probably her entire season's salary, as a bonus. If she recovered, she could rejoin them anywhere on tour.

Sibyl agreed to his terms, and it was decided that the news would not be made public until the company arrived in Chicago. Before he left, Grau inquired about her mother and particularly Mr. Terry, since the eastern papers were filled with innuendoes about a chill in their relationship. Sibyl replied that Jane had joined her sisters in Nervi and, happily, her mother was off the critical list. As for Tony, she handed Grau his latest cablegram announcing he was sailing for New York that week.

When Grau's songbirds arrived in Boston for a two-weeks' visit, rumors were already circulating that the manager and Sanderson had quietly drawn up their "divorce" papers. Reporters were astonished to observe Mrs. Stevens and Lina helping the singer off the train on the afternoon of 27 February. By the time she had been put to bed at the Hotel Vendome, it was obvious she was in no condition to appear that evening in *Manon*. *Carmen* was hastily substituted after a phone call from Mrs. Stevens. For the rest of the week, this patient companion, who never once complained of her own serious heart problem, helped Lina nurse Sibyl back to health.

Mrs. Stevens also kept the reporters away, because a scurrilous tale had burst into print that Sanderson had been seen "sulking in the tavern down the street from her hotel." Although ladies were permitted to sit at tables in taverns during this era, Sibyl was a closet drinker, so the report can be easily discredited. If she did enter that tavern, it was to order enough cases of wine to last for a month. Lina's unfamiliarity with the English language prevented her from running such errands.

By 5 March, the soprano had improved enough to receive an emissary from the *Boston Herald*. The reporter found her standing by the window in the sunset, glamorously attired in a black silk empire gown trimmed with jet and lace. Sibyl asked him to sit by the fire and confided that she would definitely sing at the Saturday matinee. She admitted that she was tired of being "cooped up" in her suite day after day idly watching traffic in the avenue below. Laughing heartlly about the puritanical furor her partially clad opera photographs had caused in America, Sibyl declined to comment about the rumor that she was leaving the company.

"A singer's life is not an easy one," she mused. "The voice is such a delicate thing to care for. It is a life, too, of so many deprivations. I have given up so much for it. . . . It has been so hard for me to come to America so full of ambition, and then fall ill and to accomplish so little of what I had hoped for."

Sanderson, however, wasn't the only artist whose adverse health was sabotaging Grau's profits. During the two-week Boston engagement, Jean de Reszke, Mauguière, and even the indestructible Emma Eames were forced to bow out of various performances because of illness.

On Saturday, 9 March 1895, the soprano was determined to go ahead with the matinee. Arriving at Mechanics Hall she discovered the filth backstage to be just as disgraceful as it had been in other American cities. Her dressing room was little more than a cramped storage closest, and, as usual, there wasn't a washbasin in the place.

Tony was due in Boston that afternoon, and Sibyl hoped he would arrive in time for the performance. A doctor was on hand to treat her throat between acts, and evidently he was successful, because the audience was extremely demonstrative. Hearty salvos of applause kept growing in volume after every act, and the soprano received a continuous string of curtain calls and cries of "Brava!"

Phillip Hale, who had not heard Sibyl sing since his student days in Paris, penned a glowing review in the *Boston Journal* on 18 March.

> Sibyl Sanderson was evidently suffering physically during the performance, and occasionally her voice was hoarse, but it carried easily in the vast hall. Many tones were often of haunting sweetness and will long haunt the memory. . . . She phrases admirably and sings with an elegance rare in these days of boisterous sopranos. She never sacrifices meaning for cheap theatrical display. . . . As an actress she is easily the first woman of the company. Why all this gossip about continual rows between Miss Sanderson and the management of the Metropolitan? Saturday she showed pluck and honesty as well as art. . . . She should have received better support. Mauguière was a walking stick, wooden in action, ineffectual in song.

When the Metropolitan's train pulled out of Boston on 10 March for Chicago, Sibyl was conspicuously absent. Maurice Grau and his staff had preceded the singers, and Sanderson was the chief topic of his interviews in the Windy City. Stressing the fact that she had not been dismissed, Grau admitted that she was ill and had been released from her contract with the understanding that she was to rejoin the company if her health improved. He also denied current rumors that Mrs. Langtry had caused a rift between the diva and her fiancé.[4]

No sooner had the national wire services relayed his comments to Boston than newsmen besieged the Hotel Vendome for a statement from the ailing artist. Because Sibyl refused to be interviewed, Mrs. Stevens read a statement that the soprano had prepared: "It is not true that I have left Mr. Grau's company for the rest of the season. As soon as I have recovered my health I shall again rejoin them and I look forward to doing so."

Although Terry had arrived in Boston on March 9, too late to hear *Manon*, he immediately went into seclusion at the Vendome to avoid reporters. The following Wednesday, 13 March, Sibyl and her party left Boston for New York. Privately, she had no intention of rejoining the company as long as Grau would not permit her to sing other roles. When the singer arrived at the St. James, newsmen were already hovering about the lobby. It took them only a few seconds to ascertain that Sanderson was "in a feeble condition." Supported on either side by Mrs. Stevens and Lina, she could hardly stand long enough to register, and her voice was "barely audible." Hoping that they hadn't surmised her state of advanced intoxication, Mrs. Stevens abruptly dismissed the reporters.

As soon as Sibyl was put to bed, a doctor was summoned. When he left her suite, he directed the desk clerk not to allow anyone but her closest friends to see her and for the porters to keep her corridor as quiet as possible. He returned the following morning to treat her again.

Not knowing Terry had taken rooms at the nearby Hotel Victoria, reporters again stationed themselves in the lobby of the St. James, waiting to pounce upon him the minute he appeared. When Lina emerged from the elevator about 9 A.M. with a note for Tony, all that the newsmen elicited from her was "Pardonnez moi, mais je ne parle pas l'anglais." By the time evening shadows had enveloped the lobby, there was still no sign of him. On Friday, reporters were no more successful when they cornered Mrs. Stevens in the lobby. She assured them that "Miss Sanderson was resting comfortably and mustn't be disturbed."

On 17 March, Sibyl received a sole reporter—from the *San Francisco Examiner*—to clarify the conflicting stories about her. She denied the calumnies that she was feuding with Messrs Abbey and Grau as well as her "dear friends Melba and Eames." She insisted her managers had treated her "most graciously" and had even released her entire salary for the year, leaving her free to depart whenever she chose.

During the same week, a journalist from Philadelphia managed to locate Terry's hotel and even cornered him for a short interview. Although he failed to learn any of the couple's plans, Terry regaled him with a colorful tale about his recent trip to Cuba, where he narrowly escaped a trap set by the Spanish authorities who planned to accuse him of secretly subsidizing the insurrectionists. An official approached him to give an undisclosed amount of money to the family of an imprisoned revolutionary. Had he done so, he would have been immediately arrested, and his estates confiscated by the government. Fortunately, his Cuban traveling companion warned him of the plot; still, they were constantly shadowed by the secret police until their departure for Tampa.[5]

Meanwhile, Terry had quietly made arrangements for the couple to sail for Europe aboard the *Gascogne* on Saturday, 23 March. Their embarkation was cloaked in such secrecy that the press was not even aware of it until four days afterward. If there was one person in America who had reason to be grateful for Sibyl's departure it should have been Mrs. Paran Stevens. Unfortunately for her, it occurred too late. Already in poor health, she had literally sacrificed her life for the soprano. Three weeks later, on 14 April 1895, Mrs. Stevens succumbed to pneumonia following a heart attack at her residence on East 47th Street. Sanderson arrived in Paris on 2 April 1895 to find her home still deserted. Her sisters remained in Italy with their mother, who was now well on the way to recovery. Although *Le Gaulois* had already announced the singer's departure from New York with Terry, so far she remained unaware that malicious gossip about her added weight had preceded her to Europe.

Sibyl's contract with the Opéra called for her to resume appearances as Thaïs on 1 June. With her bronchial tubes now inflamed, she feared this would be impossible. Always unpredictable, instead of joining her family in the warm, salubrious climate of Italy, she unaccountably fled to London, where she decided to consult some physicians. Naturally, this curious choice only added fuel to the whispers about her "secret condition." At the moment, the only dependable friend she had in the English capital was Mrs. Atherton. Constance Wilde was in no position to entertain her. With Oscar's trial at the height of its notoriety, she was preparing to flee the country. However, it is a sure bet that Sibyl did not desert Mrs. Wilde in her hour of need.[6]

A few weeks of constant rain and dampness did nothing beneficial for Sibyl's throat. Tests by the English physicians revealed that the diva was suffering from a severe bronchial infection. They forbade her to sing for the next four or five months. Massenet claimed to have learned of Sibyl's flight to England through correspondence with her sister Marion, who had kept him posted that winter about Mrs. Sanderson's illness. He even sent her a pressed flower on 16 April with "remembrances of my wife and me."

Six days later he wrote a letter telling Marion how relieved he was to learn that her mother was out of danger and on the road to recovery. Then he added:

> Winter has been cruel to you—cruel to Mlle Sibyl, your sister, who you say is presently in London also suffering. . . . When you write her, I beg of you, tell her that all of my letters addressed to her in America have been returned to me undelivered. Tell her that we have thought so often of her.

Massenet knew all along that Sibyl was in London. The mysterious Mme X, upon whom he was counting heavily to undermine Sibyl's engagement to Terry, had already followed her there, if not at his instigation, at least with his blessing. What he didn't know was the fact that Sibyl had refused to accept any of his correspondence.

Mme X appears to have been Massenet's trump card in a diabolical scheme to stop Sibyl's marriage to Tony, or any man, for that matter. Mme X was a lesbian. In a lifetime of scheming and conniving, this idea was Massenet's perverted masterpiece. If the lady succeeded in converting Sibyl to the ancient cult of Lesbos, all his worries would be over. Her voice and soul would belong to him alone. If his agent failed, he could easily deny any knowledge of Mme X's sexual inclinations with a militant self-righteousness.

Sibyl later, and perhaps unwisely, confided to Mary Garden that Massenet introduced this woman to her in his studio during the fall of 1894 "as a good friend of his wife." According to Sibyl's confession, at first she had no idea that Mme X was homosexual; she was a divorcée who seemed "so feminine, elegant, and refined." Mme X told Sibyl how delighted she was to make her acquaintance and how much she had admired her on the stage. One evening before the soprano left for America, this "good friend of Mme Massenet invited her to dinner." If the story that Mary Garden later recounted to Louis Biancolli, Carl Van Vechten, and Robert Lawrence is true, Madame got the diva drunk on her favorite wine (whose name had been so thoughtfully provided by Massenet) and seduced her. Only afterward did Sibyl learn that Massenet was not only aware of Mme X's sexual preference, but had purposely introduced them to destroy her relationship with the male sex for all time.

"I could never do to my worst enemy what he did to me," was her bitter comment upon the episode to Garden.

Sibyl was shocked by the composer's treachery, but once she knew what he was capable of, she was not surprised to discover that his wife never even knew this woman. Nor was Sibyl any less horrified at herself for succumbing to Mme X's advances so easily. How could she be so trusting, so gullible—the very qualities upon which Massenet was counting? Quickly severing her friendship with Mme X, she assured herself that her stupid mistake could easily be swept under the rug; Tony would never be the wiser; and Massenet's intrigue was doomed to failure.

But Mme X refused to be discarded so easily. Having boldly pursued Sibyl to London, she claimed that she was no longer acting upon orders from anyone; she had fallen in love with the singer against her better judgment. If Sibyl rejected her this time, she had nothing more to live for. We do not know Sanderson's reaction to Mme X's desperate entreaties. No letters exist between the two. We do know that the soprano succumbed to the temptress's spell[7] temporarily, but just how far their affair progressed will remain a mystery.

Whatever their relationship may have been in London, it must be remembered that Sibyl was still very much in love with Terry. With her faith in the male sex at its lowest point ever, it is true that she had never been more vulnerable to an experiment in Sapphic love. And it also should be pointed out that such an experiment might well have stemmed from her unswerving compassion for all persecuted outcasts of society rather than from her teenage avowal to savor every possible experience in life. Tony was due in London shortly, and with Mme X pressuring her to break off their engagement, the singer must have been overwhelmed by massive waves of anxiety.[8] Because of her rapidly escalating problems with the managers of the Opéra, the last thing she needed now was a sexual identity crisis.

By the middle of May, Bertrand and Gailhard were seriously perturbed by Sibyl's failure to respond to their notices about the *Thaïs* rehearsals. About May 18, they received a letter from the singer informing them that she was suffering from acute bronchitis and consequently must cancel all appearances for the present time. Refusing to accept her word, they demanded a doctor's statement. Sibyl immediately forwarded a certificate drawn up by her English physicians. Declining to approve it, they sent her a summons to return to Paris by 30 May for an examination by their medical authorities. Again the singer refused.

Not only were the boulevardiers enjoying this game of hide-and-go-seek, but certain American journalists were publishing their own theories about it. To protect himself from a libel suit, the *Musical Courier*'s "Raconteur" suppressed her name in his salacious exposé of 26 June 1895, but left no doubt as to her identity.

A prima donna came to America last season. She was—let us call her an American, just for the sake of argument. But to all intents and purposes, she was a Parisian. Dainty, yet well covered as to flesh, not svelte physically, but spiritually; large-eyed, with a slow, sad smile which carried conviction.

Ah! The night that she made her debut! We all enjoyed her Gallic touch, her hopelessly Parisian style, and we all said that this young woman did herself and her country proud.

Naturally, in the swirl of success the singer had many admirers. In Paris she had been the pet of a famous composer; in New York a billionaire followed her persistently. There was but one obstacle to his suit—his wife, and she most grimly refused a divorce. The pair were enragedly in love. And love has been known to smile at locksmiths. My singer was no Puritan, and thereby hangs a tale.

She broke time and time again her engagements. A doctor was kept busy writing certificates of ill health for her, and when she returned to Paris the old trouble was renewed. Will you believe me when I tell you that only last week I read in a cable dispatch that she refused to be examined by the house doctor of a certain Parisian theater. Naturally, she had her reasons. . . . Next August it is to transpire. Several people are keenly interested in the outcome—the soprano, among the rest. Query: what *will* it be?

The author of the Raconteur's column was none other than fledgling critic James Gibbons Huneker, the very man who would later claim that he slept with Sibyl Sanderson in Paris in 1900. Arnold T. Schwab, the author of his 1963 biography, neatly shot down this little trial balloon when his research proved that Huneker was never even in Paris that year.[9]

Huneker wasn't the only one who believed the pregnancy stories. Messrs Bertrand and Gailhard even sent a detective to London to shadow the singer. His reports implied that she not only appeared to be eating for two but that she had broken her engagement to Terry after a bitter row. On 16 June the Opéra sent an ultimatum ordering Sanderson to either come back to work or forfeit 90,000 francs for breach of contract.

A London correspondent for *Le Monde musical* encountered Sibyl at this time and was told that since the doctors "absolutely forbade" her to sing at the present time, she could accept "neither condition." Instead, she would return to Paris shortly and allow herself to be examined by the Opéra physicians.

The prima donna finally arrived in Paris the first week of July and lost no time in holding a press conference. Reporters were astonished to see that she was once again in possession of her svelte figure. She told a representative of the *New York World:*[10]

I had become too Parisianized to feel altogether at ease in my own country. Houses and railroad cars are kept too hot in America. I fell victim to the system and caught a fearful cold. If I could have stayed quietly at home and taken care of myself, I should soon have gotten well, but going about from town to town, exposed to heat and cold, and to the draughts of theaters, I fell ill, and at Boston was obliged to leave my companions and return to Europe. At London I consulted several physicians who forbade me to sing before I was completely restored.

I had hoped, however, thanks to the regime I was following, to have been able to resume my work at the Paris Opéra in June. Unfortunately, in June I was not in a fit state to sing. I immediately informed directors Gailhard and Bertrand, expressing my regret and sending them the certificates of my English doctors. Those gentlemen deemed the certificates insufficient proof and requested me to come to Paris to be examined by their doctor.

When questioned about the writ and summons from the Opéra directors, she replied that a medical examination had taken place that very morning. "I hope Messrs Bertrand and Gailhard will no longer doubt my good will and good faith," she added.

Reporters then confronted her with the latest scandal that had exploded in print. Unfounded stories had appeared in various newspapers throughout Europe that Sanderson had recently attempted suicide by throwing herself into the Thames during the late afternoon of 22 June only to be rescued by two barge hands. Actually, the "beautifully dressed" American woman was never identified.[11]

"That is infamous!" the diva cried.

> How can people have invented anything so abominable? That day I had been to Covent Garden. I was in excellent spirits and had never thought of dying, yet they came and aroused my sisters in Germany for information. . . . The calumnies they have been spreading lately about me are beyond belief! They have even gone so far as to say that I dared not return to Paris because I could not show myself for reasons too delicate for me to state. Well, I'm here; people can see me. I'll show myself in the Place de l'Opéra if they like. But what in the world have I done to make people talk so much of me, and above all, with so much malevolence? My mother was at Baden, very ill, when on opening a newspaper, she saw an announcement of my soi-disant suicide. Imagine her fright! At the end of this week, I shall go to Hamburg to rejoin my mother and complete my convalescence. Afterwards I hope to finish my engagement here, for I trust that the difficulty with the Opéra will be quickly arranged.

Sanderson had asked the reporters a naive question. The year was 1895, and she had flouted a sacred Victorian taboo. Not only had she been traveling with a man of whom she was admittedly enamored, but he was still married to a respected New York lady. Mrs. Stevens was dead and unable to come to her defense.

Perplexed by her startling loss of weight, one enterprising journalist even sought out Mrs. Walden Pell, a doyenne of the American colony in Paris, to inquire if Sibyl had possibly undergone an abortion.[12] Smiling enigmatically, Mrs. Pell replied, "Really, my dear, how would I know? Why don't we just cover her with the mantle of charity?"

Judge Silas W. Sanderson, Sibyl's father.
As long as he lived, he opposed her
ambition for an operatic career.
(Collection of Margaret Sanderson Nall)

The young William Randolph Hearst, circa
1882, who later became a multimillionaire
publisher. He and Sibyl were engaged to be
married, but parental pressures broke up their
romance. (Courtesy W. R. Hearst Corporation,
New York City)

Sibyl Sanderson as a teenager in San
Francisco at the time she was engaged to
William Randolph Hearst, 1881. (Collection
of Margaret Sanderson Nall)

Jules Massenet, the French
composer who was bewitched by
Sanderson and made her a star.
(From a French postcard, courtesy
Andrew Farkas)

Sibyl Sanderson wearing a glamorous lace-covered gown
of *la belle époque* and carrying a turkey-feather fan, 1889.
(Collection of Margaret Sanderson Nall)

Sibyl Sanderson making her Parisian debut in
Esclarmonde, the first opera Massenet wrote for
her, 1889. (Courtesy Bibliothèque de l'Opéra)

Photograph of Jules Massenet inscribed to
Sanderson as "the divine Esclarmonde,"
15 May 1889. He wrote the highest note in
musical history for her. (Collection of
Margaret Sanderson Nall)

Sibyl Sanderson in Act IV of Gounod's
Roméo et Juliette, 1890. (Collection of
Margaret Sanderson Nall)

Sibyl Sanderson in Massenet's *Manon,*
preparing to dance the Gavotte, a work
that was interpolated into the opera for her
in 1891. (Courtesy the Players Club, New
York City)

Sibyl Sanderson in the title role of *Manon,* the
opera Massenet was to rewrite for her, 1890.
(Collection of Margaret Sanderson Nall)

Sibyl Sanderson as Charlotte in Massenet's *Werther*,
1892. (Collection of Margaret Sanderson Nall)

Camille Saint-Saëns, the French
composer who wrote his comic operetta
Phryné for Sanderson. (Courtesy
www.cs.princeton.edu)

Sibyl Sanderson in the title role of *Phryné,*
1893. This picture was often reproduced as
calendar art during the 1890s. (Collection of
Jack Winsor Hansen)

Toulouse-Lautrec's sketch of Sibyl
Sanderson, drawn at the Opéra-Comique
during a performance of *Phryné,* 1893.
(From H. de Toulouse-Lautrec, *Treize
Lithographies,* 1901)

Sibyl Sanderson reclining in a sybaritic pose in
Thaïs, the third opera Massenet wrote for her,
1894. (Collection of Jack Winsor Hansen)

Antonio Terry, the Cuban millionaire who married Sibyl Sanderson. (Courtesy Prince Jean de Faucyny-Lucinge, grandson of Antonio Terry)

Sibyl Sanderson dressed in an evening gown designed by Jean Worth. (Collection of Jane Sanderson Herrick)

A rare photograph of Sibyl Sanderson (standing) and Mary Garden (seated) taken at Baden-Baden, Germany, in 1900. (Collection of Jane Sanderson Herrick)

Sibyl Sanderson in the Saint Sulpice scene of Massenet's *Manon*, 1890. (Collection of Margaret Sanderson Nall)

Chapter 24

Enter Madame Schmidt

A year after Sibyl's American fiasco, an anonymous older diva, probably Clara Louise Kellogg, emerged from retirement to be interviewed by the *New York Sun*.[1] As the subject concerned singers who had dazzled Europe but failed in America, the Sanderson enigma was naturally of paramount interest.

Sibyl herself had confided to the retired singer that she felt *Manon* to be jinxed on foreign soil. The senior artist admitted that she too had superstitions about appearing in certain countries in specific roles, but in Sanderson's case there were sounder reasons for not making her debut in a new land as Manon. The *Sun* account continued:

> That was the role she sang when she made an experimental debut at the Hague, and it is the part she sang most at the outset of her career. She sings it now just as she did then, with all a beginner's faults of vocal training. I have felt the necessity, as I began to learn more about the use of my voice, of restudying my old roles with the light I had gotten from later practice and experience. Nobody who has heard Sanderson sing only in *Manon* has any idea of the extent of her voice. In *Roméo, Thaïs,* and *Faust* she fills the great auditorium of the Opéra in Paris, whereas in *Manon* she seems to have a very small voice indeed. She barely fills the Comique. That is because she sings the role just as she did as a beginner, while in parts she learned later she knows how to use her voice to bring out all there is of it. But she was an ill woman when she arrived here, and she grew steadily worse. It was only the fear that he might refuse to allow her to come over that prevented her from consulting a physician.

Although she was unaware that Sibyl had caught cold only the night before her Metropolitan debut, there was insight and wisdom in the anonymous singer's statement. However, there was one important point she failed to mention. Sanderson's conception of Manon was strictly scaled to the smaller European theater, and the architect had been Jules Massenet himself. It never would have occurred to Sibyl to relearn the role later in her career. The Metropolitan performance was modeled upon the composer's blueprints for the Opéra-Comique, and Sanderson had never made a truer statement than her declaration to the Musical Courier shortly after the New York premiere that she "sang Massenet's instructions to the letter."[2]

Whatever the soprano may have lacked in adaptability, she more than made up in determination. For most of the summer of 1895 she remained with her family at Baden and Marienbad, convalescing and nursing her voice back to health. Mme X seems to have been given an abrupt dismissal, and Terry spent a few weeks with his fiancée at the Hotel National in Geneva, Switzerland, belying reports in various journals that their romance was dead. When the singer returned to Paris the first week in September, she began her vocal studies again, this time with a new teacher, Maestro Trabadello. Although Emma Eames may have been responsible for Sibyl's defection from Marchesi's fold, regrettably her exit severed all ties with the teacher who had done more for her voice than all the others combined. Eames never liked Marchesi and was prone to exaggerate Trabadello's virtues.

A flamboyant character in the Parisian musical world, the Marquis de Trabadello was a five-foot Spaniard who plastered his face with rouge to disguise some odious smallpox scars, dyed his mustache, and covered his bald pate with a long black wig. His wife, not to be outdone, affected blond wigs, huge feathered hats, and equally exotic feather boas.

Although the Trabadellos were forced to exist solely on his teaching income, their apartment at 4 rue Marbeuf abounded with magnificent vases, paintings, marble statues, and tapestries—visible reminders of a more glorious past. The Marquise de Trabadello had been the onetime mistress of the Duke of Mantua, who compensated her handsomely for her generous favors. To thwart gossiping tongues and royal displeasure, a compliant husband had to be found to give the lady a necessary measure of respectability. Trabadello, a young tenor then singing in Rome and Milan, proved to be the ideal candidate. He was even rewarded with a title, and the rain of royal largess continued until the couple moved to France.

With such a colorful background, the Trabadellos had no difficulty in adapting to the bohemian life of Paris. Neither did the Spaniard have any trouble carving out his niche among the better-known singing teachers in the capital. Trabadello was a master of bel canto. He never tired of explaining the messianic sense of duty that had called him to France to rid its native singers of their national vice, the tremolo. To this end he labored assiduously. And to show students that he never demanded anything he could not produce himself, he would walk from one end of his enormous studio to the other, starting with a pianissimo high C, swelling to a loud climax, and diminishing to a faint tone at the opposite end of the room. All in one breath.

Sibyl found his ability to teach as inspiring as his feats of breath control. When she returned to the Opéra on 9 October 1895 as Thaïs, it was still too early for the public or critics to judge her comeback. Throughout the month she kept improving, and when she sang Juliette the first week in November, even the skeptical critics were forced to admit she had scored "a signal triumph."

After her revival of *Thaïs* the following week, there was no doubt about the pronounced increase in her vocal power. Although she had returned to the Opéra too late in the year to match the number of *Thaïs* performances given the previous season, she sang the role seven out of the nine times it was performed before the end of 1895.[3] Sibyl was grateful not only for her ultimate victory over the pernicious bronchitis, but also to the man who had helped recover her vocal technique. "I am delighted with M Trabadello as a teacher," she told reporters. "I cannot express what I owe him. He is doing for my voice just what I felt needed to be done for it, which means he is the teacher for me."[4]

The following year he also became the instructor for her youngest sister. Edith Sanderson had terminated her studies with Leschetizky in Vienna with the bitter realization that she could never become a concert pianist. She had returned to Paris full of resentment and frustration. She felt doomed to a life of aridity and creative unfulfillment. Sibyl, long cognizant of her lovely soprano voice, persuaded her to study with Trabadello for the sheer enjoyment of self-expression.

It was obvious from the crowded houses Sibyl was drawing again that her American debacle had in no way affected her popularity with the French. Gailhard and Bertrand were offering all kinds of inducements to sign her to another two-year contract, but she refused to tie herself down. There were several reasons for this decision.

While Sibyl wanted to be free to accept engagements elsewhere, her principal motivation was the elusive hope of marriage to her Cuban playboy, and Terry still insisted that she retire from the stage afterward. As a matter of fact, the couple was no closer to nuptial bliss by the end of 1895 than they had been the year before. Irritated by his wife's continual stalling, Terry eventually realized that she had no intention of ever releasing him until he capitulated to all her terms for a property and cash settlement. Now he had no choice but to do the ungentlemanly thing: file for divorce himself.

On 20 December 1895, the fourth chamber of the Civil Tribunal heard the case for the first time. Maurice Travers, Tony's attorney, brought some inflammatory charges against Mrs. Terry, including drunkenness and infidelity, and demanded custody of their fourteen-year-old daughter Natica, who had been living with her mother. Because of the Christmas holidays, the hearing was adjoined for a fortnight.

Sibyl's compatriot, Marie Van Zandt, had arrived in Paris a few months earlier for talks with Léon Carvalho about her long-delayed return to the Opéra-Comique. By now the Parisians had forgiven her for the 1884 *Lakmé* scandal. Hearing that she had definitely signed to make her comeback the following season, Massenet impulsively asked her to create one of the nasty stepsister roles in *Cendrillon* (Cinderella), the current opus he was writing for the Comique. To silence gossipmongers, he hastily offered the part of the other sister to Sibyl. As yet he had not announced who would create the title role, but he kept hinting to the press that he hoped to discover an unknown musical talent when auditions were held.

The request to create a supporting role in one of his operas was a distinct affront to his onetime heroine. But there had been a decided chill in their relationship in spite of the fact that he was at the piano that fall when she gave the first performances of some of his recent songs at a state dinner in the Fontainebleau palace. Maintaining his worshipful pose at her side, he wore his mask of benign humility throughout the evening while they received compliments from visiting royalty.

Earlier that year, a violent scene had erupted between them and, if any of the later stories can be believed, resulted in a suicide attempt by the singer. However, this claim is disputed by other evidence, and the date has not been established with any certainty. According to accounts in American papers,[5] she called upon him immediately after her arrival in Paris and asked him to intercede at the Opéra about postponing her return. Massenet refused to comply, claiming that he had no authority to interfere with the schedule of the directors. To Sibyl this was a flaccid excuse. His entire life had been devoted to meddling with the careers and schedules of others.

What the papers didn't report was the fact that tension had been building between them for a long time. As tempers flared, Massenet confronted her with the pregnancy rumors only to receive indignant denials. Sibyl, in turn, accused him not only of undermining her American debut by deceitfully withholding his *Manon* recitatives, but of attempting to sabotage her engagement to Terry as well. The machinations of Mme X had failed, she stormed, and likewise his insidious scheme to turn her into a lesbian. In the midst of soaring voices and heated charges, the composer had to leave the studio on some temporary errand. When he returned, he discovered Sibyl slumped on the floor half unconscious from swallowing an overdose of aconite.

Terrified of a scandal, he promised to do what he could on her behalf at the Opéra. Then he dashed into Heugel's office, begging him to telephone a sanitarium where she might have her stomach pumped out. Because Massenet couldn't risk publicity by requesting an ambulance, Heugel ordered several of his lackeys to carry her out the side door to a private carriage and rush her to the sanitarium. The source for this story, a young man who had begun working for Heugel that year, personally related it to me many years later.[6]

Still, a letter by Massenet to Marion Sanderson (22 April 1895) appears to contradict this tale. He pointedly complains that he has had no contact with Sibyl all winter and has just learned from Marion herself that the soprano has been in London. Unfortunately, we cannot credit Massenet's epistles with any excess of veracity. They were often little masterpieces of deception and not always indicative of either his real feelings or intentions. In the absence of more concrete evidence, however, Sibyl's alleged suicide attempt in her mentor's studio must be consigned to the same limbo of uncertainty as the later one in London.

Determined to leave the Opéra in a blaze of glory, the singer decided to make her farewell appearance in Verdi's *Rigoletto*. She had expressed doubts about singing Gilda again, but her confidence was soon restored when Trabadello opened up interpretative vistas in the role that she had never suspected. This time his invaluable coaching helped her to approach the part with new insight and maturity. The baritone Noté had been cast in the title role and the tenor Affre as the duke; Mme Beauvais would sing Maddalena; and Sparafucile was to be interpreted by bass Dubulle.

On 27 December 1895, a festive crowd thronged the Opéra to hear her. When the curtain went up on the second act, Sanderson had not been onstage long before the Parisians witnessed much more than just another pretty soprano with another lovely voice. A writer for *Le Gaulois* reflected the next day: "Here is an artist who plays, who lives her character, and who infects her audience with the same love she feels for her captor, the Duke."[7]

In the third act she was recalled over and over again and after the famous quartet, the applause turned into an ovation. Gailhard was so overwhelmed by her interpretation that the papers quoted him as predicting, "She will end up a dramatic soprano if her voice keeps developing in this direction." The following Monday evening, *Aida* was canceled so that *Rigoletto* could be repeated. Again the soprano scored a triumph with a chain of ovations.

Probably the most unexpected tribute to her performances was a glowing review by Fanny Edgar Thomas in the 15 January 1896 edition of the *Musical Courier*. It reversed her earlier appraisal of the singer's abilities when she created *Thaïs*.

> The success of Miss Sibyl Sanderson in her first Parisian appearance as Gilda in *Rigoletto* was a sincere success. . . . Comment was universal as to the wonderful improvement in her voice since her return from America. . . . "Her voice is brilliant, true, and even," said one. . . . "What a relief it is to hear singing," said another, "without either howling or scooping!" . . . If I should say anything it would be that Sibyl Sanderson's was the first feminine voice in the Opera House in two years that gave me real musical pleasure. . . .
>
> That a voice creates illusion is the main object. Not one in fifty can do it. Just "singing" is nothing in opera. All opera stars "sing." So far as I am concerned, Miss Sanderson's voice carried the illusion of the *Rigoletto* story from beginning to end. It represented the flower-like youth of Gilda in all of its changing hues from care-free joy to tragic death . . . its electric tones penetrated every crevice of the Opéra. . . .
>
> Miss Sanderson's voice is not what is termed in stereotyped parlance as a "big voice." It is sincerely to be hoped that its fortunate owner may never be induced to ruin it on Wagnerian interpretation . . . but by all that is truly musical, her voice as Gilda was a ravishing one last night!

Sanderson's artistry had succeeded in winning over one of her severest critics. It was once again her artistry the French Academy honored when it voted her the Légion d'honneur a few weeks later for distinguished service to French music. An excited Massenet sent her a *petit bleu* when he heard the news. It had come as a pleasant but total surprise to Sibyl. She hadn't campaigned for the honor as so many artists did. After receiving it, she never wore it. The decoration remained in her dresser drawer along with all the uncut jewels the Russian potentates had hurled at her feet.

There had been a movement in Paris to erect a monument to the eighteenth-century writer Jean Pierre Florian. When the committee-in-charge engaged Sibyl to appear on their benefit gala, it wasn't her artistry they had in mind, rather her box-office charisma. (André) Gaston Pollonais, a longtime friend of Adelina Patti, had written some curious music to an equally curious pantomime by Georges Boyer entitled *Mirka the Enchantress*. As the role had been tailored for Patti, that formidable prima donna quickly consented to perform it. She hadn't appeared in Paris for a number of years, and there was a new, burgeoning generation to whom she was merely a legend. Sibyl was asked to play her younger sister Frida.

Various stars from the Opéra, the Opéra-Comique, and the Comédie-Française had promised to lend their talents to the program, but the majority declared themselves to be indisposed when they learned that the benefit for the dead poet was likely to turn into an homage to Patti.

On 11 January 1896, more than two thousand people jammed the Gaîté theater for the opportunity to hear Patti and Sanderson on the same program. The audience grew more impatient by the minute. Florian's comedy *Les deux billets* was frostily received. Léo Claretie, who attempted to read a tribute to the late writer, was booed off the stage. When *Mirka the Enchantress* finally commenced, there was audible giggling at the sight of a woman in her fifties playing an eighteen-year-old ingenue. To compound the absurdity, Patti's lover was an actor from the Comédie-Française young enough to be her son. Sibyl had nothing to do but mime her part and sing such deeply philosophical phrases about her costar as "Oui, mais n'est-elle pas belle?" The music turned out to be trite, the pantomime the merest amateur gesticulation.

But when the divine Adelina began to sing, the house went berserk despite the fact that time had made pâté de foie gras out of her high notes. Flowers, bouquets, and crowns were thrown at her feet. Quick to perceive that the audience hungered for more, she interrupted the performance and treated the house to her perennial encore, "Si vous n'avez rien à me dire." From that point on, she could have recited a stock market report, and as long as she did it to music, the French would have been satisfied.

Although *Le Figaro* deplored the fact that never before had Art been denigrated so cheaply, the committee to honor the dead poet now had more than 30,000 francs in its coffers.

Meanwhile, Terry's efforts to obtain his divorce had met with an unexpected setback. The court adjourned the January hearing by granting his wife four hundred dollars in monthly alimony and the right to retain custody of their daughter. Terry was furious. He ordered his attorney to appeal the verdict immediately. When the case was heard again in the spring of 1896, Mrs. Terry's lawyer had quietly done his homework. This time he introduced an explosive list of six actresses with whom Terry had committed adultery. Lillie Langtry's name received top billing. He also supplied the court with a partial inventory of the expensive gifts Terry had lavished upon them as well as dates and places of their various trysts. Upon learning that the total amount of jewelry was worth several hundred thousand francs, the judge took cognizance of this Lothario's wealth and raised the wife's alimony to eight hundred dollars a month. Again, she was awarded the custody of their daughter. Tony nearly had a heart attack. How could his wife's counsel have gotten hold of such intimate information?

How indeed? The source was right in his own backyard, but he didn't realize it at first: Mme Elena Schmidt. Mme Schmidt had been Tony's longtime mistress, to whose comforting arms he always returned between his many affairs. Born the daughter (some say illegitimate) of a Spanish grandee, she was still a handsome woman in her middle forties, with brilliant auburn hair. Having married and divorced, she had fallen upon rather hard times before Terry's amorous interest restored her to her former mode of living. From then on she was, at various times, all things to him—lover, mother, sister, nurse, private confidante, and friend. If she ever had been jealous of any of his conquests, she hid it extremely well. After all, her shoulder was always available for Tony to cry upon when the affair was over. Indeed, she researched so thoroughly the taste and habits of the famous stage beauties he pursued that she could advise him about appropriate gifts to select for them. Even more damaging, she kept a complete biographical dossier on every one of them. Of the many loves who transited his life, perhaps she deserved the right to claim that she alone understood him.

But now Sibyl Sanderson represented a totally different kind of threat. Tony was going to great lengths to procure his freedom so he could actually marry her. If this happened she would lose him for all time, and she was determined to thwart his efforts by a cleverly contrived scheme.

Mme Schmidt was aware that Grace Terry had never liked her, or had anything to do with her. Actually, it mattered little because she had won the affection of the only woman in Tony's family who counted—his mother, Señora Tomaso Terry. One reason the old matriarch doted upon Mme Schmidt was the fact that they could communicate in their native tongue. Over and over she would sigh, "Tony, Tony, Elena is such a wonderful girl. Don't ever lose her, because, outside of me, she is the only woman who will ever understand you."

Obviously, she thought Tony's wife didn't. Señora Terry had never enjoyed close relations with her daughter-in-law because she was not only unable to converse in English, she had a pathological hatred for all Americans. Mme Schmidt decided that the time had come to rectify the situation.

Fluent in English as well as Spanish, Italian, and French, Mme Schmidt made the first move to bring about a reconciliation between Grace Terry and her mother-in-law. In the beginning it was only natural that Mrs. Terry should be suspicious of her longtime rival, but she quickly succumbed to a barrage of extraordinary charm, sympathy, and sisterly advice. Mme Schmidt's many kindnesses to Natica won over the daughter as well. With Tony's wife in the palm of her hand, this female Machiavelli set out to patch up the rift between the two women. She brought Grace Terry to her mother-in-law's home and served as their translator when they conversed, cleverly manipulating their attitudes to coincide with her own. Privately, she depicted Sibyl to Tony's mother as a dangerous stage adulteress who would not only ruin her precious son but the good Terry name as well. It didn't take a lot of such lurid persuasion to send the old lady's blood pressure soaring. Teresa Terry y d'Orticos quickly donned her armor and summoned the entire clan to their battle stations. It was a sacred duty of the family to save Tony's soul from the clutches of this Protestant harlot of the stage.

After the Terrys had heard and joined in their mother's war cry, Mme Schmidt laid out her campaign strategy. Tony's wife must be provided with Terry money for the best legal advice in Paris. Meanwhile, Grace was to raise her demands so high that Tony would either capitulate or eventually tire from his futile attempts to gain his freedom. The rest of the family was to employ every tactic they could devise to talk him out of this foolish divorce. Mme Schmidt herself would supply Grace's lawyers with all the data they needed about Tony's amorous adventures. Sibyl Sanderson's name was to be kept off the list of corespondents for the time being, but a smear campaign must be instituted against her in the Faubourg-St. Germain drawing rooms—the cul de sac of Parisian society.

It was ironic that the Terrys should set themselves up as Sibyl's judge and executioner. Their own reputation was anything but unsullied. Señora Terry's late husband had been one of Cuba's most notorious whoremongers. Tony's own philandering had scandalized international circles for nearly a decade. The predilection of her son Emilio for the lavender set was well known in Paris. And the shenanigans of another son, the late Juan Pedro, hadn't exactly enshrined the family name in the Blue Book. A decade previously, no one had heard a squawk from Mamacita when he rocked international society by marrying the widow of Charles Bullard, the infamous bank robber.

At first, Tony had no idea that his former mistress, whom he still saw occasionally at his mother's home, had united the entire family against him. For the time being, even Sibyl, as well as her intimates, remained unaware of such a formidable foe. Her mother, in fact, had naively confided to friends that all it would take to untangle the situation was for Mrs. Terry "simply to step down and out." As long as Elena Schmidt remained in command of this little Cuban Armada, Grace Terry would not be allowed to jump ship.[8]

Chapter 25

Molto Simpatico

Because Sanderson was a Parisian celebrity, everything she did or said made news. *La Vie Parisienne,* a weekly gossip magazine for the boulevardiers, never tired of joking about her continually postponed marriage. During the winter of 1895–96 it published a number of humorous interviews with Yvette Guilbert, Count Robert de Montesquiou, and inevitably, the two rival beauties of the marquee, Sibyl Sanderson and Cléo de Mérode. The responses were risqué enough to cast serious doubt on their authenticity, but suggestive enough to cause Tony Terry's mother to scream for her smelling salts when Sibyl's interview was translated to her. In 1896 no respectable woman would have dreamed of uttering such a public confession.

Under the title "Phryné, The One and Only," questions were published with Sibyl's alleged replies.

Q. What are your pleasures, your habits, your distractions?
A. The cult of my own ravishing person.
Q. Are you classical or romantic in your tastes?
A. Do you think I'm going to tell?
Q. What is your favorite perfume?
A. That of the modest violet.
Q. Do you see much of your friends?
A. Horrors! [Cléo de Mérode's alleged response was "Not if I can avoid them."]
Q. Are you inclined to be talkative or silent?
A. I manage to contain myself.
Q. What is your favorite type?

A. The one I happen to favor at the moment. [Cléo de Mérode's purported reply was "My own."]

Q. What role gives you the most pleasure?

A. Those in which *je peux me décolleter.* [Those in which I can reveal the most decolletage.]

Q. Where do you like best to make love? At your house? At his? In the mountains? In the forest? At the seashore? In the country? In Paris?

A. Any place where there is soft music in the background, even in America.

Q. Of what do you dream?

A. Tony's divorce and our marriage.

Sibyl remained in the public eye that spring—in a way no more likely to endear her to Señora Terry—when *La Vie Parisienne* sponsored a contest to choose the most beautiful woman in France. Readers were asked to mail their votes to the magazine, and the boulevardiers were betting heavily on *la belle Sibylle* to win. Then an unexpected incident occurred that swung the tide in de Mérode's favor. Falguière's nude statue *La Danseuse* had hardly been unveiled at the Champs-Élysées Salon that spring when Cléo dashed off a letter to *Le Figaro* claiming that she had posed for it. Crowds descended upon the salon, only to gasp in amazement. There could be no doubt about the model. The face of the statue was framed with those ubiquitous bandeaux—the 1830 hairstyle—that had become de Mérode's hallmark. The Parisians could not have cared less about whispers that she wore her hair this way to cover a pair of deformed ears, or worse yet, that she had been born without any. There she was on public display, and it was no mystery why the Belgian king had made her his mistress.[1]

When the votes were tallied, Cléo de Mérode was the winner with 3,076, Sibyl Sanderson the runner-up with 2,295. The exotic brunette Wanda de Boncza was awarded third place with 1,884. Oddly enough, such celebrated beauties as *la belle Otero* and Emma Eames emerged with only 730 and 504, respectively. The two undisputed queens of the legitimate stage, Bernhardt and Réjane, tied at the bottom of the list with 4 votes each.

If Sibyl had any regrets about the results of the beauty plebiscite, she was more than consoled by her new contract with the Mariinsky Theater in St. Petersburg. Anxious for her to return the following spring, the Russians had offered her 100,000 francs ($20,000) for twenty appearances. Her repertoire would once again include *Esclarmonde,* as well as *Roméo et Juliette, Manon,* and her debut in the role of Elsa in *Lohengrin.* She had been studying the role that spring with Trabadello, who believed that her recent gains in vocal strength now permitted her to tackle the Wagnerian repertoire.

The soprano also felt the lure of the concert stage. A "Monsieur Wolf" (probably the agent Hermann Wolff, but spelled "Wolf" in family papers) had amassed approximately sixty offers from various European cities where audiences were clamoring to hear her in recital. Although she had not made up her mind about the tour by the time she left Paris that spring, the diva did sign a contract to appear in Vienna the following year.

Sibyl departed for a two-month rest at the Italian lakes on 17 May. She had been working every day with Trabadello, and both agreed upon the necessity for some repose. Nevertheless, she hadn't been at Lake Como for two weeks when Edoardo Sonzogno arrived at her villa. The wealthy and powerful Sonzogno was director of La Scala Opera in Milan from 1894 to 1896, as well as being head of Casa Sonzogno, the Italian music publishing house, and editor of the influential Milanese paper *Il Secolo*.

The impresario was of medium height and sparse build. His face was noted for its deep-set gray eyes that matched the color of his mustache and thinning hair. Sibyl soon discovered that his soft-spoken manner belied a will that was as sharply honed as any Damascus blade.

They had already opened negotiations before she left Paris, but certain issues remained to be resolved. Two years previously he had purchased the abandoned Teatro della Cannobiana in Milan, renaming it the Teatro Lirico Internazionale and undertaking a major rebuilding effort. Intending to produce a season of foreign, primarily French, opera once the renovations were complete, he had already signed Mme Nevada for *Lakmé,* Mme Nuovina for *La navarraise,* and Mlle Simonnet for *Mignon.* When the refurbishment of the Lirico was finished, he looked forward to relinquishing control of La Scala. The pressures would be too much for him.

Sonzogno wanted to engage Sanderson for three performances each of *Manon* and *Phryné.* Not only were these roles absolutely identified with her, but the latter would be receiving its Italian premiere. Furthermore, he promised to send her the Italian translations forthwith. But Sibyl had reservations. Unless Saint-Saëns could come to Milan to oversee rehearsals, the singer felt she must decline. Without his expertise, she feared the premiere of *Phryné* would be doomed in the hands of some native director totally ignorant of *opéra comique.* As long as Terry continued to travel with her, she knew better than to expect any assistance from Massenet. When a telegram arrived from Saint-Saëns promising that he would be at her side that fall, Sibyl signed the contract with a sigh of relief.

Tony extricated himself from the snags in his divorce suit to join her for a few weeks. It marked the first time in their romance that the long-suffering lovers were alone together. They took boat trips around Lake Como, visited the picturesque towns along its shore, and felt the southern Breva gently caress their faces. In the evening, they would often stand on the Ponte Grande, which spanned the Adda River, thrilling to a flaming Italian sunset. Sibyl could already sense something about this country that would be sympathetic to her art.

Toward the end of June, they boarded a train for Venice, which Sibyl had always wanted to see. For the next week they did all the things that every tourist does. They fed peanuts to the pigeons in Saint Mark's Square, visited the Bridge of Sighs, and took numerous boat trips along the canals. Every night they fell asleep to the splash of oars and the songs of gondoliers.

One boat trip they made down the Grand Canal was to an old residence called Casa Chiodo, where American composer Ethelbert Nevin and his wife were staying. Sibyl and Tony spent a delightful evening with the couple, and before long they had gathered on the balcony, where the soprano couldn't resist answering the songs of the boatmen below. Soon there was such a traffic jam in the canal that Nevin wrote to a friend, "You could have walked over the gondolas to the other side." As for Sibyl's vocal magic, Nevin added, "well—she *can* sing, I can tell you!"[2]

Because she would be expected to perform her Milan engagements in Italian, Sibyl knew that she must soon return to Paris for study. Trabadello had wired her that he would forgo his vacation in Trouville to work with her. Arriving home the first week of August, she found the house deserted because her family was spending the summer on the Brittany coast. Every day she studied her Italian translations with the Spanish maestro. Because she had promised various tradesmen new pictures to advertise their products, she spent several afternoons at photographers' studios posing as Thaïs. Already her ill-advised endorsement of the dangerous but highly touted Vin Mariani had been reproduced in newspapers and magazines throughout the world. Sibyl Sanderson's photographs continued to earn money for everyone but herself.

By the middle of September, the soprano and her maid left for Milan. The new season at the Teatro Lirico was scheduled to open on 27 September 1896. Sibyl took a luxurious suite in the Hotel Continental and proceeded to live up to the mystique of an international opera star. Swathed in furs, she attended the opening of the Lirico wearing a stunning Jean Worth creation and her celebrated pearls. If her appearance distracted some of the spectators from concentrating on the music, she learned a lot about Milanese audiences. They were not as quick to form judgments as the Parisians; instead they allowed an artist a couple of scenes to put her vocal ability on display. Once they made up their minds, they either became aficionados or ruthless antagonists.

The sad plight of Jeanne Boyer on opening night brutally underscored this observation. When she inaugurated the Lirico season in Godard's *Vivandière,* it soon became apparent that her singing days were over. After listening patiently for nearly two scenes, the Milanese proceeded to boo her with astonishing ferocity.

Cécile Simonnet was another French artist who journeyed to Italy that season only to shed tears. A large audience had gathered to hear her in the title role of *Mignon.* Once they decided that she was an artist of questionable merit, chants of "Ola! Ola! Fiasco!" rang through the theater. On the other hand, Mme Nuovina scored a tremendous success in Massenet's *La navarraise.*[3] Hailed by both press and public alike as the "Duse of French opera," she had been the only import so far not to feel the wrath of the natives.

Already the papers were filled with unusually pessimistic warnings to Sibyl. "The beautiful American signorina will have her hands full," predicted one. "This is not a Paris or a St. Petersburg but a public who whistle through keys to demonstrate their disapproval if necessary . . . this is the land where opera was born!"

Sibyl began rehearsals two weeks before her debut, fully cognizant that she was facing one of the greatest challenges of her career. Massenet's *Manon* had been premiered in Milan three years before by an Italian cast. How would she compare to the soprano? After all, it was the first time she would be singing the role in Italian. In addition, the opera was competing with Puccini's version of the same story. Massenet had succeeded in getting Puccini's *Manon Lescaut* banned from the repertoire of both major Parisian opera houses for the duration of his life, but in Italy he was powerless. This was Puccini's turf.

Except for Dufriche, who seemed to follow Sibyl all over Europe as her ubiquitous Lescaut, the rest of the cast were Italians. The handsome young Pandolfini, son of the famous baritone, was to be her Chevalier. Tisci-Rubini had been engaged to sing the father, and Federici would portray De Brétigny. Rehearsals revealed that Signor Ferrari, the conductor, understood that the complex subtleties of the Gallic *Manon* demanded a different approach from the far more theatrical conception of Puccini.

After being postponed twice, Sibyl's debut was finally set for Wednesday night, 28 October 1896. Terry arrived just in time to lend his favorite soprano some much-needed support. As her appearance had been widely publicized, a capacity audience jammed the Lirico to pass judgment on the American Venus at whose feet Massenet had laid his heart and pen.

For a while after her entrance in the provincial inn yard, the Milanese were somewhat baffled. Accustomed to hearing both the Massenet and Puccini versions merely warbled, they soon realized that Sanderson was a completely different entity—a woman who acted with her voice! But even the most finicky of spectators agreed that her soliloquy and love scene were, in the words of *Italia del popolo,* "outstanding, done with uncommon facility of execution." By the end of Act I those evaluating her interpretation were divided into two factions: "one weaker in numbers, enthusiastic over this complex type of artist; the other, still dissatisfied with the quantity of her voice when they had paid such high prices for tickets." By the time Act II was finished, Sanderson's witchery had equalized the two groups, and Pandolfini's exquisitely spun "Il sogno" ("Le rêve" or Dream Song) had left the audience in a trance. Once the soprano introduced her flirtatious Gavotte in the next act, she knew she had the Italians in the palm of her hand. By the time the final curtain fell, the majority realized they were in the presence of an extraordinary artist. As Sibyl and Pandolfini took their last curtain calls, there were prolonged shouts of "Brava!" for the Californian, as masses of flowers were thrown at her feet.

The Italians had never seen anything like her. When she threw off her cloak in the chapel scene to reveal a pink velvet gown blazing with diamonds that boasted a long train festooned with egret tufts, audible murmurs of incredulity rippled through the theater.

By the following afternoon it was apparent that the critics had gone down before the diva like wheat before the reaper. Tony was so thrilled with the reviews that he clipped them as fast as the papers hit the streets and sent them to Sibyl's mother.

"Not since Heilbron [sic] and Patti has any foreign singer so moved Italy by the charm and intelligence of her work," wrote the critic for *Il Secolo.* The *Rivista Milanesa* hailed the performance as receiving "the highest possible acclaim from both the press and public. Signora Sanderson has lived up to all the fame and publicity which preceded her, and what a great singer and superb artist she is!" *Il Trovatore* praised

> Signorina Sanderson's interpretation is the finest and most exquisite that one could imagine . . . coquettish or impassioned, reckless or pensive, a smile on the lips or a tear in the eye, she is mindful of the smallest detail, yet never

loses sight of the dramatic action taking place . . . her mastery of our Italian language was a marvel to behold.

The *Corriere della sera* observed that Sanderson's performance was

a real triumph for Art . . . by the end of the opera the audience had formed the conviction that Sanderson is an extraordinary artist. . . . Her success will be augmented even more in future performances . . . Sanderson requires an audience which understands her unique gifts.

According to *L'Italia del popolo:*

Sibyl Sanderson is not one of those artists to be listened to as a vocal phenomenon nor judged by mere vocal quantity, but rather by the quality of her artistic endowments . . . the Manon she gave us was of the highest artistic merit! . . . It was not with mere high notes or stressing purely beautiful phrases having no relation to the dramatic context that Sanderson impressed her audience. Rather it was her complete penetration into the personality of the character, totally at the service of the composer with all the capabilities and splendor of the human throat. The voice, itself . . . is of extraordinarily beautiful quality and rare flexibility.

Sibyl had not received such adulation since her creation of *Thaïs* at the Opéra in Paris. She admitted in a letter to Fanny Edgar Thomas, dated 1 November, that "I never was so frightened in my life at appearing before a strange audience and singing for the first time in a strange language." By the end of her second appearance, her conquest of Italy was assured. All future performances were sold out. Every night excited students gathered at the stage door to pull her carriage through the streets. Small wonder that one newspaper likened her to a nineteenth-century "Queen of Sheba."

The Milan correspondent for the *Musical Courier* wrote to his American readers on 12 November 1896 that

Miss Sanderson's immense success in Italy is incontestable . . . put beyond any question by the unanimous verdict of the press, and by the extremely flattering offers from La Scala and other houses that have been made to her as a result of popular enthusiasm . . . originally engaged for six representations, six supplemental ones have now been arranged for, all at advanced rates of admission.

Sonzogno had demonstrated his business acumen by signing Sibyl for the additional performances before she succumbed to offers from other Italian impresarios. The current managers of La Scala were anxious to sign her for a brand-new staging of *La traviata* after the first of the year. The house of Ricordi, at Puccini's insistence, proposed a new production of his *La Bohème* for the soprano, also at La Scala. Sibyl agreed to lengthen her stay if La Scala could obtain permission from the Mariinsky Theater in St. Petersburg, where she was due in February.

By the latter part of November Puccini was lavishing a good deal of attention on the prima donna. He recently had received the Illica-Giacosa libretto for *Tosca* and had begun making a few preliminary sketches as early as 22 August, according to his letter to Ricordi. Hoping that Sibyl might agree to create the title role, the handsome mustachioed composer called upon her at the Hotel Continental. He brought an autographed picture in addition to a portfolio containing Illica's libretto and some of his own sketches for Act I.[4]

It is frustrating not to know Sibyl's reactions to Puccini's offer that day, or what themes he picked out on the piano in her suite. Although she must have been flattered, even intrigued, she had no way of knowing that the work was destined to become world famous. Nor have any of his biographers ever suspected that he approached her to portray the operatic heroine of the play Sardou originally wrote for Sarah Bernhardt. However, *Le Matin* in Paris had already announced that Puccini wanted Sanderson for his *Tosca,* and in America the *Musical Courier* erred in printing that it was Giordano who was writing the opera for her.

The composer's only surviving note to her, dated 1 December, 1896 is equally intriguing.

> Signorina—
> Like the rest of Milan I remain at your feet. I urgently beg of you to consider my proposition most carefully. Please keep me informed of your future plans.
>
> Hommage sympathique,
> Giacomo Puccini

Toward the end of November, Saint-Saëns arrived in Milan to oversee rehearsals for the upcoming premiere of *Phryné.* The managers of the Grand Hotel not only gave him Verdi's personal suite, but also the royal treatment accorded to its regular occupant. They saw that it was properly filled with flowers, every candlestick held a fresh candle, and a new piece of Blanc's soap was on the washbasin every day. Sibyl was overjoyed to see the composer again. Kissing her warmly on both cheeks, he assured her that her nude statue was being transported from the Opéra-Comique warehouse to Milan especially for the occasion.

The composer's youthful vitality continued to amaze Sibyl. She observed that his fingernails were still bitten to the quick. And his eccentricities were as pronounced as ever. Saint-Saëns never carried his hotel key with him because he was able to pick any lock he wanted with a collection of cleverly carved toothbrushes that never left his pocket. Sibyl wrote to her sister Jane that he would tiptoe impishly up and down the corridors late at night, quietly opening the doors to individual suites with his toothbrushes, hoping to observe a scene that would titillate his more prurient nature.[5]

Phryné was given its Italian premiere in a translation by Galli on November 26, 1896. Young Pandolfini was again at the soprano's side to sing Nicias, while the legendary buffo artist Pini-Corsi created the lecherous Dicéphile. All of Sanderson's seductive wiles went into the performance, and by the end of the evening she had not only brought Dicéphile to his knees, but the audience as well. The Invocation to Venus had to be encored, and after the last act Saint-Saëns joined his interpreters on stage to acknowledge wave after wave of applause. The hall was literally overflowing with the Milanese elite. Composers Puccini and Giordano were in the audience, and among the aristocracy was the wildly cheering Princess Laetitia Bonaparte from Turin.

Although the reviews were divided about the artistic merits of the opera, all the papers agreed with *Il Secolo,* which acknowledged "its success was due to Sanderson's scintillating interpretation . . . her artful coquetry was never once tainted with any vulgarity in spite of the risqué subject."

Sanderson's farewell appearance took place on 5 December in *Manon.* The correspondent for the *Musical Courier* informed his American readers that

> The theater was sold out and the applause hearty and prolonged. Basket after basket of laurel wreaths and floral sprays were brought to the diva on stage while acknowledging her encore in the second act, marring the performance, but on the last night it was pardonable. . . . Her voice was more fresh and powerful than I ever heard it before, and the Italians howled with joy.

That night cries of "Do not leave us, bella donna" echoed through the Milanese streets as students pulled her carriage back to the hotel for the last time. In the midst of the excitement, some enthusiastic American hoisted the Stars and Stripes to celebrate Sanderson's triumph on foreign soil—one the singer had been denied in her native land.

Sibyl's engagement had been the artistic and financial apex of Sonzogno's season. In retrospect, there were a number of reasons for her conquest of Milan. Thanks to the excellent coaching of Trabadello, her voice was again in pristine condition. Because her sporadic bouts with alcohol were successfully being kept under restraint, the treacherous symptoms of cramps and nausea, which so often sabotaged her appearances, were absent. In addition, the open vowels of the Italian language allowed her voice to sound fuller and more resonant than the nasal French ones.

Had she lived completely for her art, she might have returned to Italy after her Russian season and devoted herself to studying and singing more in the language. It is pointless to speculate about the operas that Puccini and Giordano might have written for her. The Milanese newspapers had already extended an open invitation for her to return and make Italy her home. The Italian musical world realized that she required audiences who understood her highly personal art.

Unfortunately art was not the center of her existence, as it was for other great prima donnas. Sibyl Sanderson was a woman who wished to savor life to its limits, including all its extremes and excesses. She was quite willing to alter her priorities even if it meant art would soon be replaced by marriage. Why? Sibyl had been born a hedonist, albeit a loveable one, and she was well aware that the life of a hedonist is too often a short one.

Chapter 26

Odette-Odile

Sibyl had not been home long before she learned that the managers of the Mariinsky had no intention of postponing her St. Petersburg engagement for the special performances La Scala had requested. The schedules of too many artists on their payroll would be thrown into jeopardy. Once the soprano understood the reason for their decision, she accepted it philosophically and resumed her daily lessons with Trabadello. Meanwhile, the Sanderson household had turned its attention to one of her sisters, who was about to be married.

When Jane returned to Europe in February 1895 to be with her gravely ill mother, she had no idea whether she would arrive in time. A young couple on their European honeymoon, Mr. and Mrs. McElroy, noticed her sitting alone one night in the ship's dining room, weeping despondently. They invited her to their table, and gradually their sympathetic understanding consoled her. Upon her arrival in Italy, she was relieved to find her mother out of danger and on the road to recovery. When Margaret subsequently went to Germany to convalesce, the McElroys invited Jane to spend the summer with them on the Isle of Sark off the British coast. They had another guest, handsome Roy Durand Herrick[1] of Minneapolis, who had just graduated from Harvard University. Young Herrick's weakness was redheaded beauties, and the moment he laid eyes on Jane's copper tresses, he was lost. She, in turn, fell in love with this jovial bearded heir to one of Minneapolis's real-estate fortunes. Roy left for America that fall to attend to his father's investments, but he returned in the summer of 1896 to propose marriage. Once Jane had accepted, it was decided that they would be married the first week in March at the Sanderson residence. Sibyl was thrilled for her sister; she knew how unhappy Jane had been living abroad.

Unfortunately, Sibyl's Russian engagement would prevent the singer from being maid of honor.

Jane was way ahead of Sibyl in the matrimonial game. Tony's latest efforts to secure his freedom had made him the laughingstock of Paris. Determined to crush his wife, he had withdrawn his divorce suit from the civil courts and transferred it to the police courts because of the serious new charges he was bringing against her. Although the exact nature of the allegations was kept secret, the papers hinted at everything from sex orgies and lesbianism to drugs.

Seldom had the police court seen a more motley crew of degenerates than the parade of pimps, hustlers, and perverts that Terry's lawyer ushered into its chambers. After each one had told a more sordid story than the last about Mrs. Terry's alleged iniquities, her counsel quickly moved to discredit the fictitious testimony by a simple ruse. He introduced a half dozen women to the witnesses and asked them to identify the correct Grace Terry. Only one of the group was able to do so, and the authorities speculated that this was only by sheer accident. Several others broke down under fiery cross-examination and admitted that they were promised money if they successfully incriminated Mrs. Terry. Naturally, the case backfired in Tony's face, and the police court had no choice but to drop the embarrassing affair and let the prior verdict of the civil court stand.

While Sibyl was home in December, Massenet attended one of her mother's Sunday evenings, ostensibly to congratulate his protégée on her Italian triumphs. According to Marion Sanderson's memoirs, it was a scintillating soirée. Saint-Saëns was present and announced that he was writing another light opera for Sibyl. But the evening was particularly memorable because of a newcomer to the Sanderson circle. She was a young Scottish-born soprano named Mary Garden who had been residing in Chicago with her family. Her voice teacher, Sarah Robinson-Duff, had taken her, along with several other students, to Paris in the late summer of 1896.[2] After securing teachers for her various charges and depositing them in their respective pensions, Mrs. Duff returned to Chicago.

Garden, who was now studying with Trabadello, brought a letter of introduction to Marion, even though she was not totally unknown to the Sandersons. On her various visits to May Stevens's family in Scotland, Marion had become acquainted with some of Mary's relatives, two maiden aunts and her ambitious grandmother.

Describing her as "lovely, fresh, and blond," Marion recalled Mary singing Saint-Saëns's "Les cygnes" (The Swans) that evening, and everyone, including the composer, appears to have been charmed by her voice and ebullient personality.

A strong friendship began to grow between Sibyl and Mary.[3] The Scottish-American lass had dozens of questions to ask about voice coaches, interpretations of roles, and opportunities for singing. Sibyl was impressed by this youngster's keenly honed intelligence and by her temperament. There was a single-minded determination in Mary's cold gray eyes as well as an independent spirit that aroused Sibyl's interest. She even contacted her former colleague, Lucien Fugère, about coaching her new friend. Quick to take advantage of an opportunity, the girl perceived that Margaret Sanderson's soirees offered American students not only a congenial atmosphere away from home but also the chance to make valuable contacts in Parisian artistic circles.

For the time being, however, Mary's new camaraderie with Sibyl was to suffer an interruption. On 16 January 1897, the prima donna and her maid departed for Russia.[4] Also boarding the Paris–St. Petersburg Express that day were Tony, his valet, Adolph, and two of the diva's fox terriers, Maggie and Pippo.

If she carried out her plan to sing Elsa in Wagner's *Lohengrin,* Sibyl was facing the greatest trial of her career, for her tenor would be none other than her old flame, Van Dyck. The Mariinsky had engaged him to sing the roles of Roméo and Des Grieux opposite her as well. After the disaster in London, it was amazing that she would consent to appear with him again. Everyone was convinced that she had elected to commit artistic suicide. Sibyl, on the other hand, was willing to take the risk because she had made such remarkable gains in vocal power since working with Trabadello. For her it would be the ultimate challenge, the decisive test.

Although it was no secret to their friends that the singer and her fiancé were now living together on tour, for the sake of propriety they took separate suites at the Hotel de Paris when they arrived in St. Petersburg. Sibyl plunged into rehearsals for *Manon* at once, disregarding the invisible jinx that so often cursed a foreign debut in this role. This time, everything seemed to go smoothly. Van Dyck made a sincere effort to observe all the composer's dynamics. With the superb Vianesi imported from France to preside over the orchestra, Sibyl felt confident that the hour was fast approaching when she would even the score with her Belgian nemesis.

When the gorgeous gold curtain went up on the stage of the Mariinsky the night of 25 January 1897, a capacity crowd had assembled to welcome Sanderson back. American ambassador Breckinridge and his wife were in their box early, and the moment the czar made his entrance, the audience rose to their feet while the orchestra struck up the national anthem.

The first act went off splendidly, with Van Dyck outdoing himself to observe Massenet's sensitive nuances and blend his voice with Sibyl's. It was fortunate for him that he did. The Russians were well acquainted with this opera, and not for one minute would they have tolerated the liberties he had taken in London some years before. Although other sopranos had sung the title role in St. Petersburg, the public had never heard its most famous exponent on her previous visit because illness had forced her to cancel her appearances.

When she was summoned to the imperial box in the grand tier, it was before Nicholas II that she curtseyed this time. Since Sibyl had last seen him, he had married a German princess and ascended the throne after his father's assassination. Although his eyes still retained their kindly blue twinkle, he now wore a Vandyke beard, and his gestures seemed more authoritative. A few minutes' conversation revealed that he was no longer the bashful young prince with whom she had sung duets a few years earlier. Nicholas congratulated her warmly and confided that he had been eagerly awaiting her return. He also expressed regret that his wife, the Empress Alexandra, could not be with him because she was in retirement that season expecting their second child. Before she returned to her dressing room, the czar asked her to convey his regards to her mother.

For the rest of the evening, Sanderson and Van Dyck were feted with continuous ovations, cries of "Bravo!" and baskets of flowers. When the curtain fell on the last act, the Emperor rose in the imperial box and, like his late father, ordered a shower of jewels to be thrown to the stars. Sibyl stood before the curtain bowing to the tremendous applause while all about her diamonds, topazes, sapphires, and emeralds were falling like pellets of multicolored hail.[5] If her heart was beating wildly with pride, perhaps she could be forgiven. She had waited a long time for this night. Odette had more than held her own against the Belgian heldentenor.

The next morning an excited Terry telegraphed Sibyl's mother: 26 JANUARY 1897—ST. PETERSBURG—SIBYL WELL—SANG MANON LAST NIGHT WITH VAN DYCK—BOTH HAD GREAT SUCCESS—LOVE—TONY. Margaret was relieved to receive his wire. Massenet, who had just written her three days before, was also anxious for news.

23 January 1897

Chère Madame,

Have you any word from Mlle Sibyl since her arrival in Russia? I assure you that my thoughts are constantly in step with her triumphs. In this I suppose

I appear to be somewhat conceited in your eyes, but how can I relinquish a single day of dreaming about her Esclarmonde or her incomparable Manon? Apropos Manon, I saw my distinguished colleague of the Institute, Benjamin Constant, recently. He is the artist who will execute the four paintings on the Opéra-Comique ceilings. He wants that beautiful photograph of Mlle Sibyl in Act III of *Manon* (the scene with her in the sedan chair wearing the same costume that she wore in Paris).

> Dear, dear remembrances
> from your villain,
> Massenet

P.S. The photograph can be addressed to me, and I will forward it to him.

Despite some comment about the delicately spoken passages not carrying in the large theater, most of the Russian press joined in praise of the highly artistic collaboration that Sanderson, Van Dyck, and Vianesi had achieved. The demand for tickets was so great that the management was obliged to present the opera four nights a week at escalated box-office prices. Such a schedule was far too strenuous for Sibyl's health, but throughout her career she never objected to the exhausting demands of avaricious entrepreneurs. Not once did she consider her own health before the satisfaction of others.

The following week Sanderson and Van Dyck reduced the Russian capital to ashes with an incendiary performance of *Roméo et Juliette*. Sibyl's virtuosic rendition of the Waltz Song stopped the show, and the audience demanded that she encore it again and again. When the performance had concluded, excited spectators recalled the stars before the curtain over twenty-five times. Once more the czar ordered his personal largess to be flung at the singer's feet.

It was inevitable that gossip should arise in the capital about the young emperor's fervid admiration of the prima donna. Every time he requested her presence in the royal box, rumors began to swirl. Nicholas was quoted as admitting that not only was the beauteous Sibyl his favorite soprano, but he had never known another singer to be favored with so many gifts. No one knew just where his admiration of the artist ended and his infatuation with the woman began. Like Hearst, Massenet, and other notables before him, he, too, had succumbed to her legendary mystique.[6]

The St. Petersburg press, however, had lost none of its hatred for the Romanovs. Neither did it lose any time in attacking Nicholas for showing more attention to the California Circe than to the czarina, who was undergoing a trying pregnancy that winter at Tsarskoye Selo. Comments about his undisguised penchant for Sibyl quickly spread through the European papers.

Because of demands for additional performances of *Roméo et Juliette* as well as *Manon,* plans for *Lohengrin* were regrettably canceled. Van Dyck had commitments elsewhere after the first of March. Sibyl's contract still called for appearances as Esclarmonde and Marguerite (*Faust*) with local artists. *Esclarmonde* was being revived at the special request of the czar; it was his favorite opera. Once again the incredibly beautiful sets, which had been created for the 1892 Russian premiere, were taken out of the warehouse to transform the stage of the Mariinsky into a Byzantine fantasy world.

The revival took place the first week in March and proved to be Sibyl's third triumph of the season. A vision in a filmy white gown with a waistband of enormous sapphires around her waist, Sanderson cast her spell not only over the French knight but the sold-out theater as well. Again her Eiffel Tower cadenza (scene 6) received a tumultuous acclamation, stopping the performance for nearly five minutes before the bishop was allowed to tear off Esclarmonde's veil and exorcise her.[7]

Years later, a chance acquaintance, an elderly Mrs. Harwood, recalled to Marion Sanderson's daughter that she had seen Sibyl leave the Mariinsky. "There was great excitement at the door, and a shout went up among the fans the minute she appeared. Two gentlemen escorted her to her carriage, and they treated her like royalty. The students threw their coats down onto the street so her feet would not touch the snow. She was wearing a full-length sable cloak and still had on her stage makeup, as I remember. But I'll never forget that huge emerald ring on her finger which they say the Czar had given her. Then, the students unhitched the horses and fastened ropes from the carriage to themselves. They pulled her through the snowy streets shouting and singing."

After the *Esclarmonde* revival, Terry found a telegram from Paris awaiting him at the hotel. His attorney, Maurice Travers, had notified him that his latest divorce hearing would be held in two weeks in the civil courts. Travers was promptly informed that he would have to handle it alone. After all, he was being amply compensated for his puerile efforts. At the moment Tony had no intention of leaving Sibyl's side, being content to bask in his fiancée's reflected glory. This was his first trip to Russia and also his first opportunity to sample the legendary hospitality of the aristocracy. He had met a few of the grand dukes on their various Gallic forays and discovered that their sybaritic tastes coincided with his own—wine, women, and horses.

But even the self-indulgent Terry was amazed at the gigantic silver salvers and vats of cold sturgeon, caviar, champagne, and deviled eggs that a battery of servants kept heaping upon the tables of the Grand Duke Vladimir. The grand duke and his wife had organized a sumptuous banquet in Sibyl's honor following a private concert she gave for their guests.

Tony had not realized that the grand duke and his wife were such close friends of Sibyl's. Of course, Sibyl had told him about the czar's sister, Grand Duchess Xenia, who had paid a surprise visit to the Sanderson residence in Paris a few years before. Having admired Sibyl's wasp-waisted figure on stage, she wanted to know how the diva corseted herself. Her Highness arrived at 46 avenue Malakoff complete with escort and much éclat. As all the Sandersons stood out of respect for Russian royalty, Sibyl informed the astonished grand duchess that she never wore a corset on stage. However, she did show her several that she used in private life and gave her the address of her corsetière. After a casual conversation, the haughty grand duchess took her leave with an indifferent nod to the rest of the family—much to their relief. They had been forced to stand at attention throughout the entire visit without once being addressed.

Sibyl's farewell appearances in St. Petersburg were as Marguerite in *Faust,* a role in which she was always well received. Until now she had performed it exclusively in the Russian capital, but this time she was asked to sing it elsewhere. Savva Ivanovich Mamontov, a Moscow millionaire, had wired the Mariinsky about bringing the entire production of *Faust* to Moscow. Having successfully built the trans-Siberian railroad from Moscow to Vladivostok, Mamontov had also constructed a magnificent theater in Moscow that offered foreign as well as native operas to the public. An ardent lover of the dramatic arts, he had hired the foremost architects, painters, costumers, and directors in Europe to make his opera house the equal of anything in St. Petersburg. As he was underwriting the entire cost of the production, Sibyl agreed to come for two performances if Vianesi was engaged to conduct.

When Sibyl and Tony arrived at the Hotel National in Moscow, they were fascinated by the "City of Forty Times Forty Churches." At first, everywhere they looked, there seemed to be nothing but the gilded onion domes of church towers. The multicolored reins of the horse-drawn cabs were ornamented with the same silver and brass bangles as those in St. Petersburg. But the more they saw of the city, they began to realize that its architecture was decidedly more Slavic in style. As the transportation hub of the Russian empire, they felt it should be called the "City of Forty Times Forty Railroads." The Kremlin cast its enigmatic spell over them. This red-walled city within a city, with its strange conglomeration of towers, arsenals, fortresses, and palaces, seemed to embody all the mystery and violence in Russian history.

As Mamontov had stridently trumpeted Sanderson's Moscow debut with a massive advertising campaign, it was not surprising that her first performance, on 21 March 1897, was sold out. While the curiosity of the populace had been aroused, their approval would be difficult to win. Muscovites had heard many performances of *Faust,* and they often failed to receive singers who were lionized in St. Petersburg with equal acclaim. Artists were judged strictly on their own merits at their Moscow trial.

Amazingly, after all the concentrated singing at the Mariinsky, not to mention the exhausting nineteenth-century custom of encoring arias, Sibyl's lungs seem to have acquired an extra reserve of dramatic power. According to a dispatch to *L'Art musical,* Moscow's audiences had never before heard a singing actress of her ilk. "Sanderson's voice became a stained glass window depicting Marguerite's very soul." All the heroine's childlike innocence from betrayal to ultimate redemption was captured by the diva's interpretation. In the prison scene "the radiant purity [of her voice] soared over the famous trio."

When the final curtain fell, Sanderson received one of the most hysterical demonstrations of adulation in her career. Flowers, crowns, watches, bracelets, rings, and laurel wreaths were thrown at her feet.[8] The frenzied audience refused to let her leave the stage until she had been recalled thirty-five times. Moscow had offered her the most hallowed of gifts: its ancient, Oriental heart.

A genuinely thrilled Terry sent another wire to Margaret the next morning.

MOSCOW—22 MARCH—SIBYL'S REPRESENTATION IN FAUST LAST NIGHT GREATEST TRIUMPH OF HER LIFE—VIANESI AND I VERY PROUD OF HER—TREMENDOUS DEMONSTRATION—HUNDREDS OF STUDENTS AT STAGE DOOR FIGHTING TO PULL CARRIAGE TO HOTEL—POLICE CALLED TO STOP RIOTING—LOVE—TONY

The second performance was received with equal enthusiasm, and Sibyl agreed to postpone her stay in order to sing a benefit concert for the students at the University of Moscow. It would be her personal expression of gratitude to the idolatrous youth of the city. Although the concert took place on Tuesday 25 March, presumably with Vianesi conducting the orchestra, there is no record of what she sang—probably operatic excerpts. Only a letter written to her in French by the committee in charge has survived.

25 March 1897

Madame Sibyl Sanderson:

In giving a special concert today to raise money for the Society of Student Aid at the Imperial University of Moscow, you have shown a real concern for the needs of our university youth and a sincere desire to come to their assistance. The committee of the Society . . . will forever owe you a debt of gratitude. Kindly permit us to express our highest recognition.

President of the committee,

S. Karsakoff

That evening Mamontov threw a lavish banquet for Sibyl that was attended by all the city's millionaire merchants. Their polysyllabic names were impossible for her to pronounce, let alone remember: Shchukin, Sondatankov, Sebashnikov, to mention a few. While a battery of servants moved among the guests with trays of caviar, chicken patties, cold lobster salad, and the usual abundance of vodka, the balding construction king showed the diva and her fiancé his collection of French impressionist paintings, which was among the most extensive in eastern Europe.

Sibyl was impressed by his luxurious scale of entertainment. Mamontov personified all the virtues and faults of the nouveau riche Moscow mercantile class. Although they lacked the Continental polish of the nobility, they were intensely proud of their heritage and not ashamed to speak their native tongue. Their compulsions seemed to be but two: they were obsessed with owning the best of everything, and they were determined to outdo the "degenerate" aristocracy of St. Petersburg at every turn.

Before the evening was over, Sibyl was to witness two sides of the Russian soul—its sadness and its ferocity. She felt the first in the heartbreaking songs of the gypsy singers and dancers hired especially for the occasion. She heard the second in the raucous shouting and table pounding of the guests, which increased in volume as the dancers grew wilder and more daringly acrobatic. One look at the rapt expression on Tony's face, and she knew he was trembling with excitement. Neither of them had witnessed anything like this before.

When they boarded the train for Warsaw on 26 March, the haunting cadences of the gypsy voices, the frenzied stomping of their boots, and the crash of broken goblets still rang in their ears. A surfeit of vodka also dulled their sensibilities. Having consumed too much alcohol already in Moscow, Tony proceeded to drink heavily on the journey, defying his doctor's warning about his damaged liver. Sibyl let down her guard and followed suit, oblivious to the fact that in two days she was to make her debut in Vienna with the Vienna Philharmonic. They were already behind schedule because Sibyl had prolonged their stay in Moscow to sing the benefit concert. In addition, they had overslept that morning and were forced to catch a later train for Warsaw, where they planned to board the St. Petersburg–Vienna–Nice express. Now it would take a miracle for them to arrive in Vienna on time.

More precious time was lost changing trains in the Polish metropolis. Because they had missed their original connection with the St. Petersburg–Nice express, they were forced to stay over in Warsaw to catch the next train on which they could obtain a private car. When the train finally pulled out of the depot Friday afternoon, a disgusted Lina realized that it would take yet another miracle for the prima donna to sober up in time to perform.

On Friday night, 28 March 1897, a brilliant audience had assembled at the Musikvereinssaal in Vienna to hear the much-advertised debut of the California nightingale. They sat patiently waiting. And waiting. Backstage their beloved impresario, Albert J. Gutmann, was teetering on the brink of a nervous break-down. All day he had been praying for some word of Sibyl's arrival. The orchestra had been forced to rehearse without her. Now, after thirty-five minutes, the audience was growing restless and surly. Herr Gutmann had no choice but to go onstage and explain that Mlle Sanderson's train had been delayed, but she would appear the following evening instead. It was a blatant fabrication on his part, but he didn't want to lose one of the season's largest gates. The crowd seemed to take the news good-naturedly and departed with astonishing forbearance.

Twenty-four hours later, the same assembly convened again with great anticipation. This time a humiliated Herr Gutmann reappeared on stage to read a telegram he had just received from the singer: HAVE MADE MISTAKE IN TRAIN SCHEDULE—JUST ARRIVED IN NICE—AM INDISPOSED—VERY SORRY NOT TO BE ABLE TO SING—SIBYL SANDERSON.

After apologizing profusely, Herr Gutmann explained that all ticket money would be refunded. A storm of boos and hisses greeted this announcement. Lent commenced the following week, and there would be no possibility of reengaging the soprano then. It was a belligerent horde that left the hall on Saturday night. Sibyl's programs were ripped to shreds. Posters bearing her pictures were spat upon, torn up, and stomped. In just twenty-four hours the soprano had plummeted from quasi-divinity to public pariah.

Furthermore, it wasn't long before newsmen discovered that Sanderson had passed through Vienna shortly after midnight without stepping off the train.

They had no inkling, of course, that she was so inebriated she had no awareness of even transiting the city. Only when the train reached Nice the following day did Sibyl awaken to the awful realization of what had happened. If Lina had not been in one of her cantankerous moods, she could have done much to alleviate the situation. A pot of hot coffee always went a long way toward restoring her mistress's sobriety.

Sibyl and Tony spent a week on the Riviera drying out before returning to Paris. The singer was physically debilitated from her strenuous Russian season, but sober enough now to assess her latest blunder. It was all perfectly clear. Had she not overstayed her visit to Moscow, she would have arrived in Vienna on time. Bitterly ashamed of her conduct on the train, she vowed that her family would never hear of it. Her mistake with regard to the train schedule would have to suffice for an excuse.

But there were not enough excuses to justify her growing number of self-destructive rampages. Such impulsive abandonment of personal discipline was Odile's method of undermining Odette's achievements, and the former was becoming a dangerous threat to the latter's career. Deep in the grottoes of Sibyl's subconscious lurked the conviction that the rewards of her career did not compensate for the sacrifices she constantly had to make or the endless suffering it caused her. Therefore, Odile, her alter ego, had been conceived to destroy Odette.

The Bacchus syndrome in Tony was the perfect trigger to set off more and more of Odile in Sibyl. These two hedonistic personalities were fatally attracted to each other. As Odette had dedicated her aspirations to the ascetic—the sworn enemy of self-indulgence—Sibyl found her loyalties torn between these opposite polarities.

Gertrude Atherton seems to have been unaware of the agonies Sibyl endured because of her career. In her memoirs she laid the blame for Sibyl's fallen star squarely on the doorstep of her rampant hedonism—a partially accurate analysis at best.

> She grew more and more unbridled, yielded more and more to all the wild impulses of her nature, as the insolence of power, the freedom of her position, and flattery, incense, adulation, shattered whatever inhibitions she may have inherited. She had feared her father, but he was dead and she feared no one else on earth . . . for nearly ten years she had no rival in her own sphere, but her triumphs should have lasted for twenty . . . her early downfall was no fault of the critics.[9]

Sibyl's apprehension of tomorrow night's audience, her dread of competing with her previous performance, her worry over technical insecurity were fears far more terrifying than any fear she may have had of her father. Yet, Mrs. Atherton knew nothing of these anxieties, because Sibyl kept them concealed under a masterful facade of self-possession.

Chapter 27

Hymen's Victory

On 10 March 1897 the Reverend Washington of the American Protestant Church arrived at No. 46 avenue Malakoff to perform the marriage of Miss Jane Sanderson to Mr. Roy Herrick before twenty-four friends. Jane was a radiant vision in a pale-blue velvet gown with black chiffon sleeves and jet butterflies sewn over her bodice. It was her shining hour—for once Big Sister wasn't there to usurp all the glory.

Attired in silver-gray satin and black ostrich plumes, a glamorous Margaret Sanderson even hired her own gypsy band for the reception. The house was crammed with masses of scarlet cannas, orchids, and roses. After the nuptial dinner and endless champagne toasts, the newlyweds left for the Riviera, where they were to spend their honeymoon. By the time Sibyl arrived in Paris the first week in April, Jane and Roy had already sailed for America, where they would make their home in Minneapolis.

At last someone in the Sanderson family had gotten married. The American enclave in Paris was beginning to wonder if Sibyl would ever get to the altar. Tony's latest divorce action had been postponed until after Easter. When it was resumed, attorney Travers again requested that custody of the daughter be awarded to his client.

It was then that Mme Schmidt decided to play her trump card. If there ever was a time to introduce Sibyl Sanderson's name to the list of corespondents, it was now. After all, she and Tony were traveling across Europe together, scandalously unchaperoned. When the case was continued for another month, Mme Schmidt was confident that Tony would be thwarted again.

What she didn't anticipate was a rebellion in her own ranks. Tony's wife instructed her lawyer to add not only Sibyl Sanderson's name to the list of her husband's mistresses, but Elena Schmidt's as well. By now, Grace Terry had grown tired of being a pawn in Mme Schmidt's private war with the singer. The prospect of a divorce had never seemed more welcome.

In spite of his fatiguing marital conflicts, Tony continued to court Sibyl in his usual opulent style. Not only had he given her a diamond bracelet and each of her sisters a diamond ring, he even bestowed diamond dog collars upon her five fox terriers. Yellow diamonds, of course. They were the current rage. There was always considerable excitement on the avenue Malakoff when his splendid coach and four drove up to the Sanderson home. Blowing the clarion to announce their arrival, his coachman Célestin would be in the rear, clad in white breeches and high boots, with a tricolor cockade on his shining hat. Sibyl's sisters would hurry up the small ladder to their respective seats in the rear, while the diva sat next to Tony in front. With the ends of his mustache waxed to perfection, and a boutonniere of cornflowers in his lapel, Terry cut a dapper figure as he gripped the reins.

Sometimes they would drive out to his stud farm at Vaucreson and eat lunch along the way. Then they were off to a fling at the racetrack for the afternoon, or he would take them to the Bois de Boulogne for the five-o'clock promenade. Sometimes Tony and Sibyl would pass his estranged wife's little fiacre in the fashionable parade of carriages, or Mme Schmidt's handsome victoria—an ironic scene that never failed to amuse the spectators.

When the Terrys' divorce cross-suit was resumed with a hearing on 22 May, the fourth chamber of the civil tribunal was fed up with the entire affair. Both parties were granted a divorce on mutual grounds of adultery. Mrs. Terry was allowed a continuance of her $800-a-month alimony. On the other hand, custody of the daughter was awarded to the grandmother, who was ordered to place the girl in a convent school at Neuilly until she turned eighteen. Although her mother was allowed visiting rights, Natica was instructed to alternate between parents during her holidays. The court also found that Terry's marriage was legal under United States law, which would ensure an appropriate bearing on the property settlement in America. Tony was free at last! Rumor had it that now her subsistence was assured, his ex-wife might return to New York. The divorce had been a long and harrowing battle.

Sibyl's attempts to reach the altar, however, were still unsuccessful. The Sanderson mystique that had mowed down Europe from Paris to Moscow was halted abruptly at the doorstep of Señora Terry. When Tony requested permission to bring his future bride to 144 Champs-Élysées, Mamacita refused to receive her.

"Never!" she snapped. "Never will I receive that stage harlot! What is a divorce in the eyes of God but a worthless piece of paper? Under church law Grace is still your wife. As long as she lives, you can never marry again! To think that you went to all this expense for a stupid piece of paper!"

Tony left that maternal interview deeply shaken, His mother was right. The church would never sanction his marriage to Sibyl as long as his ex-wife lived. In the last analysis, what was his divorce but a hollow victory? The Vatican, not Elena Schmidt, still held the winning cards.

With the close of her Russian tour, Sibyl lapsed into her old social routine. Perhaps it was understandable, for this was the world into which she had been born. No ambitious parent had driven her through the portals of Art; she had entered on her own volition. More and more she had grown to resent the necessary sacrifices, the discipline she struggled to maintain. Were the rewards really worth it? Deep within her psyche Odette and Odile were in perpetual conflict over this question. By now, Odette had become satiated with triumphs, surfeited with tributes, and bored with ovations. The singer's recent season in Italy and Russia represented the pinnacle of her career. Never again would she duplicate these achievements.

To take a closer look at her values, one should read what she wrote in her sister Edith's memory book. Although undated, the entries are probably from the fall of 1897. Ironically, even a cursory look at the characteristics the soprano most admired in men would have revealed that Antonio Terry possessed none of them.[1] For Sibyl, love had obscured all his faults. As to her ideal virtue, she made a sincere effort to practice it with regard to everyone but herself.

My ideal virtue truthfulness.

My idea of beauty in nature a calm, beautiful night in the country.

My idea of beauty in art have several ideas on the subject.

My favorite study singing—mankind.

My favorite qualities in men courage, strength, honor.

My favorite qualities in women tact, honesty.

My greatest happiness being with the one I love.

My greatest misery the contrary (to the above).

My favorite amusements theaters—small.

My favorite residence Paris.

My favorite authors Ouida and de Maupassant.

My favorite poets Musset—in fact, don't care much for poetry.

My favorite musical composer and instrument Verdi—Massenet—Organ.

My favorite heroes in real life Napoleon.

My favorite heroines in real life [line left blank]

My favorite names Doris, Sarah.

My favorite animal horses, dogs, little pink pigs.

My favorite quotation Where there's a will, there's a way.

My motto [arrow drawn to her favorite quotation]

My present state of mind happy anxiety.

A letter Sibyl wrote to her mother that summer from Switzerland was typical of the few that survive in her family. Although she complained about the strain of socializing, she had little else to occupy her time. She wasn't practicing, teaching, or doing charity work. French novels made up the bulk of her limited reading interests. Like many singers, she was merely irritated by poetry unless it was set to music. In the words of Gertrude Atherton, "she refused to cultivate a remarkable intelligence into an intellect."[2]

> Geneva Switzerland
> 20 June 1897
> Sunday

Darling mother,

Are you ill or displeased with me? I was so disappointed not to have news from some of you at least. I write at least once a week. Cannot someone do the same?

Tony has almost rented a charming house with grounds on the corner of the Ave. du Bois de Boulogne and the Ave. Malakoff . . . I am delighted with it . . . We cannot have it until January. So if we are married then we will move in . . .

Of course, I am not quite sure of my plans until I receive news from Heugel and the Opéra-Comique . . . They meet tomorrow (Monday), and I shall no doubt know within a day or two. I shall let you know immediately when I can be sure. I have fully decided not to create M Saint-Saëns's operetta so I shall write to the great agent Wolf [sic] to arrange a concert *tournée,* or I may wait until January before singing . . .

I stayed until Saturday night in Paris, so as to end up matters as nearly as possible. We had Fanny Reed to dinner. She came and was as affectionate as of old. So amusing to Tony. As Laura says, "all are varnishing up" to us. It is disgusting. Saw Mattie [Mitchell], the Duchesse de La Rochefoucauld. She is a dear, true friend. The De Fiels dined with her. All are anxious for me to return to Paris [to sing]. I saw Massenet several times, also M Crozier [protocol chef] and the Bessands. They are eternally together. Juliette [Massenet's daughter] looks ill, and says she is so. Dined with May [Stevens?], Tony, Arthur Meyer [editor of *Le Gaulois*], Henri Martell [Sibyl's lawyer], and [illegible] at the Ambassadeurs and had a good dinner and a pleasant evening. Tony and I took Mary Garden to a reprise of *Werther*. Delna was in bad voice. Friday night, Arthur Meyer dined with the Count and Countess Potocka, May, Tony, and myself. A lovely dinner and afterwards we all went to the theater. So what with the days taken up at the races and the evenings out every day of the week I was tired out and only too glad to get out of the whirl and din. I am too used to quiet to be able to stand much excitement anymore.

I am awfully annoyed in a way about our trip to Carlsbad. The King of Milan has the appartment [sic] reserved for the Duc at Phripps [hotel?]. I cannot have it until the 12th or 14th. And out of this I must be there by the 6th or 7th of July as people have it engaged. So we have decided to cross the Simplon Pass into Italy and kill time in this roundabout way. That is a slow five-days' trip. . . . I am feeling better and all tell me I am looking better than I did when I made my debut at The Hague. I owe it, I feel sure, to boiled milk and water. Tony looks well and handsome. He is on water.

Good night mamma darling, *do, do write*. I am anxious to receive news of Jane's impressions of Roy's house. . . . I hope she is quite, quite happy. . . . Do write her that I shall write as soon as possible. I have been too tired and busy to do so before . . . Deep, deep love to you, also love to the girls.

Your own
Sibyl

Although the letter revealed that Sibyl was making vague plans to return to the Opéra-Comique the following winter, there was no mention that Tony was seriously considering petitioning the Vatican to have his former marriage annulled. It would be a difficult step, in terms of both the expense and the possible consequences. He had wed Grace Dalton Secor, a baptized Catholic girl, in a prominent New York Catholic church. In addition, the marriage had been consummated. These two facts irrefutably damaged any case he might present. If the request was granted, the decision might render his daughter illegitimate. On the other hand, it would be one way to outmaneuver his meddlesome family. When Señora Terry had heard recent newspaper reports of a secret marriage to Sibyl, she threatened to disinherit him if he dared to marry "that woman" outside of the church. Sadly, Tony assured her that the stories were untrue.

If the diva found herself caught up in a futile whirl of social pursuits, she still continued her beneficent deeds. The support that she gave a young American woman recently released from a French prison demonstrated that no one could have a more loyal friend. Mme Jonquières, a New Orleans–born Creole and wife of a prominent French admiral, had been a tragic victim of her era. For a few years after her marriage, the American girl was very happy with her new life in France. Then her husband took a mistress. The lovely Creole was so stunned and hurt that she, in turn, entered into a hasty affair with a young French army officer from Toulon. Unfortunately, their relationship was not a discreet one, and Mme Jonquières soon found herself pregnant. Her decision to have an abortion brought swift legal recrimination. She and her lover were arrested and put on trial. After a scandalous court case, both of them were convicted and sent to prison, the young officer having been stripped of his rank. Meanwhile, social pressure had forced the admiral to divorce his wife.

Early in 1897 Mme Jonquières was released from prison, a wreck of a woman, penniless and shunned by society. Sibyl was notified of her pathetic condition, and she immediately joined a few other friends in giving her money and finding an apartment for her in Paris. Knowing that the admiral and his onetime wife still retained fond memories of each other, she helped to arrange a reconciliation between the two, and the couple remarried in the fall of 1897.

Although Massenet had asked Sibyl and Marie Van Zandt to create the stepsister roles in the upcoming production of *Cendrillon* at the Opéra-Comique, Carvalho wanted some little sign of contrition from his former box-office queen for her behavior during the *Thaïs* episode before he sent her a contract. After endless auditions, he and Massenet had selected a pretty young soprano, Julia Guiraudon, for the role of Cinderella.

By the first week in September, differences between singer and director were evidently resolved, because Carvalho dispatched a contract to the Sanderson residence. Only twenty-four hours after Sibyl and her paramour arrived in Paris on the 9th, a higher court than the French civil tribunal was to alter Tony's matrimonial dilemma. On 11 September 1897, international cables flashed the news that Mrs. Antonio Terry had died suddenly of "cerebral congestion" the previous day. She had returned to Paris from Tréport only two days earlier. It was an unjust end for the beautiful, tragic Grace Terry. Barely thirty-four years old, she deserved a better fate than her wretched marriage to a notorious philanderer.

No one bothered to notify her daughter at the convent school until afterward. Natica arranged for a quiet funeral and burial in Paris. "They came and told me my mother was dead," she later said. "We hadn't been getting along in her last year; there was nothing I could do but see she was given a decent burial."[3]

While Sibyl and Tony were moved by his wife's sudden demise, they were relieved, nonetheless, that all obstacles were now removed from their path to the altar. On 12 September, the Hearst syndicate, ever eager to capitalize on international romance, began a three-part story, drenched in bathos, about the long tribulations their love had endured. "Was there ever such a keeping apart of two lovers who wished to be one? All Europe sympathized with them. Such fidelity. Such patience. It must meet its reward some day." European newspapers, too, were in agreement that Terry had served his seven years for his bride. The question remained: when would he claim her?

The answer remained veiled in mystery. *Le Matin* announced that of the two contracts that lay at the feet of *la belle Sibylle,* she obviously preferred the one that assured her of a fortune for life—marriage. The other, an offer from the Opéra-Comique for a mere six hundred francs a night, had been regretfully returned with a statement that the prima donna planned to retire from the stage permanently.[4] In October, the anonymous columnist Le Passant wrote a poignant farewell to Sibyl in *Le Figaro* asking the public to permit their idols to leave the footlights and enjoy a private life of their own.

If Parisians hoped to see their beloved Sibyl once more at the Opéra-Comique, they would have to be content with Benjamin Constant's portrait of her on the ceiling as Manon. Two other divas were represented beside her: Célestine Galli-Marié as Mignon and Emma Calvé as Carmen.[5] Sibyl was the only American ever to be enshrined in such a fashion in a French state theater, and the honor plainly bespoke the love and veneration the French bore for her.

After the birth of their second child, Czar Nicholas II and Empress Alexandra paid a state visit to Paris that fall. A grand ball in their honor was given at the Opéra, and it brought out the entire beau monde, including the czar's favorite soprano and her fiancé. If friends were wondering why their wedding preparations had been lagging, one look at the pair should have sufficed to satisfy their curiosity. Fanny Edgar Thomas was shocked to see Sibyl resembling "a ghost of her former self." Tony was reported by *Town Topics* as "looking wretchedly ill of late." Obviously, the Cuban's long-standing liver complaint had flared up again.

Tony had leased a magnificent apartment at 104 Champs-Élysées, where the couple planned to move after their marriage. Because details about the approaching nuptials were kept so secret, *Le Figaro* complained that the entire affair was being handled with "the usual odious American reserve." On 30 November, Sibyl, who had been taking instruction in Catholicism, braved a bizarre fog to make her first communion at the Convent of the Blessed Sacrament. Fortunately, it was close by; the seven-day fog had already caused eleven fatalities.

On 1 December 1897, at 11:05 A.M., the singer emerged from her home, followed by her mother, two sisters, Terry, and one of his compatriots. Five landaus were waiting. So was a reporter from *Le Figaro* who obviously had been tipped off by the old newspaper crone whose stand was a few paces away. He described the bride-to-be as "highly rouged with eyes demurely downcast, and wearing a chestnut walking suit trimmed with sable." Tony's mustache, bereft of its usual jet dye, was less charitably depicted as "the color of sheepskin." Evidently, the fog had lifted.

Ten minutes later, the wedding party arrived at the mayor's office in the Passy district for the civil ceremony. Dr. Marmottan performed the ritual, which was not without its peculiarities. There was no mention of the engaged couple having notified their respective progenitors of their marital intentions three times. Instead, the civil documents simply declared that Monsieur Terry and Mademoiselle Sanderson, both being over thirty, were allowed by the laws of their respective countries to marry without observing this old Gallic custom. The *Le Figaro* reporter noticed that none of the bridegroom's family was present. Tony's witnesses were his solicitor Maurice Travers and Dr. Iscovesco. American painter Henry Howard and the lawyer Henri-Auguste Martell stood for Sibyl.

At ten minutes after twelve, the cortège departed for the convent of the Blessed Sacrament on the avenue Malakoff. At this exclusive retreat, every precaution had been taken by Mother St. Paul to keep the wedding a secret. Reporters were barred from the premises. Father Odelin performed the religious rites in the chapel, which was decorated with baskets of chrysanthemums and orchids. At 12:30 P.M., the ceremony was concluded, and everybody returned to the bride's home, where Sibyl's mother had prepared a lunch for a dozen intimate friends. None of the Terrys showed up, but Margaret hadn't expected them.

Newspapers in Paris and abroad continued to print their observations about the long-delayed nuptials. Most Parisian journals tactfully omitted all references to the boycott by the Terrys, but the Italian papers took a sadistic delight in revealing the hostility of the bridegroom's family toward the soprano. In the United States, commentators seemed frankly relieved that the holy rites of matrimony had finally turned a notorious stage siren into a respectable society matron. Yet, even they had to admit that Sibyl's marriage ended a meteoric career that, as *Town Topics* observed, "far outshone those of her American contemporaries in Europe."[6]

Accompanied by three servants, Lina, Adolph, and Célestin, Monsieur and Madame Antonio Terry left for the Riviera the next day by train. With the sudden and mysterious death of Tony's first wife, fate seemed to have made all the dreams of the long-suffering couple come true. Sibyl had given up stardom for domesticity—the very decision Massenet had dreaded for so long.

Fanny Legrand, the seductive artists' model in his current opus, Sapho, would have made an ideal vehicle for Sibyl. Having been apprehensive about her intentions for several years, Massenet never disguised the fact that he was writing the part for Emma Calvé. The woman he had discovered and catapulted to fame had broken her wedding vows to Art, and thus to him. For this he could not forgive her.

No mutual admiration existed between Terry and Massenet. A short time before the diva's marriage, *Town Topics* reported that a lovely young English girl had encountered Sibyl at a reception and sought her advice about studying with Massenet. "Before the singer could answer, Tony supposedly interrupted with an almost paternal solicitude, 'Oh, don't go to that old man, Mademoiselle. All his pretty pupils—he invariably turns them into mistresses.'" Those who witnessed the scene observed that "Terry's naive horror was equaled only by Miss Sanderson's pained surprise that such a thing could be spoken of—and in her presence."[7]

Strange as it may seem, Sibyl's image of Tony still resembled that of Prince Charming in Perrault's fairy tales. He had arrived just in time to save her from the insidious spell that Massenet had cast over her. She was perfectly willing to sacrifice her career at his request. The more that career made her suffer, the more she saw herself as a frail Antonia and Massenet as her evil Dr. Miracle. The agony of competing with last night's performance would be over at least. There would be no more audiences to fear, no longer any reason to seek courage in a bottle. She refused to accept the fact that her knight in shining armor was an alcoholic like herself, waging his own futile battle against self-destruction.

Having abandoned her routine of serious practice after the Russian tour, she gradually discontinued her lessons with Trabadello also. When her voice suddenly failed her in the middle of a concert in Nice that fall, she shouldn't have been nearly as surprised as the audience. An artist, like an athlete, is only as good as her most recent training. Jaded from adulation, she had willingly closed the door on her operatic triumphs. Now she wanted to savor the joys of marriage and rearing a family. No amount of applause would ever mean as much as the cry of her firstborn child.

According to the Raconteur's column in the *Musical Courier* of 8 December 1897, there was one woman in Paris who supported her decision wholeheartedly:

> In conclusion, let me hasten to add that the Massenets were not at the wedding feast. Jules was busy with his *Sappho* [*sic*] and his wife was not invited. But she was there *in spirit,* of that there can be no doubt![8]

Chapter 28

Unhappily Ever After

It was the morning of 24 December 1897, and the depot in Nice was a scene of hectic activity. The train from Paris had arrived shortly before 8 A.M.jammed with passengers anxious to spend the Christmas holidays on the Riviera. Among the disembarking travelers was a small, sixteen-year-old girl wearing a navy-blue cloak over her convent dress and struggling to maintain an appearance of casual disinterest. Brilliant red hair framed her fragile oval face, with its impertinent turned-up nose and pale ivory complexion. Although she could never be classified as a beauty, her most attractive feature was a pair of enormous hazel eyes that blazed with emerald streaks in the sunlight. Making her way through the crowd with an air of feigned indifference, she suddenly found herself buried under an armful of roses and swept off her feet in a paternal embrace. Antonio Terry was reunited with his daughter. Once Célestin had taken charge of her luggage, the pair left the depot arm in arm.

Outside was a long line of cabs, landaus, and victorias. As they approached her father's landau, the girl knew this was the moment she had been dreading. There sat the new Mme Terry. Poise and dignity were what she needed now to meet the crisis. After all, what difference did it make if her father chose to remarry? Her parents had been separated for years before her mother died.

His eyes beaming with pride, Tony introduced his daughter to Sibyl. The girl made a perfunctory curtsey and mechanically intoned, "Although my name is Natividad, Papa calls me Natica, but you may call me Nattie if you wish. All my friends do at school." The new Mme Terry squeezed the proffered hand warmly and flashed a magnetic smile. "Your father and I are so happy you could join us for the holidays. Now, come up here and sit beside me. I've been looking forward to meeting you so much."

Sibyl was delighted that Tony had agreed to invite his daughter for the holidays. If she succeeded in winning the girl's friendship, she would have one ally, at least, in enemy territory. During the ride back to her father's villa, Natica kept stealing glances at her celebrated stepmother. Yes, she was certainly pretty, and far lovelier than the photographs she had seen. But the singer wasn't nearly as tall as her pictures indicated, and her mouth appeared to be provocatively set a trifle out of line. When her father casually lighted the woman's cigarette, the girl quickly averted her eyes. The only members of her sex who even contemplated smoking in public were known to be tarts and stage hussies. Whatever conflicts Natica may have experienced in categorizing her new stepmother, there could be no doubt about the woman's figure. Only one word properly described it: voluptuous.

But she was so warm and outgoing, so genuinely interested in other people. And Natica had never seen her father so happy. He was constantly joking and laughing. It had been years since she heard him laugh. The strange tormented look that she used to notice in his eyes was gone.

By the time they arrived at their villa and Lina unpacked the girl's luggage, Natica had abandoned her original pose of indifference. Sibyl made her feel perfectly at ease, and her father had outdone himself to give her a festive reception. Masses of roses, bouquets of jonquils, violets, and carnations were on every table, stand, and mantel.

After dinner on the terrace, they went to midnight mass at the cathedral. On Christmas day they strolled along the Promenade des Anglais, watching the boats in the harbor. And wherever they went, music was sure to follow. Natica thrilled to hear her father accompany himself on the guitar as he relaxed on their terrace, singing Spanish and Cuban songs. At other times, Tony would blend his untrained, high tenor voice with Sibyl's golden soprano in impromptu renditions of French or American songs. The delighted teenager informed her stepmother that she had studied piano for seven years and currently was taking lessons with the distinguished organist and composer, Francis Joseph Thomé.

There was no end of social activities. Lunches at Beaulieu on the terrace of the Hotel Réserve. Lunches at Villa Belvedere, which belonged to her father's good friend James Gordon Bennett, the tall, bewhiskered editor of the *New York Herald*. Bennett's eccentricities were legend. She had heard of his drunken high jinks in Parisian nightclubs and his practical jokes, if not his scandalous orgies with prostitutes. Last but not least, she had recently learned of the social disaster that made him a pariah in the United States. Having arrived at his fiancée's

New York reception flagrantly intoxicated in 1877, he proceeded to entertain the guests by urinating in her grand piano. Her cancellation of their impending marriage was the least of the repercussions. The doors of every Fifth Avenue mansion were slammed shut to him permanently.

After an objective assessment of the situation, Bennett decided to move the hub of his operations to the more sympathetic climate of *la belle France.* In Paris he continued as the editor of the *Herald,* hiring and firing at will, amassing a fortune, hobnobbing with royalty, and even publishing an English edition for the American colony. Now an international playboy and famous yachtsman, he often spent time with Antonio Terry organizing horse races, regattas, and even bicycle races, all thrilling innovations to the French. At night the two often partook of the grape together in various Parisian dens of iniquity.

Whatever his shortcomings, the magnificent sinner won a lifelong fan that winter when he gave Tony's daughter a bicycle. For the rest of her vacation, the excited girl would arise at dawn and cycle down the cobblestone streets, eager to explore every new path. These ten days rapidly became the most enchanting she had ever known.

At night she joined her father and Sibyl at the Casino Municipal in spite of her moral reservations about gambling. Natica was overwhelmed by all the glamour—white ties and tails, diamonds, exotic perfumes, and a trail of ermine. There were German barons, Russian grand dukes, American millionaires, and Italian countesses. Tony and Sibyl seemed to know them all.

Tony himself had never seemed more buoyant and carefree. He was delighted to watch two of the three people he loved most becoming fast friends. Sibyl was so kind and sympathetic to the lonely girl he had shamefully neglected. If only his mother could see the warmth and companionship the soprano was bringing into his daughter's life. Obstinate, resolute Mamacita. In his heart Tony knew she would never receive her new daughter-in-law.

As for Mlle Terry, she soon found herself adoring her stepmother. Sibyl seemed like a big sister. Natica decided her father's family had seriously misjudged his new wife, and upon her return to Paris, the girl was determined to refute their malicious accusations.

But just as she was about to become Sibyl's lone champion in the alien camp, she was inadvertently cast in a far different role by a horrid twist of fate. On the evening before her departure, Natica joined her father and stepmother on the terrace of their villa for a game of blind-man's buff. Having caught Sibyl, Natica promptly blindfolded her and began to whirl her around, when the latter suddenly lost her balance and fell. Emitting a shriek of terror, Tony rushed to his wife's side, picked her up gently, and carried her inside the villa. Only after Sibyl had been put to bed did he break the news. Her stepmother was approximately five months pregnant. Natica was stunned. Now the girl's heart beat wildly. Guilt and remorse overwhelmed her.

Natica found herself timidly entering Sibyl's bedroom to ask forgiveness. Sibyl smiled sweetly at her and murmured, "There's nothing to forgive. You didn't know. It's my own fault. I shouldn't have been so careless." After the doctor left, Tony remained at Sibyl's bedside for some time praying fervently. Natica was very moved. She had never seen him reveal this serious side of his character before, and only now did she realize how much he wanted another child.

The next day no change was detected in Sibyl's condition, and as her father drove Natica to the depot, the girl felt utterly devastated. What had begun as such an idyllic vacation had turned into a nightmare. Before he put her on the train, Tony kissed away a tear in her eye and reminded her of the old Italian proverb, "Che sarà, sarà." She knew he was bravely trying to mask his real emotions.

On her way home, Natica had time for a little contemplation. Pregnant? They had been married less than a month. Like most convent-bred girls of her era, she had been kept so ignorant of sex education that for a while she entertained the widely believed teenage theory that a girl could become pregnant by merely kissing a boy on the lips. It was only recently that she and a few classmates were able to correct their misconceptions, thanks to some illustrated literature one of the girls had smuggled into the school.

Sibyl's pregnancy shouldn't have been a surprise anyway. She knew that her father and the singer had been living together for more than a year. Sexually, they had obviously thrown caution to the winds shortly before her mother died. When Natica arrived at the convent in Neuilly, she found that her father's wire had already preceded her. With trembling fingers, she opened the telegram. SIBYL MISCARRIED LAST NIGHT—PROMISE YOU WILL SAY NOTHING TO ANYONE—LOVE, PAPA.

In 1958 Natica recalled that she had felt like a murderer. She would have to live with this emotional scar for the rest of her life. And her father's reference to "anyone" meant Grandmother Terry and the family. Natica vowed to keep her lips sealed. If they discovered that Sibyl was pregnant before her marriage, the Terrys would have additional ammunition with which to further sully the ex-diva's reputation. How Tony would keep the news from them was his business. Sooner or later they were certain to find out.

If Sibyl had been blessed with a normal recovery, the Terrys might never have learned of it. Perhaps no one would have, but the furies seemed determined to prevent the former lyric queen from knowing any marital happiness. Serious complications arose about six days after Sibyl's miscarriage. An acute pain struck the calf of her right leg, and within twenty-four hours the limb began to swell, glowing a hot, waxen pink. Next, she was racked with a peculiar fever that rose and fell erratically. A blood clot was discovered in her right leg, and doctors diagnosed crural phlebitis, better know as milk leg. She was ordered to remain absolutely immobile in bed. Any movement whatsoever might send the clot on a terminal course toward her heart.

Since time immemorial milk leg had been a troublesome and frequently fatal problem that followed childbirth, but in the nineteenth century there were no miracle drugs to dissolve the clot. Nature had to be relied upon to perform the task, and its healing process was a slow one. Every day the doctors came to observe the patient, treat her fever, and carefully ascertain whether there had been any movement in the clot. Lina and Tony took turns bathing Sibyl's forehead with cold compresses, and the worried husband kept Margaret informed about the latest developments with a series of telegrams. He also made certain that his wife's bedroom was always filled with bouquets of roses and violets. Upon hearing of the death of Léon Carvalho, the longtime director of the Opéra-Comique, Tony sent a telegram of condolence to Carvalho's family at Sibyl's request.

Meanwhile, society on the Riviera was buzzing. Why had the newlyweds suddenly dropped out of circulation? Dozens of rumors were popping up in print, from a myth about the Terrys embarking upon a secret American visit to a vicious canard that the former star was already disillusioned with her playboy husband and was expected to walk out on him at any moment.

James Gordon Bennett had promised Tony that he would keep the news about Mme Terry's illness suppressed in the *Herald* as long as other journals didn't get wind of it. Ironically, the San Francisco *Call,* thousands of miles away, was the paper that first received rumors of Sibyl's indisposition, undoubtedly from Americans wintering on the Riviera. On Saturday, 19 March 1898, it broke the news that she was seriously ill and bedfast in Nice. The doctors were said to have had "the greatest difficulty in preventing her malady from developing into brain fever" and "at present she is in very delicate condition with paralysis of the lower limbs." Bennett immediately decided that if he reprinted the story in the *New York Herald* he still could not be accused of breaking his word. On Monday, 21 March 1898, his Paris edition carried the same version on its front page, and other Parisian and American journals followed suit with similar accounts. At least Bennett had kept quiet about the miscarriage.

René Wisner wrote a sympathetic tribute to Sibyl in *L'Écho de Paris* entitled "The Horror of Destiny," lamenting that of the many artists who have been carried to such lofty heights, "she, least of all, deserved to be cut down by such insidious destiny." In a long and moving article in *La Presse,* Louis de Gramont admitted that he was "close to despising Nature, which seems to have taken a sadistic delight in creating such a rarely gifted person as Sibyl Sanderson only to strike her down so cruelly on a bed of pain." Both writers expressed their fervent wish that the former prima donna would make a complete recovery and return "to charm both our eyes and ears."

Stacks of get-well messages were pouring into the villa every day. There were none, however, from Massenet. He and his wife had visited Nice for a brief respite in February, but it is doubtful whether he called upon his ailing goddess.

By 13 April, the blood clot in Sibyl's leg had stabilized sufficiently to permit her to return to Paris. Célestin and Adolph carried her onto the train in a stretcher under Tony's nervous supervision. Once back in their sumptuous Champs-Élysées apartment, the former diva was allowed to sit up in bed, but, as yet, was deemed too weak to stand on her feet. There was never any danger of Sibyl suffering from cold or dampness, because Terry had installed central heating.

All Paris called upon its stricken favorite. Everyone from such stage celebrities as Emma Eames and Jeanne Granier to longtime friends like the Dreyfuses— everyone but Señora Tomaso Terry. Her name was conspicuously absent from the cards that blanketed the singer's residence. Tony knew better than to expect any sympathy from the rest of his family.

Spending lavishly on flowers and nurses, he continued to humor his wife's every wish. When Sibyl expressed a desire to hear music again, Tony arranged with actress Jeanne Granier to secure the services of her gifted protégé, violinist Jacques Thibaud. He insisted that Thibaud move into their home for about six weeks and, when not performing with the Colonne orchestra, amble through the apartment playing everything from Bach unaccompanied sonatas to gypsy airs. The solicitous Cuban assured the young virtuoso that he would be handsomely compensated.

Next Terry engaged Edouard Colonne's orchestra and enough singers from the Opéra-Comique, including the entire chorus, to perform a concert version of *Esclarmonde* in his wife's bedroom. Paris was titillated! No one from the beau monde had indulged in such delectable extravagance since Boni de Castellane had financed—with his wife's fortune, of course—his huge costume fete in the Bois a few years before. The boulevardiers were wagering that such a prodigal undertaking would cost the Latin spendthrift anywhere from 35,000 to 50,000 francs. But Terry continued to rationalize his impulsive expenditure. This was the opera in which he had heard his future wife for the first time, and the role that forever endeared her to him. It might be the last chance either of them would have to hear it.

On the day of the performance, folding chairs were set up in the spacious gallery where the orchestra was to play. Colonne would stand in the doorway, where he could be seen not only by his musicians and the chorus, but also by the soloists who were to sing opposite Sibyl's magnificent Louis XV bed. A few select friends were invited to the concert, and the ex-star, glittering in Tony's canary diamonds, was propped up on pillows in a glamorous peignoir. After the conclusion of the opera, the entire cast bowed in unison to the invalid. Tears of joy streamed down Sibyl's face. The emotional rapture of this experience would remain with her forever. Upon her insistence, all the participants, from chorus to orchestra, filed past her bedside so she could thank each one individually. A grateful kiss and an affectionate embrace awaited Colonne, who found himself the hero of the hour. Equally feted was Mlle Nardi, now a German baroness, who had come out of retirement to sing her original role of Parséïs. Massenet had been expressly invited to the concert, but there is no record of his attendance. More than likely he used his frenetic rehearsal schedule as an excuse not to attend.

It seemed that everyone else in Paris, however, called upon the stricken favorite. On Sundays after the races the apartment was often crowded with prominent Americans, such as Madeleine Mitchell, the beautiful Duchesse de La Rochefoucauld, one of Sibyl's most faithful friends. Sunday was also the one day that Natica was allowed to spend with her father and stepmother. The girl was delighted to see Sibyl walking a few steps with the aid of a cane. Adolph or Célestin would carry her into the grand salon, where she now received her guests.

Natica was always in awe of the theatrical celebrities who called upon Sibyl. Since many of them were singers, she eagerly looked forward to the marvelous impromptu performances that often took place. One Sunday it might be Lucienne Bréval, the statuesque brunette soprano from the Opéra, or the ravishing Mlle Brandès from the Comédie Française, exquisitely gowned in pale gray and wearing a violet toque. The next weekend it might be the famous Emma Calvé who dropped by. "Sibylle," she would tease, "I am so-o-o-o jealous of you. You receive more flowers in bed than I ever have on the stage." Years later, Terry's daughter recalled Calvé singing melodies from Bizet's *L'Arlésienne* for the guests.

The famous actor Coquelin and singers Bartet and Van Dyck were also familiar faces. When Van Dyck sang Wagner's "Winterstürme" from *Die Walküre,* the Terry girl was so overcome by his magnificent voice that she stopped accompanying him and sat in a trance at the Steinway grand.

Eventually Massenet put in a belated appearance, without his wife as usual. When he asked Natica about her nationality, her reply that she was half Cuban and half American prompted one of his standard retorts: "Well, Mademoiselle, one thing is certain; no one can call you half pretty." Natica recalled that later that afternoon he sat down at the piano, playing and singing a group of songs that he called *Chansons grises* (Songs in Gray). Although the composer seemed to be the height of affability, Natica noticed that he never took his eyes off Sibyl. She wondered: what were his *real* thoughts and feelings? So did Tony. He never stopped watching the man who was covertly scrutinizing his wife. In private, Terry always referred to Massenet as *el viejo* (the old man), even though the composer was only fifty-six that year. But in front of the guests he remained the perfect host, deferring to Massenet's every request.

Massenet, however, was not the only composer who called. Natica always looked forward to the visits of Augusta Holmès, one of France's most distinguished female composers, because she adored Miss Holmès's song *Sans moi* (Without Me), which Sibyl often sang. It was also on one of those Sunday visits that Natica first met her stepmother's younger sisters, mademoiselles Marion and Edith. Although the girl decided that Marion was the reigning beauty in the family, her first impression of them was one of chilly reserve. They seemed very self-conscious and ill at ease. And she hoped it was just her imagination, but she sensed in them a silent hostility toward Sibyl.

With all the visitors coming and going at 104 Champs-Élysées, it was inevitable that the truth about Sibyl's miscarriage would surface. The second week in April her name was again on the lips of every boulevardier because of the revival of *Thaïs* at the Opéra. Lucy Berthet, Sibyl's former understudy, had been cast in the title role. In addition to many changes in the score, the composer had made two important additions: the Oasis Scene and a brand new ballet. Metamorphoses were occurring offstage as well. Mme Massenet was finally emerging from her cocoon. She even announced to the press that she would be attending the opera for the first time. On the first night of the revival, Massenet had never seemed more jovial, laughing and joking with his many female admirers. Before they left the Opéra, his wife gave reporters another choice morsel for the boulevardiers to savor. The morning papers quoted her as saying that she couldn't imagine "anyone giving a more perfect interpretation of the title role than Mlle Berthet."

Unfortunately, the critics did not agree with her. Though they welcomed the oasis tableau as "a memorable interpolation" in the score, they considered the revival an unmitigated catastrophe. Fanny Edgar Thomas summed up current opinion in the 18 May 1898 issue of the *Musical Courier:*

> While the news is just beginning to leak out that the ravishing California-Egyptian is not at all afflicted with paralysis, but by a much more simple and natural malady,[1] Mlle Berthet has been called to stand in comparison with her memorable predecessor and to show how the concept of love for an apostle differs in the mind of the Belgian and the Californian . . . an habitué of the Opéra, speaking of the two characterizations, says, 'There is absolutely no comparison possible. Sibyl Sanderson, as Thaïs, was simply perfection! Nothing else can be said. She fairly shook us with frissons [chills]. Her effect upon the audience was, as she was, *indescribable* . . . she was not playing Thaïs, she *was* Thaïs . . . There is no danger of Mlle Berthet being suppressed for playing havoc with the emotions. She has not a tiger in her make-up, mental or physical . . . and never for one moment is she filled with the passionate ardor which makes Thaïs such a thrilling dramatization! She is audacious at the beginning of the opera instead of feline and merely monotonous at the end.

Massenet fever had swept Paris that year. With works again playing at both opera houses, the composer was constantly being feted and eulogized. Furthermore, since her husband's lyric goddess was now in retirement, Mme Massenet had finally abandoned her self-imposed exile from the public eye. The worm had turned. Mme Massenet's recent laconic statements to the press were notable for their thinly veiled hostility to Sibyl.

Every day Sibyl continued to grow stronger, walking more and more with the aid of a cane. Ironically, while his wife was steadily convalescing that spring, Tony's health was slowly deteriorating. Recent dispatches from Cuba about the Spanish-American War heralded catastrophe. His sugar cane fields had been razed to the ground. All the months of anxiety about Sibyl and now the loss of his plantation were taking its toll. The spoiled child of Bacchus had never known the meaning of worry before, and he found himself unable to cope with the emotion. He had strayed from the strict diet imposed by his doctor. Once again he was indulging in fatty foods, rich sauces, and—even more disastrous for his liver ailment—bottle after bottle of Bordeaux wine. His family's attitude toward the new Mme Terry was another festering sore upon his heart. His own mother lived just down the street at 144 Champs-Élysées, and yet he was forbidden to bring the woman he loved—the woman he had married—across her threshold. His entire family was slowly poisoning him with their bigoted hatred of Sibyl. More and more he suffered from shortness of breath and chest pains. He found himself dropping things. He began to move like a zombie.

Tony was convinced he did not have much longer to live, and in May 1898 he ordered his Paris and New York lawyers to draft his final will. He was further depressed by the constant rain that had inundated the French capital for two successive months. Dr. Iscovesco suggested that he go to Aix-les-Bains to try the waters for his long-standing liver trouble. Tony knew that although half of fashionable Europe came trouping to the spa every summer to take the cure, only a handful left feeling any beneficial results. Still, he was in no position to reject the proposal. With Tony's vacationing daughter and a retinue of servants, the Terrys left for the resort in the middle of July and took a suite at the Grand Hotel. Since Natica had always wanted to visit the mountains around Chambéry, Tony encouraged her to make the trip because she would quickly become bored at the hotel with nothing to do.

No sooner had Natica departed than Sibyl felt a compulsive urge to write to the Massenets about her recovery. The letter arrived on 24 July 1898, at Pourville by the sea, where the composer and his wife were spending the summer.

> My convalescence is even more complete than I dared to hope for . . . it seems like a miracle but I am now able to walk without a cane and go everywhere . . . mama and my sisters are spending the summer at Dinard although we expect her and Edith to join us shortly in Aix . . . if only Tony can improve, my joy will be complete.

Massenet was so moved that he sat down the following day and dashed off a note to Margaret, noting "how overjoyed my wife and I are to learn of Mme Terry's recovery." How overjoyed Louise Massenet may have been was a matter of speculation.

One genuinely thrilled friend was Gertrude Atherton, who had stopped in Aix-les-Bains to visit Sibyl. The novelist was now making her home in England, since the British had been the first to appreciate her work. Mrs. Atherton was curious to know how Sibyl was enjoying her long-awaited marital bliss. In a frank discussion, the ex-diva mentioned the unwarranted persecution she had endured from the Terrys. Gertrude sympathized with her; after all, she had suffered some minor ostracism when she first married into her husband's Chilean family. She even recalled with amusement how opposed her Spanish mother-in-law had been to her literary ambitions. Although she had never approved of the Cuban playboy, Mrs. Atherton now was alarmed when she saw him. His eyes were sunk in dark, sagging ruts; his complexion seemed to be growing more jaundiced every day.

When Tony showed no improvement after a few weeks of daily immersions at Aix-les-Bains, Sibyl encouraged him to try the waters at Brides-les-Bains. There they were rejoined by Natica, and even she was shocked by the dramatic deterioration in her father's condition. Not only was his face the color of a harvest moon, but his heart was seriously malfunctioning as well. Every inhalation and exhalation caused an excruciating pain in his chest. Even the simple task of walking had become a nightmare. The much-hoped-for improvement at the second spa was not forthcoming either. Terry's desperate pilgrimage to save his health had failed. Now death seemed to be the inevitable dénouement.

By the time the family returned to Paris in September, Terry was so weak that Célestin and Adolph had to help him onto the train, almost six months after a similar ordeal with Sibyl. With heavy heart, Natica returned to the convent school at Neuilly, knowing that her father would remain more or less bedfast until the end. Tony, however, insisted that his wife again take up her vocal studies with Trabadello. He couldn't bear to see her constantly worrying about him.

Sibyl reluctantly obliged, and the little maestro was so delighted to welcome her back that he and his wife gave a dinner party in her honor that fall. After the dinner the former lyric queen sang four of her host's songs and was enthusiastically received. Although Sibyl was touched when Trabadello dedicated one of his compositions to her, her husband's daily decline made it impossible to concentrate on practicing. Early in August she had written her mother not to come to Aix, but now she desperately needed some maternal comfort and support. When was Mama coming home?

When indeed? Ordinarily the Sandersons returned to Paris by the second week in September, but this time they remained at Dinard the entire fall. Sibyl never suspected that her sisters were determined not to allow their mother even to set foot in the depot. From Sibyl's reports, they expected their brother-in-law to expire before the end of the year, and cognizant of the pathetic situation, they were determined to shield their mother from it—and particularly from Sibyl's emotional scenes.[2] Marion and Edith were fully aware of how upset Margaret became when she was around the family star for any length of time. Dr. Iscovesco had recommended the Carlsbad cure, but as Tony's heart was failing so rapidly, the physician now advised Mme Terry not to attempt the journey.

Since it was imperative that Tony's family be notified about his condition, Sibyl sent a desperate wire to Dinard begging Marion to be with her in her hour of need. She also mentioned that she was "ill." The word ill carried only one possible connotation. Sibyl had broken down under the strain and was drinking again. The family couldn't possibly allow the Terrys to see the former diva on one of her alcoholic sprees. Marion quickly packed her bags and sped to her sister's side. With so much volatile temperament now simmering under the Terry roof, she hoped that she would arrive before an explosion took place. Edith would remain with their mother.

Anxiety can be a cohesive agent to bind opposing forces together. In the case of the Terrys and that "stage hussy," it was inevitable that their mutual concern would effect a temporary truce.

Marion arrived to discover most of the Terrys encamped at either 104 Champs-Élysées or close by at their mother's residence. Tony was in a semicomatose state by the end of November, and Célestin, his faithful coachman, was in constant attendance, sleeping on a lounge at the foot of his employer's bed.

Drawing a deep breath, Marion met the opposition for the first time: Tony's elderly mother, Doña Teresa; his sister, the Baroness Blanc; and his brother's family, the Alfonso Terrys, with their beautiful daughter Natalie. Other members of the family were making daily appearances, including Tony's brother Andres, his sister Mme Perina, and her son, Luis. Another sister, Mme Martinet, was married to a Parisian doctor, who was often called in for consultation. Surprisingly, they all showed Marion the greatest deference, but the only one who offered any help was Tony's homosexual brother Emilio.

Fortunately for her sister, Marion proved to be a catalytic angel in the enemy camp.[3] Every night the Terrys assembled in the enormous gallery that ran through the apartment, and Emilio helped Marion provide them with comfortable chairs. They took turns kneeling in prayer at Tony's bedroom door. Whether they were praying for his life or his wealth Marion was unable to determine, but for the moment she had little time to indulge in any speculation. She was always trying to offer hope and courage to the family. At midnight she had to see that coffee and sandwiches were served.

Dr. Iscovesco, who was constantly at the apartment, shuttled between Tony's room and Sibyl's, and then back to Marion to determine whether any new instructions were needed for the nurse. As he had already pronounced Terry's condition hopeless on 5 December, the family anticipated the end, so there was precious little sleep for anyone. By 2 A.M. Marion and Natica would retire to the latter's bedroom, utterly exhausted.

On Saturday, 10 December, Terry's heartbeat had become so weak that Father Odelin was summoned to administer the last rites. Dr. Iscovesco kept the two main women in his patient's life at arm's length by sedating Sibyl most of the time, although he had no luck with her mother-in-law, whose melodramatic scenes echoed up and down the gallery. She would begin screaming hysterically at the sight of a hypodermic syringe.

Tony continued to have intermittent moments of consciousness and on 13 December asked to see Sibyl once more. According to the 15 December edition of the *New York Tribune,* he begged her to sing the air that he had first heard her perform at her Parisian debut.[4] Terry was alluding to an aria from *Esclarmonde,* but its identity cannot be determined. Sibyl began to sing it softly but soon broke down sobbing and had to be taken back to her room.

On 14 December, the morning of his death, Tony was conscious again for a few moments and tried unsuccessfully to communicate with Sibyl's sister. "Marion, Marion," was all she could understand from his incoherent whispering before he sank into a final coma. When the nurse informed her that his pulse was growing fainter every minute, Marion tried to ring Dr. Iscovesco at 11 A.M. but failed to elicit a response. A similar attempt to contact Tony's brother-in-law, Dr. Martinet, proved equally unsuccessful. Everyone who had stayed overnight gathered in his room, and at 11:40 A.M. Antonio Eusebio Terry quietly passed away.

The minute the nurse announced that his pulse was gone, Sibyl threw herself on his body and began kissing him on his open lips. When her sister and a few of the Terrys tried to pull her away, she turned on them like a frenzied beast. She hissed, snarled, kicked, clawed, and struck at them with an unparalleled ferocity. In a letter to their mother dated 16 December 1898, Marion related that she was "as strong as a giant and savage toward us all!"[5] She remained with Tony in this primitive ritual for nearly an hour, refusing to let anyone approach him. When the rest of the family finally arrived, it took six bruised and bleeding males to pry the deranged widow off her husband's body. They locked her in the petit salon, with Marion promising to remain at her side. After the corpse had been washed and dressed, the Terrys opened the door and let her into

Tony's room again. Confusion was rampant. Everyone was sobbing, and in spite of all efforts to keep Tony's mother out of the room, there stood the old lady screaming for God to take her life instead of her son's. By nightfall she still refused to go home, so Marion and Emilio made up a bed for her in the grand salon. An emotionally exhausted Sibyl eventually quieted down and spent the remainder of the night at Tony's side with Lina and Marion taking turns watching her.

The following day, Tony's body, now attired in an elegant black suit, was placed in the coffin. Velvet cloth was draped over it and candelabras were lighted. Throughout the day and night, two Catholic Sisters of Charity remained praying at his side. Weeping softly, Sibyl placed some violets over his heart beside her miniature ivory portrait. Entering his room, the Terrys were greeted with what must have been a pathetic sight—the family infidel on her knees begging the nuns to instruct her in the use of her rosary. During this crisis Sibyl yearned to practice her adopted religion, if only to be closer to Tony. It was the first time in her entire life she had ever felt the need for any religious or spiritual comfort. Even as a girl, she had never taken her Sunday school instruction seriously. Now she desperately sought the solace of the Catholic faith, but the results only temporarily alleviated her moods of despair.

Massive floral tributes were pouring into the apartment, and the entire gallery as well as Tony's room was filled with enormous wreaths. Terry's mother had insisted that her son be given a lavish funeral *de première classe*—a luxury in France, reserved only for cardinals, presidents, cabinet ministers, and generals. Marion was aghast at the idea and some of the other family members were no less mortified, but not wanting to defy her, they all capitulated. On Terry turf, as Marion was quick to learn, Mamacita's word was law! The funeral was scheduled for December 16 at the Cathedral of St. Philippe de Roule with Abbé Odelin, the same priest who had married Tony and Sibyl just a year before, officiating.

On Friday morning, 16 December, the family arose early for the private rites at the home, as French tradition prohibits the widow from appearing at the public funeral. Everyone was present except Tony's mother. On the night before, her son-in-law Dr. Martinet had somehow managed to slip her such a powerful sedative that she slept through the entire day blissfully unaware of what was going on.

No sooner had the service begun than Sibyl was seized by some kind of "convulsive fit" that Marion later described in her memoirs as a *crise de nerfs*. Her entire body stiffened as though in a seizure, her eyes staring into space, and her mouth twisted to one side dribbling saliva.[6] This time she docilely allowed herself to be removed from the room, and little by little Dr. Iscovesco was able to restore her to normal by his artful use of hypnotism. When the ceremony was over, a stream of friends began pouring into the home. Fanny Fetridge, Emma Eames's secretary, promised to return right after the funeral and remain with Sibyl for the rest of the day.

The carriages had lined up now in front of the house, and as various family members began entering them, Sibyl was taken upstairs to watch the procession from her bedroom window, which overlooked the Champs-Élysées. This proved to be a mistake. When the coffin was carried out, she again went berserk. Suddenly opening the window, she threw herself out onto the balcony, screaming, "Oh, Tony! Tony! Take me with you!" Looking up from below, Marion froze in horror while Tony's family watched in macabre fascination. Before Sibyl could jump, Lina, the nurse, and Mme Iscovesco seized her and dragged her back into the house. Heaving a deep sigh of relief, the Terrys relaxed, and the cortège started for the church. Crowds were already congregating along the Champs-Élysées, as policemen wearing black armbands and riding horses draped in black closed the avenue to all traffic. Many ignorant bystanders wondered if the president had died. It was first class all the way. Mamacita would have been proud.

At the cathedral the funeral was carried out with equally grandiose ceremony. The church was heavily draped in black, with funeral braziers at each side of the rostrum and the catafalque surmounted by a heavy metal baldachin. Guards in medieval costumes seated the mourners by invitation only. Fanny Fetridge had magnanimously corralled several of Sibyl's former colleagues at the Opéra-Comique and persuaded them to perform. Lucien Fugère, Edmond Clément, and Badiali volunteered to sing religious works of Steenman, Stradella, and Mozart. Composer Francis Joseph Thomé, Natica's music teacher, was at the organ. Yet, it was violoncellist Joseph Hollmann who incited an epidemic of weeping by a stirring performance of Bach's Aria in A Minor.

After the service was over, the funeral cortège began the slow, lugubrious journey to the enormous family crypt at Père Lachaise. About forty members made the trip on foot, following the coffin. There were many more men than women in Antonio Terry's funeral procession, including the esteemed James Gordon Bennett, but most of the lady loves in Terry's life retained their various diamond souvenirs by which to remember him.[7] After a short graveside ceremony, one of the Continent's most flamboyant playboys was laid to rest.

As for hyperbolic tributes, Bennett outdid himself in his Paris *Herald* editorial on 15 December 1898. He praised the late Antonio Terry extravagantly as a man of "magnificent, rare, and charitable qualities" and lauded his accomplishment of introducing the first trotters to French racetracks.

At Dinard on a chilly winter day, Edith Sanderson closed her diary entry with a far more accurate assessment: "14 Dec. 1898. Poor Tony is dead—died this morning at 11:40. It is all too, too sad—what a throwing away of life."

Chapter 29

Phantom Legacy

The week of 14 December 1898 was the most catastrophic in Sibyl's life. Not only had she lost her Prince Charming, she was about to lose his castle and estates as well. After a reading of the will on 19 December, the widow returned home in a state of shock. She knew her husband had suffered severe financial reverses in Cuba during the past year, but she was unaware that his staggering legacy of debt totaled more than two million francs. Nor did Sibyl realize that because Tony had mortgaged his Cuban estates to his mother for several million dollars, Señora Tomaso Terry now held the title to most of his Caribbean holdings.

It wouldn't have occurred to Sibyl that her former fiancé, William Randolph Hearst, whose hawkish jingoism had helped push the United States into the Spanish-American War, was the man indirectly responsible for the destruction of her husband's cane fields. Just how much of Heathcliff Hearst may have had in his psyche will always remain a matter for speculation. She had been too excited to notice Hearst's reaction to Terry the night they met in her Metropolitan dressing room, but her sister Jane had observed the icy greeting that the newspaper mogul extended to the sugar king. Hearst had continued to call upon Sibyl before her marriage every time he visited Paris.

The widow was alone in the huge Champs-Élysées apartment and grieving bitterly. Her stepdaughter had returned to the convent school in Neuilly and only came to spend Sundays with her. Natica knew they no longer needed her father's horses at the Vaucreson stables, and promptly put them up for sale.

Hearst's *New York Journal* learned of the impending transaction and reported early in January 1899 that Terry's fortune had been greatly overestimated. Most of what remained would go to his mother and daughter. Other newspapers began the exposé of the Terry millions, and on 22 January, the *New York World* disclosed the smoldering family feud. Under the shocking headline: SIBYL SANDERSON FORCED TO RETURN TO THE STAGE, it revealed:

> When the beautiful singer married Antonio Terry it was said she would never sing in public again. Now that Terry is dead, it seems that he and his bride have spent his birthright prodigally, and the bulk of the estate is controlled by Sibyl's mother-in-law, a strict Roman Catholic, who objected strenuously to her son's predilection for the songstress while the first Mrs. Terry was still alive. Even after her divorce, she antagonized Sibyl, and now nothing but a slender annuity will be paid Terry's widow if the elderly Mrs. Terry can prevent it. Mme Sanderson-Terry's own family asserts that despite the enormous sum received by the wonderful songstress, her total income never equaled the sum she expended in training her voice and providing the costumes for her while she was on the operatic stage.

Sibyl actually had made every effort to keep the lines of communication open with her mother-in-law. One Sunday not long after Tony's demise, she and her stepdaughter paid an unannounced visit to the family monarch at 144 Champs-Élysées. The widow was dressed in a long, black mourning ensemble with dramatic crepe veils dragging on the floor. They were ushered into the drawing room to behold the family matriarch swathed in yards of black crepe also. The two women eyed each other apprehensively; Tony's death had only intensified their rivalry.

Señora Tomaso Terry received her daughter-in-law coldly as Sibyl and Natica confronted her with the fact that they desperately needed a loan against Tony's Cuban estates to meet his mountainous debts.

The old lady's black eyes narrowed to two slits of fiery jet. "Tony would be alive now," she snapped, "if he hadn't insisted upon marrying an immoral woman of the stage! It was God's curse upon you both, but Tony wouldn't listen to me. This terrible sin has caused you to lose your child, and now my son has paid for it with his life! Repent your *pecados* to God!" hissed the angry dowager.

Her voice trembled with emotion when she told Sibyl how their concupiscence had caused the Lord's malediction to fall upon her as well as themselves. She was doomed to live out her remaining days without ever gazing upon her "baby" again. Now the family empress had no intention of releasing any of Tony's Cuban properties to help Sibyl pay off his debts; they would be held in trust for Natica's dowry. She proudly revealed plans to erect a colossal monument over her son's grave in Père Lachaise. It would consist of a handsome Renaissance chapel with four statues executed by the artist Lenoir. But there would be no place in the burial plot for the singer. Señora Teresa Terry never regarded the star as Tony's real wife in spite of their Roman Catholic marriage.

Sibyl and Natica left that audience completely shaken. The girl, who had been doing the translating, was furious with her grandmother for being so "ignorant and hostile," as she later recalled in a personal interview. The minute they stepped out on the street, Natica exploded. "That self-righteous old hypocrite! Did she feel morally justified in scheming to disinherit some of my uncles and aunts back in Cuba who just happened to be illegitimate? My grandfather provided for all of them in his will . . . the ones she hated the most were the issue of my grandfather's liaison with some actress in Cienfuegos. She's loathed the stage ever since!"

To get away from the tragic memories of that apartment, Sibyl decided to spend a few weeks on the Riviera. When she read American newspaper stories about herself she cabled Hearst from Nice on 13 January 1899:

> It is so short a time since my husband's death that I have not been able to fully decide the grave question of returning to grand opera. My health . . . is now sufficiently good to permit my return, but one must await a becoming time. Massenet counsels my return, and I am sure the Parisian public will receive me well as they have always done . . . But if I take up my calling again it will be more for artistic than financial reasons, although Mr. Terry was not quite as rich as he was supposed. He had to make a provision for his daughter, a young lady of sixteen. Let me add that the sale of Mr. Terry's horses takes place not simply because we need the money, but simply because we do not need seventy horses.

In the spring of 1899 *Town Topics* revealed that Terry had mortgaged his estates for ready cash one year before his death. The will was filed for probate on 6 May in New York. It announced that the exact value of the Cuban estates was unknown, but that it was somewhere in the vicinity of two million dollars, and the decedent left estates in both Cuba and France. The heirs were his wife, Sibyl Sanderson Terry, and his daughter, Natividad Marta Mercedes Dolores Terry. Francis E. Webb of 32 Wall Street in New York was appointed guardian of the daughter. To Mr. Webb and his Parisian lawyer Maurice Travers Tony left 90,000 francs each. He directed that all his horses and stables in France be sold. To his coachman Célestin Menendez he left 25,000 francs. To Mr. Weeks, the manager of his stud farm, he bequeathed 15,000 francs. His valet, Adolph Bonnet, received 25,000 francs. Certain charitable bequests of 25,000 francs each were left to the General Society of Shipwrecked Sailors of Paris, the Aid Society for the Families of Shipwrecked Sailors, and the Little Sisters of the Poor at Tours.

Under the terms of the will, Terry left his entire estate to any children that might be born to himself and Sibyl Sanderson Terry on condition that a life estate be created for his wife as in the marriage settlement. The will also prohibited his wife from disposing of any personal possessions—furniture, paintings, bronzes, tapestries, marbles, silver, china, and crystal—within twenty years of his death. He further stipulated that if any legatee should contest the will such legatee was to be cut off without any bequest. An additional codicil ordered his daughter, Natividad Terry, affectionately known as "Natica," to live with his wife in their Parisian home. The daughter's life interest amounted to half the estate, and Terry bequeathed an annual interest of $10,000 to each of his heirs. If either the daughter or the wife were to die first, the survivor was to receive all the remaining income. Also, if the widow chose to remarry, her yearly stipend would immediately revert to the daughter. At the time Sibyl had no idea that Tony's will would cruelly chain her to his ghost for the rest of her life.

The source of Sibyl and Natica's joint interest was one sugar plantation still in Tony's name, Aguadura a la Caudal, but its total output that year was perilously close to nil because most of Terry's fields had been razed to the ground. Sibyl must have realized she would not receive a cent from his other estates because Mamacita now held the title to most of them. The will had originally left the annual $20,000 income to Sibyl, but the previous May she had foolishly insisted that Tony revise it and divide the annuity between her and Natica. This would soon prove to be a disastrous blunder on her part.Of all the abrupt changes that had marked the ex-Californian's life, none was more pronounced than her transition from marriage to a highly touted millionaire to widowhood on $10,000 a year. Within twelve months she had gone from a life of luxury to one of comparative penury.

Dr. Iscovesco and his wife often invited Sibyl and her stepdaughter to their country cottage on the weekends, trying to cheer them up. Dressed in deepest mourning, Mme Terry arrived at Aix-les-Bains that spring to try the waters for her liver and kidney problems. After a week or so, she failed to discern any improvement. What was worse, ill health and nervous tension over the past year had caused her hair to turn white and fall out by the handful. At present, her hairdresser dyed what strands were left and artfully concealed the loss.

At the hotel she encountered another American star she had known casually in Paris, the colorful fire dancer Loïe Fuller. Born near Hinsdale, Illinois, Loïe hadn't gotten very far in the legitimate dance world before she developed her famous "gimmick," the serpentine fire dance.[1] Ever since her sensational debut at the Folies Bergères in 1892, Fuller had repeated her Parisian triumph throughout the major European capitals. Loïe was a very charitable person and listened sympathetically to Sibyl's troubles. She advised the former singer to go to Carlsbad at once, for its medicinal waters were considered by many to be the finest in Europe for liver troubles and problems caused by uric acid..

Fin-de-siècle Europeans believed there was no problem of body or mind that could not be relieved by the waters of a spa, including ailments for which they would later turn to Freudian psychiatry. With Natica, her maid, and a new chestnut-colored wig, Sibyl set off for the celebrated resort hoping for a miracle.

Carlsbad was nestled tier above tier on the steep pine-forested hills that bordered the valleys of two rivers. The seventeen warm mineral springs rose from a common reservoir known as the Sprudelkessel. Although the waters had been used as medicinal baths since at least the fourteenth century, it was during the second half of the nineteenth century that hotels, hospitals, and hospices began springing up around the city.

Natica found the hills and forests around Carlsbad enchanting. She would arise in the morning and stroll into the woods to have her breakfast—a glass of the famous mineral water, a roll, honey, and superb café au lait—in a quaint Bohemian inn. At noon she would join her stepmother for lunch on the terrace beside the lake, where they invariably ordered blue trout, the most delicious in Europe. In the afternoon Sibyl took the mineral baths swathed in sheets like a mummy. She wrote to her mother that the waters were "cold, so very cold." After several weeks of daily immersion and copious quantities of mineral water, the widow began to feel rejuvenated. She felt a sense of harmony and tranquility that she had not known in years.

One day when Sibyl and Natica were entering their carriage in front of the hotel, the Prince of Wales, who had arrived in Carlsbad, came over to pay his respects. Sibyl stood up in the carriage to greet him, and Natica, not knowing what to do, stood up also. Then feeling too conspicuous, the embarrassed teenager stepped down onto the sidewalk, leaving her stepmother to curtsey before the future King Edward VII.

Sibyl felt so much improved that she and Natica planned a little tour of Central Europe before they returned home. When they arrived at the Hotel Hungaria in Budapest, the sun was setting, and gypsies played in the lobby all evening before the enchanted guests. Both of the new visitors were so overcome by the romantic spell of the music that they were unable to sleep. Slipping into their peignoirs, they tiptoed out of their rooms and leaned over the giant horse-shoe balcony to listen in a trance. Next, the pair traveled to Vienna where Sibyl took the girl to hear her first performance of Wagner's *Die Walküre* at the Hofoper. Natica described her reaction as being "fried crisp with boredom."

After the two pilgrims returned to Paris, Natica reentered the convent school at Neuilly, and Sibyl decided to visit her mother and sisters at the seashore. For the past several years Margaret had no longer spent her summers in Switzerland. Instead, she had been renting a house at St. Énogat, on the coast of Brittany near Dinard. Named Villa Plaisance by the Sandersons, it commanded a spectacular view of the ocean from a high bluff and yet was sheltered from the turbulent sea winds by massive hawthorn hedges. A narrow path led from the terrace through the bushes, down to the white, sandy beach.

Jane Sanderson Herrick and Roy had come that summer for a visit, and there were parties, picnics, and swimming. Edith appeared to be the belle of the social circuit, attending costume balls, playing charades, and capturing the attention of the distinguished French writer Marcel Prévost. Friends from America such as the Hammonds and the Crockers dropped by. But the Terry widow remained in bed for most of the day. She seldom ventured any farther than the terrace of her mother's villa and always dressed in mourning.

Americans at Dinard, eager to catch a glimpse of Mme Terry, attributed her desire for the companionship of her kin to be a lack of funds. It was true—she had spent the earnings of her halcyon days with the same profligate reckless-ness as Tony had spent his inheritance. One reason for her fatal attraction to the Latin hedonist had been his defiant disregard for money. Her own father had foreseen her financial predicament years before, when he perceived that, even in her teens, the girl exhibited no pecuniary sagacity whatsoever. He had constantly chastised her in his letters for her lack of business acumen, but his admonitions fell on deaf ears. Money to Sibyl was some primeval substance that flowed from the bank with the same magical spontaneity of artesian spring water flowing from the ground.

By pooling their individual incomes from Tony's estate, however, Sibyl and Natica found they could manage for the present. How the widow was going to deal with her husband's debts was another question. For the time being, this accursed inheritance hung around her neck like an albatross, and the problem was beyond her ability to cope.

Chapter 30

Birth of a Star

That fall Sanderson began to wrestle with the problem of returning to the stage. Every time she gave it serious consideration, she invariably reverted to alcoholic despondency. Albert Carré kept trying to woo her back to the Opéra-Comique. Massenet was growing irritated with her continual delays. These terse, philosophical comments, though undated, were sent to her by the composer, probably during this period:

> A few thoughts to express your place in the theater:
> It is the individual who charms the poet
> You *had it all!* Why settle for a part?
> There are a great number of stones at the base of the pyramid, but only one
>   at the top
> The nightingale sings alone on the flowering shrub, but the geese fly in
>   flocks

Massenet had no conception of what it had cost Sibyl to be the stone at the top of that operatic pyramid. She was paying for it bitterly every day with the mental and physical agonies caused by her craving for alcohol, developed in her attempts to cope with stage fright. It never occurred to him how much damage he had inflicted upon her voice during those lengthy, torturous sessions on his *Esclarmonde* score. Massenet was typical of composers who do not understand the price exacted by the performer's art: the relentless competition to outdo oneself every time. The distinguished German composer Paul Hindemith gave it serious thought during his Harvard lectures some decades ago and expressed it most succinctly:

To spend a life's work and, again and again, your heart's devotion and your mind's ambition in performances, with conviction that you did your best only when you and your work disappeared behind the piece performed; gone and forgotten the moment you climbed to the highest summit of perfection and self-denial—this seems to me the essential tragedy of the performer's existence.[1]

Rumors were drifting about Paris that Sanderson would return to the Opéra-Comique in March 1900 for an important new creation. On 8 December 1899 she received a reporter from the *New York Journal* who asked the singer to verify some of the stories circulating about her. She told him she would return to the stage, but only the concert platform at first. She fantasized about being "completely rehabilitated" since her "miraculous cure at Carlsbad," not realizing that all the world's medicinal waters were powerless to satiate the alcohol-starved centers of her brain.

My life has been the husk of pleasure around a heart of sorrow . . . but my return to the stage will help me bear my great sorrow. . . . The only inheritance left me by my husband is his beautiful young daughter. My devotion to her for her father's sake makes my sorrow all the keener.

Sanderson did not mention another charitable impulse that was claiming her attention at the moment. A few weeks before, she had been out for a stroll in the Bois one morning when she ran across a very dejected Mary Garden. Sibyl had not seen her for over a year. More recently, Mr. and Mrs. David Mayer, Garden's wealthy sponsors in Chicago, had received some anonymous letters from Paris informing them that the girl had given birth to an illegitimate child. After the necessary inquiries they cut her off without a penny. Mary now owed more than a month's rent on the rue Chaldrin, and the concierge was on the point of throwing her into the gutter. Garden described that chance meeting with Sanderson in her 1951 autobiography—an encounter that marked the turning point in her life:[2]

As I was thinking, there passed me by a lady in deep mourning, with great crepe veils that were dragging all the dead leaves behind her. I can still hear the rustling of those dead leaves. And with her were five little white terriers. I knew the dogs. I had seen them at the house of the great American singer Sibyl Sanderson . . . I recognized the heavily veiled lady by her terriers as she

322

passed me by and walked on. But I gave no sign of recognition. She went a little way, turned, and came back, and we were soon face to face.

"Why, Mary Garden!" she exclaimed, lifting her veil. "What are you doing out at this time of day?" . . .

"Oh, I'm trying to work out something very tragic in my life," I said.

"Well, come into the carriage and have a drive with me."

When we got in, Mme Sanderson put her hand very gently on mine and said: "What is the trouble?" That was the first kind word spoken to me in my moment of panic. I burst into tears and told her the whole story. . . .

"You call *that* trouble?" she said.

"Well, Mme Sanderson, it's trouble for me, because I don't know where to turn."

She looked at me gravely.

"I have trouble too, my dear, but my trouble will never be settled—I have lost my husband."

And then she began to cry too, and we both sat there in the carriage on that cold November morning holding hands and crying our hearts out.

Although Garden vehemently denied in her memoirs that she had given birth to any child, Amy Leslie wrote an exposé in the *Chicago Daily News* on 25 March 1909 informing its readers not only that Mary had become the mother of a baby boy, but that the Mayers had finalized their decision to cut off her allowance after their representative had visited her and her offspring in Paris.[3] Miss Leslie had been a freelance reporter and critic in Paris in 1899–1900 and claimed that her informant was none other than Sibyl Sanderson herself. It is doubtful that Sibyl would have shared such confidential information about her protégée with any newspaper correspondent, but it would have been perfectly natural to tell her stepdaughter, which she did. Since the story was widely circulated throughout the American expatriate colony at the time, Leslie would have had no difficulty in picking up details of the twice-told gossip. Miss Leslie's article revealed that the child's father was "a little, no-account Gascon drummer" (slang for salesman) with whom Mary had been living.[4]

Mary did not take a walk from the rue Chaldrin to the Bois on that particular day only to ponder her dilemma. She knew full well that all of Parisian society could be seen there promenading in their carriages at about 11 A.M. and then again 4 P.M. It was common knowledge that if a pretty girl wished to find an affluent sponsor, ranging from middle age to dotage, the Bois provided the perfect rendezvous with lonely widowers as well as lecherous roués.

Sibyl invited Mary home to lunch that day, and they discussed the latter's situation. Upon learning that the girl was about to be thrown out of her lodgings, Sibyl rang for Célestin and ordered him to go at once to Garden's address, pay her overdue rent, and bring her possessions back to the Champs-Élysées apartment. It was one of Sanderson's most compassionate acts of charity, particularly when she was in no position to help anyone in Garden's predicament.

When Natica came home the following Sunday she discovered that the Scottish girl, "skinny as a reed," had been given her bedroom. Sibyl then moved her stepdaughter to her father's bedroom, opposite her own, facing the boulevard. She explained to Natica that Mary had had a child, which she had placed in a Catholic orphanage.[5] Natica surveyed this newcomer to the Terry household with discernment far beyond her years. There was something of Sarah Bernhardt in the girl. Mary had the same cold, calculating eyes, the same boyish, almost androgynous figure, an identical catlike intensity, and the same ruthless ambition.

The day after Mary was installed in the apartment Sibyl asked her to sing. Nearly two years had passed since Mme Terry had last heard her. Mary explained that although she was officially working with Trabadello and Fugère, she had learned the most from Fugère's expert accompanist, Jules Chevalier. In addition, Bertin had been providing her with diction lessons.

After Mary had sung, Sibyl proposed that they invite Albert Carré over to dinner so Mary could meet him. Carré was then about forty-eight and balding, with only a thin ridge of black hair left above his ears, a small dark mustache, and a pair of benign eyes whose sympathetic expression could change in a second to wrathful indignation. He had done wonders for the prestige of the Opéra-Comique in his two years at its helm. He had recently been divorced and was not averse to younger female companionship.

In her memoirs, Garden dated that dinner party to the early part of January 1900.[6] She did not mention other guests, but Sibyl's two sisters were there, and Marion has left a record of the occasion. Carré asked Sibyl if she knew of anyone who could understudy the heroine of Charpentier's *Louise,* which was then in rehearsal at the Comique. Sibyl turned to Mary and remarked, "Voilà! My little American friend here could easily sing the role." Carré kept his eyes on Mary for the rest of the evening, evidently impressed with her sponsor's recommendation. He told Mary that he didn't have time to audition her at the moment but that after the premiere of *Louise* he wanted to hear her sing.

Before he left, Sibyl asked him, "Could I take Mary with me to a rehearsal, Albert?"

"By all means, come down tomorrow. It might be a good thing for both of you."

At two the following afternoon, patroness and protégée were driven to the Opéra-Comique. The widow was elegantly swathed in furs and wearing a dramatic black hat, having formally discarded her mourning ensemble. Scarcely daring to breathe, her ward sat beside her in the dark auditorium, completely transfixed by the rehearsal. When Carré came over to greet them, Mary exclaimed that she would love to study the opera. He immediately sent for a copy of the score and presented it to her.

As of that day, *Louise* also moved into the Terry apartment, and everyone got along famously for a while. Sibyl, who had been so lonely, now had the daily companionship of her young friend. The Steinway grand was no longer mute, for Mary spent every minute she could at the piano learning the new role. Each weekend Natica would accompany her, until she believed that she, too, knew the score by heart.

Music had indeed returned to the Terry household. When Natica was on vacation, Sibyl took her, as well as Mary, to another rehearsal of *Louise*. Mlle Terry was equally thrilled by the story of the young dressmaker who abandons her bourgeois family for free love in Montmartre. The plot was so contemporary that she and countless young people of her age could easily relate to it. Charpentier's work was an excellent example of the growing popularity of opéra verismo, which dealt with realistic situations and social problems of the day.

Sibyl herself returned to music, too, if only informally. Her two wards were constantly begging her to sing their favorite airs: "L'Amour est une vertue rare" (*Thaïs*) and "Pensée d'automne." Natica would accompany her stepmother at the piano except when she sang the latest ragtime hits from America. For these, Sibyl would improvise her own clever accompaniments.

But even *Louise* did not have the power to soothe the beast that stalked Sanderson's psyche. If anything, it agitated this unseen monster. In Sibyl's mind the drudgery of concentrated practice was so synonymous with alcoholic escape that Mary's daily routine began to upset her as if it were her own. Unconsciously identifying with her protégée, the former star kept reliving her own youthful hours spent in the service of the muse. It was not long before she was plagued by manic-depressive episodes and confined to bed.

These spells had been occurring long before Mary appeared on the scene and showed certain predictable patterns her stepdaughter later recalled. Several days before an attack, Sibyl would exhibit signs of extreme nervousness and irritability. Her speech would accelerate until her brain could no longer regulate it. As a result, her sentences were often jumbled, incoherent, and as fragmented as her uncoordinated gestures. This hyperarousal would not allow her to sleep at all, and her craving for alcohol would become insatiable. When the climax arrived, it manifested itself either in hysterical screaming and shaking, or in wanton destruction, with Sibyl throwing and breaking things around her. Her muscles would stiffen as rigidly as if she were suffering from epilepsy. After the inevitable sweating, or occasional vomiting, the attack usually abated, and she would grow weak and lethargic. The final stage would see her reverting in speech and action to the behavior of a repentant little girl, with Lina playing the role of the forgiving mother.[7]

One day Garden came home rather dispirited, having seen a handsome dog run over by a cab. She was wearing a new hat that she had just bought, and before she could remove it, Lina appeared and announced that Sibyl wished to speak with her. Mary had wondered for some time whether her practicing disturbed her benefactress, and now she fully expected to see it curtailed. She also had been alarmed to discover that her patroness was drinking.

When she opened the door to Sibyl's bedroom she found the widow to be in a highly agitated state. However, Mme Terry's attention was diverted by Garden's new acquisition, and her mood changed abruptly.

"Mary! What an adorable hat! Let me see what I look like in it."

Sibyl sat up in bed modeling the hat before a looking glass. Then she smiled at her ward. "Mary, it's a dream, and you may practice as long as you wish." From that day on, however, Mary tried to limit her routine at the piano. She would take her score into the bedroom and go over it carefully, humming it to herself, as she tapped out the rhythms on the floor with her foot.

The Scottish soprano claimed in her autobiography that she was again living in her little pension when she made her unexpected debut in *Louise*. She explained that Sibyl had been advised by her doctor to close the Champs-Élysées apartment and spend the rest of the winter on the Riviera. Garden's desire to create a dramatic story of the poor student slaving alone on her score of *Louise* was just part of a larger fantasy she later concocted about her debut.

According to the reminiscences of both Marion Sanderson and Natividad Terry, Mary continued to reside at 104 Champs-Élysées until the end of April 1900. Sibyl had taken her stepdaughter to Nice over the Christmas holidays, and did not depart for the Riviera again until a few weeks after Garden's debut.

The premiere of Charpentier's *Louise* took place on 2 February 1900 and was enthusiastically received by the Parisians. The roles of the dressmaker and her lover were created by Marthe Rioton and Adolphe Maréchal, with Mme Deschamps-Jehin and Fugère portraying Louise's parents. Garden had been engaged by Carré as an employee of the Opéra-Comique at the end of January 1900 with a postdated contract to sing Micaëla in the fall. As unofficial understudy for the title role in *Louise,* she was granted the privilege of attending all rehearsals at the Comique—a dispensation of which she took full advantage. She mutilated her score with hundreds of notes about blocking, orchestral tempi, and the conductor's cues. When the opportunity came for Mary Garden to go on in the middle of the opera, she was ready, although she claimed she had never had an orchestral rehearsal.

In his biography of Mary Garden, Michael Turnbull states that the Opéra-Comique register shows she did have an orchestra rehearsal on 5 March.[8] However, the rehearsal was more than likely with an assistant conductor whose duties included working with understudies. It is unlikely that she had more than one, because Cathérine Mastio was the official understudy for the title role, and opportunities to rehearse would have been awarded to her first. Certainly, the Scottish soprano would have had her share of piano rehearsals because these were required of all the understudies as well as the principals.

Mary's dramatic coup de théâtre was an event of tremendous excitement but evidently not exciting enough for her. Later she was to glamorize it with further embellishment, fabricating for it a date of Friday, 13 April, and an assigned seat number 13. She repeated this canard for decades in countless interviews (including her conversation with me), and also in her 1951 autobiography. Friday, 13 April just happened to be Good Friday in 1900, and every state theater in Paris was closed for the religious holiday. The soprano actually skyrocketed onto the operatic horizon on Tuesday, 10 April.

According to Marion Sanderson's memoirs, Sibyl received a telephone call from Albert Carré requesting that Mary be at the theater early that night because Mlle Rioton had informed him she was suffering from throat trouble but would still try to go on that evening. Apparently Mlle Mastio, the regular understudy, was also ill. Sibyl began arguing that the circumstances were too risky for her ward, but Garden grabbed the receiver from her hand and announced she would be ready to stand by.[9] Sibyl paid for a cab to drive Mary to the theater early, and the excited understudy informed the staff that she would be in the Sanderson box.

The first two acts of *Louise* went fairly well, with Rioton showing little signs of trouble. But during intermission the heroine was suddenly seized with constricture of the vocal cords, and, panicking, ran out the stage door into the night.

Mary was conducted backstage to discover that the queen ant's disappearance had thrown the entire colony into an uproar. The whole production staff was running around in circles. Everybody was shouting at everyone else. Even the stagehand who had been sent to find the runaway soprano had not returned. Just as everything was beginning to resemble the card scene from *Alice in Wonderland,* Carré emerged from the chaos to ask Mary if she could finish the opera. Garden, realizing this moment was the chance of a lifetime, assured him she knew the part thoroughly.

André Messager, the conductor, protested vigorously to Carré in his office. This little foreigner had never had an orchestral rehearsal with him, and no professional experience whatsoever.[10] The performance would be a disaster. He urged the director to refund the audience's money rather than risk failure.

Carré stood firm against the conductor's dissension, his faith in the little Scottish-American girl unshaken. The director informed Messager that if he declined to conduct for the newcomer, his staff would immediately call another conductor to replace him. Carré's will prevailed, and Lucien Fugère, who was singing Louise's father, went onstage just before the third-act curtain to announce that "a Mlle Garden would assume the role of Louise for the remainder of the opera."

Marion Sanderson, who was with Sibyl in her box, described the rest of the performance in her posthumous papers:

> We all piled into some fiacres and arrived at the Opéra-Comique late—just in time for Mary to go on the stage with no orchestra rehearsal or preparation. It was an unheard-of thing to do, and she did it magnificently! She wore her own outfit, a tailored skirt, a chemise shirtwaist, and tie; subsequently they became the standard costume for the opera. People rushed to our box after the third act to ask Sibyl where she had found her and commented upon what a lovely voice she had and what an excellent actress she was. But what a dreadful accent—it was pure Scotch!

Fifty years later in her private memoirs Natividad Terry de Lucinge recalled her thrill at Mary's success.

> One Sunday I came home and learned of the tremendous event which had taken place: Mary had made her debut in *Louise.* They had asked her to come early, because the star had a cold. She didn't know what to wear, and by chance Sibyl gave her one of my blouses of mauve-colored silk in the pleated

shirt-waist style which I often used for bicycling. Mary wore her own skirt . . . she had to go on at the beginning of the third act just in time to sing "Depuis le jour," the most difficult aria in the opera. She made a tremendous success. . . . As for my part, I, who had accompanied her a thousand times in the past at the piano, was overjoyed for her.

After the third act, Messager was so impressed that he asked the orchestra to stand in recognition of Garden's extraordinary achievement. That same night the publicity department of the Opéra-Comique quickly dispatched press releases to all the newspapers about the exciting birth of a new star.[11]

Sibyl was thrilled at Mary's triumph, but her own health was in a precarious state. Her episodes of manic depression often confined her to bed. Dr. Iscovesco recommended that she leave Paris for a while and relax on the Riviera. The expenses of maintaining the luxurious Champs-Élysées apartment had become overwhelming. Both Sibyl and Natica reluctantly decided to give it up. At the end of April Sibyl returned Mary to her little room on the rue Chaldrin, rented a piano for her, and paid six month's rent in advance—none of which she could afford.

Chapter 31

Storm over the Namouna

With Mary safely placed in her former pension, Sibyl and Natica closed the Champs-Élysées apartment. The furniture, paintings, antiques, and objets d'art were put in storage, but the bittersweet memories of that place would remain with Sibyl forever.

Once their bags were packed, the two boarded a train for Nice. Again they rented a villa at Beaulieu, not far from James Gordon Bennett's Villa Belvedere. Every sunrise found Natica up early, trying to rediscover all her old hiking and cycling trails. There were plenty of friends on the Riviera and no end of invitations. But Sibyl seldom rose before the middle of the afternoon. It wasn't long before Natica realized that the change of scene hadn't done anything for her stepmother's state of mind. She was drinking in her bedroom, as unremittingly as she had in Paris. Worried about Sibyl's persistent attacks of depression, the girl voiced her concern to Bennett one day.

Gallantly, the editor, known to friends as "the Commodore," invited them to lunch on his terrace. In the middle of dessert the unpredictable bachelor made a surprise proposal. How would they like to accompany him on a little cruise of the Mediterranean to Greece? It would do them both a world of good. He told the widow she was too young to mourn the past. This is not what Tony would have wanted. She needed to climb out of her rut of self-pity and relate to people again. The two women talked it over briefly. Sailing to Greece would be something different and amusing. Natica was overjoyed when Sibyl agreed to accept the invitation.

Bennett planned to invite a few other friends also. Foremost among them were Mrs. John Leishman, wife of the American minister to Turkey, and her daughter Martha. Mrs. Leishman, née Julia Crawford, had married John

Leishman when he began as a humble "mud clerk" supervising the unloading of steel barges. Thanks to a little wedding largess from his affluent in-laws, he soon obtained his own steel furnace. He abandoned it shortly to form an iron and steel brokerage, Leishman and Snyder. It was at this time that he caught the eye of Andrew Carnegie, who persuaded him to become vice president of the Carnegie Brothers Company when he was only twenty-nine. Within two years, Carnegie's young protégé was the obvious choice to be the next company president. In 1897, President McKinley appointed Leishman minister to Switzerland. There Mrs. Leishman still lived, even though her husband had recently been appointed minister to Turkey. As yet, Julia could not bear to leave her friends for "that barbaric place," Bennett explained; so she would stay for the time being and join her husband later. Her escort on the voyage would be a young German baron named von Graffenried.

By the middle of May everyone was packed and aboard Bennett's nine-hundred-ton floating palace, the *Namouna,* which his staff had sarcastically labeled the "Pneumonia." The Commodore's crew was meticulously clean-shaven as usual. He insisted that his nautical employees emulate the British navy, where mustaches and beards were forbidden. It would be the last voyage for this vessel, as Bennett was having another built at Dunbarton, Scotland—the larger and faster *Lysistrata.* As it turned out, the *Namouna* would be more than ready for dry dock once this cruise was over.

The first night at sea Bennett arranged for an al fresco dinner party on deck. It was a splendid evening. The Mediterranean sky had never been a deeper amethyst, with flotillas of sea clouds drifting at a lazy pace. Everyone was in a festive mood. Sibyl wore a striking décolleté gown and a new auburn wig. Natica had not seen her stepmother so charming or alluring since her father's death.

Mrs. Leishman, too, was a handsome woman. Natica learned that she was the mother of three daughters, one of whom, Nancy, was to become the Duchess of Croy. She wondered why a middle-aged lady would have such an intriguing young Lothario escorting her instead of her husband. Her youngest daughter, Martha, who had accompanied her, was about Natica's age, and the two girls liked each other immediately.

If relations between the young people were cordial, those between the diplomat's wife and the widow were definitely cooler. Natica noticed that the baron was becoming more and more attentive to Sibyl, and, even worse, her stepmother was encouraging him. The baron was kissing her hand at every opportunity, lighting her cigarettes, and helping her up from the table, while an irritated Julia Leishman was being ignored. Every day her stepmother's gowns grew more revealing, and the ex-star herself more seductive. In less than a week the pair had thrown discretion to the winds and begun trysting in the privacy of Mme Terry's cabin. The news electrified everyone on board. Natica was stunned.

The next day Mrs. Leishman's temper hit the boiling point, and tensions exploded on deck at teatime. In front of the guests and her own astonished daughter, Julia Leishman candidly informed Madame Terry that the baron was her lover and she paid him handsomely for his favors. With a mocking laugh, Sibyl reminded Mrs. Leishman that she was a married woman who ought to be in Turkey at her husband's side that very minute, helping him represent the Stars and Stripes. Insults, sneers, and threats were exchanged before a fascinated group of spectators. Then Julia Leishman threw down the gauntlet and flung the contents of her teacup at Sibyl. Seconds later, the two adversaries were hurling china and silver at each other. The hurricane had struck.

Seizing his deranged benefactress by the arm, the baron tried to placate her, but she turned on him with a stinging barrage of invectives. "Let go of me, pig! You low-down scum! You really deserve that cheap has-been!" she screamed as she struggled to free herself. Then in a surprise move, she suddenly raked the fingernails of her free hand across his eyes with a savage swipe. A howl of pain greeted this unexpected attack, and the baron released her with a jerk. Reeling like a comet in erratic orbit, Julia Leishman lost her balance and—as luck would have it—collided with Sibyl! Both women toppled to the deck but not before dragging the tablecloth, with the rest of the tea service, down upon them.

Before the brawl could send the *Namouna* to the bottom, Bennett stepped into the melee. Roaring like a rogue elephant, he ordered the decks cleared immediately. "That does it! Goddam! Get below, everybody! Now! Move your asses!" The Commodore was livid; his language, vermilion! At first he had been intrigued by the scene (hadn't his own drunken tantrums wreaked havoc on many nightclubs?), but seeing his yacht undergo free and unsolicited redecoration, Bennett had to halt the donnybrook once and for all. As Natica was helping Sibyl up, she heard him bark a command to her. "And YOU! Tell your damned stepmother to straighten her fucking wig!"[1]

That night an eerie silence pervaded the yacht. At dinnertime Bennett ate alone; no one else appeared. No one even unbolted his or her door. Next day the Commodore called his guests on deck and pronounced sentence. The cruise was over! The *Namouna* would be putting into the nearest Italian port.

Martha and Natica consoled each other. Their youthful sensibilities had been grievously wounded.

"My father's family warned me about her, but I wouldn't listen," Natica sobbed.

"What do you think of *my* mother?" wailed an equally chagrined Martha. "She's nothing but a *libertine!* I often wondered why mother and daddy spent so little time with each other, and I was naive enough to believe this slimy baron was just my mother's escort. Why, he's only a common gigolo! I'm so ashamed, I could just die!"

"I've never known a gigolo or a libertine before," Natica pondered, "but I've heard my family talk about such people."

"Then pity me," Martha sniffed. "I've been living around the real thing, but after being brought up so properly in private schools, I'd never recognize it in my own backyard."

The girls concluded that they must remain poised and dignified in spite of their personal tragedies. Deeply hurt but still loyal, Natica decided she ought to forgive and forget if her wayward stepmother would promise to mend her ways. She mustered up enough courage to knock on Sibyl's door and present an ultimatum.

When the cabin door opened, it revealed a defiant widow looking more disheveled than alluring in a peignoir that reeked of spilled alcohol.

"Well, Nattie, what's on your mind?"

"Sibyl," the girl began, "I'm willing to forgive you for what has happened if you'll just promise me one thing. The yacht will be putting into port tomorrow, and if we're going to continue living together, I expect you to give up the baron."

"And if I don't?" came the sarcastic query.

"Then I'll be forced to go back to my father's family. I'm sure they would not want me to stay with someone whose company is not a respectable influence."

"You're free to leave anytime you wish," Sibyl snapped, "but don't you ever tell me whom I can and cannot see!"

The widow became increasingly indignant. What right did a teenager, who knew nothing of life, have to pass moral judgment on her? At present she had no intention of renouncing the baron's company. An ugly row ensued, leaving Natica more hurt than ever. This was their first major quarrel. Having painted herself into a corner, she now had no choice but to go to Martha's mother and ask for sanctuary. Mrs. Leishman couldn't have been more maternal, more understanding. Of course, she'd see that Mlle Terry returned safely to Paris;

they both would accompany her. Martha was delighted with her mother's decision.

"We'll always be friends," the girls promised each other—a vow they kept until Martha's death many years later.

After the guests had been dumped unceremoniously on Italian soil, Bennett ordered his crew to sail the *Namouna* back to Cannes minus its passengers. The Leishmans, true to their word, escorted Natica home to Paris on the train. The girl was determined not to return to her grandmother's house, so the first thing she did upon arrival was to call her cousin Natalie and ask for temporary shelter with her parents, Alfonso Terry and his wife. When Natalie learned of Natica's predicament, she immediately offered her a room in their home. Now, at least, Tony's daughter had a roof over her head, albeit a transient one. Her relatives were shocked when they surveyed the girl's wardrobe. Up to now it had consisted of mostly convent garb. Sibyl's contributions amounted to little more than shirtwaists and skirts. If they were going to introduce her in society, Tony's daughter must have some fashionable evening gowns to wear. Before she knew what was happening, Natica found herself transported to the salons of famous couturiers for fittings.

It was 1900, the year of the Exposition, and all Paris was celebrating. Natalie invited her cousin to go everywhere with her and her fiancé, Count Stanislaus de Castellane. They were among the most popular couples in Paris, and their company was in demand at the most exclusive functions. There were balls and receptions every night. As Stanislaus was Boni's younger brother, Natica was often invited to the fabulous Palais Rose by Boni and Anna. It was her unofficial "coming out" into Parisian society, and the girl entered into the spirit of every ball as if it might be her last.

Crowds thronged Paris for the Exposition that summer. Visitors might take in the American exhibit and see the latest horseless carriage on display. Or there was the palace of electricity with its glittering wonders. One might go to the Indonesian exhibit and see the dancers perform with their exotic orchestras. Then there was the Russian exhibit, where tourists could examine the exquisite enamels of Carl Fabergé. Restaurants were jammed and the boulevards mobbed. At night immense crowds swarmed into the theaters. Loïe Fuller's fire dance was the sensation of the moment.

It was 1889 all over again, and the thought was constantly on Massenet's mind. He had fallen ill with uremia in May, but he was still propped up in bed working diligently on his latest creation, *Grisélidis*. Yet, there were hours when his thoughts drifted to Sibyl. It had been only eleven years since her unforgettable debut during the last exposition. And what was the divine Esclarmonde doing now except idle socializing? Whom was she seeing? Was she practicing? He penned a few lines to Mrs. Sanderson.

> Fond thoughts to all of your family—the 15th of May in 1889 was the premiere of *Esclarmonde* in Paris. I thought of that on Tuesday evening. It was also the Paris Exposition. I have been ill for three weeks—and sad—
>
> Massenet

At the bottom of the note he drew a staff and notated a motif from *Esclarmonde*. Yes, Sibyl was definitely in his thoughts. Why hadn't he heard from her? She hadn't bothered to inquire about his health or even send him a card. It was a somewhat childish composer, filled with self-pity, who wrote another note to Mrs. Sanderson on 18 May 1900.

> Dear Madame:
> It is very painful not to have any news of Mme Sibyl Terry in spite of my letters and not one word of friendly remembrance. Naturally there is no reason to address a letter to 104 Champs-Élysées. Also, I come to you who would *never forget either my wife or me.* I beg of you to tell her when you write that we remain her faithful friends of bygone days.
> To you my dear lady, my *fervent and true remembrances!*
> Massenet

At the moment, her mentor's health was the last thing on Sibyl's mind. The widow had invited Baron von Graffenried back to her rented villa in Beaulieu, where they could savor each other's company under more private conditions. They had stopped in Milan for a few days to make the rounds of the theaters, where her resplendent gowns overwhelmed the Milanese public. The Italian press described her as "more beautiful than ever," and she announced to reporters for the umpteenth time that she was "now ready to return to the stage."

However, the romance that had bloomed at sea was withering on land. The baron's ardor was souring as he watched his new sponsor prefer her alcoholic bouts to his particular brand of recreation. When he learned that she was in debt up to her wigline, he wondered if it wasn't time to seek his fortune in some other boudoir. As for the ex-diva, it didn't take her long to discover that the baron was a bore. She wondered what Julia Leishman ever saw in him. He had sprung from an undistinguished line of German gentry, and his bourgeois attitudes and tastes weren't likely to elevate it any further. By the time the widow returned to Paris at the end of June, the baron had been given his dismissal. Since the Champs-Élysées apartment was closed, Sibyl had no place to go except her family's home on the avenue Malakoff.

When Natica explained why she had left her stepmother, the Terrys must have raised their eyebrows in unison and responded simultaneously, "we told you so." They had always disapproved of Sibyl; now what combustible fuel they had for her funeral pyre! It wasn't long before all Paris was informed of the ex-star's gala matinee on the Bennett yacht. The solicitous Terrys told the family orphan that under no circumstances was she to return to Sibyl. The woman was unfit to be her guardian. But Natica knew her father's will dictated otherwise. If she didn't stay with her unpredictable stepmother, she had to return to her grandmother's jurisdiction. That was worse than being banished to Devil's Island; she would have no freedom at all.

A spirited quarrel over Sibyl erupted one night between the two Terry heiresses. The piously smug Natalie, who loathed the diva in true Terry fashion, began a recital of her iniquities. The woman was "a drunken, selfish, morally irresponsible trollop"—after all, everyone in Paris knew that if "she hadn't been Massenet's mistress, she never would have had any career at all." She thought Natica must be slightly demented to even consider going back to her.

But the girl found herself defending her stepmother. She knew how much the singer had loved her father, how devastated she had been by his death, and the loneliness she had suffered. Her grandmother and all of her father's family had treated Sibyl shamefully. Everyone had a right to make a mistake once. The woman was far more sinned against than sinning. Natica was surprised to discover she not only liked her stepmother, she was still loyal to her. The argument reached an impasse. Having exhausted her supply of defamatory adjectives, the raven-haired Natalie shrugged her shoulders and flounced out of the room.

Natica retired for the night still torn by indecision. But sleep would not come. She tossed fitfully for a few hours and then knew what she must do. She arose, dressed, and quietly packed her bags. Tiptoeing downstairs, the girl called for a fiacre. Without awakening anyone, she crept out of her uncle's house in the early-morning hours. In a short time she had arrived at 46 avenue Malakoff. Even though she had roused the Sandersons from their slumber, Margaret welcomed her like a long-lost daughter.

Natica adored Mrs. Sanderson, whom she considered "a kind, warm-hearted American mother with the exquisite manners of true gentility." She would later observe that "the bohemian life of her famous daughter had upset her for years." It pained the girl to explain the incident on the Bennett yacht, which was the talk of Paris by now. When she told Mrs. Sanderson about Sibyl's drinking at both the Champs-Élysées apartment and the Riviera villa, Margaret admitted she had tried to keep it a closely guarded secret for a long time. It can be assumed that Sibyl and her stepdaughter went through the motions of a half-hearted reconciliation.

Natica was keeping a diary that summer. As she got to know Sibyl's sisters better, she began to record her impressions. In one entry she described them as "extremely puritanical, frigid in personality, and very reserved." They were ice to their sister's fire. In her journal Natica classified them as "premature old maids." It wasn't long before she discovered that antipathy toward Sibyl was not the exclusive prerogative of the Terry clan; it was incubating in the Sanderson household as well. Marion and Edith were obviously not overjoyed at having their older sister home again.

The girl had a chance to discuss her stepmother more fully when they went to Dinard in July. Sibyl and Natica rented a cottage next door to Mrs. Sanderson's Villa Plaisance at St. Énogat. Marion, the tallest, loveliest, and most sensitive of the sisters, decided it was time to have a little heart-to-heart talk with the Terry girl. She candidly admitted that the lives of both her and her sisters had been blighted by the shadow of Sibyl's fame. They had suffered deprivation and sacrifice. She was aware of *Town Topics*'s cruel description of them as "fully mature damsels" still going by "the courtesy title of girls."[2] Her own achievements had never been taken seriously in artistic circles. Even worse was the fact that she had begun to doubt her own ability and to destroy some of her canvases. "Marion suffered for me," Natica observed, "and worried that the same self-doubt and anxieties would cloud my life."

A similar fate had befallen Edith. She had closed the lid of the piano because she lacked the confidence to perform in public. She had refused to take any more voice lessons with Trabadello. She was becoming extremely cynical about life and contemptuous of society. More and more she began championing such radical causes as free love in order to shock the conservative bluenoses with whom her family mingled. Jane was the fortunate one. She had refused to remain with the family in Paris once Sibyl's career had taken wing. She had broken away, traveled, met new people, and now was residing happily back in the States as Mrs. Roy Herrick of Minneapolis.

Natica listened to their long list of Sibyl's paramours and transgressions. She was amazed to discover Massenet's name strangely absent from the record of the prima donna's horizontal accomplishments. Quite naturally, she had accepted what the entire Terry tribe was so eager to believe—that her step-mother had once been Massenet's mistress.

The girl decided Marion and Edith were jealous of their sister. Fifty years later she wrote: "they envied her beauty, her joie-de-vivre, and her artistic success. Above all, they envied the extraordinary magnetism by which she held the male sex captive." In later years she felt that they were partially responsible for turning her against Sibyl.

The girl was more determined than ever that no stepmother was going to dominate *her* life. She went bicycling, swimming, and picnicking. On the week-ends she attended dances at the American Club in Dinard. Five o'clock tea was a ritual on the terrace of Villa Plaisance. Natica was enchanted with the ter-race's magnificent exposure to the sea and invigorating air. Mrs. Sanderson was delighted when she learned that the young lady had captured her first beau. Marion and Edith waited maliciously for their older sister's reaction to this development.

The ex-star was not exactly reassured to observe the male sex now noticing Mlle Terry instead of herself. She knew Natica had the one asset she no longer possessed—youth. Every time a man flirted with her stepdaughter it was a cruel reminder that she was now a generation older than the ravishing teenager who had left a trail of broken hearts back in San Francisco. She grew morose and sullen. Every day she found something new to criticize about the girl: her hair, her voice, or what she wore. Every day their quarrels escalated. Sibyl began drinking despondently and took to her bed.

Natica found herself dreading the moments she had to spend in the cottage. Except for her own room, the shutters were always closed. No sunlight was permit-ted to enter. "It hurts Madame's eyes," Lina muttered cantankerously. Even she seemed out of sorts. Every niche in the place was permeated by a doleful gloom.

One day, in a state of questionable sobriety, Sibyl stumbled into Natica's room looking for something. Quite by accident, she came across the girl's open diary lying on her dressing table. She began reading a series of devastating comments about herself and her family. Natica returned from swimming that day to dis-cover clouds of cigarette smoke issuing from her room. From the doorway she observed Sibyl seated before the dressing table in a loose-fitting peignoir, puff-ing savagely on a cigarette. Beside her lay the open diary. One glance at her stepmother's face, and Natica saw that she was smoldering.

"Nattie, is *this* really what you think of me? Is it my fault that my sisters can't find husbands? They've been given every opportunity. Do you actually believe I'm a modern Messalina?"

"Well, they're my observations at present."

Shocked and wounded, the former diva flew into a rage. She accused her step-daughter of ingratitude, infidelity, and every other character defect that flashed into her mind. Natica defended her grievances against Sibyl with the stubborn self-righteousness of youth. She reproached Sibyl for pursuing the identical course of self-destruction her father had taken. Her stepmother's soul seemed to encompass two opposite personalities: one that radiated kindness, joy, and gen-erosity; the other bloated with self-pity, morbidity, and hedonism. As far as the girl could determine, the positive one had been buried in Père Lachaise beside her father, because all Sibyl had exhibited for the past half year was the perni-cious side.

"You miserable little ingrate!" her stepmother spat, then picked up the diary and flung it through the window. The explosion of shattered glass was only a prelude to the violent scene that followed. With one sweep of her hand, she sent the entire contents of Natica's dressing table crashing to the floor. This was the final confrontation—and both women knew it.

But the irate widow had met her match in the eighteen-year-old Terry girl. Summoning all her strength, Natica seized her stepmother by the arms and hurled her onto the bed. The impact left Sibyl momentarily stunned. When she regained her equilibrium, she was staring into a pair of hazel eyes blazing with emerald fire. Natica screamed that she could no longer live with her another minute; she demanded to be put on a train for Paris that very day. Sibyl wrath-fully enumerated a few other places she could go. The room echoed with invec-tives and denunciations.

Sobbing hysterically that she never wanted to see Sibyl again, Natica ran out of the cottage and down the path to Villa Plaisance. The distraught girl wept in Mrs. Sanderson's arms, pouring out the details of the terrible clash. She could not go back to Sibyl. A sympathetic Margaret Sanderson unhappily agreed. Her daughter was not fit to be a guardian in her present con-dition.

Sibyl was infuriated to discover her mother and sisters solidly united behind Natica's decision. Accusing her own family of forming a cabal against her, the paranoid widow ordered Lina to pack her bags and stormed out of the cottage for the depot. She refused to stay at St. Énogat any longer. On the train to Paris, Sibyl had more time for reflection. If her stepdaughter left her permanently this time, half her income from Tony's estate would be gone also. She would be the loser, and her husband's creditors, not to mention her own, would soon be camping on her doorstep.

Natica moved into Margaret's villa for the remainder of August. Sadly, she wrote to her uncle, the Baron Blanc, in Savoy, asking if she could seek refuge with him once Mrs. Sanderson returned to Paris. The baron concurred, and in September the Sandersons put her on the train for Paris, where she would change again for Savoy. Natica never dreamed it would be the last time she was to see them. With tears streaming down their cheeks, Margaret and the Terry girl kissed each other good-bye forever at the little depot in Dinard.

Once she arrived at her uncle's estate in Chambéry, Natica confided to him the terrible impasse she had reached with Sibyl. For some time the baron had suspected their relationship was deteriorating. He immediately wrote her guardian, Mr. Webb of New York City, that his niece could no longer remain with her irresponsible stepmother. The Wall Street barrister was determined to carry out the provisions of the will and ordered her to return to her grand-mother's home. Natica heard the clatter of the glass coach pulled by the white mice. It was midnight. The ball was over.

She reluctantly returned to 144 Champs-Élysées to take up a drab existence with her grandmother. There would be no more parties, no more beaux; life would be duller than any monastic existence. Occasionally, her cousins would invite her out and rescue her temporarily from the emptiness of *la vie en gris*. But in general she knew what to expect. There would be the usual tête-à-tête every evening, the same boring drive in the Bois at four every afternoon, her grandmother's same vapid remarks about the weather. Not even a book or mag-azine to read, except for the Bible. Life would take on a deadly predictability. With Sibyl, at least, one never knew what to expect next.

Chapter 32

Ill-Fated Tour

One day in the fall of 1900 a letter from Frank Webb arrived at 46 avenue Malakoff. Even before reading it, Sibyl could guess its contents. Webb had sent her official notification that Mlle Terry was being consigned to her grandmother's care. The letter, of course, mentioned nothing about Sibyl's escalating alcoholism as the reason for their irreparable rift. Mr. Webb had simply pronounced his verdict in favor of Señora Tomaso Terry. The two women would each continue to receive half of Tony's annuity. Sibyl's survival was entirely her own affair.[1]

But surviving had become a serious problem. Sibyl knew she could not continue to live with her family. Their steadily deteriorating relationship had finally come to a head that summer at Dinard. Now she was forced to sell a few objets d'art that she had kept from the Champs-Élysées apartment. Yet, with the exception of her Louis XV bed and Tony's grand piano, she couldn't even have her husband's furniture repossessed, because it had been put in storage under Natica's name. The man who had treated her so indulgently in life cruelly held her hostage in death.

The widow found an apartment in a handsome gray stone building at #1 avenue Bois de Boulogne[2] with a lovely view of the park. She borrowed some of the surplus antique furniture stored at her mother's home and soon began to give a series of small dinner parties, singing for her guests.

Romance was never absent long. Even in mourning, Sibyl continued to exercise a hypnotic spell upon the male sex. At Dinard, either that summer or the year before, she had met Henrick Voisin, a dashing Swedish artist who was more than fourteen years her junior. A true son of the North—tall, blond, handsome, and athletic—he was the perfect target for the widow's wiles. Her mourning ensemble gave her delicate complexion a kind of ethereal allure, a fragile vulnerability that the twenty-year-old artist proposed to capture on canvas. It wasn't long before the young Swede had become romantically ensnared by his model. Reports in the New York and Parisian papers intimated their engagement would be announced at any time.

Sanderson herself refused any public comment about her ardent Viking, realizing their relationship was threatened by too many obstacles. According to nastier whispers in the French capital, Henrick's wealthy parents were fighting the liaison with every weapon at their disposal, ostensibly because their son was secretly betrothed to the daughter of another Scandinavian family. Besides being too old for him, Mme Terry had been a woman of the stage and its loose morality—in Victorian eyes, a stigma tantamount to leprosy.

In spite of parental opposition the two continued to see each other all year; still, Sibyl knew marriage was out of the question. Tony's diamond bracelet that never left her arm, the canary diamonds on her finger, the diamond dog collars on her fox terriers—all were a visible reminder of the mountainous heritage of debts he had bequeathed her. And now gossip had it the Voisins were threatening to disinherit their son if he should marry the ex-opera star. Assuming the rumors were true, it was a reprise of Sibyl's long-ago clash with the Hearsts.

The summer of 1900 found Massenet in the country recuperating from his attack of uremia. Earlier that year he had purchased a sixteenth-century stone-turreted château in the small town called Égreville, not far from Fontainebleau. Aside from his passion for expensive book bindings, it was a rare indulgence for this penurious apostle of song. There had been a series of domiciles constructed on this site by local barons since the tenth century, with houses constantly being razed and rebuilt by various owners, including the Duchesse d'Étampes, onetime mistress of Francis I. Here Massenet was to spend the remaining summers of his life, either relaxing in his garden or laboring feverishly on his scores.

Yet he found time to beg everyone who came to visit him for news about his former muse. He must have heard stories about young Voisin earlier in the year and, by now, at least a half dozen versions of the ex-diva's gala matinee on the Bennett yacht. The composer was still at Égreville working on his *jongleur de Notre-Dame* when he realized the summer was quickly passing without any letters from her. He laid down his manuscript temporarily to write another pathetic note to Sibyl's mother on 6 September 1900.

My very dear Madame:
I would like to have word

I would like to have news of Mme Terry
I do not wish to be forgotten
I, myself forget nothing
As always your faithful
and fervent friend.

Massenet

For once he was direct enough to omit his standard cliché, "My wife and I." Pygmalion had been hurt by the callous indifference of his Galatea. He felt discarded and no longer needed. Massenet had a neurotic need to be needed. He had made this woman into a star—the most brilliant on the European horizon—and now she was casting him aside with casual nonchalance, like last week's newspaper. Massenet could cope with hostility, but he could not bear indifference.

After Sibyl had installed herself in the new apartment, she contacted her neglected mentor, and Massenet lost no time in calling upon her. No record of his private observations is available to us, but he must have been shocked to see how she was aging. Her once alabaster skin had turned sallow from her liver problems and resembled grainy parchment. Her entire face was shellacked with makeup. Violet circles under her eyes now matched the famed rainbows within them.

Neither had time stood still for the composer. His once handsome black hair had vanished, and the remaining silver-gray strands were combed back over his ears, revealing a considerable bald area. He was growing stout and more stooped. Although his speech was as rapid as ever, his gestures were not as nervous as in former years. However, he still smoked incessantly when excited or apprehensive.

Sibyl explained that her health had improved sufficiently for a return to the stage. Not to opera right away but rather the concert platform. She requested a new art song from him. The Frenchman was overjoyed to oblige her. Édouard Colonne was planning an all-Massenet festival in the spring of 1901, and the composer wanted her to appear on the program with him. It would be like old times. He left a copy of his oratorio *La terre promise* (The Promised Land) and asked her to learn the soprano part. He was revising his *Esclarmonde* score into a symphonic suite and intended to conduct it personally. Massenet's heart must have beaten a little faster when he left the Terry apartment. At last! She needed his pen again. Had the nightingale finally returned to the flowering shrub?

Since more and more threatening letters from the Terry creditors were appearing in the mail every month, Sibyl realized she could procrastinate no longer. She signed a contract with the Opéra-Comique to make her long-awaited comeback the following spring. Massenet was not the only composer offering encouragement. Reynaldo Hahn called upon her frequently that winter.[3]

Hahn was writing a new opera, *La carmélite,* for her return to the stage. The libretto had been created by Catulle Mendès, a distinguished author who also collaborated with Massenet. Hahn knew he would have to pay 10,000 francs to the Opéra-Comique to have the opera performed. This time he was hoping that Mme Terry could help defray some of the expenses—after all, the leading role of Louise de la Vallière was being written for her.

Sibyl generously assured him that when the time arrived she would do everything she could to assist him. At the present she had no funds. The important thing for Hahn to do now was to play a few scenes for Albert Carré and ascertain his impressions. Happily, Carré's reaction was favorable. He not only accepted the incomplete manuscript "with pleasure," but assured the young Venezuelan that Mme Sanderson-Terry would create the soprano role. The production date was left open until the work was finished.

By now the creditors of Sibyl's late husband were baying at the door in unison. She fully realized that the maximum salary of the Opéra-Comique (600 francs per night) would never make a dent in those enormous debts. Neither could she expect any financial help from her family. Calling upon her former agent Wolff, she urged him to book a concert tour throughout the European capitals. The object was to make as much money as the shrewd manager could squeeze out of the local impresarios.

When Wolff discovered that Sibyl Sanderson's mystique still retained its old box-office allure, he speedily obtained dates in Vienna, Budapest, Warsaw, Moscow, and St. Petersburg. But he didn't stop with these engagements. Knowing that the Wintergarten Music Hall in Berlin was interested in attracting stellar names, Wolff told his client he had a chance to book her into that establishment, where she would earn more money in two weeks than at the Comique in two months. In addition, he had already engaged Cléo de Mérode to perform her usual program of kindergarten pirouettes there, and the dancer hadn't felt it demeaning in the least. Neither did Sibyl, even though she knew she would be the first opera star ever to appear in a Berlin variety hall. Moreover, if she failed to fulfill her engagements, her fees would be forfeited.

Sanderson decided to try out her voice in the salons first. On 23 January 1901 she sang at the soirée of Gustave Worms, a retired actor of the Comédie-Française, and was warmly received by the guests. After essaying several

Massenet songs, she was joined by famed tenor Francesco Tamagno for a duet from Verdi's *La forza del destino.*

Albert Carré asked her to sing a group of solos at the 7 February 1901 benefit for retired members of the Opéra-Comique—an annual event he had originated. The great actor Coquelin, tenor Maréchal, and other stars would appear on the program. Alexandre Luigini would conduct the orchestra. Sibyl agreed, thinking this would be an excellent opportunity to test not only her vocal dependability but also the climate of Parisian favor.

The house was packed with an elite crowd. The first half of the program was devoted to various actors from the Comédie-Française and their routines. Mme Sanderson-Terry was scheduled to appear after intermission. The moment she stepped onto the stage, the applause was deafening. The audience seemed overjoyed to see her again at the scene of her former triumphs.

She sang two of Massenet's songs: "Pensée d'automne" and the premiere of his "Amoureux appel," which the critics hailed as "a jewel among his finest efforts." Still, it was her coloratura technique in Juliette's Waltz Song (Gounod) that stopped the show. The audience cheered her wildly, giving her eight curtain calls, refusing to let her leave the stage until the aria was encored. Later for the grand finale, she was joined by all the stars of the Opéra-Comique in singing Gounod's "Ave Maria."[4]

Wolff had been a busy agent. Besides sending press releases to the New York papers about her brilliant reappearance on the Parisian stage, he was planning a major publicity campaign for her upcoming tour. There would be posters throughout the cities where she was appearing, reams of newspaper releases, and new photographs for the billboards. Famed couturier Jean Worth was contributing his talents too. He had designed twenty-four sensational gowns for the soprano and generously sold them to her on credit.

Sanderson was scheduled to begin her season in Vienna on 22 February 1901. The Viennese appearance would be followed by others in Budapest and Warsaw; then she would return to Paris briefly to sing at the all-Massenet concert with the Colonne orchestra on 10 March. After that, it was off to Berlin, followed by concerts in St. Petersburg and Moscow. Once she was home to stay in April, the Opéra-Comique was beckoning for her comeback in *Manon.*

Sibyl knew the tour would demand all her physical stamina. The question was, did she have enough reserve strength to cope with its rigors? Events were already following a familiar pattern. The week of departure she came down with her inevitable cold. Having succumbed to periodic drinking bouts, she continued to be plagued by attacks of insomnia.

On 19 February 1901 Mme Sanderson-Terry boarded the train with her maid, two fox terriers, and a mountain of trunks to begin her perilous comeback journey. She arrived in Vienna the following day to find her suite at the Hotel Bristol crammed with floral offerings from every part of the Austro-Hungarian Empire. Obviously, she had not been forgotten. Nor was Lina long in discovering that the city abounded with illustrated posters whose boldly printed captions read: FEBRUARY 22—FRIDAY NIGHT—THE DEBUT OF MME SIBYL SANDERSON FROM THE PARIS OPÉRA. Wolff had done a splendid job of marketing Sibyl, but he was guilty of a slight misrepresentation. The soprano hadn't set foot on the stage of the Opéra in six years.

Sibyl's long-awaited debut with the Vienna Philharmonic Society was scheduled for the Musikvereinssaal; Gustav Mahler would be her distinguished conductor. Her co-artist was the young pianist Mark Hambourg, who would be soloist in the Liszt *Hungarian Fantasy* with the symphony.

Sanderson planned to open her program with "Depuis le jour" from Charpentier's *Louise,* the first Viennese performance of the aria. This would be followed by three songs by Massenet: "Passionnément," "Pensée d'automne," and "Amoureux appel." The next group would consist of a song by Reynaldo Hahn between two operatic arias: the Waltz Song from Gounod's *Roméo et Juliette* and the grand air "Regardez ces yeux" from *Esclarmonde,* also a Viennese premiere. Coughing and clearing her throat, the soprano apologized for not being in her best voice during rehearsals with the symphony, but since she didn't want to disappoint the Viennese public this time, she was determined not to cancel.

On Friday night, the famous Musikvereinssaal was crowded to capacity. The boxes were filled with the Viennese crème de la crème; the names of the occupants read like a Who's Who of the Austro-Hungarian Empire. Among them were archdukes, princes and princesses, and counts and countesses, including the ex-diva Marie Renard, now the Countess Kinsky. Theodore Leschetizky, the mentor of Mark Hambourg, Sanderson's co-artist, was sitting quietly in the orchestra.

While the orchestra was tuning up, a nervously perspiring Albert J. Gutmann dropped by Sibyl's dressing room to wish her luck. Before he left he made his usual speech about maintaining one's dignity at all times before the Viennese public. The soloist seemed to be receptive, but anyone who knew her well could perceive that mentally she was light years away. Sanderson was less than fully sober when she arrived at the theater that night.

The stage was festooned with floral bouquets, and when Sibyl made her entrance, "she did not bow but stood quietly, very beautiful and imposing, and superbly gowned."[5] Lorgnettes went up, and after a moment's scrutiny the audience gave her a warm welcome, evidently not holding any grudge against her for missing their city four years before.

Applause, however, was tepid after "Depuis le jour." It was obvious the soprano would have to do some extraordinary singing to win such a critical house. Little by little the audience began to thaw through the succeeding numbers, and after Juliette's Waltz Song, the reception was enthusiastic enough to justify an encore. But disaster struck a few minutes later. In the middle of the Hahn number, Sibyl suddenly broke down, stopped, and said to the audience, "Je ne peux pas chanter. Croyez moi, c'est mieux." (I am unable to sing. Believe me, this is best.). With a shrug of her shoulders she walked off the stage, leaving an astonished conductor to put down his baton before an equally astonished audience. Herr Gutmann rushed out on stage to explain that Mme Sanderson was "temporarily indisposed," but a storm of hisses, boos, and catcalls drowned him out. The offended Viennese considered her behavior to be totally unprofessional.

After a brief conference between Mahler and Gutmann, a violinist in the orchestra, Marie Soldat-Roeger, was asked to fill in and play some solos until Mme Sanderson could recover. Her impromptu renditions were greeted with enthusiastic applause. Finally, the erratic soprano reappeared to finish the program, just in time to save the distraught impresario from nervous collapse. By now the mood of the audience had plunged to glacial temperatures. The hall had become a frozen tundra.

Emil Steinegger wrote to the editors of San Francisco's *Town Talk* that not only was Sibyl "a flat failure," but "she was not even given a hand."[6] Mark Hambourg was also coldly received, perhaps because the Viennese were notoriously prejudiced against any pupil of Leschetizky.

After the calamitous concert the singer should have returned to her hotel and retired, but instead she was determined to go ahead with plans to entertain friends in her suite. Too often the socialite in her preempted the artist. But this time there was a better reason not to throw a party. Her excited gestures and rapid, incoherent speech were familiar danger signals.

As could be expected, everyone was having a wonderful time except Sibyl. There was the sound of laughter, spurious compliments, and the tinkle of glasses, and the guests stayed far too late. At first Sanderson's spirits were buoyed by the superficial praise, but it wasn't long before she became aware of her emotional and physical exhaustion. No one could understand the anguish she had suffered on the stage of the Musikvereinssaal. Now it seemed unreal. It hadn't happened. What was she doing in this hotel suite with these people who meant nothing to her? What was she doing back on the stage? She had never wanted to return. Her spirit had died with Tony. Why did her body go on living posthumously?

A cloud of negative thoughts was whirling through her mind, and she realized too late that she was caught in the insidious grip of manic depression. Her nerves were raw and inflamed—burning, constricting, and torturing her until she could no longer stand it. She was gasping for breath and already felt herself beginning to shake. How long would it be before she began throwing things, screaming, hitting her head repeatedly against a wall, or jumping out of a window to escape this unbearable torture? What was she to do? She couldn't let the guests see her in this state.

All at once, Sibyl dashed into the bedroom to gulp down some sleeping medicine. On the bedside were two bottles similar in appearance. One contained a liniment for massage, the other, a sedative. Not bothering to light the lamp or measure the contents, she grabbed the wrong bottle and impulsively swallowed half the liniment. As soon as she perceived her mistake, Sanderson collapsed on the bed screaming, suddenly overwhelmed with a desire to cling to life.

A panic-stricken Lina rushed into the room followed by the guests. When they discovered the prostrate soprano writhing in pain, they notified the hotel management immediately. Since a doctor could not be speedily summoned at that hour, the Vienna Ambulance Corps was summoned.

Between the wail of the ambulance siren and the arrival of the mounted police, the hotel was in an uproar. Guests hurried into the corridors in varying states of undress. Sometime in the early morning hours Sibyl was carried out on a stretcher and rushed to the hospital to have her stomach pumped. As Princess Metternich had been one of her guests, the hotel management and the hospital were sworn to secrecy.

A day or so later, friends arranged to spirit her quietly out of the city and up into the mountains to Semmering, where she could rest and recover in a private chalet. Lina immediately sent a telegram to Sibyl's mother about the "accidental" poisoning. Margaret could not possibly have been deceived by its contents. She knew Sibyl had been ordered by her doctor always to measure the sleeping medicine carefully in a spoon. There could be little doubt that her daughter had planned to effect a painless demise by emptying the entire bottle. What saved her was the fact that she had seized the wrong bottle.

Another telegram was dispatched to Édouard Colonne canceling her performance in Paris (the Massenet festival) on 10 March. Mme Auguez de

Montalant was engaged to substitute for her by a puzzled conductor and an equally baffled composer. Sanderson remained in the mountain resort for about ten days of recuperation. So far, no word of her folly had leaked out in the press.

The singer was well enough to return to her Vienna hotel on 4 March—the very day that news of her "suicide attempt" hit the papers. Not the Viennese but the Budapest papers. No one had sworn them to secrecy. It was printed that she tried to take her own life and was recovering in a hospital. Her condition was said to be "uncertain." The international wire services jumped to the conclusion that since the story broke in Budapest, it was there that she had tried to commit suicide. Erroneous reports seared the American and Parisian papers on 5 March 1901.

Margaret loyally sprang to her daughter's defense and sent an indignant cable to William Randolph Hearst in New York on 5 March:

Special cable to the editor of the New York Journal:

Dear Mr. Hearst:

Will the Journal kindly show its wonted American and chivalrous spirit by protecting my daughter Sibyl Sanderson-Terry against the slanderous statement that she attempted suicide. My daughter is working hard to win fame for herself and her country. She took the wrong medicine by mistake. Is now so well that she sings tonight in Vienna.

Margaret Sanderson

Hearst printed her plea under a big reproduction of Ernest Frederick's portrait of the prima donna and another paragraph commenting about the confusion in the cables. The first woman he had wanted to marry possessed one redeeming quality. She was always a good subject for scandal and gossip.

Complicating the situation even further, agent Wolff sent his own releases to the New York papers, saying she had arrived in Vienna from Semmering on 4 March "hale and hearty," and would "sing in the Hungarian capital on Friday." Because the American press still believed that Sanderson had attempted suicide in Budapest, it assumed that the two capitals were reversed in Wolff's cables. Therefore, the New York Tribune and the New York Herald both announced that she "had just arrived from Budapest and will sing in Vienna on 5 March." The concert to which Sibyl's mother alluded in her telegram was a private soirée that night in Vienna.

Unhappily, her run of bad luck in Vienna was not over. On Wednesday, 6 March, after the trunks were packed, the soprano and her maid attempted to defect from their hotel without paying the bill. Sibyl admitted to the manager that it was embarrassing but she was temporarily out of money. If he could oblige her by sending the bill to Paris, her attorney would take care of it. The manager promptly informed her that hotel policy forbade extending credit. Until the account was settled in full, he had no choice but to withhold her luggage.

It never occurred to Sibyl that the expense of her luxurious hotel suite had mounted astronomically during the ten days she was recuperating in the Austrian Alps. In her entire life she had never known what it was to be stranded anywhere without money. Now she was forced to telegraph her lawyer in Paris for funds. Travers wired the necessary amount the following day, and only then would the hotel release her trunks.

It was the middle of Thursday afternoon before the humiliated singer and her maid boarded the train for Budapest. Fortunately, the journey was not long, and she still would have ample time to rehearse with her accompanist on Friday afternoon. The Viennese nightmare was finally behind her.

But the nightmare refused to stay buried. When Sibyl arrived at the Hotel Hungaria, she discovered the lobby was swarming with reporters just waiting to swoop down upon her. Brushing them aside, the singer refused to be interviewed until after her concert.

On Friday evening, 8 March 1901, Sibyl Sanderson made her debut in the Hungarian capital before a packed house seething with curiosity. There was no symphony orchestra to accompany her this time, only a pianist. Her program followed the same basic plan as the one in Vienna, with two exceptions. She replaced her *Esclarmonde* aria with the "Bell Song" from *Lakmé* and ended the program with a group of songs by Reynaldo Hahn and Cécile Chaminade

Telegraph dispatches to the Paris *Herald* announced that the concert had been sold out, and her audience "utterly enchanted." It is quite possible that Sanderson did receive a warm reception in Budapest, because tremendous rivalry existed between the two capitals of the empire. Also, she was now over her cold and able to do herself justice.

The report stated that "the three arias aroused the enthusiasm of the audience, particularly her coloratura work in the 'Bell Song' which had to be encored." As for the art songs, "Massenet's 'Pensée d'automne' was greatly appreciated." Tribute was also paid to "the most beautiful and simple style" in which Chaminade's "L'anneau d'argent" was rendered.

On the day after her concert Sibyl consented to receive some members of the press, which was anxiously seeking comment about her alleged suicide attempt. She indignantly denied the story to the *Minneapolis Tribune* correspondent,

> I had been ill for some time and could not sleep. My physician prescribed a sleeping potion for me. On my table were two bottles identical in appearances; one containing a rubbing liniment which I was accustomed to use and the other contained a sleeping potion . . . instead of measuring the medicine I put the bottle to my mouth. No sooner had I swallowed the medicine than I discovered my mistake. Even if I had taken the whole of it, it would not have resulted fatally. The sensation was awful, though. It made me deaf for almost two weeks. But the story that I attempted suicide is simply absurd!

Although the soprano ridiculed the report that she was unable to pay her Viennese hotel bill, the *New York World* correspondent was distrustful enough to check with the Hotel Bristol authorities, who indeed confirmed his suspicions.

She also refused to discuss her affairs of the heart when reporters asked about her relationship with Henrick Voisin and a few other suitors in Paris. She did admit that trouble with her late husband's family had caused serious financial problems but would not elaborate. Newsmen left with one more fabrication:

> Nothing that would part me from my present life could possibly induce me to commit suicide or marry again.

Chapter 33

The Comeback

Sanderson remained a few days in the Hungarian capital to be indulged by society, warbling for friends at the Paris Club. On 12 March, she reluctantly canceled a performance in Vienna at the palace of Princess Metternich because it was imperative she depart for Berlin.

The German capital had been inundated with posters announcing the appearance of the American opera star at the Wintergarten. Once Sanderson arrived, she discovered the famous variety hall to be an atrocious, tasteless monstrosity. Walls, doors, pillars, and ceilings were all disfigured by hideous excesses of pseudo-rococo ornamentation, compounded by a ton of gilt. However, the orchestra turned out to be surprisingly good, and the directors, Messrs Dorn and Baron, assured her that she would be a hit. On the night of 15 March 1901, more than a thousand spectators packed the hall to hear her debut.

No Berlin music critic attended. They had attacked the prima donna for even setting foot in such a place. It was nothing short of sacrilege to a large segment of the European press—the divine Esclarmonde, the incomparable Manon appearing in a music hall.

For the moment the divine Esclarmonde could not have been less concerned. The management was paying her handsomely. She had to sing only two songs an evening, and the first night the public even refrained from smoking while she was on stage. During her two-week engagement she wore fourteen Worth gowns, treating the German burghers to a fashion parade.

Artistically speaking, the results were less impressive. The acoustics of the hall proved to be as abominable as the decor, and in a few nights the audience was talking and laughing indifferently while she struggled to project her voice through a stagnant haze of cigar and cigarette smoke.

The Berlin correspondent of the *Musical Courier,* who had been so curious to hear her, sent a blistering review back to the States:[1]

> Yes, it's come to that. The once famous American singer, the possessor of the 'Eiffel Tower notes,' whom I heard and more or less admired as Esclarmonde during the 1889 Exposition, is now singing at the Koster and Bial's of Berlin. And what is worse, she didn't even make a success here with the not overly musically fastidious audience. . . . The high notes are no longer as high as they used to be, for a C is produced only with the greatest of effort, and the quality of tone is as piercing and shrill as a locomotive whistle.[2]

Rumors that Sanderson had canceled the rest of her tour were leaking out in various European newspapers. She admitted to reporters they were true. She was in bad health and could not continue. The singer's previously announced return to the Opéra-Comique in April had to be retracted. Carré hoped it was only temporary.

What Sibyl didn't confide to the press was the fact that she was drinking incessantly in her hotel suite and shunning food. It was not a new development; she hadn't eaten properly in years. Now, after her Berlin engagement was over, it was mandatory that she return to Paris for rest and prompt medical attention.

The facts were cruel and inescapable. Sanderson's tour had collapsed and with it her short-lived aspirations for a comeback. Her hotel and medical bills in Vienna had cost far more than she earned. While she was able to recoup some of her losses in Berlin, most of her fees would go to repay her lawyer for his loan.

Physically, Sanderson was exhausted. Her health had been in a precarious state at the beginning of the tour. On the concert circuit it deteriorated rapidly. She was continually plagued with liver trouble. Strange rashes would erupt periodically on her body and then gradually fade away.

Once home in Paris it was imperative that she arrest her unbridled progress toward self-destruction. Without decent health, her vocal cords were worthless, and at this moment she desperately needed them for a livelihood. No dark angel was going to rescue her from that millstone of debts. She had to settle them herself: carriage makers, couturiers, jewelers, upholsterers, doctors, nurses, hairdressers, florists, wig makers, antique dealers, lace makers—the list was endless! She, who once had been enumerated among "the elect of destiny," was now suffering bitterly for all her husband's extravagances as well as her own.

In April, the soprano entered a Parisian sanitarium for medical help. Little by little she gained temporary control over her compulsive drinking. Next, she submitted to a series of beauty treatments at Mme Merle Valentin's salon, which specialized in rejuvenating aging stars. Her health improved. By the end of May the Opéra-Comique announced that Mme Sanderson-Terry would definitely make her comeback in a revival of Saint-Saëns's *Phryné* on 11 June. She had signed for six performances with the original cast—Clément and Fugère. Sibyl knew she would have to prove herself all over again. It was the perennial curse of any artist's life. But this time she had a new and urgent motive for returning to the footlights: money.

All Paris flocked to the Opéra-Comique on the night of 11 June 1901. Tensions were high and expectations mixed. Curiosity reached its peak when André Messager made his entrance into the orchestra and lifted his baton. (Alexandre Luigini took over subsequent performances.) Once more the bassoons were sneering at the corrupt Greek magistrate. Once again the choruses were extolling the wicked excesses of youth. Then came the anxiously awaited moment: the entrance of the courtesan while the chorus chanted: "C'est elle, la divine Phryné."

When the heroine appeared on her portico, a murmur of astonishment rippled from one end of the theater to the other. In spite of her recent tribulations, *la belle Sibylle* didn't look a day older than when she had first created the role (thanks to a superb make-up artist). The *New York Herald* observed that "emotion dulled her voice for a little while but this was to be expected." Once those silvery tones began to ring through the hall, the audience realized that she had lost none of her old sorcery. For a moment many eyes were moist with memory; then the entire Opéra-Comique reverberated with a tumultuous welcome. Again and again the soprano was showered with bouquets. Her "Invocation to Venus" stopped the show, evoking enthusiastic cries of *"Brava!"* and *"Bis!"* (Encore!). After the performance ecstatic friends wept as they embraced her in the flower-banked artists' loge. After kissing her on both cheeks, her director, Albert Carré, remarked, "Like Caesar of old, you have returned to subjugate Gaul."

The next morning all the Parisian papers jubilantly agreed that she had been "fully equal to the part." The critic on *Le Matin* admitted that "the perilous task of an operatic comeback was triumphantly carried out." "Her wonderful singing showed she has lost none of the charm exercised in former days," proclaimed the Paris critic of the *New York Herald*. "Last night's return to the Opéra-Comique was a triumph!" *Le Figaro* declared that "the theater was literally crammed, and the audience repeatedly gave way to its enthusiasm with cries of brava!" Hailing the diva's comeback as "a brilliant return to the stage," *Le Ménéstrel* added, "the Opéra-Comique these days is decidedly the theater for sensational evenings!"

Henri de Courzon paid the following tribute to the artist in *Le Guide musical:*[3]

> Sibyl Sanderson has never been replaced as Phryné. That rare purity of voice, that finesse of utterance, accompanied by such natural grace and gesture are qualities of which one is never satiated . . . Everyone was overjoyed to find her once again on the scene of her former triumphs, and everybody wishes that this exquisite apparition, so enthusiastically welcomed back, will remain on the stage with us.

Letters of congratulation deluged the singer's residence, but if there were any from Massenet, they have not survived. Reynaldo Hahn paid her the following homage:

> Tuesday
> You were faultless—
> Absolutely exquisite—
> and I send you all of my heart.
> It looks as if I will have to put
> on my old gloves again
> to applaud you.
> > Yours devotedly,
> > Reynaldo Hahn

Mme Terry's operatic return was a major topic in the world of European theater. Her indisputable victory had won the Gallic heart from its current favorites, but that wasn't enough for agent Wolff. Forty-eight hours later he informed the world of the secret terror that had purportedly reigned backstage.

Among the floral tributes passed over the footlights on June 11 was one "containing a dagger," according to agent Wolff's dispatch to the *New York Telegraph*. Sanderson was rumored to have discovered it hidden among some roses with the word "duplicate" scrawled on it. Upon later examination, the singer's friends told reporters that the dagger was not a jeweled work of art but just an ordinary weapon.

They speculated it might be a message from "some known crank who was constantly writing love letters to her" or a message from "a vengeful rival." At any rate, the word "duplicate" implied that another knife was held in reserve by the sender. For the next few days she was "carefully guarded from all fans seeking autographs."

Refusing to discuss the dagger in an interview with the *New York Herald,* Sibyl confided that she felt "no emotion, whatsoever," upon her return to the Parisian stage. "So far as nervousness is concerned," she explained, "I might have been a stone—that is at first. It was really only after I had been on the stage several minutes I began to realize the presence of the audience."[4]

Demand for tickets was soaring, so the soprano agreed to double her six performances. Since the Opéra-Comique closed its doors at the end of June, it meant that Sanderson would be singing three nights a week for the rest of the month. Amazingly, she came through the ordeal without missing an appearance.

Subscribers, meanwhile, were clamoring to have *Thaïs* transferred from the Opéra to the Opéra-Comique for the role's creator. Massenet took the hint and made a fruitless attempt to plead the case with Gailhard, the Opéra manager. The composer argued that it had received insufficient performances at the Opéra to remain in its repertoire. Gailhard refused to relinquish the work, claiming that the addition of the Oasis scene and the ballet had created a new score, and that he thus had a legal right to keep it. This very year, he reminded the composer, he had brought it out of mothballs, alternating Marguerite Carrère and Lucy Berthet in the role of the Egyptian courtesan.

"So I have noticed," retorted Massenet with a sardonic smile, "and they are playing to half-empty houses."

The composer left Gailhard's office smarting with defeat. He had made a sincere effort to have *Thaïs* transferred back to "chez Carré" for the woman who created the title role. He had demonstrated that he was still her "faithful friend," even though he had become almost apoplectic when his "incomparable Manon" appeared in a Berlin music hall. Pygmalion feared that Galatea was no longer interested in maintaining their artistic relationship. He repeatedly moaned to various colleagues, "Mme Terry doesn't care about my wife and me anymore."

Massenet's suspicions were not wholly inaccurate. Presently Sibyl was faced with threats of legal action from her creditors, and she knew better than to ask him for a loan. At the moment she was courting the attention of another man who had come back into her life: Maurice Grau.

Chapter 34

Desperate Gamble

The spurious improvement in Sibyl Sanderson's health was partly the result of a questionable experiment by an unknown doctor. Sibyl's personal physician, Dr. Iscovesco, was probably not the culprit.

After her ill-fated spring concert tour, Sanderson placed herself in a Parisian sanitarium for a few weeks. It is more than likely that certain preliminary tests were initiated at this time. The doctor in question had conceived a horrifying plan that was at best a gamble. As an alternative to her craving for alcohol, he suggested a series of morphine injections, tightly controlled under his strict supervision. He assured her he would inject just enough of the drug to get the desired reaction. Her entire being, he promised, would be bathed in a spiritual reverie. Addicts have poetically described the sensation as "a sunbeam trapped in the body." She would never again desire hard liquor, and would glow with a sudden rebirth of health. Then the physician would cut off the drug before she had time to become addicted. Even the celebrated Dr. Semelaigne had not been afraid to recommend the practice for consumptives. It is quite possible that Semelaigne was the party guilty of persuading Sanderson to participate in this hazardous undertaking, for she had institutionalized herself in his sanitarium at about this time.[1]

Sanderson was desperate. She had tried spas, sanitariums, and even hypnosis to arrest her alcoholism, all without success. Now she grasped at straws. The doctor's daring scheme might be worth a try. He assured her that under his scrupulous control there should be no undue risk—only a minimum of danger. Innocently—naively—Sibyl Sanderson agreed to this dangerous plan, and in so doing signed her own death warrant.

Early results of the experiment seemed to have the desired effect. The initial injections produced a sudden warm flush throughout her body with a concentrated intensity in the vaginal area. Engulfed in alternating waves of exhilaration and preternatural quiescence, she was able to relax and sleep deeply for the first time in years. She no longer needed the fiery stimulation of alcohol. It seemed too good to be true. Had she finally found salvation? Was this at last the long-sought panacea?

Sanderson left the sanitarium filled with an illusion of well-being. She threw herself into her comeback with renewed vigor. Her brilliant return to the Parisian stage appeared to be a scintillating testimonial to the doctor's daring ingenuity; in truth, he was about to unlock Pandora's box. Emotionally and physically, she now felt well enough to cope with other problems. At the moment the major storm cloud on the horizon was the threat of legal action from her creditors.

Maurice Grau was in Paris that month auditioning new talent for his upcoming American tour. Hearing that his itinerary included San Francisco, Sibyl decided to call upon him at his hotel. The thought of touring the United States again was thoroughly repugnant to her, but the prospect of being dragged through the French courts was even more so.

Grau received her with a patronizing smile and a gallant kiss to the hand. How delighted he was to learn of Mme Terry's operatic comeback. Swallowing her pride, Sibyl lost no time in launching her proposition. She was "anxious" to return to America and had long dreamed of singing in the city of her youth. She was equally candid in admitting that her late husband's creditors were pressing her. If only she could earn $20,000 in America and hand it over to them upon her return to France, what a relief it would be.

Grau was undeniably interested but remained reserved. He could afford such an attitude, for this time their situations were reversed. Now it was Sibyl Sanderson who needed him, not the Metropolitan that was wooing her. True, he could use another lyric coloratura, as Melba would not be with the company this season. Also, Sanderson ought to be a potent drawing card in her native state. But there was the question of her health. The 1895 fiasco was still a burning scar on Grau's memory, not to mention his ledgers. He warned her that she would not receive a cent for any time lost to absenteeism on this tour.

Sibyl was in no position to bargain. Money was what she had to think of now, any sum at all. Negotiations continued through the month of June. Grau finally offered her a contract of twenty performances at five hundred dollars each, half of what she had asked. In return, he would engage her for the roles of Manon, Juliette, Gilda (*Rigoletto*), Micaëla (*Carmen*), Marguerite de Valois (*Les huguenots*), and Thaïs. He agreed to give the American premiere of the last-named work in New York during the upcoming season.

Sanderson signed the contract with the full realization that Maurice Grau had outwitted her at every comma. Still, it was comforting to know that this time she would have the role of Juliette to herself. The impresario, on the other hand, felt that during her three weeks in San Francisco she ought to bring in more money than her fees for the entire season. Grau stroked his beard and congratulated himself. Whatever his artistic limitations were, he had few peers in the realm of negotiating business deals.

Sibyl was well aware of the gargantuan task looming before her. She had demonstrated enough stamina to weather twelve performances of *Phryné* in a month, but the singer knew she would need every ounce of reserve power to withstand the rigors of Grau's coast-to-coast campaign in the fall. Everything depended upon her health and her ability to control her compulsive drinking. Unless she exhibited extraordinary self-control, the American expedition could very well meet with the same type of disaster that had claimed the European tour.

On Sibyl's scale of priorities, however, it was still of paramount urgency to be equipped with a resplendent wardrobe for her American return. Jean Worth was commissioned to indulge himself in a veritable orgy of opulence. It mattered little that her full remuneration from the tour could not possibly cover such extravagance. Of far greater importance was the necessity to show her compatriots that she was still the undisputed queen of glamour.

Flushed with her newly acquired contract and feeling once more enthroned at the Opéra-Comique, Sibyl decided to spend the summer in southern France—and in the grand manner befitting a prima donna. Her family had already left for St. Énogat, while her sister Jane and husband Roy would be staying temporarily in her apartment after their arrival from America. Accompanied by her maid and the dogs, the soprano rented a château near Aix-les-Bains, on the edge of Lake Bourget.

Behind the château was a beautiful garden with an arbor beyond the hedges, and the grapevines swept all the way down to the lake itself. Sibyl found the interior to be something out of the *Arabian Nights*. The great hall displayed such a comical profusion of styles—everything from wicker divans to wolf skin area rugs—that it reminded her of Sarah Bernhardt's Parisian home. How the previous tenants had coped with the lack of sanitation facilities was not known, but Célestin was quickly dispatched to town and directed to bring an adequate supply of chamber pots.

Sibyl rented a grand piano so she could practice for her forthcoming American tour. The diva had invited Mary Garden to stay with her when the latter made her debut in the Aix-les-Bains premiere of *Thaïs* on 25 August 1901. All summer Sibyl had been coaching Mary: how to move seductively, how to display the *contrapposto,* and how to control those high notes that were so difficult for her.

When Garden stepped off the train with her conductor (and new paramour), none other than composer-conductor André Messager, Sibyl was impressed. Mary should go far at the Opéra-Comique under such an influential aegis. At the time Messager was married to his second wife, Irish composer Hope Temple, who was a friend of Sibyl's.

A week before Mary's debut Célestin arrived with the new automobile Sibyl had bought on credit. She wanted him to drive her and Lina on a scenic excursion into the Swiss Alps. According to postcards she sent her family, the five-day trip proved most relaxing, and she expected to be back in Aix by 21 August for the dress rehearsal of *Thaïs*. A card to her brother-in-law revealed her true feelings about her approaching return to the United States: "Oh! that hateful trip to America!"

On the night of 25 August, Sibyl swept into Garden's dressing room to wish her luck. In a sudden impulsive gesture so typical of her, she removed her fabulous ropes of pearls and threw them around her pupil's neck. "Mary," she exclaimed, "Thaïs must have pearls!"

After the performance Mme Terry brought her old friend King George of Greece backstage to congratulate her protégée. The Greek monarch predicted that the work would become world famous one day. As the pearls were again fastened about her neck, Sibyl announced that she expected to create the title role for the American premiere during the coming season in New York, sadly unaware it was not in her destiny to sing the role ever again.

The time was drawing close for the diva's departure to America. As soon as she returned to Paris, Jean Worth summoned her for the final fittings. And he had more than lived up to his reputation. Sibyl was ecstatic over his breathtaking creations. Both star and designer were aware that such a wardrobe would totally annihilate the toilettes of her female colleagues. Even more encouraging were the couturier's generous assurances that Madame should not think about paying him until after her return from America.

Worth was not flattering himself when he predicted to a *New York Journal* reporter that his costumes for Mme Terry would cause a sensation in New York. Rapturously he showed them to American photographers and newsmen. For

Thaïs he had designed a seductively clinging robe of pink crêpe-de-chine covered with white silk gauze, while white tulle galloon, embroidered with diamonds, crisscrossed the dancer's breasts. When the courtesan ran down the stairs in Nicias's palace, the audience would see her cloaked in a Nile-green mantle of crêpe-de-chine.

In *Rigoletto* Sanderson would be attired in white crêpe-de-chine shot through with pink. As Micaëla she was to wear a pale-blue fleurs-de-velours gown, "demure yet alluring," as Worth described it.

For the role of the Queen in *Les huguenots,* Worth paraded two sumptuous costumes before the reporters that would have dazzled Marguerite de Valois herself. First he had designed a yellow satin dress with a long train and a diadem of matching canary diamonds. The skirt was cut away showing a front of white satin decorated with silver and pearls. The yellow satin bodice and high collar also glittered with incrustations of pearls. Two satin scarves fell from the shoulders to the bottom of the skirt in back to complete this sun-flooded picture.

The other creation was a black stamped-velvet marvel with a gold-embroidered skirt. The black velvet bodice opened in front to show a pink satin underbodice also outlined in gold. A high queen's collar flared upward dramatically in stiff silver over pink velvet. Completing the ensemble was a small beige velvet cloak.

"Here is a gown which Madame will wear in *Roméo et Juliette,*" Worth purred to the newsmen as he brought out the pièce de résistance of the collection. "*Regardez!* A fantastic pink stamped-velvet ball gown ornamented with silver and cream lace. The entire front of the skirt is adorned in garlands of pearls . . . The sleeves are fashioned of contrasting blue satin and embellished with emeralds and diamonds. Never did my father design anything like it for Mme Patti!" The other Juliette costumes were no less astonishing, ranging from an incredible lilac velvet creation completely spangled with silver to a white damask vision embroidered with gold and pearls.

With these weapons of war arrayed before her, the onetime queen of the lyric stage foolishly prepared to go forth to battle, when her most valuable piece of artillery should have been her voice.[2]

Chapter 35

The American Return

With twelve trunks full of clothes, the cantankerous Lina, and a flaming red wig, Mme Sanderson-Terry sailed for her native land on the *Savoie* on 28 September 1901. The American press had widely trumpeted her return.

"Sibyl Sanderson Comes to Dazzle" "Sails with Gowns That Are Marvels" chorused the newspapers. Photographs of her fabulous operatic creations had been paraded through the Sunday supplement section of the *New York Telegraph.* Even blasé New Yorkers took notice.

Three months earlier, Nicolet's gossip column in Paris's *Le Gaulois* had leaked the news of Sanderson's return to the Metropolitan even before she signed the contract. It was only a matter of hours before the international cables ignited with dispatches. From then on, East Coast society was avid with curiosity, and American dailies crammed with speculative stories. Unfortunately, America's attitude toward its lyric expatriate had not changed. "Sibyl Sanderson is forced to return to the stage," announced the *New York World.* "Absolute necessity, it is said, compels her to seek her livelihood."[1]

"Undaunted by the fact that the Metropolitan stage is unsuited to her voice and also that her roles do not especially appeal to New Yorkers, Sibyl Sanderson is promised at last in *Thaïs,* which Maurice Grau intends to produce in New York," sneered *Town Topics.*[2]

Hobart Burr took a more analytical view in *Cosmopolitan* magazine.

> Should there be a change in public taste in America, by which the operas in which she is queen become fashionable, she can return and score an overwhelming triumph. As it is, America needs some preliminary education in that field of operas which lies between the levels of light and grand operas.[3]

Before the eve of departure, the bustle of packing, the farewells of friends, and the advice of a solicitous mother had occupied the singer's attention. Margaret may have been too old to accompany her anymore, but was never old enough to be free of anxiety about her. Now on the voyage Sibyl had more time for introspection. Self-doubt and worry nibbled away at her composure. Although her health had improved superficially that summer, in the long run the morphine injections had failed to arrest her alcoholism. Nor had her voice come back with the amplitude for which she hoped. How dependable would it prove to be? If it betrayed her this time, her career was finished in the United States. And how would American audiences react to her waning beauty? Every time she picked up her looking glass, the furies of self-destruction returned her gaze.

On 5 October, Mme Sanderson-Terry descended the gangplank in New York. A balmy autumn day greeted her as she set foot on native soil for the first time in more than six years. The Manhattan skyline was splashed with sunshine as huge puffs of smoky white clouds drifted lazily over the horizon.

Six-and-a-half years. In 1895 she had arrived fresh from her Parisian triumphs, the empress of the French footlights, the indisputable queen of glamour, and the fiancée of a Cuban millionaire. Now she returned as a weary, insolvent widow attempting a comeback. Did anyone still care?

Once she had registered at the Hotel Savoy, the city lost no time in acknowledging her arrival. Messengers knocked constantly at the door of her suite bringing telegrams, bouquets, floral sprays, and cards. Reporters and fans clamored for interviews and autographed pictures. Sibyl Sanderson was home again and she was remembered!

Surrounded by an embankment of flowers from admirers both in America and abroad, Massenet's ex-muse held a press conference the day after her arrival. Merely a half-dozen years had elapsed since her last visit, but to colleagues and friends the change in her appearance was appalling. Her skin, once sparkling with youth, was now flabby and porous. Although her face was plastered with cosmetics, circles of dissipation still underlined her eyes. A copper-colored wig covered the film of white peach fuzz which was all that remained of her once abundant hair. Still, her irresistible personality seemed as natural as ever.

The fading siren faced a bombardment of questions that kept her constantly on the defensive. She labeled accounts of the czar's romantic penchant for her as "absurd" and the rumors of her alleged "Budapest suicide attempt" as "pure nonsense." Stories of trouble with her mother-in-law and stepdaughter were emphatically denied.

"Mr. Terry's mother and I are on the best of terms; the Countess de Castellane has been caring for his daughter ever since I decided to go back on the stage," she prevaricated. Regarding her late husband's phantom legacy and her return to the footlights because of financial pressures, she declared, "I have gone back on the stage because I must do something."

She defended her right to sing in a Berlin music hall if she chose and chatted about her forthcoming creation of the title role in the Hillemachers' *Circé*, which was to have its Parisian premiere in the spring of 1902. Sanderson didn't bother to explain that the Hillemacher brothers, Paul and Lucien, were two promising young French composers who had won the Prix de Rome after their musical apprenticeship in Massenet's classroom. Having been longtime admirers of the singer, they had written the opera together especially for her. Gazing into the future, she mused, "If my audiences in San Francisco give me as enthusiastic a reception as they did for Mme Nevada, I fear I shall just sit down in the middle of the stage and cry . . . I hope the Americans will like me."

The next few days were hectic ones. Sibyl enjoyed a reunion with other artists who were converging upon the city from all over the world. Maurice Grau had assembled a galaxy of stars that was being advertised as the greatest array of stellar names since the days of P .T. Barnum and Jenny Lind.

In the soprano realm, Mmes Gadski, Sembrich, Eames, and Calvé were the four queens of song with whom Sanderson would share bouquets until the arrival of Milka Ternina in December. Mme Schumann-Heink and Louise Homer were the grand duchesses from the contralto kingdom. The leading tenors included such renowned artists as Van Dyck, Dippel, Salignac, and Gibert. Alvarez would join the company upon their return to New York. Antonio Scotti, Marcel Journet, David Bispham, and Andrés de Segurola were among the famous singers of the baritone and bass provinces. Édouard de Reszke would join them at the end of October.

The three principal conductors among whom the repertoire would be divided were Walter Damrosch, Philippe Flon, and Armando Seppilli. Flon was given charge of the French operas and Seppilli the Italian, and Damrosch assumed responsibility for the German repertoire. A host of lesser lights such as Fritzi Scheff, Suzanne Adams, Carrie Bridewell, Adolph Mühlmann, and Mathilda Bauermeister completed the roster.

Sibyl's new leading tenor was a Frenchman, Thomas Eustace Salignac. She found his mock-heroic gestures amusing, and he used them to good effect. He was of diminutive stature and, like many tenors who wished to appear taller, wore specially constructed high heels. Massenet later became so enthralled with his interpretation of Jésus in a revival of *Marie-Magdeleine* that the composer surpassed himself in his effusively autographed pictures: "To Salignac who is more like Jesus than Jesus himself." After such heady praise, it was fortunate for Salignac that no one asked him to walk on the surface of the Mediterranean.

The artists knew this tour would be the most spectacular marathon Grau had ever organized. His agenda called for 145 performances of thirty operas throughout the United States and Canada—a record-breaking schedule. The company would have a private train of seventeen passenger cars consisting of five sleepers for the stars, two tourist cars for the orchestra, one more for the chorus, another for the corps de ballet, a diner, and seven drawing-room cars, plus seventy-eight freight cars. One special freight car was to be shipped directly to San Francisco for the Wagnerian productions.

Because of overcrowding in the diner, most of the stars refused to use it. Their servants invariably had to pick up provisions of canned food for the long runs, as lunch counters in the small-town depots were often deemed inadequate by the singers' standards. Dinners on the train always remained highly improvised affairs.

A voice worth a thousand dollars a night was as carefully guarded as the crown jewels in the Tower of London. When a vocal luminary had sung one night and was not to appear until several nights later in another city, she was sent on ahead of the company in the drawing-room car of a regular train to rest before the troupe arrived.

Grau's lyric armada pulled out of New York's Grand Central Station on 7 October 1901, bound for Canada. After one performance in Albany, the season would officially open in Montreal on the 8th with the irrepressible Emma Calvé as Carmen.

Manon was booked for a matinee on the 10th. With Flon in the pit, Salignac was to sing the Chevalier Des Grieux, and the cast would include such old colleagues as Dufriche in the role of Lescaut and Decléry playing the Count Des Grieux. Everyone in the company was waiting to see if Massenet's ex-goddess would finally score her long-dreamed-of conquest on New World soil.

Wednesday, 10 October, was an ominous day for Sibyl's professional return to the North American continent. Storm clouds that hovered menacingly over the city broke just after midday, and rain came down in torrents. The furies did not have long to wait. Nevertheless, an audience of twenty-five hundred Québecois who had purchased their tickets weeks in advance was not going to be cheated out of its first performance of Massenet's most famous opera. The thoroughly soaked spectators pushed and shoved their way into the Montreal (skating) Arena, where the Metropolitan company was appearing.

Sibyl discovered that the dressing rooms were ludicrously improvised; furthermore, her Chevalier was in bad voice. Still worse, the dilapidated roof of the Arena leaked copiously on the singers. The Gambling Scene and Des Grieux's two other arias had to be omitted because of a cold, for which Salignac begged the indulgence of the audience. Sibyl, though, was in excellent voice and, according to the cables, "sang with much dramatic effect." Her reception was enthusiastic, and she received four or five curtain calls after each act with repeated ovations for her superb work in the Saint Sulpice scene. A wildly cheering audience even gave the ill-starred lovers seven curtain calls after the death scene.

The Canadian premiere of *Manon* had been a victory in spite of Salignac's below-par condition, and if the triumph of the day belonged to the California nightingale, her conquest of Montreal was not complete without its absurd aspects. Enthusiastic fans insisted upon hurling soggy flowers at the feet of an already bespattered Manon. The prima donna retired to her hotel suite flushed with the first taste of success. The next morning she awoke flushed with a fever. Her throat was raw, and her nasal passages were swollen shut. She had caught cold in that dripping arena.

A feeling of horror chilled Sibyl to the bone. Would this misfortune herald a reprise of the bronchitis that wrecked her American tour in 1895? At that time she had provoked the disaster herself; here in Montreal, after the most solicitous precautions, she had succumbed to forces beyond her control. Had the furies already snatched true victory from her grasp and handed her a Pyrrhic one instead?

For every success she would be cursed with a corresponding adversity.

Two days later in Toronto, where she was to have sung her first Juliette, she was still indisposed. Camille Seygard, the Belgian soprano who became her unfailing lady-in-waiting throughout the tour, went on instead. By the time the company returned to the States, Sibyl had recovered sufficiently to sing a matinee of *Manon* on 14 October in Rochester. Her claim to fame in that town seems to be the distinction of having been responsible for Maurice Grau's all-time box-office nadir. The total gate was only $332, a low never equaled since in the annals of the Metropolitan.

After reappearing on native soil only to earn this dubious honor, Sanderson began to lapse into spells of depression. Grau had informed her during their contract negotiations that he intended to use her repertoire primarily for his matinee offerings. Flatteringly, he observed that her Dresden-china femininity ought to be a valuable drawing card for her own sex, which dominated these audiences. Furthermore, Grau had not forgotten that her cancellations in 1895 cost him a small fortune in nocturnal receipts. His many years of experience had taught him to put his trust only in orthodox operas for evening engagements—and in reliable troupers.

Sibyl had not objected. Given the desperate need for money that was her principal reason for rejoining the Metropolitan, she would have sung at four in the morning if ordered to do so. But now it was becoming obvious that neither she nor her mentor were exactly household names at some of the whistle stops on the tour. The only French operas Grau ever scheduled for evening productions were his veteran warhorses, *Faust* and *Carmen*. It would be up to her to campaign for her mentor and the new school of French opera.

The date of 19 October found Sibyl in Buffalo making her third appearance as Manon, and at night for a change. This time Decléry assumed the role of Lescaut, and Journet had arrived to sing his first Count Des Grieux. The night before, Sibyl had invited Emma Eames and her longtime secretary Fanny Fetridge to dine with her in her hotel room. In the midst of a very feminine tête-à-tête, a disheveled young man suddenly staggered into Sibyl's chambers muttering incoherently about wanting a drink. Suspecting him of being a reporter, Mme Eames ordered him to leave, but instead he lurched toward Sibyl. Eames immediately sprang to her defense. Seizing him by the shoulders, she spun him out of the room. Apparently, the tipsy intruder was too uncoordinated to resist.

A more sympathetic Sibyl, aroused by curiosity, rushed to the door a moment later to discover his identity. She watched him emerge from his own room across the hall shortly afterwards, leaving the door unlatched, and wander downstairs, presumably for that drink he so desperately craved. After he was out of sight, she tiptoed across the hall and peeped into his room. On the bed sat a young woman dissolved in tears. Sibyl learned that her mysterious interloper was not a reporter at all but a nervous bridegroom celebrating his wedding night by getting as intoxicated as possible. Between paroxysms of sobbing, the deserted bride explained that she had not eaten and was in despair over the antics of her wayward spouse. Sibyl came to her rescue at once, inviting the girl into her room, where both prima donnas shared their dinners with her.

After the performance, the Metropolitan entourage steamed out of Buffalo to invade the South, with Louisville, Kentucky, being the first stop. Nashville and

Memphis, Tennessee, were to follow. With a large portion of the Mississippi Valley's populace pouring into Memphis for the performances, the local impresarios, Messrs Pernell and Kronberg, decided to book the company into the huge stone-turreted auditorium instead of the opera house because of the former's larger seating capacity. *Lohengrin* and *Faust* were both sold out. *Manon* was scheduled for a Saturday matinee on 26 October.

Sanderson had not withstood the trip well. Insomnia continued to torment her. She had written her mother that she was unable to sleep because of the constant jolting and weaving of the train cars. Nevertheless, she attempted a brave descent for the photographers when the caravan pulled into Union Station on Friday at 10 A.M.

If ever there was a reminder that she was no longer an international siren, it was that merciless photograph taken at the Memphis depot. Decked out in an enormous picture hat, furs, and ropes of pearls over a sagging bust, the prima donna had all the external trappings of glamour, but her inner misery betrayed her. The eyes were dull and listless, sunken in deep, swollen folds, the lids heavy from sedation. Her entire face was bloated, and suffused with an expression of such weariness that it should have served as an augury of the bizarre events that were to follow.

With three hundred members of Grau's company all talking and shouting in four different languages, the station was a polyglot of confusion. The voices of Pernell and Kronberg were hopelessly lost as they struggled to assign the various stars to their hotels. Mme Schumann-Heink, Salignac and his wife, Fritzi Scheff, Dippel, Giuseppe Campanari, Walter Damrosch, and the David Bisphams were among those allotted rooms at the Fransioli. Sanderson's cab driver failed to understand Kronberg's direction to take her to the Clarendon and, instead, followed the other carriages to the Fransioli. In the meantime, her trunks were dispatched to their original destination.

For the rest of the day no one knew what had happened to the missing baggage. In desperation Sibyl telephoned her impresario. Grau immediately ordered his assistants to scout the city for it. When the trunks were finally discovered at the Clarendon, the management refused to release them until a ten-dollar claim was paid. After all, they had not been notified that her reservation was canceled.

Sibyl was in a fractious state. She could not rest; her insomniac furies pursued her relentlessly. On Saturday morning she felt like a wretched Prometheus, devoured by an unseen vulture. How could she possibly sing *Manon* in the afternoon? By the time she and her maid arrived at the auditorium, an insidious rumor was in circulation backstage that the prima donna was inebriated.[4]

It was no secret to the company that Sanderson had been drinking on the tour. It was impossible to keep such dissipation a secret when traveling under such overcrowded conditions. No one in Grau's company—with the possible exception of Emma Eames—had any idea that she was suffering from persistent bouts of manic depression, and the latest one would be cresting shortly. Only Lina watched helplessly as the tension continued to accelerate. In 1901 the disease was not understood at all. In America it was categorized with other undefined nervous disorders under the general classification of "nervous prostration," and ignorant doctors often prescribed alcohol-based drugs indiscriminately to treat them.

Not long after the opera commenced, it became apparent the heroine was in no condition to perform. "She seemed to pause for a moment," reported the *Commercial Appeal* "as if lost and exclaimed in a whisper, distinctly heard by those in front, 'I cannot sing!'" As soon as the first-act curtain[5] had been rung down, an announcement was made from the stage that "Mme Sanderson was ill and unable to complete the performance." The first-act intermission lasted over forty minutes and gossip was running riot through the house.

In the midst of the crisis Camille Seygard was summoned to go on in Sibyl's place. The audience rallied and gave the substitute courtesan three curtain calls for saving the day. For the rest of the afternoon critical laurels were divided between the new Manon and Dufriche's Lescaut. Tribute was also paid to Salignac for sustaining the burden of several important scenes until Mme Seygard could assume command of her role.

Summing up the tumultuous events of the day, the critic on the *Commercial Appeal* concluded, "It was a matter of congratulation that Seygard was substituted since it was clear to everyone in the first act that Sanderson was very ill and never on key." There was no mention in the paper of the spurious tale that Mrs. August Belmont perpetrated in New York for decades. According to theatrical legend, Sanderson recovered later in the opera and staggered out on the stage in the middle of the Saint-Sulpice scene to compete with her substitute for the personal affections of a bewildered Salignac. The alleged incident would have been the only time in operatic history that the Abbé Des Grieux was pulled in opposite directions by two courtesans, each claiming to be the true Manon, each determined to drag him back to her own secular world of sin.

Quite to the contrary, the pathetic soprano was taken back to the hotel by her maid and put to bed immediately. Cables flashed across the country about her

Memphis breakdown, and baritone Campanari fanned the flames by informing newsmen that "Mme Sanderson was in critical condition and completely hysterical." The Fransioli brothers immediately summoned a doctor to her bedside, and it can only be assumed that injections of morphine were administered to quiet her. By nightfall her screams had evidently subsided, for inquisitive reporters found the corridors to be silent. The next day she was much improved, and friends in the company warded off journalistic predators with assurances that "she had been suffering only from severe nervous prostration and would be herself in a few days."

When Grau's barnstormers pulled out of Memphis for Atlanta Sunday night, Sibyl had recovered sufficiently to join them. By now, however, the company had journeyed far enough to realize that Massenet's ailing muse could not bear the strain of constant travel and work. Sleep continued to elude her. Colleagues noticed that her eyes were dull and lifeless. According to Mrs. Adolph Mühlmann, whose husband was singing in the German productions that season, she would stare inexpressively at people well known to her in former years. By 1901 Sibyl Sanderson had become a pitiful shell of the woman friends once knew.

The Metropolitan tour arrived in Atlanta concurrently with the execution of Czolgosz, President McKinley's assassin. Fortunately, the sensational publicity that surrounded the event did not affect ticket sales in the least. The *Atlanta Constitution* proclaimed that "full dress would be worn on the main floor by all Atlanta belles for *Lohengrin* and *The Barber of Seville*." Georgia society was determined not to be cheated out of its finest hour by the death of a political maniac.

Manon was slated for the 29 October matinee, but Sanderson was seized by a superstitious whim and refused to sing the role. Haunted by the trauma of her recent disaster in Tennessee, she had more than enough justification. The management agreeably changed the bill to *Roméo et Juliette*.

There was nothing strange about the fact that Gibert, who hadn't sung opposite Sibyl since their early days in Paris, should be cast as her first American Roméo. Theatrical annals abound with such coincidences. Mme Bauermeister was chosen for the nurse; Dufriche would play the Duke of Verona; Decléry was picked for Mercutio, and Journet was assigned his first American Friar Laurence. More skeptical members of the company waited in the wings to see if the unpredictable soprano would get through her first American performance as Juliette.

The curtain went up promptly at 2 P.M. before an exquisitely gowned audience. Bouquets were in every lap, flowers in all coiffures. A stir of audible approval crisscrossed the house when Juliette's dazzling pink ball gown wafted onto the stage. To the surprise of the cast, Sibyl floated through the afternoon, enchanting her audience with a sparkling and exceptionally youthful interpretation of the role. When the final curtain fell, Atlanta society gave her a long and enthusiastic reception, showering her with bouquets.

If the critic for the *Atlanta Journal* complained that Sanderson's "coloratura work was neither smooth nor facile," he had to admit that "her dramatic portrayal of the part was very good." In contrast, the reviewer on the *Constitution* lauded her voice as "a lyric soprano of agreeable quality and its culture is of the happiest type . . . though by no means robust, it lasted bravely and well through the long Gounod opera . . . Miss Sanderson's best work was done, indeed, during the last act."

That evening in the hotel as Sibyl and Emma Eames were relaxing after dinner, they were puzzled by the strange, winged visitors whizzing in and out of the dining-room windows. When they asked a waiter about them, he chuckled and offered a startling reply, "No ma'am, dem ain't no hummin' birds. Dem's flyin' cockroaches."

In 1901 Atlanta was not the grande dame of Southern sophistication. That honor belonged to New Orleans—the last bastion of old French culture still lingering in the United States. By the time Grau's caravan approached the shores of Lake Pontchartrain, opera fever in Louisiana had reached the proportions of an epidemic. Hundreds of tourists and natives alike mobbed Toulouse Street to watch the long succession of wagons transporting the giant stage sets from the depot to the French Opera House.

The singers could hardly wait to go sightseeing along the narrow streets and picturesque shops in the old French Quarter. Fritzi Scheff, Louise Homer, and Carrie Bridewell purchased new shirtwaists in department stores on Canal Street. New arrival Édouard de Reszke joined Messrs Scotti and Dippel in a gastronomical tour of the quaint Italian and French restaurants along the waterfront. Elsewhere, newsmen were interviewing various stars about their impressions of the tour and future plans.

At the Saint-Charles, Sanderson wearily changed into a glamorous gown of pink silk to receive the emissary from the *Times-Picayune*. "Please excuse my apparent nonchalance," she explained to the reporter as she reclined in a large easy chair. "I have passed through a most horrible experience on the train. I feel tired and weak spirited. I passed another wretched night.[6] I do not know if it is due to the fatigue, the trip, or the late arrival, but I am not my normal self." After a moment's pause, she added, "It is passing though, and I am ready to sing tomorrow in *Manon*."

Sibyl confided that she intended to visit the historic sights of the French Quarter. She reminisced that she had been a mere teenager when she visited New Orleans with her father almost twenty years before. She also announced she would not go to Texas with the rest of the company but would take a special car to California ahead of time. When asked which parts she preferred, the artist replied, "I have no favorite role. I love to sing and always try to identify as much as possible with the character I impersonate."

Eames and Van Dyck inaugurated the opera season with *Lohengrin,* while *Manon* was booked for the usual matinee Saturday, 2 November. Since New Orleans had its own French opera company, most of the contemporary Gallic works had already been presented there, even the exotic *Esclarmonde,* which had been given its American premiere in 1893. Massenet, for once, was not an entity unknown to the public.

Sibyl faced the unenviable task of convincing opera aficionados why the composer had once chosen her to be the keeper of his lyric flame. For this reason, the audience was expected to be unusually critical. In the court of public opinion an artist's career remains a continuous succession of retrials year after year. She had arrived to discover her reputation already approaching the proportions of a legend. Just how would the onetime toast of the Paris Opéra measure up to New Orleans's own exponents of the French repertoire? More and more she was relying upon her phenomenal histrionic ability to aid her in creating the greatest artifice of all: the illusion that she could still sing, when, in actuality, her middle register was deteriorating.

The 2 November matinee turned out to be an unqualified victory for the opera, its cast, and the composer. Sanderson managed to score a triumph in the title role, and on Sunday the *Times-Picayune* extolled her in rapturous headlines: GREAT DAY FOR GRAU AND COMPANY—SANDERSON SHINES AT THE-MATINEE.

The soprano was showered with superlatives. "She is unique in her style . . . her beauty of face and form, her sensuous grace, her charm, and, above all, her unquestioned histrionic ability combine to make her a most attractive personality . . . her gowns are triumphs of art and good taste . . . her voice is a pure lyric soprano of high quality . . . her enunciation and phrasing are exquisite . . . she is, above all, a diseuse . . . were she only to speak the lines and not sing them, she could still thrill an audience . . . she can be in turn coquettish and tragic . . . in the Saint Sulpice scene, where she lures Des Grieux away from his vows, she was a veritable siren."

The *Picayune* critic was so carried away with the performance that he even forgave Salignac for "a common-place Dream Song" earlier in the opera. Commenting on the ovation given to the Saint Sulpice scene, he observed that "the tenor rose to unexpected heights and fairly electrified the hall." Journet was praised for being a "dignified and elegant Count Des Grieux."

There was no mention in the papers of the consternation backstage before curtain time. The chorus girls' dressing room was located in the basement underneath those of the stars, and a covey of half-dressed women suddenly ran upstairs screaming about an invasion of rats in their quarters. To help solve the dilemma, Sibyl generously offered her dressing room to some of the cast.

Manon had made its first American conquest at last and, not surprisingly, on old French soil. New Orleans was the only stop on Grau's circuit where the opera was not a novelty, and the audience was all the more difficult to impress. Yet, the Queen of the South held one advantage over all other American cities. It had the only tradition of *opéra comique* in the New World and truly understood the meaning of the spoken word with musical accompaniment.

The impresario himself, however, most assuredly did not. Throughout the tour Maurice Grau was afraid to gamble evening performances upon Massenet's exotic exponent, primarily because of her unfamiliar repertoire. *Manon* was simply too Parisian to ever develop the universal appeal of *Faust*. Besides, the California siren was a security risk. So far, Sanderson had earned the dubious distinction of being queen of the matinees.

Now that his lyric cavalcade was heading toward the West Coast, this situation would change. There Sanderson was a legend. Her career and her romances had been avidly followed by Californians ever since her family had departed for Paris. The Bay Area public was already clamoring for tickets, and at last she would be given her shining hour on the nocturnal agenda. It would be up to her to sell Massenet's reputation—so far he was known only in the newspapers as her mysteriously lurid Svengali. This time the burden of proselytizing would fall upon his undependable Trilby. Meanwhile, Grau and his staff would be left to ponder a disturbing question: with the recent decline in her health and voice, just how capable was Sibyl Sanderson of campaigning for Massenet's music?

Chapter 36

A Prophet Without Honor

Before the Metropolitan company departed for Texas, Mr. Grau dispatched his assistant Max Hirsch to San Francisco on a special train carrying scenery for just the California productions. Sibyl was also aboard. She knew that she would be facing her greatest challenge on the Pacific slopes. It was the potential to sell Sanderson to her compatriots that persuaded Grau to re-sign her with the Metropolitan in the first place. Sibyl had no illusions about this. It was here that her reputation as a success or failure on tour would be decreed—at the hand of her own people.

San Francisco was ablaze with publicity. The homecoming of the "California linnet" had created a furor. Newspapers had congratulated Maurice Grau for bringing their expatriate daughter back to them. The train stopped in Sacramento to pick up Sibyl's aunt Mrs. John Yost and her daughter Mabel. Upon arriving in Oakland on 8 November shortly before 9 A.M., Mme Sanderson-Terry and entourage took the ferry across the bay and reached the Palace Hotel by cab. There she retired to her suite and slept until the middle of the afternoon.

Reporters were milling about the hotel lobby before noon only to find that they would have to wait for interviews. Max Hirsch, who was handling Sibyl's press arrangements, asked them to return at three o'clock, explaining that some canned nourishment taken on the train had upset the star's digestion. By 3 P.M. representatives from the *Examiner,* the *Chronicle,* and the *Bulletin* were champing at the bit. Mrs. Yost led them into the suite, explaining that her niece was extremely fatigued and not looking her best. The reporters made themselves comfortable on the settee in the flower-crammed parlor.

Ashton Stevens, the ambassador from the *Examiner,* surveyed the room. There were American Beauty roses on the center table, banks of violets on the mantel, and bouquets of roses and carnations everywhere. Most prominent was another rose that sparkled and danced with a half dozen diamond pins. This rose was at the bosom of a soft, clinging blue tea gown with tapered angel sleeves. Stevens looked up into a pair of heavy-lidded rain-blue eyes.

"Well?" queried the eyes, and their owner repeated the interrogation out loud.

"I-I was just thinking to myself what a remarkable likeness you bear to your photographs."

"That's not particularly flattering," came the reply. "I'm not a bit fond of my photographs. They all make me out to be so big and gross. They positively vulgarize me with size."

Stevens agreed that she was not buxom in the least and then asked her how she prepared on performance days. Sibyl explained that she always slept late and after eating a big breakfast trusted "to luck and pluck for the rest."

> Please tell my friends not to expect a great big voice when I sing to them for the first time. They won't hear it because it would be entirely out of keeping with the part. Manon does not show my voice at its best. . . . The role is an acting part, and the way I play her in each act Manon is really a different woman. They like the opera very much in Europe but in this country it has never been a great favorite. Perhaps *Roméo et Juliette* would be better for my debut, but still I love *Manon* and I am going to try and make my friends love her too.

Sibyl confided that she had promised to take Mme Eames to a night at the minstrels as soon as the soprano arrived. Stevens explained that most of the old minstrel shows were no more.

The inevitable question was raised about how Sibyl liked returning to the stage after approximately four years of social idling. "Don't talk 'society' to me," she scoffed. "When I was married and was out of opera I tried society. It was awful! I had to stand in line and wait my turn in the shops. Dressmakers said they could arrange to fit me next week. Now I'm back in the harness, and there is no waiting in line."

She laughed heartily over the story about the dagger in the roses at the Comique. Neither had she attempted suicide in Budapest, nor was the czar in love with her. "I live a very simple, quiet life," she reflected. "There is nothing sensational about me, and I hope my friends here will understand that I am just the same little Sanderson girl who went away long ago, except that I am older, a good deal wiser, a good deal sadder, and—they say—a better singer."

San Francisco was humming with opera fever. *Lohengrin* with Eames and Van Dyck opened the season on November 11 before a brilliantly bejeweled audience that included Mrs. George Hearst, conspicuously attired in an elegant ruby velvet gown. The dress circle sparkled with diamond necklaces, corsages, bracelets, and stickpins.

Sibyl wisely absented herself from most social activities. "After *Manon*" was the official answer to all invitations. On 13 November she gave a small tea in her suite for some old friends whom she introduced to Mme Eames. That evening she joined her aunt, cousin, and baritone David Bispham for an evening at the theater. Several people recognized her and the whisper "There's Sibyl Sanderson!" swiftly crisscrossed the theater. At intermission an *Examiner* reporter insisted upon an interview.

"This is my only dissipation since I arrived home," she told him. "I am not going to risk taking cold because I want to sing Saturday night." On 14 November Mayor Phelan's carriage called for her, and she was his guest at a luncheon given in her honor at the Cliff House. Friday the 15th passed with a brilliant production of Wagner's *Die Walküre*. The Morosco Opera House was still reverberating from the tremendous applause when the first edition of the Saturday *Examiner* hit the newsstands. It contained a pathetic plea from a panicky artist to her people.

> Manon is one of my favorite roles and I hope it may please my audience tonight. I am very anxious to please my old friends in my old home and I hope they will like me. I sincerely hope that this, my first appearance, will not be a disappointment either to myself or my friends, or the patrons of grand opera. To the critical ones I only wish to say that they must expect more of quality than quantity in my role of Manon, and when it is over I wish only that everyone will love me, as this is my home.

Sanderson may have been worried about the premiere of a delicate, subtle French opera following the heels of a bombastic German one, but she had committed the unpardonable sin of begging her compatriots for approval.

All day long on 16 November delegations were arriving from Sacramento, and throngs were queuing up in front of the opera house throughout the chilly afternoon. Every seat had been sold. By nightfall the city was enveloped in a murky cowl of fog. But this was no ordinary night. A goddess—a legend—had returned.

When the doors of the opera house finally opened, the largest crowd in the history of San Francisco poured in. Maurice Grau was purring over the most colossal box office receipts of his tour. People stood against the back wall and three deep around all sides of the theater. They sat down three deep in the dress circle aisles, violating the local fire ordinance. The Bohemian Club had sent a huge basket of violets and carnations surmounted by a stuffed brown owl. Mayor Phelan, who had also sent flowers, entered his box fifteen minutes before curtain time. Sibyl's colleagues Madames Eames and Gadski and Antonio Scotti had arrived. Everyone from the social register was there except for Phoebe Apperson Hearst.

When the curtain went up Salignac was again the Chevalier Des Grieux, Marcel Journet, his father. By the time it fell on the last act, both the heroine and the opera itself had truly died, along with Sibyl's hopes for a triumphant reception. What happened at the ill-fated homecoming was best summarized by Geraldine Bonner, writing in the *Argonaut* of 2 December 1901.

> It is a curious conclusion to have arrived at, but the audience seemed to have gathered with the intention of disapproving. For some reason its own special prima donna did not seem to be in the city's good graces. San Francisco had made up its mind beforehand that it was going to be disappointed and that it wanted to be disappointed. A few perfunctory curtain calls were given her, and two bouquets thrown by Emma Eames and Mrs. Maurice Grau were all that San Francisco greeted her with. After that the house sits chilly and stolid, while she throws her high notes against that staring wall of coldness for five more scenes. Her vivacity openly dies away. She sings with effort, her voice as it were flattened against the frozen indifference of the vast, motionless audience. When it was over one felt relieved; it must have been hideously difficult to sing to the dead unresponsiveness of such a house.

After the performance, reporters mobbed Sibyl's dressing room to procure a statement from the exhausted soprano. She reflected sadly:

> San Francisco is apparently not greatly pleased to see me. My impression is that everyone came tonight with a simple desire to see and criticize. . . . It is the story of the prophet without honor in his own country. The Lord did not give me a voice for Wagnerian roles . . . but in opéra-comique, which is evidently not understood here, I have been very successful in other countries.

However, I do not wish to criticize my audience. They have seen me, heard, and I hope are satisfied. In some other part I may, probably will, be more pleasing. *Manon* is not known here, and I suppose that has something to do with the lack of appreciation.

The gala homecoming had turned into an icy wake. Ned Hamilton reported that the diva cried herself to sleep. It had been a devastating experience from which she would never recover.

The next morning revealed that two critics, at least, strove to be polite. Ashton Stevens wrote in the *Examiner* that Sibyl achieved "a distinctive success in her cozy little boudoir voice." He found *Manon* to be "character acting and singing of the most intimate and unoperatic kind." As to her singing, he concluded:

> Taken as an instrument the Sanderson voice is not great. It is free and facile and compact and extremely expressive, but there is none of that ineffable inner tone that telegraphs up and down the vertebrae, and while fully adequate in power to the demands of this part, it does not suggest much of a reserve force for a more strenuous effort.

The *Chronicle* described Sanderson's voice as "pure of note, not of passionate quality, but of more warmth and color than we had expected . . . the upper register is clear and smooth, and when Miss Sanderson took the dramatic scenes last night, she displayed considerable dramatic power, which in the beginning she hardly promised."

On the other hand, criticisms from her own sex were downright hostile. Josephine Phelps, writing in the *Argonaut* on 25 November, observed that Sanderson's days as a reigning beauty were over: "There is an inward weariness in the expression in her eyes . . . her smile is sweet but mechanical . . . neither temperamentally nor vocally is she built on the proper colossal scale to charm the musical susceptibilities of her fellow countrymen. She may please but never thrill . . . we are a practical people and want much for our money." Mrs. Phelps had naively pinpointed the fact that in 1901 *opéra comique* was hopelessly misunderstood and unappreciated in America.

The most brutal review of the lot, however, belonged to Blanche Partington of the San Francisco *Call,* who twisted the edge of the scalpel deeply into both the opera and its exponent:

The opera was Massenet's chocolate creamy Manon Lescaut, opera-comique they call it in Paris. Its lightsome loves and airy sorrows came with an almost profane comicality after *Die Walküre* and left one with that curious feeling that the average person has after swallowing a vegetarian banquet. . . . There is nothing "to" the opera . . . judging from her work in *Manon* last night, Mme Sanderson cannot sing now, whatever she may have done once. The voice is gone, the control is gone, and only once—in her duet in the chapel at Saint Sulpice with Des Grieux—did her song give any evidence of the kind of thing that drew Paris and St. Petersburg to her feet but a few years ago. There she was at her best vocally, but though she is "of ours," it must be regretfully owned that Sibyl Sanderson has no place in grand opera and that even *Manon* overweighs her as far as voice is concerned. What is left of the voice shows that it was once worthwhile, but as a singer Sibyl Sanderson does not count.

On Sunday morning Sibyl read the *Call* review in a state of shock and disbelief. Seriously wounded by Miss Partington's rapier-edged prose, she drafted an indignant reply, but the Metropolitan management forbade her to send it.

In the afternoon she was driven by friends to the Crocker House, where the Princess Poniatowski had invited thirty guests to a tea for her. When she left she was again waylaid by reporters panting to promote a feud between the diva and the critics. "I have read the criticisms," she answered candidly, "and my friends have told me that *Manon* was not disliked. I shall sing Juliette tomorrow and then the public may judge my musical ability better."

Throughout Sunday she was the target of a smear campaign. Rumormongers predicted that she would capsize as Juliette on Monday night. "Melba couldn't make a go of that opera last year, Sibyl Sanderson will be a disaster" was one of the current sneers that found their way into print.

With all the adverse auguries it was a wonder that anyone turned out for her second appearance on 18 November. Salignac was cast as Roméo, Journet as Capulet, and Édouard de Reszke as Friar Laurence. Contrary to reports in the New York papers the cold autumn winds did not whistle through an empty theater. When the curtain went up, according to Ned Hamilton, the spectators "saw the most beautiful Juliette they had ever laid their eyes on." Sanderson's sensational pink brocaded-velvet gown, which glittered with thousands of pearl-encrusted figurations was described as "the finest specimen of the dressmaker's art ever seen in this city" by the San Francisco *Call,* which reported that it "created audible gasps of admiration."

No sooner had Sanderson finished scaling the famous coloratura passages of Juliette's Waltz Song than Hamilton reported "people began nudging each other, asking in amazement, 'Who said she couldn't sing?' " There was a huge burst of applause and throughout the evening she received a steady stream of spontaneous ovations and bravas. The enthusiasm of the limited audience seemed to be San Francisco's belated apology for its frigid behavior on Saturday night. After the final curtain, reporters again stormed the soprano's dressing room only to find her flashing one of her most irresistible smiles.

"The audience was small, but it was a good one. I am very happy San Francisco people are now convinced that I can sing. I was a bit piqued Saturday but I must attribute that to the fact that the audience did not understand *Manon*. For the benefit of the critics I sang the Waltz Song in its higher and original key, G major. Today no other singer attempts this."[1]

By the next morning the court of critical opinion had reversed its verdict unanimously. Not only were the newspaper sultans wearing "egg on their faces," their reviews were dripping with it. Blanche Partington spent half her review on the defensive for having written forty-eight hours earlier that Sanderson could no longer sing. In discussing the enigma of why Grau did not present the prima donna first in *Roméo et Juliette*, Miss Partington lamented, "It was a mistake, and a big one." She had no way of knowing it was Sibyl's own ill-fated decision to open in *Manon;* the artist had been too timid to risk a comparison with Melba's previous interpretation of Juliette. Miss Partington went on:

It was different last night . . . *Roméo et Juliette,* though not a great opera is at least worthy and in parts strikingly beautiful. . . . Miss Sanderson's voice at its best, as heard last night, is a high, light soprano of sweet though uncertain quality, flexible, and well cultivated. But it is worn and only safely used in the lighter voice, the loss of quality being immediately apparent when the singer attempts anything fuller than a mezza voce. But she sang the Waltz Song with a great deal of charm and throughout the evening showed a vocal competency that gives her a place not with singers of first rank, but with others who come a quite respectable second. She enunciates beautifully, every word being clearly distinguishable all over the house. . . . As to Miss Sanderson's dramatic conception of the role, it is by far the most satisfying I have ever seen. It is very French, unusually animated, but full of charm, tenderness, and girlish grace. She is quite worth the money to look at, but she acts the part too and is the only singer I have ever heard who puts the tenor in the shade from the standpoint of dramatic interest. Melba as Juliette created the most languid enthusiasm here in spite of her marvelous vocal gifts, but Miss Sanderson last night roused the house to a genuine enthusiasm for the role and the singer, and justly so by the virtue of the truth and poetry of her conception.

Ashton Stevens admitted in the *Examiner* that he enjoyed Mme Sanderson's interpretation of Juliette "way beyond" his expectations.

I had no idea that she was so shrewd an artist. . . . She was delightful in the balcony scene singing those long mezza voce passages without a shade of strain and with an unaffected sympathy . . . the performance in its entirety was above and beyond and all around the one of the same opera that opened the last Grau season, even though there was no Melba for Juliette and no Plançon for Capulet. Where a year ago it was irresolute and broken, last night it glided on glass thanks to Sibyl Sanderson.

Stevens even found a few words of praise for Salignac, hailing him as a "really poetic Romeo." He lauded de Reszke's characterization of Friar Laurence as one of "superb conviction" whose "dignity and poise held the house in a hush that was the next thing to reverence."

Sanderson had galvanized the entire cast into giving a superb perform-ance.[2] At the same time she had taken a great step toward reversing San Francisco's negative judgment of her in *Manon*. It was imperative that she redouble her efforts at self-discipline because her next appearance, as the Queen in Meyerbeer's *Les huguenots* the following Sunday, could turn the tide of public opinion unanimously in her favor. But she blithely began to accept a torrent of social invitations. On Tuesday night, gowned in a form-fitting black, low-cut sheath, with a corsage of violets, the artist joined Mr. and Mrs. Maurice Grau in their box for Eames's performance in Mozart's *The Marriage of Figaro*. She also raised eyebrows because she was escorted by childhood friend Shafter Howard, whose wife was visiting the East Coast that week.

According to Mrs. Fremont Older, who met her at this performance, the "wear and tear of stage makeup" was blamed at the time for her ravaged com-plexion. Recalling her appearance in 1962, she remarked, "Her skin was coarse and hard as leather and the color of a harvest moon. Her pores were flabby and large. Her entire face was plastered with makeup, but it couldn't hide the dissi-pated look she had. There wasn't a shred of beauty left. It was rumored that she was an alcoholic. . . . Thinking about it now, it was obvious she had all the symptoms of liver disease."

The following afternoon Sanderson was given a large reception by Mrs. George Boardman and won the hearts of all the Mrs. Grundys by asking naively, "Really, I had no idea people would criticize me because I went to the theater last night with Shafter Howard. Do you think I shouldn't have?" Her godmother, Mrs. John F. Swift, was touched by such a display of innocent contrition. "Why Sibyl, you are an artist," Mrs. Swift answered, "and they do things I suppose other young ladies would not approve of. What did you do in Paris?"

"I never went anywhere without mama—not even to the theater. The only exception I ever made was Mr. Terry, and I fell in love with him and he became my husband." That ingenuous response assured all the Victorian ladies that Judge Sanderson's little girl was still a credit to American womanhood.

On Thursday night Sibyl pleaded indisposition as pretext for avoiding a dinner party given by Mrs. Easton, mother-in-law of longtime Sanderson friend Charles Crocker. Instead, she and Emma Eames slipped off to a minstrel show and had the time of their lives. The next morning Sibyl was awakened by fits of persistent coughing and sneezing; she had caught cold, thanks to her foolish escapade. Unfortunately, the consequences were catastrophic to her West Coast success. Her third and crucial San Francisco appearance had to be canceled. Suzanne Adams went on in her place.

Actually, it was amazing that she had been home two weeks before succumbing to the elements. Every day the damp fog and chilly winds permeated every room in her hotel suite because she insisted upon leaving a few windows open at all times. The deceptive climate that season in San Francisco also played havoc with the throats of Calvé and Van Dyck, but they had the resilience to overcome it. Sanderson's resistance was constantly being sapped by her private dissipations. She was scheduled for the role of Micaëla in *Carmen* on 4 December, but again Suzanne Adams had to substitute.

In Sanderson's life one setback was invariably followed by others. Next, she broke out in one of her periodic rashes. Dr. Selfridge publicly diagnosed the curious ailment as "poison oak," although how she could have contracted this menace in late fall except through inoculation remains a mystery. It is possible that these rashes were the toxic reaction of a weakened constitution trying to combat a dangerous onslaught of morphine and alcohol.

"I can now account for my hoarseness," Sibyl explained in a press statement on 24 November. "Besides my cold I have been afflicted with poison oak, so, all in all, my visit here has been full of mishaps. However, I expect to be well enough to sing Juliette again on the Thursday matinee."

Needless to say, she wasn't. The San Francisco papers soon informed their readers that she was suffering from what singers called "a knot in the throat"; Dr. Selfridge would perform some minor surgery on it. The doctor announced that she would have to forgo all public performances for three weeks and forbade her to sing until the company opened in Cincinnati.

Sanderson's dreams of conquering her native state were now completely crushed, and the furies had scored a mortal victory.

Chapter 37

Romantic Interlude

On 5 December 1901 the Metropolitan caravan pulled out of the Oakland depot and headed for Kansas City. Knowing that Sanderson would not be on hand to open in *Roméo et Juliette* on 9 December, Grau penciled in Camille Seygard. On 11 December, Seygard again went on in the same opera in St. Louis. Grau was nervously counting on the ailing diva to catch up in Cincinnati as she had promised. When the train arrived on the banks of the Ohio River, there was no sign of the delinquent soprano, so Grau's staff again requested Mme Seygard to assume the role. Meanwhile, the Metropolitan office in New York was sending press releases to the Gotham papers announcing that Sanderson was scheduled to sing Juliette at the 28 December matinee. But the puzzle remained: where had the singer vanished?

Ostensibly, Sibyl remained in San Francisco for treatment, but it is doubtful whether she submitted to any throat operation. Instead, she left the Palace Hotel for the privacy of her aunt's home. There a solicitous Mrs. Yost spent the next few weeks helping Lina nurse a bedridden, severely depressed alcoholic back to health. In spite of the fact that she had been nervous enough to rely on the prompter occasionally, Sanderson knew she had brought no discredit upon Massenet's masterpiece. Nonetheless, Odette had been severely wounded by the arrows of her own townspeople. Now she lay grieving, unable to cope with rejection anymore.

The arrival of a mysterious telegram from Paris, however, proved to be a fortunate antidote for the artist's despair. A flurry of exchanges quickly followed. At Sibyl's request, her aunt cabled New York for hotel accommodations. As soon as she had recovered sufficiently, both singer and maid secretly boarded a train in Oakland for the cross-country trip.

Although Sanderson was despondent over her string of mishaps in her native state, she was the one songbird in Grau's aviary who could offer no excuse for not being cognizant of the treacherous Bay Area climate. Pathetically, after the disastrous West Coast campaign, all her vaporous attempts at self-preservation were abandoned.

Even the editorial in the *Sacramento Daily Record-Union* on 20 November 1901, entitled "A Chance for Justice," was small consolation. It not only damned the San Francisco critics as spurious and ignorant in their judgment of the lyric prodigal, but extended a personal invitation to Sanderson to appear in her native city and be accorded a worthy reception. Of course, the Sacramento editor had no way of knowing that Sibyl continued to sing *Manon* all her life in the cozy, intimate Opéra-Comique style upon which Massenet insisted. She refused, or did not know how, to readjust her voice in the role to the larger American theaters.

On the train, Blanche Partington's scurrilous phrases must have echoed in Sibyl's tortured brain. *Sanderson cannot sing now—cannot sing now*—over and over the words repeated themselves with every turn of the wheels. *The voice is gone—voice is gone*—again and again the phrases tore into her wounded psyche like a frenzied whip. Scene after scene of white desolation pierced by occasional lonely windmills passed before her eyes. She counted the hours, the minutes, until her contract with Grau would be over, and she could leave this cultural wasteland forever. She would never sing *Manon* again, she told herself.

As soon as the train arrived in New York on 15 December, they went directly to the suite Mrs. Yost had reserved for them at the Manhattan Hotel. Two days later a tall, handsome stranger registered at the same hotel and appeared to be extremely attentive to the soprano. He spoke excellent English with only the slightest trace of an accent, but no one knew who he was.

When the Metropolitan Opera Company pulled into New York a few days before Christmas, Grau was surprised to receive a message requesting him to call upon her at the Manhattan. When Grau arrived at her hotel he was shocked at the singer's deteriorated condition. She admitted that she was in bad health and wanted to rest before her solitary appearance at the Metropolitan. He was rumored to have offered her a deal to stage *Thaïs* in New York if she would stay past her contract deadline and make up some of her missed performances, but this has never been substantiated. At any rate, Sibyl told him any future engagement with the Metropolitan would have to be postponed to the following year because she was due at the Opéra-Comique in February to begin rehearsals in the Hillemachers' *Circé*. As Grau closed the door to her suite, both of them knew that unless there was a dramatic change in her lifestyle, Sibyl Sanderson was finished in America.

Tristan and Isolde with Ternina and Van Dyck opened the New York Metropolitan season on 23 December before a large, elegantly dressed audience. Alvarez had arrived from France for his appearances in *Roméo et Juliette*, in which he was scheduled to sing opposite Eames on Christmas day and with Sanderson at the Saturday matinee on 28 December. Sibyl had not sung with him since they portrayed the ill-starred lovers in 1894, and she knew she would need all her strength to hold her own against his huge, stentorian voice. Since it was announced this would be Sanderson's only New York appearance for the 1901–02 season, there was a tremendous rush for tickets. If Grau had lost any sleep over the soprano's recent cancellations, he should have been pacified by the soaring box-office sales.

Saturday afternoon arrived in an ominous flurry of cold winds and an overcast sky. Snow threatened, and coat collars were turned up high in the large crowd gathering in front of the Metropolitan. With such figures as the Perry Belmonts, Mrs. August Belmont, Mrs. Charles Alexander (Hattie Crocker), and her guest Lady Algernon Lenox in the audience, the social register was well represented.

At a quarter of two the callboy went to the star's dressing room to give the usual fifteen-minute warning. He received no answer. Pushing the door open he discovered the prima donna was nowhere to be seen. Her maid had been there, and had left her costumes in the closet and cosmetics on the dressing table. As Lina had temporarily disappeared, it was assumed she had gone to search for her mistress.

When word circulated backstage that the diva had not yet arrived, consternation prevailed. Messengers were dispatched immediately to her hotel, and nervous telephone calls were placed. In the midst of the pandemonium, a doorman reported there was a strange lady at the wrong door of the opera house who might be Miss Sanderson. The stage manager rushed frantically to the designated door. There stood the prima donna in a beautiful gown, very décolleté, draped with her sable cloak, which was not even buttoned at the collar. The cold winter winds blew her skirts about her feet, and snow was falling on her exposed neck and throat. Yet, she appeared to be totally unconcerned as she scolded the cab driver for bringing her to the wrong entrance.

"Miss Sanderson, do come in!" yelled the stage manager, blinking with disbelief. "We have just notified Mme Seygard to come and sing your part. Do hurry! You have less than fifteen minutes before curtain time."

"Is it really so late?" she asked with a faraway smile. "I had no idea of it."

By the time she was dressed and made up, the performance began a half hour late. But Sanderson was a radiant vision as she floated down the stairs to be introduced at the ball by Capulet, and her gossamer Waltz Song received tremendous applause. Then the intermission after the first act lasted over fifty minutes because the diva was seized with throat trouble, and the Metropolitan physician had to be summoned to treat her. Somehow the doctor worked a miracle. Through the remainder of the performance, the enthusiasm of the audience for her youthful and highly animated interpretation turned into a series of ovations and curtain calls for the soprano. The furies momentarily relaxed their pursuit of the hapless artist; it was amazing that she survived the afternoon. She had foolishly ignored the elements twice now in New York, risking her health and reputation.

Reviews were mixed. The sage of the *New York Herald* rhapsodized, "She was a surprise to her friends who had come to hear her in fear and trembling . . . certainly she has never sung or acted so well in this city . . . in beauty of tone and power her Juliette has excelled anything she has previously done . . . in the balcony scene and in all that follows she has never appeared here to better advantage."[1] Alvarez was chided for one of his old failings, singing off pitch in the sotto voce passages, "but throughout he acted and sang with such spirit that the house repeatedly called him before the curtain with Mme Sanderson."

Critically, there was no commotion in either the *World* or the *Journal* the next day; the reviews were so identical they could have been written by Siamese twins. The magistrate on the *Journal* observed that "in personal appearance Sanderson is the ideal Juliet. . . . She suggested the extreme youth of the part, and it needed no special power of imagination to justify Romeo's feeling for her. . . . Her voice was agreeably sweet when singing in mezza voce . . . but singing with full voice, it was often unpleasantly hard and cutting."

The pundit on the *World* added that "her voice is too thin in volume, too thin in quality, its middle and low registers too worn to be effective in the big auditorium." However, even he had to admit that "her Waltz Song was a finished piece of vocalization" and "in the florid passages she pipes forth the sweetest of high tones, clear and silvery; she trills and twists top notes with the delicacy of a songbird, and runs scales that suggest threaded pearls." He was also impressed by the fact that "Sanderson's personal magnetism evokes a curious sympathy for her that is of no little value" and agreed the reason for this had to be "her intelligent and expressive acting."

New York had finally heard Sanderson's Juliette for the first time and seemed to be amazed at the display of a more brilliant vocal technique than the one she used in *Manon.* All the reviewers agreed on one other point: "her intelligent and expressive acting."

After the performance, Sibyl and her tall, distinguished escort attended a supper party given for her by Mrs. Charles Alexander and other friends at Sherry's. She introduced him as Count Henri de Fitz-James of Paris. Rumors were circulating that the two would wed that weekend, but she fended them off with tongue-in-cheek denials.

The singer Giovanni Perugini né Jack Chatterton wrote her the following lines:

> I had such pleasure in witnessing your great improvement as to your voice the other afternoon when I heard you for the first time as Juliette, but even more the exquisite diction, style, and your real triumph as an actress—attributes which our so-called critics here do not let play sufficient stress in writing about you.

The following evening, accompanied by Count Fitz-James and her old friend Grace Mosher Wood, she left for Philadelphia to make her farewell American appearance. Reporters were already waiting in the lobby when she arrived at the Hotel Walton, but she asked them to return the following afternoon. On Monday, 30 December, representatives from a half dozen New York papers as well as local ones were fidgeting impatiently in her parlor. The heavy brocade drapes had been pulled back, and winter sunlight was streaming through the windows.

"Should I speak?" mused the prima donna turning to the count and Mrs. Wood as she toyed with a superb diamond ring. "My mother has not been told of it yet. Ought I not to wait until I have received her blessing? What do you think, Count?"

The count agreed it would be proper to inform her mother first. "Oh, tell it," Mrs. Wood urged. "You can't keep such things secret. Everybody will know it tomorrow morning anyway!"

"Yes, I am engaged," Sibyl slowly confessed, "to marry Count de Fitz-James, a French nobleman in Paris, next month. I have known him for some years, but he says he came to America for no other purpose than to ask me to marry him. Silly, wasn't it?"

"I made up my mind I would have it settled, and so I came to America. and shall never cease rejoicing that I did," the Count interrupted.

Sanderson announced they would sail on 4 January, first for England where the count had some business to transact.

"I shall continue on the stage, not because I have to," she explained, "but because I am happy on the stage. I have already made the count promise that he will never attempt to interfere with my ambition." Then she added, "I am going to marry again because I want a congenial companion. I have been dreadfully lonely." The singer denied having to forfeit an interest in the Terry estate upon remarriage. She also admitted that she had been deeply hurt by the manner in which her former townspeople had received her on the West Coast.

The count introduced himself as the second son of Édouard, Duc de Fitz-James, born in 1855 and descended from the English family of James Fitz-James, illegitimate son of James II and Arabella Churchill. The family had resided in France for over two centuries, and his home was the Château de Benais on the Loire. The count related that he had been a cavalry officer on the staff of General Boulanger and had spent the year 1883 traveling in the United States. He admitted he was not a wealthy man but said he had lately embarked upon a mercantile enterprise in French Guiana that he hoped would thrive. Then he explained that he had been divorced for some years from his first wife, Adèle de Sontaut-Biron. Not one reporter thought to ask him whether his status as a divorcé would affect the couple's future marriage plans.

On the evening of 31 December, Sanderson sang her farewell performance in America, again as Juliette to Salignac's Romeo at the Philadelphia Academy of Music. The diva was on time for this appearance, but the large New Year's Eve crowd arrived late.

One reviewer wrote that the early coldness of the house plainly affected the singer. "The first act seemed pinched, but as the audience grew more appreciative, more warmth came into her voice . . . in the balcony scene her voice suddenly opened like the south wind on a flower and continued to grow in warmth until in the long, passionate duet in Act IV she conveyed her romantic fervor most beautifully."

The same critic blamed the director for cutting the Act IV aria "Dieu! Quel frisson court dans mes veines" and for dropping the curtain as soon as Juliette had swallowed the sleeping potion, unaware that this was the traditional version of the Paris Opéra. The writer did not consider Salignac's Romeo "inspired" and awarded all the laurels to Sanderson, "who received hearty rounds of well-deserved applause afterwards."[2]

When the diva and her fiancé returned to New York the next day, the count was forced to correct an erroneous headline in the *New York Sun* announcing that their wedding would be postponed for two years. "Business will detain us in London for about a fortnight, and then we shall go directly to Paris," he told an impromptu news conference. "We both prefer to have our marriage solemnized there."

On the cold, gray morning of 4 January 1902, the star and her fiancé bade farewell to friends who had gathered at the pier. She wore all black, dress and toque, and a sable jacket to match her sable muff. The count had bought her some flowers that Lina apathetically pinned on her shoulder to add a little color.

Reporters were also there to request a few departing words. "It was my desire to be married in America," the prima donna confided, "but my mother, who could not be present, cabled me to wait until we arrive in Paris, so we shall go to see her at once on our arrival.[3] The wedding will take place during the latter part of February, and we shall later travel for some time on a honeymoon in Europe. I shall return to America, I hope, next season and certainly have enjoyed my visit here ever so much."

As the *Kronprinz Wilhelm* steamed out of the harbor, Sanderson watched the New York skyline blur, then vanish into gray oblivion. And with it faded her ties to opera in her native land. She had time now to assess her American adventure, a tour that had been undertaken with great hopes but had fizzled into a disaster. Engaged for twenty performances she had been able to fulfill fewer than half of them—nine to be exact. Still, Grau had been kind enough to pay for her Memphis appearance despite her pitiful breakdown there. She had hoped to make enough money in America to pay her creditors. Now she was facing bankruptcy.

Was she not emotionally and physically bankrupt as well? Her health and her voice had undergone steady deterioration, yet she had become less and less disciplined in her vocal practice. She could no longer listen to herself with a critical ear. She had become appallingly careless in her personal discipline and behavior, arriving at the Metropolitan only fifteen minutes before curtain time on a wintry day—and dressed for a summer garden party—when it was imperative that she do her best. She could no longer endure any serious self-introspection. She had become a prematurely old woman at thirty-seven, a weary woman with a worn voice. Even looking into the mirror had become an agonizing ordeal. Life was bearable only through the haze of alcoholic euphoria. Every empty bottle, every empty flask pushed her a little closer to the precipice.

The singer was unaware that a friend who knew her well had written these lines to Will S. Monroe on the day she sailed from New York.[4]

Sibyl Sanderson leaves her native country today for Paris, a broken-hearted woman. The cruel blow that came to her in San Francisco has undermined her courage and spirit, and disappointment and discouragement have affected her health. For the present, at least, she is unfitted for operatic work; and in her delicate, sensitive condition I fear the blow may end her artistic career.

But the journalistic savants in San Francisco weren't the only ones who had written that her voice was strident and worn in different registers. The New York critics had made the same unhappy observation. Her contemporaries Eames and Melba, whose fame she had eclipsed in Paris, were soaring to the heights of their careers. Sibyl's wings were sadly soiled and broken.

Chapter 38

Walpurgis Nights

Icy sheets of winter rain greeted the arrival of the *Kronprinz Wilhelm* at Southampton on 11 January 1902. Clutching her fiancé's arm, Sibyl struggled not to lose her balance as they inched their way down the gangplank. Once their voluminous luggage was collected, they boarded a train for London, where their rooms were reserved at Claridge's. It had been a dreary crossing, and the singer was not looking forward to their stay in England with much enthusiasm.

Sanderson's arrival had been duly noted in all the London papers, and journalists were eager to learn the latest developments in her nuptial plans. On Monday, 13 January, she received a large delegation from the press in her parlor. She feigned both pleasure with her American season and anticipation about returning the following winter—although she admitted to disliking "the frequent changes and long jumps from place to place."

"Think of appearing in Montreal and a few days later in New Orleans!" she mused. "No wonder Mr. Grau's artists are always laid up with colds."

The reporters, however, were not interested in generalities. They wanted to hear her version of the debacle in San Francisco.

> Well, if you wish me to tell my candid opinion of the so-called opera critics in San Francisco, I must say I don't think they know much about criticism. Why, when they said I was 'too Frenchy' in *Manon,* fancy such criticism of French opera. . . . Do you know while singing Manon, I was asked to sing 'Home, Sweet Home,' as some of the audience would appreciate that more. Still, I should not be afraid to return there to sing. They liked *Romeo and Juliet.*

To the question about the audience she liked most, she replied, "the Philadelphians, I think . . . I also had a warm reception in Atlanta and at the Metropolitan in New York, where I sang only once."

Sibyl announced that she would create *Circé* by the Hillemacher brothers about 1 March, with her engagement at the Opéra-Comique running until the end of June. She also emphasized that she would never again sing *Manon* in the United States, as she was convinced Americans did not appreciate the work.

"I think I should like to sing Elsa and Mimì as American audiences like *Lohengrin* and *La Bohème*," she added.

When asked if Americans were more appreciative of opera than formerly, she agreed that they were. "Still, I must say Americans prefer quantity to quality. They would rather listen to a voice of volume than to a smaller one of better cultivation."

Fitz-James explained that he had entered into a land-speculation project in French Guiana and needed to procure financial backing. In fact, he spent most of his week in London trying to persuade bankers and investors to loan him the necessary capital. He painted a rhapsodic picture of the undeveloped country for them. Within those mosquito-infested swamps lay enormous deposits of rich minerals. He and his partners planned to develop gold mines, grow rubber trees, and even build a railroad. By the time the couple left for France a week later, the count had been singularly unsuccessful in demonstrating any Midas touch.

Gales of icy rain and snow had struck Paris that month. On 22 January, the day after Sibyl and her fiancé arrived home, a reporter from the *New York Herald* braved a sleet storm to interview them. The conversation followed the same basic trend as the one in London. Fitz-James reiterated that he would not force his fiancée to renounce her career after their marriage: "My wife will finish out her season at the Opéra-Comique. Then she will join me in South America for which I plan to depart no later than 15 April." The singer refrained from any comment on this statement, but she did contradict a report in *Le Figaro* that she would abandon the operatic stage the next year for a fling in operetta.

For once she was listening to her mother, who had borne down hard upon her. Marriage, Margaret argued, was out of the question. It was for this reason that she had cabled Sibyl in New York to postpone any foolish plans until after her return to France. With a tremendous burden of debts to be shouldered, how could Sibyl even consider renouncing her small annual stipend from the Terry estate for a next-to-penniless count? Already Sibyl's solicitors were preparing their briefs for an impending court clash with her creditors. They explained to her that she and Fitz-James could be married only civilly. The Roman Catholic Church would never unite them in any religious ceremony because of his divorce.[1]

Sibyl knew her mother was right. Everywhere she turned, her late husband's will kept her in perpetual bondage. Sadly, she sat down at Tony's Louis XVI desk—a desk she wasn't allowed to sell—and wrote a note to James Gordon Bennett's office at the Paris *Herald*.

> Monsieur,
> I wish you would do me the favor of publishing this note as soon as possible in your journal. "The marriage announced between Count Henri de Fitz-James and Mlle Sibyl Sanderson will not take place." You would do me the greatest courtesy by publishing this note without further comment.
>
> Please accept my salutations and best wishes,
> Sibyl Sanderson

Reason prevailed; Mrs. Sanderson had won. The Paris *Herald* published the retraction on 26 January but printed the entire letter instead of just the information requested. In a matter of minutes transatlantic cables were humming with the news. "Sibyl Sanderson Breaks Her Engagement—We Told You So," chorused the American newspapers in unison. Operatic circles were relieved to know that the California nightingale would not outrank her colleagues socially for the time being.

On 27 January, Sibyl received a representative of the Associated Press to discuss the reasons for her broken engagement. She explained that when she and the count became engaged in America, they did not realize that his divorce would be such a "serious obstacle" toward any religious marriage in the Catholic Church.[2] As they could only be married civilly, this would be unacceptable to the Fitz-James and Sanderson families. Therefore, they agreed to terminate their nuptial plans and remain "the best of friends." The count would leave for South America immediately, and she would undertake "a short tour of Belgium and Holland" before returning to the Opéra-Comique to create Circé on 15 March.

"It is better to break engagements than hearts," she added. "Marriages are sometimes broken off by mutual consent, and it sometimes happens that engagements bring people so close together that they find they are not compatible. There is more tragedy than comedy to life, and life at its best is but the husk of pleasure around a heart of sorrow."

The collapse of her impending marriage was only the first in a series of devastating reverses. What Sibyl's mother had predicted soon came to pass. On 4 February, Camerino, a lacemaker from the avenue de l'Opéra, brought suit for three unpaid bills totaling 18,951 francs ($3,800).

Maurice Travers, Sibyl's attorney, told the court that when these antique Murano laces were shown to Mme Terry, in 1899, she was suffering from a "nervous complaint." Camerino had called upon her and insisted upon displaying them, even though she wasn't interested at that time. According to Travers, once the exquisite fichus, tablecloths, and scarves had been displayed, the insinuating tradesman refused to take them away. Mme Terry insisted that she could not afford them, but her tempter told her she could pay him "when and how she pleased."

"Eve sampled the apple and bought the laces, but she needs time to acquit herself of the debt," Travers explained. "She requests the court for ten years to pay off the debt because she is insolvent. Furthermore, my client asks that the court appoint an expert to appraise the laces, because it is Mme Terry's opinion that M Camerino had unduly raised the price." The counsel for the plaintiff denied that the price had been hiked and insisted that the overdue bill be paid at once.

As expected, judgment was against Sanderson. The fifth chamber of the civil tribunal ruled that the damage was to be reduced to 15,900 francs ($3,180), but she was ordered to pay 5,000 francs ($1,000) immediately, and the balance in three annual installments. Camerino's lawsuit was the first boulder to fall. A landslide was soon to follow.

The next blow was the cancellation of her new opera, *Circé*. Debussy's *Pelléas et Mélisande* was to be given its world premiere that spring, and already its supporters were heralding it as a revolutionary work of genius. André Messager, the powerful conductor-composer at the Opéra-Comique, was leading the Debussy claque. He had successfully recommended his mistress, Mary Garden, to Carré for the title role, and Debussy had approved her also. Rehearsals for *Pelléas* were already in progress by February. Infected with Messager's enthusiasm for the score, Carré was determined to give the opera extraordinary attention as well as rehearsal time. All other new productions were shelved for the rest of the season.[3]

Sanderson had no concerts scheduled in either Belgium or the Netherlands. Instead, she promised her mother that she would enter another sanitarium for treatment. An insatiable craving for continual morphine injections seemed to be the only alternative to her need for alcohol. She had gone through the earlier stages of sleep, nausea, vomiting, and headache. Now her body cried for relief from this strange, new pain. Her head seemed to be a hollow drum reverberating savagely. During a bout with manic depression, her skin would feel as if it had been doused with kerosene and set afire, but this is also a symptom of seriously ill cirrhotics.

Alarmed by these new and baffling symptoms, her physicians tried their usual ritual of cutting her drug intake using various douches and tonics. Doctor after doctor, not specialists in drug addiction, tried different cures without success. Once the effects of morphine subsided, an uncontrollable desire for alcohol would return.

Despite the lack of any progress in finding a cure, Sibyl left the sanitarium early in March determined to resume her career. She had no other way to pay off her creditors. On 21 March, she gave a dinner party to celebrate the reopening of her home. Among the guests were many prominent Americans, including the Duchess de La Rochefoucauld and Mme Jonquières. Sibyl, superbly gowned in black velvet with a corsage of camellias, managed to create an offstage illusion of a buoyant and happy Violetta. No allusion was made to her broken engagement, nor did she volunteer any explanation. Most of her smiles were reserved for a young Belgian playwright who was never far from her side.

Massenet and his wife had not been home much of the winter. They had spent February in Monte Carlo, where the composer had supervised the world premiere of his first opera with an all-male cast, *Le jongleur de Notre-Dame* (The Juggler of Notre Dame). Immediately afterward, they boarded a train for Brussels to oversee the Belgian premiere of *Grisélidis*. In March they attended the centennial performance of *Manon* in Vienna, where, after much festivity, Massenet was given a bronze laurel crown and decorated with the official order of the Austro-Hungarian Empire. According to various press announcements, he planned to be back in Paris the last week in March to attend his ex-protégée's return to the Comique.

The Parisians had long considered Sibyl Sanderson to be the woman who re-created *Manon,* and newspaper journalists were constantly asking her to revive it. In spite of the fact that a host of newer sopranos had undertaken the role, none of them had ever replaced the incomparable *Sibylle*. With the popular young tenor Maréchal eager to portray her Chevalier, and Fugère once again his father, she found it impossible to refuse.

An excited audience packed the Opéra-Comique on Wednesday night, April 2, 1902, to welcome her back. She was warmly greeted upon her entrance to the country inn, and after the first-act love duet the artists received an enthusiastic acclamation. *Le Figaro* reported unanimously flattering comments in the foyer during intermissions.[4]

"*Très bien,* Sibyl Sanderson, *très bien!*" "The voice is as beautiful as always." "What do you think of those jewels she's wearing tonight?" "They say that dazzling diamond collar she wore in the last scene [Cours-la-Reine] and her other jewels amount to almost one million francs!" "Really?" interrupted an elderly gentleman behind *Le Figaro*'s Serge Busset. "That million you spoke of is not what she is wearing around her neck, it is in her throat instead."

When the bravos for the Saint Sulpice scene had died away, friends rushed to the *petit foyer des artistes,* where Massenet was congratulating his interpreters. Although the composer had seldom seemed more congenial, no one knew what he was really thinking about his ex-goddess's appearance and voice. He was well aware of Sanderson's glacial reception in San Francisco, but he made no queries about it.[5] The composer wore his mask of exquisite humility throughout the evening, carefully concealing his real emotions.

"I was so upset earlier this evening," a smiling diva confided to Serge Busset. "It seemed to me that something kept tearing and tearing inside of my throat. I was frantic with concern, but of course the idea of reappearing before the Parisian public is always so unnerving and exciting!"

Back in her dressing room Sanderson received reporter Ratteau from *L'Écho de Paris* for a brief interview.[6] He was nearly overcome with the heady aroma of roses that two maids were pinning onto her gown and diamond aigrette. To a query if she was satisfied with her Parisian reception, the soprano replied that she dearly loved the French public, who had always been so wonderful to her. Sanderson confided to the reporter that she was feeling "terribly tired" that evening. "No one knows how poorly I feel." Mr. Ratteau encouraged her by observing, "The tremendous applause you are receiving indicates the pleasure you are giving your audience tonight." As a warning gong interrupted their conversation, Sanderson's mood changed abruptly, and she emitted a few sparkling notes from the fourth-act waltz that she would soon sing.

Neither Massenet nor Carré had any regrets about Sanderson's successful Parisian comeback in *Manon.* She had brought the maximum box-office receipts of the season into the Opéra-Comique—more than 9,000 francs. Paris was still loyal to its spoiled American child, but now it was the celebration of a personality, a legend.

While the press complimented her as "still the loveliest and most seductive of Manon's many interpreters," Henri de Courzon observed on 20 April in *Le Guide Musical* that "she atones for the weakness in her middle register by a spirited and unusually animated performance." The fact that Maréchal had received even more applause than the heroine was also noted. By 1902, it was obvious, even to the French, that Sanderson's voice had seen its best days.[7]

For the next two weeks, her extraordinary charisma continued to draw capacity audiences. Paris was feverishly renewing a love affair with its former darling when an announcement appeared in the papers on 17 April that Mme Sanderson had suddenly been taken ill by "influenza." Marie Thiery and Vera Courtenay would share the role with Mary Garden.

Sanderson's strength had collapsed, and her voice had treacherously betrayed her. There was no breath to support it. Her alcohol and drug addictions were fast destroying her career, and she felt powerless to fight them. On 4 May the Parisian papers informed the public that the Opéra-Comique had granted her a leave of absence until 20 May to sing "some concerts in England." Certain musical sophisticates were astute enough to guess there were no concerts anywhere.

Sanderson was to remain ill for nearly two months, and it is doubtful if she was able to attend a star-studded retirement party at the Comique for Laurent Grivot on 1 May.[8] Nevertheless, she made a convenient "return from England" to appear at the Trocadéro on 10 May, where the Ministry des Beaux Arts staged a spectacular festival to commemorate the history of the Opéra-Comique. Albert Carré had commanded an assembly of artists, chorus, machinists, dancers, and orchestra members for the event. Massenet and Saint-Saëns were among the many conductors on the podium. Over-rouged and underdressed, Sanderson somehow survived the gala evening, but she seemed hopelessly ill at ease with the new stars. It was obvious to everyone that if a drastic change didn't occur soon in her lifestyle, she would have to leave the stage.

The soprano felt as though her entire body had been cannibalized by her addictions during that two months' nightmare. Hideous phantoms seemed to swirl about her at intervals, clutching and tearing at her flesh and sinews. Her legs, arms, and head continued to throb in agony. Her heart felt horribly oppressed, palpitating so weakly she could scarcely breathe, while her glands had gone berserk, causing uncontrollable sweating and tearing and a constant runny nose. Gradually, however, she grew stronger as she gained temporary control over herself. Little by little her appetite increased. When her pulse and heartbeat finally stabilized, she discovered her breath control was also returning.

On 19 June, she finally felt strong enough to return to *Manon*, this time with Edmond Clément as her chevalier. *Le Figaro* declared that the hall was crammed and "the audience cheered her with the wildest enthusiasm." There had been a good crowd, but the theater was not sold out. The time of year had arrived when the beau monde closed its houses and departed for the country or the seashore.

It was a strange phenomenon. The former star could no longer compete with younger sopranos, yet the public cherished every lyrical moment she shared with them, sensing that their mutual love affair was to be an ephemeral one. To the Parisians she was an exotic dragonfly whose prismatic wings shimmered and reflected colors from the footlights. If they turned aside for one moment, that gossamer whir of rainbows in the air would be gone forever.

Sanderson sang three more performances with Clément on 23 and 28 June and 1 July 1902. Although the Opéra-Comique usually shut its doors at the end of June, there was unusual demand to hear her, and Carré was encouraged to extend the season an extra week. He wanted to close it with a performance of *Manon* on 5 July for which he had engaged the great Pol Plançon as Comte Des Grieux. Once again she was unable to appear, and the bill was changed to Godard's *Vivandière*.

Reluctantly, the singer had returned an unsigned contract for the following season. It meant giving up creations of *Circé* and *La Carmélite,* two operas that had been written for her, but the tragic decline in her health left her no choice. Albert Carré sadly accepted her decision. Both knew that unless a miracle occurred, Sibyl Sanderson would never appear at the Opéra-Comique again.

Sanderson had received an offer from Pathé studios that spring to collaborate with Massenet in recording some of his operatic arias. Regrettably, she declined the opportunity with the excuse that she preferred to wait until improvements were made in their recording techniques. Her action deprived future generations of ever hearing her sing, and yet from another standpoint she made the right decision. By 1902 Sibyl Sanderson knew she would be doing herself a grave injustice to leave posterity any souvenir of her deteriorating voice.

After her illness she probably would not have returned to the Comique to fulfill her contract if it hadn't been for the encouragement of a new admirer. All her life the soprano had been so immersed in male adulation that she felt desiccated without it. She could not exist for long without an admirer, a companion, or a lover. It remains a mystery to this day, however, to what extent Francis de Croisset fulfilled these functions.

Born Franz Werner, or Weiner, in Brussels in 1877, he was the son of a Belgian family with a distinguished history in diplomacy and the military.[9] Young Franz rebelled against his parents' wish that he pursue an army career and at the age of seventeen ran away to Paris, where he decided to study for the bar. After graduating from law school, he practiced for a while in Paris, even though his heart never belonged to the profession. His secret passion was the theater, and he spent all his spare time on its periphery. Having already written plays for amateur theatrical groups, he soon found the professional stage beckoning for his pen. Once his light, frothy comedies became box-office hits, famous actresses such as Cécile Sorel and Jeanne Granier vied to appear in them. It wasn't long before he was facing a major decision: whether or not to forswear his legal practice for a full-time career in the theater.

Sibyl had met the budding playwright a year or so before she became seriously attracted to him. Any number of friends, including Jeanne Granier or Madeleine Lemaire, could have introduced them. They were both on intimate terms with the Parisian artist's world—everyone from Reynaldo Hahn to Robert de Flers, with whom de Croisset would later collaborate. Although rumors abounded about de Croisset's sexual preferences, one thing was certain: he had a positive genius for cultivating influential people.

Even more of a curiosity is what attracted Sibyl to him in the first place. He was about thirteen years her junior, and while nothing flatters an aging beauty more than the attentions of a young man, he was the least handsome of her suitors. Someone described him as "having the mundane face of a footman though admittedly one in a high-class establishment." If his jutting nose and angular jaw prevented him from ever being labeled an Adonis, he was certainly determined to emulate Beau Brummell in his immaculate tailoring.

Quick tempered and sensitive, he had challenged a journalist on *Le Figaro* to a duel that winter for making a few unflattering remarks about his manhood. When his seconds arrived, the cowardly reporter lied to them, saying the dramatist had just called him to announce he was canceling the duel. This so infuriated de Croisset that he charged onto the premises of *Le Figaro* and thoroughly thrashed his antagonist in person. The injured scribe promptly retaliated by hauling the playwright into court, and on 9 February 1902, he was fined 1,000 francs for assault and battery.

De Croisset perceived that Sibyl was lonely, vulnerable, and ripe for the plucking. He had already noted that his scintillating conversation and wit were making her laugh again. Dinner invitations from the widow led to theater invitations from the playwright. She had been one of his guests earlier that spring at the Théâtre du Vaudeville to see Mme Réjane star in his *La Passerelle*. In return, the diva frequently invited him to share her box at La Cigale, where they could relax and laugh at the clever and satiric—and often risqué—stage reviews.

405

It wasn't long before their relationship developed into something more serious. De Croisset still pondered giving up his law practice and devoting himself to a full-time career in the theater, but his royalties were not yet sufficient to cover his living expenses. Sibyl not only encouraged him to make the break, but volunteered to help support him. Quick to take advantage of her offer, de Croisset gallantly assured her of his lifelong devotion. Sometime in the spring of 1902 they began secretly living together.

Natica Terry drove down the avenue Bois de Boulogne every afternoon with her grandmother and occasionally would see the dramatist entering or leaving Sibyl's residence. She recognized him from his pictures in *Illustration* and *Le Théâtre*, two magazines she read at her cousin's home. Fifty-six years later, Antonio Terry's daughter was still convinced that Francis de Croisset had played her stepmother for a fool. "I will go to my grave believing that he took her for what little she had left," the Princess de Faucyny-Lucinge reflected in 1958. "In spite of the fact that he later married a very wealthy heiress, his attitude towards women remained one of total cynicism."[10]

It is always possible that Sanderson and de Croisset were genuinely fond of each other and that at first the dramatist not only sympathized with the soprano's battles with her insidious alcoholism but tried to help her. Sibyl was very proud of her talented protégé. She felt that he had brilliant potential; with the right sponsorship he could become the Oscar Wilde of France. If she was no longer well enough to pursue her own career, she could still thrill vicariously to de Croisset's accomplishments.

In his biography of Massenet, James Harding quoted the ridiculous rumor that Sanderson spent "four hundred thousand francs launching de Croisset's career."[11] With new lawsuits from dressmakers, upholsterers, and florists looming on the horizon after Camerino's victory, Sanderson's insolvency was a matter of public record.

One particular play by de Croisset intrigued her as having fascinating possibilities for an opera scenario—*Le chérubin.* The plot was an expansion of the romantic escapades of the character Cherubino in Mozart's *Marriage of Figaro.* It had gotten as far as a public dress rehearsal at the Comédie-Française on 1 June 1901, with the teenage hero being created by a female singer. After considerable uproar over this from various reactionary circles, the ministry of fine arts intervened and banned any public performances. A year later it was scheduled to be performed at the Porte-Saint-Martin theater, this time with an adult male creating the title role of the amorous lad. Sanderson felt strongly that it should not be altered and encouraged de Croisset to delay plans for the revival until Albert Carré could meet him and discuss the possibility of an operatic adaptation.

The meeting took place at a private dinner party in her apartment in late June of 1902, and de Croisset gave Carré the script to read. On 10 July *L'Écho de Paris* announced that the previous afternoon Carré had invited both of them to his office for further discussion. Carré liked the script and was willing to produce it if he could be guaranteed proper financial coverage. The diva seems to have been hallucinating when she assured him that she would come up with the necessary 10,000 francs. However, she was thoroughly pragmatic in her insistence that Mary Garden was the only female member of the company who had the figure to play the male lead.

When Massenet next appears on the scene is not clear at all. In his unreliable memoirs, he totally fabricated his initial meeting with de Croisset, claiming he had attended the *représentation générale* of *Chérubin* at the Comédie-Française in 1901 and had dashed to de Croisset's house two days later to ask him for the work [not likely]. Shortly afterward, according to Massenet's fictional account, he came to an agreement with the author as the pair strolled down the Champs-Élysées after attending the unveiling of the Daudet monument—a ceremony that didn't occur until a year later, 31 May 1902.

Massenet makes no mention of Sanderson having a hand in the project, but there is some evidence that she suggested Carré commission a younger composer to write the operatic score—a commission she volunteered to underwrite. If she did, this would have infuriated Massenet (whose spies kept him informed), and he would have gone to unparalleled lengths to bargain privately with de Croisset for the musical rights to the work. The Parisian papers announced on 15 October 1902 that Massenet would compose the opera shortly after the Porte-Saint-Martin revival that fall.[12] In retrospect, Massenet need not have worried about any younger competitor; there wasn't a banker in Paris foolish enough to loan Sibyl Sanderson the money.

A few days after her meeting with Carré, Sibyl attended the funeral of an Opéra-Comique official and then departed with her maid for Aix-les-Bains in a despondent state of mind. Their rooms had been reserved at the Hôtel de l'Europe. Aix-les-Bains, the summer playground for the international set, was jammed with tourists as usual. Sanderson had been engaged for one performance in *Phryné* followed by another in *Manon*.

Phryné was given on Sunday night, 20 July, and the Théâtre du Grand Cercle was sold out. Extra chairs were placed in the aisles and at the back of the last row of theater seats to accommodate the overflow crowd, but a large number of latecomers were admitted to standing room only.

According to Pierre Weber's dispatch to the Paris *Herald* on 21 July, Sanderson sang very well and received tremendous applause, but outside of a nod to Léon Jehin's sympathetic conducting, he never mentioned the rest of the cast. The audience was crammed with international celebrities including American millionaires J. Pierpont Morgan and Charles Knoedler; the Portuguese Duke of Oporto; José Paz, the Brazilian publishing magnate; the composer Bemberg; and numerous French counts and barons.

The next day the soprano wrote a short note to Serge Busset of *Le Figaro* announcing that she had recently signed a contract with Monsieur Chatonet in Paris to be her exclusive agent. Chatonet was the former director of the General Agency of French Theaters and had powerful connections not only on his native turf but also abroad.

On 24 July the Hôtel de l'Europe feted the arrival of Sibyl's friend King George I of Greece with a sumptuous al fresco banquet. The gardens were brilliantly illuminated and decorated with hanging Chinese lanterns. A band of Neapolitans sang rollicking Italian songs as they strolled among the fifty-some tables of guests. Sanderson was seated at the table of Count d'Harcourt next to King George's aide-de-camp, Colonel de Kergariou. The Greek monarch was as cordial to her as always and told her he was looking forward to hearing her next performance.

The following week saw heavy rains hitting Aix-les-Bains, curtailing some races and many of the out-of-doors social events. The showers certainly contributed to the downward spiral in Sanderson's mental health. As a gruesome episode of manic depression enveloped her, she began drinking heavily in her hotel room between *Manon* rehearsals. Colleagues in the production were alarmed by her erratic behavior. Her memory kept failing her; she stumbled from scene to scene. She had no breath control: she felt as if molten strands of barbed wire were constricting her so tightly she couldn't breathe. The incessant pounding in her temples was maddening. She was unable to sleep.

By Saturday night, 2 August, fair weather had returned, and a capacity crowd poured into the Théâtre du Grand Cercle to hear the diva in her most famous role. The orchestra kept tuning interminably while the audience waited and waited. Finally, the curtains parted ominously, and Monsieur Gandrey, the manager, appeared to announce that Mme Sanderson was ill and "not quite well enough to sing this evening. It is hoped that she will soon recover and be able to sing next Tuesday. All tickets will be honored at that time." As a disgruntled audience left the theater, odious rumors were in circulation about the prima donna's condition. Backstage, a sobbing, humiliated soprano was helped into a cab and driven to her hotel, where an equally disgruntled Lina put her to bed.

For the next week she remained in her room under a doctor's care, suffering from severe despondency. Tuesday evening passed, and the singer was still unable to fulfill her *Manon* commitment. A 6 August dispatch to the Paris *Herald* announced that Mary Garden, who was due for rehearsals the following week in a Messager operetta, was hastily summoned to replace her.

It was a strange irony that as Sanderson's star was falling out of the operatic firmament, her protégée's was rising so rapidly. Just eleven years earlier at Aix-les-Bains, Sibyl's Saint Sulpice scene in *Manon* had reduced the audience to tears. Now, after her bitter struggle with Odile, Odette lay grievously wounded, afraid to raise her head and look up. She knew the sword of Damocles was hanging by a thread.

Chapter 39

The Labyrinth

As usual the Sandersons had been spending their summer at Villa Plaisance on the Brittany coast. There were masked balls thrown by social doyenne Mrs. Hughes Hallett, Mrs. Carl Weinberg's tea parties in Dinard, and no end of invitations to dinner parties.

Marion was entertaining a serious suitor, Dr. Edwin Nall, whom she had met on her American voyage in 1900 to visit Jane and Roy. They had been corresponding for over a year and were now enjoying each other's company immensely. Every weekend they went dancing at the American Club in Dinard and were usually the last couple to leave.

Edith, too, was receiving a longtime beau—Hypollite Dreyfus, who would later surprise society by marrying Alice Barney, sister of the notorious American lesbian Natalie Barney. Both mademoiselles could breathe easier knowing their alcoholic sister would not be around to embarrass them.

In fact, Sibyl had become a colossal embarrassment. The Sandersons never knew how to cope with her manic-depressive attacks or her rampant alcoholism. In one of Marion's letters to Jane that spring, she confessed, "We are having a terrible time with Sibyl!" She mentioned that just being near the family drunk gave her "awful headaches." Both she and Edith had their hands full keeping their mother away from her. Margaret Sanderson's primary goal for her old age had been peace of mind, but there could be no peace around an alcoholic daughter whose moods vacillated from defiant fits of screaming and weeping to heartbreaking despair.

The Sandersons awoke one day in early August to discover Sibyl's troubles in Aix-les-Bains had been deposited right at their doorstep. She had sent her mother a wire desperately pleading for $1,200 to pay the hotel and doctor bills;

she had no money. It was just the kind of news the family needed to spoil their vacation. To compound the situation, this was one time Margaret could not lay her hands on that large a sum. She was forced to cable her bank in San Francisco and ask for a loan. She directed the funds to be dispatched immediately to Mme Terry at her hotel in Aix-les-Bains. Evidently, the money arrived on 9 August, because the local papers reported on the 10th that Mme Sanderson-Terry had left the hotel the previous day for Switzerland. She had already made an appointment to enter a sanitarium there for treatment.

A few weeks earlier Massenet stepped off the train in Dinard on his way to Heugel's nearby villa and unexpectedly encountered Mrs. Sanderson at the depot. Writing to Jane, Margaret observed, "I never knew that eyes could say more than words." His sorrowful expression revealed how much Sibyl had been on his mind. He had agonized over her rejection of a contract for the coming season at the Opéra-Comique, but at the same time he was aware of the pitiful condition of her health. Later that summer, he sent Margaret a note from his château at Égreville and enclosed a flowering sprig from one of his trees.

20 August 1902
Égreville

Chère madame:
From one of my windows I send you the faithful memories of an old friend from 1887 to 1902. Fifteen years.
Esclarmonde
Manon
Thaïs

J. M.

Just a few words, but they spoke volumes. Of course he had heard the gossip about Sibyl and de Croisset; the item was well circulated in theatrical circles. Privately, Massenet knew it would take more than another lover to save her from her disastrous course. He had stopped writing to her. She never responded. If he had something to communicate, he did it through her mother.

According to the Princess de Lucinge, Sibyl never kept her date at the Swiss sanitarium but took de Croisset to Nice instead for the rest of the summer—at least this was the story circulated about her in the exclusive Faubourg St. Germain set.[1] Perhaps the tale was true, but a thorough investigation of the

Nice society columns of August and September 1902 reveals no mention of Mme Sanderson-Terry's visit, and a search of the hotel registers, published weekly in local newspapers, likewise turns up a blank. It is possible she rented a private villa in the area, on credit of course, since her insolvency wasn't public knowledge on the Riviera. At any rate, the princess confided that reports of incessant quarreling between Sibyl and her lover were rife in Nice, and that de Croisset finally packed up and walked out on her. He had to be back in Paris by September anyway because his *Les deux courtisanes* was scheduled to open later that month.

For years rumors continued to surface as to why de Croisset left her. Some say they split because of the dramatist's predilection for his own sex. Others maintain this wouldn't have disturbed his patroness in the least—stories about her public solicitation of young women in ladies' restrooms were prevalent that year. There were those who insisted he deserted her once the money was gone. The Princess de Lucinge belonged to the latter group, yet she understood the agony that spawned his decision. Having walked that Via Dolorosa with Sibyl, she had seen first hand how Odile could torture Odette.

"De Croisset was too fastidious in his personal hygiene," the Princess observed, "to tolerate some boozing mistress who lay half conscious in a bed reeking of vomit and urine" (because Lina would go on one of her periodic rebellions and refuse to change the sheets).

Sooner or later de Croisset had to reach the inevitable conclusion that he could no longer remain Sibyl's male support figure and keep his sanity. They both knew she needed to be institutionalized, and ultimately she had to make this decision herself. Undoubtedly, de Croisset urged her to take this step because he knew it was her last chance to save her life. An ill-equipped Theseus without a weapon, he was powerless to do battle with the Minotaur she harbored in the labyrinth of her subconscious.

No letters between the two have come to light. The dramatist carefully burned all correspondence between them and displayed a guarded reluctance to discuss their relationship years later when questioned by Carl Van Vechten.[2] One of his few observations to the American author resembles a sinister gravestone epitaph: "She had a rendezvous with self-destruction."

Returning to Paris in September, Sibyl was determined to try one more cure. It meant placing herself in one of the most forbidding institutions in France. Every time she considered the idea in the past she had postponed the decision. Now she knew there was no choice; more procrastination was tantamount to suicide.

Her goal entailed raising a considerable amount of money. If only she could get hold of Tony's effects and sell them. Those bronzes, marbles, paintings, rugs, and tapestries should bring a handsome sum. He had left her two million francs in debts and at the same time drafted a will that forbade her the remotest chance of attaining solvency. It seemed as though Terry wanted to shackle her permanently to him, even beyond the grave.

Sibyl decided to defy her late husband's will. She would have to proceed with extreme caution so that her stepdaughter did not find out. On 7 July 1902 Natica had wed Prince Guy de Faucyny-Lucinge, a Parisian aristocrat years older than herself. She was now the second granddaughter of Tomaso Terry to "purchase" an ancient French title. Sibyl knew that Mamacita must have been thrilled. Undoubtedly, the old lady would siphon a small fortune from Tony's estate into Natica's dowry.

In a none too sober state, Sibyl called upon a prominent antique dealer and explained that she wanted to dispose quietly of her late husband's personal estate. Handing him a list of contents and the address where Tony's possessions were located, she admitted they were stored under her stepdaughter's name. Naturally, there was no reason for Natica to know anything about the transaction. "She might hesitate to part with certain items for sentimental reasons," Sibyl prevaricated.

The dealer seemed interested in the sub-rosa project, but he was no fool. He had heard enough gossip from his wealthy clientele to learn that an irreparable schism existed between Mme Terry and her stepdaughter. Because the treasures of the late Antonio Terry were in storage under his daughter's name, the dealer decided to call upon the Prince and Princess de Lucinge and disclose Mme Terry's recent visit.

Natica was aghast. Sibyl must be desperate for money to commit such an infraction of her father's legacy. An irate Prince de Lucinge immediately procured a copy of the will to show the dealer that the late Antonio Terry's possessions were not to be sold for the next two decades. Needless to say, Sibyl's scheme was quickly aborted when the prince and princess forbade the sale.

Before the dealer left, Natica motioned him aside and asked, "Was she sober?"

"Please believe me, Madame, when I say she had been drinking heavily," he replied.

Now that her plan had been thwarted, Sibyl was forced to seek alternate avenues for money. Although her mother offered to pay part of the treatment, even with small loans from friends like the duchess de La Rochefoucauld (Mattie Mitchell) she still had not procured the necessary amount. Since she knew better than to approach her miserly mentor, she had no alternative but to sell some of her furs to raise the balance.

The date when Sanderson entered the Château de Saint-James in Neuilly is not known for certain.[3] If Blanche Marchesi's chilling account is accurate, it must have occurred sometime in late September 1902. Having tried cure after cure in vain, Sibyl voluntarily committed herself to an asylum spoken of only in whispers. Toulouse-Lautrec had undergone treatment there a year before and sarcastically referred to it as "Madrid-les-Bains." The institution housed some of the most dreadfully incurable cases in France. One paid for the entire treatment in advance and signed an agreement: 1) not to prosecute the management for sequestration; 2) not to ask for a refund if one should decide to quit the cure by the second or third day; 3) to hold the establishment guiltless no matter how much one suffered.

In the language of the layman it was the terrible "cold turkey" cure, considered passé by twenty-first-century psychiatry. The doctors cut the patient off from all drugs and stimulants for five days, letting the victim's body struggle for salvation in a nightmare worse than the tortures of the Inquisition. If the patient survived the horrendous agony of the first week, a two-month period of excruciating weakness followed. Those who survived the cure preferred suicide to a possible repetition. Sibyl, rather than risk a reccurrence of her previous failures, finally summoned the courage to place herself in this dreaded institution.

Dr. Sollier, the proprietor, had done everything possible to disguise the fact that his handsome villa housed wealthy patients who were suffering from mental illness in various degrees. They were always referred to as "guests." Some of them had two- or three-room apartments as well as their own private gardens. The drawing room resembled the salon of an elegant mansion, with a grand piano and damask chairs and sofas. However, its luxurious furnishings were strictly a façade. A doleful gloom permeated the dimly lit halls, while the grilled doors of the individual apartments looked unhappily like those of prison cells. Only the occasional shrieks or moans of the patients broke the lugubrious silence of those narrow corridors. Visits were always limited; appointments for visitations had to be made in advance, if the particular inmate was allowed such a luxury. Outside, the caretakers made sure that the beautiful hedges and shrubbery were neatly trimmed and that the huge iron gates were always locked.

Honored to have such a celebrated "guest," the charming Dr. Sollier made unheard-of exceptions in Sibyl's favor. Because she was an artist of extraordinary sensitivity, she was to be "let down" gradually, as much as his cure would permit. Unfortunately, no records are available to show how much her daily intake of alcohol was reduced, or how much it was supplemented by equally treacherous doses of morphine and other drugs.[4] We know only that she went through all the terrible hallucinations, deliria, and cramps of the first stages of withdrawal. Writing to Jane, Marion observed that although she had taken Sibyl flowers, "she doesn't seem to know I'm there."[5] An attendant slept in the room next to her, constantly on call. Perspiration poured from her wasted skin, soaking her nightgown and bedsheets. Wracked with horrendous spasms and gut-wrenching cramps, her body became a relief map of enormous blue welts, although periodic injections of various drugs would usually mitigate her vomiting and diarrhea. Apparently, Dr. Sollier realized that they had to be administered on some kind of a systematic basis, because she wasn't strong enough to survive the "cold turkey" cure.

Gradually, the agonizing feelings of suffocation and violent cramps subsided along with her screams. She grew stronger. It was no longer necessary to place a cardboard between her teeth to keep her from biting her tongue and lips to shreds. As she appeared to improve, she began to fantasize about returning to the stage. Fantasy now became her only refuge. Never did she relinquish her dream of making a comeback and paying off her debts.

According to Blanche Marchesi, "it was toward the end of this last effort that she wrote to Massenet asking him to come to see her and hear her again, so as to decide whether she could, yes or no, face the Parisian public."[6] Marchesi continued:

> Édouard Colonne told me about this last tragic interview when he came to London to conduct an orchestral concert. Massenet wrote asking Colonne to accompany him to St. Cloud [sic] to see Sibyl Sanderson as he had not the courage to go alone, knowing her to be seriously ill. It was arranged between them that if Sibyl could still sing, Colonne would engage her for one of his concerts, thus to present her again to the Paris public.
>
> The sight of the house, the sound of the doorbell, the melancholy of the bare parlour walls of the house where incurable nervous cases were treated fell upon their souls like a shroud. Massenet was breathing heavily when the door opened and the once-beautiful Sibyl came in. She was still beautiful, but there was something unspeakably sad about her, and when she stretched out both of her hands to Massenet and said, "maître, sauvez-moi de moi-même, rendez-moi à l'art et la vie," ["Master, save me from myself, take me back to

art and life"] his eyes closed, and he turned white, biting his lips, unable to utter a single word.

"Come, let us sing," exclaimed Colonne, cutting short the painful scene, and in saying so, he opened the piano striking some chords from *Manon,* thinking that she would feel more at home in her favorite part than in anything else . . . it was not so. She could not remember a single note; not a word would come back to her memory. Some passages of agility still came out brilliantly like sudden flashes peering through dark clouds, and she would throw them into the air to show these men that the voice was still there but of *Manon* there was no more trace in her memory.

When Massenet realized it, he remained motionless, leaning against the piano, the tears flowing over his cheeks. Seeing this, she was seized by a hysterical fit and began to laugh at the top of her voice. "Et voilà, c'est l'histoire de Manon Lescaut," ["And that is the story of Manon Lescaut."] she screamed—the very words with which the opera ends. After this, she began to cry desperately on the floor. Massenet, seized with terror, grabbed his hat shouting, "Partons, Colonne, partons avant que je deviens fou!" ["Let's get out of here, Colonne, before I go crazy!"] He took Colonne by the arm, and they fled the woman who had been the ideal Manon.[7]

As far as we know, this surreal scene was Massenet's final encounter with Sibyl Sanderson.

The cure was no more successful than their bizarre meeting. After five weeks in which all rules of the normally strict house were broken in her favor, Sibyl renounced the treatment and left the asylum in despair. As the iron gates clanged shut behind her and Célestin helped her into her carriage, she knew she was doomed to a permanent liaison with failure.

Once again a fog of alcoholic stupor enveloped her, distorting space and time. The voice and touch of the people closest to her seemed farther away than the most distant steeple on the Paris skyline. Night after night sleep eluded her. She was reaching a state called "sub-delirium" by doctors of her era. Gradually she no longer shrank in terror. More and more she welcomed the end. Like Sisyphus, she felt condemned to roll an enormous boulder uphill for eternity. For every meter of ground gained by her efforts, the rock rolled back at least three the minute she relaxed.

Communicating with the dead occupied increasing importance in her thoughts. It is not known if she attended any séances in 1902, but earlier that year she wrote to Fred Sharon, an old California friend interested in the occult, about finding a certain Parisian address where such meetings were held. Her handwriting, always bold and determined, had now become large, haphazard scrawls.

In spite of the Stygian haze that clouded her existence, she still had a few comparatively sober days. Realizing that she had no more money to pay her servants, let alone her creditors, Sibyl began to formulate a desperate scheme. On 2 November 1902, she visited a chic jewelry shop on the rue de la Paix. Selecting a beautiful diamond-and-sapphire necklace for purchase, she explained to the owner, Goudstikker, that she did not have the funds—150,000 francs—at present to pay for the jewels. Since she was a former customer, would he be kind enough to sell her the jewels on credit? Amazingly Monsieur Goudstikker, who should have known better, agreed, but he made her sign a promissory note that included a high rate of interest due every three months.

Sibyl swore Lina to secrecy about this new acquisition. No one must ever know about it, not even her family. One can only speculate as to what happened next because Lina destroyed most letters promptly after Sibyl's death, but some mysterious correspondence between certain jewelers and pawnbrokers in Brussels probably occurred. In December Sibyl's agent Chatonet sent news releases to the Parisian papers that Mme Terry was in Brussels "recovering from laryngitis" and would soon leave for Nice, where she had some engagements.

What she really was doing in Brussels wasn't published, but one can be sure it had nothing to do with any treatment for laryngitis. The singer had informed her family that she was undergoing therapy at a Belgian sanitarium, and this may have been the truth. On the other hand, if she decided to dispose of the diamond necklace in Brussels, one can only conjecture that it was sold privately. There is also a possibility that she agreed to have the stones cut up and sold to agents for the Amsterdam black market. This would eliminate any trace of the necklace. Lastly, Sanderson could have visited the diamond district of Antwerp instead of Brussels. Assuming that she sold the jewels, it has never been learned how much Odile raised from this fraudulent transaction, but she could always claim a fictitious robbery later on.

The December press release was accurate at least in one area: she had been engaged for a late winter appearance at the Casino Municipal in Nice. Margaret had consulted Sibyl's physician about her terrible fits of melancholia, and Dr. Iscovesco recommended that Mrs. Sanderson send her daughter to the Riviera a few months before the performance to relax and socialize. She could also be treated for cirrhosis of the liver as an outpatient in a private sanitarium in Nice. Margaret agreed to cover the expenses if Sibyl would promise to follow the doctor's regime.

The singer returned to Paris shortly after Christmas and spent the rest of the week selecting clothes for Lina to pack and visiting with her family. Not a word was said about the mysterious diamond necklace. Sibyl and her maid arrived at the Hotel Luxembourg in Nice 6 January 1903. Fortunately, a letter she wrote to her mother has survived. Revealing her faltering memory, she dated the letter 1902 instead of 1903.

15, January 1902

Only a short line, mother dear. Have been in Nice a week. The Mistral is blowing, so cold—out in an auto with Mrs. Whitney to Monte Carlo. Friends of Joe Redding are here—drove along the Corniche Road from Monte Carlo to Menton under a full moon. Have been invited to the races but will not go. I have gone so often, and besides I have one of my oft-repeated blue days. A party of us leave Sunday for Genoa to see Ned Porter off to Japan—if the wind ceases, it will be delightful. Saturday I go with the Count and Countess Arthur de Gabriac and Count de Mornay to the first night of the opera—De Lara's *Messalina* [*Messaline*]. I may want a society woman to go about with me later—you see, I am taking the bull by the horns—Thank God, I sleep well, thanks to hypnol, but, of course, I am far from happy. Mary Garden is in Monte Carlo alone—looks awful. Mary and Mrs. Whiting arrived Tuesday separately. We had a good dinner and afterwards went to the casino . . . am still in the hands of the doctors. I tire easily, but that is because I generally go out so little. The auto does not tire me but the air stupifies [sic] me. I feel as though I must tumble into bed as soon as I reach the hotel. Lina is in one of her nasty moods and as thoroughly *nasty* as only she can be. Shuts herself up in her room all day and appears not even to know I am here. She will not go on errands, even the shortest, unless she is driven. Her room is 20 frs. And food 8 frs. Per day. She scarcely deserves [illegible] . . . Received a funny note from Laco and also one from Miss Fetridge [Eames's secretary]. I wish she wouldn't write, for I cannot answer. A fond loving kiss to you, and love to both [sisters].

Sibyl

Although Sibyl admitted she was "far from happy," the letter not only displayed coherency but showed a definite mental improvement. If she expressed surprise at how "awful" Mary was looking, Garden was equally shocked by Sibyl's pathetic decay. Amazed at how stout Sibyl was growing, Mary later recalled the texture of her skin to Carl Van Vechten as "sallow and coarse as leather."

Tension had been brewing between the two women for a long time, and a showdown was inevitable. Sibyl had approached Mary about a loan several times in 1902 only to be put off with the most vapid excuses. The subject was brought up as late as November, but Mary apparently postponed any decision until after the first of the year. There had been no communication between them when Sibyl was in the asylum, and Garden must have been surprised to encounter her in Nice that January. Now the two prima donnas were face to face. One's star was in blazing ascendancy; the other's light had been all but extinguished.

Having followed Mary's career with pride, Sibyl often wondered why her protégée never offered to help her. Three years before, she had picked Mary up from the gutter, paid her bills, and launched her on the path to stardom. Now their circumstances were reversed. It was the fallen angel who desperately needed to be rescued.

When they met to resolve the issue, Mary evaded the subject at first. Other topics were discussed. It gave Sibyl no pleasure to learn that Emma Calvé's recent creation of Louise de la Vallière in *La Carmélite* [the opera Reynaldo Hahn had written for Sanderson] had been such a critical failure that she fled Paris after several performances. Finally Sibyl interrupted the idle chatter to ask for a loan.

According to a documented conversation Garden later had with Carl Van Vechten, she was aware that Sibyl had been in various sanitariums for treatment.[8]

"If you had seen the way that woman was destroying herself, you'd have understood why I didn't have the heart to go see her," Garden confessed to Van Vechten. She continued:

> I told Sibyl I'd like to help her but I just wasn't able. I wasn't earning much money then, and I sent part of it home to my father who managed my finances for me. He allowed me only so much for living expenses, and I remember times when I could hardly make it from month to month.

If Mary really said this, Sibyl must have been astonished at such prevarication. She knew that Mary's salary had increased dramatically as she rose to the top echelons of the Opéra-Comique. She also was aware that André Messager gave Mary considerable sums from time to time from the royalties of his operettas. Not once did Sibyl ever think of betraying Mary by informing Mme Messager about their liaison.

Tempers flared. Voices rose in a shrill crescendo. The dispute invariably focused upon Sibyl's dissipations. Mary's onetime role model was committing suicide day by day, and she would not be the one to grease the path. Sibyl, in turn, branded her former protégée as an opportunist of the cheapest kind. Then, if what Garden told Van Vechten is true, a forgotten chapter from Sibyl's past underwent an ill-timed resurrection.

Garden: I admitted I'd been avoiding her, but not because I was afraid she'd ask me for money. I'd heard ugly stories about her private life. Up to that time I had always defended her and dismissed them as vicious gossip. Eventually, I had to confront her with them. It was all over the Comique that she had become a lesbian. Some say de Croisset was the one to blame [for converting her]. You know . . . he liked men.

Van Vechten: What was Sibyl's reply?

Garden: She took a deep breath, threw back her head, and admitted it was true. She was a lesbian and had been one for years, long before she met de Croisset. I was so shocked, I couldn't think of anything to say.

Before an astonished Mary Garden could open her mouth, Sibyl explained how Massenet had been so jealous of Tony Terry that he was determined to stop her marriage at all costs. Without mentioning Mme X's name, she confided that Massenet had arranged to have a lesbian seduce her.

Van Vechten: You mean Massenet set her up?

Garden: Yes, Sibyl was sure of it. I remember she burst into tears and said to me, "Mary, he knew all the time she was a lesbian. He had introduced her to me as a good friend of his wife. And later I found out his wife never heard of her. He did it deliberately! He even gave her the name of my favorite wine. . . . If anyone had done the same thing to Juliette [his daughter] he would have killed him!" . . . She said she had no one to turn to. She couldn't tell her family, and she didn't dare tell Tony. He might have left her, and Massenet would have won. She insisted that she had loved Tony more than anyone else in this world. . . . She told me she would marry again even though she was doomed to go through life wanting a woman from time to time. She insisted she was no longer ashamed of her lesbianism, but before we parted she asked me to keep our conversation secret.

Van Vechten: Were you able to help her out?

Garden: I told her I'd try to in the spring, but then she died that spring. I promised her [that] her secret was safe with me, but after what she admitted, I couldn't afford to be seen with her in public any more. My God! We said some terrible things to each other that day. . . . It took courage to admit what she was; if only she could have shown that same courage in fighting her vices! I felt so sorry for her afterwards.

If Garden told the truth to Van Vechten, Sibyl played right into her hand. She had given Mary the perfect excuse to avoid her. Now it was obvious her ex-protégée felt no moral obligation to pay back any of the money Sibyl had spent on her.[9] But the Scottish diva did keep her vow of secrecy for a number of years until she disclosed the incident to Carl Van Vechten circa World War I. During the following decades she also confided it to baritone Barre Hill, conductor Robert Lawrence, and Louis Biancolli, the coauthor of her autobiography, although she asked the latter to keep it confidential until after her death.

How much faith can we put into Garden's disclosure? Van Vechten believed her, and so did Lawrence and Biancolli. But Quaintance Eaton, who gave little credence to anything Garden said or wrote, warned against accepting it at all. Having interviewed all the sources above, I am impressed by the fact that Garden's later versions do not deviate from her earlier interview with Van Vechten.[10]

If her account is true, we know she had another motive for keeping Sibyl's confession secret—her own reputation. Because she had lived with Sibyl during the winter of 1899–1900, there was always the possibility of vicious gossip arising about their relationship.[11]

As could be expected, the quarrel left Sibyl feeling so emotionally ravaged that she was determined never again to ask Mary for any assistance. Nor was Lina's bitter "I told you so" any consolation. Sibyl recalled how her maid had seemed to stiffen every time Mary approached her at the Champs-Élysées apartment.

When the widow once asked her why she seemed so cold to Garden, Lina had replied, "Madame, it's strange but I don't understand her. I've watched her. She studies you all the time. She observes how you walk, sit and every gesture you use. I've even caught her mimicking you when she thought no one was around.

It's as if she were preparing to take over your identity, and you're not even aware of it."[12]

"Oh, Lina don't be silly!" came the naïve response. "Don't you know imitation is the sincerest form of flattery?"

Now Sibyl was not so sure. In a rare moment of self-analysis, she wondered if her maid wasn't a more adroit observer of human nature than she was.

For the next few weeks the singer's health fluctuated precariously. Occasionally she could be seen ambling about the casino like some disembodied spirit pitifully searching for its host. Constantly hounded by her furies, she began to feel that everyone she had loved, trusted, or befriended had betrayed her in some way. Toward the end of the month she wired her family that she had been too depressed to write and confessed to having fallen and hurt her foot. Needless to say, she maintained strict silence about her rupture with Mary Garden. Neither did her telegram mention any contact with Massenet, who had arrived in Nice on 25 January, to oversee the final rehearsals of *Marie Magdeleine* at the opera house.

In February she returned to Aix-les-Bains, where she was asked to sing a few numbers at a local charity concert. She always felt better, at least superficially, after taking the waters, but this time there was another reason for the unexpected upswing in her mental health.

Earlier that month she had met a tall, bearded Russian, at least ten years younger than herself, and devastatingly handsome. He was never seen without his ominous black cloak. His card read simply "Count Paul Tolstoy." He claimed to be a cousin of the famous Leo Tolstoy, but his reputation was shrouded in mystery.[13] There were some who sneered that he was no relation to the Russian novelist nor was he any count.

A reputed international fortune hunter, he began an ardent pursuit of Mme Terry, and within a month they had fallen in love. Gossip had it that she was covering his gambling losses, but this canard is too absurd to merit comment. He already belonged to several elite men's clubs on the Riviera and was well connected socially, so apparently this was not his first visit to the area. Sibyl desperately needed another male figure for support, a fearless knight to protect her from her unseen furies. Impervious to negative gossip about him, she planned to marry her young cavalier in the summer of 1903.

Whatever powers her enigmatic suitor may have had, they kept the soprano remarkably sober during the rehearsals of *Phryné*. Henri Carvalho, the manager of the Casino Municipal Theater and son of the late Léon Carvalho, had assembled a first-class production for the Riviera premiere. Edmond Clément was engaged to sing Nicias, and the splendid baritone Soulacroix would interpret the roguish Dicéphile.[14] The conductor, Lebornes, proved to be far more than just another time-beater. Until the curtain of the casino theater rose on Friday evening, 13 March, however, everyone in the production remained on tenter-hooks. Sibyl had jeopardized her physical strength by embarking upon an ill-advised diet to recapture her former figure.

When Phryné appeared on her portico, time stood still for a while. An ageless apparition from Sanderson's past had come to life again, and it held her audi-ence in thrall. Amazingly, the furies allowed Odette to savor success one last time. After the final curtain fell, she received a prolonged ovation and armloads of flowers just like the accolades of her halcyon days. The theater was filled with a select representation of international society, including old friends such as Princess Metternich and such colleagues as tenors Andreas Dippel and Van Dyck, who was in Nice to rehearse *Die Walküre* at the opera house.

Constantine Roche, the critic on *L'Éclaireur de Nice,* pronounced the perform-ance "a sparkling triumph" the next day—everything from the beautiful harp effects to the excellent offstage chorus. Lauding the superb interpretations of Clément and Soulacroix, he noted that the stellar trio received such vocifer-ous applause it had to be encored. The following tribute was paid to Sibyl's interpretation:

> Yesterday, we joyfully heard Mme Sibyl Sanderson again, this time on the stage of the Casino de Nice . . . the role of Phryné fits her like a tailor-made gown. She not only sings the part, but brings the character to life as well. It was only necessary to hear her first aria which she minutely delin-eated with a practiced voice and mimed it with all of the inimitable allure of her sculptured posing. . . . She commandeered her role to perfection even down to the slightest details.

The critic on *La Vie mondaine* also hailed the premiere on 19 March as "a great success for Mme Sibyl Sanderson" and heaped encomiums on everyone in the cast as well as the conductor. Sibyl was so thrilled with her reviews that she clipped a few and immediately sent them to her mother—something she hadn't done in several years.

With all the congratulatory messages and social invitations pouring into her hotel, Sanderson was riding a dangerous high at one extreme of the bipolar spectrum. She saw no more need for her diet or her medical regime. She felt consumed by waves of boundless energy. Her mind was swarming with ideas for the future. She sensed the heady stamina of an Olympic runner. Andreas Dippel took her to lunch and proposed some lofty if vague plans for an opera season he was negotiating to direct. Defying the Mistral, she joined friends for a trip to Genoa in an open automobile. On 24 March she was supposed to attend the opening of an exhibit, "Des oeuvres des Crêches," with her fiancé. When the day arrived she found herself in bed coming down with the grippe. "Count" Tolstoy attended the ball without her. Odette was now paying the price for ignoring her doctor's counsel. It was to be a fatal one.

Chapter 40

Full Circle

On a balmy afternoon early in May 1903, the butler opened the front door of the de Lucinge mansion to the venerable Prince de Sagan, an uncle of the de Castellanes. Monocled as usual and wearing a top hat, gray gloves, and a velvet-collared waistcoat, he crossed the threshold with an unmistakable air of old Second Empire elegance.

When the elderly caller was settled in the drawing room, he inquired about the young princess's health. His host informed him of some exciting news. He and his wife were expecting their first child. After conveying his congratulations, the Prince de Sagan had something less exhilarating to impart. He turned toward Natica and said to her gravely, "Do you know that your stepmother has been bedfast and seriously ill ever since they brought her home from Nice last month? I am told she has been drinking uncontrollably all winter."

There was a moment of silence. "Is it to be fatal?"

"That is what they say."

"I am sorry to hear it. She has chosen to die the same way as my father," came the pensive reply. "Perhaps I should go to her again. I would not want her to die with any bitterness in her heart toward me."

"Why?" her husband interrupted caustically. "You and she have severed all ties. She has elected to commit suicide. You were unable to stop her. You don't belong there now, especially after she tried to sell your father's furniture behind your back."

"Do the Massenets know?" asked the princess.

"Of course," the old gentleman answered, "but it is so painful a subject he refuses to speak about it. And what is more pathetic is the fact that her mother is said to be ill and cannot come to her side."

"At least I should be grateful to her for one thing," mused the princess. "She insisted I have a half share in my father's estate, when he originally left everything to her."

"That's probably because she wasn't sober at the time and didn't know what she was doing." Her husband's acerbic observation trailed off into mocking laughter. "No! I forbid you to have anything to do with her again. You can't help her now, and you know that your family would support me in this decision wholeheartedly."

Natica knew only too well. It was just the kind of patronizing opinion the Terrys would have seconded. But Natica did not smile. She could only remember the glow in her father's eyes the first time he introduced her to Sibyl at Christmastime in Nice. She had never seen them shine like that.

It was true; the rumors had reached 46 rue du Général Foy. Massenet had heard that his onetime muse was dying, but he refused to think of it. She was no longer the radiant young vision who had mesmerized his heart and his imagination. Now she was a depraved creature who repulsed him. He could never erase from his memory that ghastly image of her in the asylum: groveling at his feet, clutching his ankles, screaming the final words of his own opera at him!

The whispers had not only filtered into the Faubourg-St. Germain bastions of the aristocracy, they also were circulating through the American colony. Gossip and rumor proliferated. The tall, mysterious stranger in a black cloak who visited the invalid every day was said to be William Randolph Hearst. He was whispered to be stealing away from his new bride a few hours every afternoon to see his first love.

Strangely enough, Hearst did arrive in Paris the week Sibyl died. Just a short time before, he had married the lovely Millicent Willson on 28 April 1903 in New York City, and the couple sailed for Europe on their honeymoon.[1] But Hearst was not the mysterious stranger in the black cloak. That gentleman was Sibyl's fiancé, "Count" Paul Tolstoy. The "Count" continued to be conspicuously devoted to the dying diva after he and Lina had brought her home to Paris. He visited her every day, bringing flowers. Even on her deathbed, Sibyl Sanderson continued to cast her spell over the male sex.

Tolstoy is mentioned in the 30 April 1903 letter Marion wrote to her sister, Mrs. Roy Herrick, in Minneapolis.

> Mama has more time than the rest of us, so she keeps you regularly posted as to Sibyl's condition. Yesterday, when Edith went over she seemed very exhausted, *very yellow,* eyes rather too glistening and no desire to talk or

have anyone near . . . [there is] inflammation in lungs—has difficulty in breathing—and leeches were applied. It appears this is a natural turn of things in this malady. Her stomach is *enormous* and she is *very* weak—and yet feels interested enough in things at times to wish to be put on the chaise longue at the window to see the King of England (Edward VII) pass by the Ave. Bois de Boulogne in two days.

She considers herself engaged to be married to Russian Count Paul Tolstoy, who is a good-for-nothing, as the report goes. He is handsome and appears a gentleman and is certainly devoted, spending hours quietly near her. It is allowed, as she loves him, and it gives her pleasure to have him near, and we hate to deny her this now. Poor, poor, girl. She never says how she feels . . .

But yesterday, she cried some and I fear she is beginning to suffer *morally.* There is so little we can do for her. She is troubled in our presence. We feel it gives her no pleasure to see us, and yet we cannot stay away. It is all very, very sad. No money either [to pay the servants]. So tied up. . . . We can make no plans for the summer. To sum it up, I consider Sibyl's case just like Tony's and very serious, but it may be a long time before death comes . . .

Before Sibyl sank into a coma, she asked Lina to call Mary Garden. She wanted to make up with Mary before she died. Garden did not mention their quarrel in her autobiography, but instead described her last visit to the bedside of the pathetic singer.[2]

> I went up to Sybil's [*sic*] apartment and when I walked into the room, I had a strange experience. I had not seen Sybil for a month or two, and now I suddenly saw the death mask on her face. I had never seen a death mask before in my life, but as I stayed with her it slowly disappeared. Then there was a man sitting in a corner smoking a big, black cigar in the bedroom of a dying woman.
>
> Poor Sybil had baskets over her because she couldn't stand a sheet touching her body, which was all swollen and discolored. And I remember her maid came in to feed her. She had pieces of raw meat covered with salt, and the maid opened Sybil's lips because her lips were as hard as wood, and put these little pieces of meat between her teeth with little toothpicks. That was all she ate.
>
> Then I turned to this man sitting in the corner with his cigar and I said, "Don't you think you should smoke somewhere else?"
>
> And I saw Sybil making a gesture to me, and I went over and put my ear to

her, and I heard her say, "No, Mary, let him smoke; he's my fiancé."

So I went home feeling very wretched.

Garden didn't mention that she also left with the promise of more than when she arrived. Her dying patroness had bequeathed her a unique gift: the diamond-topped walking stick that Manon always carried in the Cours-la-Reine scene. Sibyl felt Mary would be her logical successor in French opera and had no way of knowing that Garden, in the course of her long career, would drop the role shortly after she left France for America.[3]

On 9 May, Sibyl's colleague Emma Calvé, despondent over a rift with her latest lover, unsuccessfully attempted suicide with an overdose of aconite. When her sisters informed Sibyl of the incident, she whispered to them, "Death would be a merciful release to life's sufferings."

Marion's letter to Mrs. Herrick on 14 May 1903, described the serious deterioration of Sibyl's condition.

> I am watching with Edith over poor Sibyl. It is 11:15 P.M. She is almost always unconscious now . . . talking continually in her sleep and always of "auntie and uncle" . . . anyone who sits by her bedside becomes "auntie" and all night long she asks her questions. She has only mentioned mama once . . . we go from night to night not knowing when the end will come . . . the doctor assures us that Sibyl is not suffering, but I feel that restless brain is troubled . . . Mama caught cold coming to Sibyl and has been quite ill, but we got her a night nurse as we might be freer and now she is nearly herself but still in bed and weak. She knows Sibyl is at her worst, there is no hiding it. She bears up wonderfully. Poor mama! Her husband, mother, and daughter—all will have died without her seeing them.
>
> Jennie, as I sit beside Sibyl and gaze at that poor, yellow, tired body and eyes nearly dimmed, I want to take her in my arms and help her, but she doesn't know me nor does she want to be touched except by the nurse whom she calls "auntie." Edith has gone to lie down in the library. I cannot write more. I must go to Sibyl. Her moans go to my heart. . . . Her words are now, "oh, auntie. I'm giving you a lot of trouble." She repeats it about twenty times . . . I love her now as I never have. She is to be cremated, Jennie, it is her wish.

The letter is heartbreaking not only because of the description of Sibyl's condition but for the obvious conflict of emotions within Marion. She and Edith had suffered the worst—far more than Jane—from eclipse by Sibyl's fame. For all their repressed envy and jealousy, and perceptions of parental neglect, the two sisters still maintained an intense loyalty to Sibyl. Marion now had a young American doctor as a steady beau, but unfortunately his job as a shipboard physician kept him from being with her during this agonizing period. Edith, on the other hand, had found her lifelong cause: championing the Bahai faith. Her total commitment would eventually involve translating many works of its leaders into English and French for the first time.

It is interesting to note that Marion makes no mention of the doomed Sibyl's request, reported by Blanche Marchesi, that a small stand be constructed at her bedside.[4] She purportedly asked for some old mementos of her career to be placed upon it—faded laurel wreaths, crowns, the little red shoes of Manon, the mantle of Thaïs, the veil of Esclarmonde—all covered with a muslin sheet. According to Marchesi, when she felt herself expiring, she begged the nurse to remove the sheet so she might die gazing at the weathered souvenirs of her past triumphs. Although the anecdote would have been characteristic of the soprano, the incident could not have occurred during her last few days, because Marion's letter indicated that Sibyl had lapsed into a coma before 14 May.

On the night of Friday, 15 May, Marion and Edith were alarmed by new signs of serious deterioration in the condition of their dying sister. Around midnight her body suddenly became wracked with terrible, unexplained agonies. Her eyes were open, staring into space, but she recognized no one. Her screams resembled those of a mortally wounded animal.

Dr. Iscovesco was hurriedly called, but after an examination, he pronounced her condition hopeless and baffling.[5] This wasn't the way terminal cirrhotics expired. The symptoms suggested poison to him, but the doctor soon rejected this theory as "impossible." Later, when Mary Garden asked him if Sibyl was conscious before she died, he confessed, "Her screams were so frightful I couldn't tell whether she was conscious or not. I hope she wasn't."[6]

Sibyl remained semiconscious until after 3:30 Saturday morning. Her agonizing cries gradually subsided, and for the next half hour she slowly regained serenity. At four o'clock the singer breathed her last.

Dr. Iscovesco completed the death certificate declaring that Sibyl Sanderson-Terry had died that morning at 4 A.M. of pneumonia and listed cirrhosis of the liver as well as eight other diseases as contributing factors. Lina and Célestin were immediately dispatched to the mayor's office with the report.

Scouts for the Hearst syndicate learned of Sanderson's demise at 4:30 A.M. and, pursuing the news with bloodhound persistence, roused Mary Garden from her slumber an hour later. Garden quickly dressed and joined a reporter to go to Sibyl's apartment. Once they arrived, the reporter was denied admittance.

The *New York Tribune* quoted her in an interview later that day as saying:

> I saw poor Sibyl yesterday . . . she could hardly be recognized . . . her once famous beauty was gone, and her body cruelly distorted . . . in the passing of Sibyl, the world of music has lost someone unmatched in talent and beauty. But if Sibyl is gone, her interpretations of the three great roles—Manon, Phryné, and Thaïs—which she created have passed into tradition, and thus Sibyl is immortalized.[7]

By the morning of 16 May, the international wire services had informed the world that the California nightingale was dead. Leaders of French theatrical circles and many Americans called at the Sanderson apartment over the weekend to inscribe their names in the visitor's register.

Albert Vizentini, assistant stage director of the Opéra-Comique, paid tribute to the deceased as "one of the foremost figures in French opera during the present generation. Her *Esclarmonde* was a triumph of the 1889 Exposition, and she was recognized in France as the leading exponent of *Manon, Phryné,* and *Thaïs*—the lark, the robin, and the nightingale—now they are gone forever."[8]

"Poor Sibyl," said one colleague at the Opéra-Comique who had known her for years, "she was like some beautiful butterfly whose wings were broken and soiled in the struggle for life."[9]

American reporters besieged Massenet's apartment that weekend for interviews, but "he was out to all callers." At least the French newsmen had had enough respect not to intrude upon his privacy. This was the moment he had been dreading. All the emotional armor he had donned to protect his vulnerability had suddenly disintegrated. He could not bear the thought of a personal visit to #1 avenue Bois de Boulogne; the corpse would be laid out there. He could not trust his emotions to remain under control at the moment he viewed the body. It would be painful enough to appear at her funeral. Dignity was what he must strive for now. Dignity and propriety. His wife, who had boycotted the singer's performances for years, would stay home again.

At 6 P.M. on 16 May, he forced himself to send the following petit bleu:

To Mlle Marion Sanderson at 46 Ave. Malakoff:
Yes, we are with you. We are with you. We learned of the death so cruel. We

are profoundly shaken and moved so much for your poor mother and you, all of you! My wife and I wish to see you, but your affliction is so terrible that it is not wise to disturb you in these terrible moments. From us both the most tender and faithful remembrances.

Massenet

Although the composer had adroitly excused himself from the moral responsibility of going to comfort his onetime adopted family, this hitherto unpublished message is memorable for another reason—the tiny, delicate handwriting along the edge of the note: "To your mother and all of you with all our heart.—Louise Massenet."

Auguste Germain, in the 17 May edition of *L'Écho de Paris,* described Sibyl as "one of the most adorable apparitions in theatrical history" and exhorted all who had heard her to cover the grave with "an avalanche of violets—she loved them so."

In *Le Gaulois* the anonymous scribe called "Tout Paris" conjured a radiant souvenir:

> I remember her as Thaïs . . . Thaïs of the sculptured poses, for she was always the "princess of the beautiful poses"—those marvelous shoulders, those ravishing arms—Manon leaving her sedan chair, completely bejeweled, with that rare and beautiful allure which is never studied or acquired—they are gone forever . . . Paris, guard well your memories of this vision, for the likes of her will not pass this way again.[10]

On 23 May in *L'Illustration* André Fagel recalled a different memory of her. It was a summer garden party at the country villa of a famous writer. As twilight was falling, a Romanian orchestra played languorous waltzes behind a massive bank of lilacs. Suddenly, a fresh, pure voice arose in the air. According to Fagel, it harmonized so perfectly with the serenity of the hour that no one could resist its sensuous allure. The dancing ceased, and everyone rushed across the green to the house. There at the piano by an open window was Jules Massenet accompanying an American girl "whose astonishing beauty was enhanced by a simple muslin gown." He seemed to be playing in a trance, "utterly lost in the dreamy eyes of the soprano."

> She *was* Manon—Phryné—Thaïs. She seemed born to recreate all of the enchantresses of history . . . but I shall no longer remember her from any

scene in the theater. I shall only recall the salon of the country villa in which she sang that evening. There she still stands by an open window singing to a sky gilded with the last rays of sunset and joyfully inhaling the fresh odors of the summer air.

Few of the French journals made any allusion to Sanderson's fatal vices, of which many must have been aware. Only *Le Gaulois* hinted at the subject when it described her life as "an *Adventure* out of a bizarre tale." The New York press, quite to the contrary, was more realistic about Sanderson's demise. Occasional references to her "dangerous habits" and "tragic life style" could be found in various accounts of her life. The *New York Dramatic Mirror* reflected sadly that "her career was . . . a peculiarly pathetic one . . . the personal happiness for which she yearned constantly eluded her. European triumphs that she valued lightly came easily to her. The success in her native country that she most desired was denied her."[11]

Neither French nor American reporters, however, knew of the poignant mass that weekend in the late singer's bedroom where her two last suitors—Count Fitz-James and Count Tolstoy—were clasping hands in mutual grief over Sanderson's body.

On Monday morning, 18 May, the church of Saint Honoré d'Eylau was jammed with the Parisian elite. The funeral was scheduled for 11 A.M., and the procession left the late singer's residence at 10:40 A.M. Crowds, unable to gain entrance to the cathedral, lined up in the Place Victor Hugo to watch the rich and famous enter its portals: composers Massenet, Saint-Saëns, and Hahn; stage stars Eugene Mandick and Jeanne Granier; opera singers Jean Delmas and Jacques Mouliérat. High society was represented by the Duchess of Rochefoucauld, British ambassador Sir Austin Lee and his American-born wife, French admiral Jonquières and his wife, and artist Madeleine Lemaire. Paul Viardot, son of contralto Pauline Viardot, and Sir Austin Lee volunteered to join the pallbearers. Ironically, not one of the Parisian papers mentioned Mary Garden among the prominent mourners. With all the celebrities in attendance, it was almost like one of the diva's opening nights except for the heart-numbing sorrow that shrouded the scene. This was a final testimonial from Paris to its lyric queen.

Francis de Croisset later confessed to Carl Van Vechten that he chose to stay home, and there were other conspicuous absences as well. Mme Marchesi did not attend, and, of course, none of the Terrys were there. When interviewed in 1958, the Princess de Lucinge expressed her regrets.

If it happened today, I would go. I wanted to, but you know how much my family disapproved of Sibyl. I was young then, so naïve, and completely dominated by my husband who opposed the idea. . . . It must have been so hard on her to cope after I took my share of the estate and left.

Inside the church the floral offerings were so profuse that the coffin was literally buried beneath them. Among the most spectacular tributes were wreaths sent by the Bohemian Club of San Francisco, the French Association of Dramatic Artists, and the Artists and Management of the Opéra-Comique.

By a strange coincidence, cellist Joseph Hollmann found himself with the sad task of performing at both Tony's and Sibyl's funerals; this time he played Massenet's famous *Élégie*. Other beautiful music was heard as well. The cathedral choir performed a Kyrie by Niedermeyer, the Pie Jesu by Stradella, and the Ego Sum by Gounod. Tisserand, a Parisian tenor, rendered the De Profundis.[12]

Marion sat next to the coffin with Édith de Klée, a family friend, trying to stifle an attack of the hiccups that always plagued her during moments of terrible emotional stress. Edith stayed home with their mother. Although Marion's memoirs made no mention of Mary Garden sitting beside her, the Scottish soprano later insisted she did.

"I've often heard people say . . . 'My heart is breaking' and it always seemed such a silly exaggeration to me," Garden wrote in her autobiography.[13] "But while I was sitting at that service next to the coffin of that great dear friend of mine, I said to myself, 'I understand how a heart can break.' I thought I never would get out of the church for pain and sorrow."

When the service was over, Sibyl's faithful retainer Célestin went up to the coffin and removed Tony's diamond bracelet, which Sibyl had never taken off her arm. Then the ceremony of blessing the dead began. The first mourners were given a small vessel containing holy water to sprinkle on the coffin and then pass to the next in line, until everyone in the procession completed the ritual. Dr. Iscovesco was first, followed by Marion and Édith de Klée. Then came Massenet and Albert Carré.

According to a personal interview with Garden in 1953, the composer was shaking with emotion. Tears streaming down his face, a trembling Massenet nearly dropped the vessel of holy water, but he quickly gained control of himself and averted his gaze. There were no scenes.[14]

As the mourners departed from the church, they saw the place Victor Hugo swollen with an enormous throng of silent fans. People were standing bareheaded on benches and holding up children to glimpse the procession. Eight

435

years later, Massenet was to record the scene in his serialized *Souvenirs* with moving tenderness.[15]

> A large, silent, meditative crowd gathered at the passing of the cortège which bore Sibyl Sanderson to her last resting place. A veil of sorrow seemed to be over them all. Albert Carré and I followed the coffin. We were the first behind all that remained of her beauty, grace, goodness, and talent with all of its appeal. As we noted the universal sorrow, Albert Carré interpreted the feeling of the multitude toward the beautiful departed . . . "She was loved!"

According to the *San Francisco Call,* thousands followed the funeral cortège to the cemetery (Père Lachaise). Marion was not among them; Édith de Klée drove her home. French custom dictated that the family refrain from participating in the cortège or accompanying the mourners to the grave for the last rites. This time, however, the mourners did not enter the cemetery because there was no grave, and no last rites. Sanderson's body was, according to her request, cremated, and thus burial in consecrated ground at Père Lachaise was forbidden to her by state and religious law. Her ashes could only be interred in the crematory among those of convicts and other social outcasts.

Emotionally exhausted, Marion was more than ready for a nap, but while the stranger-than-fiction drama of her sister's life continued to unfold posthumously, there could be no rest. The doorbell rang late that afternoon. When the maid answered, a tall, rather nervous man requested to speak with Mrs. Sanderson. After trying to explain that she was confined and not receiving visitors, the maid promptly roused Marion, telling her of an American stranger at the door. She went downstairs to greet the gentleman who stood in the foyer with a huge box under his arm. Although Marion had not seen him in some years, she would have known him anywhere. It was William Randolph Hearst.

Apologizing for his intrusion upon this moment of grief, Hearst explained that he and his bride were in Paris on their honeymoon and had been unable to attend the funeral that morning. He was profoundly moved to learn of Sibyl's death and wished to convey his condolences. He also had brought a huge wreath of violets; he remembered that she loved them so. Would Marion see that it was placed on the grave? Unable to read the French newspapers, Hearst was not aware that Sibyl had been cremated earlier that day. Marion thought it was a beautiful gesture, and she was touched. With this final return of her first love, Sibyl's life had come full circle.

Epilogue

Aside from its phenomenal range, was the Sanderson voice a great one? Apparently, she was not born with one of the world's great lyric instruments, any more than 90 percent of other opera stars were—Dorothy Kirsten, Bidú Sayão, Grace Moore, Kiri Te Kanawa, Teresa Berganza, Helen Jepson, Lucrezia Bori, Mary Garden, Rose Bampton, Jean Madeira, to name a few. They all worked tremendously hard to develop promising amateur voices into finely tuned mechanisms of operatic quality. Sanderson, however, belonged to a special category of lyric interpreters: she was a consummate singing actress. In this area, according to Carl Van Vechten, "there is no doubt that she was one of the great ones." The Italians as well as the French considered her to be a great artist whose interpretations "penetrated the entire character of the heroine." Huneker bestowed the title officially upon Mary Garden. Nonetheless, the singing actor had originated in nineteenth-century Italian, Russian, and French opera—particularly the latter, where such composers as Offenbach and Bizet were writing parts that opened new vistas for character interpretation, sometimes assigning a singer multiple roles in one opera.

Sanderson was among the first in the school of great singing actors and actresses that included such superb artists as Galli-Marié, Talazac, Emma Calvé, Lucien Fugère, Mary Garden, Geraldine Farrar, and more recently, Jennie Tourel, Regina Resnik, Tito Gobbi, Beverly Sills, Maria Callas, and Catherine Malfitano. To these performers, employing the voice to express the character's emotions and thoughts was the first and foremost priority. For these artists, pouring forth beautiful tone for the sake of mere voluptuous sound was an outdated, and even repugnant, mode of performing.

No opera star of her generation ever approached her capacity to create illusions in the realm of characterization through her singing, not to mention the transformation of a very pretty woman into a ravishing beauty. Even offstage, during the last two pathetic years of her life, she managed to camouflage her personal problems with illusions. Leading couturiers sold fabulous creations to her on credit. She had no doubt that Parisian bankers would loan her the necessary funds to produce the de Croisset opera. Servants were so devoted they were willing to work for her without remuneration during her last half year. One suitor was so enamored he was willing to travel across the ocean to propose marriage.

The only possible explanation for this phenomenon was that she believed in her own illusions. Her entire life had been predicated upon one grand illusion: she was destined to have it all—a brilliant career, adoring fans, courtship by and marriage to a storybook prince, followed by living happily ever after in his castle with all the money in the world. And she never completely let go of her illusions—even on her deathbed, Sibyl would whisper to visitors that she wanted to return to the Opéra-Comique and create Nedda in the French premiere of Leoncavallo's *Pagliacci*.

Because Sanderson was on the operatic stage less than a decade before her marriage, her repertoire was not a large one. Nevertheless, in the short period before her marriage she sang an astonishing number of performances: over 300 of *Manon,* 125 of *Esclarmonde* (100 of which were consecutive), 34 of *Thaïs,* and 43 of *Phryné,* in addition to roles in *Werther, Roméo et Juliette, Faust, Lakmé, Rigoletto, The Magic Flute,* and *Mireille.* These statistics do not include additional appearances she made as Phryné, Manon, and Juliette during her comeback in the years of 1901 and 1902.

If only her talents had been harnessed by self-control, there is no telling to what greater heights her star might have risen. But the pressures of her career outgrew her ability to cope. She did not know how to shield herself from a greedy public, a neurotically possessive Svengali, ignorant critics, avaricious managers, and eventually her most dangerous enemy—her self-destructive alter ego. After she retired from the stage she became the victim of malevolent and bigoted in-laws, blundering doctors, dishonest lawyers, and deceitful friends. They all must bear their share of culpability for her tragic demise.

In her memoirs Blanche Marchesi asserted that "what was lacking in her was strength of character. With strength and will power she could have fought the deadly narcotics."[1] This is only partially correct. The medical help available to alcoholics at the turn of the twentieth century was hopelessly primitive. There were no organizations such as Alcoholics Anonymous and none of the excellent drugs now available to treat the emotional problems that made her turn to alcohol.[2] The administration of narcotics to counteract her desire for alcohol was a disastrous medical experiment by ignorant doctors. Obviously, Marchesi did not know that all the will power in the world wouldn't have been enough to fight the toxicity they created in Sanderson's system.

For several weeks after her death Sanderson continued to be eulogized in various European journals. Although Henri de Courzon felt she always lacked a certain "style" in her interpretations, his tribute to her in *Le Théâtre*, June 1903, was an eloquent one.

> She had all the seductions. The beauty first, regal, radiant; then the voice, brilliant, light, with an exceptional high register; then the natural grace, without affectation . . . the gifts were rare and magnificent.

> Everything in her was charm itself, as well as sparkling and vigorous youth, coquettish and provocative vivacity, the enchanting smile, the inborn allure of elegance . . . that certain capricious nervousness which has been described to us by those who knew her best as the reflection of a complex and spontaneous spirit, strongly responsive to life. . . . She had experienced great joys and great sorrows, and had retained her benevolence always, which was abundant. . . . No doubt death wished to leave intact, and without time's inevitable tarnish, this radiant apparition which we shall remember now only through a halo of youth.

While Europe mourned her passing, America seemed bent on analyzing the reasons for her premature demise. Sanderson's death had left many unexplained mysteries, and some of her contemporaries held tenaciously to their own ideas about it. There were those who agreed with Will S. Monroe when he wrote to the *Musical Courier* (21 May 1903) that her cruel treatment in San Francisco was really the final blow. The editors promptly rebutted this allegation on 27 May with their own theories:

> It is a delicate matter to connect Miss Sanderson's death . . . with her San Francisco fiasco. Sibyl Sanderson had seen her best vocal days when she came here for the season of 1901–02. She could hardly have hoped to repeat here her Parisian triumphs gained in the heyday of her youth, beauty, and vocal ability. . . . In a measure, her early success was responsible for some of her

439

later misfortune. She lived not wisely like Patti, Sembrich, and Lehmann, and other women who sing at fifty and over. It is perhaps not the kindest thing to make Sibyl Sanderson's career a moral lesson for young singers. For us it will be a grateful remembrance to think of her only as one of the greatest coloratura singers of her day and as the woman who inspired the gifted Massenet to some of his best efforts.

There could be no doubt that Sanderson had suffered a devastating experience in California; neither can there be any uncertainty that the San Francisco catastrophe haunted her to the end.[3] Even when she was dying, San Francisco weighed on her mind, and anyone at her bedside became "auntie" (Aunt Mary) or "uncle" (Uncle John), relatives who cared for her during her West Coast illness.

Although Dr. Iscovesco listed pneumonia on his certificate as the official cause of death, he had long treated her for liver disease. She suffered from all the classic symptoms: the jaundiced complexion, the stomach pains, the bloated belly, weakness, and in the end, coma. Under normal circumstances she should have slipped away quietly as her husband had done. What happened to her on the night of her death was wholly foreign to cirrhosis victims. New and horrendous agonies wracked her entire body causing heartrending screams and violent thrashing—reactions totally different from those of terminally ill cirrhotics. When Dr. Iscovesco arrived at her apartment, he was so baffled by her symptoms that he could think of only one diagnosis at first—poison.

Even though the doctor mentioned it as a possibility to Sibyl's sisters as well as to the international wire services, he later publicly dismissed the theory as preposterous. Neither did he endorse the stories in the American papers that Sanderson had suffered a stroke in her last hours. Even though the immediate cause of death was to remain an unsolved puzzle for the rest of his life, the poison hypothesis lingered in his mind for a long time. Her deathbed symptoms didn't suggest any other conclusion.

A week after Sanderson's passing, San Francisco's *Town Talk,* on 23 May, boldly revealed its own theory. The writer printed the rumor that Sibyl Sanderson had tried to commit suicide the last night of her life by swallowing a bottle of cologne next to her bedside. Two things were wrong with the story: there was no bottle of cologne next to the bed, and Sanderson had been unconscious for the last three days of her life.

If it wasn't suicide or a stroke, then we are forced to return to the poison hypothesis. Sibyl's sisters could be ruled out immediately. Not only were they incapable of such a desperate act, they didn't know how to prepare food, much less concoct poison. The woman who had not only the opportunity but also the motive and the experience was Lina Bournie, Sibyl's maid. She alone fixed Sibyl's food. She had a good amateur knowledge of poison and administration of antidotes. Having weathered various suicide attempts of Sibyl's, she had helped to save the singer's life on several occasions. By May 1903 she realized that her mistress was beyond salvation. Rather than see her linger day after day, week after week, drifting in and out of comas as Antonio Terry had done, she could have decided to end Sibyl's suffering by a mercy killing. It would have been so easy.

Edith and Marion weren't benefiting from their sister's estate but Lina was, and knew exactly what she was to receive thanks to Sibyl's oral bedside will: the huge cabochon emerald ring that Alexander III had given the singer, the czar's emerald bracelet, the pearl necklace, and some antique furniture. There would be enough for Lina to buy herself a room in a retirement home when she became too old and infirm to work anymore. As Sibyl had already left orders to be cremated, once the doctors signed the death certificate, the maid knew there would be no reason for an autopsy.

Quiet, demure, ultra precious Lina, so full of deep but conflicting feelings toward her mistress. Who would ever suspect her? Theirs had been a love–hate relationship for years. As Francis de Croisset later observed to Carl Van Vechten, her neurotic devotion to Sibyl was not normal. No normal woman would endure what Lina had been forced to go through. But de Croisset had no conception of how Lina had worshipped the diva during her halcyon years. They had traveled the world together. She had seen the rich, the famous, and the great in Sibyl's dressing rooms. She had vicariously lived many thrilling lives through Sibyl's operatic heroines. When the soprano's career began to slide, her adoration turned to disgust and contempt, and eventually to pity.

Circumstantial evidence points strongly to Lina as the one who gave Sibyl the fatal dose of aconite or arsenic on the night of May 16.[4] Once her mistress was out of her misery, Lina would be free to pursue her new vocation: nursing invalid patients. She told Marion that she wanted to leave the apartment as soon as possible, but the Terry lawyers, Webb and Travers, appointed her temporary custodian of the estate until they could arrange for an auction of the late singer's effects. Nothing was supposed to be touched.[5]

Perhaps it was fortunate for the Sandersons that Lina was forced to stay on the premises that summer. She managed to smuggle the czar's turquoise-and-silver necklace, the diamond dog collars, the full-length sable cloak, Massenet's various gifts, and a few of Tony's jewels to them. Terry's enormous canary diamond ring, his diamond bracelet, and most of his jewelry were to go to Natica by the terms of his will. Webb and Travers had ordered Lina to put them all in the bank vault for safekeeping, but the perverse Mlle Bournie was as uncooperative as usual.

No sooner had Sibyl been cremated than the vultures began to circle over the spoils. Less than twenty-four hours after the funeral Mary Garden was the first to swoop down upon the late singer's family. Announcing that Sibyl had given her the Manon walking stick, she further demanded her pick of Sibyl's wigs, costumes, and stage jewelry. Marion and Edith explained that the lawyers had ordered Sibyl's operatic wardrobe and stage effects to be held for auction that fall. They were shocked that this cold-blooded woman, who owed everything to Sibyl, could be so avaricious at a time when they were in mourning.

After the funeral, Massenet sank into a state of despair. He had lost his incentive to compose—the worst possible torture that could be inflicted upon him. He returned to his studio the day after Sibyl's funeral because he had a long-standing appointment with a young American soprano from Berlin—the beautiful Geraldine Farrar. She had come to Paris to coach *Manon* with him for the Berlin premiere that fall. Farrar found him in tears.

"The musical world knew of their long and tender attachment," she wrote in her autobiography. "And I felt somewhat embarrassed that this particular moment should find me an observer of his grief. However, perhaps a sorrowful heart had its consolation in reviewing *Manon*—one of her own successful roles at the Opéra-Comique—for the long consultation embraced as much the topic of Sibyl as it did his operatic heroine."[6]

Early in June the Parisian papers announced that Massenet was vacating his longtime residence at 46 rue du Général Foy and moving to the corner of the rue de Vaugirard and the rue Ferou. Perhaps he felt that he needed a clean break from the past, a complete change of scene. By the end of the month, he and his wife were ensconced in a large front apartment on the mezzanine at 48 rue de Vaugirard whose windows overlooked the Luxembourg Gardens.

In addition to helping his faithful valet, Michel, unpack more than six thousand books and scores in record-breaking time, he had gone to the Opéra-Comique once to hear the American soprano Vera Courtenay sing *Manon*. It was his first public appearance since Sanderson's funeral. On 28 June he realized that he had made no effort to contact Margaret since Sibyl's death. That evening he wrote her a letter and for once omitted any reference to his wife.

Chère Madame,

It is *toujours* with profound emotion that I write to you—I hope that you are recovering although I know how much you have suffered morally—I am compelled to recall the thoughts of a friend from the rue de la Trémoille—then the rue Lincoln—a friend and companion on our trip to Holland—I feel so sad—then the friend of the Ave. Malakoff—It seems necessary that these thoughts, as I have said, should fly to you and your other children—with all of you suffering the maximum afflictions that exist in the world.

> To you tenderly,
> respectfully,
> J. Massenet

The letter was addressed to the avenue Malakoff, because Massenet did not know that Margaret had recovered sufficiently to leave for her summer cottage at St. Énogat. Before she left, Nellie Melba called upon her. It was a joy for the Sanderson family to see Melba again after so many years. According to Marion's reminiscences, Melba spoke very tenderly to their mother about her warm affection for Sibyl.

During the summer of 1903 Massenet's path again crossed the Sandersons'. He had made a business trip to Heugel's summer villa near Dinard, when he unexpectedly encountered Marion at the depot in St. Énogat. She described their poignant meeting in her letter of 11 September to Jane.

I was at the station returning from Dinard the day he arrived, when I turned and saw him standing beside me, trembling, unable to speak, his eyes streaming with tears. He held both of my hands tight and said nothing—a great lump came up in my throat and we parted—but he said volumes, far more than if he had spoken. What a beautiful nature, so full of sentiment!

Sentiment indeed. Such an opinion was not only typical of Marion, but all the Sandersons. For the rest of their lives they continued looking at Massenet through rose-colored glasses. He had good reason to be grief-stricken. He had a great deal on his conscience.

To the end of his days he held himself blameless for Sibyl Sanderson's tragedy. He maintained that, like a father, he had tried to guide her career and protect her from adversity. Even after she retired from the stage, he claimed, he never turned his back on her. His wife believed likewise. She steadfastly supported him through all the virulent gossip that surrounded his unstable relationship with the ill-fated singer.

Massenet was far from faultless. His sins—of ignorance, avarice, jealousy, and selfishness—contributed emphatically to Sanderson's early downfall. She had mortgaged her soul to him for stardom, and the price she paid was a tragic one. By writing a cruelly difficult opera for her debut that she wasn't ready to sing, he had quite possibly signed the death warrant for her vocal career. He never realized the damage done to her vocal cords during all the hours she forced her voice in those strenuous *Esclarmonde* rehearsals. He was oblivious to the dangers as she strained nightly to reach the highest cadenzas in operatic history. The fact that she sang a hundred performances of the work within nine months remains one of the truly amazing feats in the operatic annals.

Once her career took wings, he greedily saw her as the goose that laid the golden eggs. He never lifted a finger to protect her from the dreadful exploitation to which impresarios subjected her; after all, her name guaranteed sold-out houses. If it is true that he connived to turn her into a lesbian to keep her from marriage, this was the most dastardly act he committed. Knowing how desperately she needed money during her last years, he never offered to loan her a sou, in spite of the fact her career had helped make him a millionaire. Mme Massenet, who insisted that Sibyl Sanderson had destroyed herself, was undeniably correct, but her husband had created some propitious conditions for the soprano's premature demise.

For the rest of the summer Massenet forced himself to labor on de Croisset's *Chérubin*. On 23 December, he wrote to Margaret apologizing for not having called upon her all year, but 1903 had been "such a cruel year for us both." It wasn't until 1904 that the composer found the courage to see her again.

Meanwhile, the Paris *Herald* announced on 23 September that Antonio Terry's will had finally been admitted to probate in New York. As long as Sibyl lived, her mother-in-law would not release a cent to help Sibyl pay the two million francs in debts that Tony left her, but his daughter Natividad, now the sole heir, would inherit a quarter of a million dollars. In her letter of 29 September to Jane, Marion remarked that "Natica is now a very rich young woman. . . . The prince she bought with the Terry money must be doubly happy. I hear she is to have a baby soon."

The public exhibition of Sanderson's possessions didn't open at the Hotel Drouot until 12 November and was advertised throughout Paris as "a sensational auction." It drew enormous crowds eager to see how the American star had lived. Pushing his way through hoards of curiosity seekers, a *Figaro* reporter encountered the last woman he expected to see—Louise Massenet. Had he been acquainted with a few intimate friends from the diva's past, he would have noticed another elegantly dressed lady—Mme X. There were 120 gowns on display, including some of her designer dresses and her fabulous theater costumes. Also included in the sale were furniture, objets d'art, and her stage jewels, as well as a good deal of personal costume jewelry. Although the papers announced her automobile would also be auctioned, there is no record of this occurring. It may have been sold privately or repossessed.

When the bidding began on Friday, 13 November, with the exception of an embroidered Juliette gown of antique brocade, both her personal wardrobe and theater costumes achieved disappointing results, with many of them being purchased by secondhand dealers. The veil of Esclarmonde and Juliette's cloak went for a song. On the other hand, her jackets of sable, ermine, and Persian lamb fetched high prices. Her antique lace and muslin table service soared to 3,400 francs.

Startling revelations were made on 15 November. A few days before the sale, Mme X had tried unsuccessfully to persuade officials to withdraw the jewelry she once gave Sibyl. She now produced the old receipts necessary to prove ownership and announced she had only "loaned" them to her. She demanded the money from their sale, and auction officials had no choice but to honor her claim. Two brooches of brilliants, pearls, and sapphires, a pair of sapphire drop earrings, and a bracelet of brilliants brought her the sum of 8,340 francs. There was considerable grumbling among the buyers because none of Sibyl's top-quality jewels had been put on the auction block.

The sale of her objets d'art fared poorly, with the exception of her gold-bronze and marble clocks. Some of the Directoire furniture fetched decent prices, but the most hotly contested items on the last day of the sale were her musical scores.[7] When the auction closed on Tuesday, 17 November, the total proceeds of her estate had brought 86,680 francs.[8]

The year 1904 was a far happier one for the Sandersons. Marion and Dr. Edwin Nall were to be married in the summer, and Jane insisted their nuptials be performed in her Minneapolis home. Margaret was anxious to accompany them on the voyage, as she had not set foot on native soil since 1886. Before the Sanderson party left for America, Marion received a pleasant surprise in the mail. It was a charming letter from Louise Massenet expressing her delight over Marion's upcoming marriage and wishing her all "you want in happiness for the rest of your life."

After the wedding, Marion and Edwin planned to make their home in New York City, where Dr. Nall would practice medicine. Margaret returned to Paris with Edith in the fall of 1904, never to see her native land again. She had lived in France for so many years that she felt more at home there than in her own country. Without realizing it, she had become the typical American expatriate; there were now more than forty thousand living in the French capital.

Yet, even in Paris she was not allowed any peace. Sibyl's ghost was shortly to be exhumed for a posthumous scandal. On 7 November 1905, Mr. Goudstikker finally brought suit against her estate for the unpaid diamond necklace valued at $30,000. *Le Figaro* took delight in reporting all the sensational revelations of the trial, while Arthur Meyer, who had been a friend of Sibyl and her husband, ordered *Le Gaulois* to suppress it.

Margaret was heartsick over the situation. She wrote to Jane the same week:

> I am sad over the newspapers. Poor Sibyl's illness is now known to the world all over. . . . All will be cabled to New York . . . Jennie, you will be sick over it . . . it all comes from that thief of a jeweler selling her 145,000 francs of diamonds and having her sign papers to pay an interest, culpable on the jeweler's part, every three months.

Margaret's predictions came true before her daughter ever received the letter. The case hit the New York papers on 12 November, and the *Morning Telegraph* printed the following dispatch:

> The sad history of the American soprano, Sibyl Sanderson, was recalled with all of its painful details in the Civil Tribunal of the Seine yesterday, when the executor of the dead singer resisted a claim for $30,000 made against her estate by a jeweler from the rue de la Paix for an unpaid bill. The bill was dated a month after the singer's last appearance on the stage in Nice at a time when she was known to be insolvent.
>
> The administrator of her estate contests the claim on the grounds that there is no evidence of her ever having had possession of such jewels, or of her selling them again, or of pawning them, in fact, no trace of the jewels has been found. He further argues that an experienced tradesman, such as the plaintiff, would scarcely be so unwise as to sell $30,000 worth of jewels on credit to the singer at such time, and therefore the supposed bill is really a moneylender's note of hand.

In reply, the plaintiff's counsel refers the defendant to the bill itself, signed by Sibyl Sanderson, herself, promising "to pay 145,000 francs for value received in goods." The jeweler further disputes the administrator's right to object to his bill and declares that Sibyl Sanderson's orders, signed by herself, were neither forbidden nor furnished by a guardian. Judgment will be given in two weeks.

For the case to be fully understood, Monsieur Signorino, the Sanderson lawyer, had no choice but to reveal the circumstances of Sibyl's tragic life in court. The attorney explained:

This admirable artist, with a voice like crystal, had never been able to overcome stage fright and sought artificial courage in alcoholic stimulants. The habit grew upon her after she left the boards . . . and [she] died of cirrhosis of the liver brought on by this cause. On the death of her husband, Señor Emilio [sic] Terry, a rich Cuban, she was left a life interest in his fortune of $10,000 a year. Being accustomed to a life of luxury she was unable to live on this small income and in consequence, after two years of widowhood, found herself financially ruined and beset by creditors. Hoping to make a comeback on the operatic stage, she decided to return to the footlights in the fall of October 1902 (one month before the date of the bill).

Appearing as "Esclarmonde" in Massenet's opera which she originally created, she appeared at the Nice Opera House in 1902. It is ironic she should make her reappearance in a part that had brought her fame originally at the Opéra-Comique. Few who witnessed her return will forget that day, for the once celebrated singer had completely lost her voice, and her reception was so cold, she only got through the first act with difficulty. The performance had to be stopped and the unfortunate singer was taken to her hotel where she remained seriously ill from a liver attack and confined to her bed for the rest of the month.[9]

Signorino disclosed that when she died the following spring, she was over $100,000 in debt. Her creditors included prominent tradesmen from all over Paris. He further claimed that the auction of her personal estate brought only $2,000, which, coupled with her annuity from her husband's estate, barely made $12,000 to appease her creditors.

Either Signorino was afflicted with a temporary memory loss or he flagrantly perjured himself in the Parisian court. There was no performance of

Esclarmonde that fall. The doors of the Nice Opera House opened with *Aïda* on 24 November 1902.[10] Sanderson's only appearance in Nice that season was in *Phryné,* in March 1903 at the Casino Municipal. It is possible that Signorino based this fictitious onstage breakdown on Sanderson's inability to appear in *Manon* at Aix-les-Bains two months earlier. In any event, she had no date to perform *Esclarmonde* anywhere that year.

Neither did Signorino tell the truth about the results of the auction. Assuming that the Hotel Drouot took the usual 20 percent of the total 86,680 francs, this still should have left a balance of roughly 70,000 francs. Surely, the lawyer didn't bleed the remaining income of a shocking 69,560 francs (approximately $14,000).

When the court reconvened two weeks later, Sibyl Sanderson's signature was declared genuine, and judgment was in favor of Goudstikker. Whether he ever collected any money from her estate is doubtful. Most, if not all, of the proceeds must have been parceled out to her other creditors by this time.

What happened to the vanished necklace is another tantalizing mystery. Lina Bournie was the only person who really knew what became of it. Assuming that the signature on the jeweler's bill was not a forgery, she lied to Signorino about having no knowledge of such jewels. This devious woman knew about all Sibyl's confidential transactions, and she accompanied the singer on her mysterious trip to Brussels less than a month after the purchase.

After devoting a long life to nursing, the enigmatic Lina died about 1950, taking more than her share of secrets to the grave. She spent her last years in a home for the elderly, where she had purchased a room with Sibyl's legacy. Thirtysome years after the trial, still garbed in floor-length dresses from the turn of the century, she would occasionally call upon Edith Sanderson with some of her inheritance hidden under her long sleeves and high collars. No one ever saw whatever bracelet or necklace she claimed to be wearing because she was paranoid about a possible robbery. It gave her a secret thrill just to whisper to Edith Sanderson's maid, "Esther, I am wearing some of Madame's jewels today."[11] Perhaps one of them was the diamond necklace.

Throughout his remaining years, Massenet kept in touch with Mrs. Sanderson. In 1911, before the composer's memoirs began to appear serially in *L'Écho de Paris,* he sent the galleys of his first six chapters to her with an affectionate note as always. It must have made her very proud to read the chapter devoted to Sibyl ("A Star"), in which he called her the "ideal Manon" and "a never to be forgotten Thaïs."[12] It didn't matter to Margaret that the chapter abounded in inaccuracies and that the composer concealed more truth than he chose to reveal.

Because Sibyl's demise had been such a terrible blow to him, he refused to allow any revivals of *Esclarmonde* during his lifetime. "After I am gone," he told his biographer, Marc Delmas, "one can do with the score whatever one chooses."

Honor continued to be piled upon honor during his last years. In the final winter of his life, 1911–12, having grown old and frail, Massenet held one of his last Sunday receptions. Garbed in a long cassock, he was seated in a huge Renaissance armchair as guests continued to pay homage. News had just arrived from America that day about Mary Garden's continued success in *Thaïs,* a fact that never ceased to amaze him. He turned to soprano Minnie Tracey and remarked, "You know how I wrote it for the exquisite Sibylle . . . little by little it has grown in public favor until today, perhaps with *Manon,* it is the work that brings me the greatest amount of royalties."[13]

Reminiscing about the opera that day, his eyes filled with tears as he made his final public statement about the legendary woman he had loved: "She was Thaïs, the exponent in flesh of all that was poetical, earthly, and divine in love. In this role she has never been equaled and certainly will never be surpassed." On 13 August 1912 at a Parisian hospital Massenet quietly joined his muse in death.

Margaret Sanderson survived him by little more than a year. It was perpetually offensive to her that Sibyl's remains lay among those of anarchists and criminals in the Père Lachaise crematorium because of the Catholic Church's ban on cremation. Ironically, the soprano's fox terriers received the rite she was never accorded. As they died, one by one, Célestin Menendez would bury them in the pet cemetery beside Père Lachaise. As of 1960, their graves were still marked "the dogs of the American singer, Sibyl Sanderson" and cared for by the French government. Before she died, Margaret left a note requesting that her daughters exhume Sibyl's ashes and rebury them in some other place in Paris, where a proper monument could be erected.

This never happened. After Mrs. Sanderson's death on 22 October 1913, Mrs. Roy Herrick brought her mother's remains and Sibyl's ashes to Minneapolis, where they were interred in a Sanderson family plot. Today, with the exception of the judge, the entire family is reunited in the Minneapolis Lakewood Cemetery.

In death, as in life, the unexpected continued to happen to Sibyl. Somehow it seemed natural that her earthly remains should find permanent sanctuary in a city she never knew. Nor would her unquiet spirit have cared. During her brief thirty-eight years she had soared like Icarus to unparalleled heights and plummeted to depths not even he had known. She had savored life to its extremes. The words that Goethe breathed into the dying Werther could as easily have been hers:

> If holy ground be not for one who dies as I have died, then let some desolate valley be my exiled refuge, my grave . . . and the shedding of a stranger's tear, my blessing.

Manon–Phryné
To Sibyl Sanderson

—by Edmé Paze

Goddess of harmony, you whose voice
   sings
With more sweetness than a crystal
   chime,
You were the exquisitely touching
   love
For whom the Chevalier spilled his
   blood.

You were the Manon, tenderly
   clinging
And possessing a charm most
   powerful,
The adorable Manon whose supple
   enchantment
Resembles a song of love that delights
   in cradling.

But years of perfecting, still the work
   unfinished,
Irresistible and ever the daughter of
   Genius
Whose bird has engraved her voice in
   Carrara marble.

Déesse d'Harmonie à vous dont la voix
   chante
Avec plus de douceur qu'un cristal
   bruissant
Vous fûtes l'amoureuse exquissement
   touchante
Pour qui le Chevalier eut versé son
   sang.

Vous fûtes la Manon tendrement
   attachante
Et possédant en elle un charme tout
   puissant
L'adorable Manon dont un souple
   enchante
En semble un *lied* d'amour qui ravit en
   bercant.

Mais ans de parfaire encore l'oeuvre
   béate,
Irrésistible à jamais et Fille d'un
   Génie
Dont l'oiseau du Carrere la voix a
   buriné.

From Le Figaro, *12 October 1893, translated by John Bolinger and Jack Winsor Hansen.*

Notes

Preface

    1. *Le Gaulois,* 17 May 1903.

Chapter 1

    1. His brother Elnathan was prospecting for gold not far from there. It can be safely assumed that they were reunited, although Elnathan's diary, still in the Sanderson family's possession, lacks the pages for these months.

    2. Shuck 1875, 1011.

    3. Edith Wharton, "Xingu," *Scribner's Magazine* 50 (December 1911), 684–696.

    4. Silas Sanderson to his wife, 28 May 1886.

Chapter 2

    1. Conversations with Evelyn Wells and Marion Davies.

    2. Older 1936, 36. However, Marion Sanderson told her daughter, Sibyl's niece, the truth, and the true reasons for the split also appeared in an article about Sibyl in *Munsey's* magazine in February 1899.

    3. In several of her later letters to her daughter Jane, Margaret Sanderson alludes to Mrs. Hearst's private talk with Sibyl (for example, "Sibyl and I are not getting along, she is making me nervous. If only dear Mrs. Hearst was here to reason with her again").

    4. Tebbel 1952, 58.

    5. Swanberg 1961, 23.

    6. Marion Davies to author, 1960.

Chapter 3

    1. This was the Left Bank bastion of perhaps the oldest, most aristocratic families in Paris.

Chapter 4

1. *The Call-Bulletin* (San Francisco), 31 October 1947.
2. Emma Nevada, née Wixon, 1859–1940.
3. Atherton 1932, 118
4. Years later Edith Sanderson remarked to her niece, Margaret, that Sibyl's fame had unjustifiably overshadowed their father's.
5. When Lone Mountain Cemetery was later demolished to make room for urban reconstruction, the city's dead pioneers were reburied elsewhere under rows of concrete blocks marked only by number.

Chapter 5

1. The Dreyfus girls were overwhelmed by the exquisite Sanderson sisters. They could not agree upon who was the more beautiful. Once when Sibyl and Marion stayed overnight at the Dreyfus home, the four sisters conducted a unique investigation to satisfy their curiosity. Just after sunrise, they quietly piled a series of books on several chairs outside the bedroom in which Sibyl and Marion were sleeping and peeped through the open transom at the sleeping beauties. Votes were taken, and Marion won unanimously.
2. See Marguerite Cassini's memoirs *Never a Dull Moment* (Harper 1956) for a more detailed indictment of de Reszke's teaching methods. The suicide of soprano Bessie Abott, despondent over the loss of her voice, was laid at de Reszke's doorstep. Mme Nellie Gardini, longtime head of the vocal department at the Chicago Musical College, told me that she left de Reszke just in time to save her voice. These singers worked with him at the close of the nineteenth century, when he was still actively performing. By the time he was teaching Edvina, Teyte, and Sayão, he had retired from the stage and modified his methods and approach to the female voice, according to Sayão.
3. Nellie Gardini, personal communication.

Chapter 6

1. New York Public Library, Massenet file, undated clipping.
2. Irvine 1994, 310.
3. Fortunately, her civil marriage documents exist and give her name as Constance Louise de Gressy. In all her letters to the Sandersons, she never refers to herself as Ninon, always Louise.
4. Thomas did bring his doctor to look after Massenet, and the doctor happened to be the emperor's physician as well.
5. *Musical Courier,* 9 December 1899 and London *Times,* undated clipping.

6. Mary Garden, "Of Me I Sing," *Collier's Magazine,* 4 March 1933.

7. *Le Gaulois,* 11 October 1891.

Chapter 7

1. The letter belongs to the Biblioteca Cantonale of Locarno, Italy.

2. Massenet 1912, 174.

3. Massenet also noted on the holograph of *Werther,* which he later presented to Sibyl, that she had worked on the role of Charlotte at the same lesson.

Chapter 8

1. Marchesi 1923, 54.

2. The main reason for Sanderson's fantastically high voice was a set of unusually short vocal cords. All her photographs reveal that she had a short neck; and the shorter the cords, the faster the vibration, and the higher the sound. Once she had mastered a light adjustment of the vocal cords, she possessed the secret for her effortless control. There was no comparable voice in the twentieth century of which I am aware, with the exception of the late Mado Robin.

3. According to Octavia Hensel in the *Musical Courier,* Sanderson took the part back to Sbriglia and worked on it with him. She denied this in later interviews.

4. She signed two holographs that day: the manuscript Massenet gave her and his own personal one as well.

5. Eames 1927, 66.

6. Even the Sandersons were among the spectators. Marion has recorded that they sat next to a very excited Julian Story, the painter, and Eames's fiancé.

7. Mrs. Atherton learned of Massenet's miserliness when he invited her to attend a performance of his oratorio *Marie-Magdeleine* with him. She had to pay for her own ticket.

8. Atherton 1932, 155.

Chapter 9

1. In private life Willy was Henri Gauthiers-Villars.

2. Atherton 1932, 157.

3. A short, rapid-delivery message dispatched through underground pneumatic tubes in major French cities.

4. Carré 1950, 243.

5. London *Times,* 16 May 1889.

6. I have rendered names as they appeared in newspapers of the day. When a critic has since become known by a different name, I have included both versions: Jean (Johannès) Weber was Jean at the time. Similarly André Pollonais was referred to at the time as Gaston Pollonais; thus in this book he appears as (André) Gaston Pollonais.

7. There is far more of Berlioz than Wagner in both the choral and orchestral writing in the third act.

Chapter 10

1. Sanderson wrote on her photograph, "To the master of Esclarmonde, Souvenir Affectueux." Massenet inscribed his, "To the divine Esclarmonde, with homage of recognition and admiration."

2. Irvine's date of conception, 24–25 September 1887, would be somewhat after their original meeting in the summer. Massenet mentions in his running diary on the holograph of *Esclarmonde* that he prepared this manuscript, notated for voice and piano, on 12 May 1888 after a dinner at the Sanderson home. For its publication, Massenet transposed it a major third above the original key of F major.

3. *The American Musician,* 24 August 1889.

4. *New York Herald,* 26 September 1889.

5. Massenet was fantasizing when he wrote that, not expecting to find a voice comparable to Sanderson's, he had been forced to make "numerous changes" in his score which "perverted" the work. Any analysis of the holograph he gave Sibyl shows that many technically easier passages had been purposely altered in favor of far more difficult vocal acrobatics for her voice. All he had to do for other sopranos who would sing the role was to revert to his original conception.

6. Elson 1896, 217.

7. Perhaps the most convincing evidence that the relationship between the singer and her mentor remained a platonic one was the disclosure by Sanderson's stepdaughter, the Princess de Faucyny-Lucinge, that Sibyl occasionally flaunted her lovers before her properly offended Victorian sisters. As the Princess observed, "the fact that no love letters have survived between the two means nothing. She and Massenet had plenty of opportunity for intimacy in his office at Heugel's [sic]--and Sibyl would try anything once--but she never included his name when she would enumerate her various sexual conquests to Marion and Edith. Had there been a relationship, this would have been extremely unlike her. She was a liberated woman--years ahead of her time."

8. Benoist 1978, 28.

9. Carré 1950, 243.

10. Massenet had good reason to try to keep Sanderson off the marriage market. She was the first singing actress to bring glamor to a European operatic stage long overcrowded with herds of hippopotami who had swallowed nightingales. Her sold-out houses had brought him unprecedented profits, and as she went on to champion his works throughout Europe, her Midas touch was to help make him a millionaire.

11. Rimsky-Korsakov recorded his impression of the event in his autobiography. Massenet reminded him, as he had Mary Garden, Emma Eames, and so many others, of "a crafty fox." He attended one of Sanderson's performances in *Esclarmonde* and described it as "excellent."

Chapter 11

1. The temperamental Lina Bournie, whom Sibyl brought along as her personal maid over Margaret's objections, must have had a room on the réz-de-chaussée also, but there is no record of it.

2. Margaret Sanderson to Jane, 12 November 1890.

3. Throughout her career in Europe and America, Sanderson was often compared to the famous actress Anna Judic. It is not known whether she ever saw Judic on stage in San Francisco, but the lady appeared there periodically on her American tours.

4. Writing to the *American Musician* on 12 November 1890, *Chicago Tribune* reporter Henry Haynie commented, "Sanderson achieved a great success . . . I know, for I went up to Brussels to hear her with Mlle Adiny from the Paris Opera . . . in the St. Sulpice scene she was recalled four times alone after the rest of the cast . . . when attired in those marvelous costumes, ladies audibly sighed in the audience . . . I should not like to say how much that Watteau court robe of satin cost, but I do say her notes were pure, her phrasing perfect, and her acting splendid."

5. *L'Indépendance belge,* 3 December 1890.

6. *Le Guide musical,* 27 December 1890

Chapter 12

1. Both Oriental heroines prefer death to dishonor after betrayal by their Western lovers. However, Lakmé's father, the Brahmin priest, admires her suicide to appease the gods.

2. After the funeral the court physicians were to propose still another expla-

nation: "death due to internal variola, a recently discovered disease."

3. *L'Indépendance belge,* 3 February 1891.

4. *Chronique belge,* 3 February 1891.

5. *Gazette de Bruxelles,* 3 February 1891.

6. *Le Ménéstrel,* 8 February 1891.

7. Massenet kept it a secret during his lifetime but privately recorded the deed on the holograph of the song.

8. Lesourd 1934.

9. Jean Clément, intimate of the royal family, to the author.

10. Louis Clément, Belgian career diplomat and friend of King Albert's son, Prince Charles, verified the account in a personal interview.

Chapter 13

1. Actually, the Carl Rosa company had premiered it several weeks earlier in Liverpool before the company returned to the capital to give the London premiere.

2. Fortunately, in a few days the composer received a telegram informing him that Henri Heugel and his nephew had purchased Hartmann's entire inventory. The composer was to enjoy twenty-one years of felicitous relations with his new publishers.

3. Lahee 1898, 87.

4. George Bernard Shaw, "Garrick to the Life," *London World,* 27 May 1891.

5. *Monthly Musical Record,* 1 June 1891, 139.

6. The critic on *Vanity Fair* had remarked that "the music is so refined, so delicate, and so perfumed that one feels inclined to put on a pair of white kid gloves before listening to so dainty a score."

7. *Punch,* 16 May 1891.

8. Instead of campaigning for a return engagement to Covent Garden, according to a letter from Margaret to Jane, Sibyl used the lunch time to crusade for Nellie Melba who had not been appreciated in London so far. Lady de Grey was so impressed by Sibyl's impassioned plea for Melba, that she promised to use her influence upon Augustus Harris to extend Melba's contract. The result was the beginning of a lifelong love affair between Melba and Covent Garden audiences. Unfortunately, Sibyl's extraordinary generosity was seldom reciprocated by its beneficiaries.

9. A fascinating legend still exists about Sanderson's meeting with the famous palmist Cheiro in London. He is said to have gazed at both of her palms and remarked about their differences. One expressed some of the noblest aspi-

rations of character he had ever witnessed; the other was the hand of a woman who would destroy herself. "I have seen only one other pair so similar to yours," he purportedly remarked and, when queried as to the owner, whispered sotto voce, "Oscar Wilde's." If this story has any validity, Cheiro had already forecast the future conflict between her two personalities, Odette and Odile.

10. Sibyl's sisters learned about her sexual encounter with Van Dyck from their mother after the soprano subsequently renewed her affair with him in Paris. At the turn of the century, when Edith and Marion were nursing deep-seated hostility toward Sibyl, Marion decided to tell the entire story to Sibyl's stepdaughter, Natividad Terry, who related it to me.

11. The king originally was a member of the Danish royal family.

Chapter 14

1. Interview with Pierre Monteux, 1 July 1959, Ravinia Festival.

2. *Le Temps*, 13 October 1891, reported that Nellie Melba jumped up in her box impetuously screaming, "Brava, Sibyl!"

3. *L'Indépendance belge*, 17 May 1903.

4. *New York Herald* (Paris edition), 17 May 1903.

5. *Le Ménéstrel*, 18 October 1891.

6. Discussing Sanderson's interpretation in 1955, Philipp recalled her portrayal of Manon's different personalities as if it were yesterday, adding, "No one I have ever seen even approached her in the role." He confided an observation Massenet later made to him about Sibyl that struck me as especially adroit: "She is the eternal child in a woman's body, and it is these characteristics which make her Manon so tantalizing and irresistible."

7. *La Revue des deux mondes*, November 1891.

8. "L'âme des fleurs" remains the perfect example of why Massenet's songs rank so far below those of Chausson and Fauré. Too often they were hastily written for commercial purposes and received his leftover inspiration.

9. Hahn 1946, 57.

10. According to Massenet's notes on his manuscript, the first changes were made for Sanderson as early as 20 November 1887.

11. At The Hague in 1888 Sanderson added one of her interpolations, a stunning descending coloratura cadenza against a rising orchestral line in "À nous les amours et les roses" (Act IV, measures 86–90). Massenet curiously did not include it in the revised edition.

12. "Sibyl Sanderson at Last," *Boston Herald*, 6 March 1895.

13. In an interview in 1987 Bidù Sayão recalled, "My teacher, Jacques

459

Isnardon, often sang the Count Des Grieux with her. He told me how extraordinarily musical and perceptive she was. . . . Every soprano who has sung Manon owes this woman a debt of gratitude."

Chapter 15

1. Fanny Reed may have been the one who first suggested that Sibyl take a glass of wine before a performance. In her memoirs Emma Eames labeled her "a most unwise friend to Sibyl Sanderson as friends can be."

2. Kshesinskaia 1961, 37.

3. Review from [*Journal*] *Petrogradskaia* reprinted in *Le Guide musical*, 21 February 1892.

4. *L'Art musical*, 19 January 1892.

5. A dated photograph of this gown is still in the possession of the Sanderson family and appeared in a number of European journals, including the French weekly *L'Illustration*.

6. Every time his perennial favorite, an actress named Baletta, appeared in public displaying her sensational diamond necklace, the St. Petersburg gossips would caustically remark, "she's wearing our Pacific fleet again."

Chapter 16

1. Since the recent discovery of Massenet's 1892 letter to Leoncavallo (see chapter 7), I am convinced Sanderson was not fantasizing when she told California reporters in Paris that Leoncavallo was responsible for her introduction to Massenet.

2. Döme later retrained himself as a tenor with the help of Giovanni Sbriglia. He even sang Parsifal at Bayreuth. In 1896 he married the American prima donna Lillian Nordica, but their duet didn't last for life. After stormy years in which he did his best to make the soprano's life miserable, she finally divorced him.

3. Massenet 1912, 167.

4. Lucien Solvay, Brussels report, *Le Ménéstrel*, 8 May 1892.

5. May Palmer shared an art studio with Marion Sanderson but always claimed to be without funds when the rent came due. In a few years her fortunes would change drastically when she married multimillionaire Chauncey DePew.

6. The alarming prophecy of Count Robert de Montesquiou, uttered when he heard that his cousin was about to marry below her social station, must have thoroughly chilled Edith's class-conscious sensibilities: "What is one month of

ecstasy compared to forty years at the end of the dinner table?"

7. Pierre Monteux did not think she was a bona fide coloratura; agreeing with him was a Belgian critic who had written about her Queen of the Night aria after a Brussels concert, "This work is decidedly not for her."

Chapter 17

1. Delna had already signed a contract with the Opéra-Comique to appear shortly in Berlioz's *Les troyens* (The Trojans).

2. She was replaced by a Mlle Arnaud.

3. Augé de Lassus, quoted in Rhodes 1984, 4.

4. Bonnerot 1923, 79.

5. Perhaps the *Musical Courier* made the mistake of taking seriously the tongue-in-cheek remark that Carvalho made to the Parisian press: "To portray the queen of porn in ancient Greece, I have chosen the reigning queen of porn in decadent Paris--Mlle Sanderson, herself."

6. Rhodes 1984, 4.

7. *Le Journal des débats,* 27 May 1893.

8. Hughes Imbert, *Le Guide musical,* 4 June 1893

9. Rhodes 1984, 4.

10. Rudolph Ganz personally related the following incident that occurred between Sarah Bernhardt and his brother-in-law, a popular American actor named Arthur Forrest, upon their first stage appearance together. Bernhardt told him: "Tonight, young man, you are going to learn a lesson from me in technique. At the very moment of my most impassioned scene, when I have the audience in tears, when I pretend to tear my heart out and offer it to them as a live sacrifice, I will turn to you and secretly thumb my nose at them. This is the only way a star can remain on the stage and survive."

11. Maurice Halperson, "Manons I have Heard," *Musical America,* 15 July 1916.

Chapter 18

1. De Croisset 1929, 34.

2. Oddly enough, Adolph Ederer, in a more recent article in *Le Théâtre,* credits Mme Massenet with first bringing the idea to her husband's attention. She purportedly read a review of *Thaïs* by Paul Desjardin in which he suggested that the story would make the perfect operatic subject for a composer like Massenet. I believe Mme Massenet would not have been so foolish as to call her husband's attention to the article even if she had read it. She would have known only too well whom he would visualize in the title role.

3. Oudin produced the first English translation of Massenet's songs in 1888 for Schirmer Music Company in New York. As a visitor to the 1889 Paris Exposition, he first met Sibyl Sanderson that year and more than likely Massenet as well.

4. Massenet 1912, 195.

5. A distraught Massenet evidently failed to enlist Mrs. Sanderson to chastise Sibyl for her selfish and unprofessional behavior, because Margaret defended her. Angrily, the composer wrote to his wife on 7 May 1893 that "the Sandersons are positively insufferable, the mother even more than the daughter."

Chapter 19

1. Alexander McArthur, "Paris Letter," *Musical Courier*, 16 August 1893.

2. Massenet may have added the Fabliau ("Oui, dans les bois"), a difficult coloratura aria, for the bicentennial performance. Demar Irvine and others have written that the piece was composed for the much-married Georgette Bréjean-Silver, who was to assume Sanderson's role a year later, in September 1894, at the Comique under her first husband's name, Gravière. However, Bidú Sayão told me that according to her teacher, Jacques Isnardon, who often sang the Comte Des Grieux opposite both Sanderson and Bréjean-Silver, the Fabliau was composed expressly for Sibyl. French soprano Alice Verlet, who coached the role of Manon with the composer, told the late American painter Carroll Kelly that the Fabliau was written for the bicentennial performance at Sanderson's request. Jean-Christophe Branger, in his recent book *Manon de Jules Massenet,* disputes Irvine's statement that Bréjean-Silver premiered the Fabliau in Brussels. According to him she first performed the aria on 17 November 1898 in concert in Paris with Massenet at the piano, and *Le Ménéstrel* published a concert version of it for voice and piano a month later. It had, however, already appeared in the appendix of the revised 1895 edition of *Manon.* [Quotation from author interview with Pierre Monteux.]

3. *Musical Courier,* 29 November 1893.

4. *L'Illustration,* 8 March 1894.

5. Fanny Edgar Thomas, "Paris column," *Musical Courier,* May 1898.

6. *Town Topics,* 14 October 1897.

7. In his memoirs Massenet wrote, "Never have I so regretted letting myself go in a moment of disappointment . . . could I foresee that I should again observe this same score of *Thaïs,* dated 1894, in the salon of Sibyl Sanderson's mother on the piano at which that admirable artist, long since no more, studied?" Massenet 1912.

8. In the vision sequence, the foreground of the monks' shanties was plunged into darkness, and a spotlight was focused on a scrim at the back of the stage to reveal Thaïs (actually clad in a flesh-colored body stocking) dancing on a pedestal before the populace.

9. *L'Écho de Paris,* 14 March 1894

10. De Mérode 1955, 37.

11. *Le Temps,* 19 March 1894.

12. *Le Journal des débats,* 17 March 1894.

13. *La Revue des deux mondes,* 17 March 1894.

14. *Le Figaro,* 17 March 1894

15. *La Revue de Paris,* 2 April 1894

16. *Le Petit journal,* 17 March 1894

17. *La Revue des deux mondes,* 17 March 1894.

18. Rosita Mauri assumed the role of the soul's destruction which was tormented by the corps de ballet representing man's various sins.

19. Sibyl Sanderson, according to personal accounts by Mrs. Maley and others, remained onstage during the Méditation. Immediately after the curtain descended upon the first scene in Act II, a spotlight was thrown onto a scrim that was dropped a little ways in front of the curtain. It revealed Thaïs walking slowly to and fro, pondering the monk's promise of eternal life. Regrettably, Massenet left no directions for this important pantomime when he copyrighted his revised edition in 1898. In my lifetime only one director--Tito Capobianco-- had the insight to realize Thaïs must remain onstage during the Méditation. He created a remarkable tableau of mirrored cubicles for Beverly Sills to glimpse her life from youth to the rotting skeleton revealed in the last compartment.

20. "La nouvelle étoile," *Le Figaro,* 14 March 1894.

Chapter 20

1. "The Lillian Russell of Paris," *Musical Courier,* 4 September 1894.

2. Brooklyn *Eagle,* 27 May 1894.

3. The recitatives remained hidden among Massenet's effects until discovered in the 1980s and given their American premiere in the Metropolitan's 1987 production. Ironically, a Metropolitan official confided to the New York papers that they were probably written "late in Massenet's life."

Chapter 21

1. In the first installment, 13 September 1897, the *New York Journal* presented its readers with an erroneous description of the lovers. It depicted Sanderson as

a "magnificently tall, dark-haired Greek goddess" and Terry as "small, very dark, rather unhandsome--not at all the sort of boy who would grow up to be a rival for a beautiful woman's favors with czars and kings."

2. "The pig!" she snarled as a ruined Count Chevedolé blasted the gory remnants of his head all over her bedroom. "He has soiled my finest silk sheets!"

3. Terry was always supporting penniless painters and musicians, among them a Spanish composer named Mario Costa.

4. It would seem that Terry loved to spin endless variations on the Rudyard Kipling tale.

5. Armstrong 1922, 129.

Chapter 22

1. The St. James Hotel was located at 29th and Broadway.

2. *Rhode Island Gazette,* 11 January 1895.

3. *New York World,* 12 January 1895; *Musical Courier,* 23 January 1895.

4. Interview with Muriel Atherton Russell, 1956.

5. A typical example could have been the following excerpt from the *New York World,* January 15, 1895: "Rumor and gossip have placed the fair Californian so much in evidence, so much romance has been woven about her, her beauty so exploited, its charms of figure so pictured and described, her taste in dress so often emphasized, that every woman in New York yearns to be present."

6. "Mother was very proud of her profile and considered it far superior to Sibyl Sanderson's," Mrs. Russell confided. "Every chance she got that evening she would try to catch my eye and then pose next to Sibyl's profile for comparison. Mother could be so vain at times."

7. According to Mrs. Atherton's second article on Sibyl in the San Francisco *Call-Bulletin* 1 November 1947, after tramping up and down in her bedroom slippers through the whirling snow for twenty minutes, Sibyl returned to her suite soaked to the bone. Exhausted and tearful, she decided to call Tony's suite one more time. To her amazement she woke him from a sound sleep. Since the Athertons had left, it is assumed Jane briefed Mrs. Atherton on the dénouement the following night.

8. New York did not hear it until the following season when the title role was sung by Nellie Melba.

9. *Manon* contained far more spoken dialogue than New Yorkers were accustomed to hearing. Both *Faust* and *Carmen* had been performed at the Metropolitan with recitatives that had replaced the original passages.

10. All the reviews quoted from the New York papers are dated 17 January 1895.

11. In Paris *Le Ménéstrel* had already accused both men of being "ferociously Wagnerian."

12. When I interviewed Bidú Sayão in 1987, she was perplexed as to why Henderson could have written that Sanderson's voice was "much too small for the Metropolitan." "She must have had a far larger voice than I have," Mme Sayão admitted. "I could never have sung Esclarmonde. I didn't have the range or the power. That cold you speak of must have seriously impaired her debut." Sayão did not realize that by the time she made her debut at the Metropolitan singing *Manon,* the New York critics had heard innumerable performances of the work in its revised edition and had learned to appreciate its delicate subtleties and nuances.

13. Two years before, New York critics had welcomed Emma Calvé's passionate interpretation of Bizet's *Carmen,* but Calvé sang the musical recitatives Guiraud had written for it. These recitatives turned *Carmen* into conventional opera, in total contrast to the intimate style of spoken recitatives Massenet employed for *Manon.*

14. *New York Journal,* 20 January 1895.

15. *Musical Courier,* 23 January 1895.

16. *Philadelphia Ledger, Philadelphia Times,* 23 and 24 January 1895.

17. Probably the Brooklyn *Eagle.* The newspaper title was torn in Sanderson's scrapbook.

Chapter 23

1. Grau's letter of request is still preserved in the Sanderson family memorabilia. Yet as it turned out, Melba seems to have performed all her *Rigoletto* engagements.

2. *Washington Post,* 24 February 1895.

3. *Washington Times,* 24 February 1895.

4. According to the *San Francisco Examiner,* 27 March 1895, Mr. Grau was quoted as saying, "The truth is Mr. Terry did meet Mrs. Langtry once, and that brief occasion caused him more regrets because of the reports growing out of it . . . He had merely been presented to Mrs. Langtry by a common friend in a hotel corridor and had only spent a few minutes in her company. This was the only occasion when he met or saw Mrs. Langtry and out of that incident came the story of Miss Sanderson's . . . ill health because of a broken heart."

5. *Philadelphia Press,* 25 March 1895.

6. Although Constance Wilde's family had some financial as well as social connections, it is very possible that her staunch American friend, Sibyl Sanderson, gave her an undisclosed sum of money to help spirit her two children out of England that month. When Vyvyan Holland, the second son of the Wildes, wrote his memoirs in 1954, he admitted that he was too young to know how his mother obtained the money to act as fast as she did. The winter of 1895 found Mrs. Wilde and her children living temporarily in Nervi, Italy, less than three miles from where the Sandersons were staying. Marion Sanderson, in her private reminiscences, seemed at a loss to understand the devoted friendship between Sibyl and Mrs. Wilde. The latter had visited Sibyl in Paris, and the diva had arranged for her sisters to stay overnight several times with the Wildes on various trips to England. Yet, when she was writing her memoirs ca. 1939, Marion remarked that Mrs. Wilde seemed so "plain and unassuming" that it was hard to remember what she looked like.

7. Muriel Atherton Russell, Gertrude Atherton's daughter, confided to author Evelyn Wells that her mother was severely upset by Sibyl's open involvement with "some lesbian in London" and told her she refused to have anything more to do with her until "she came to her senses." This lesbian must have been Madame X.

8. Stories of Sibyl's alleged lesbian entanglement eventually reached Paris. In 1958 Antonio Terry's daughter, the Princess de Lucinge, observed, "I can only repeat to you what I was told some years later. I do not know whether my father ever learned of it, but I don't see how he could have kept from it. Imagine my chagrin when I discovered everyone else in the family had heard at least one version."

9. Schwab 1963, 256.

10. *New York World*, 7 July 1895.

11. If Sanderson did try to commit suicide in London, one can only speculate that her recently discovered, or perhaps admitted, bisexuality may have been at the root of her emotional turmoil. She was perhaps closer to a nervous breakdown than at any other time in her life. Since the extent of her relationship with Mme X is unknown, any postulation about her bisexuality must remain purely speculative.

12. Various American journals continued to hint at a pregnancy. *Kunkel's Music Journal* titillated its readers by revealing that Sanderson was hiding in the French countryside that summer (1895) until the blessed event transpired in August. In September of 1895, the *Musical Courier* announced to the world that its mystery prima donna had given birth to twins. When I discussed this possi-

bility with Antonio Terry's daughter, the Princess de Lucinge snorted, "Rubbish! There was no illegitimate child or any abortion! Sibyl would have given anything to have had a child, and had she given birth to twins, she and my father would have adopted them after their marriage. Besides, no financial provisions were ever made for such mythical children."

Chapter 24

1. *New York Sun,* 6 December 1896
2. "Sibyl Sanderson in New York," *Musical Courier,* 23 January 1895.
3. Lucy Berthet, Sanderson's understudy, sang the other two before Sibyl's return to the Opéra.
4. To show her gratitude, Sibyl insisted that he share a curtain call with her after her second appearance of the season.
5. New York *Sun, Journal,* and *Herald,* 17 May 1903
6. When interviewed in 1958, this source requested that his anonymity be respected.
7. *Le Gaulois,* 28 December 1895.
8. Gertrude Atherton had just passed her ninetieth birthday when she wrote two articles about Sibyl, printed in the San Francisco *Call-Bulletin* on 31 October and 1 November 1947. In them she admitted to being "a trifle hazy" about a public altercation between the two women in Terry's life. According to Mrs. Atherton the first Mrs. Terry espied Sibyl exiting a store on the rue de Rivoli one afternoon and attacked the singer with her parasol. After Sibyl recovered, she merely straightened her hat and walked on "with an expressionless face." One may wonder whether Grace Terry, who had grown indifferent to her husband's many affairs since the days of Sadie Martinot, would have bothered. More likely, the woman who attacked Sibyl was Mme Schmidt, who was far more hostile toward the singer.

Chapter 25

1. In a 1958 interview de Mérode vehemently denied the age-old rumor that she had been the Belgian king's mistress. She maintained that every time she had been in his company, her mother had been present. She was at a total loss to explain why the monarch's enemies insisted upon labeling him "King Cléopold."
2. Thompson 1913, 183.
3. Massenet arrived to supervise the final rehearsals of *La navarraise,* but there is no record of his remaining on the scene for Sibyl's rehearsals.

4. It is possible he played a sketch of the duet for Tosca and Cavaradossi beginning "Mia gelosa," since three different versions of this music still exist, suggesting that it predates the final lyrics.

5. Sibyl's letter to her sister Jane, 21 November 1896.

Chapter 26

1. Roy Herrick was a first cousin to Myron Herrick, the longtime, much beloved American ambassador to France.

2. One of them was the young American soprano and future opera star Fanchon Thompson.

3. In a letter to her patron, Mrs. Mayer of Chicago, she described Sibyl as "simply charming, beautiful, fascinating, and clever."

4. A photograph of the singer boarding the train that day shows her to be garbed in a fur-trimmed velvet cloak with a high fur collar, and a feathered fur toque on her head.

5. Although he had been apprised of this ancient Oriental custom, Tony later told his daughter, Natividad, that he was agog witnessing the spectacle for the first time.

6. Among the gifts from Nicholas II to Sanderson was a large artist-signed Russian enamel-on-silver necklace interspersed with beautiful medallions of turquoise.

7. Unhappily, dispatches to the French and American musical journals of this period do not list the casts of her Russian performances, but there is a good chance the native tenor Mikhailov was once more her Roland in *Esclarmonde*.

8. Sibyl quickly learned that after the heat of the moment had cooled, Muscovites could be notorious Indian givers. It was customary for them to call at the box office the next day and reclaim their personal effects.

9. Atherton 1932, 158, 159.

Chapter 27

1. In an interview in the 1950s, Mary Garden described Terry as a "handsome, dissolute, good-for-nothing playboy."

2. Atherton 1932, 119.

3. In 1958 the Princess de Lucinge seemed reluctant to discuss her mother's mysterious "stroke." She admitted that they had not been getting along, and I decided to forgo questions about the rumor that Mrs. Terry was a cocaine addict and had died from free basing the drug.

4. Sibyl's decision meant she would not appear in Massenet's *Cendrillon*. Coincidentally, Marie Van Zandt, who was to create the other stepsister, married at about this time and also retired from the stage.

5. These portraits were removed in the 1950s when a new administration of the Opéra-Comique decided upon complete redecoration.

6. *Town Topics,* 12 December 1897.

7. *Town Topics,* 14 October 1897.

8. So was Jules, whether he knew it or not. Margaret Sanderson had had a huge photographic image of Massenet stenciled on one of her dining room walls. Nothing in that room escaped his surveillance--at least by proxy.

Chapter 28

1. Rumors of Sibyl's miscarriage were now fairly common in Paris, but obviously Miss Thomas was not aware that Sibyl's life had been threatened by crural phlebitis.

2. As Natica was unaware of this in our 1958 conversations, she pondered why the Sandersons failed to come to Sibyl's side. "My family may have disapproved of Sibyl," she commented, "but I know they would have liked the Sandersons immensely if they could only have met them."

3. In one of her letters to Jane, Marion admitted she never really loved Sibyl until the last month of Sibyl's life. Terry's daughter, the Princess de Lucinge, observed that both Marion and Edith were secretly jealous of their oldest sister.

4. Terry was quoted as saying to Sibyl, "Dearest, I know I cannot escape this heart disease which makes me suffer so much. Please sing the air in which I heard you for the first time, as from that day on I have always loved you."

5. Marion mentioned in her letter that "Sibyl kissed him again and again on his dead, open mouth making my terrible dream come true." This sentence evidently refers to a premonition of Tony's death scene that she had already confided to her mother.

6. In retrospect, this strange "convulsive fit" was probably the climax to one of Sibyl's ever-increasing number of manic-depressive episodes.

7. The newspapers made no mention of Elena Schmidt's attendance, so it is not known whether Terry's longtime mistress was present. Since the family considered her practically a member, she undoubtedly received an invitation.

Chapter 29

1. The center section of the stage was removed and replaced with glass

blocks through which a mechanical apparatus below flashed dazzling arcs of colored lights on to the swirling panels of Loïe's costumes.

Chapter 30

1. Hindemith 1952, 145.
2. Garden and Biancolli 1951, 22.
3. The David Mayer family, who sponsored Mary's studies, were owners of Schlesinger and Mayers' department store (later to become Carson, Pirie, and Scott) in Chicago. After they cut off Mary's allowance, the only thing they offered her was a steamship ticket home. She was thrown out of her pension and had to find cheap lodging on the upper floor of a boardinghouse. Her studies came to a halt, and for six months her life was a desperate struggle for survival. Although she sold her jewelry and most of her personal effects, she was now down to her last few centimes and facing another eviction notice. Presumably, her child, if she had one, was living with her.
4. It is interesting to note Garden was in America in 1909 and chose not to bring suit against the paper for slander. A year or so later the Mayers threatened to file a $20,000 lawsuit against her that included all the compound interest from the intervening years. Contrary to Garden's tale as quoted in Michael Turnbull's 1997 biography, she wasn't given twenty-four hours to settle the account. According to the version Mary told Louise Hamill, her longtime Chicago confidante and childhood playmate, the Mayers allowed her one week to come up with the cash. Her father's lawyer entered into some fast wheeling and dealing with the Mayers' attorneys. Once Mary had settled the account in full, Mrs. Mayer would issue a formal statement to the press admitting she had been misinformed about Mary having a child. "It was the old-fashioned trade-off, tit for tat," Garden confided to Miss Hamill, "but it closed the book on my stupid indiscretion and got those dreadful Mayers off my back." Louise Hamill told her niece, Margaret Hamill Stewart, Garden's confidential disclosure, which strongly supports the information Sanderson shared with her stepdaughter. Mrs. Stewart, who died in 1996, was a close friend of mine for many years. She related that the Gardens and the Hamills had been next-door neighbors living at 59th and Dorchester on Chicago's once-chic south side. She first met Garden in the early 1920s at her aunt Louise's apartment.
5. According to my interviews with the Princess de Lucinge, Sibyl asked her to keep the story of Mary's illegitimate child confidential, and Natica complied. "I never once mentioned it to her," the Princess confided, "and everything was completely entente cordiale between us. I'm sure she surmised that I

knew. . . . Some years later, after she became such a big star, I occasionally wondered if that boy grew to manhood ever learning that Mary Garden was his real mother. . . . Catholic orphanages in France keep very private records. When they are sealed, they're sealed for life. . . . Years later I ran into her one night in Monte Carlo at the casino and reintroduced myself to her. When I recalled the delightful times the three of us had, she seemed so distant and aloof, as if she barely remembered me. I don't know if this act was prompted by not wanting to recall the painful circumstances under which Sibyl took her in, but if she hadn't Mary would have been forced to sell her body in order to survive. If Mary Garden ever owed her life to anyone, it was to Sibyl; yet a few years later when Sibyl was desperate for money, I'm told she refused to lend her a sou."

6. Garden told me that Carré was actually a dinner guest at Mme Sanderson Terry's home about three times that winter. She said that she met more important people in Sibyl's home in five months than she had during the three previous years she lived in Paris. She further confided that Fugère, although a great artist, couldn't teach "worth a damn." Each time Chevalier would have to explain to her what Fugère was trying to impart.

7. Natica seemed to be the only one who noticed that these manic-depressive spells often paralleled Sibyl's three-week menstrual cycle. When she mentioned this curious observation years later, premenstrual syndrome was still not common knowledge.

8. Turnbull 1997, 21.

9. In an interview with Gustav Kobbé for his *Opera Singers* (1913), Garden repeated Marion Sanderson's version almost word for word.

10. According to the Princess de Lucinge, Mary had had a limited number of rehearsals with piano at the Opéra-Comique, but none with orchestra. Neither had she been privy, as she claimed, to Messager's protests, because they occurred privately in Carré's office. Carré himself related the altercation to Garden the next day when he signed her to a new contract.

11. Garden claimed in her autobiography that the role of Louise became exclusively hers and Marthe Rioton never sang it again. Any perusal of the *Annales de l'Opéra-Comique* (1900) will show that Mlle Rioton returned the following week to reclaim her role once her vocal problems had abated.

Chapter 31

1. All conversation is quoted from my 1958 interviews with the Princess de Lucinge. She remarked that she would never forget that night as long as she lived.

2. *Town Topics,* 19 August 1899.

Chapter 32

1. In 1958 Natividad Terry de Lucinge recalled Mr. Webb with a certain amount of animosity. She accused him of having secretly bled her father's estate for years.

2. Later the street was renamed avenue Foch after the French World War I general.

3. Hahn's lover Marcel Proust may have accompanied him on some of these visits. One of his notes to Hahn, declining a dinner invitation at Mme Terry's because of a previous commitment, has survived.

4. This was probably the only time Sanderson and Mary Garden were on the stage singing together.

5. Newcomb 1921, 146.

6. San Francisco unfortunately learned of the disastrous Viennese concert nearly eight months before Sanderson returned to appear there. It is a matter of conjecture how much Steinegger's report may have prejudiced the Californians against their own diva.

Chapter 33

1. *Musical Courier,* 17 April 1901

2. Koster and Bial was the leading variety hall in New York City at the turn of the century.

3. *Le Guide musical,* 23 June 1901

4. *New York Herald,* 16 June 1901.

Chapter 34

1. In 1960 Dr. Semelaigne's son refused to share his father's records on Sibyl Sanderson, claiming that French law prohibited him from doing so for anyone who was not a relative of the deceased.

2. On 27 August 1901 she wrote to Massenet, giving him a synopsis of her American schedule and asking him to hear her Manon once more. Since no response has been found in the Sanderson memorabilia, it is questionable whether Massenet answered her.

Chapter 35

1. *New York World,* 22 June 1901.

2. *Town Topics,* 28 September 1901.

3. *Cosmopolitan,* August 1901.

4. Sanderson would not have had to leave the Fransioli Hotel to purchase a case of hard liquor. There was an enormous saloon on the first floor, complete with "tables for ladies."

5. A photograph of the asbestos stage curtain that rose on that ill-fated matinee has been preserved in the New York Public Library. A kaleidoscope of colloquial advertising, it boasted such backwoods crudities as "I will be blamed if he ain't smokin' a long staple five cent SEGER from MOSELEY'S SEGER FACTORY" and "best damned LICKER in the South--your own TENNESSEE BREWING COMPANY."

6. Quite possibly Sanderson suffered another bout of manic depression on the way. The Metropolitan train had arrived ten hours late in New Orleans because Buffalo Bill's personal train was derailed on the same track.

Chapter 36

1. All other twentieth-century sopranos have sung it in the transposed key of F major.

2. A young man named Edward Bowes, later to become radio's beloved Major Bowes, was in the audience. In a letter to Marion Sanderson Nall, dated 1940, he fondly recalled Sibyl's performances.

Chapter 37

1. *New York Herald,* 29 December 1901.

2. Among the well-wishers in her dressing room after the performance were Mary Garden's grateful parents, Mr. and Mrs. Robert Garden. They had been alarmed to read in the *New York Herald* on 16 December a lurid article about Mary's mysterious disappearance from the Opéra-Comique. As soon as Sibyl was informed, she thoughtfully telegraphed them not to worry because Mary was singing in Monte Carlo that week.

3. Mrs. Sanderson had cabled Sibyl, desperately trying to stall her matrimonial plans. Such a foolish marriage would cut off her daughter's small but steady income from Terry's will.

4. When Will S. Monroe published this letter in the 27 May 1903 issue of the *Musical Courier,* he did not reveal the author's name.

Chapter 38

1. It is altogether possible that Sanderson and Fitz-James consulted some authorities of the Anglican Church while in London about a conversion and subsequent marriage by the Church of England.

2. Obviously, Sanderson did not tell the truth, because she and her fiancé could not have avoided being aware of the problem from the beginning. She had lived with the identical situation before the first Mrs. Terry died.

3. As it turned out, *Circé* had to wait until after Sanderson's death, when Geneviève Vix created the title role in 1907 at the Opéra-Comique.

4. *Le Figaro,* 3 April 1902

5. The wealthy DeYoungs, who were in Sibyl's San Francisco audience that night, spent the Christmas holidays in their Paris home afterward. They related the sad story to Fanny Reed and others, who lost no time in informing Massenet.

6. *L'Écho de Paris,* 3 April 1902.

7. Edgar Mills, an old musical colleague of Sibyl's from California, heard her Manon in April 1902. Judging from an undated letter he wrote her mother, her voice still had some good days left: "I was led to look for wonderful high notes, but I did not expect such an admirably balanced medium and carrying power of the low notes. Her mezza voce is delicious, her attack clean and pure, her phrasing a delight to hear . . . Miss Sanderson most kindly took me backstage, but there were so many who wished to offer congratulations, that only the faintest expression of my pleasure was possible . . . I hope you will tell Mme Terry how delighted I was."

8. Laurent Grivot had sung innumerable character roles at the Comique during his long career and countless performances of Guillot Morfontaine, the role he created in *Manon. L'Écho de Paris* announced she would attend the event even though, according to *Le Figaro,* she was in England to sing some (fictitious) concerts.

9. Born of a German Jewish father and an English Protestant mother, de Croisset learned English as a child and spoke it fluently.

10. In 1910 de Croisset married Marie de Chevigny, daughter of the Countess de Chevigny, among the richest women in France, by whom he had two children.

11. Harding 1971, 156.

12. The premiere of Massenet's opera *Chérubin* didn't occur until 14 February 1905 in Monte Carlo and the following May at the Opéra-Comique. Meanwhile, the original theater version was playing in capitals all over Europe.

Chapter 39

1. It is entirely possible that Sanderson did spend a few weeks in the Swiss sanitarium before leaving to join de Croisset in Nice.

2. De Croisset departed this world in 1937 maintaining a lifelong silence

about his relationship with Sibyl Sanderson. Van Vechten did not have a high opinion of the Belgian playwright, finding him a "shallow, self-centered bore."

3. In her memoirs Blanche Marchesi erroneously placed the location in St. Cloud.

4. The asylum was closed in 1921.

5. From an undated letter written sometime in the latter part of 1902.

6. Marchesi 1923, 54–55.

7. Actually, the final words of the opera are "Et c'est là, l'histoire de Manon Lescaut."

8. Garden asked Van Vechten to keep their conversation confidential, but in 1962 he gave me his notes, which unfortunately weren't dated. The closest Van Vechten could come to dating them was to say that the conversation occurred shortly after World War I.

9. Garden remarked self-righteously to Van Vechten, "Why should I loan her any money when all she would have done is spend it on more booze?"

10. When interviewed, Robert Lawrence admitted that while he greatly admired some of Massenet's operas, he had no respect for him as a human being. "Don't ever think that Massenet was a nice man," Lawrence intoned, "he was pure bastard! Do you know he turned Sibyl Sanderson into a lesbian?" Once he learned that I was aware of the situation, we compared Garden's disclosures in both instances, to discover they remained the same. On the other hand, Quaintance Eaton insisted Garden was a closet bisexual as well as a notorious prevaricator and related a confidence about her making a pass at a student who later became one of America's most celebrated sopranos.

11. Apropos this subject, the Princess de Lucinge made the following remarks: "They could have tried it once, but I doubt it. There certainly was no affair between them. For years I heard Sibyl enjoyed sexual relations with women, but during the two years I lived with her, I never caught her in bed with any. Later on, a jealous Mme Carré, in her smear campaign to drive Garden from the Opéra-Comique, circulated the story the two had been lovers. But it wasn't true. I ought to know; I lived with them."

12. Conversation with Esther Leger, a Sanderson retainer, January 1978.

13. I have tracked Paul Tolstoy's travels in Western Europe as far as Lucerne, Switzerland, where he was mentioned among the socially prominent visitors in August 1902. Evidently, he had some kind of monthly stipend from Russia, or wherever his homeland was, that allowed him to visit the fashionable resorts.

14. I suspect this was the same cast that sang *Phryné* at Aix-les-Bains with Sibyl the previous summer.

Chapter 40

1. On board the same ship was Hearst's old enemy, Fremont Older, editor of the *San Francisco Bulletin,* and his wife, Cora. Before the end of the voyage, they had not only patched up their feud but promised to see each other often in Paris. It was the beginning of a lifelong friendship, according to conversations with Mrs. Older.

2. Garden and Biancolli 1951, 57.

3. Fortunately, the walking stick was used by other Manons. Garden gave it to Grace Moore, who in turn bequeathed it to Dorothy Kirsten.

4. Marchesi 1923, 55.

5. Garden related in her interviews with American newsmen that Sibyl had suffered paralysis to the right side of her face and body during her last hours, but Dr. Iscovesco made no mention of any stroke in his public statements about her.

6. Garden and Biancolli 1951, 58.

7. *New York Tribune,* 16 May 1903. (Sanderson did not create Manon.)

8. *New York Tribune,* 16 May 1903.

9. *New York Sun,* 17 May 1903.

10. *Le Gaulois,* 16 May 1903.

11. *New York Dramatic Mirror,* 25 May 1903.

12. British author Arnold Bennett used Sanderson's obituary in his *The Book of Carlotta,* originally published in 1911.

13. Garden and Biancolli 1951, 58–59.

14. Saint-Saëns paused to stroke her cheek for a second when his turn came and kept murmuring "ma pauvre Phryné" as tears ran down his face.

15. Massenet 1912, 180.

Chapter 41

1. Marchesi 1923, 55.

2. Buspar, Revia, Librium, Ativan, to name a few.

3. Some thirty-five years later, Marion Sanderson underscored Monroe's observation when she wrote, "Sibyl's reception in her native state . . . almost broke her heart, leaving forever in her mind a sad remembrance of her native country."

4. I discussed my poison theory with the late Dr. George Anteblian, husband of Sanderson's niece. He concurred strongly and had long suspected it himself, but in spite of Marion's and Edith's cautious opinions on the subject, the Sandersons still maintained lifelong ties to Mlle Bournie. If "dear Lina" was the

deathbed angel, the family felt it was an errand of mercy. The Anteblians even visited her on their trips to France after World War II and always brought her chocolate, which she so adored.

5. One mysterious souvenir of Sibyl remained elsewhere. When Massenet returned to Paris from supervising the Milan premiere of *Thaïs* that fall, he found a petit bleu from Margaret inquiring as to the whereabouts of the mystery item. In a prompt reply dated 25 October 1903, he assured her "the keepsake remains exactly in its hiding place--it is with a cruel emotion that I thank you for your concern." Whatever it was, whatever its significance, neither party wished to mention it by name. Mme Massenet, it can be assumed, knew nothing about it.

6. Farrar 1938, 63. Marion Sanderson and her fiancé, Dr. Edwin Nall, met Farrar during her Paris visit. It was the beginning of a lifelong friendship.

7. These did not include the original edition of *Manon* or the Massenet holographs.

8. Perhaps the most pathetic items auctioned were the lace-fringed baby garments that Terry bought for their ill-fated child. Sibyl had never found the courage to dispose of them.

9. *Le Figaro,* 8 November 1905.

10. After years of researching the Nice newspapers, I acquired the invaluable services of the chief archivist of Nice, Mme Mireille Massot, who provided me with the complete dates and casts of the opera season. Both of us came to the conclusion that the Sanderson attorney had fabricated a highly dramatic but erroneous tale.

11. Conversation with Esther Léger, January 1978.

12. Massenet 1912, 179.

13. *Daily Mail,* 16 August 1912.

Bibliography

For a summary of unpublished sources, see the preface.

Books

Altrocchi, Julia. 1949. *The Spectacular San Franciscans.* New York: Dutton and Co.

Annales de l'Opéra-Comique, Noel et Stoullig. Paris: Charpentier.

Armstrong, William. 1922. *The Romantic World of Music.* New York: Dutton.

AthertonAbb 1932. *Adventures of a Novelist: My Autobiography.* New York: Liveright.

———. 1946. *My San Francisco: A Wayward Autobiography.* New York: Bobbs-Merrill.

Augé-Laribe, Michel. 1951. *André Messager.* Paris: La Colombe.

Bellaigue, Camille. 1891, 1893. *L'année musicale.* Paris: Charpentier.

Benoist, André. 1978. *The Accompanist.* Neptune City, New Jersey: Paganiniana Publications.

Bonnerot, Jean. 1923. *Camille Saint-Saëns: Sa vie et son oeuvre.* Paris: Durand.

Bouvet, Charles. 1929. *Massenet.* Paris: Lauriens.

Brancour, René. 1931. *Massenet.* Paris: Librairie Alcan.

Branger, Jean-Christophe. 1999. *Manon de Jules Massenet.* Paris: Serpenoise.

Cammaerts, Émile. 1935. *Albert of Belgium: Defender of Right.* New York: Macmillan.

Carré, Arthur. 1950. *Souvenirs de théâtre.* Paris: Plon.

de Croisset, Francis. 1929. *Our Puppet Show* (Nos marionettes). New York: Harper.

Dandelot, Arthur. 1930. *Saint-Saëns.* Paris: Dandelot Press.

Davidson, Gladys. 1956. *Opera Biographies.* London: T. Werner Laurie.

Delmas, Marc. 1932. *Massenet.* Paris: Édition de la Jeune Académie.

de Mérode, Cléo. 1955. *Le ballet de ma vie.* Paris: Pierre Horay.

Dobie, Charles Caldwell. 1939. *San Francisco: A Pageant.* New York: Appleton-Century.

d'Ydewalle, Charles. 1935. *Albert and the Belgians.* New York: Morrow.

Eames, Emma. 1927. *Some Memories and Reflections.* New York: Appleton Press.

Eaton, Quaintance. 1956. *Opera Caravan: The Metropolitan on Tour, 1883–1956.* New York: Farrar, Straus, and Cudahy.

Elson, Louis C. 1896. *European Reminiscences, Musical and Otherwise.* Philadelpha: T. Presser.

———. 1901. *History of Opera.* Boston: Page.

———. 1903. *Women in Music.* Boston: Page.

Farrar, Geraldine. 1938. *Such Sweet Compulsion.* New York: Greystone Press.

Février, Henri. 1948. *André Messager: Mon maître, mon ami.* Paris: Amoit-Dumont.

Garden, Mary, and Louis Biancolli. 1951. *Mary Garden's Story.* New York: Simon & Schuster.

Hahn, Reynaldo. 1933. *Notes: Journal d'un musicien.* Paris: Plon.

———. 1946. *Thèmes variés.* Paris: J. B. Janin.

Harding, James. 1971. *Massenet.* New York: St. Martin's Press.

Hervey, Arthur. 1894. *Masters of French Music.* New York: Scribner.

Hindemith, Paul. 1952. *A Composer's World.* Cambridge, Massachusetts: Harvard University Press.

Howe, Granville L., and W. S. B. Mathews. [1889] 1970. *A Hundred Years of Music in America.* Reprint, New York: AMS Press.

Huret, Jules. 1901. *Loges et coulisses.* Paris: Éditions de la revue blanche.

Irvine, Demar. 1994. *Massenet: A Chronicle of His Life and Times.* Portland: Amadeus Press.

Johnson, Allen, ed. 1935. *Dictionary of American Biography.* New York: Scribner.

Kobbé, Gustav. 1913. *Opera Singers.* Boston: Ditson.

Kshesinskaia, M. F. 1961. *Dancing in Petersburg.* Trans. Arnold Haskell. Garden City, New York: Doubleday.

Lahee, Henry Charles. 1898. *Famous Singers of Yesterday and Today.* Boston: Page.

Lesourd, Paul. 1934. *Le roi Albert: Homme de devoir.* Paris: Éditions des Portiques.

Lewis, Oscar, and Carol Hall. 1939. *Bonanza Inn.* New York: Knopf.

Loewenberg, Alfred. 1943. *Annals of Opera, 1597–1940.* Cambridge, England: W. Heffer and Sons.

Loisel, Joseph. 1922. *Manon de Massenet.* Paris: Mellotte.

Malherbe, Charles. 1890. *Notice sur Esclarmonde.* Paris: Fischbacher.

Marchesi, Blanche. 1923. *A Singer's Pilgrimage.* Boston: Small and Maynard.

Marchesi, Mathilde. 1897. *Marchesi and Music*. London: Harper.

Martin, Sadie. 1891. *The Life and Professional Career of Emma Abbott*. Minneapolis: Kimball.

Massenet, Jules. 1919. *My Recollections*. Trans. H. Villiers Barnett. Boston: Small, Maynard. Originally published as *Mes souvenirs* (Paris: P. Lafitte, 1912).

McClatchy High School Seniors. 1949. *Early Sacramentans*. Student publication.

Newcomb, Ethel. 1921. *Leschetizky As I Knew Him*. New York: Appleton.

Older, Mrs. Fremont. 1936. *William Randolph Hearst, American*. New York: Appleton.

———. 1961. *San Francisco, Magic City*. New York: Longmans, Green & Co.

Paderewski, Ignacy, and Mary Lawton. 1938. *The Paderewski Memoirs*. New York: Scribner.

Rhodes, John. 1984. *Notes on Phryné* (for MRF Records). Paris.

Rimsky-Korsakov, Nikolay, and Carl Van Vechten. 1923. *My Musical Life*. New York: Knopf.

Schneider, Louis. 1908. *Massenet, l'homme—le musicien*. Paris: L. Carteret.

Schwab, Arnold T. 1963. *James Gibbons Huneker*. Stanford University Press.

Shaw, George Bernard. 1932. *Music in London*. Vol. 1. London: Constable.

Shuck, Oscar. 1875. *Sketches of Leading and Representative Men of San Francisco*. London: London and New York Publishing; New York: News Companies.

Sichel, Pierre. 1958. *Jersey Lily: The Story of Lillie Langtry*. Englewood Cliffs, New Jersey: Prentice-Hall.

Solenière, Édouard de. 1897. *Massenet: Étude critique et documentaire*. Paris: Charpentier et Ollendorf.

Swanberg, W. A. 1961. *Citizen Hearst*. New York: Scribner.

Tebbel, John. 1952. *The Life and Good Times of William Randolph Hearst*. New York: Dutton.

Thompson, Oscar. 1937. *The American Singer: 100 Years of Success in Opera*. New York: Dial Press.

Thompson, Vance. 1913. *The Life of Ethelbert Nevin from His Letters and His Wife's Memories*. Boston: Boston Music.

Turnbull, Michael. 1997. *Mary Garden*. Portland, Oregon: Amadeus Press.

D'Udine, Jean. 1931. *L'art du lied et les mélodies de Massenet*. Paris: Heugel.

Van Vechten, Carl. 1915. *Massenet and Women*. New York: Schirmer.

———. 1917. *Interpreters and Interpretations*. New York: Knopf.

Wells, Evelyn. 1939. *Champagne Days of Old San Francisco*. New York: Appleton-Century.

Worth, Jean. 1928. *A Century of Fashion*. Boston: Little, Brown.

Periodicals and Newspapers

American Art Journal. 1889–1897

The American Musician. 1889–1894

The Argonaut (San Francisco). 1883–1903

L'Art musical (Paris). 1890–1897; 1901–1903

Atlanta Constitution. 1901, 1903

Atlanta Journal. 1901, 1903

Baltimore Sun. 1895

La Bataille (Paris). 1889

Billets du matin (Paris). 1889

Boston Herald. 1895

Boston Musical Herald. 1889–1891

The Bulletin (San Francisco). 1901, 1903

The Call (San Francisco). 1901, 1903

The Call-Bulletin (San Francisco). 1947

Chronique belge (Brussels). 1890–1891

Chronique Bruxelles (Brussels). 1890–1891

Collier's Magazine. 1933

Commercial Appeal (Memphis). 1901, 1903

Corriere della sera (Milan). 1896, 1898

Cosmopolitan. 1901

Daily Alta California. 1885.

The Eagle (Brooklyn). 1894–1895

Éclaireur de Nice (Nice). 1892, 1903

Le Figaro (Paris). 1888-1897; 1901–1903

Freund's Music Journal. 1889–1897

Gallery of Players (New York). 1895, 1901

Le Gaulois (Paris). 1889–1897; 1901–1903

La Gazette de Bruxelles (Brussels). 1891–1892

La Gazzetta musicale di Milano (Milan). 1896

Le Guide musical (Paris). 1889–1898, 1901–1903

The Illustrated American. 1891–1895

L'Illustration (Paris). 1889–1894, 1901–1903

L'Indépendance belge (Brussels). 1890–1892, 1903

The Inter-Ocean (Chicago). 1895, 1901–1902

L'Italia del popolo (Milan). 1896, 1898

Le Journal des débats (Paris). 1889–1897.

Kunkel's Musical Journal. 1889, 1894–1895

The London Music Review. 1891

The London Post (A.M. and P.M.). 1891, 1895

The London Star. 1891

The London World. 1891

The Looker-On. 1895, 1896

Le Matin (Paris). 1889–1897, 1901–1903

Le Ménéstrel (Paris). 1889–1898, 1901–1903

Le Monde musical (Paris). 1891–1897, 1903

Monthly Musical Record (London). 1891

Munsey's. 1895, 1897–1899

Musica (Paris). 1903, 1907

Musical America. 1903, 1905

Musical Courier. 1889–1903

The Musician. 1901

The New York Dramatic Mirror. 1896–1897, 1901, 1903

The New York Herald (New York and Paris editions). 1888–1903

The New York Journal. 1895–1903

The New York Sun. 1893–1903

The New York Telegraph. 1895–1903

The New York Times. 1888–1903

The New York Tribune. 1888–1903

The New York World. 1889–1903

The Opera Glass. 1895

Le Panorama (Paris). 1895–1896

Le Petit journal (Paris). 1889, 1891–1894

Petrogradskaia (St. Petersburg). 1892

Le Peuple (Brussels). 1891

Philadelphia Ledger. 1895

Philadelphia North American. 1895, 1901

Philadelphia Press. 1895

Philadelphia Times. 1895, 1901

Piccadilly Portraits (London). 1891

Punch (London). 1891

Le Radical (Paris). 1894

La Reforma. 1890

La République française (Paris). 1889, 1893, 1894

La Revue des deux mondes. 1889, 1891, 1893, 1894

La Revue de Paris (Paris). 1889–1897, 1902–1903

The Rhode Island Gazette. 1895

Rivista milanese (Milan). 1896

Sacramento Daily Record-Union. 1888–1889, 1901, 1903

San Francisco Chronicle. 1901, 1903

San Francisco Examiner. 1881–1903

Saturday Review (London). 1891

Scribner's Magazine. 1911

Il Secolo (Milan). 1896,1897, 1900

Le Temps (Paris). 1889, 1892–1894, 1903

The Theater. 1900–1901

Le Théâtre (Paris). 1892, 1894, 1901, 1903

The Times (London). 1889, 1891, 1903

Times-Picayune (New Orleans). 1901

Town Topics (New York). 1888–1903

Vanity Fair (London). 1891

La Vie mondaine (Nice). 1903

La Vie parisienne (Paris). 1889–1902

Index